Organization Diagnosis, Design, and Transformation

Baldrige Users Guide

(BUG)

Seventh Edition

2015 – 2016

John Vinyard

American Society for Quality, Quality Press, Milwaukee, WI 53203

© 2015 by ASQ.

All rights reserved. Published 2015.

Printed in the United States of America.

20 19 18 17 16 15   5 4 3 2 1

Library of Congress Cataloging-in-Publication Data

Application in progress

Vinyard, John, author.
Organization Design, Diagnosis, and Transformation: Baldrige User's Guide/John Vinyard.

ISBN 978-0-87389-911-6 (softcover: alk. paper)

Publisher: Lynelle Korte
Acquisitions Editor: Matt T. Meinholz
Managing Editor: Paul Daniel O'Mara
Production Administrator: Randall Benson

ASQ Mission: The American Society for Quality advances individual, organizational, and community excellence worldwide through learning, quality improvement, and knowledge exchange.

Attention Bookstores, Wholesalers, Schools, and Corporations: ASQ Quality Press books, video, audio, and software are available at quantity discounts with bulk purchases for business, educational, or instructional use. For information, please contact ASQ Quality Press at 800-248-1946, or write to ASQ Quality Press, P.O. Box 3005, Milwaukee, WI 53201-3005.

To place orders or to request ASQ membership information, call 800-248-1946. Visit our Web site at www.asq.org/quality-press.

∞ Printed on acid-free paper

Quality Press
600 N. Plankinton Ave.
Milwaukee, WI 53203-2914
E-mail: authors@asq.org

ASQ The Global Voice of Quality™

Table of Contents

Dedication

This book is dedicated to my father-in-law, Jack Olson

He has led life in a manner which always made others feel valued and significant.

I am proud he is my father-in-law, and will remember and
learn from his integrity, dignity and consideration for others the rest of my life.

He is a great example of the old axiom:

"You cannot delegate being a role model."

Acknowledgements

A special acknowledgement goes to Dr. John Latham. Much of his work, from previous editions, remains in this seventh edition. John is one of the great thinkers on the topic of Performance Excellence, and I am privileged to have him as a friend.

This book is the product of the thousands of "person years" (not only from the author, although it feels like it) which have gone into the development of the Baldrige model and Baldrige Assessment Process. The Malcolm Baldrige National Quality Award (Baldrige) began with a dream in the mid 1980's which ultimately resulted in legislation in 1987. Baldrige was designed to make United States organizations more competitive, but its impact has been worldwide. It has been more widely accepted than any of the original authors could have ever predicted. Since 1988 organizations of all kinds have discovered the power of using the Baldrige Criteria to dramatically improve their performance.

The Baldrige Team

In its third decade, the Baldrige Process has been a dynamic force in world competitiveness. Not only is this process used in the United States, but I have had the opportunity to travel the globe to work with organizations which have a burning desire to improve - at an unusual rate. They use the Baldrige Criteria to drive their organizational performance. I hope each of them will use this book to continue to advance their competitiveness.

I am indebted to a number of key people who helped make this book possible. Putting a book like this together reminds me of all the people who have really made a difference. This list of contributors starts with Curt Reimann, Harry Hertz, Bob Fangmeyer and the entire Baldrige Team (The Baldrige Performance Excellence Team at The National Institute for Standards and Technology – NIST). These are some of the most professional and dedicated employees in our country. They are making a difference to our lives, our nation, and the quality of life for employees worldwide. The NIST Baldrige Team is helping to improve our nation in a manner which will impact our children and grandchildren. These words were true for previous editions of the book, when there were 40 Baldrige Staff. It's even more true now, when there are only 20 staff. Each of them makes a difference – Thank You.

Looking back to the beginning of the Baldrige Office, Curt Reimann was such an incredible force that many thought he could never be replaced. When Harry Hertz came in as an Assistant Administrator in 1992, it was unclear if anybody could fill Curt's shoes! Harry became the Administrator in 1995 and served for 18 years, taking Baldrige to new heights.

Once again, it seemed like nobody could replace the Baldrige Administrator. Bob Fangmeyer became the Administrator in 2013, and certainly had big shoes to fill. Nevertheless, Bob has taken the helm in an admirable way.

He has tried to keep what works, but has applied the improvement mentality to the Baldrige Office as well. He has taken on specific areas, and has listened to all stakeholders and improved:

- Examiner Training
- Examiner Selection
- The Application Process
- The Site Visit Process
- The scope of the Baldrige products and services
- The scope of the outreach to the various sectors
- The comprehensiveness of their communication to stakeholders
- The breadth and depth of the criteria development and validation process to make it more inclusive and expansive

Organizations which have embraced, and are using, the Criteria for Performance Excellence are more competitive in the marketplace, and are better places to work. Those of us who have been fortunate enough to have worked closely with the NIST Baldrige Team have benefited every day from that association. Not only are they gifted professionals, but they tirelessly share their knowledge and experience to help others. They are always there for help or advice. I feel privileged to be their friend.

Baldrige still needs support from our hearts and wallets. Nevertheless, they have made significant improvements to become more self-funding and have added several funding sources. Where staff was reduced 50% through a comprehensive organizational redesign, expenses were reduced 60%, and they have doubled revenues.

Taking their own advice from the 2015 – 2016 criteria, they have expanded and clarified the Baldrige Brand.

Kudos, Bob Fangmeyer and the entire Baldrige Team

****

The use of this model is pivotal to organizational performance. At a time when many organizations want a hand-out from the government, I have not heard about any of those wanting a 'hand-out' who are focused on the eleven core values of Baldrige, or using this model to try to turn their organizations around. I hope they see the value of the processes which Baldrige helps an organization to define, and the improved metrics those processes drive. That insight would help our nation and the world.

I wish to thank all of the organizations who have contributed knowledge and examples to this book. Without their lessons learned this book would not be as valuable to the user.

I also thank my office support staff – Jane Sonnet and Megan Jordan. The time spent on this edition of the book was significant and without their support, the book would not have come to pass. Many times this was an active role of reading, rereading, rereading, rereading... and other times it was simply showing heroic tolerance as the author spent hours on the phone, hours on the computer, or hours sending emails.

Last, but certainly not least, I thank my wife JoAnn who's love and support have been pivotal.

As with any list of acknowledgements, I know my list has the risk of not mentioning someone who has been key to the development of my thoughts. In that vein, I thank all those who have worked with me over the years and have shared their lessons learned, knowledge, and wisdom. I feel those clients, coworkers and friends are some of the most talented individuals in the world, and they are generous with their wisdom. Just look at the organizations who have contributed examples to this book.

From my heart -- Thank you! I could not have written this without your excellence, your attitude of sharing, your friendship, and your help.

About the Author

John Vinyard

John is the Managing Partner and Co-Founder of Genitect, an organizational diagnosis, design, and transformation firm with offices in Atlanta and New York.

Genitect is passionately dedicated to helping client organizations improve their performance and competitiveness. This is achieved through effectively assessing organizations, and working with leaders to design and implement change.

John has worked with numerous clients in the United States and international firms in Europe, the Middle East, India, Asia and the Pacific Rim. He specializes in working with leadership teams to help transform their organizations. He has worked with twelve Baldrige recipients during their journey (and over 40 state and other award recipients), and has helped them use the Baldrige Model to significantly impact their competitiveness and bottom-line results.

John has over 40 years experience working with organizational improvement at all levels. He focuses on helping executives design and lead strategic change initiatives from the strategy down to results. Focus areas include: strategic leadership, execution excellence, and organizational learning. John has consulted to help twelve organizations become Baldrige Award Recipients. He has experience in health care, commercial, nonprofit, education and government organizations including the following 14 Baldrige Organizations:

- Pewaukee School System (2013 Recipient)
- Baylor Regional Medical Center, Plano (Announced as a 2013 recipient)
- Advocate Good Samaritan Hospital (2010 Baldrige Recipient)
- VA Cooperative Studies Program Clinical Research Pharmacy Coordinating Center (2009 Baldrige Recipient)
- Poudre Valley Health System (2008 Baldrige Recipient)
- Sharp Healthcare (2007 Baldrige Recipient)
- Northern Mississippi Medical Center (2006 Baldrige Recipient)
- PRO-TEC Coating Company (2007 Baldrige Recipient)
- Monfort School of Business, University of Northern Colorado (2004 Baldrige Recipient)
- Boeing Aerospace (2003 Baldrige Recipient)
- Clarke American (2001 Baldrige Recipient)
- Ritz-Carlton Hotel Company (1999 Baldrige Recipient)
- Boeing Airlift & Tanker (1998 Baldrige Recipient)
- Corning Telecommunications Products Division (1995 Baldrige Recipient).

John has worked with over a twenty health care clients, some of which are hospitals, and other are large health care systems. Other clients have included the U.S. Army, the U.S. Air Force, Eaton Corporation, Lanier Worldwide, Cessna Aircraft, Shorts Brothers LLC, TATA Sons Ltd. (over 18 different divisions of Tata - India), InfoSys (India), Bekaert Corporation (Belgium – the first recipient of the European Foundation for Quality Management (EFQM) Award), and many others.

John is licensed by the Federal Aviation Administration (FAA) in Airframe and Powerplant Maintenance (A&P License).

John is on the Board of Directors of Navicent Health, Macon, Georgia.

He has held positions as:

- Director, Engine Maintenance, United Airlines
- VP Quality and Manufacturing Operations, GenCorp Polymer Products
- Group VP, Manufacturing, Cadmus Communications
- President and CEO of Bekaert Associates, Inc.
- His first job was as a Quality Engineer for Pratt & Whitney Aircraft

Awards Include:

Distinguished Achievement Award- Los Angeles Council of Engineers and Scientists

Fellow (FIAE) - The Institute for the Advancement of Engineering

Distinguished Interprofessional Engineering Achievement Award - Society of Professional Engineers

Distinguished Productivity Engineering Achievement Award - California Council of Industrial and Business Associations

Health Care Foreword

Dr. Ken Davis

Baldrige principles can serve as the absolute "go to" framework for any organization or business that is committed to standards of excellence. During the past twenty years of my career as a physician executive I've seen the Baldrige processes at work. These processes positively impacted health care at North Mississippi Health Services (National Baldrige Award Winner, 2006, 2012), and at Methodist Healthcare in San Antonio (Baldrige Texas Award for Performance Excellence Recipient, 2014).

John Vinyard's books highlight the complexities of the Baldrige model but also offer practical examples that any organization can employ as a guide for continual improvement. Organizations that are prepared for the relentless process design, deployment and improvement necessary to sustain a Baldrige culture will find this seventh edition indispensible.

In the health care organizations I've been privileged to help lead, we have and continue to use John's systematic processes to re-design our business, from organizational governance to creating a data and process-driven culture focused on multiple customers' needs. With physicians as "partners," we use this guide to greatly improve patient outcomes, physician and staff satisfaction scores and the financial bottom line.

This text will be heralded as an invaluable reference for practical application of the Baldrige criteria.

Ken Davis, MD, MSc. HP&M, FACP

Chief Medical Officer
San Antonio Methodist Healthcare

Note: Dr. Davis became a Malcolm Baldrige National Quality Award Judge in 2015

Education Foreword

Dr. JoAnn Sternke

To be honest, I think we're all on a continuous improvement journey. Seriously, who would say, "We're a mediocre organization and I want it to stay that way"? No! We all want to get better. What separates those of us on a continuous improvement journey is how systematic we are in pursuing improvement.

A map helps us be more systematic on this journey to improvement. So I ask you, "How well is your map guiding you on your continuous improvement journey?" What map do you use? My guess is that if you're reading this book, you are looking for a better map. And I'm here to tell you that you are looking in the right place!

The Baldrige Criteria for Performance Excellence became our map to continuous improvement in the Pewaukee School District. The Baldrige Criteria asks such tough yet important questions. It does chart a course to excellence. Using the Criteria as our map helped us navigate a pathway to improvement. Yet when we began on this journey, it all felt like a foreign language we entitled "Baldrigian". As we continued to answer those tough questions presented in the Baldrige Criteria, we got to know our organization better and we then began to improve processes. The Baldrige User's Guide helped us to better understand those really tough questions asked of us in the Baldrige Criteria. It helped bring meaning to complex yet important improvement principles in the Baldrige Criteria. Simply put, it made the map more readable. The Baldrige User's Guide also helped us learn to diagram our key processes in pictorial form, and better see how things worked – or at times, didn't work. That's how we grew and continue to grow on our improvement journey.

Lo and behold, over time we started to reach higher and higher levels of student achievement and organizational effectiveness. Our Baldrige "map" was indeed pointing us in the right direction on our continuous improvement journey. Using the Baldrige Criteria for Performance Excellence and the Baldrige User's Guide by John Vinyard, I am confident that you, too, will better understand your organization and, in turn, better serve your stakeholders. And that's what continuous improvement is all about. Read on – you've found a great map.

Happy journeying! You're on the right track!

Dr. JoAnn Sternke
Superintendent of Schools
Pewaukee School District
Baldrige National Quality Award Recipient 2013

Business Foreword and

A Tribute to Don Chalmers

The Original Foreword by Don Chalmers for the previous (Sixth) Edition:

John Vinyard has helped Don Chalmers Ford develop systematic approaches to our quality systems. Through the 10 years we have been working with John our results have continued to go north and are performing well above our Benchmarks.

The introduction of the Baldrige Users Guide (BUG) over 5 years ago accelerated our ability to respond to the Baldrige Criteria and develop the appropriate systems and processes to beat our competition. This occurred during one of the worst recessions in our nation's history. We are able to build a more sustainable company by utilizing the Baldrige criteria and the BUG's blueprints for success.

The alignment to our culture is seamless and supports our core competency: The Don Chalmers Ford Experience Real Value (outcomes), Real People (our key stakeholders) and Real Simple (Processes).

I would recommend the BUG to any organization interested in pursuing their state or the Malcolm Baldrige National Quality Award.

Don Chalmers

Dealer Principal
Don Chalmers Ford
2008 & 2012 Baldrige site visited

Don passed away in 2014.

It was prophetic that he passed on Easter Day since many of his employees would refer to WWDD (What Would Don Do?). Similar to WWJD (What Would Jesus Do), WWDD meant do the right thing, no matter what!

This foreword was kept in the Seventh Edition of the Baldrige Users Guide as a tribute to a man who helped thousands of people during his lifetime.

In walking through his dealership everyone had a story about how Don impacted their life – and frequently their entire family's lives. These stories were not publicized or published, but were universal. In the years I had the privilege to work with Don, I saw him 'correct' many problems. He always corrected them with care and love for his coworkers, which made him the role model for servant leadership.

He believed the Baldrige Journey would help his organization and make it a better place to work as they provided an exceptional experience to customers.

He actually made me like a car dealer. **Thank you Don**

The **Baldrige Criteria for Performance Excellence (CPE)** model was created by Public Law 100-107, the Malcolm Baldrige National Quality Improvement Act, signed by President Reagan on August 20, 1987. The purpose of the legislation is to help improve the quality and productivity of American companies by promoting an awareness of performance excellence as an increasingly vital element in achieving a competitive edge.

According to Heaphy & Gruska (1995), "when the first set of Criteria was released in 1988, the intention was to get this material in the hands of industry leaders, university professors, government organizations, and others looking for guidance on defining the elements of total quality leadership...the government never intended to have thousands of companies applying for the Award, but rather to have them use the Criteria for self-improvement" (p. 20).

Millions of copies of the criteria have been distributed, and over 1,000 organizations have applied for recognition at the national level since the award was created. Additionally, many thousands of organizations have applied for their local or state awards as a stepping-stone to applying for the award at the national level. The award is managed by the Malcolm Baldrige National Quality Award (MBNQA) Office, under the National Institute of Standards and Technology (NIST), within the Department of Commerce.

To find out if this original objective was being met, several researchers inquired into how organizations are using the CPE model. According to Bemowski & Stratton (May 1995):

- 44% survey respondents said they used the criteria for *department-wide informal* self-assessment
- 41% said they used the criteria for *department-wide written* self-assessment
- 37% said they used the criteria for *company-wide written* self-assessment
- 35% said they used them for *company-wide informal* self-assessment
- **Only 24% of the respondents were using the CPE to apply for an award (p. 43)**

Knotts, Parrish, and Evans (1993) experienced similar results with a survey sent to the CEOs of Fortune 500 industrial and service firms and a survey sent to 120 small manufacturing and 120 small service firms. They found, overall, that:

- 44% of the respondents used the criteria for internal assessment
  - 88% of the Fortune 100 Industrial firms
  - 48% of the Fortune 101-500 industrial firms
  - 31% of the Fortune 500 Service firms
  - 17% of the small manufacturing firms
  - 8% of the small service firms

used the criteria as an internal assessment instrument (p. 50).

More recently, a study conducted by Booz Allen Hamilton (2003) found that "more than 70 percent of leaders surveyed among Fortune 1000 companies said they are likely to use the Criteria for Performance Excellence" (p. 3). Ultimately, the motivation to use the CPE model to improve organizational performance is based on the expectation of improved results.

Several researchers have investigated the impact of using the CPE model on organizational results including financial performance. Evans and Jack (2003) confirmed the linkage between system improvement and results. In addition, Hendricks and Singhal (1997) found that "overall, the results provide strong evidence that firms that have won quality awards outperform a control sample on operating income-based measures. Over a ten year period, starting six years before to three years after the year of winning the first quality award, the mean (median) change in the operating income for the test sample is

107% (48%) higher than that of the control sample (p. 1271)." More recently, Jacob et al. (2004) found that "award winners are more successful firms and are valued higher by investors. However, the award itself has not created value, since it did not create any value differences subsequent to the firms receiving the awards (p. 911)." These research findings, along with the financial and market results (levels, trends and comparisons) of the individual award recipients, support the conclusion that organizations that are **effectively** using the CPE model enjoy the associated benefits of improved financial performance.

Looking to the future, Thompson Reuters found that "65% of hospitals are likely to use the Baldrige Criteria for Performance Excellence as a systematic framework for performance improvement or as an internal assessment tool by 2018." Although they may not use the Baldrige Criteria itself, if they do not use the principles it embraces, they may not survive against those who do use those principles.

The use of the CPE to improve performance has increased worldwide. This has not only spread to additional sectors, such as education, healthcare, non-profit, and government organizations, but also has spread around the world. According to NIST, in the United States, there are 49 active CPE-based award programs in 41 states. In addition, approximately 79 award programs are located across the world. For example, in addition to the Deming Prize, there is a CPE-based award in Japan. Elements of the CPE are also used in the European Quality Award (EFQM) and Canadian Awards for Excellence (NIST 2004 Presentation). Given the growth in both the types of organizations and the geography, we conclude that the CPE have truly become a global benchmark, and the CPE have become accepted as a worldwide standard for performance excellence.

For example, some of the fastest growing, most profitable and largest companies in India are using the CPE as their basis for improvement. It is so pervasive in some corporations there, that if some of their division CEO's cannot score well on this scale, they are no longer allowed to use the corporate identity!

The definition of success for organizations of all types (profit seeking, non-profit, and government) is continuously changing and increasingly complex. From the mid 1940s to the 1970s the limited global competition allowed business leaders in the United States to focus mainly on financial results. The "party" ended sometime around 1980 when Xerox woke up to a situation where the Japanese were selling copiers in the US for what it was costing Xerox to make them (Kotter and Heskett, 1992).

During the 1980s quality became a key success factor and was directly linked to market and ultimately financial success. In the beginning many proposed that high quality was simply too expensive. However organizations eventually discovered that high quality resulted in reduced cost and increased market share or as Phillip Crosby wrote in a book by the same title - *Quality is Free*! As the service industry and in particular the knowledge worker industries increased in size and importance they discovered that talented passionate people are also a key to high quality and financial performance.

During the 1990s successful organizations became quite good at "connecting the dots" or as FedEx called it - "people, service, profit" (AMA 1991). The "bar" is being raised once again to include sustainable results in three key areas - financial, environmental, and societal or as Elkington, Emerson, and Beloe (2006) call it - the triple bottom line.

Recently, and looking into the future, Truvan (Previously Thompson Reuters) stated: "According the latest research, "65% of hospitals are likely to use the Baldrige Criteria for Performance Excellence as a systematic framework for performance improvement or as an internal assessment tool by 2018.

Clearly, financial results alone are not enough to ensure a successful (and sustainable) organization. This is one of the reasons the holistic view of an organization, represented by Baldrige is attractive to these visionary organizations.

The CPE Framework

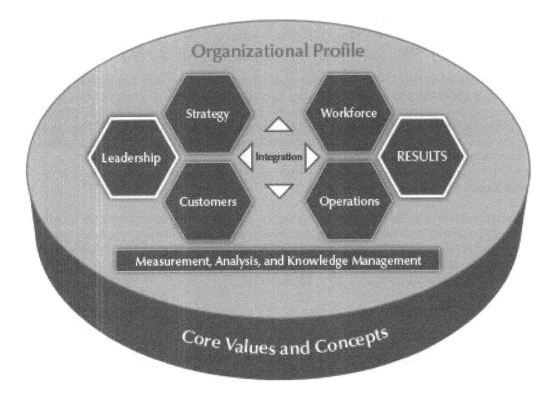

Source: NIST (2015 - 2016, p. 1)

The CPE framework, or "hamburger chart" as it is frequently called, provides a high-level or "category" view of the holistic nature of the CPE. Seven categories are shown in the diagram. Within these 7 categories and the organizational profile there are 40 areas to address. There are 5 areas to address in the Organizational Profile, 29 areas to address in the first six process categories and finally 8 areas to address in the results category.

This book is written to address the most detailed level of the criteria — the 42 Areas to Address.

This book is organized into five parts and is designed to help leaders and organization architects understand: (1) the fundamentals or key design concepts of performance excellence; (2) their organization's unique context as it relates to the design of organization systems and a comprehensive scorecard; (3) organization systems including strategic leadership, execution excellence and organizational learning and support systems; (4) the organization scorecard including comparisons to other world class organizations; and (5) the path to performance excellence including organization diagnosis, design, and transformation.

Part 1: Design Concepts

The first step in to understand the fundamentals of performance excellence. The design concepts are the underlying 11 core values and concepts of performance excellence. They are cross cutting through the organization's management systems and define performance excellence for the organization. It is possible that, in certain circumstances, not all design concepts are equally *relevant* and *important* to all organizations or management systems. Consequently, each organization should consciously examine and consider prioritizing the concepts based on their unique context and strategy prior to designing or redesigning the business systems.

Part 2: Organization Context

The key organizational factors establish the unique context of the specific organization. They help to determine what is **relevant** and **important** to the particular organization. This includes establishing the factors which will become the 'golden threads' of the organization, such as: employee groupings, customer groupings, external challenges, internal strengths, and other factors. The design principles (a.k.a. core values and concepts) are the key characteristics of high performing organizations and the desired characteristics of the management systems.

Part 3: Organization Systems

Performance excellence is achieved by focusing on the design of the organization as an interdependent grouping of large systems and the supporting processes, activities, and practices that make up the three essential competencies - strategic leadership, execution excellence, and organizational learning. Part 3 focuses on the 15 systems necessary to achieve and sustain performance excellence. Part 3 includes the 28 process areas to address that make up the 15 systems.

Part 4: Organization Scorecard

Part 4 addresses the comprehensive organization scorecard. This scorecard is composed of seven areas to address including products and services, operations, strategy implementation, customer-focus, workforce, governances, societal and environmental and financial and market results. The focus of this section is on the actual results including the current levels, trends and comparisons.

Each of the 42 area to address sections in Parts 2, 3 and 4 follow a similar pattern of:

- **Foundation** – What does the criteria mean, in plain English
- **Examples** – What have leading organizations done in this area
- **Questions** – The Baldrige Criteria
- **Worksheets** - If you can fill out these templates, you have written an application
- **Assessment** – Questions to ask if you want a quick look at your status
- **Blueprint** – The interrelationships between the Baldrige Criteria
- **System integration** – A description of the linkages
- **Thoughts for leaders** – Why leaders should care about or focus on this portion of the criteria

Each section begins with a **foundation** which is an introduction to the basics of the particular area to address. This is a common sense description of what the CPE questions in the particular area to address are asking.

Following the foundation, a mix of business, healthcare, and education **examples** are included to help "bring alive" the key elements of the particular areas to address. These tangible real world examples are included courtesy of the individual Baldrige Award recipients and other world-class organizations.

For the convenience of the reader, the actual **CPE questions** are presented verbatim. This is provided through the courtesy of:

- The Baldrige Performance Excellence Program, 2013. 2013–2014 Criteria for Performance Excellence. Gaithersburg, MD: U.S. Department of Commerce, National Institute of Standards and Technology.

"Fill-in-the-blank" **worksheets** are provided to help writers and assessors collect and organize information about the organization's context, systems, and scorecard. Completing these worksheets will help the writing team develop responses to the CPE in the form of an award application. After the team has filled in the worksheets, assessment questions are provided to help the team quickly "take the temperature" of the organization by providing a rough estimate score.

The **blueprints** provide a "visual version" of the CPE. These flowchart style diagrams depict the logic flow and relationships of the elements found in the particular area to address as well as linkages to other CPE areas to address (context, systems, and scorecard).

The **system integration** section supports the blueprints by describing the nature of the relationships (linkages) to other areas to address. This section provides descriptions of the linkages depicted in the blueprint and their relationships to other CPE areas (context, systems, and scorecard).

Thoughts for leaders are included for each section and typically use brief anecdotes to bring the concepts alive for the leaders of the organization. In some cases, they provide leaders a view of why this portion of the criteria should be important to them.

 ## FOUNDATION

Foundation – Each section begins with an introduction to the basics of the Area to Address. This is a common sense description of what the CPE in the particular Area to Address are trying to achieve. The introduction focuses on what the CPE actually mean and not just the questions in the CPE.

This focus will help new and experienced users gain a better understanding of the CPE, their background as well as their meaning.

 ## EXAMPLES

Example Key Context Factors, Systems, and Scorecards – A mix of business, healthcare, and education examples are included to help "bring alive" the key elements of the particular CPE Areas to Address. These tangible real world examples are included courtesy of the individual Baldrige Award recipients and other world-class organizations.

Typically these examples include graphics and descriptions of best practices from the contributing organizations.

CRITERIA QUESTIONS

CPE Questions - *The actual Malcolm Baldrige National Quality Award Criteria for Performance Excellence (CPE) is presented verbatim. Included are the actual questions and notes (explanations) from the CPE.*

This is provided through the courtesy of:

- The Baldrige Performance Excellence Program, National Institute of Standards and Technology (NIST), United States Department of Commerce, January 2015, Criteria for Performance Excellence, Gaithersburg, MD.

WORKSHEETS

Worksheets – The "fill-in-the-blank" worksheets help writers and assessors collect and organize information about the organization's key context factors, systems, and scorecard. Completing these worksheets will help the writing team develop responses to the criteria in the form of an award application. The worksheets are structured and aligned in a manner that will help the user understand the breadth and depth of what the CPE address.

The worksheets presented in the book are condensed to save space, but full-size editable (landscape) format worksheets are available on the CD-ROM included with this book in **unprotected** Microsoft Word files.

ASSESSMENT

Diagnostic Questions – These diagnostic questions help the organization quickly "take the temperature" of the organization by providing a rough estimate score.

This portion of the book can also be used as a survey across different groups to understand how they feel the organization is currently performing. A complete set of the questions is available in one file on the CD-ROM.

BLUEPRINT

Blueprints – The blueprints provide a "visual version" of the particular CPE area to address. These flowchart diagrams depict the logic flow and relationships of the components found in the particular area to address as well as linkages to other areas to address (context, systems, and scorecard).

 SYSTEM INTEGRATION

System Integration (a.k.a. Linkages) – The system integration sections support the blueprints by describing the nature of the relationships and linkages to other areas to address. This section provides descriptions of the linkages depicted in the blueprint and their relationships to other CPE context a.k.a. key factors, system of processes, and the results.

 THOUGHTS FOR LEADERS

Thoughts for Leaders - Thoughts for leaders are included for each Area to Address and typically include a brief anecdote to bring the concepts alive for the leaders of the organization. In some cases, they provide leaders a view of why this portion of the CPE should be important to them.

Regardless of whether an organization is working toward an award or simply interested in improving performance, 7 Categories (plus the Organizational Profile = 8 sections), 17 Items (plus the Organizational Profile =19) and the 41 sections (Areas to Address) on the CPE model are the basis for organization diagnosis (self-assessment), design (planning for improvement), and transformation (successful implementation) described in Part 5.

Part 5 – The Path to Performance Excellence

Reading the criteria can be challenging; many people have difficulty understanding what all the elements mean on their first (or 10th?) reading. For those who become Baldrige Examiners, the criteria often "come alive" in their third year as an examiner. In that third year, the flow becomes clearer, the linkages make more sense, and the overall process is more evident. Many people and organizations, however, do not have three years to study and wait. Organizations entering this process need tools that can help them understand the CPE model and process quickly. Part 5 is focused on making the process of understanding, diagnosing, designing (and redesigning) and transformation using the CPE easier.

The path to performance excellence is one of learning. This is true for both the organization and every individual in the organization including leaders. Ford and Evans (2001) and Latham (1997) found that the CPE self-assessment and improvement cycle is essentially an organizational learning cycle.

There are no "silver bullets" or quick fixes to achieving performance excellence for any organization. Part 5 discusses how to conduct a self-assessment (diagnosis) of the organization's processes and results, redesign the systems and processes using a design studio approach and framework, and lead the transformation to successfully implement the new designs. The diagnosis chapter describes a process for developing a written application for either an award process evaluation or an internal or third party evaluation. The design chapter describes a three phase approach (discovery, diagnosis, and design) and framework to design or redesign the management systems. The transformation chapter describes the implementation of the new designs to transform the organization.

The learning cannot be delegated to the quality or performance excellence department, consultants, or middle management. While senior leaders do not need to be 'experts' in the criteria, they must be able to read it, ask questions, and lead the learning in order for the organization to achieve and sustain performance excellence.

What organization characteristics are most important to the future success of your organization? The design concepts are the underlying core values and concepts of performance excellence. They are cross cutting through the organization's management systems and define performance excellence for the organization. It is possible that, in certain circumstances, not all design concepts are equally *relevant* and *important* to all organizations or management systems. Consequently, each organization should consciously examine and consider prioritizing the concepts based on their unique context and strategy prior to designing or redesigning the business systems.

The performance excellence system is based on 11 core values and concepts. Think of these values as design concepts or the desired characteristics of the systems and processes identified. While Collins (2001) limited, for practical reasons, the definition of "great" to financial performance, specifically sustained stock price improvement, the performance excellence model proposes a more comprehensive definition that includes creating value for multiple stakeholders. A great or **excellent** company, according to the performance excellence model, demonstrates the 11 characteristics found in the table below.

Design Concepts

Good Performance	Performance Excellence
1. Directive Leadership	1. Visionary Leadership
2. Product/Service-Driven	2. Customer-Focused Excellence
3. Meet Standards or "*status quo*"	3. Organizational Learning & Agility
4. Suppliers and Unions as Adversaries	4. Valuing People
5. Respond in Time Allotted	5. Managing for Innovation
6. Focus on Next Quarter's Results	6. Focus on Success
7. Employees Follow Procedures	7. Ethics & Transparency
8. Management by Intuition	8. Management by Fact
9. Compliance with Regulation	9. Societal Responsibility
10. Focus on $ "*bottom-line*" Exclusively	10. Delivering Value & Results
11. Functional Perspective	11. Systems Perspective

A key point to keep in mind is that the characteristics of an **excellent** organization do not necessarily replace those of a **good** organization. Rather, many of them build upon the good characteristics and, in some cases, transform them. While the CPE model proposes that all 11 core values and concepts are important, it is possible that some of these concepts might be more important than others depending on the organization's situation and vision.

While the concepts can apply to all parts of the system, some concepts seem to be more applicable to certain areas than others. The design concepts are integrated through each of the three competencies of performance excellence:

- Strategic Leadership
- Execution Excellence
- Organizational Learning

In Strategic Leadership, an organization must have visionary leaders who can focus on the future as well as the present. Within that visionary leadership, leaders must understand the integrated systems of the company and show a responsibility for social issues.

Within Execution Excellence, the organization's overall performance must be driven by what customers need, expect, and are willing to pay for. This drive is found in employees who are agile and focused on the results customers expect.

Lastly, Organizational Learning cycles need to be driven from organizational and personal learning, managing by fact, and innovation to create competitive advantage. The linkages to each competency are described in the individual sections on each principle.

Visionary Leadership

While directive and transactional leadership can achieve high performance in a good organization, transformational leadership sustains high performance in an excellent organization. According to Bass (1990), however, transformational leadership augments and is compatible and complementary with transactional leadership (p. 220). Later in this section we discuss how leaders must focus not only on running the business but also changing the business, although these two roles often call for different leadership styles.

Visionary Leadership – CPE Core Value

Your organization's senior leaders should set a vision for the organization, create a customer focus, demonstrate clear and visible organizational values and ethics, and set high expectations for the workforce. The vision, values, and expectations should balance the needs of all your stakeholders. Your leaders should also ensure the creation of strategies, systems, and methods for achieving performance excellence, stimulating innovation, building knowledge and capabilities, and ensuring organizational sustainability.

The values and strategies leaders define should help guide all of your organization's activities and decisions. Senior leaders should inspire and encourage your entire workforce to contribute, to develop and learn, to be innovative, and to embrace meaningful change. Senior leaders should be responsible to your organization's governance body for their actions and performance, and the governance body should be responsible ultimately to all your stakeholders for your organization's and its senior leaders' ethics, actions, and performance.

Senior leaders should serve as role models through their ethical behavior and their personal involvement in planning, providing a supportive environment for taking intelligent risks, communicating, coaching and motivating the workforce, developing future leaders, reviewing organizational performance, and recognizing workforce members. As role models, they can reinforce ethics, values, and expectations while building leadership, commitment, and initiative throughout your organization.

NIST (2015 - 2016) p. 39

Visionary Leadership - *Application to System Design*

The corner stone of strategic leadership is visionary leadership, leadership that looks beyond the present toward a vision of the future and develops the employees and the organization to achieve that vision. This leadership is an integral part of setting direction and establishing values and creating a culture in Item 1.1, developing a clear and achievable strategy in Item 2.1, and creating a customer focus based on segmentation and customer and market knowledge in Item 3.1. Evans and Ford (1997) found that the leadership value had a high or medium importance to two categories - leadership and strategic planning. Their findings support the notion that this value is more important to strategic leadership than the other competencies (p. 26).

Visionary leadership needs to permeate all levels of the organization in order to transform the organization. In short, there must be leaders at all levels. It is one thing for the organization to have a vision and quite another for the organization to work toward that vision at all levels in the organization. Visionary leadership is an integral part of employee development in Item 5.2c, the workplace in Item 5.1, process management and improvement in Item 6.2, and improved customer relationships in Item 3.2. In Item 1.1, where the criteria asks for a *Leadership System*, this system needs to be usable by all leaders at all levels.

Visionary leadership sets the agenda for learning. While all learning might be good in general, the direction and priorities set by visionary leaders help to establish the priorities for measurement, analysis, knowledge, and learning, which are all key parts of Category 4 (Measurement, Analysis, and Knowledge Management) as well as Category 7 (Results).

Customer-Focused Excellence

Good organizations focus on creating and delivering high quality products and services. Excellent organizations focus on creating and delivering products and services that the customers want, and more importantly, are willing to pay for. The customer excellence movement has been around in the United States for more than 25 years.

In the years following World War II, it was fairly easy to be successful in running a business in the United States. The economy was booming, there was little competition from overseas, and the demand for goods and services was greater than the supply. This environment, however, led to two problems for American business: (1) hubris reinforced by success and (2) a general lack of appreciation or caring for the customers. Eventually, the hubris of American corporations allowed other companies around the world to catch up and surpass them, not only in quality but also in price. Many American businesses had taken for granted the customers and their willingness to buy most anything.

Customer-driven excellence is not just another business concept; it is a necessity for business success. All organizations have customers even if they sometimes call them by different names such as patients, families, students, parents, or simply primary beneficiaries. The CPE model is based on the assumption that the organization exists to serve some group of people or another organization.

It does not matter whether the customers actually pay for the services directly. What does matter is that excellence is defined by the customers, and, if the customer is not satisfied (or even better – if they are not engaged) the customer's use of your product of services will be shifted to another organization (i.e., to one of your competitors).

Customer-Focused Excellence – CPE Core Value

Your customers are the ultimate judges of performance and quality. Thus, your organization must take into account all product and service features and characteristics and all modes of customer access and support that contribute value to your customers. Such behavior leads to customer acquisition, satisfaction, preference, and loyalty; positive referrals; and, ultimately, the sustainability of your business. Customer-driven excellence has both current and future components: understanding today's customer desires and anticipating future customer desires and marketplace potential.

Many factors may influence value and satisfaction over the course of your customers' experience with your organization. These factors include your organization's customer relationship management, which helps build trust, confidence, and loyalty. Customer-driven excellence means much more than reducing defects and errors, merely meeting specifications, or reducing complaints. Nevertheless, these factors contribute to your customers' view of your organization and thus are also important parts of customer-driven excellence. In addition, your success in recovering from defects, service errors, and mistakes is crucial for retaining customers and engaging them for the long term.

A customer-driven organization addresses not only the product and service characteristics that meet basic customer requirements but also those features and characteristics that differentiate the organization from competitors. This differentiation may be based on innovative offerings, combinations of product and service offerings, customized offerings, multiple access and outward communication mechanisms, rapid response, or special relationships.

Customer-driven excellence is thus a strategic concept. It is directed toward customer retention and loyalty, market share gain, and growth. It demands constant sensitivity to changing and emerging customer and market requirements and to the factors that drive customer engagement. It demands close attention to the voice of the customer. It demands anticipating changes in the marketplace. Therefore, customer-driven excellence demands a customer-focused culture and organizational agility.

NIST (2015 - 2016) pp. 39 - 40

Customer-Focused Excellence - *Application to System Design*

Not surprisingly, Evans and Ford (1997) found that **customer-driven quality**, as it was called in 1996, was of high or medium importance to four categories, including Customer, Strategy, Operations, and Measurement, Analysis, and Knowledge Management (p. 26).

Customer-driven excellence is both an input to strategy development and an output in the form of strategic objectives (Items 2.1 and 2.2). It is also central to setting direction and priorities in Item 1.1. Finally, there is an obvious direct connection with customer and market knowledge (Item 3.1).

Customer-driven excellence is central to the design, execution, and measurement of the design of work systems and processes (Items 6.1 and 6.2). In addition, the development of the people that serve the customers (Item 5.2c) should include any appropriate customer service training. Finally, customer-driven quality is an integral part of the customer relationship management approach (Item 3.2).

Customer-driven excellence is one of several topics included in the measurement and analysis approaches described in Item 4.1 and in Item 3.1. In addition, Item 4.2 addresses how knowledge is transferred to and from stakeholders, including the customers. Results on how well the organization is doing from a customer's perspective are addressed in Items 7.1 and 7.2.

Customer-driven excellence is threaded throughout all categories of the performance excellence model and should be integrated into the design of the approaches that address these areas.

Organizational Learning and Agility

Good organizations meet standards. Excellent organizations continuously learn and improve. This concept is woven throughout the various components of the CEP including the context or profile, the process and results Items and the maturity models (scoring system). The organization that can learn fastest will achieve and sustain a competitive advantage. Using the CPE model to assess and improve is part of this learning process (Ford & Evans 2001; Latham 1997).

Organizational Learning & Agility - CPE Core Value

Success in today's ever-changing, globally competitive environment demands continual organizational learning and agility. Agility requires a capacity for rapid change and for flexibility in operations. Organizations face ever-shorter cycles for introducing new or improved products and
services, and nonprofit and government organizations are increasingly being asked to respond rapidly to new or emerging social issues. Disruptive events are occurring more frequently. They can be triggered by innovative technologies or product introductions, economic upheaval or stress, major weather events, or social or societal demands. Organizations must be capable of making transformational changes on an ever-shorter cycle time. Major improvements in response times often require new work systems, the simplification of work processes, or the ability for rapid changeover from one process or one location to another. A cross-trained and empowered workforce and effective management of up-to-date organizational knowledge are vital assets in such a demanding environment.

Organizational learning includes both continuous improvement of existing approaches and significant change or innovation, leading to new goals, approaches, products, and markets.

Learning needs to be embedded in the way your organization operates. This means that learning (1) is a regular part of daily work; (2) results in solving problems at their source (root cause); (3) is focused on building and sharing
knowledge throughout your organization; and (4) is driven by opportunities to effect significant, meaningful change and to innovate. Sources for learning include employees' and volunteers' ideas, research and development, customers' input, best-practice sharing, competitors' performance, and benchmarking.

Organizational learning can result in (1) enhanced value to customers through new and improved products and customer services; (2) the development of new business opportunities; (3) the development of new and improved processes or business models; (4) reduced errors, defects, waste, and related costs; (5) improved responsiveness and cycle-time performance; (6) increased productivity and effectiveness in the use of all your resources; (7) enhanced performance in fulfilling your organization's societal responsibilities; and (8) greater agility in managing change and disruption.

A major success factor in meeting competitive challenges
is design-to-introduction time (the time it takes to initiate a product or service feature) or innovation cycle time. To meet the demands of rapidly changing markets, your organization needs to carry out stage-to-stage integration of activities from research or concept to commercialization or implementation.

All aspects of time performance are now more critical, and cycle time is a key process measure. Other important benefits can be derived from this focus on time; time improvements often drive simultaneous improvements or changes in your work systems, organization, quality, cost, supply-chain integration, productivity, and ongoing success in a challenging economy.

> Organizational learning and agility can also be achieved through strategic partnerships or alliances, which might offer complementary core competencies that allow entry into new markets or a basis for new products or services. Partnerships might also permit you to address common issues by blending your organization's core competencies or leadership capabilities with partners' complementary strengths and capabilities, creating a new source of strategic advantage.
>
> NIST (2015 - 2016) pp. 40 - 41

Organizational Learning and Agility - *Application to System Design*

Both the leadership system (Item 1.1) and the strategy development and deployment system (Items 2.1 and 2.2) are learning cycles. Inputs are gathered, plans and directions are developed and determined, action plans are executed, performance reviews are conducted to study progress, actions are either validated or refined, and the cycle begins again. Item 3.1 Voice of the Customer is designed to support not only the strategic leadership processes but also the execution excellence processes.

It is interesting that the connection between learning and strategy development and deployment was not identified by the participants in the Evans and Ford (1997) study. They found the importance of the continuous improvement value, as it was called in 1996, of high or medium importance to four categories, including Customer and Market Focus; Process Management; Measurement, Analysis, and Knowledge Management; and Human Resource Management (p. 26).

Learning is also a key element of the approaches to people and process. As the title suggests, there is a direct connection with area to address 5.2c Workforce and Leader Development. Improvement of the work processes is explicitly called for are to address 6.2b.

It might seem obvious, but there is also a direct connection with the organizational learning competency. The measurement, analysis, and knowledge management all directly support organizational and personal learning.

Valuing People

Good organizations manage their suppliers, partner relationships, and employees to ensure adequate performance. Unfortunately, this management often is accomplished through an adversarial relationships with suppliers and unions. This approach, coupled with a short-term focus, results in suppliers that often offer the lowest prices but fail to provide the lowest overall cost of ownership. Deming (1986) proposed that this approach to suppliers was actually more expensive (pp. 35 – 44). When suppliers are constantly squeezed on price, they do not have the extra resources to spend on improvement.

In particular, improvement that would help an organization to achieve their strategic objectives. Heskett, Sasser, and Schlesinger (1997) link the loyalty, satisfaction, and capability of employees with the value created for the customer and customer satisfaction and, in turn, revenue growth and profitability. They term this linkage the "Service Profit Chain" (p. 12). The conclusion, improving employee satisfaction, loyalty, and capability are not only the right things to do, but also the profitable things to do.

Valuing People - CPE Core Value

An organization's success depends on an engaged workforce that benefits from meaningful work, clear organizational direction, the opportunity to learn, and accountability for performance. That engaged workforce must also have a safe, trusting, and cooperative environment. The successful organization has a culture of inclusion that capitalizes on the diverse backgrounds, knowledge, skills, creativity, and motivation of its workforce and partners. Such an organization values all people who have a stake in the organization, including customers, community members, stockholders, and other people affected by the organization's actions.

Valuing the people in your workforce means committing to their engagement, development, and well-being. Increasingly, this may involve offering flexible work practices that are tailored to varying workplace and home life needs. Major challenges in valuing your workforce members include (1) demonstrating your leaders' commitment to their success, (2) providing motivation and recognition that go beyond the regular compensation system, (3) offering development and progression within your organization, (4) sharing your organization's knowledge so that your workforce can better serve your customers and contribute to achieving your strategic objectives, (5) creating an environment that encourages intelligent risk taking to achieve innovation, (6) developing a system of workforce and organizational accountability for performance, and (7) creating an inclusive environment for a diverse workforce.

The success of your workforce members—including your leaders—depends on their having opportunities to learn. This learning includes preparing people for future organizational core competencies. On-the-job training offers a cost-effective way to cross-train and to link training more closely to your organization's capacity needs and priorities. If your organization relies on volunteers, their personal development and learning are also important to consider.

To accomplish their overall goals, successful organizations build internal and external partnerships with people and with other organizations. Internal partnerships might include cooperation between labor and management. Forming internal partnerships might also involve creating network relationships among people across work units and locations or between employees and volunteers to improve flexibility, responsiveness, and knowledge sharing.

External partnerships might be with customers, suppliers, and education or community organizations. All of these people can contribute to your organization's ongoing success.

NIST (2015 - 2016) p. 40

Valuing People - Application to System Design

One of the better examples of a company that lives this value is FedEx. FedEx focuses on what they call their People, Service, Profit philosophy (PSP). This philosophy permeates all aspects of the organziation. As their founder, Fred Smith says, "Customer satisfaction begins with employee satisfaction" (AMA, 1991, p. 15).

Valuing employees and partners starts with the direction set by the leadership and the values of the organization (Item 1.1). In addition, the strategy development and deployment can incorporate this value in two ways (Items 2.1 and 2.2). First, employee and partner input can be used to develop strategy. Second, the strategic objectives and action plans should include goals that address employees and partners.

There is a direct connection between valuing employees and the Workforce Focus Items 5.1 and 5.2. In addition, the work processes should be designed to leverage the capabilities of the people and partners and to create value for the people and partners. Evans and Ford (1997) found that the importance of the employee participation and partnership development value, as it was called in 1996, was of high importance to the human resource focus category and of medium importance to the process management category (p. 26).

The main connection between valuing employees and partners is what the organization learns about employees and partners. In other words, the measurement and analysis system needs to include both employee and partner measures. The result is a better understanding of their capabilities and requirements in both planning and execution.

Managing for Innovation

In good organizations, employees follow procedures. In excellent organizations, employees not only follow procedures but they also look for new and innovative ways to accomplish the work. In some cases, these innovations result in new procedures. Following procedures is expected in order to control work processes and achieve predicted results, particularly in situations such as aviation, space, nuclear power, etc., where disasters and loss of life can occur when procedures are not followed. However, by themselves, procedures are insufficient to achieve and sustain performance excellence and a competitive advantage. Innovation goes beyond fact-based analysis and the scientific method. An innovation is a new way of doing something, a new product or service, a new way of delivering a product or service, or a new feature or function. Innovation requires creativity.

Drucker (1985) proposed that "systematic innovation means monitoring *seven sources* for innovative opportunity" (p. 35). Four of these sources are inside or close to the organization, including: (1) the unexpected (success, failure, outside event); (2) incongruities (reality vs. what it is assumed to be or ought to be); (3) process need; and (4) changes in market industry structure. The other three sources are external to the organization and are more global in nature, such as: (5) demographic changes; (6) changes in perceptions, moods, etc.; and (7) new knowledge (p. 35). The key question is how the monitoring of these seven sources is integrated into the three competencies of strategic leadership, execution excellence, and organizational learning.

Managing for Innovation - CPE Core Value

Innovation means making meaningful change to improve your organization's products, services, programs, processes, operations, and business model, with the purpose of creating new value for stakeholders. Innovation should lead your organization to new dimensions of performance. Innovation requires a supportive environment, a process for identifying strategic opportunities, and the pursuit of intelligent risks.

Innovation is no longer strictly the purview of research and development departments; innovation is important for all aspects of your operations and all work systems and work processes. Your organization should be led and managed so that taking intelligent risks becomes part of the learning culture. Innovation should be integrated into daily work and be supported by your performance improvement system. Systematic processes for identifying strategic opportunities should reach across your entire organization.

Innovation may arise from adapting innovations in other industries to achieve a breakthrough in your industry. It builds on the accumulated knowledge of your organization and its people and the innovations of competitors. It may involve collaboration among people who do not normally work together and are in different parts of the organization. Therefore, the ability to rapidly disseminate and capitalize on new and accumulated knowledge is critical to driving organizational innovation.

NIST (2015 - 2016) p. 42

Managing for Innovation - Application to System Design

The connection to strategic leadership lies in two key areas - the environment that leadership creates and the strategy that is developed. The approach to leadership and creating an environment for innovation is addressed in Item 1.1. The strategy needs to include innovations to products, service, and operations that touch the customer in order to achieve and maintain a competitive advantage (Item 2.1). Several of the sources of innovation that Drucker (1985) identifies can be integrated into the strategy development process during the SWOT analysis, including changes in market industry structure; demographic changes; changes in perceptions, moods, etc.; and new knowledge.

Innovation is directly related to work process improvement (area to address 6.2b). Sources to consider adding to your improvement process include unexpected successes and failures, incongruity, processes needs, and new knowledge.

The measurement, analysis, and knowledge management approaches all should ideally support an environment for innovation. An environment of fear will inhibit innovation. Thus, it is important to design the organization performance review process in a way that creates a supportive environment.

Focus on Success

While good organizations focus on running the business, excellent organizations focus on both **running** the business and **changing** the business. This concept requires leaders at all levels to allocate their time between running the organization (execution) and improving the organization (changing the business). Imai (1986) proposes that the amount of time allocated to changing the business increases as an individual moves from front line worker to top management (p. 5). Workers spend the majority of their time on execution and a small percentage of their time on improvement. Supervisors spend less time than workers on execution and more time on improvement. This trend continues to the most senior leaders who spend most of their time on changing the business and only a small percentage of their time on execution. However, the ability to do both - run the business and change the business - is central to achieving and sustaining high levels of performance and competitive advantage.

Focus on Success - CPE Core Value

Ensuring your organization's success now and in the future requires an understanding of the short- and longer-term factors that affect your organization and its marketplace. Ensuring this ongoing success requires managing uncertainty in the environment, as well as balancing some stakeholders' short-term demands with the organization's and stakeholders' needs to invest in long-term success. The pursuit of sustained growth and performance leadership requires a strong future orientation and a willingness to make long-term commitments to key stakeholders—your customers, workforce, suppliers, partners, and stockholders; the public; and the community. It also requires the agility to modify plans when circumstances warrant.

Your organization's planning and resource allocation should anticipate many factors, such as customers' short- and long-term expectations; new business and partnering opportunities; potential crises, including changing economic conditions; workforce capacity and capability needs; the competitive global marketplace; technological developments; changes in customer and market segments; new business models; evolving regulatory requirements; changes in community and societal expectations and needs; and strategic moves by competitors. Your strategic objectives and resource allocations need to accommodate these influences. A focus on success includes developing your leaders, workforce, and suppliers; accomplishing effective succession planning; creating a supportive environment for taking intelligent risks and encouraging innovation; and anticipating societal responsibilities and concerns.

NIST (2015 - 2016) pp. 39 - 42

Focus on Success - Application to System Design

Clarke American is a Baldrige recipient who has *threaded* the dual concept of run the business and change the business throughout their processes and scorecard. This concept is designed into the processes from strategy development to the scorecard and results.

The future is an integral part of setting direction in Item 1.1, developing strategy in Item 2.1, and understanding the needs, wants, and desires of potential customers in Items 3.1 and 3.2. Evans and Ford (1997) found that **long-range view**, as it was called in 1996, was of medium importance to the strategic

planning category although it was of low importance to all other categories. This finding supports the notion that long-range view is important to strategic leadership (p. 26).

Focus on the future and a balance of short- and long-term objectives is essential to the continuous improvement of processes and the development of people. Focus on the future is an integral part of acquiring people in Item 5.1a, developing them in Item 5.2c, and ensuring their well being in Item 5.1b. In addition, Item 6.2b asks how processes are improved.

Focus on the future is not as directly linked to organizational learning as it is strategic leadership and execution excellence. However, the measurements and the analysis of the data do need to be forward looking in order for it to support a fact-based approach to setting direction and developing plans for the future.

The organization needs to be able to forecast their own performance, but they also need to forecast the performance of key competitors to ensure that their plans will help them achieve and sustain a competitive advantage.

Ethics and Transparency

While good organizations comply with the laws and regulations designed to protect the public, the environment, etc., excellent organizations go beyond mere compliance and focus on being good corporate citizens. The CPE model proposes that you cannot be a high performing organization if you ignore the environment, conduct business in an unethical manner, or put the public at risk. High performance organizations figure out how to serve their customers in a way that is socially responsible and profitable.

While being a good corporate citizen might not ensure success, being a bad corporate citizen will ensure failure.

The Glossary includes a Wikipedia© definition of Corporate Transparency.

Ethics & Transparency - CPE Core Value

Your organization should stress ethical behavior in all stakeholder transactions and interactions. Your organization's governance body should require highly ethical conduct and monitor all conduct accordingly. Your senior leaders should be role models of ethical behavior and make their expectations of the workforce very clear.

Your organization's ethical principles are the foundation for your culture and values. They distinguish right from wrong. Clearly articulated ethical principles, along with your organizational values, empower your people to make effective decisions and may serve as boundary conditions for determining organizational norms and prohibitions.

Transparency is characterized by consistently candid and open communication on the part of leadership and management and by the sharing of clear and accurate information. The benefits of transparency are manifold. Transparency is
a key factor in workforce engagement and allows people to see why actions are being taken and how they can contribute. Transparency also is important in interactions with customers and other stakeholders, giving them a sense of involvement, engagement, and confidence in your organization.

Ethical behavior and transparency build trust in the organization and a belief in its fairness and integrity that is valued by all key stakeholders.

NIST (2015 - 2016) p. 43

Ethics and Transparency - Application to System Design

Ethics and Transparency is an integral and specific part of Item 1.2. Ideally, it is addressed by the strategic management system (Items 2.1 and 2.2) as not only part of the strategic objectives but also an integral part of achieving the strategic objectives. Evans and Ford (1997) found that **corporate responsibility**, as it was called in 1996, was of medium importance to the leadership category although it was of low importance to all other categories. It would be interesting to see the survey results if it were repeated today. The notion that this value, corporate responsibility, is most important to the strategic leadership competency is supported by the findings (p. 26).

Ethics and Transparency is an integral part of acquiring and developing people (Items 5.1 and 5.2). In addition, the approaches to motivation, incentives, and compensation should be consistent with and encourage socially responsible behavior. Value creation and support processes should be designed in a way that will be environmentally safe and ethical while avoiding putting the public at risk.

The linkage with organizational learning is primarily focused on the measurement and analysis of key areas of social responsibility including ethical behavior, environmental performance, community involvement, and public safety. Learning in these areas supports continuous improvement in these areas.

Management by Fact

Good organizations have smart people who manage by intuition. Excellent organizations have smart people who manage by intuition "turbo-charged" with facts. The model does not pretend that an organization can ever have perfect knowledge, but it does assume that the more an organization knows about key variables and relationships the more prepared the organization is to identify leverage points and set priorities that will have the greatest impact on overall organizational success.

Management by Fact - CPE Core Value

Management by fact requires you to measure and analyze your organization's performance, both inside the organization and in your competitive environment. Measurements should derive from business needs and strategy, and they should provide critical data and information about key processes, outputs, results, outcomes, and competitor and industry performance. Organizations need many types of data and information to effectively manage their performance. Data and information may come in many forms, such as numerical, graphical, or qualitative, and from many sources, including internal processes, surveys, and social media. Performance measurement should include measurement of customer, product, and process performance; comparisons of operational, market, and competitive performance; supplier, workforce, partner, cost, and financial performance; governance and compliance results; and accomplishment of strategic objectives.

A major consideration in performance improvement and change management is the selection and use of performance measures or indicators. The measures or indicators you select should best represent the factors that lead to improved customer, operational, financial, and societal performance. A comprehensive yet carefully culled set of measures or indicators tied to customer and organizational performance requirements provides a clear basis for aligning all processes with your organization's goals. You may need measures and indicators to support you in making decisions in a rapidly changing environment. By analyzing data from your tracking processes, you can evaluate the measures or indicators themselves and change them to better support your goals.

Analysis means extracting larger meaning from data and information to support evaluation, decision making, improvement, and innovation. It entails using data to determine trends, projections, and cause-and-effect relationships that might not otherwise be evident. Analysis supports a variety of purposes, such as planning, reviewing your overall performance, improving operations, managing change, and comparing your performance with competitors' or with best practice benchmarks. To facilitate analysis, data may need to be aggregated from various sources. Data may also need to be segmented by, for example, markets, product lines, and workforce groups to gain deeper understanding.

NIST (2015 - 2016) p. 42

Management by Fact - Application to System Design

This design concept is common to most elements in the CPE model. Consequently, it is not surprising that Evans and Ford (1997) found that the importance of **management by fact** was high or medium for five categories, including Measurement, Analysis, and Knowledge Management; Strategic Planning; Customer and Market Focus; Process Management; and Human Resource Focus (p. 26).

The connection to strategic leadership is fact-based strategy (Item 2.1). The assumption here is that strategy based on solid evidence and facts from the market and the organization is better than a strategy that is based solely on intuition. Again, the CPE model does not assume that strategy can be mechanized to the point where human involvement is not important. Human intuition and creativity are key elements of strategy development. The model does assume that creative humans with strong intuition will be better prepared to develop strategy when armed with facts.

Fact-based management is important to both the people processes and the work processes. The effectiveness of attracting, acquiring, developing, and retaining employees is increased when the systems are designed and managed using fact v. myth. The same is true for the design, management, and improvement of work processes (Item 6.2).

Without facts, learning cannot take place. Both quantitative and qualitative facts are essential for a valid scientific method or learning cycle. While we have not yet achieved a completely valid, accurate, and unbiased measurement of social science issues, such as those associated with organizations, the goal here is to obtain the most valid, least biased, most accurate information economically possible.

Societal Responsibility

While good organizations comply with the laws and regulations designed to protect the public, the environment, etc., excellent organizations go beyond mere compliance and focus on being good corporate citizens. The CPE model proposes that you cannot be a high performing organization if you ignore the environment, conduct business in an unethical manner, or put the public at risk. High performance organizations figure out how to serve their customers in a way that is socially responsible and profitable. While being a good corporate citizen might not ensure success, being a bad citizen will ensure failure.

Societal Responsibility - CPE Core Value

Your organization's leaders should stress responsibilities to the public and the consideration of societal well-being and benefit. Leaders should be role models for your organization and its workforce in the protection of public health, safety, and the environment. This protection applies to any impact of your organization's operations, as well as the life cycles of your products. Also, your organization should emphasize resource conservation and waste reduction at the source. Planning should anticipate adverse impacts from the production, distribution, transportation, use, and disposal of your products. Effective planning should reduce or prevent problems; provide for a forthright response if problems occur; and make available the information and support needed to maintain public awareness, safety, and confidence.

Your organization should meet all local, state, and federal laws and regulatory requirements and should also treat these and related requirements as opportunities to excel beyond minimal compliance. Considering societal wellbeing and benefit means leading and supporting—within the limits of your resources—the environmental, social, and economic systems in your organization's sphere of influence. Such leadership and support might include improving education, health care, and other services in your community; pursuing environmental excellence; being a role model for socially important issues; practicing resource conservation; reducing your carbon footprint; performing community service and charity; improving industry and business practices; and sharing nonproprietary information. For a role-model organization, leadership also entails influencing other organizations, private and public, to partner for these purposes.

Managing societal responsibilities requires your organization to use appropriate measures and your leaders to assume responsibility for those measures.

NIST (2015 - 2016) pp. 42 - 43

Societal Responsibility - Application to System Design

Social responsibility is an integral and specific part of Item 1.2. Ideally, it is addressed by the strategic management system (Items 2.1 and 2.2) as not only part of the strategic objectives but also an integral part of achieving the strategic objectives. Evans and Ford (1997) found that **corporate responsibility**, as it was called in 1996, was of medium importance to the leadership category although it was of low importance to all other categories. It would be interesting to see the survey results if it were repeated today. The notion that this value, corporate responsibility, is most important to the strategic leadership competency is supported by the findings (p. 26).

Social responsibility is an integral part of acquiring and developing people (Items 5.1 and 5.2). In addition, the approaches to motivation, incentives, and compensation should be consistent with and encourage socially responsible behavior. Value creation and support processes should be designed in a way that will be environmentally safe and ethical while avoiding putting the public at risk.

The linkage with organizational learning is primarily focused on the measurement and analysis of key areas of social responsibility including ethical behavior, environmental performance, community involvement, and public safety. Learning in these areas supports continuous improvement in these areas.

Delivering Value & Results

Good organizations focus on the bottom line. High performing organizations focus on creating value for multiple stakeholders. While financial performance may be the "life blood" of the organization, it is not the only reason for its existence. Organizations exist to serve the needs of multiple stakeholders. The CPE model focuses on the systems perspective and the natural linkages between the stakeholders. Highly qualified, passionate employees serve loyal customers who keep coming back and bringing their friends. The result is revenue growth and profitability, making for satisfied investors. This approach does not assume a "zero sum game" where scarce resources are allocated among the stakeholders. Rather, it assumes a system that generates increasing value for all stakeholders.

The measurement of value for multiple stakeholders is specified in the results category, which is broken into six components collectively representing the interests of various stakeholders. Kaplan and Norton (1996) propose a four-perspective scorecard that they have termed a "Balanced Scorecard." This scorecard includes financial, business process, learning and growth, and customer results. The CPE scorecard addresses seven perspectives (a.k.a. results areas to address). The seven perspectives included in the CPE scorecard include three of the Kaplan and Norton perspectives of financial, process (operations), and customer. The CPE scorecard also explicitly addresses human resources, product and service outcomes (predictors of customers satisfaction), and leadership and social responsibility. The CPE scorecard actually incorporates the Kaplan and Norton learning and growth perspective into all seven perspectives by focusing on not only the level of performance but also the trend.

Delivering Value & Results – CPE Core Value

Results should be used By delivering value to key stakeholders, your organization builds loyalty, contributes to growing the economy, and contributes to society. To meet the sometimes conflicting and changing aims that balancing value implies, your organizational strategy should explicitly include key stakeholder requirements. This will help ensure that plans and actions meet differing stakeholder needs and avoid adverse impacts on any stakeholders. A balanced composite of leading and lagging performance measures is an effective means to communicate short- and longer-term priorities, monitor actual performance, and provide a clear basis for improving results.

Your organization's performance measurements need to focus on key results. Results should be used to deliver and balance value for your key stakeholders—your customers, workforce, stockholders, suppliers, and partners; the public; and the community. Thus results need to be a composite of measures that include not just financial results, but also product and process results; customer and workforce satisfaction and engagement results; and leadership, strategy, and societal performance.

NIST (2015 - 2016) p. 43

Delivering Value & Results - Application to System Design

Not surprisingly, Evans and Ford (1997) found that the importance of **results orientation**, as it was called in 1996, was of medium importance to five categories, including Strategic Planning; Customer and Market Focus; Process Management; Human Resource Focus; and Measurement, Analysis, and Knowledge Management, placing it in a similar situation with customer-focus as a cross-cutting value that should ideally permeate the entire enterprise (p. 26). The setting direction and developing strategy is based on measurable outcomes that address the needs of multiple stakeholders. How customers define value is addressed in Item 3.1 Voice of the Customer. Creating value for multiple stakeholders is a key consideration in the design of all processes. Process should be designed so that they serve the customers, are enjoyable to execute by the employees, make the most of partnerships and suppliers, protect the interests of the public and, at the same time, are profitable. The approaches to acquiring, developing, motivating, and retaining employees should also be designed with these multiples stakeholders in mind. The measurement, analysis, and knowledge management approaches need to include results that address the needs of the multiple stakeholders. The bottom line is that planning, processes, and learning all need to be designed to create results and value for the multiple stakeholders identified in the organizational profile.

Systems Perspective

While good organizations focus on functional excellence, excellent organizations focus on the system. The systems perspective has grown in popularity and utility over the past several decades. It is based on the work of several notable contributors from General Systems Theory to more recent concepts and theories, such as those proposed by Jay Forrester, Russell Ackoff, W. Edwards Deming, and Peter Senge, to name just a few. As our understanding of the organization system increases, so does our ability to identify the key leverage points that have the greatest impact on overall system performance. When evaluating and redesigning organization systems, focus on the system integration notes and the linkages identified in the blueprints.

Systems Perspective - CPE Core Value

A systems perspective means managing all the components of your organization as a unified whole to achieve your mission, ongoing success, and performance excellence. Successfully managing overall organizational performance requires realization of your organization as a system with interdependent operations. Organization-specific synthesis, alignment, and integration make the system successful. Synthesis means looking at your organization as a whole and incorporates key business attributes, including your core competencies, strategic objectives, action plans, and work systems. Alignment means using key organizational linkages to ensure consistency of plans, processes, measures, and actions. Integration builds on alignment, so that the individual components of your performance management system operate in a fully interconnected, unified, and mutually beneficial manner to deliver anticipated results.

These concepts are depicted in the Baldrige Criteria overview (page 1). When your organization takes a systems perspective, your senior leaders focus on strategic directions and customers. Your senior leaders monitor, respond to, and manage performance based on your results. With a systems perspective, you use your measures, indicators, core competencies, and organizational knowledge to build your key strategies, link these strategies with your work systems and key processes, and align your resources to improve your overall performance and your focus on customers and stakeholders. The core values and concepts, the seven Criteria categories, and the scoring guidelines are the system's building blocks and integrating mechanism.

NIST (2015 - 2016) p. 39

Systems Perspective - Application to System Design

The systems perspective helps the organization understand how the various pieces and parts work together to produce overall outcomes. Part of developing strategy is determining where to focus limited resources and efforts to improve the overall performance. This focus allows the organization to identify the key strategic objectives identified in Item 2.1 and the key action plans in Item 2.2.

The systems perspective also helps the organization develop a system or people and processes that work together as a congruent and internally consistent system. Well-intentioned people improving processes in the organization can actually reduce the overall performance of the system. The systems perspective is needed by all people at all points in the organization in order to achieve and sustain execution excellence.

The concept of systems perspective is an important enabler of organizational learning. The essence of scientific knowledge is the ability to predict. In order to predict the results of certain actions, the organization must first understand the causal relationships involved. While measurement and analysis in the early stages of the performance excellence journey might be focused on individual aspects of the organization (e.g., processes, people, finances, customer satisfaction), the focus turns to understanding the system as the organization matures. This shift, in turn, supports both strategic leadership and execution excellence.

How can you avoid "book of the month club" management fads? Design custom organization systems and scorecard that fits your unique organization like a "glove." The focus on the organizational key factors provides a design "guidance system" by establishing the organization's unique context and, in turn, requirements and priorities for the design of the organizational systems and scorecard. The Criteria for Performance Excellence (CPE) organizes the context factors into five Areas to Address including:

- P1 – Organizational Description
  - o P1a - Organizational Environment
  - o P1b – Organizational Relationships
- P2 – Organizational Situation
  - o P2a – Competitive Environment
  - o P2b - Strategic Context
  - o P2c - Performance Improvement System

These factors define what is **relevant** and **important** for the custom design of the leadership and management systems and processes.

Organization Context

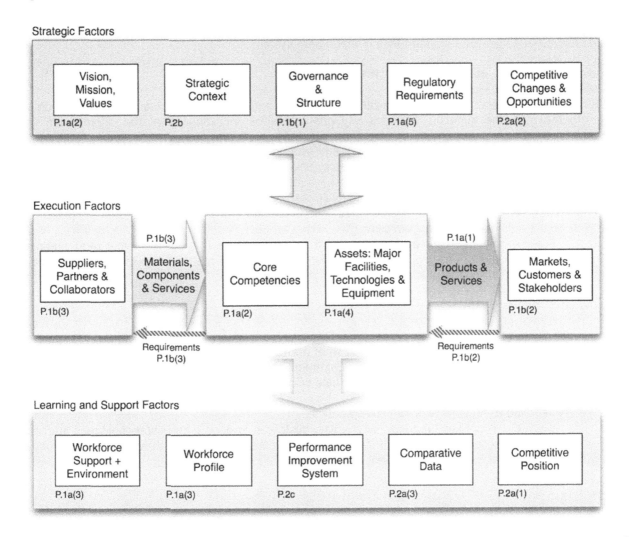

Why is the context of the organization so important to the design of the management systems? The CPE model is a non-prescriptive, context dependent model. In other words, the appropriate approach to a particular aspect of the model (e.g., strategic planning) is dependent on the unique situation or context of the organization. For example, the appropriate strategy development and deployment process for the local "Mom and Pop" grocery store is likely to be a bit different than a multi-national Fortune 500 company with operations in over 40 countries.

Ask any executive in any organization and chances are they will tell you that their organization is unique. Answering the Organizational Profile questions provides a common understanding of the organization's unique context in a way that will be useful to diagnose and design the management systems. According to NIST (2015 – 2016, P. 4), "Your Organizational Profile is the most appropriate starting point for self-assessment and for writing an application. It is critically important for the following reasons:

- It helps you identify gaps in key information and focus on key performance requirements and results.
- You can use it as an initial self-assessment. If you identify topics for which conflicting, little, or no information is available, use these topics for action planning.
- It sets the context for your responses to the Criteria requirements in categories 1–7. (NIST)

The Organizational Profile sets the context for the way your organization operates. Your organization's environment, key working relationships, and strategic situation – including competitive environment, strategic challenges and advantages and performance improvement systems - serve as an overarching guide for your organizational performance management system.

Know yourself and your environment (P.1a)

The first step is to know your own organization and environment. This first component asks what defines the organization. The question pinpoints key characteristics, including: what the organization does (products, services, and operations); why it does it (mission & purpose); how it does it (culture and values); who does it (employee demographics); and what tools they have to do it (technology, equipment, & facilities). In addition, the operating and regulatory environments are included in this section.

> Note: Two aspects of this are particularly critical:
> - Your product and services – if these are not clear, an assessment (internal or external) is not possible.
> - Your workforce segments and their requirements (of you, NOT your requirements of them) – they will be key throughout your assessment, and should be reported against in your results.

Know your friends (P.1b)

Two major types of external relationships exist; those with customers and those with supplier partners. Who are the organization's key customers and what are their requirements? Who are the major supplier partners and what are the key supply chain requirements? What methods does the organization use to build and maintain the relationship and communicate with the supplier partners?

> Note: One aspect of this is particularly critical:
> - Your key market segments, customer groups, and stakeholders, and their requirements (of you, NOT your requirements of them) – these constitute over 20% of the total assessment score in Items 7.1, 7.2, and others.

Know your enemies (P.2a)

Who are the key competitors, and how good are they? How does the organization compare to these competitors? It helps if you understand some reference point, such as market share trends.

What performance factors will make the greatest difference with the customers in the industry? How do the core competency, strategic challenges, success factors, strategic objectives, and action plans link to each other?

Know your strategic context (P.2b)

What are the main challenges the organization faces with respect to winning in the marketplace? What are the most significant operations, people, and global challenges? What advantages does the organization posses?

> Note: Two aspects of this are particularly critical:
> - What is coming at you from the outside (Strategic Challenges)?
> - What are the linkages between the Strategic Challenges, and what you have to be good at (in your industry), what you are good at (Strategic Advantages) and what you will continue to improve (Strategic Objectives)?

Know how to improve (P.2c)

Finally, the last component asks about the system that the organization uses to evaluate and improve the organization's management systems and processes and share that knowledge throughout the organization.

> Note: One aspect of this is particularly critical:
> - Your approach to improvement – is it one technique, or do you have different techniques for different needs? This will resurface in 4.1c, 6.1b(3), 6.2d, and anywhere improvement is discussed. Different techniques are good if it is clear why different techniques are used and when each should be used. There is nothing more confusing than multiple improvement techniques if nobody knows when to use each of them.

The Organizational Profile is used by several "players" to diagnose, design, and transform the organization:

- **Leaders** - to determine, finalize, and clarify key aspects of the business and to communicate these consistently throughout the organization;

- **Writers** – as a starting point for self-assessment and for writing an award application;

- **Examiners** (internal and external) – during the application review process including the site visit, to understand the organization and what is relevant and important; and

- **Management System and Scorecard Designers** – to help determine priorities and appropriate improvements and where the key processes or measures need to be linked.

The Organizational Profile provides the organization with critical insight into the key internal and external factors that shape its operating environment. These factors, such as the mission, vision, values, competitive environment, and strategic challenges, impact the way the organization is run and the decisions they make. As such, the Organizational Profile helps the business better understand the context in which it operates; the key requirements for current and future business success; and the needs, opportunities, and constraints placed upon the organization's performance management system. A detailed description of the context is described in the profile sections P.1a through P.2c.

 THOUGHTS FOR LEADERS

One weekend in the 1990's, the manufacturer of an industrial product had a serious problem — it was almost out of stock, but its production lines were still running. These types of production lines are very costly to shut down. In a panic, the manufacturer called the supplier's plant in Arkansas, but could only reach the night guard. The night guard called somebody in accounting (at home), somebody in shipping (at home), and a number of hourly employees came into the plant.

The individuals called the trucking line, shipped products to the customer, and cut the appropriate invoice. No one in management even knew this situation had occurred until Monday morning. When the plant manager did find out, HE NEVER ASKED "WHY DIDN'T YOU CALL ME." He proudly told the story to everyone who would listen. Later that year, when that plant received their State Quality Award Site Visit, the plant manager used this example to show the level of employee empowerment. What the example **really** demonstrated was:

1. The pride and trust the leadership had in their team
2. Everybody knew the priorities
3. Everybody knew their job – starting with the night guard
4. Everybody was empowered
5. The relationship with the supplier – sure we could talk about how they should have scheduled 'in advance,' but in reality, this is an example of how groups worked together, and problems can always occur

What was the organization's culture? In that plant, the level of empowerment and teamwork was clear — do what the customer needs. This level of empowerment was possible because the employees understood the business, the relationships, and the priorities. More importantly, however, they trusted that leadership would support them in doing whatever was necessary to support a customer. What was *really* important in that organization was clear – customers and their people.

A key question for leaders is:

"Do employees clearly understand the business and their personal level of empowerment?"

In most instances, leaders feel that this question is silly because their response is typically "of course they do!" When you ask employees the same question, however, the level of their personal empowerment is often unclear – they will give you an answer, but it will not be a clear delineation of their level of empowerment. In these circumstances what will employees do? They will only do what they know is safe! Most times that means they will do nothing or do less than what is required to meet the spirit and intent of the customer's requirements.

The Organizational Profile (OP) is the very heartbeat of your application. Cherish the time spent building the OP - you will never regret it.

Robb Schwartz

> *Culture is what is left after everything we have learned has been forgotten. It consists of a deepened understanding, a breadth of outlook, an unbiased approach, and a heart that has deep sympathy and strength of courage.*
>
> **G. Bromley Oxnam**

 ## FOUNDATION

The **Organizational Environment** portion of the Organizational Profile is focused on the internal aspects of the organization, including: key product offerings (products and services); organizational culture; people; major technologies, equipment, and facilities; and the regulatory environment that the organization must operate within. The first question typically asks what the organization produces (e.g., products and services). In the Criteria For Performance Excellence, NIST (in the 2011-2012 edition) changed the definition of "products" to include "'product offerings' and 'products' refer to the goods and services that your organization offers in the marketplace. Mechanisms for product delivery to your end-use customers might be direct or through dealers, distributors, collaborators, or channel partners. Nonprofit organizations might refer to their product offerings as programs, projects, or services" (p. 5). In many places in this book (particularly in the Worksheets) the terms "products and services" are still used to remind the user that it is not just the products that are being addressed.

Subsequent questions ask for a description on the internal characteristics of the organization. These descriptions will be used later to assess whether the organization is focusing on the most important aspects of their internal environment. For example, if there are several employee groups, and one is in a nationwide shortage, the organization would be expected to take action to attract and retain employees in that particular group.

Product Offerings

Sometimes the identification of the products, services, and operations is easy and straight forward, and sometimes it is not. For example, for the local coffee shop entrepreneur, some might say that coffee is the central product while others might say that a forum for the exchange of information is the primary product or service and coffee is simply an enhancer. If the primary product is the latter, the coffee shop might offer free wireless internet along with a variety of coffees and snacks. How these products and services are delivered is another decision. This portion of the criteria also asks about the delivery mechanisms. How the products are delivered may have a significant impact on most of the organization's actions, including communication, planning, deployment, measures, improvement cycles, and other actions. For the local coffee shop, delivery might be in the form of counter service, a drive-up window, and maybe even internet ordering and mail delivery for coffee beans and accessories.

One of the key questions asked in this area is 'the relative importance of each to your success' (NIST, 2015 - 2016, p.4). Without understanding the importance of each product and service (both now and in the future), an organization cannot leverage the right decisions, take the right risks, and may not succeed. Conversely, if an examiner does not understand these, then they do not understand the basic business model of the organization being assessed, and they will not have an understanding of what is more or less important.

Vision and Mission

The culture of the organization is a critical enabler to the organization's direction and internal environment. If the culture is characterized by an open collaborative and creative operating style known for its innovation, then detailed procedures on information sharing might not fit. For example, at the local coffee shop, the desired environment may require a culture of teamwork focused on creating an atmosphere for personal information exchange, a place where as a customer, "everybody knows your name."

The culture and purpose of the organization, along with its vision and values, help establish the areas of greatest importance (as viewed by the leadership) to the organization's success. Consider ownership, for example. If the owners are the same as the customers, the central purpose of the organization may be different than if the owners are investors in a for-profit company. In this example, the cooperative type organization (where owners are customers) is typically focused on the greatest benefit to the members at the least expense.

The *Mission* is the overall function of the organization, the *Vision* is the desired future state, and the *Values* are the guiding principles. Most organizations have lofty beliefs and values. The key, however, is the ability to turn these beliefs and values into actions and behaviors. To do this, some organizations have taken the values and translated them into behaviors which are expected of every employee in every transaction with every stakeholder. More advanced organizations have even taken the behaviors and expanded the definition of them to include behaviors which are not acceptable, and (if you demonstrate one of the unacceptable behaviors) how you can recover. Some behaviors, however, cannot be recovered from (such as a breach of integrity).

The organization should also be clear on their Core Competencies and the relationship to the Mission. Beyond this basic linkage required at this point in the criteria, the organization should also be able to link the Core Competencies to the Success Factors, Strategic Challenges, Strategic Objectives, Strategic Advantages, Metrics Tracked, and the Action Plans. See the Glossary for the definition of each of these terms.

Workforce Profile

Now that we know what work is to be accomplished as well as the culture (beliefs, norms, values, behaviors, symbols) to accomplish it, who is going to do the work? What type of employees does the organization use to accomplish the work? What is the breakdown of the knowledge, skills, and abilities required of the workforce? The employee demographics will impact the types and methods of measurement needed to acquire, develop, utilize, evaluate, and promote the workforce uniquely suited to the business. These demographics form the employee profile. The same types of employees, in different work environments, however, may have different requirements, and need to be classified differently. For example, a secretary in an office environment will have different safety requirements than a secretary in a factory. Also, we can control the work environment for a nurse in a hospital, but we may not be able to control the work environment for a home-care nurse.

For the local coffee shop, the workforce might consist of supervisors who are full-time employees and workers who are part-time employees and full-time students. The bigger question, of course, is what these two groups of employees need to be successful. In each case, the organization needs to understand the requirements for each position, so the steps necessary to meet these requirements can be included in the organization's plans.

Assets

After the work, the culture, and the employees are determined, the next question is, "where are we going to do the work, and what kind of equipment do we need?" Specifically, what are the organization's major technologies, equipment, and facilities? The technology, equipment, and facilities will influence what is important to measure, how best to measure it, and how best to aggregate the data. The answer to this question, of course, varies widely depending on the type of business. A Fortune 100 "high tech" firm with operations around the world will have a very different answer to this question than the local coffee shop. The local coffee shop may only need a shop with furniture, some coffee making equipment, and high speed wireless Internet.

Regulatory Requirements

The last element of the organizational environment is the regulatory environment. What external rules and regulations does the organization have to comply with in order to do business? The regulatory environment is a key variable to understanding the most important measures in anticipating issues and preventing problems with areas of public well-being. This element, of course, is again very different for a nuclear power plant than it is for the local coffee shop down the street.

Most organizations are regulated by the financial (IRS) and environmental (EPA) agencies, but it is important to also understand the regulatory agencies unique to the organization's industry. For example, a hospital is regulated by numerous groups and agencies which would not be important to an aerospace firm. Conversely, an aerospace firm may be regulated by the Federal Aviation Administration (FAA) laws and regulations that would not apply to the hospital. Once again, these regulatory agencies are important because the training, measures, goals, objectives, and actions should address the regulatory environment. The organization should seek to meet or exceed all regulations applicable to their operations.

As outlined above, the organizational environment is the first major component of the organization's context. It consists of five major elements: products and services; culture and philosophy; employees; technology, equipment, and facilities; and the regulatory environment in which the organization operates. A clear understanding of the internal environment is a critical foundation for diagnosing, designing, and transforming the organization.

Note: The ability to describe an organization simply is very important to both the organization and the external examiners. In too many cases, the organization describes itself in terms so complex that the reader cannot understand and, in fact, the employees in the organization cannot clearly agree on the key processes, the inputs, outputs, requirements and resources. To do this the authors recommend that an organization develop a one-page graphical description of their business. This works for all sectors, public sectors, health care, and even government or not-for profit. This model can also be the basis for the organization's approach to process management. For example, the one page description (or "stadium chart" because it describes the entire business as one view of the "stadium") shows many of the key components of the business which can be broken-down further into the various levels of processes.

EXAMPLES

PRO-TEC Coating Company (Baldrige Recipient 2007)

Organizational Environment

A small business centrally located to the American automotive industry in northwest Ohio, PRO-TEC Coating Company (PRO-TEC) provides world-class coated sheet steel products and services primarily to the quality-critical automotive market.

It was established as a 50/50 joint venture partnership in 1990 by two global leaders in steel technology – U.S. Steel Corporation (USS) and KOBE Steel (KOBE) of Japan. The partnership agreement was designed to ensure organizational sustainability with an assured substrate (raw material) supply from USS as well as 'shared services' type of external support services. Finally, USS provides the interface to the final customer (supported by PRO-TEC, particularly where there is a processing or technical issue).

This model has allowed all participants to leverage their strengths. For example, KOBE is a world leader in advanced steel technology and processing requirements, USS is a product and technology leader within the United States, and has a marketing presence throughout North America, and PRO-TEC is a leader in process control, and innovative approaches to bringing new products to market.

In many ways, this partnership is viewed as a global alliance which is a model for many future organizations.

PRO-TEC Enterprise Model

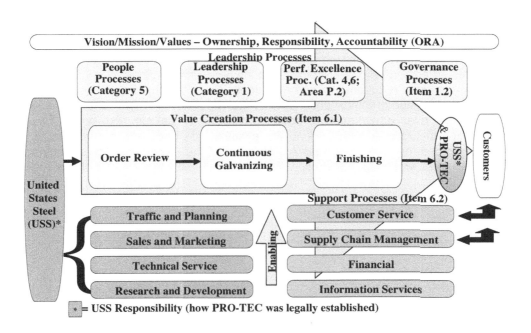

Lafayette General Medical Center – LGMC (Lafayette, Louisiana)

> *Note from the Author: Walking into Lafayette General Medical Center*
> *you quickly feel the positive atmosphere.* **This place feels different!**
> *The behaviors they embrace (shown below) are comprehensive, and are well*
> *known by everybody. They are even posted in a main hallway.*
>
> *In working sessions, it is difficult to tell "who represents which function,"*
> *because the ownership for success is universal. For example,*
> *NOBODY EVER SAYS "that's not my job."*

Employee Service Standards Of Behavior

As an employee of Lafayette General Health, I believe that there is no higher responsibility than to provide and ensure high quality and a caring environment for our patients, customers and coworkers. I know that I am only one person, but I also know that it only takes one person to make a difference, either positive or negative. When I choose to work within this system, I am choosing to embrace the following SERVICE standards and behavioral values in order to promote the mission and vision of our system. I will be both committed to and accountable for demonstrating supportiveness, etiquette, respect, vibrancy, integrity, communication and excellence in service delivery by adhering to the behaviors specified in this document.

Supportiveness

- I will welcome new employees to the system.
- I will be a team player and work collaboratively to help others, including those outside of my department.
- I will avoid using the phrase, "That's not my job."
- I will recognize, praise and thank my fellow workers as well as my customers and patients.
- I will have a mentor and be a mentor.
- I will promote confidence in LGH by speaking well of my co-workers, medical staff and any part of our system, especially but not only, in front of patients.

Etiquette

- I will use AIDET always.
- I will use proper phone etiquette by identifying myself & the department, followed by a pleasant greeting.
- I will follow the 10/5 rule: acknowledging the person at 10 feet away with a smile, saying "hello" at 5 feet away.
- I will allow patients, customers & guests on and off an elevator first.
- I will help lost guests and new employees by escorting them to their destination. I will avoid merely pointing in a general direction.

Respect

- I will dress to reflect respect and professionalism. I will be mindful of what my appearance portrays by wearing clothes that are clean, neat and in good repair.
- I will respect my coworkers by ensuring that my workspace is clean, neat and organized prior to leaving each day or night.
- I will respect my patient's dignity. I will knock before entering patient rooms and appropriately cover patients being transferred or transported.
- I will respect religious and cultural diversity, as well as those with special needs.

Vibrancy

- I will make a conscious decision to have a positive, willing and flexible attitude each day.
- I will be attentive and alert, ready to help at all times. I will promptly acknowledge people who approach me or my desk.
- I will wear my name badge properly on the upper part of my body where it proudly communicates who I am and what I do.
- I will promote a nurturing, healing and safe physical environment by removing clutter, ensuring cleanliness and keeping equipment in working order. I will report any damaged equipment or unsafe situations immediately.
- I will care for my own health, well-being and emotions so that I can better care for others.
- I will embrace change by contributing & being open to new ideas & approaches. Further, I will avoid using phrases like, "But that's how we've always done it."

Integrity

- I will lead by example.
- I will ensure the privacy and validity of all medical records, correspondence and confidential dialogue.
- I will proactively seek opportunities for continued learning, as well as professional and personal growth.
- I will be fiscally responsible by not wasting hospital time, resources or equipment.

Communication

- I will explain things in a way people can understand.
- I will remember that body language is a powerful communicator. I will smile and demonstrate an open, friendly posture.
- I will take the time to listen — to employees, patients, customers, administrators, guests, etc. - making eye contact when possible.
- I will give and receive constructive criticism in a timely manner and turn it into an opportunity to improve.
- I will take the time to read hospital and system communications (emails, flyers, bulletins, policies, electronic boards, etc.) to stay informed of responsibilities, changes and events. I will avoid repeatedly using the phrase, "I didn't know."
- I will ensure that employees and patients are informed and updated about changes. Further, I will foster participation in decision making to the greatest extent possible.
- I will avoid using communication devices (cell phones, text, internet, iPod) for personal reasons during work time. (Policy V-D7)

Excellence (in service delivery)

- I will convey concern and compassion as well as a willingness to serve.
- I will respond to all calls for assistance in a timely manner (1-2 min.) and provide periodic progress reports.
- I will know and utilize the ACT Complaint Resolution/Service Recovery Policy when presented with any complaint(s) from patients, visitors, employees, vendors and medical professionals. (Policy II-U) -

Poudre Valley Health System (Baldrige Recipient 2008)

Poudre Valley Health System (PVHS) is a locally owned, private, not-for-profit organization that provides care to residents of northern Colorado, Nebraska, and Wyoming. Headquartered 60 miles north of Denver in Fort Collins, Colorado (service area population 500,000), PVHS dates back to 1925, when Poudre Valley Hospital (PVH) opened its doors as a 40-bed hospital on the outskirts of Fort Collins. Recognizing that "Baldrige saves lives," PVHS chose to use the Baldrige Criteria for Performance Excellence in 1999 and started participating in the Colorado Performance Excellence (CPEx) program in 2001. PVHS remains the sole recipient in any industry of the CPEx Peak Award, Colorado's top Baldrige-based recognition, and has received consecutive Baldrige site visits since 2005. On this Baldrige journey, PVH has expanded and diversified into PVHS - a regional medical hub with a service area covering 50,000 square miles (roughly the size of Florida).The organization's goal remains the same: to provide world class health care, with a mission to remain independent while providing innovative, comprehensive care of the highest quality, always exceeding customer expectations.

PVHS offers a full spectrum of healthcare services, including emergency/urgent care, intensive care, medical/surgical care, maternal/child care, oncology care, and orthopedic care. PVHS' unique focus areas include: 1) Colorado's third largest cardiac center; 2) the only Level IIIa Neonatal Intensive Care Unit between Denver and Billings, Montana; 3) Level II and III trauma centers; and 4) a Bariatric Surgery Center of Excellence. PVHS also offers role model community health programs that prevent injury or illness and help the medically underserved.

The PVHS model of patient- and family-centered care drives delivery of healthcare services. The process for involving patients in their care begins with facility and service design and continues throughout key healthcare processes. PVHS uses two primary care delivery mechanisms - partnerships and interdisciplinary teams.

Partnerships - A decade ago, in support of its mission and vision, PVHS made a commitment to provide a lifetime of care for its community. To achieve this goal while avoiding costly service duplication and ensuring optimal outcomes, PVHS strategically evaluated whether to provide a service on its own or through partnerships with other organizations. At a time when physician-owned specialty facilities began to threaten traditional community hospitals, PVHS led the industry in **physician joint ventures**. With best practices learned from these early relationships, PVHS expanded its partner base beyond physicians to include entities such as home health agencies, a long-term care provider, community health organizations (1.2c) and a health plan administrator (United Medical Alliance) - a partnership that saves local employers $5 million each year.

In an historic innovation, PVHS partnered with Regional West Medical Center (RWMC, Scottsbluff, Nebraska, population 15,000) in PVHS 'newest hospital, Medical Center of the Rockies (MCR). Traditionally, rural hospitals such as RWMC have faced the dilemma of establishing their own specialty programs (i.e. cardiac surgery) or sending their patients elsewhere for specialty care. If they refer their patients elsewhere, they lose the income associated with that care. However, if they keep their patients at home, their small volumes do not give physicians and staff enough experience to ensure optimal clinical outcomes. Now, as part owner of MCR, RWMC is able to offer their patients world-class care and keep some of the income associated with that care.

Poudre Valley Health System – Global Path to Success

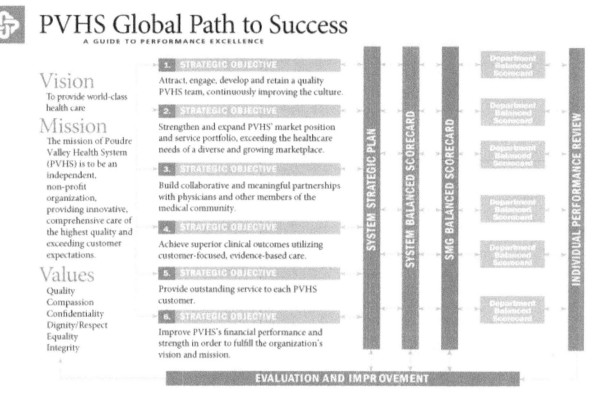

Interdisciplinary Teams - From design of new facilities and services to provision of bedside care, PVHS engages teams to meet patient and other customer needs. Teams throughout the organization work together to provide the best possible care, participate in strategic planning, monitor quality indicators, and coordinate systematic improvements. A culture of engagement and innovation is the foundation of the PVHS strategy for providing world-class health care. Senior leaders began systematically building this culture a decade ago, by asking staff, "What makes you want to jump out of bed and come to work in the morning?"

The PVHS Global Path to Success (GPS, Figure P.1-1) provides a leadership system and framework for this culture, incorporating: 1) the performance management system, which links individual goals to organizational goals through each employee's personal goal card; and 2) the Code of Conduct, Behavior Standards, and Leadership Competencies, which outline specific behaviors that support organizational values, key customer requirements, and key workforce requirements. Members of the workforce understand and demonstrate the Vision, Mission, and Values (V/M/V) and, through their goal cards, focus on how they can help the organization provide world-class care. PVHS defines "world-class"- a term commonly used to mean "the best" - as striving for results in the 90th percentile or top 10 percent of available national comparative databases. If external comparative data are not available, PVHS uses internal, historical data to set stretch goals that will drive performance improvement and innovation.

PVHS continues to receive external verification of its progress toward its world-class vision through recognition, most recently, as: 1) the nation's No. 1 hospital for nursing care (PVH: American Nurses Association and National Database for Nursing Quality Indicators, 2007); 2) the nation's No. 1 hospital for overall patient satisfaction (MCR: Avatar, 2007); and 3) a Thomson Top 100 Hospital for five consecutive years (PVH: one of only seven U.S.hospitals).

Monfort College of Business (Baldrige Recipient 2004)

Products and Services

The University of Northern Colorado's (UNC) College of Business was established in 1968 as an autonomous, degree-recommending unit, with a primary mission to provide graduate and undergraduate business education. The College's evolution through the 1970s paralleled a national trend for business schools of explosive enrollment growth and a proliferation of program options for students. By 1984, the College's 50-person faculty was serving more than 2,000 students enrolled in a wide range of undergraduate, masters, and doctoral degree programs.

A Quality Journey Begins. In 1984, the College took dramatic steps to make program quality its top priority. At the time, UNC's business program was generally regarded as average and largely overshadowed by a number of key competitors within a fifty-mile radius. With its competitors and most U.S. business programs opting for a growth strategy of degree program assortment and further proliferation of graduate programs, UNC's business administrators and faculty chose an opposite approach. A vision was cast for becoming Colorado's best undergraduate business program—a goal it was agreed would not be possible without making undergraduate business education the College's exclusive mission. Within two years, a revolutionary plan commenced for eliminating all graduate programs, including a Ph.D. degree program and Colorado's largest MBA program. Additional changes were made at the undergraduate level, with the elimination of all but one degree program—the Bachelor of Science in business administration. Future business students would declare business as a major and choose from six emphasis areas: accounting, computer information systems, finance, management, marketing, or general business. The College adopted two long-term strategies to guide its actions: (1) a program delivery framework of *high- touch, wide-tech, and professional depth*, and (2) a positioning strategy of high-quality *and* low-cost (i.e., exceptional *value*). The College became known for providing a "private school education at a public school price."

Quality Milestones. By 1992, following numerous curriculum and faculty upgrades and a $5+ million renovation of Kepner Hall (its instructional facilities), the College's revised

---

A singular focus on undergraduate business excellence

MCB's Mission
Our mission is to deliver excellent undergraduate business programs that prepare students for successful careers and responsible leadership in business.

MCB's Vision

Our vision is to build a reputation of excellence in Colorado and beyond for preparing future business leaders and professionals.

MCB's Values - Each MCB value statement is held within an overall framework focused on the pursuit of excellence; a philosophy of continuous improvement guides employee behavior.

Instructional Values—We value excellence in the *courses* we offer and seek to provide reasonable class sizes; outside-of-class assignments; faculty availability and student interaction beyond-the-classroom; and exercises to develop logical/creative thought processes.

We set standards to assure *faculty* are academically prepared and professionally experienced; are of high integrity; maintain high standards for student performance; and offer students opportunities to interact with business professionals and community leaders.

We value excellence in the business *curriculum* and seek to assure it is current; a reflection of emerging trends; built on a liberal arts foundation; incorporates the role of technology; reflects best practices of ethical and moral standards; a recognition of the global economy; and assists in the transition to a lifetime of learning.

We value excellence in the activities of our *students* and seek to assure they maintain high levels of integrity; and build/improve skill sets in written and oral communication, interpersonal, teamwork, leadership, and they develop professional habits and appropriate behaviors.

Scholarship Values—We value excellence in faculty *scholarship* and seek to assure it is relevant, classroom-enriching, develops faculty as a resource; publishable in peer-recognized academic/ professional outlets; and enhances the development extension, and clarification of knowledge bases in business professions.

Service Values—We value excellence in *academic service* and seek to assure that faculty governance is conducted in a thoughtful, constructive, and innovative environment; and participants act responsibly, creatively, and collegially.

We value excellence in faculty *professional service* and seek to assure such activities challenge theory against practice; enrich teaching and scholarship; assist in identifying and cultivating employment opportunities for students; encourage participation that aids business growth and improvement; and support business/professional disciplines and organizations.

mission was paying significant dividends. The College reached its first major quality goal by earning accredited status from AACSB International—The Association to Advance Collegiate Schools of Business (AACSB). UNC became the first public university in Colorado to be accredited by AACSB in both business administration *and* accounting.

In 1999, in conjunction with a $10.5 million commitment from the Monfort family, the College's name was changed to the Kenneth W. Monfort College of Business (MCB). The gift was designed to provide a "margin of excellence" for the College. A Greeley native and long-time supporter, Mr. Monfort was widely known as a pioneer whose commitment to innovation and quality through ethical business practice was legendary.

In 2000, the College was recognized by the Colorado Commission on Higher Education (CCHE) as a Program of Excellence (POE)—a highly selective and prestigious award given to programs demonstrating widespread excellence and a readiness "to take the next step toward national prominence." MCB is the only business program in Colorado to ever earn the POE award.

The Journey Continues. Today, the Monfort College of Business (MCB) is housed within UNC, a publicly- supported residential university of 11,611 students, offering a wide range of graduate and undergraduate degree programs in five academic colleges. Located on UNC's 236-acre campus in Greeley, Colorado (2000 census pop, 76,930), MCB's primary service is offered to its 1,090 undergraduate majors. Half of the 120-credit degree program is dedicated to non-business topics, including general education subjects and liberal arts electives. The other half is dedicated to business subjects, including the business core, business emphasis classes, and business electives. The College's educational services are delivered almost exclusively through a resident, on-campus learning mode of face-to-face student/professor contact. Class sizes (average of 30) are designed to enhance student/professor interaction. Distance educational delivery through technology is limited to the role of augmenting resident student classroom experience through use of ancillary techniques (e.g., threaded discussions for extended class discussions, Web-recorded lectures for post-class reviews, and course-based Web sites with portals to related information sources).

Culture – Mission, Vision, Values

The uniqueness of MCB's chosen mission/values combination (see P-1) stems from its singular focus on pursuing excellence in *undergraduate-only* business education—a unique position among its regional and national peers. The College remains as one of just five undergraduate-only programs nationally to hold AACSB accreditations in business and accounting. Additionally, MCB holds a unique position within the regional marketplace. A leader in value when compared to its competitors, MCB's product quality and learning environment also exceed those peers. The *Denver Post* described the College as "possibly the best bargain in business education anywhere in the U.S." In addition to price, MCB's commitment to a program strategy of *high-touch, wide-tech,* and *professional depth* has made it a value leader in undergraduate business education anywhere in the U.S.

High-Touch. Smaller class sizes are designed to facilitate faculty-student interaction in the classroom. No "mass sections" are permitted to ensure this interaction occurs across the entire curriculum. Smaller class sizes also allow for experiential, hands-on learning techniques to be employed and are designed to increase active learning levels within the student population. Each professor maintains student office hours to increase student access.

Wide-Tech. Since the Kepner renovation in 1987, MCB has invested millions of dollars in its technology infrastructure to support a curriculum that exposes students to a wide array of existing and emerging business technologies, enabling graduates to make a seamless transition into the workplace. The curriculum integrates technology within course content, and MCB prides itself on incorporating the most current versions of industry-standard technologies.

Professional depth. MCB values professional business experience as a selection trait for its instructors. The College also utilizes an innovative *executive professor program* to strengthen classroom currency and ties with the employment community for graduates. Many of these professors are regionally- or nationally-known executives teaching in-residence, while others are brought to campus as visiting lecturers. The College also has developed partnerships with the business community to provide students with additional opportunities to gain real-world experiences through course components (e.g., business plans, advertising campaigns, market research, and portfolio management).

Faculty and Staff

MCB's faculty and staff include a total of 34 full-time faculty (including dean), 8 administrative staff (including technology and external relations directors) and 13 part-time adjunct faculty members. No graduate assistants teach in MCB's classrooms. The non-unionized faculty is spread across rank and type, with senior professors and executives making up the majority. All but one tenured/tenure-track faculty member holds a doctorate in discipline. The remaining lecturers and executive professors hold a Ph.D., M.B.A., or J.D., and many held senior positions in industry immediately preceding their hiring. The full-time faculty is 76.5% male and 79.5% Caucasian, and the largest minority group is Hispanic (11.8%), with Asian and Native American percentages at 5.9% and 2.9%, respectively. The only new tenure-track hire for 2003-04 was Hispanic and female. Of the seven staff, four are assigned to an academic department, primarily as clerical and customer service support. Two are assigned to the dean's office for overall program support, and one directs the College's advising center.

Major Technologies Equipment, and Facilities

MCB is housed in Kepner Hall, a learning facility built in 1910 and fully-renovated in 1987. A regular maintenance program has kept the building in excellent condition. Kepner houses all business classrooms, faculty and student support offices, computer labs, and special use facilities. More than 95 percent of the space is dedicated to MCB use. Kepner contains 14 classrooms, ranging in seating capacity from 25 to 60. Each classroom is wired to the College's 400-station, Ethernet LAN. Two open student technology labs are available an average of 80 hours weekly and house approximately 100 Pentium IV workstations, CD RW CD-ROMs, and high-speed laser printers (including color). Each workstation contains access to the latest discipline-specific software applications and commercial databases. Students also have access to a 21-station electronic meeting laboratory, 16-station finance trading center, three high-tech team practice rooms, a graphics media lab, and a 10-station cyber café provided through a partnership with university dining services. A wireless PC network (A&B technologies) supports authenticated PC notebook access throughout the building. The showcase 196-seat Milne Auditorium was updated in 2002, receiving $100,000 in technology and furnishings upgrades. Milne provides high-tech presentation space for special events, including executive speaker presentations that allow the attendance of multiple classes at once.

Regulatory Environment

MCB is governed by University of Northern Colorado policies and procedures underneath a larger umbrella of policies mandated by the CCHE, whose mission is to provide access to high-quality, affordable education for all Colorado residents. CCHE adopts statewide admissions standards, policies for academic planning, degree approval, financial aid and transfer/articulation policies. CCHE also recognizes a statutory and fiduciary responsibility to ensure institutions manage the system's capital assets effectively. As a UNC college, MCB is subject to CCHE governance and policies and is committed to complying with federal regulations applicable to institutions of higher education, including ADA, FERPA, and OSHA.

MCB's primary accreditation agency that requires mission-driven periodic assessment is AACSB. In order to maintain its accreditations, MCB must attend to each standards area, including faculty composition and development, curriculum content and evaluation, instructional resources and responsibilities, students, and intellectual contributions. On-site inspection occurs on a five-year cycle, with written reports submitted annually to assure standards compliance and continuous improvement.

Source: Monfort (2005)

CRITERIA QUESTIONS

In your response, answer the following questions:

a. Organizational Environment

(1) **Product Offerings** What are your main product offerings (see the note on the next page)? What is the relative importance of each to your success? What mechanisms do you use to deliver your products?

(2) **Mission, Vision, and Values** What are your stated mission, vision, and values? What are your organization's core competencies, and what is their relationship to your mission?

(3) **Workforce Profile** What is your workforce profile? What recent changes have you experienced in workforce composition or your workforce needs? What are:

- your workforce or employee groups and segments,
- the educational requirements for different employee groups and segments, and
- the key drivers that engage them in achieving your mission and vision?

What are your organized bargaining units (union representation)? What are your organization's special health and safety requirements?

(4) **Assets** What are your major facilities, technologies, and equipment?

(5) **Regulatory Requirements** What is the regulatory environment under which you operate? What are the applicable occupational health and safety regulations; accreditation, certification, or registration requirements; industry standards; and environmental, financial, and product regulations?

Notes:

P.   Your responses to the Organizational Profile questions are very important. They set the context for understanding your organization and how it operates. Your responses to all other questions in the Baldrige Criteria should relate to the organizational context you describe in this Profile. Your responses to the Organizational Profile questions thus allow you to tailor your responses to all other questions to your organization's uniqueness.

P.1a(1).   Product offerings and products are the goods and services you offer in the marketplace. Mechanisms for delivering products to your end-use customers might be direct or might be indirect, through dealers, distributors, collaborators, or channel partners. *Nonprofit organizations might refer to their product offerings as programs, projects, or services.*

P.1a(2).   Core competencies are your organization's areas of greatest expertise. They are those strategically important capabilities that are central to fulfilling your mission or provide an advantage in your marketplace or service environment. Core competencies are frequently challenging for competitors or suppliers and partners to imitate and frequently preserve your competitive advantage.

P.1a(2). Core competencies are one example of concepts that are woven throughout the Criteria to ensure a systems approach to organizational performance management. Other such concepts include innovation, use of data and information to review performance and create knowledge, and change readiness and management.

P.1a(3).   Workforce or employee groups and segments (including organized bargaining units) might be based on type of employment or contract-reporting relationship, location (including telework), tour of duty, work environment, use of certain family-friendly policies, or other factors.

P.1a(3).   Organizations that also rely on volunteers and unpaid interns to accomplish their work should include these groups as part of their workforce.

P.1a(5).   Industry standards might include industrywide codes of conduct and policy guidance. In the Criteria, industry refers to the sector in which you operate. *For nonprofit organizations, this sector might be charitable organizations, professional associations and societies, religious organizations, or government entities—or a subsector of one of these.* Depending on the regions in which you operate, environmental regulations might include greenhouse gas emissions, carbon regulations and trading, and energy efficiency.

NIST (2015-2016) pp. 4 - 5

Author's Note: The regulatory environment in which the organization operates places requirements on the organization and impacts how the organization manages the business.

Understanding this environment is key to making effective operational and strategic decisions. Further, it allows one to identify whether they are merely complying with the minimum requirements of applicable laws and regulations or exceeding them.

Exceeding minimum requirements is a hallmark of leading organizations.

WORKSHEETS

P.1a(1) – Product Offerings

	Caution: The area below is one of the critical factors to be considered in the Organizational Profile. If the products, services and delivery mechanisms are not simple and clear, the organization cannot ensure they are focused on the appropriate processes, measures or improvements. If an external assessor cannot understand what is important, they will not understand what they should emphasize in the assessment, and certainly will not understand the organization's business model.

Main Products Offerings	Delivery Mechanisms	Relative Importance To Your Organizational Success

P.1a(2) – Mission, Vision and Values

Mission	Values (and associated behaviors)	Other Descriptors Of The Culture
Vision		
Core Competencies (one or more)		

⚠	Caution: The area below is one of the critical factors to be considered in the Organizational Profile. The Baldrige Criteria includes the reference to the Core Competency in several places. It has been our experience that organizations that have several core competencies are not as well focused as organizations which have one (or at the most two). Additionally, the core competency should clearly match the definition of what a core competency should include (see the Glossary at the back of the Baldrige Criteria or the Baldrige Users Guide©.

Core Competencies (One or More)	Relationship of Core Competency To The Mission

P.1a(3) – Workforce Profile

⚠	Caution: The area below is one of the critical factors to be considered in the Organizational Profile. The Baldrige Criteria includes each of the factors in the worksheets below. The workforce groupings should be driven by the requirements each of the workforce groups has of the organization (and NOT the organization's requirements of them. Those requirements from each group must be addressed in the Category 5 processes and in the Category 7 (Item 7.3) Business Results.

Workforce or Employee Groups, Segments, or Job Type	Number and/or %	Special Health and Safety Requirements, Expectations, or Benefits	Key Drivers Which Engage Them In Accomplishing Your Mission and Vision	Workforce or Job Diversity Group	Number and/or %

Job Type	Education Levels	Recent Changes In Composition or Needs	Number or Percent Of Workforce

Note: Include in the breakdown any Bargaining Units, Contract Employees, Volunteers and other groups who have unique health, safety or job requirements, unique rights or critical capabilities.

P.1a(4) – Assets

Major Assets (Do Not List All Minor Details)	
Facilities	
Technologies	
Equipment	

P.1a(5) - Regulatory Requirements

Regulatory Agencies or Bodies under which you operate:	Regulations From Those Groups, including: - Occupational Safety & Health - Accreditation, Certification, Registration Requirements - Relevant Industry Standards - Environmental, Financial and Product Regulations	**Impact** on the Organization – This can include industry - wide codes of conduct and policy guidance. The number of employees impacted, importance to the product or service, importance to the customer, or the impact of 'not' meeting these regulatory requirements.

BLUEPRINT

P.1a Organizational Environment

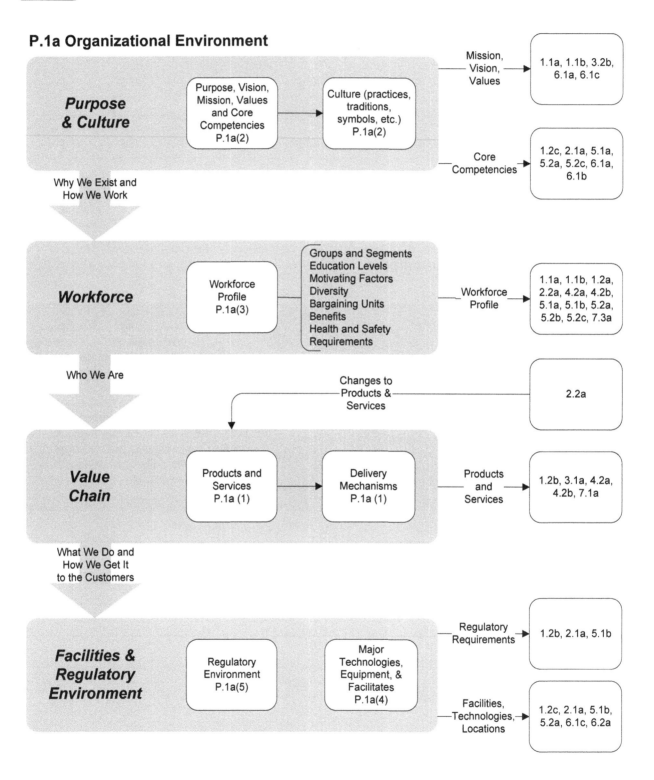

SYSTEM INTEGRATION

Systems

Mission, Vision, Values

P.1a > 1.1a Mission, Vision, Values - The "setting" of organizational values and direction including short and long-term expectations in 1.1a should be consistent with and include the purpose, mission, vision, and values described in the profile P.1a.

P.1a > 1.1b Mission, Vision, Values - Creating a focus on action (performance and strategies) in 1.1b should be consistent with and support the mission, vision, and values of the organization described in P.1a.

P.1a > 3.2b Mission, Vision, Values – Building customer relationships in 3.2b should be consistent with the overall organization mission, vision, and values described in P.1a. One issue that organizations often run into when developing a customer-focused culture is the tendency to sacrifice other stakeholders and their needs in order to serve the customers. While this can be a useful strategy in the short-term, it is seldom a sustainable strategy for the longer-term.

P.1a > 6.1a Mission, Vision, Values - The mission, vision, and values of the organization set the parameters of organization operations and products and services. This is an important input to the identification of core competencies which should be consistent with the mission, vision, values of the organization. If the core competencies are not consistent with the mission, the organization has two choices - adjust the mission or the core competencies.

P.1a > 6.1c Mission, Vision, Values - The nature of the mission also is an important consideration when determining the requirements for the emergency readiness system. Some organizations can shut their doors for a week or even a month without much impact on their customers. However, some organizations such as hospitals need to be able to conduct business and provide critical services during emergencies.

Core Competencies

P.1a > 1.2c Core Competencies - The organizations core competencies are an important consideration when deciding on the areas of emphasis for supporting key communities. For example, an organization that designs and manufactures computers might support the local community center by providing computers and training for the local citizens.

P.1a > 2.1a Core Competencies - The organizations core competencies are a key input to strategy development. Core competencies is a strategic concept made popular by C. K. Prahalad and Gary Hamel in a 1990 *Harvard Business Review* article titled: The Core Competence of the Corporation. In this article they propose that core competencies provide the organization with a competitive advantage a key element in an effective strategy.

P.1a > 5.1a Core Competencies - The assessment of the workforce capability and capacity should include their capability and capacity relevant to the core competencies. Not only does the workforce need to continually develop the knowledge skills and abilities related to the core competencies, ensuring that the organization attracts, retains, and manages the workforce to ensure it has sufficient capability and capacity associated with the core competencies.

P.1a > 5.2a Core Competencies - The organization's core competencies are key inputs to the performance management system. Core competencies are a key part of the "success criteria" and the subsequent planning, evaluation, and reinforcement of the knowledge, skills, and behaviors that result in the workforce achieving the success criteria.

P.1a > 5.2c Core Competencies - The workforce has to continuously develop and improve their knowledge, skills, and abilities related to the organization's core competencies. Consequently, the core competencies should be part of the needs assessment process that drives the workforce and leader development system described in 5.2c.

P.1a < 6.1a Core Competencies - The core competencies described in the profile (P.1a) are determined using the process described in 6.1a. The core competencies are also a critical input to the work placement strategy. It is difficult to maintain a competency and the associated competitive advantage if the organization outsources activities associated with the core competency.

P.1a > 6.1b Core Competencies - The organization's core competencies are also an important input to the identification of the key work processes.

Workforce Profile

P.1a > 1.1a Workforce Profile - The workforce profile is a key input to developing, deploying, and reinforcing the mission, vision, and values. In addition, the workforce profile is also a key input when creating the organization environment for innovation, agility, etc.

P.1a > 1.1b Workforce Profile - The workforce profile is a key input to the design and selection of methods to communicate with and engage the workforce. First, employees are one of the stakeholders of the organization and as such their needs should be considered when setting expectations that create value and balanced the needs of customers and stakeholders. Second, the workforce profile is an input to setting the direction and empowerment and motivation of the workforce.

P.1a > 1.2a Workforce Profile - The workforce profile (job types, employee education, etc.) are key inputs to the design and selection of organizational governance processes that protect the interests of stakeholders and stockholders.

P.1a > 2.2a Workforce Profile - The workforce profile is an important input to developing realistic action plans, the associated human resource plans, and deploying those action and human resource plans.

P.1a > 4.2a Workforce Profile - The number, type, and nature of the workforce described in the workforce profile (P.1a) is a critical input to the design of the data and information processes and systems that makes the right data available to the right employees. The goal is to design the system to ensure that the appropriate information is available for all employee groups.

P.1a > 4.2b Workforce Profile - The number, type, and nature of the workforce described in the workforce profile is a critical input to keeping the data and information processes and systems current with the changing needs of the workforce.

P.1a > 5.1a Workforce Profile - The workforce segments identified in the profile together with the organization's requirements will determine the gaps that need to be filled with new employees. These can be gaps in technical skills, diversity, education and so forth. In addition, the employee profile describes the current available labor pool.

P.1a > 5.1b Workforce Profile - The workforce profile is a key input to the nature of employee segments, groups, work units, and work environments which, in turn, influence the design of the processes, measures, and goals to create the desired work environment. In addition, the workforce profile (groups and needs) is a key input to the design of the services, benefits, and policies (support system) tailored to the various segments' and groups' needs, wants, and desires.

P.1a > 5.2a Workforce Profile - The workforce profile is an important input to the determination of the workforce segments. The profile provides demographics that can be useful in determining the segments that differ in their requirements for satisfaction and engagement.

P.1a > 5.2b Workforce Profile - The workforce profile identifies the number, type, and characteristics of key employee segments. The description of the employees in the profile should correspond to the segments used to determine key factors, processes, and measures for workforce satisfaction and engagement.

P.1a > 5.2c Workforce Profile - The workforce profile is an important input to the workforce development needs assessment process. The needs will often vary depending on the type of employees, their education level, etc. For example, employees handling hazardous cargo will have additional development needs vs. those working in the office. In addition, the workforce profile – is an important input to the leadership development needs assessment process. The type of leadership development that is needed at each level can vary depending on the make up of the existing workforce.

Products and Services

P.1a < 2.2a Change to Products and Services - Action plans often call for additions, changes, and improvement to products, services, and the processes that create them. In this case, the work system and processes are refined or changed to assist in accomplishing the strategic objectives and the description of the products, services, and operations in the profile (P.1a) should be refined to reflect these changes.

P.1a > 1.2b Products and Services - The most important input to area 1.2b is the description and nature of the products, services and operations identified and described in the profile P.1a. Since this area is focused on the public concerns, risks, and regulatory and legal issues related to the firm, the type of products and services are the central driving factor that determines what is relevant and important. For example, if the products are eaten by the consumers then the FDA will be part of the regulatory environment. Some of the risks associated will be health risks to consumers, and there are public concerns to deal with, such as the case of Mad Cow disease. The design of the processes to address these areas will likely be different for a business consulting firm than they will be for an airline.

P.1a > 3.1a Products and Services - Customer listening and learning methods should be designed to include specific feedback on the products and services described in the profile (P.1a).

P.1a > 4.2a Products and Services - The types and nature of the products, services, and operations are key inputs to the information system characteristics and the types of data and information needed by the workforce, suppliers and partners, customers, etc.

P.1a > 4.2b Products and Services - The nature of the products and services can be an important consideration in the information systems characteristics (e.g., reliability, security, user friendliness). For example, a government customer with high technology products might require an unusually high degree of security to ensure the protection of classified documents, etc.

Regulatory Requirements

P.1a > 1.2b Regulatory Requirements - A key input to legal and ethical behavior (1.2b) requirements, processes, and measures is the description of the regulatory environment described in the profile (P.1a). This environment is largely driven by the nature of the products, services, and operations, but other factors can also drive this environment including the nature of the ownership, the employees, and so forth. This is a key input to the identification of regulatory and legal requirements called for in area 1.2b.

P.1a > 2.1a Regulatory Requirements - The regulatory environment described in the profile (P.1a) is a key input to strategy development and should be included in the SWOT analysis. The regulatory environment establishes parameters for the industry that can limit the strategic options that an organization can legally pursue. In addition, changes in the regulatory environment can impact the profitability of certain products and services.

P.1a > 5.1b Regulatory Requirements - The regulatory environment is a key consideration when determining the requirements, practices, processes, and measures for workplace health, safety, security, and ergonomics.

Facilities, Technologies, and Locations

P.1a > 1.2c Facilitates, Technologies, Locations - While the CPE do not specify that an organization has to be involved and support every community where they have an office, it does expect that the key communities will be determined from the major operating locations and possibly the locations where their products and services are used, which might be different from the production facilities. So, the communities that are considered by the processes that support key communities should include those identified in the profile (P.1a).

P.1a > 2.1a Facilitates, Technologies, Locations - The analysis of facilities and locations along with technology changes and key innovations described in the profile are key inputs to strategy development. The SWOT analysis should be designed to include or address these issues and in particular the major technologies described in the profile (P.1a).

P.1a > 5.1b Facilitates, Technologies, Locations - The location and type of facilities and the nature of the technology used in the facilities is a direct input to the safety and security approaches. In other words, the safety and security threats differ depending on location and the nature of the technologies used. In addition, the facilities and industry impact the workplace health and ergonomics requirements, practices, processes and measures.

P.1a > 5.2a Facilitates, Technologies, Locations - The location of the facilities as described in the profile determines the nature and make up of the local communities. The demographic profile of the local communities influences the approaches to capitalize on the diverse ideas, cultures, and thinking of the local communities.

P.1a > 6.1c Facilitates, Technologies, Locations - The types of facilities, technologies, equipment, and locations will make a big difference in the threat assessment and the identification of requirements for the emergency readiness system. For example, organizations that handle hazardous materials have different emergency preparation and COOP requirements than do organizations that provide internet services. In addition, location will drive the type of environmental threat (weather, earthquakes, etc.) that an organization should prepare for.

P.1a > 6.2a Facilitates, Technologies, Locations - The facilities (type, layout, etc.) along with the technologies and locations are key inputs to the design of the work processes.

Scorecard

P.1a > 7.1a Products and Services - The results presented here should be those associated with the products and services identified in the profile P.1a.

P.1a > 7.3a Workforce Profile - The workforce profile is a key input to determining the workforce segments that are appropriate for the various workforce results including engagement, satisfaction, well-being, dissatisfaction, learning, etc. In addition, the employee profile is a key input to the identification of the key factors for employee engagement, well-being, satisfaction, and motivation which should also be measured and the results reported for the key factors by employee segment.

THOUGHTS FOR LEADERS

Workforce segmentation is one of the critical factors to be considered in the Organizational Profile. Successful leaders clearly understand and define the businesses they are in and define employee groups based on their needs from the organization, and their contributions to the different business needs. In very simple terms, they "line up" the following logic chain:

Organizational Purpose ⇨
  ⇨ External Influences/Needs ⇨
    ⇨ Internal Processes ⇨
      ⇨ Internal Measures ⇨
        ⇨ Employee Capabilities ⇨
          ⇨ Employee Goals ⇨
            ⇨ Performance Reviews ⇨
              ⇨ Development Plans and Execution ⇨
                ⇨ Other Actions To Adjust To Current Performance And External Influences

Although this alignment may seem like an obvious part of running a complex organization, many organizations have not made these linkages clear. Employees, who do not understand the organization's purpose and a clear linkage to their own goals, will not be able to contribute most effectively to the organization's success. Without clear knowledge of foundational issues, the employees will not operate the organization smoothly.

Conversely, if the organization does not understand the needs of various employees, the organization will not be able to effectively meet those needs. This can result in employees who do not want to (or who do not have the capability to) meet the organization's needs. These needs should be clearly defined for each employee group, and matched to the contribution they are expected to make to the organization's success.

Additionally, the relationship between the core competencies and the mission, success factors, strategic challenges, strategic objectives, strategic advantages, metrics tracked, and the action plans should be defined and made clear in the Organizational Profile. If this is not clear within the organization, it is very difficult for the organization to focus on the appropriate plans, actions, and improvements.

A LIGHTER MOMENT:

> *It's pretty clear now that what looked like it might have been some kind of counterculture is, in reality, just the plain old chaos of undifferentiated weirdness.*
>
> **Jerry Garcia**

> **The price of greatness is responsibility.**
>
> Winston Churchill

 ## FOUNDATION

With the internal environmental context of the organization established in (P.1a), the key relationships which impact the internal operations of the organization (P.1b) are reviewed.

Organizational Structure

The first question inquires about the organizational structure and governance system. More specifically, what are the reporting relationships among the board of directors, senior leaders, and parent organization (if there is one)? Who are these people, what do they want, and how does the organization interact with them? The answer to this question varies widely depending on size of the organization, ownership structure, and the level of autonomy of the organization. For example, a single owner Limited Liability Company will have a very different board of directors than a publicly traded corporation.

Note: this area is an opportunity to clearly describe a number of aspects of the organization, including:

- The organization structure (chain of command)
- The relationships with other key groups (such as Nursing Shared Governance Councils or Medical Committees in Health Care)
- The parent organization (including key committees and shared services, as appropriate
- Although it is not specifically asked for in the criteria, this is a good place to describe other factors which can help to understand the organization, such as:
  - Membership in key committees which are referenced in the application
  - Membership in key governing or leadership groups
  - Level of education or commitment of the leaders in the Baldrige Journey:
    - Leaders trained in Performance Excellence (as a side note, it is always interesting to assess an organization on a Performance Excellence when their leaders have had little or no formal experience with the criteria, processes, systems, or practices)

Customers and Stakeholders

Key customer segments or groups are the second type of external relationships. These groups are typically determined by the differences in customer requirements. In other words, each segment should have different needs, wants, and desires. The organization, therefore, prioritizes their needs, wants, and desires differently for each segment. For example, the local coffee shop might have several schemes for segmenting customers, including the "on-the-way-to-work" crowd, the traditional conversation crowd, and the technology crowd. The first two segments might not rate the wireless Internet as important to their experience, but the technology crowd probably would. The traditional conversation crowd might not rate speed of service as important, but the "on-the-way-to-work" crowd probably would. Thus, each segment may drink coffee and have similar coffee requirements (temperature, taste, etc.), but may have very different "experience" requirements. The processes used to segment customers should be described in Item 3.2. The requirements for each segment show in this area should be reflected in the results reported in Area to Address 7.1a (this is particularly true for Health Care applicants, many of which only focus on their clinical results in Item 7.1, and do not report against the customer's requirements). The customer satisfaction, dissatisfaction and loyalty for each segment should be reported in Item 7.2.

Some organizations segment their customers by their profitability or contribution to margin. For example, airlines often classify customers into cheap-fare infrequent leisure flyers; business full-fare flyers; and frequent flyers at various fares - the relationship mechanisms differ for each segment. Access to information, seating, etc. varies with the status of the customer. The airlines spend less time impressing the infrequent super-saver passenger than they do the frequent business passenger. This strategy is simply a matter of allocating limited resources to areas having the greatest impact on the top line in a highly competitive environment. Service levels are appropriate for what the consumer is willing to pay for. Infrequent leisure travelers are generally not loyal to a particular airline; however, business travelers who are members of clubs and benefit from status, etc., are often loyal to a particular airline.

Suppliers and Partners

Finally, suppliers are key to the quality of any organization's value chain. An old computer programmer saying warns, "garbage in, garbage out." If our suppliers do not provide quality products and services, then most organizations will not be able to provide excellence to their external customers. An old supply chain saying warns, "we no longer compete company-to-company; we compete supply chain-to-supply chain."

What roles do suppliers and distributors play in your value creation processes? This contribution to your success will be different for virtually every organization. Nevertheless, the effective integration of the supply chain into an organization's integrated value chain is critical in today's marketplace. For example, in a coffee shop, you can make lousy coffee from good beans, but you cannot make good coffee from lousy beans. In addition, if the Internet works only half the time then the experience for the technology crowd will suffer. Finally, how do you build relationships and communicate with customers and suppliers?

Supplier partners will be important to almost every organization in the next decade or so. As organizations excel at focusing on their core competencies, they will increase their outsourcing of the other functions. The need for relationship management with key suppliers, partners and collaborators will grow. It is difficult, however, to successfully outsource key operations using the traditional *us vs. them* procurement processes and relationship techniques.

The future of the integrated supply chain network will require close relationships and increased sharing of information. The scope and magnitude of your supplier, partner, and collaborator network will determine what is necessary to measure and how it can be used to improve performance of the entire supply chain system.

EXAMPLES

Don Chalmers Ford - (Baldrige Site Visited Company – Small Business 2008, 2012)

The retail customers Don Chalmers Ford (DCF) serves may need either products or services. Specifically, they may wish to:

1. buy a vehicle or
2. service a vehicle.

Accordingly, DCF has determined their market segments to be:

1. New Vehicle Sales
2. Used Vehicle Sales
3. Vehicle Maintenance and Repair Service
4. Vehicle Body Repair

Figure P.1-6 summarizes the key customer requirements for each of these groups. Additionally the requirements and expectations are shown for the other Stakeholder segments.

This table clearly shows the linkage between the Segments and Key Requirements and Expectations and the Business Results Figure Numbers presented in Category 7. This is one of the most critical linkages in the CPE model, since it impacts 25% of the total score! (Item 7.1= 10 %; Item 7.2 = 7 %; and Category 3 [which defines how the customers were segmented] is worth 8 %).

Segment (P1b2)	Key Requirements & Expectations (In priority order) (P1b2)	Requirements Results (Item 7.1)	Satisfaction Results (Area 7.2a[1])	Loyalty Results (Area 7.2a[2])
Customer Market Segments				
New Vehicle Sales	1. Real value in products & services 2. Total satisfaction	Figures 7.1-1 thru 7.1-7	Figure 7.2-2	Figure 7.2-8
Used Vehicle Sales	1. Real value in products & services 2. Total satisfaction	Figures 7.1-8 & 7.1-9	Figure 7.2-4	Figure 7.2-10
Vehicle Maintenance & Repair	1. Real value in products & services 2. Total satisfaction 3. Fix it right the first time	Figures 7.1-10 thru 7.1-18	Figure 7.2-5	Figure 7.2-11
Body Repair	1. Real value in products & services 2. Total satisfaction	Figure 7.1-19	Figure 7.2-7	Figure 7.2-14
Other Key Stakeholders				
Workforce	1. Positive work experience	Figures 7.4-2	Figures 7.4-3,	Figure 7.4-11

Segment (P1b2)	Key Requirements & Expectations (In priority order) (P1b2)	Requirements Results (Item 7.1)	Satisfaction Results (Area 7.2a[1])	Loyalty Results (Area 7.2a[2])
	2. Compensation growth	7.4-7	7.4-6 & 7.4-10	
	3. Work at DCF a long time	7.4-4		
Community		Figures 7.6-7	Figures 7.6-7	Figures 7.6-7
	1. DCF leadership in philanthropy	7.6-7	7.6-7	7.6-7
	2. Provide funding	7.6-6	7.6-7	7.6-7
	3. Actively partner w/the community	7.6-4 & -5	7.6-4	7.6-4
Ford		Figures 7.4-5, 8 & 9	Figures 7.4-5, 8 & 9	Figures 7.6-1
	1. Provide competent, trained personnel			
	2. Meet dealership's assigned market share for Ford car & truck sales	7.3-18 & 7.3-19 7.1-1 thru 19	7.3-18 & 7.3-19 7.2-1	7.6-1
	3. Provide customer satisfaction	7.3-4	7.3-4	7.6-1
	4. Provide necessary & supportive working capitol	7.3-1	7.3-1	7.3-5
	5. Provide profitability			7.3-1
Share-holders	1. All other stakeholders are satisfied	All Above	All Above	Above
	2. Shareholder ROI	Figure 7.3-1	Figure 7.3-1	Figure 7.3-1

Figure P.1-6 - Key Customer & Stakeholder Segments Requirements, Expectations & Results

Source: Don Chalmers Ford

Sharp Healthcare (Baldrige Recipient 2007)

Sharp identifies patients as their key customers, and notes focus efforts on attracting key market segment customers, identified through research to be vital to sustaining their presence as the market leader.

Target audiences include insured women, between the ages of 25 and 54, who make the majority of health care decisions for themselves and their extended families; seniors age 65 and over, who are covered by traditional Medicare or a Medicare managed-care health plan; and the Hispanic population, which currently represents over 32 percent of the San Diego market.

Sharp also notes that they also strive to build relationships with businesses, health plans, brokers, and legislators. These customer relationships and key requirements are included in a table format, with a cross reference to results which illustrate their degree of success.

Customer Segment	Customer Requirements	Performance	Patient-Centered Satisfaction	Loyalty
Inpatient	Safe	This table in the application provides cross references to the results items which illustrate the degree to which the customer requirements are being met	This table in the application provides cross references to the results items which illustrate the degree to which each customer segment is satisfied	This table in the application provides cross references to the results items which illustrate the degree to which each customer segment is likely to return or recommend, and also to market share
	Evidence-based			
	Timely			
	Efficient			
	Equitable			
Outpatient	Safe			
	Evidence-based			
	Timely			
	Efficient			
	Equitable			
Emergency Department	Safe			
	Evidence-based			
	Timely			
	Efficient			
	Equitable			
Stakeholders (Brokers, Payors, Suppliers)	Accurate			
	Timely			

Monfort College of Business (Baldrige Recipient 2004)

Governance

UNC is governed by a Colorado Governor-appointed Board of Trustees. The board manages within a Colorado higher educational system headed by the CCHE. The UNC president supervises three vice presidents, including the provost/vice president of academic affairs, who supervises the colleges' five academic deans (See Organizational Chart, page xi).

The MCB dean serves on an Academic Affairs Council, Deans Council, President's Council, and University Planning Council, representing the College and its interests within each of these policy-recommending bodies. The MCB assistant dean serves on the UNC Assessment Committee and the Technology Advisory Committee. MCB utilizes a system of shared governance.

The College's Administrative Council (ADMC) includes an associate and assistant dean and chairs of the five academic departments. It serves as the College's primary mission review and strategic planning group, the College's assessment group, and is a primary recommending body to the dean. MCB has four key faculty committees and a Student Representative Council (SRC).

Students

MCB's student population origin is concentrated in Colorado (86.7%), with the remainder representing 31 states. Within Colorado, 18.7% are from the Greeley area, with a large proportion of the remainder from Denver and surrounding areas. International students account for .9% of the total. The student population is 58.6% male, has an average age of 21.5, is enrolled on a full-time basis (89%) and works at least part-time (over 80%). The student population is 82% Caucasian, 7% Hispanic, 4% Asian/Pacific, and 2% African-American.

MCB's student customers originate from three sources: high school graduates, external college transfers, and internal changes-of-major. The College partners with the UNC Admissions Office to target high school students during their junior/senior years and community college students preparing for transfer. To recruit internal changes-of-major, the College partners with the College Transition Center which serves UNC's undeclared majors. By design, the majority of MCB's program is delivered to upper-division students (i.e., third and fourth years of program). Therefore, the College's student customers tend to be similar in experience levels, age, and expectations as they move into the majority of curriculum completion. As a result, the College's single degree program is targeted to its one key market, business majors (see P-2).

Figure P-2
MCB's Key Market Segment—Business Majors
Key Requirements/Expectations
▨ Strong reputation of College and/or faculty
▨ Outstanding educational value
▨ Strong reputation of major/area of study
▨ Financial feasibility (affordability)
▨ Financial aid/scholarships (assistance)
▨ Accessibility of high-quality instructors
▨ Outstanding facilities/technology
▨ Extra-curricular options (student clubs, speakers, conferences, and competitions)
▨ Course availability (scheduling)
▨ Outstanding placement for graduates
▨ Interaction with practitioners

In addition to students, MCB's other key stakeholder groups are alumni, employers, faculty, and staff. The College works to address each group's key requirements and expectations (see P-3).

Suppliers and Partners

A number of MCB's partners (see P-4) play an important supporting role in delivering its educational services. Each partner listed plays a direct role in the College's learning-centered processes as pertaining to students.

Figure P-3
MCB's Key Stakeholder Groups—Requirements/Differences
▨ **Alumni**—Enhanced program reputation for adding value to MCB business degree
▨ **Employers**—Access to well-prepared business graduates (employees)
▨ **Faculty & Staff**—Fair compensation and opportunities for professional growth and development

MCB's most important requirements for its suppliers (e.g., Dell, Gateway, Barnes & Noble, and curriculum support organizations like Microsoft, Bloomberg, *The Wall Street Journal*, and McGraw-Hill/Irwin) are timeliness and reliability for orders placed and received, as well as fair market pricing and current high-quality product assortments.

Although business majors select any of six academic emphasis areas, each has identical requirements as to program size, advising processes, and class scheduling. Majors are surveyed (e.g., MCB Student Survey, EBI Undergraduate Business Exit Study) at selected times during their academic career to assess and prioritize areas for potential improvements, and MCB uses a variety of communications mechanisms to inform its students (i.e., electronic monthly newsletters, MCB weekly student listserv, Web site, customized mail-merge advising letters, required advising sessions, a student representative council government system, an MCB Listens electronic feedback system, and foyer-based, customizable information ticker).

University-wide, department and committee meetings, employee Web portals, and a comprehensive e-mail system, constitute the major formal communication mechanisms for faculty and staff. The majority of MCB's 10,000+ alumni resides in Colorado and is communicated with through mailings (e.g., annual report publication), Web portals, and personal thank you letters or hand-written cards for financial gifts to MCB.

The College initiated a formalized system with its primary partners that involved frequent one-on-one meetings between the dean and key partner representatives (i.e., admissions assistant director, career services director, and foundation development officer). The purpose of such meetings is to share information and examine opportunities for improving joint performance. A similar meeting pattern now exists for the technology director and an IT representative. A business reference librarian holds regular office hours away from Michener Library in a Kepner Hall satellite office to improve communications between the two units, as well as to improve service levels to students and faculty.

Figure P-4   **MCB's Primary Partners and Their Roles**
Admissions—works with MCB in recruiting students with outstanding learning potential.
Career Services (CS)—assists in student degree path selection via career choice instruction; assists in internship identification/employment preparation (e.g., CAP program for juniors & seniors); assists in building relationships between MCB and key employers.
College Transition Center (CTC)—assists in advising qualified undeclared students (i.e., pre-business) in making the transition to business as a major.
Foundation/Alumni—assist MCB in building a financial resource base to support learning initiatives; assists in communications and database support for graduates.
Information Technology (IT)—maintains technology infrastructure to support instruction and research; works with MCB technology director and assistant dean through university committee structures.
Library—helps select and maintain instructional resources; works with faculty and students in classroom; research support (e.g., satellite office space in Kepner).

Source: Monfort (2005)

CRITERIA QUESTIONS

In your response, answer the following questions:

b. Organizational Relationships

(1) Organizational Structure What are your organizational structure and governance system? What are the reporting relationships among your governance board, senior leaders, and parent organization, as appropriate?

(2) Customers and Stakeholders What are your key market segments, customer groups, and stakeholder groups, as appropriate? What are their key requirements and expectations of your products, customer support services, and operations? What are the differences in these requirements and expectations among market segments, customer groups, and stakeholder groups?

(3) Suppliers and Partners What are your key types of suppliers, partners, and collaborators? What role do they play:

- in your work systems, especially in producing and delivering your key products and customer support services; and

- in enhancing your competitiveness?

What are your key mechanisms for two-way communication with suppliers, partners, and collaborators? What role, if any, do these organizations play in contributing and implementing innovations in your organization? What are your key supply-chain requirements?

Notes:

P.1b(1). *For some nonprofit organizations, governance and reporting relationships might include relationships with major funding sources, such as granting agencies or foundations.*

P.1b(2). Customers include the users and potential users of your products. *For some nonprofit organizations, customers might include members, taxpayers, citizens, recipients, clients, and beneficiaries, and market segments might be referred to as constituencies.*

P.1b(2). Customer groups might be based on common expectations, behaviors, preferences, or profiles. Within a group, there may be customer segments based on differences and commonalities. You might subdivide your market into market segments based on product lines or features, distribution channels, business volume, geography, or other factors that you use to define a market segment.

P.1b(2). The requirements of your customer groups and market segments might include on-time delivery, low defect levels, safety, security, ongoing price reductions, the leveraging of technology, rapid response, after-sales service, and multilingual services. The requirements of your stakeholder groups might include socially responsible behavior and community service. *For some nonprofit organizations, these requirements might also include administrative cost reductions, at-home services, and rapid response to emergencies.*

P.1b(3). Communication mechanisms should be two-way and use understandable language, and they might involve in-person contact, e-mail, social media, or the telephone. For many organizations, these mechanisms may change as marketplace, customer, or stakeholder requirements change.

NIST (2015 - 2016) pp. 4 – 5

 WORKSHEETS

P.1b(1) - Organizational Structure

Organizational Structure:

Note: This should include the governance board, the parent organization, the leader of the organization, and at least one more level down the organization.

P.1b(1) Continued - Governance System

Positions	Roles & Responsibilities	Reporting Relationships		Audits	
		Reports To:	Supervises:	Internal	External
Governance Board:					
Parent Organization:					
Senior Leaders:					

P.1b(2) – Customers and Stakeholders

	Caution: The area below is one of the critical factors to be considered in the Organizational Profile. The customer requirements must be addressed in the Category 3 processes (how the groups were determined and how they are addressed) and in Category 7 Business Results (Area 7.1a for your internal measures of meeting customer requirements, and Item 7.2 for Customer Satisfaction, Dissatisfaction and Engagement).

Key Market Segments, Customer Groups and/or Stakeholder Groups	Key Requirements Or Expectations For Your Products, Customer Support or Operations (In Priority Order For Each Group Or Segment)
	1.
	2.
	3.
	1.
	2.
	3.
	1.
	2.
	3.
	1.
	2.
	3.
Note: Performance Against The Above Segments For Customer Satisfaction, Dissatisfaction and Loyalty Should Be Reported In Item 7.2	Note: Performance Against The Above Requirements Or Expectations (Grouped By Customer Segment) Should Be Reported In Area 7.1a.

Other Stakeholders or Market Segments:	Key Requirements & Expectations (in priority order for each Stakeholder)
	1.
	2.
	3.
	1.
	2.
	3.
	1.
	2.
	3.
	1.
	2.
	3.
	1.
	2.
	3.

P.1b(3) – Suppliers and Partners

Key Suppliers, Partners, and Collaborators and	Most Important Requirements and Expectations You Have Of Them	Role They Play In Your Work Systems	Role They Play In The Producing and Delivering Your Key Products and Support Services	Role They Play In Enhancing Your Competitiveness

Your Most Important Supply Chain Requirements
•   •   •   •

Key Supplier, Partner And Collaborator Relationships	Two-Way Communication Mechanisms Used	Their Role In Contributing And Implementing Innovations In Your Organization

BLUEPRINT

P.1b Organizational Relationships

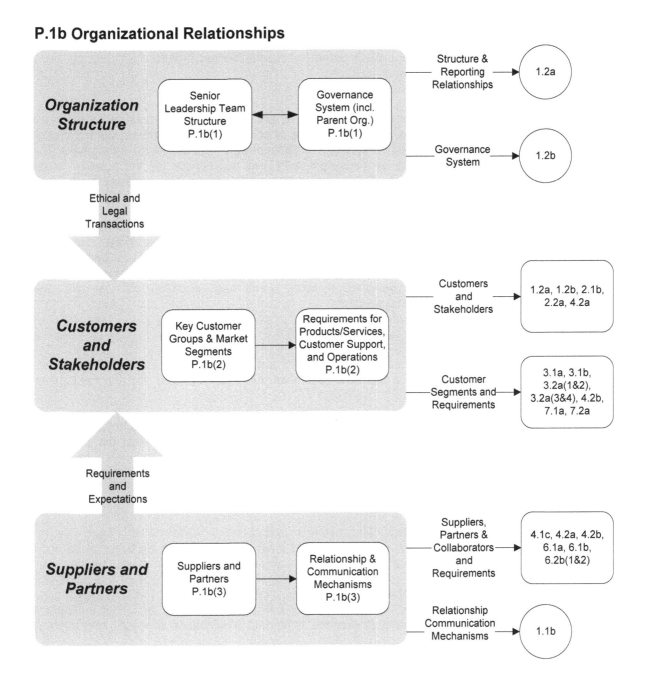

SYSTEM INTEGRATION

Systems

P.1b > 1.1b Relationship Communication Mechanisms - The creation and communication of the values, directions, and expectations to all employees, suppliers, and partners should include the communication mechanisms described in the profile (P.1b). In addition, the expectations should balance the needs of the customers and multiple stakeholders and those stakeholders are identified in P.1b.

Governance System

P.1b > 1.2a Structure and Reporting Relationships - There are two key factors to consider when diagnosing or designing a governance system – first the structure and governance system and second the reporting relationships among the board of directors - both of which are described in the profile (P.1b). The approach to governance should be consistent with and appropriate for the specific situation described in P.1b. This can vary widely depending on the history of the organization, the ownership model, and the legal status of the organization (incorporated, 501c, etc.).

P.1b > 1.2b Governance System - The processes that ensure ethical interactions also need to be designed to work within the governance system described in the profile (P.1b). All too often organizations will create processes and structures that are different and distinct from the main systems of the organization. While this might be appropriate for processes that require "third party" status to be effective (e.g., ombudsman) they should be designed to work within and be consistent with the overall management systems and organizational structure.

Customers and Stakeholders

P.1b > 1.2a Customers and Stakeholders - The customers and stakeholders identified in P.1b should be addressed by the governance processes and practices identified in 1.2a for the protection of "stakeholder" and stockholder interests.

P.1b > 1.2b Customers and Stakeholders - The customers and stakeholders identified in the profile (P.1b) should be the same groups addressed by the processes and practices to ensure ethical interactions.

P.1b > 2.1b Customers and Stakeholders - The test to determine whether the strategic objectives balance the needs of the key stakeholders is based in part on the customers and stakeholders and their needs identified in the profile (P.1b).

P.1b > 2.2a Customers and Stakeholders - The customers and stakeholders identified in the profile (P.1b) should be addressed by the measures that track progress toward accomplishing the action plans and the overall strategy.

P.1b > 4.2a Customers and Stakeholders - The number, type, and nature of the customers, groups, segments and stakeholders described in the profile are critical inputs to the design of the data and information processes and systems that makes the right data available to the right customers and stakeholders.

Customer Segments and Requirements

P.1b > 3.1a Customers Segments and Requirements - The listening and learning methods described in 3.1a should address the customer segments, groups, etc. identified in the profile (P.1b).

P.1b > 3.1b Customers Segments and Requirements - The customer satisfaction determination processes should be designed to capture the satisfaction of the key customer and market segments and groups identified in the profile (P.1b). In addition, the mechanisms used to capture this information should also include the ability to capture the demographics of the segmentation scheme as described in P.1b and in 3.2a.

P.1b <> 3.2a(1&2) Customers Segments and Requirements - The processes and practices described in 3.2a(1&2) to determine product and service offerings and features should be consistent with the customer segments and requirements described in the profile (P.1b).

P.1b > 3.2a(3&4) Customers Segments and Requirements - The customer segments and requirements identified in the profile (P.1b) are key inputs to the customer segmentation and requirements determination processes and practices described in 3.2a(3&4). In addition, if this process modifies the customer and market segments then that should be reflected in an updated profile.

P.1b > 4.2b Customers Segments and Requirements - The number, type, and nature of the customers, groups, and segments described in the profile are critical inputs to the design of the data and information processes and systems that makes the right data available to the right customers. There should be processes to ensure the appropriate information system is reliable, secure, and user friendly for all customer segments and groups.

Suppliers and Partners

P.1b > 4.1c Suppliers, Partners, Collaborators - Suppliers, partners, and collaborators identified in the profile (P.1b) should be addressed when determining the appropriate or most effective methods to deploy the organization's priorities for continuous and breakthrough improvement and opportunities for innovation.

P.1b > 4.2a Suppliers, Partners, Collaborators - The number, type, and nature of the suppliers, partners, and collaborators as described in the profile (P.1b) are critical inputs to the design of the data and information processes and systems that makes the right data available to the right suppliers, partners, and collaborators.

P.1b > 4.2b Suppliers, Partners, Collaborators - The number, type, and nature of the suppliers, partners, and collaborators as described in the profile (P.1b) are critical inputs to the design of the data and information systems (reliability, security, user friendliness).

P.1b > 6.1a Suppliers, Partners, Collaborators - The suppliers, partners, and collaborators identified in the profile (P.1b) are key inputs to the work placement strategy (6.1a). Core competencies constitute strategic advantage and as such would not be candidates for outsourcing. Where to place work (inside or outside the organization) is directly influenced by the nature of the work, if it is part of a core competency, and the capability and capacity of the suppliers, partners, and collaborators identified in the profile (P.1b).

P.1b > 6.1b Suppliers, Partners, Collaborators - The suppliers, partners, and collaborators identified in the profile (P.1b) are key inputs to both the requirements determination process a key input into the design of the processes (6.1a). In addition, the suppliers', partners', and collaborators' capabilities and needs should be part of the requirements process to ensure that the supply chain works as an integrated system.

P.1b > 6.2b Suppliers, Partners, Collaborators - Suppliers, partners, and collaborators are often engaged in and an integral part of the work processes. In addition, suppliers, partners, and collaborators are often key inputs to the work process management activities. In fact, they often work side-by-side or even accomplish key tasks by themselves.

Scorecard

P.1b > 7.1a Customers Segments and Requirements - Customer segments and the associated requirements as described in the profile (P.1b) are key inputs to determining and segmenting the key product and service results that are "proxies" for customer satisfaction (7.1a).

P.1b > 7.2a Customers Segments and Requirements - Customers, customer groups, and market segments along with the associated requirements described in the profile (P.1b) are a key input to determining and segmenting the customer focused results presented in 7.2a.

 THOUGHTS FOR LEADERS

It is critical that senior leaders and the governing board (as applicable) of the organization clearly define the governance of the organization and structure all activities to fit within that governance system. For many business issues, a leader's governance decisions may determine whether or not the organization performs well on key financial (and other business) metrics, or even survives. We have seen several instances of leaders who clearly defined the "right ethics and culture," but were not able to translate these into the actions of every employee. In either the public sector or the private sector, the result of this leadership shortcoming can be that the organization is no longer viewed as being viable by their employees, owners, customers, the public, or other stakeholders. While strong governance and transparent behavior might not ensure success, unethical behavior (or a failure in governance) will frequently guarantee failure.

A clear definition of the various customer groups and their requirements is another key part of this portion of the organizational profile. This is one of the most critical definitions any leadership team should develop. Every leadership team we have worked with feels that this definition "is clear." Arguments begin, however, if you ask them to show you the definition, or if you ask the members of the leadership team to agree on the customer groups and their requirements (for products, services, and support).

The fact is, many organizations have not clearly defined (or segmented) their customer groups based on the **customer's requirements.** Until these customer segments or groups are clearly defined, and until every employee understands what the customers' require, the organization will have a difficult time aligning their processes to the customer's requirements. Furthermore, the organization will not be able to align every employee's measures, goals, and actions to meet those requirements.

In simple terms, an organization must understand what drives their customer's behavior. Understanding the linkage between customer requirements ⇨ organizational performance ⇨ customer satisfaction ⇨ customer engagement (loyalty) is critical to understanding customer behavior and may even be critical to organizational survival.

A LIGHTER MOMENT:

> *People will buy anything that is one to a customer.*
>
> **Sinclair Lewis**

> *There is a tendency among some businesses to criticize and belittle their competitors. This is a bad procedure. Praise them. Learn from them. There are times when you can co-operate with them to their advantage and to yours! Speak well of them and they will speak well of you. You can't destroy good ideas. Take advantage of them.*
>
> **George Matthew Adams**

 ## FOUNDATION

The first two Areas to Address of the Organizational Profile focused on the organization itself - the Organizational Description, and those they directly interface with, such as customers, suppliers and partners. The remaining three Areas to Address, in the Organizational Profile, focus on various aspects or the external environment in which the organization operates, and the methods used to continuously learn and improve to meet the challenges of that environment - the Organizational Situation.

Competitive Position

This begins with where the organization stands in relation to their competitors. Who are their competitors? How fast is the market and industry growing? What factors will determine who wins in the marketplace? How the organization and the competitors doing against these key success factors? How does the organization know?

Our experience has shown us that these are critical questions that are applicable to all organizations, even Not-For-Profit or Governmental organizations. Even these organizations can be hurt competitively if they do not keep pace with the changes in the competition or changes in the products and services they provide.

Why are these questions important? In the **For-Profit** free marketplace, the answers to these questions are critical when developing strategies to ensure continued success and sustainable results. For example, the local coffee shop's position might be head-to-head competition with the local Starbucks. When Starbucks came to town, however, the customers loyal to the local coffee shop put bumper stickers on their cars that read "Friends don't let friends drink Starbucks." While Starbucks might make a fine cup of coffee, something else was at work here. The *free* wireless internet at the local shop might have had something to do with it, but there were clearly other factors, including personal relationships between the customers and the owner of the local coffee shop. The good news may be that both coffee shops are thriving, perhaps because they serve different markets or customer groups. Each of them, however, is focused on their particular product and service offerings and they are not trying to beat the other at their own game.

A key question is how would each coffee shop know how they were doing against each other?

Years ago I worked with Boeing in Ft. Walton Beach, Florida. One of the history books about the region told the story of two theatres in town who were arch rivals. The owner of one theatre always ensured his son was first in line to buy a ticket at the <u>competitor's</u> theatre every morning. In the evening his son would run across town to buy the last ticket of the day. His dad would look at the two ticket numbers, and calculate (through a sophisticated analysis technique called *subtraction* using the serial numbers on the tickets) how many customers his competitor had attracted that day. Nevertheless, some more sophisticated businesses don't even do this level of reconnaissance of their competitors. How can they make valid decisions if they don't know what their competitors are doing?

Competitiveness Changes

Once the competitive position is understood, the next understanding which is reviewed is critical. In previous years, the criteria asked "what are the principal factors that determine your success relative to your competitors?" These were called Success Factors.

We recommend that organizations do not lose sight of the Success Factors for their industry. In these few words, a question is asked which very few organizations can really answer. In simple terms it asks, what are the few things that drive your competitive advantage? These are the things anybody in your industry needs to be good at in order to succeed. The organization should benchmark the organizations that are the best at these things. These are the things the organization should invest in improving and these are the things leaders should consider as the *lifeline* of the organization. This need to understand what is critical to your success is also true in **Not-For-Profit**. For example, one of our clients stores 500,000 part number and processes thousands of shipments each week. They MUST be good at: 1) record accuracy; 2) storage discipline; 3) preparing orders for shipment; and 4) partnering with shipping and freight forwarding organizations. If they are not good at one of these things, nothing else can make up for that shortcoming. Although this has been taken out of the criteria, we think it is still be a critical question, and can be very beneficial in helping an organization determine their strategic advantages.

The criteria now asks what are the key changes taking place which affect your competitiveness. Again, it can help an organization to determine the industry's principal factors that determine success as a step toward determining the changes taking place and/or the opportunities for innovation and collaboration to favorably impact your competitiveness.

Comparative Data

Performance measures and competitive comparisons provide evidence to increase the understanding of the competitive environment. Today's competitive environment requires advanced customer knowledge and understanding. It is one thing to understand the customers' stated wants and needs and it is quite another to understand what drives their behavior and what they will actually pay for. If the organization understands what drives their customer's behavior better than the competitors, and they align the organization's processes to address that behavior, they will often win in the marketplace.

Performance measures can certainly be influenced by competitors. These are some of the areas of greatest importance for comparison. Comparison measures can provide a relative measure for comparing performance levels and trends. Comparisons help organizations and their leaders to understand gaps in performance and the magnitude of these gaps. They also help the organization to set realistic, but meaningful, targets.

The danger in comparisons is that they can limit the organization's improvement efforts to continuously *catching up*, rather than leaping beyond its competitors with innovative products, services, and processes. This is the comparison trap. Jim Collins warns that comparison is, "the cardinal sin of modern life. It traps us in a game that we can't win. Once we define ourselves in terms of others, we lose the freedom to shape our own lives." Organizations are no different. Apple Inc. doesn't win in the marketplace because they are chasing their competitors' products and services. They win by carving their own unique path and leading in the marketplace. Comparisons can help to drive an increased sense of urgency, but they need to be tempered with an understanding of the rate of change required to be a leader.

A competitive environment can be critical to future survival - it certainly will impact whether an organization merely *survives* or *thrives* in the future. Tang and Bauer, in their book *Competitive Dominance*, identify several competitive positions from "dead" to "follower" to "dominance." Knowledge of the competition and their performance, particularly through the customers' eyes, is key to developing strategies to overtake the competitor's position and dominate the market.

As we will see later in Part 4, performance relative to competitors can be categorized into four categories. Two of these categories require little to no action while the other two require fundamental shifts in the organization's mindset, methods, and rate of improvement. This area is particularly difficult to address for many non-profits and government organizations. For one thing, they are not designed primarily for a competitive market. Moreover, many of their competitors are only a "potential" threat and may not be currently in the same product offering arena.

 EXAMPLES

Clarke American - (Baldrige Recipient 2001)

Market Performance
- *Clarke American has outperformed the market in the FI check supply industry over the past five years.*
- Another source of competition to the FI check industry is direct mail competitors with 20 percent of the US check market. Their growth has come as a result of lower prices and consumer awareness of the variety of check styles offered through mail circulars. Three major players exist in this market.

Growth
- *Our growth is attributable to our refined, consistent FIS strategy of partnering with Financial Institutions (FIs) to provide best-in-class check printing and check-related services and products to enhance their businesses.*
- During the early 1990s, aggressive competitive pricing drove all check providers to significantly reduce costs. Clarke American increased investment in the emerging **FIS** approach to ensure improvement in quality, products and services. This committed strategy of differentiating through **FIS** is the principal factor in determining success.

Source: Clarke (2002) p. 5

Advocate Good Samaritan Hospital (Baldrige Recipient 2010)

GSAM serves patients in a highly competitive market with eleven (11) hospitals within 20 miles of GSAM; three (3) of these hospitals (Hinsdale, Edward, Elmhurst) are considered primary competitors. The primary competitors are all not-for-profit hospitals ranging from 311 to 427 licensed beds and either have, or have plans to add, private rooms. Private rooms have become a differentiator in the marketplace; however, GSAM is constrained by limited availability of private rooms in the Medical/Surgical areas. To respond to this disadvantage, they leverage their core competency of *building loyal relationships* and have launched a redesigned model of care both of which create an environment that makes GSAM the hospital of choice. While each of these competitive hospitals has a stronghold in the community in which they are located, many of the surrounding communities have loyalties that are shared with at least one other hospital. In addition to hospitals, large multi and single specialty physician groups provide competition for outpatient and ambulatory services throughout the market.

This highly competitive environment creates intense and beneficial competition between hospitals in DuPage County to provide superior health care outcomes and service. It also results in large competitive capital expenditures. Yet despite this intense competition, GSAM:

- Continues to be the market share leader in its primary service area (PSA) and has grown market share over the last three (3) years. 'Market Share' measures the increase, decrease, and total number of inpatient cases in the PSA for each hospital.
- Has grown overall physician loyalty. Physician loyalty is tracked on a monthly basis to determine the percent of medical staff admissions that come to GSAM compared to their three (3) competitors. This percentage increased from 57.8% in 2007 to 62.2% in 2009, a 7.6% increase in new volume directed by the physicians on our medical staff.

This growth has been accomplished through significantly improving health outcomes, engaging and building loyal relationships with physicians, and offering exceptional service to patients making GSAM their hospital of choice.

Figure P.2-1 Primary Service Area Market Share and Key Competitors

Hospital		Bed Size	2006 Market Share	2009 Q2 Market Share	Variance
GSAM		333	20.0%	22.3%	11.5%
Competitors	A	427	10.1%	9.6%	(4.9%)
	B	311	18.8%	17.5%	(6.9%)
	C	354	12.6%	10.5%	(16.6 %)

Advocate Health Care © 2010

North Mississippi Medical Center (Baldrige Recipient as a Hospital in 2006, and as a Health Care System in 2012)

NMMC notes that the competitive environment for their tertiary services differs from the environment for their outpatient and general acute care services. Therefore, these may be expected to be addressed as separate segments of their patient population.

NMMC is in an unusual competitive situation by virtue of its relative geographic isolation. Tupelo, Miss., (population – 35,000) is the hub city of this sparsely populated, 7,500 square mile, 24-county rural region in which 2-lane roads dominate. The nearest hospitals of comparable size, and offering a comparable range of services, are headquartered in urban locations at least 100 miles away (Memphis, TN; Birmingham, AL; and Jackson, MS). However, NMMC's primary competitors for providing specialized outpatient and acute care services are two of the Baptist Memorial System's medical centers in Oxford and Columbus, Miss. (NMMC's secondary service area). The Baptist Hospitals in Columbus and Oxford have 20% and 18% market share, respectively, of NMMC's secondary service area.

NMMC collaborates with Le Bonheur Children's Medical Center in Memphis, which provides neonatal cardiology consults, and the Good Samaritan Free Clinic (GSFC), which provides health care services to the working poor. NMMC has established referral relationships to other facilities for those services it does not provide. Some of the information for the NMMC competitive environment is addressed in the opening paragraph of their profile, setting the expectation that they will compare themselves to other large, rural medical centers throughout the country.

There was a time when being last, or close to it, stopped surprising or even disappointing residents of Mississippi. For too long, Mississippi placed last or near last among the nation in education, income and health. No longer. North Mississippi Medical Center (NMMC*), established in 1937 as Tupelo's solitary "hospital on the hill," is now a health care organization prepared to inspire all health care organizations in the United States to higher levels of performance. Nestled in a rural community, NMMC is driven by the passion to break through the barriers of low expectations that have allowed us to provide and accept less than what is possible. Through our relentless commitment, we have successfully and distinctively become a compassionate operational, clinical, and technological organization of excellence.

NMMC, as the region's dominant health care provider, has embraced the responsibility to commit the entirety of its $706 million in assets and its annual operating revenue of more than $443 million to provide the most accurate, safe, and sensitive health care for the people whose lives and livelihood depend on us. NMMC's commitment to higher performance transcends the challenge from our competitors. Rather, it is based on the simple idea: people deserve the best health care services professionals can provide. Not less. Period.   Source: NMMC (2007) pg v

University of Wisconsin - Stout (Baldrige Recipient 2001)

There are two competitive considerations essential to achieving UW-Stout's goals: (1) competition for faculty, and (2) competition for students. Mission-similar universities and business/industry compete for skilled and qualified faculty.   Competitive differentiators for faculty include: participation in the university decision-making process, quality of laboratory and other facilities, technology infrastructure, peer recognition, campus atmosphere and image, and opportunities for research and professional and career development. Competition for students comes from other UW System universities, public universities and colleges in the State of Minnesota (because of reciprocity agreements), and other national and international private and public universities.

Business and industry are also competitors for high school and technical college students. Since our primary market is Wisconsin (72 percent of students), the other UW System campuses are the major competition. Twenty-eight percent of students are non-residents and come to UW-Stout because of its unique mission and curriculum. UW-Stout's outreach initiatives with high schools, businesses, alumni, and Friends of Stout are effective methods to compete for students.   Competitive differentiators for students include: UW-Stout's image and focused mission, career focus and placement success, student services, and active learning facilities.

In order to achieve leadership in these key competitive factors, UW-Stout compares its performance with the other UW System campuses and with a selected set of nationally recognized universities with similar missions and/or curriculums, including California Polytechnic State University–San Luis Obispo, Ferris State University, and the New Jersey Institute of Technology. These comparisons provide data to assess leadership performance levels within the market of opportunity and for mission differentiation. To build and sustain its reputation and image nationally and internationally, UW-Stout also uses major national university benchmarks to compare its performance in key areas of student satisfaction, diversity, and financial management. This year, the universities selected for comparison are from states attaining A-B scores in the 2000 "Measuring Up" National Education Survey. Wisconsin was one of only three states attaining "A" or "B" scores in all five categories.   Source: UW-Stout (2002) p. 186

Pewaukee School District (Baldrige Recipient 2013)

Our strategic advantages heighten PSD's (Pewaukee School District) sustainability and support attainment of our Mission. They influence our core competencies. Strategic challenges are addressed in our SP Strategies and by our core competencies. Strategic challenges and advantages (Figure P-10) are identified in the Environmental Scan (ES) and SWOT analysis conducted in our SPP (Strategic Planning Process), addressed in our SP (Strategic Plan), and reviewed by the AT (Administrative Team).

Area	Strategic Advantage	Strategic Challenge	SP Integration
Educational Programs & Services	High student achievement Comprehensive curriculum & extra-curricular offerings Innovation in academic programs and use of technology	Teaching 21st century skills Increasing student achievement for all students Increasing student & stakeholder engagement using technology Growing community partnerships	Teaching & Learning Technology Communication
Operations	Safe campus setting and small size	Operating with increased efficiency	Facilities & Operations
Societal Responsibilities	Fiscal stability & growing enrollment	Changes in WI education funding system and changes to collective bargaining due to Act 10	Facilities & Operations
Workforce	Talented & professional workforce Strong leadership Strong collaborative culture	Engaging & developing our talented staff	Workforce Engagement & Development

Figure P-10 Strategic Advantages & Challenges

CRITERIA QUESTIONS

In your response, include answers to the following questions:

a. Competitive Environment

(1) **Competitive Position** What is your competitive position? What are your relative size and growth in your industry or the markets you serve? How many and what types of competitors do you have?

(2) **Competitiveness Changes** What key changes, if any, are affecting your competitive situation, including changes that create opportunities for innovation and collaboration, as appropriate?

(3) **Comparative Data** What key sources of comparative and competitive data are available from within your industry? What key sources of comparative data are available from outside your industry? What limitations, if any, affect your ability to obtain or use these data?

Notes:

P.2a. *Like for-profit businesses, nonprofit organizations are frequently in a highly competitive environment. Nonprofit organizations must often compete with other organizations and alternative sources of similar services to secure financial and volunteer resources, membership, visibility in appropriate communities, and media attention.*

NIST (2015 - 2016) p. 6

WORKSHEETS

P.2a(1) - Competitive Position

Industry or Market Group Served	Size of Your Group	Growth of Group	Key Competitors and Size	Key Collaborators

P.2a(2) – Competitiveness Changes

Industry or Market Group Served	Key Changes Taking Place That Affect Your Competitive Position	How The Key Changes Impact Innovation and Collaboration

* These factors should include opportunities for innovation and collaboration, as appropriate. The drivers of each of these may be internal or external factors, such as the knowledge gained from your external customer listening posts.

P.2a(3) – Comparative Data

Sources of Comparative or Competitive Data	Measures	Limitations in Obtaining Data
From Within The Industry:		
From Outside The Industry:		

BLUEPRINT

P.2a Competitive Environment

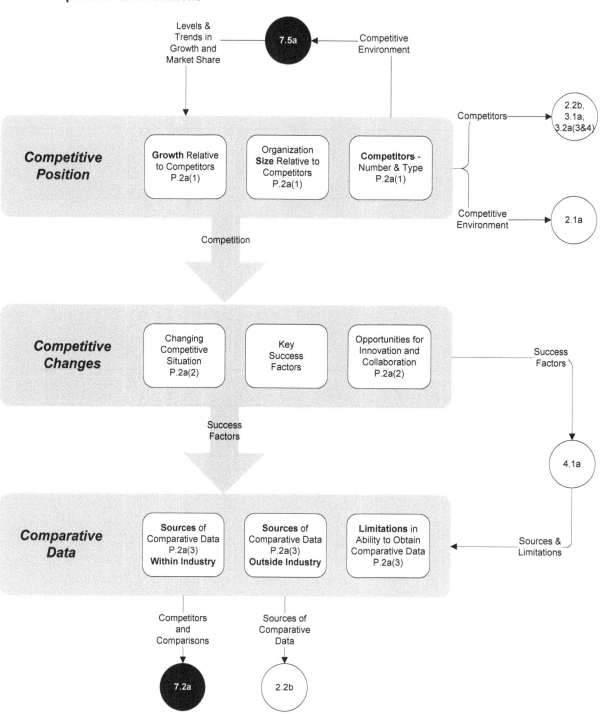

SYSTEM INTEGRATION

Systems

P.2a > 2.1a Competitive Environment - The competitive environment including the growth relative to competitors, size relative to competitors, and the number and type of competitors described in the profile (P.2a) are key inputs to strategy development and should be a central component of the SWOT analysis.

P.2a > 2.2b Competitors - The competitors identified in the organizational profile (P.2a) are key inputs to determining the appropriate comparisons to include with the performance projections in 2.2b.

P.2a > 2.2b Sources of Comparative Data - The sources of comparison data described in the organizational profile (P.2a) will drive the types of comparisons that are available for inclusion with the performance projections described in 2.2b.

P.2a > 3.1a Competitors - The customers of the competitors identified in the profile (P.2a) are an input to the listening and learning processes and practices described in 3.1a. The listening and learning processes not only address current customers but also those of the competitors identified in the profile (P.2a).

P.2a > 3.2a(3&4) Competitors - The customers of the competitors identified in the profile (P.2a) are an input to the process of identifying customers, customer groups, and market segments described in 3.2a(3&4).

P.2a > 4.1a Success Factors - The key success factors for the key markets and competitive environments along with the competitors described in the profile (P.2a) are key inputs to the selection of comparison information measures and sources described in 4.1a. This is particularly important in areas that are linked to market performance.

P.2a < 4.1a Sources and Limitations - The selection of comparison information to support the analysis of all facets of organizational performance is limited due to barriers to sharing of competitive information and the cost of collecting comparison information. The profile describes both the sources of comparison information and the limitations to collecting comparisons that the organization faces. Both of these should be derived or outputs from the processes and criteria used by the organization to select comparisons as describe in 4.1a.

Scorecard

P.2a > 7.2a Competitors and Comparisons - The comparisons presented in the customer-focused results (7.2a) should be consistent with the competitors and comparison sources identified in the profile (P.2a).

P.2a > 7.5a Competitive Environment - The competitors (number and type) are key inputs to the results in 7.3a Financial and Market Results. The actual results should include the level of performance or size of the organization relative to competitors and the trends in the results indicating the growth relative to competitors.

P.2a < 7.5a Levels and Trends - The levels and trends in the growth and market share are an input to the competitive position described in the profile (P.2a).

THOUGHTS FOR LEADERS

For any organization, it is key to clearly gauge the competitive environment and their own organization's competitive advantage. This should include an understanding of what the organization must (and what the organization can) do better than anyone else. Without this understanding, how can leaders and employees make the right decisions?

Domino's Pizza, in their early years, for example, did not make the case that their pizza was the best. Most likely, banks were not willing to finance a business model that said their pizza was better than all the rest. Instead, Domino's emphasized **time sensitive delivery**. In the early years, they guaranteed that customers would receive their pizzas in 30 minutes or less, or the pizza was free. Their core competency and competitive advantage was consistent timely delivery.

An organization's list of competitive advantages should not include dozens of competencies. Competitive Advantages should include the handful of things (4 - 6?) that the customers feel are the organization's competitive advantage, and for which they are willing to pay. It is surprising, however, how many organizations you can visit who do not clearly define, communicate, develop and measure the small number of things they have to be good at in order to succeed. Without this understanding the leaders and the employees will not know what areas to protect and what areas to improve.

A LIGHTER MOMENT:

Without the spur of competition we'd loaf out our life.

Arnold Glasow

> *There are two ways of meeting difficulties:*
> *you alter the difficulties, or you alter yourself to meet them.*
>
> **Phyllis Bottome**

FOUNDATION

The strategic challenges focus on four main areas - business challenges and advantages, operational challenges and advantages, societal responsibility challenges and advantages, and human resource challenges and advantages. Strategic challenges are those things coming at the organization from the outside which the organization does not control. The organization, however, must take internal action (normally through the strategic objectives and the associated action plans) to address these challenges if the organization is to remain competitive and sustainable. This is even true for non-profit organizations. Not-for-profit is a tax status, not a business model! The strategic advantages are the areas where the organization has a competitive advantage, and the factors which drive the competitive advantage are typically in the organizational objectives and are continuously strengthened and reviewed.

Business Challenges

Business challenges vary depending on the nature of the organization (for profit, non-profit, government, etc.), but they often include how to keep black ink on the books! For example, local coffee shops are not the most highly capitalized firms in the country. Consequently, the business challenges are often focused on how to keep the cash flowing.

Operations Challenges

Operational challenges, on the other hand, generally focus on the organization's ability to meet the demands of the customers while efficiently and safely meeting or exceeding regulatory requirements. This challenge can get even more complicated when there are multiple customer groups with a range of needs or demands. For example, at the coffee shop, satisfying the demands of the on-the-way-to-work crowd might be difficult when the line is also filled with other customer groups, such as the group that lingers for conversation and often orders food to go with their coffee.

Societal Responsibility Challenges

Societal responsibility challenges address the needs of the community (which can be defined as local, state or national). These, for most organizations, are changing frequently. Some of the changes are optional (supporting a local program) while others may be broader in scope and mandatory (nationally mandated programs).

Workforce Challenges

Finally, there are human resource challenges. These can be at the heart of what can make an organization thrive or struggle. For example, with a coffee shop, how do they keep well-trained, motivated employees when the industry pay is relatively low and student workers graduate and create turnover on a regular basis?

Competitive Advantages

These are the things which the organization has been given, or has created, which provides them an advantage in the competitive marketplace. This advantage could be internally with their cost, schedule or quality, or externally with their customer's perception of their value. For example, the notional coffee shop had a geographic advantage before Starbucks moved to the neighborhood. No competitor nearby sold top quality coffee. Once the geographic advantage was gone, the leaders of the coffee shop needed to understand what else would drive the customer's behavior. That advantage (or differentiator) could be either products or services, but must be something which was valued by the customer.

 EXAMPLES

Charleston Area Medical Center (Charleston, West Virginia)

The figure below shows Charleston Area Medical Centers (CAMC's) alignment and integration of the key healthcare service, operational, societal responsibility and human resource strategic challenges and advantages with our strategic plan.

⇨ **Strategic Challenges:** Understanding what is coming at us from the outside which we must address, but do not control

    ⇨ **Success Factors:** Understanding what anybody in our business needs to excel at if they wish to remain competitive today

        ⇨ **Strategic Advantages:** Understanding our organization's strengths vs. the competitors

            ⇨ **Strategic Opportunities:** Understanding what is happening in the marketplace (or internally) which is an opportunity the organization can leverage.

                ⇨ **Strategic Objectives:** Understanding what we will be stronger in once our objectives are achieved.

In linking of these factors, some are addressed in Area to Address P2b and others are addressed in Category 2.

Figure P.2-3 Alignment of Pillars, Strategic Challenges, Success Factors, Advantages, Strategic Objectives

Mission	CC	Vision Pillars	Pillar Key Result Area	Strategic Challenges	Key Success Factors (Healthcare)	Strategic Advantages	Strategic Objectives (4 year long term)	TCT	CC Improve Health	Improve Economics
Striving to provide the best health care to every patient, every day.	Transforming Care Together to improve the health and economics of our community	Best Place to Receive Patient Centered Care	•Patient engagement •Quality •Safety	•Governmental pressure on continuously increasing quality and decreasing cost •Safety Net requirements and funding •Aging and inadequate facilities •Recruiting and retaining competent staff	•Evidence-based and cost effective care •Value Based Purchasing results •Service and clinical outcomes •Competitive cost structure •Integrated IT infrastructure	•Performance improvement culture and infrastructure •Scope of services •Cost effectiveness •Image /reputation	•Improve HCAHPS patient experience results to top quartile •Achieve top quartile performance on clinical care outcomes	x	x	x
		Best Place to Work	•Employee engagement	•Governmental pressure on continuously increasing quality and decreasing cost •Recruiting and retaining competent staff •Talent/skill set availability	•Integrated IT infrastructure •Workforce capability and capacity •Loyal / aligned relationships with patients, physicians and employees	•Performance improvement culture and infrastructure •"Grow our own" •Learning culture	•Improve employee satisfaction and engagement to "Employer of Choice"	x	x	x
		Best Place to Practice Medicine	•Medical Staff alignment	•Governmental pressure on continuously increasing quality and decreasing cost •Safety Net requirements and funding •EHR and MU requirements •Recruiting and retaining competent staff	•Service and clinical outcomes •Workforce capability and capacity •Loyal / aligned relationships with patients, physicians and employees	•Performance improvement culture and infrastructure •Scope of services •Highly competent / capable medical staff •"Grow our own" •Learning culture	•Ensure adequate medical resources to meet the needs of current and evolving service delivery and reimbursement models •Create the capability and capacity to respond agilely to healthcare reform	x	x	x
		Best Place to Learn	•Learning organization •Grow our own	•Governmental pressure on continuously increasing quality and decreasing cost •Recruiting and retaining competent staff •Talent/skill set availability	•Fully integrated IT infrastructure •Workforce capability and capacity	•Performance improvement culture and infrastructure •"Grow our own" •Learning culture	•Ensure integrated education and research systems and academic partnerships that address workforce needs of our community •Promote organizational and individual learning, innovation and performance improvement	x	x	x
		Best Place to Refer Patients	•Market share •Funding for the future •Competency for healthcare reform	•Governmental pressure on continuously increasing quality and decreasing cost •Aging and inadequate facilities •Expectations / entitlement for health services •Accountability for total population health •Recruiting and retaining competent staff	•Service and clinical outcomes •Cost of capital •Success in impacting the continuum of care •Loyal community relationships •Loyal / aligned relationships with patients, physicians and employees	•Scope of services •Market dominance •Partners in Health network	•Grow market share in primary and secondary service areas •Establish competencies for success in the health care reform environment		x	x

Pewaukee School District (Baldrige Recipient 2013)

Competitive Environment

Viewed as a high performing school district in a county that is home to eleven high achieving K-12 school districts (with three school districts participating in our state level Baldrige program), PSD is reaching increasingly high levels of excellence positively impacting our competitive position. In 2009 Business Week Magazine rated the City of Pewaukee as the #1 affordable suburb in the nation, citing quality schools. Money Magazine ranked Pewaukee in the top 100 places to live in the nation in 2010, also citing the quality school system. Milwaukee Magazine rates Pewaukee High School an over-performer and one of the top 20 area prep schools and Pewaukee a Top Ten community in which to reside.

When comparing size, PSD has the smallest K-12 student enrollment in Waukesha County and ranks 91st largest of the 424 school districts in WI when comparing enrollment size. PSD's operating budget is $28.6 million and our comparative cost per pupil is $11,688 which ranks 294th out of 424 school districts in the State. Unlike 2/3 of the school districts in WI, PSD is experiencing steady enrollment growth, greatly impacting a more favorable budget picture when compared to our competitors. In terms of market share, PSD holds 87% of resident students who elect to attend PSD schools over private/parochial or home school options, a percent greater than area districts. At one time PSD had a negative OE trend, sending more resident students to other schools than attracting non-resident students to PSD. This trend has changed dramatically.

We currently have 220 incoming OE students and 65 outgoing OE students with 153 OE applications for seats we cannot fill. PSD's key competitors are the Waukesha County (WC) public schools, in particular the schools with whom we share a border, that we compete with for market share. In analyzing student achievement, PSD elects to benchmark with six high performing WI public schools due to their high levels of student achievement; we call these "Aspiring" school districts. These schools provide us stretch goals we aspire to reach.

Competitive changes that may affect PSD's competitive situation and provide opportunities for innovation and collaboration include:

- Our partnership with CESA 1 and the Innovation Lab which is propelling our SP Action Plan in Personalized Learning, an innovative instructional strategy. We are viewed as a leader in personalized learning throughout our state.
- State legislation which is increasing opportunity for students to elect non-public school options using vouchers to attend parochial school or attend independent charter schools.
- The passing of Act 10 which changes the WI State budget & funding formula and collective bargaining practices presents challenges but also results in the development of innovative approaches to fiscal responsibility and operational practices that may better support student learning, and staff recruitment and retention. Our core competencies facilitate our being both strategic yet agile at a time of educational change in WI.
- Educator Effectiveness, a WI-mandated teacher evaluation system to be implemented by 2015, will change how we evaluate teachers and potentially how we compensate staff.

PSD utilizes comparative and competitive data (Figure P-6) as part of our core competency of creating a culture of continuous improvement. Since we are a small organization with very limited data assessment staff, we primarily use available public data as our source of comparative and competitive data with much found on the DPI Wisedash/WINNS web site. Many competitors do not collect data with the same depth in areas other than student achievement, so benchmarking opportunities are challenging in our support work process areas. PSD strategically identifies "stretch providing" benchmarking opportunities in our Academic work process area, electing to benchmark with high performing WI schools whose student achievement we aspire to attain.

University of Wisconsin-Stout (Baldrige Recipient 2001)

Guided by its vision, values, and mission, UW-Stout's objective is to be the school of choice for the 21st century. To achieve this objective, campus direction is guided by seven strategic goals with specific action plans deployed through its annual budget planning process involving the entire campus. This process enables UW-Stout to respond to its strategic challenges with constancy of purpose and consistency of actions, avoiding year-to-year major shifts in direction. UW-Stout's strategic challenges and goals are:

1. *Offer high quality, challenging academic programs that influence and respond to a changing society.* UW-Stout's challenge is to keep its programs continually renewed and refreshed. Strong stakeholder contact processes are employed to keep current on changing requirements. These relationship processes are complemented by Program Directors who use an effective Program Development Process to refine existing programs and to design new programs that cut across the three Colleges and strengthen UW-Stout's mission. Key indicators of success include: (1) curriculum renewal, (2) employer assessment of graduate readiness and job performance, and (3) increased level of academic challenge.

2. *Preserve and enhance our educational processes through the application of active learning principles.* Hands-on, minds-on student learning capabilities have differentiated UW-Stout in the marketplace as demonstrated by its superior job placement success. The challenge in maintaining this reputation is to continue to lead in the percent of instruction provided in laboratories and to increase the number of experiential learning opportunities through cooperative relationships with industry. Key success indicators include: (1) increased level of student engagement (collaborative learning, student interactions with faculty, and enriching experiences), (2) targeted computer competencies for students, and (3) job placement success.

3. *Promote excellence in teaching, research, scholarship, and service.* The campus promotes and facilitates research and developmental opportunities to attract, retain, and develop UW-Stout's faculty and staff. Even though UW-Stout is primarily a teaching university, its objective is to be a leader among the UW System comprehensives in federal grants and in budget allocated for professional development. Key indicators of success include (1) faculty engaged in research grants, (2) professional development expenditures, (3) number of sabbaticals and professorships, and (4) distance education offering growth.

4. *Recruit and retain a diverse university population.* To support the increasing requirement for students to operate effectively in a globally diverse environment, UW-Stout deploys initiatives to retain and graduate all student groups, has strengthened multicultural student services, and implements specialized academic support programs and new cultural-specific courses. New study abroad programs and additional foreign language requirements for graduation are also being implemented. Key success indicators include (1) recruitment of minority faculty and staff, (2) freshman retention rate, (3) graduation success, and (4) scholarship growth for diversity recruiting and academic quality.

5. *Foster a collegial, trusting, and tolerant environment.* The challenge in achieving this goal is to make shared governance effective by integrating the Faculty Senate, the Senate of Academic Staff and the Stout Student Association (SSA) in planning and decision-making processes. Success indicators include (1) faculty/staff morale, (2) employee turnover, and (3) student retention and satisfaction.

6. *Provide safe, accessible, effective, efficient, and inviting physical facilities.* UW-Stout implements effective capital and budget planning processes and innovative methods of funding new technology plans to continually improve its physical facilities in an environment of constant budgetary challenges. This commitment to up-to-date, safe facilities and services has enabled UW-Stout to achieve leadership in student morale in national surveys. The Stout Foundation leads universities its size in fund raising, and strong industry partnerships provide additional sources for state-of the art laboratory technology. Key success indicators are (1) student satisfaction with the college environment, (2) safety and security, and (3) Stout Foundation financial growth.

7. *Provide responsive, efficient, and cost-effective (educational support) programs and services.* UW-Stout must continuously improve and refine internal capabilities to: (a) strengthen its attraction as a leading academic institution; (b) optimize its support programs and services to best meet the needs of its students and stakeholders; and (c) ensure that budget priorities are allocated to instruction. In order to achieve this goal, UW-Stout systematically evaluates its support process effectiveness, efficiency, and satisfaction as described in P.2 c. Key success indicators include (1) percent of budget allocated to instruction; (2) student evaluation of support programs and services; and (3) energy use.

Source: UW-Stout (2002) pp. 186 - 187

QUESTIONS

In your response, include answers to the following questions:

b. Strategic Context

What are your key strategic challenges and advantages in the areas of business, operations, societal responsibilities, and workforce?

Notes:

P.2b. Strategic challenges and advantages might relate to technology, products, finances, operations, organizational structure and culture, your parent organization's capabilities, customers and markets, brand recognition and reputation, your industry, globalization, climate change, your value chain, and people. Strategic advantages might include differentiators such as price leadership, design services, innovation rate, geographic proximity, accessibility, and warranty and product options. *For some nonprofit organizations, differentiators might also include relative influence with decision makers, ratio of administrative costs to programmatic contributions, reputation for program or service delivery, and wait times for service.*

P.2b. *Throughout the Criteria, "business" refers to a nonprofit organization's main mission area or enterprise activity.*

NIST (2015 - 2016) p. 6

WORKSHEETS

P.2b - Strategic Context

	Caution: The area below is one of the critical factors to be considered in the Organizational Profile. The relationship between the Core Competency, Strategic Challenges, Strategic Advantages and the Success Factors (from an earlier versions of the criteria – see the Glossary at the back of The Baldrige Users Guide) should be described. This framework forms the foundation for much of the application and links: 1) The Organizational Profile; 2) Category 2; and 3) Business Results in Category 7. These should relate to the strategic plans, strategic objectives, improvements, and all aspects of process management.

Strategic Advantages Achieved By The Initiatives	Strategic Challenges (Typically External Influences on the Organization)	Initiatives to Address the Challenges (linked to Strategic Objectives)
	Business Strategic Challenges:	
	Operational Strategic Challenges:	
	Societal Responsibility Strategic Challenges:	
	Human Resource Strategic Challenges:	

BLUEPRINT

P.2b Strategic Context

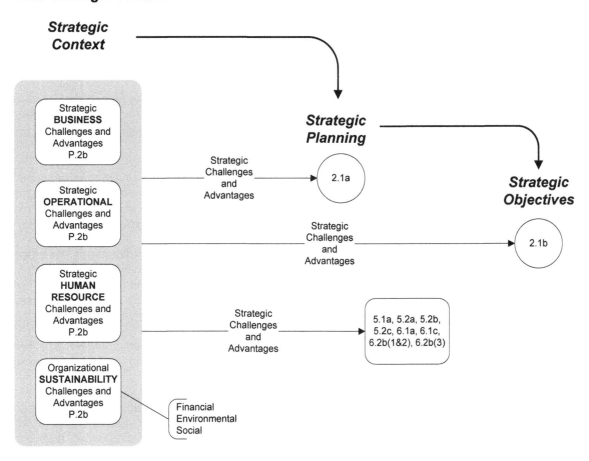

SYSTEM INTEGRATION

Systems

P.2b > 2.1a Strategic Challenges and Advantages - The strategic challenges and advantages identified in the profile (P.2b) are a direct input to the strategy development process and should be an integral part of the SWOT analysis. In addition, the strategic objectives that are developed as an output of this process should reflect and address these challenges and advantages.

P.2b > 2.1b Strategic Challenges and Advantages - The criteria ask how the strategic objectives identified in 2.1b address the strategic challenges and advantages identified in the profile (P.2b). Consequently, there should be an explicit linkage and alignment between the challenges and advantages in P.2b and the objectives identified in 2.1b.

P.2b > 5.1a Strategic Challenges and Advantages - The strategic challenges and advantages described in the profile (P.2b) are important inputs to the workforce needs assessment process. Both challenges and advantages are important considerations when determining the gaps in the actual v. the desired workforce capability and capacity to overcome the challenges and to sustain or enhance the advantages.

P.2b > 5.2a Strategic Challenges and Advantages - The strategic challenges and advantages described in the profile (P.2b) are key inputs to the overall workforce enrichment and engagement system including: (a) the identification of key factors; (b) the creation of a high performance culture; and (c) the performance management system. The challenges and advantages should be addressed by each of these processes and practices.

P.2b > 5.2b Strategic Challenges and Advantages - The strategic challenges and advantages described in the profile (P.2b) are key inputs to the identification of key issues and factors to measure regarding workforce satisfaction and engagement.

P.2b > 5.2c Strategic Challenges and Advantages - The strategic challenges and advantages described in the profile (P.2b) are in important part of the workforce development needs assessment process (5.2c). Both the challenges and advantages are important considerations when deciding what areas to emphasize in workforce and leader development to overcome the challenges and to sustain or enhance the advantages.

P.2b > 6.1 Strategic Challenges and Advantages - The identification of core competencies is directly influenced by the strategic challenges and advantages described in the profile (P.2b). By definition, "the organization's core competencies are those strategically important capabilities that provide an advantage in your marketplace or service environment. Core competencies frequently are challenging for competitors or suppliers and partners to imitate, and they provide a sustainable competitive advantage" (NIST 2007 p. 66).

P.2b > 6.1 Strategic Challenges and Advantages - The strategic challenges and advantages described in the profile (P.2b) are important considerations when determining the threats and the requirements for the emergency readiness system. In some cases, the ability to operate during emergencies might be a competitive advantage.

P.2b > 6.2 Strategic Challenges and Advantages - The strategic challenges and advantages described in the profile (P.2b) should be considered during process implementation and management 6.2b so that the implementation can be accomplished in a way that addresses the challenges and potentially leverages the advantages.

P.2b > 6.2 Strategic Challenges and Advantages - Most organizations have more opportunities for improvement than they have the resources (time and money) to work on at any given time. Consequently, the priorities for process improvement 6.2b(3) should be influenced by the strategic challenges and advantages identified in the profile (P.2b).

THOUGHTS FOR LEADERS

To begin any planning process, leaders need a clear understanding of the challenges facing them. These challenges can be both external and internal, but the focus is frequently on the challenges which the organization does not control. The CPE calls these challenges the **strategic challenges**, and they are primarily external to the organization.

To define an organization's strategic challenges, think of the problems facing the organization that come from each of the stakeholder areas. For example, think of the challenges from competitors, customers, the community, etc. Once an organization can clearly define their external influences, which they do not control, their internal plan of attack for the strategic objectives becomes much clearer.

Additionally, leaders must clearly understand the advantages they have. Each of us can cite personal examples of when someone providing us a product or service "changed" and we never went back. That product or service provider did not understand what we valued.

Understanding the following flow and linkage is critical:

⇨ **Strategic Challenges:** Understanding what is coming at us from the outside which we must address, but do not control

⇨ **Success Factors:** Understanding what anybody in our business needs to excel at if they wish to remain competitive today

⇨ **Strategic Advantages:** Understanding our organization's strengths vs. the competitors

⇨ **Strategic Opportunities:** Understanding what is happening in the marketplace (or internally) which is an opportunity the organization can leverage.

⇨ **Strategic Objectives:** Understanding what we will be stronger in once our objectives are achieved.

With an understanding of this linkage, determining Strategic Objectives is clearer and easier.

> ### *A LIGHTER MOMENT:*
>
> *A man's worst difficulties begin when he is able to do as he likes.*
>
> **Thomas Huxley**

> *There isn't a plant or business on earth that couldn't stand a few improvements – and be better for them. Someone is going to think of them. Why not beat the other fellow to it?*
>
> **Roger B. Babson**

 FOUNDATION

Performance Improvement System

This Area to Address focuses on the continuous improvement processes that are used throughout the organization. How does the organization systematically and continuously improve and stay current with the changing needs of the key stakeholders? When we "boil down" the essence of most of the approaches to improvement, we find that they all follow the scientific method proposed by Shewhart, and later refined by Deming. The scientific method includes four main steps or phases - Plan, Do, Study, Act (PDSA). The "study" step at one time was referred to as "check" (PDCA). This step, however, was changed by Deming to "study" to better reflect the meaning of the step, which is to study the results and learn from them as a basis for further action.

Examples of four applications of the PDSA cycle can include:

- Leadership System;

- Strategy Development and Deployment;

- Organization Transformation (Baldrige Assessment and Improvement); and

- Process Improvement (Continuous Process Improvement, Six Sigma, Lean, etc.).

These approaches, in order to create sustainable change, must incorporate culture, individual, and information improvement, as needed. Any one of these, without the others will not result in change which is lasting.

The improvement approach selected needs to be one that is used throughout the organization. Although the criteria do not **specifically** ask for a specific type of improvement approach (such as Plan-Do-Study-Act), the examiners typically expect to understand what approach is used and why. It is reasonable to use different approaches for different applications, but the reasons "why" each approach is used should be clear. Once the improvement approach or technique is understood, the criteria specifically ask for the process used to maintain an overall focus on performance improvement.

Note: Area to Address P.2c asks how the organization improves. Many responses make one of two mistakes, either:

- They describe improvement at such a high level that the reader cannot understand what the organization **specifically** does, or

- They list so many different types of improvement tools that the reader is confused as to what is used, when, and why?

It is key that performance improvement is used throughout any organization. It does not bode well for an organization if they are proud that they adopted a trendy technique early, have trained everybody, and nobody is using the technique. Everybody should be using the improvement techniques endorsed by the organization, and not just a few employees.

The business example following this section uses several different improvement tools and when each is used is clearly understood by the employees. This starts with individual employees, and goes all the way up to major changes which require Senior Leadership and/or Board approval.

 EXAMPLES

Don Chalmers Ford (Baldrige Site Visit 2008 and 2012)

A systematic organizational focus is Don Chalmers Ford's (DCF's) approach to performance improvement, accomplished by using Find opportunities for improvement from analysis in performance reviews, Organize an improvement plan and implement potential solutions, Review the results and Document the change (FORD figure below).

DCF uses the FORD Improvement Process to achieve better performance, reduce variability and improve services when needed. Every work process improvement goes through this process. Improvements may be simple no-brainers or process discipline where the work is fine but not being followed as designed. Improvements are the result of data from employees via the Driving Forward Board (Item 4.1c(1), meetings and performance analysis reviews highlighted by the 20 Group reviews. Data and trends are used to determine if the process is performing as expected before an improvement is attempted and (early in the process) whether the improvement should continue.

Once a decision is made to continue, the process owner reviews the idea, issue, and data, and determines whether the results are due to process discipline or if a process improvement is needed. Sometimes the process design is appropriate and just needs retraining. Once a determination is made to continue, the process owner is assigned to follow through and provide recommendations. When the process improvement proceeds, the design and innovation process is followed. The change is documented in the in-process on line process system. Baldrige system changes require SLT approval: any other process can be approved by the process owner.

Periodically, a technology change in DCF's computer system is needed to facilitate the dealership's improvements and track current performance. Example: DCF management contacted UCS for an automated update of online service repair order status. The computer automatically updates the vehicle's status, and an e-mail is sent immediately to the customer with a hot link to the web site so that the vehicle status can be tracked.

Once the design is completed, improvements are communicated in e-mails, meetings, and in-process updates, as necessary. The process owner and/or manager are responsible for coordinating changes, which are reviewed, recommended, and updated, as appropriate. Improvements are shared with other departments through implementation, documentation, and training.

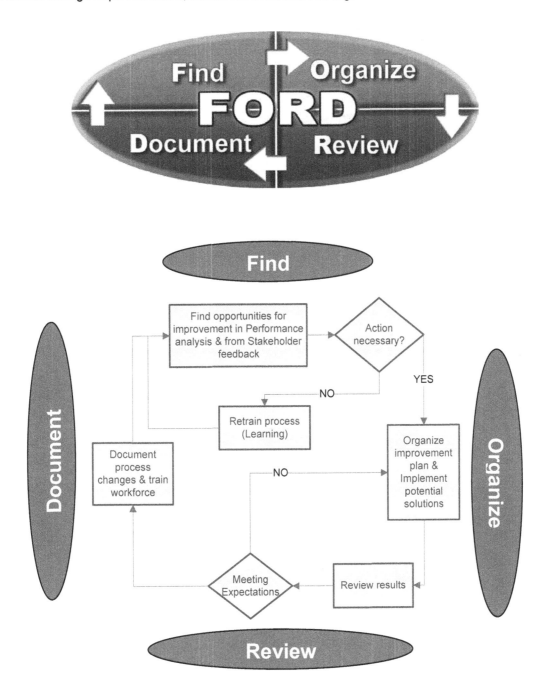

PRO-TEC Coating Company (Baldrige Recipient 2007)

The overall approach to continuous improvement methods is illustrated in Figure P.2-2, with methods contingent on the complexity and scope of an opportunity. The cornerstone of improvement at PRO-TEC is "I-to-I" or *Initiation-to-Implementation.* Although "I-to-I" is a subset of the fully integrated continuous improvement process, for simplicity sake the overall approach is referred to henceforth as "I-to-I." This begins with every associate and goes up to the leadership team or beyond.

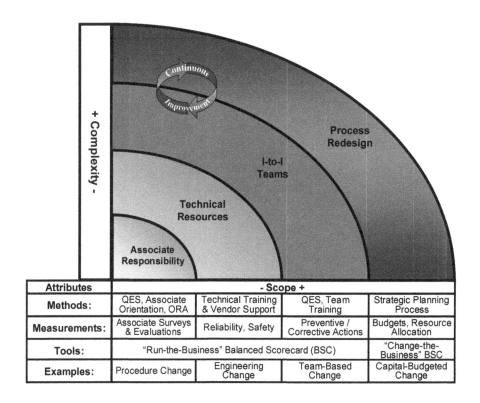

Attributes	- Scope +			
Methods:	QES, Associate Orientation, ORA	Technical Training & Vendor Support	QES, Team Training	Strategic Planning Process
Measurements:	Associate Surveys & Evaluations	Reliability, Safety	Preventive / Corrective Actions	Budgets, Resource Allocation
Tools:	"Run-the-Business" Balanced Scorecard (BSC)			"Change-the-Business" BSC
Examples:	Procedure Change	Engineering Change	Team-Based Change	Capital-Budgeted Change

Associate Responsibility is fostered by teaching Associates to fix problems as they are identified and empowering them to do so. Organizational learning and sharing starts with the initial Associate selection process and continues through new employee orientation, assigned mentors, cross-training, cultural (Ownership, Responsibility, and Authority – ORA – personal empowerment) training, management system training, and through team interactions that serve to develop Associate responsibility.

Technical Resources or subject matter experts have been developed and designated (internally or by vendor support) to support opportunity definition and resolution. These resources are essential to support a 24x7 operation with self-directed work teams to ensure process and product reliability as well as Associate safety. Associates can ask for technical help at any time, based on their own assessment of the need.

The **Initiation-to-Implementation** (I-to-I) process for continuous improvement of team-based changes provides the means and methods for organizational learning and sharing, with its resource committee meeting twice a month to monitor, allocate resources as required, evaluate, and improve the process. The activities of these cross-functional teams are posted on bulletin boards and on the intranet, and typically at least one team activity is presented at each monthly plant management review meeting.

The **Process Redesign** corresponds to strategic planning changes requiring capital budget funding and significant project management requirements. The supporting activities are monitored and tracked on the recently developed "Change the Business" balanced scorecard.

This improvement cycle begins with each employee's ORA level of authority. In simple terms, if they see a problem "we just fix it." If they need help they can access the necessary technical resources. If the scope and complexity is even greater, they can initiate an "I-to-I" or *Initiation-to-Implementation* team who conducts a systematic assessment of the issue using defined problem solving techniques. If the scope and complexity is even greater then it is referred to the leadership team who has the ability to approve the capital (if required) or to integrate it into the short- or longer-term plans.

Each level of improvement uses specific methods to ensure that the approach used is consistent across the organization. Each level also has measurements and can be tracked through the two balanced scorecards. The 'Change the Business' Scorecard is fully integrated with the 'Run the Business' Scorecard and with lower-level individual and team goals and objectives.

North Mississippi Medical Center (Baldrige Recipient as a Hospital in 2006, and as a Health System in 2012)

North Mississippi Medical Center describes their cycles of learning and improvement related to their performance improvement system, and also notes that they have already been identified as a role model for their current process, not only within their state award program, but also nationally. Further, they point to their results to show the maturity of their performance excellence journey.

In 1983, NMMC implemented Quality Circles, which were succeeded by Quality Improvement Teams and the implementation of the PLAN-DO-CHECK-ACT (PDCA) model as the overall approach to improvement efforts. In 1992, NMMC developed the Clinical Practice Analysis (CPA) process, which provided physicians with individualized performance profiles of their care management and outcomes that were compared to local and national benchmarks. Sharing comparative data engaged physicians in performance improvement, and set the stage for the development of the Care-Based Cost Management (CBCM) approach. CBCM links health care quality and cost containment by looking beyond traditional cost drivers (people, equipment, supplies) to the care issues that have a much greater impact on the actual cost of care, namely: practice variation, complications, and social issues. The CBCM approach has produced significant results (7.1), has been featured in numerous national forums and has resulted in national recognition and awards, including the 2003, 2004 and 2005 Solucient's 100 Top Hospital Performance Improvement Leaders and first prize in the 2005 American Hospital Association McKesson Quest for Quality Prize.

In 1996, NMMC began using Baldrige Criteria to identify Opportunities for Improvement (OFIs). The state of Mississippi Baldrige program awarded NMMC the Excellence Award in 1997 and the Governor's Award in 2000. NMMC continues to use Baldrige criteria to critically examine its approaches and processes.

NMMC's systematic evaluation and improvement of key processes have evolved from our Baldrige-based performance analysis. Senior Leadership teams meet monthly and use Performance Score Cards (PSCs) to assess performance. Each team's PSC is organized by the Critical Success Factors, and each key process indicator has a target and a benchmark and is tracked (monthly in most cases).

In addition, each SL and department produces a monthly Budget Accountability Report (BAR) that incorporates the unit's revenues, expenses and productivity into an overall measure. If the measure is below the established threshold, then an Action Plan (AP) is required. NMMC also uses the PSC system for organizational learning by routinely sharing these results and the lessons from them with the staff and Board of Directors.

Source: NMMC (2007) p. vi

 CRITERIA QUESTIONS

In your response, include answers to the following questions:

c. Performance Improvement System

What are the key elements of your performance improvement system, including your processes for evaluation and improvement of key organizational projects and processes?

Notes:

P.2c. The Baldrige Scoring System (pages 30 – 35 in the Baldrige Criteria) uses performance improvement through learning and integration as a dimension in assessing the maturity of organizational approaches and their deployment. This question is intended to set an overall context for your approach to performance improvement. The approach you use should be related to your organization's needs. Approaches that are compatible with the overarching systems approach provided by the Baldrige framework might include implementing a Lean Enterprise System, applying Six Sigma methodology, using Plan-Do-Check-Act (PDCA) methodology, using standards from ISO (e.g., 9000 or 14000), using decision science, or employing other improvement tools.

NIST (2013-2014) p. 6

WORKSHEETS

P.2c - Performance Improvement System

	Caution: Below is one of the critical factors to be considered in the Organizational Profile. The approach to improvement described here should be used throughout the application. If several improvement approaches are used, describe when each approach is used and how they relate to each other.

Approach Used For Performance Improvement Throughout The Organization
Evaluation And Improvement Method(s) Used (e.g., Plan, Do, Study, Act - PDSA) – Note why and when each method is used if there is more than one method described.
Other Organizational Or Leadership Methods Used To Maintain A Focus On The Importance Of Performance Improvement.
Other Organizational Or Leadership Methods Used To Maintain A Focus On Organizational Learning.
How You Evaluate Needed Improvements, And Learn From Improvements (Including Innovation):
Larger-Scale (Possibly Longer Time-Frame) Assessments Used To Validate Systematic Improvement Of Key Processes - Such As: 1) Scientific improvement method (PDSA); 2) Performing A Baldrige-Based Assessment; 3) a Strategic Assessment Cycle; and 4) Benchmarking to drive more aggressive improvement.

Caution:
Although not specifically required by the criteria, the organization may wish to ensure that improvements are being accomplished at several organizational levels. For example, in some organizations each employee is involved in a small scale improvement. At the organization level, however, improvement can take on a broader scope and complexity, and may include innovation and the following factors:

Improvement Phase	Larger-Scale Assessment Approach			
	PDSA	Baldrige Assessment	Strategic Assessment	Benchmarking
Plan				
Do				
Study				
Act				

BLUEPRINT

P.2c Performance Improvement System

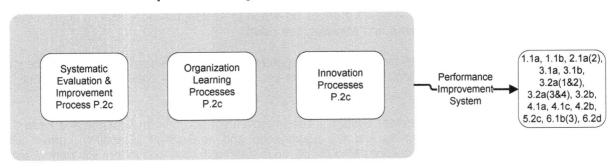

Note: Performance improvement should be used throughout the organization. It is typically not enough to have a few teams or a few projects and have the majority of the organization not involved in improvement. The deployment of an improvement mentality and the use of improvement tools is one of the easiest factors to verify on a site visit.

SYSTEM INTEGRATION

Systems

P.2c > 1.1a Performance Improvement System - The performance improvement system described in the profile (P.2c) should be consistent with the environment that is created to support employee and organizational learning and performance improvement.

P.2c > 1.1b Performance Improvement System - The performance improvement system described in the profile (P.2c) is a key enabler of the ability to focus on action to accomplish performance improvement, the organization's strategic objectives, and ultimately the vision.

P.2c > 2.1a(2) Innovation. The manner in which the organization drives innovation must begin at the top. This is a necessary part of the strategy development process, as leaders create an environment for innovation.

P.2c > 3.1a Performance Improvement System - The improvement activities to evaluate and keep the approaches to listening and learning and the aggregation and analysis of complaints current with changing business needs and directions should be consistent with and based on the performance improvement approaches described in the profile (P.2c).

P.2c > 3.1b Performance Improvement System - The performance improvement system described in the profile (P.2c) should be a key input to the methods used to evaluate and keep the approaches to determining customer satisfaction and engagement current with changing business needs and directions.

P.2c > 3.2a(1&2) Performance Improvement System - The performance improvement system described in the profile (P.2c) should be a key input to the methods used to evaluate and keep the approaches to product and service offerings and customer support and access mechanisms current with changing business needs and directions.

P.2c > 3.2a(3&4) Performance Improvement System - The 3.2a improvement activities based on customer satisfaction should be consistent with and based on the performance improvement system described in the profile (P.2c).

P.2c > 3.2b Performance Improvement System - The performance improvement system described in the profile (P.2c) should be a key input to the methods used to evaluate and keep the approaches to the customer focused culture and the building and management of relationships current with changing business needs and directions.

P.2c > 4.1a Performance Improvement System - The process that the organization uses to evaluate, improve, and keep current the performance measurement system should be consistent with and based on the improvement approaches described in the profile (P.2c).

P.2c > 4.1c Performance Improvement System - The improvement activities described in 4.1c should be consistent with and based on the performance improvement system described in the profile (P.2c).

P.2c > 4.2b Performance Improvement System - The processes for keeping the data and information availability processes and systems current with changing business needs and directions should be based on the overall performance improvement system described in the profile (P.2c).

P.2c > 5.2c Performance Improvement System - The processes for evaluating and improving the workforce and leader development programs and keeping them current with changing business needs and directions should be based on the overall performance improvement system described in the profile (P.2c).

P.2c > 6.1b(3) Performance Improvement System - Process improvement methods and approaches described in 6.2b(3) should be consistent with the overall approach to performance improvement described in the profile (P.2c).

P.2c > 6.2d. Innovation Management – Innovations can be at all levels or the organization, but must be driven at the top with significant organizational breakthroughs. This is clearly aligned with innovation in the strategy process (2.1a[2]).

THOUGHTS FOR LEADERS

In the end, the only sustainable competitive advantage for any organization is the rate of their improvement.

Of the 1899 top ten Dow Jones companies, only one company is still on top. Number six on the 1899 list was GE, and they are still an extremely dominant company in the 21st century. What has kept them on top for over 100 years? Certainly great leadership and leadership development is part of the equation, but another part is that GE is passionate about improvement. They have invested in the tools to improve, and, more importantly, it is culturally unacceptable to be stagnant at GE. Every leader has a strong mandate to improve, regardless of the company's current competitive position.

When companies use a variety of improvement tools, it should be clear to the employees why each tool is needed, and when each tool should be used. If this is not clear, the proponents of the various tools will invariably get into a political battle to prove their tool is best, rather than trying to understand the fit for each tool. The key is to understand the fit (if the tools are truly different and used for different circumstances) and optimize the synergy between tools. That can allow the organization to use the various tools where they fit.

Finally, organizations need to evaluate whether the continuous improvement tools they have are truly being used. In reviewing this within an organization a number of situations can be observed:

- People do not know which tool to use and when.
- The tools are not actually being used.
- The results from using the tool is not being measured, quantified, and the benefit used to spur the continued use of the tool.
- The various tools (and their champions) are fighting for which one is "right" for the organization.
- The tool which everybody has been taught does not have a mechanism to ensure that it is used on an ongoing basis, and the knowledge of how to use the tool fades fast.
- Everyone thinks we are using tool "X" for improvement throughout the organization and only 20 percent of the employees have been trained in the effective use of the tool – it is not being used.

A LIGHTER MOMENT:

A man who truly wants to make the world better should start by improving himself and his attitudes.

Fred DeArmond

A systems approach to organizations is not really a new idea. It has been around for at least 2,500 years.

"Whoever pursues a business in this world must have a system. A business which has attained success without a system does not exist. From ministers and generals down to the hundreds of craftsmen, every one of them has a system. The craftsmen employ the ruler to make a square and the compass to make a circle. All of them, both skilled and unskilled, use this system. The skilled may at times accomplish a circle and a square by their own dexterity. But with a system, even the unskilled may achieve the same result, though dexterity they have none. Hence, every craftsman possesses a system as a model. Now, if we govern the empire, or a large state, without a system as a model, are we not even less intelligent than a common craftsman?"

Mo-Tze (a.k.a. Micius) approximately 500 B.C. (Wu, 1928, p. 226)

Organization Systems

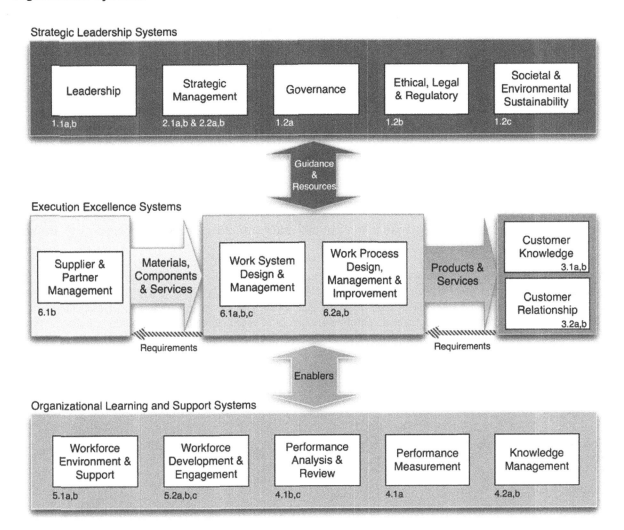

How can your organization work as an integrated high-performance system? In the last few decades, there has been an increasing interest in "the systems" perspective and approach to understanding organizations. This interest seems to have been largely driven by dissatisfaction with organization's inability to create the desired overall results and outcomes by focusing on improving the separate individual components of the organization. This frustration is compounded by the unintended consequences and outcomes that result from changing the individual pieces of an organization. Key contributors (e.g., Forrester, 1975; Senge, 1990; and Deming 1994) have proposed that the organization, when viewed as a system, is a powerful "lens" to understand, diagnose, improve, and sustain performance that creates balanced results for the key stakeholders (customers, employees, investors, supplier and partners, society and the natural environment).

The systems perspective has allowed some organizations to look beyond the immediate goals or desired outcomes and find key leverage points in the organization to achieve their objectives. For example, there is a company that does not have any explicit financial goals. No financial goals are unheard of in business, right? Instead, the organization had employee satisfaction and customer satisfaction goals. The notion was that if they focused on attracting, developing, and retaining a turned on, engaged, and empowered workforce - a workforce that is focused on creating happy customers - then the money would follow. As the president of the company used to say, "you don't make many baskets while looking at the scoreboard." While money is critical to survival and is the "life blood" of the organization, it was not the *only* reason the organization existed. Like a basketball team, the organization focused on how the team worked together to move the ball down the court and put the ball through the customer's "hoop" time after time. The more they put the ball through the hoop, the more satisfied the customers were, the more they requested their services (repeat business), and the more they told their friends about the organization (referral business). Consequently, the organization enjoyed exponential growth. There are 29 organization systems or "process" **Areas To Address** in the 2013 - 2014 CPE. Part 3 Organization Systems includes a section for each of these 29 processes.

What is a Process?

The term "process" refers to linked activities with the purpose of producing a product or service for a customer (user) within or outside your organization. Generally, processes involve combinations of people, machines, tools, techniques, materials, and improvements in a defined series of steps or actions. Processes rarely operate in isolation and must be considered in relation to other processes that impact them. In some situations, processes might require adherence to a specific sequence of steps, with documentation (sometimes formal) of procedures and requirements, including well-defined measurement and control steps.

In the delivery of services, particularly those that directly involve customers, *process* is used more generally to spell out what delivering that service entails, possibly including a preferred or expected sequence. If a sequence is critical, the process needs to include information that helps customers understand and follow the sequence. Such service processes also require guidance for service providers on handling contingencies related to customers' possible actions or behaviors.

In knowledge work, such as strategic planning, research, development, and analysis, *process* does not necessarily imply formal sequences of steps. Rather, it implies general understandings of competent performance in such areas as timing, options to include, evaluation, and reporting. Sequences might arise as part of these understandings.

Process is one of the two dimensions evaluated in a Baldrige-based assessment. This evaluation is based on four factors: approach, deployment, learning, and integration.

Source: NIST, 2015 -2016, p. 52

In its simplest form, a process step has five characteristics: inputs, activities, outputs, requirements, and resources. The generic process model below expands this basic concept to show the measurements and the SIPOC flow of a process (**S**upplier, **I**nputs, **P**rocess, **O**utputs, and **C**ustomers). This SIPOC concept is widely used to map process flow, requirements, and measures. Processes are typically designed in reverse order (instead of managing the SIPOC, you design the process with COPIS), starting with the customer.

Generic Process Model

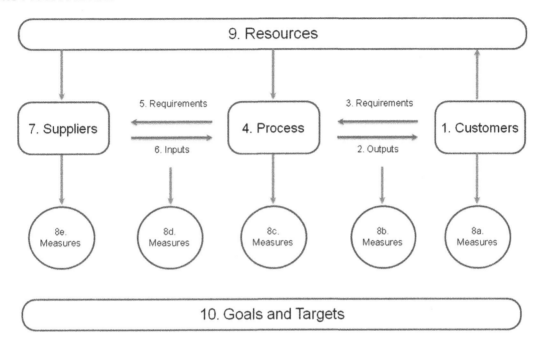

Ideally, a "systematic process" is one that incorporates ten key characteristics:

1. Customers, Customer Groups, and Market are defined.

2. Outputs and Outcomes (a.k.a. deliverables) are clearly defined.

3. Requirements for the outputs or deliverables are clear and explicit and drive the design of the process.

4. Process steps and activities are clearly defined and understood (activities and their internal and external relationships described).

5. Requirements for the inputs or the process activities are clear and explicit. This includes a work placement decision – make or buy.

6. Inputs are clearly defined – these are the supplier and partner deliverables. These can be internal from another part of the organization or external from a supplier outside of the organization.

7. Suppliers are identified (internal and external).

8. Measurements are identified for the various components. Results levels, trends and comparisons are measured at several places along the value chain or process.

9. Resources are allocated (people, capital, technology, etc.) to make the process work.

10. Goals and perofrmance targets are set and compared to actual performance.

What is Systematic?

> The term "systematic" refers to approaches that are well-ordered, repeatable, and exhibiting the use of data and information so that learning is possible. Approaches are systematic if they build in the opportunity for evaluation, improvement, and sharing, thereby permitting a gain in maturity.
>
> Source: NIST, 2015 - 2016, p. 53

Process Maturity

The CPE model includes two maturity frameworks or models to evaluate the organization – one for **processes** and one for **results**. In CPE terms these are the scoring scales or rubrics that convert qualitative descriptions of the maturity level into a quantitative score. The process maturity model is based on four dimensions – approach, deployment, learning, and integration (ADLI) and incorporates six levels of maturity 1 through 6. Although some practitioners and scholars of the CPE have proposed that these do not necessarily follow in this precise order, a few key concepts should be considered:

- If Approach does not come first, the organization doesn't have anything to deploy, improve, or integrate.

- If Deployment does not come second, the organization doesn't have anyone using the process, and it is difficult to mature (improve) the process based on the lessons learned from its use.

- While learning should occur at all stages during the design and deployment of processes, it also should be a "built in" continuous process based on experiences and results after the process is deployed. Many organizations will test a new or redesigned process in one location before it is rolled out to all applicable groups and locations.

- Integration also should occur at all stages during the design and deployment process. However, integration among the various management systems is also a continuous process that is based on experience and results after the initial deployment.

Approach

"Approach" refers to how the process addresses the Item requirements - the method(s), practices, and processes that form the particular management system.

The factors used to evaluate approaches include:

- evidence of explicit methods used to accomplish the process;

- evidence of the appropriateness of the methods to the CPE requirements and the organization's unique context (organization profile and key factors);

- evidence of the effectiveness of use of the methods; and

- evidence of the degree to which the approach is repeatable and consistently applied.

Caution!
The fundamental question for Approach is: "Is it an explicit, repeatable, systematic process or simply tacit knowledge that is not repeatable or easily teachable?" A systematic process should be defined, measured, stabilized and improved. A systematic process should be simple enough to teach to all the participants who need to use the process.

Deployment

"Deployment" refers to the extent to which the approach is applied to the appropriate areas and activities in the organization. The extent to which:

- evidence the approach is applied in addressing Item requirements relevant and important to the organization;

- evidence the approach is applied consistently; and

- evidence the approach is used by all appropriate work units.

Caution!
The most fundamental question for Deployment is: "Is this approach used by those who should be using it?" Full deployment does not mean that everyone is using the process. Some employees, department, or locations may not need the particular process.

Learning

According to the glossary, the term 'learning' refers to new knowledge or skills acquired through evaluation, study, experience, and innovation. The Baldrige Criteria refer to two distinct kinds of learning: organizational and personal. Organizational learning is achieved through research and development, evaluation and improvement cycles, ideas and input from the workforce and stakeholders, the sharing of best practices, and benchmarking. Personal learning is achieved through education, training, and developmental opportunities that further individual growth.

To be effective, learning should be embedded in the way your organization operates. Learning contributes to a competitive advantage and sustainability for your organization and workforce.

For further description of **Organizational And Personal Learning**, see the related core value and concept. Source: NIST, 2013 - 2014, p. 47

Learning is one of the dimensions considered in evaluating process items.

For further description of organizational and personal learning, see the related core value in Part 1 – Design Concepts.

Factors to consider when determining the maturity level for learning include:

- evidence of refinement of the approach through cycles of evaluation and improvement;

- evidence of the organization encouraging breakthrough change to the approach through innovation; and

- evidence of sharing refinements and innovation with other relevant work units and processes in the organization.

Caution!
The most fundamental question for Learning is "Is the *process itself* being improved?"
Many times people want to describe how the *output* of the process has improved, without describing how the process was improved. The improvement of the output may be a one-time event, while process improvement will result in better outputs every time the process is executed.

Integration and Alignment

The last dimension of the process maturity model is a combination to two related concepts - integration and alignment. According to NIST (2013 – 2014, p. 47), "The term 'integration' refers to the harmonization of plans, processes, information, resource decisions, actions, results, and analyses to support key organization-wide goals. Effective integration goes beyond alignment and is achieved when the individual components of a performance management system operate as a fully interconnected unit.

Integration is one of the dimensions considered in evaluating both process and results items. For further description, see the Scoring System (NIST, 2015 – 2016, p. 30).

Factors to consider when determining the maturity level for integration include:

- evidence that the approach is aligned (from the top of the organization all the way down) with the organizational needs identified in other CPE Item requirements;

- evidence that the measures, information, and improvement systems are complementary across processes and work units (integrated); and

- evidence that the plans, processes, results, analysis, learning, and actions are harmonized across processes and work units to support organization-wide goals (integrated).

Alignment is a state of consistency among the plans, processes, information, resource decisions, actions, results, and analyses that support key organization-wide goals. Effective alignment requires a common understanding of purposes and goals. It also requires the use of complementary measures and information for planning, tracking, analysis, and improvement at three levels: the organizational level, the key process level, and the work unit level (NIST, 2013 – 2014, p. 42).

Alignment of performance review inputs contributes to making decisions that align actions with goals. Alignment of actions and goals requires that measurements and incentives are also aligned and provide a bridge between vision and behavior.

According to the maturity model, a high degree of alignment is associated with more mature organizations. On the maturity scale "integration" does not appear until maturity level 5 which is a very high level. Organizations typically improve the components of the management systems and then bring it together as they move up into the upper levels of the maturity model. The good news is it does not have to be this way. Alignment and integration can be designed into the management systems at every maturity level.

Unfortunately, alignment does sometimes conjure up images of an overly mechanistic or rational view of organizations. However, the author proposes that it is the application or misapplication of alignment techniques and practices that determine if the system is mechanistic. Creating consistency of guidance across the organization can be accomplished in a way that allows for flexibility in interpretation appropriate for the particular business unit, department and so forth.

Alignment does not have to involve a high degree of control. If goals, measures, and initiatives are aligned and communicated these priorities will drive decisions and behavior at all levels. If each level is free to act, measure, reflect, and revise, then each will learn the specifics that lead to the greatest contribution to the overall organization system. Alignment will contribute to the efficiency and effectiveness (impact) of execution and improvement efforts. By aligning the strategy with measurement and action plans early in the journey the organization can accelerate the development of the organization up the maturity model levels.

> **Caution!**
> The most fundamental question for Integration is "Is the *process itself* linked up and down (alignment) and across (integration) the organization?" This is important to the fundamental operation of the process (through the appropriate linkages to other processes and internal customers and suppliers) and to help drive the sharing of the improvements in the process.

Maturity Levels

The process maturity model includes six stages of development from no systematic process to the benchmark. The beginning stage (Stage 1 – No Systematic Process) is the least mature and the last stage (Stage 6 – Highly Refined Benchmark) is the most mature.

Level 1 – No Systematic Process

At this level, a systematic process does not exist. The performance of the organization is dependent on smart people doing cool stuff. Improvements are based on the person who is making the improvement and the approaches are not explicitly defined in a way that would enable the organization to share or improve those practices.

Level 2 - Reacting to Problems

Operations are characterized by a collection of activities rather than systematic processes. The activities are primarily responsive or reacting to immediate needs or problems. Very little of the approach used is focused on future organizational performance or on building on the approach to achieve sustainable improvement or benefits.

Level 3 - Early Systematic Approach

The organization is at the beginning stages of conducting operations using repeatable systematic processes. At this level, evaluation and improvement cycles are in the early stages of development. In addition, there is some coordination among organizational units and evidence of the early stages or alignment (up and down) or integration (across) the organization.

Level 4 -Aligned Approach

Operations are characterized by processes that are repeatable and regularly evaluated for improvement. Where there are process improvements, the lessons learned are shared among organizational units.

Level 5 - Integrated Approach

Operations are characterized by processes that are well defined, measured, stabilized and improved. The processes are commonly used and repeatable. The processes are regularly evaluated for change and improvement in collaboration with other affected units. Efficiencies are systematically sought and achieved up, down and across the organizational units.

Level 6 – Benchmark

The final level is reserved for those highly refined processes that are truly benchmarks and have few, if any, opportunities for improvement. While processes can always benefit from cycles of continuous improvement, major breakthroughs may not be possible with level six processes. These processes perform at such a high level that most other organziations can use the performance of the process as a comparision metric and learn from many of the processes approaches.

Process Maturity Model – (a.k.a. Process Scoring Guidelines for use with Categories 1- 6)

Points	Approach	Deployment	Learning	Integration
Level 6 90%, 95%, or 100%	**An effective, systematic approach,** fully responsive to the **multiple requirements** of the Item, is evident.	The approach is **fully deployed** without significant weaknesses or gaps in any areas or work units.	Fact-based, **systematic evaluation and improvement and organizational learning** through innovation are key organization-wide tools; refinement and innovation, backed by analysis and sharing, are evident throughout the organization.	The approach is well **integrated with your current and future organizational needs** as identified in response to the Organizational Profile and other Process Items.
Level 5 70%, 75%, 80% or 85%	An **effective, systematic approach,** responsive to the **multiple requirements** of the Item, is evident.	The approach is **well deployed,** with no significant gaps.	Fact-based, **systematic evaluation and improvement and organizational learning,** including innovation, are key management tools; there is clear evidence of refinement as a result of organizational-level analysis and sharing.	The approach is **integrated with your current and future organizational needs** as identified in response to the Organizational Profile and other Process Items.
Level 4 50%, 55%, 60%, or 65%	An **effective, systematic approach,** responsive to the **overall requirements** of the Item, is evident.	The approach is **well deployed,** although deployment may vary in some areas or work units.	A fact-based, **systematic evaluation and improvement process** and some organizational learning, including innovation, are in place for improving the efficiency and effectiveness of key processes.	The approach is **aligned with your overall organizational needs** as identified in response to the Organizational Profile and other Process Items.
Level 3 30%, 35%, 40%, or 45%	An **effective, systematic approach,** responsive to the **basic requirements** of the Item, is evident.	The approach is **deployed,** although some areas or work units are in early stages of deployment.	The **beginning of a systematic approach to evaluation and improvement** of key processes is evident.	The approach is in the **early stages of alignment with your basic organizational needs** identified in response to the Organizational Profile and other Process Items.
Level 2 10%, 15%, 20%, or 25%	The **beginning** of a systematic approach to the **basic requirements** of the Item is evident.	The approach is in the **early stages of deployment** in most areas or work units, inhibiting progress in achieving the basic requirements of the Item.	**Early stages** of a transition from **reacting to problems** to a **general improvement** orientation are evident.	The approach is **aligned with other areas** or work units largely through joint problem solving.
Level 1 0% or 5%	**No systematic approach** to Item requirements is evident; information is anecdotal.	**Little or no deployment** of any systematic approach is evident.	An **improvement orientation is not evident**; improvement is achieved through reacting to problems.	**No organizational alignment** is evident; individual areas or work units operate independently.

Source: NIST (2015 - 2016) p. 34

Determining the Maturity Level of a Process

In assigning an overall maturity level or score to a process or an Item in the criteria, first determine the maturity level for each of the four dimensions (ADLI). Once the maturity for the four dimensions is determined, determine the overall level of "best fit." The overall best fit does not require total agreement with each of the statements (dimensions) for that particular scoring range.

It is recommended that when assigning the four individual dimension maturity levels that one enter the scale at level 4. If the process or Item response meets most of level 4 then move up to level 5 and see if that level best describes the maturity level of the process. If the maturity level does not meet the level four descriptions then move down to level 3 and see if that level best describes the maturity of the process.

This approach results in greater scoring accuracy for the least amount of effort. First, it will help to prevent artificially inflated or deflated scores. When examiners start at the bottom of the scale and work their way up they tend to score lower than the actual score. When examiners start at the top of the scale and work down they tend to score higher than is warranted. Second, this approach requires the least effort. At the most the examiner has to move up or down one or two levels.

If the examiner starts at the end of the scale they potentially might have to read and evaluate 6 levels. Keep in mind that a Process Item score of 50 percent represents an approach that meets the overall objectives of the Item and that is deployed to the principal activities and work units covered in the Item. Higher scores reflect maturity (cycles of improvement), integration, and broader deployment.

THOUGHTS FOR LEADERS

A LEADER'S VIEW OF PROCESS MANAGEMENT

A lot of leaders ask, "Why should I embrace process management and processes, won't they restrict the way I lead?" The simple answer is: Only if the leader creates mechanistic processes that are not easily changed.

A leader's presence in an organization is like sticking your hand in a bucket of water. It takes up a lot of room, you can make a big difference when you splash, you can make waves, you can splash water out of the bucket, but when you pull your hand out of the water, there is no evidence that you were ever there.

Putting processes into organizations is like putting cement in the water - you put your hand in, and when you pull your hand out, the impression (or leadership legacy) stays. Embedded systematic processes along with developed people and a high performance culture are the legacy a leader leaves behind. This is the reason many privately owned business have adopted the CPE. They are attempting to leave a legacy for their children who will follow them into the family business.

As you reflect on your career, you may remember some extremely dominant leaders who lead with their own styles. However, the day they left the organization it was like they were never there. Their legacy was a personal style which left with them, and the 'process' was to 'ask the boss.'

You may also remember other leaders who "built sustainable roads." For this discussion, leaders can be categorized into two types:

> 1) those who conquer the empire (save the organization from ruin through a turnaround based on personal skill); and
>
> 2) those who build the sustainable roads (e.g., establish the processes). The leader who builds the roads, and leaves the processes behind, leaves a legacy. You may find that those processes still exist years and years after the leader has left. The culture the leader has built lasts and stands the test of time.

Very few leaders can point to buildings or other concrete things they are going to leave behind. Every leader, however, should be able to leave behind processes and a culture supportive of the people, one that is focused on customers and has mature processes that will improve and keep the organization viable. In short, the leader can leave behind an organization that embraces (and has implemented) the processes that are based on the 11 CPE core values and concepts.

> *As soon as a man climbs to a high position, he must train*
> *his subordinates and trust them. They must relieve him of all*
> *small matters. He must be set free to think, to travel, to plan,*
> *to see important customers, to make improvements,*
> *to do all the big jobs of leadership.*
>
> **Herbert N Casson**

FOUNDATION

This Area to Address initiates an entire organization's focus on performance excellence as an effective business model (such as a focus on the use of the Criteria for Performance Excellence - CPE). If the leaders are not involved in the journey it will not work as a viable business model. They cannot delegate the commitment to the journey and expect anything tangible or valuable to happen down through the organization. Everyone down the organization knows what the boss values – look at their calendar – where do they spend their time?

This Area to Address starts with what the senior leaders (the head of the organization, and that person's direct reports) believe, do, and verify.

Vision and Values

Clearly, senior leaders must define where the organization is headed, what they want the organization to be, the organization's values (and other beliefs), and acceptable behaviors during that journey. Frequently the shortcoming is not the lack of values as many organizations have beautiful plaques on the wall touting a fairly routine set of values or beliefs. The shortcoming is the inability to translate the beliefs and values into behaviors and practices and then have the discipline to practice those behaviors every day in every transaction. This is where the development of a Leadership System is key. It is not intuitive what a 'systematic approach to lead' might include, but through a Leadership System the organization can begin to ensure that every leader, at every level, leads in the manner the senior leaders endorse. See the Examples, below.

The senior leaders must, at all times, role-model the behaviors they want to see throughout the organization. When senior leaders role-model these behaviors, they must also ensure that leaders at all levels in the organization are role models 100% of the time for these foundational beliefs to be taken seriously. If the leaders do not act as role models all of the time, the behaviors and culture changes they desire in the organization will not take place.

Everyone will clearly understand that what the leader says and what they do, or will tolerate, are two different things. As one Baldrige Recipient CEO put it, "when I asked why the people were not making the changes necessary to transform the organization, the answer I got back was, 'we'll change when the

CEO changes!'" Put more simply, "a leader's actions MUST speak so loudly that nobody can hear what they are saying." No leader can get away with the old axiom "do as I say, not as I do."

Promoting Legal and Ethical Behavior

Once leaders set the organizational beliefs, vision, mission, values, purpose, or other foundational factors, they must communicate them so clearly that all employees understand what the organization stands for, what the organization believes, their role, and how they are expected to act. The organizational environment must foster, require and measure legal, regulatory, and ethical compliance of each leader and employee.

With the foundational beliefs established, leaders must set the direction. This direction must be set for both short- and long-term time horizons. Additionally, the overall direction and each group's or person's responsibilities for moving in the desired direction must be clear for the organization to be effective and sustainable. Ensuring this sustainability is a key job of senior leadership. The direction set must ensure that the organization will remain viable and sustainable both operationally (short-term) and strategically (long-term). For an organization to be sustainable it must plan so, as an ongoing concern (and through disasters), it can ensure that there will be adequate people, critical skills, money, data, facilities, equipment, and an adequate supply chain. Without every one of these (and many more things) which each organization needs and must determine for itself, the organization will not be sustainable nor will it be able to withstand disasters.

Creating a Successful Organization

Once leaders have established a foundation of beliefs, set the direction of the organization, and clearly established and communicated expectations, it is then their responsibility to create an environment where people can do their best in achieving their objectives. Leaders need to implement specific processes to ensure empowerment, that employees understand their level of empowerment and that they have the opportunity (even the responsibility) to improve, innovate and learn. These processes must create an environment for organizational, personal and workforce learning, innovation, and competitive and role-model performance. To achieve this, leaders (at every level of the organization) must drive organizational agility. This can only be accomplished if those leaders use defined processes (and the associated decision criteria within those processes), review performance and drive actions at short intervals. One area where leaders must be role models is in their assessment and improvement of their personal leadership skills. If leaders do not try to improve themselves, why should anybody else try to improve? These senior leaders must also guide the development of future organizational leaders, and participate in succession planning.

To be a short-term success, an organization must ensure they have:

- people,
- critical skills,
- money,
- data,
- facilities,
- equipment,
- an environment of safety, and a
- supply chain.

If one of these is missing, the organization will fail quickly.

To be a long-term success, an organization must embrace the aspects of the criteria in 1.1a(3). This includes the leaders:

- creating an environment for the achievement of your mission,
- improvement of organizational performance,
- performance leadership,
- organizational learning, and learning for people in the workforce;
- creating a workforce culture that delivers a consistently positive customer experience and fosters customer engagement;
- creating an environment for innovation and intelligent risk taking,
- creating an environment for the achievement of your strategic objectives,
- organizational agility; and
- participate in (effective) succession planning and the development of future organizational leaders.

If one of these is missing, the organization will fail over the longer-term.

Summary

All of Item 1.1 focuses on the responsibilities of senior leaders to establish the right culture in an organization. Item 1.1 outlines the actions a senior leader must model if they want the other layers of the organization to perform effectively. The leaders must also ensure that these actions will be adopted throughout the organization. This is true for all of Item 1.1, but is particularly true for Area to Address 1.1a, where the leaders establish a foundation for all other leadership responsibilities.

 EXAMPLES

Don Chalmers Ford (Baldrige Site Visit 2008 and 2012)

With role model leadership at the wheel in Don Chalmers personal dedication to community service and organizational sustainability, each employee has been given the key to empowered high performance and outreach. An initial holiday visit to the Children's Cancer Unit at the University of New Mexico Hospital by a few employees has led to a dealership wide, manager driven effort of each department's unique contributions and volunteer skills to support the fundraising, gift wish list, shopping, wrapping and room by room delivery of presents not only to the children in the Cancer Unit, but to the healthcare practitioners who nurture them. This servant leadership philosophy permeates the workforce, motivating employees to think not only of others, but beyond their own limits, towards sustainable practices in both life and work, modeled by the leadership of Don Chalmers himself.

With an emphasis on sustainability, Don Chalmers Ford (DCF) goes beyond determining stakeholders by the assigned Ford market share to focus on community partnerships. Don Chalmers and the Senior Leadership Team (SLT) developed the vision and values with exemplary key requirements and expectations that achieve the company's purpose "To Satisfy Key Stakeholders".

DCF's systematic Leadership System (LS) (Figure below) has matured over its 10 years to achieve organizational sustainability through The DCF Experience by identifying Stakeholder expectations, setting direction based on those expectations, linking the LS to leadership training, and evaluating the LS in the Strategic Planning Process (SPP). The LS is validated from beginning to end with integration to related figures throughout the application indicated in the chart. Leaders use Steps 1-5 for all key decision-making and to implement the SPP to align individual and department objectives with DCF's foundational elements. The LS begins with key Stakeholders, and all key actions encourage two-way communication between the Stakeholders and each step's process owner. Key Steps 2-5 enable leaders to accelerate their departments and workforce forward through a system of aligning to the company vision and values, fulfilling the goals of the annual plan, evaluating and learning, and using results to move the company to a new level of organizational sustainability and performance excellence. Key actions A-D are used to implement decisions and initiate communication. The LS employs strategic tools unique to DCF such as benchmark with NCM 20 Group (20 Group) data, resulting in actions from simple adjustments to get back on track, to broad-sweeping organization-wide decisions.

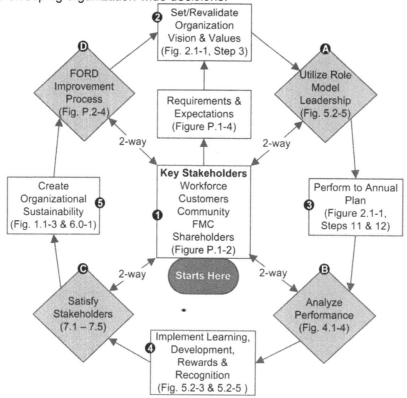

Figure 1.0-1 Leadership System

The Senior Leadership Team (SLT) uses the Strategic Planning Process to set the organizational vision and core values, and to re-validate them annually as necessary. SLT members attend a weekly leadership meeting representing all departments where they can modify the vision and values to respond quickly to innovation and Stakeholder needs.

Deployment of the vision and values to all Stakeholders takes place through communication in written format, face-to-face meetings, "How I Connect" tool, management-by-walking-around (MBWA), DVDs, the website, community involvement, and personal actions. The "How I Connect" tool was developed after an Opportunity for Improvement (OFI) in the Baldrige 2008 site visit feedback report indicated that the DCF experience had some gaps in deployment. DCF tailored a page that 2009 Baldrige winner AltantiCare used that includes the core values, stakeholders, mission and vision. It is included in new employee orientation and used as an annual re-engagement tool. One side includes a picture of the integrated DCF experience and the other side has fill in the blank items that ask the employee to personalize it to their job and their team. Two question examples are "what can I do to improve customer satisfaction" and "what can we do to improve customer satisfaction". This is repeated for the rest of the core values. DCF deploys and verifies the organizational values to the entire workforce, key suppliers and partners, customers, the community, and other stakeholders through organized communication.

PRO-TEC Coating Company (Baldrige Recipient 2007)

In the PRO-TEC organization, senior leadership is defined as the President and their direct reports. Eight leaders represent this senior Leadership Team. The PRO-TEC Coating Company leadership system is used throughout the organization as the fundamental model for their ORA-based (Ownership, Responsibility, Accountability) leadership process.

Leaders use the six disciplines of the leadership model to guide and sustain the organization. This supports strategic planning, alignment of goals and objectives, deployment, measurement, and communication in the culture of self-directed work teams. Mission, vision, values, and strategic position have been set by the Leadership Team as a foundation, and they are reviewed and renewed annually.

Mission, strategic position, and vision. A diverse multi-disciplined group created the mission statement in 2002. It has become embedded into the culture. The mission is on the business cards, is displayed prominently throughout the PRO-TEC facility, is included in most printed material, and is very much a part of the character of the company. The mission statement and strategic position (core competency) are used to cast a very general and long-term view of where the company is headed and what we believe.

The vision statement is more specific and is used by senior leadership to communicate to all stakeholders a more concrete picture of what the company will look like in ten years in pursuit of the mission and strategic position. Frequently the senior leaders refer to the mission and vision when explaining decisions and direction. When tactical decisions must be made, it is common for a leader to ask, "What do the mission and vision say?"

The Leadership Team has identified as a priority the safety and wellness of the Associates and all stakeholders. This priority is communicated to everyone in the six key success factors under "Associate Quality of Life." The hierarchy of priorities (Integrated Contingency Plan) lists preservation of human life and safety as the first priority, and the President, through every communication method, identifies safety as a key focus. Two-way safety communication is systematically encouraged, documented, and tracked within PRO-TEC through communication meetings, Associate satisfaction surveys, safety audits, and anonymous e-mail feedback tools offering direct communication to the President and Human Resources Manager.

PRO-TEC Leadership System

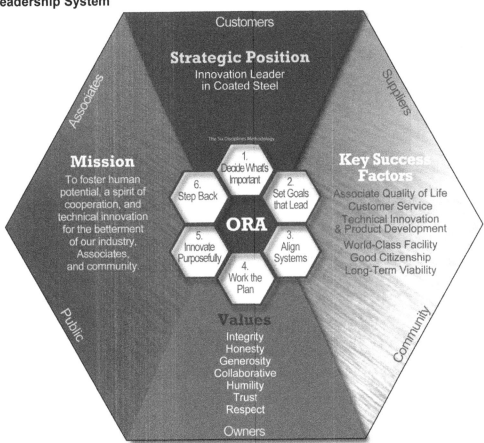

In the culture of self-directed work teams, it is essential that every Associate be a leader. Therefore, the core values were created to support defined leadership behaviors. Senior leaders conduct annual workshops within their areas of responsibility to align and integrate goals and renew commitment to mission, vision, values, and strategic position. These workshops conducted in individual areas of responsibility achieve two-way communication and alignment. Senior leaders demonstrate commitment to organizational values through their personal actions by aligning the outcomes of these individual workshops to the annual strategic planning activity. The Leadership Team uses the leadership system to create a sustainable organization at all levels. The leadership system identifies mission, strategic position, core values, stakeholders, and the six disciplines leadership cycle.

The leadership system begins with **"Deciding What's Important"** so that every Associate understands and connects with the direction. This is accomplished by leaders identifying and supporting projects that are strategic to the success of the company. Leaders revise and recommit to the mission, vision, core values, and strategic position in step 1 of the leadership system. Through performance reviews we ensure that deployment of these initiatives is a part of each Associate's ORA.

"Set Goals That Lead" defines goals and initiatives that lead Associates to take actions that align with "what's important" to the organization. Through annual SWOT activity in step 6 of the leadership system, objectives aligned to the key success factors are evaluated and reset. We then define measures and targets, build consensus around these objectives, seek input from Associates on direction, and finalize the direction.

"Align Systems" is an effort to have every Associate's work aligned and integrated to meet the goals of the company. We seek to have every Associate understand their role as related to the role of others and demonstrate leadership in a commitment to achieving the company goals. To ensure that this alignment is accomplished, goals are communicated to all Associates through quarterly communication meetings, printed newsletters, and intranet objective and performance updates. All Associates are welcomed and encouraged to attend Leadership Team meetings. These Monday, Wednesday, and Friday meetings (and monthly plant management meetings) focus on communication, alignment, integration, and oversight and are well attended by Associates from throughout the organization. Figure 1.1-2 shows this communication and oversight tool. There is structure to these activities that ensures communication of goals, measurement to the balanced scorecard, corrective action implementation, follow-up, and communication of tactical initiatives. We believe that Associates at every level practicing ORA within the structure of this leadership review process is a very tangible measure of understanding, two-way communication, and effectiveness of the efforts to align systems and resources.

Leaders sustain the organization on a daily basis by **"Working the Plan."** This simply stated means, "achieve your goals." The desire is to have every Associate connect what he or she does on a daily basis to the goals of the company. To ensure that we accomplish this, the strategic plan is implemented and tracked and results are communicated on a regular basis. We strive to create an environment that fosters involvement, participation, and ownership of the plan by communicating the goals and identifying the linkage between goals and individual Associate activities. When the scorecard indicates that objectives are not being met, corrective action is implemented that often requires the deployment of additional resources. When impacted by both external and internal conditions, the plan is adapted and realigned.

Senior leaders have established an environment for continuous improvement and Associate learning, **"Innovate Purposefully."** While working the plan on a daily basis, we attempt to tap every Associate's creative ability to achieve continuous improvement and organizational excellence. We achieve this by creating an atmosphere that encourages continuous improvement and change. We provide information and business knowledge to understand opportunities for improvement. Leaders make the linkage between the agility and innovation in developing new products and processes to the success and long-term viability of the company. Specific job-related training and a strong emphasis and support for formal continuing education clearly demonstrates leaders' commitment to foster human potential.

Senior leaders personally update the succession plan annually for the highest levels. Leaders throughout the organization support and drive I-to-I, the formal continuous improvement process. Commitment to continuous improvement, personal development, and performance excellence are emphasized and reinforced by performance reviews and the internal job selection processes.

In **"Step Back,"** senior leaders commit to annual reassessment of external and internal factors that are essential for setting direction for the company. They promote broad involvement from the organization in gathering information and processing this information for the purpose of "Deciding What's Important." Leaders ensure that these important activities occur by committing to the cycle of improvement strategic planning process (Figure 2.1-1). Leaders conduct annual SWOT analysis in functional areas feeding into a consolidated SWOT analysis for the purpose of annual strategic planning. Leaders encourage the organization to pursue continuous and breakthrough improvement initiatives to enhance the impact of the SWOT analysis effort. Leaders model desired behavior by taking on challenging tasks and committing themselves to continuous improvement.

Reasonable risks are taken in setting stretch targets and working toward the achievement of these targets. Leaders benchmark other excellent organizations and "steal" ideas that will improve our organization. The balanced scorecard (BSC) provides senior leaders a method to review key measures on a regular basis. The performance measures are determined through the strategic planning process, communicated to the workforce and stakeholders, and reviewed monthly using the green, yellow, red designation for compliance. At risk BSC measures require action, and the action is monitored through a formal management review process at the monthly plant management meeting. These same metrics are reported monthly and reviewed three times a year with our parent companies at Management Committee meetings.

Value creation for customers and stakeholders is a component of the consolidated SWOT activity. In "Step Back" of the leadership system, the integration of insights from the SWOT analysis into the strategic plan are essential for prioritization of the many planning initiatives. This prioritization through consensus building creates a manageable set of objectives that are best aligned with our mission, vision, values, and company goals. Senior leaders personally update the succession plan annually for the highest levels of the organization. This is performed in unison with the joint venture partners.

Advocate Good Samaritan Hospital (Baldrige Recipient 2010)

The *GSAM Leadership System* (GSLS) ensures that all leaders at every level of the organization understand what is expected of them. The GSLS is reviewed annually and has undergone multiple cycles of improvement, the most recent of which mapped the system to their leadership competencies and supporting leader development. The GSLS aligns and integrates their leaders at all levels by providing them with the tools to model the GSAM values and lead consistently. The GSLS is deployed to every leader through the on-boarding process, Leadership Development Institutes (LDIs), and in monthly 1:1 supervisory meetings.

GSAM's patients and stakeholders are at the center of their Leadership System❶. Driven by the Mission, Values, and Philosophy (MVP) all leaders must understand stakeholder requirements❶a. At the organizational level, these requirements are determined during the *Strategic Planning Process* (SPP) Step 3 (SWOT Analysis) and are used to set direction and establish/cascade goals ❷ and ❷a. Action plans to achieve the goals are created❸, aligned, and communicated to engage the workforce❸a. Goals and in-process measures are systematically reviewed and course corrections are made as necessary ensuring performance to plan❹. This focus on performance creates a rhythm of accountability❹a and leads to subsequent associate development through the *Capability Determination/Workforce Learning and Development System* (WLDS) and reward and recognition of high performance❺. Development and recognition ensures associates feel acknowledged and motivated❺a. Stretch goals established in the SPP and a discomfort with the status quo prompts associates to learn, improve, and innovate❻ through the *Performance Improvement System*. As leaders review annual performance, scan the environment, and re-cast organizational challenges, communication mechanisms (1.1 b1) are used to inspire and 'raise the bar'❻a.

GSAM's parent company, Advocate Health Care (AHC), sets the enterprise vision and values incorporating inputs from GSAM leaders. AHC sites are encouraged to re-shape and define the vision to fit their culture and business environment. The GSAM EXECUTIVE TEAM (ET) / Senior Leaders (SL) evaluate the vision annually during the SPP Step 4 (Visioning) and deploys it through the GSLS. In 2007, the ET, through a cycle of improvement, refined the vision to strengthen the focus on excellent outcomes and service ensuring an even greater alignment with G2G, GSAM's initiative to establish a culture of excellence. The vision and values are deployed through the GSLS ensuring that the requirements of all stakeholders are addressed. Deployment mechanisms include both one way and two way approaches. Every leader at every level is responsible for role modeling the MVP and Standards of Behavior. ET members are evaluated against their personal demonstration of the values in their individual performance reviews. Deployment of the vision and values is validated through a specific question on the associate survey, the number of MVP nominations, and leader rounding. SL reflect a commitment to the organization's values through modeling the Standards of Behavior. ET members also are personally engaged through their service on community boards and broad participation in community organizations and initiatives.

Advocate Good Samaritan Leadership System

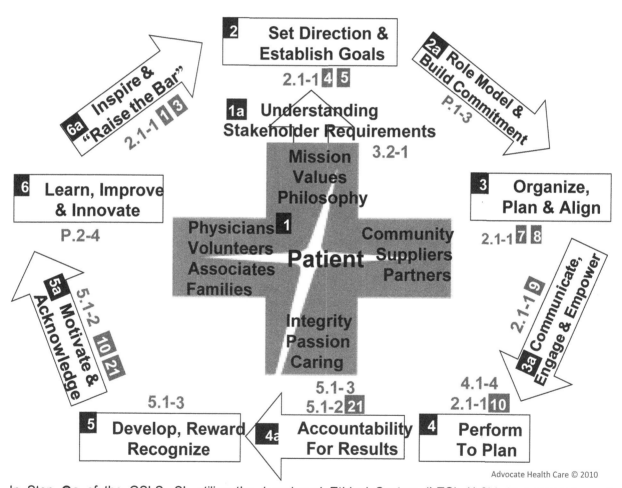

Advocate Health Care © 2010

In Step ❷a of the GSLS, SL utilize the *Legal and Ethical System* (LES) (1.2b) to personally and proactively promote a legal/ethical environment that requires and results in the highest standard of ethical behavior. These processes and SL behaviors include:

- The participation of five (5) SL on the BUSINESS CONDUCT COMMITTEE,
- Legal/ethical discussions through communication mechanisms
- Internal legal/ethical audits,
- Taking personal responsibility for follow up and response to any/all ethical issues identified through the Business Conduct Hotline, and
- Ensuring all associates are trained in and review the Business Conduct Program and HIPAA Privacy Disclosure during the *Performance Management System* (PMS) (5.2a3).

In addition, in healthcare settings, complex ethical issues often deal with life and death issues for those delivering care at the bedside. To address this, the CNE established a NURSING ETHICS COUNCIL to provide a forum to discuss, evaluate, and understand these issues.

Virtua Health (Baldrige Site Visit 2009)

The Virtua Leadership System (VLS), was developed by Senior Leaders (SL) in a retreat in February of 2004 to ensure that leaders at all levels of the organization would understand what is expected of them. In the same retreat the mission, vision and values (MVV) were reviewed and validated. These are annually reviewed in the Strategic Planning Process. Through a cycle of learning and improvement the President's Group (PG) and the senior leaders (SL) mapped this process to the vision and values to improve alignment, integration and more easily teach new managers this key process for success in providing the core competency (the Outstanding Patient Experience - OPE). The improved VLS was deployed to all levels of the organization at the STAR launch meeting in January 2009. Every leader at every level has the responsibility to deploy MVV and support the STAR standards of behavior and measures. The overall direction for the organization with supporting metrics and plan are developed to meet the stakeholder requirements.

Virtua Leadership System

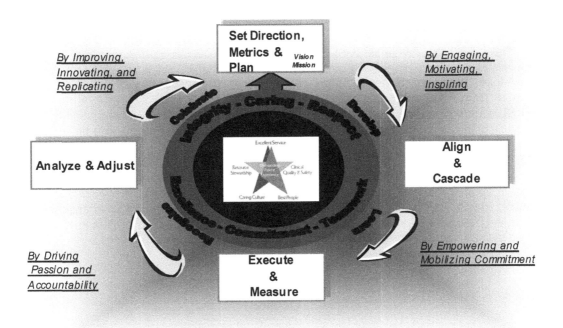

Performance is continually measured by the STAR Standards of Performance and the achievement of the Goals and Objectives (G&Os). The VLS is highly integrated with the SPP. SL deploy the MVV though multiple processes. Strategic imperatives (Strategic Objectives) and global goals are set during the SPP and the VLS. They are then cascaded to all levels of the organization in the SPP and then done by all leaders at all levels in the VLS. Everyone is held accountable for performance and results through a standardized process directly measured by the points of the STAR.

VH systematically communicates its MVV with all partners and suppliers during the contracting process following which each they are paired with an internal VH administrative contact who ensures that the partner/ supplier understands the MVV, strategic direction and how they align with the STAR and support the outstanding patient experience. Meetings are systematically scheduled throughout the year. We communicate the MVV to patients and other key stakeholders through a wide variety of mechanisms, starting with posting of the MVV in public access areas of all of the facilities, at the bedside through the Get Well Network (GWN), on the website and in key publications such as the Virtua Voice. Leaders drive each STAR Behavior and have formal reviews of Goals and Objectives (G&Os) specific to the points of the STAR from the Chief's Executive Council (CEC) and the Operations Management Group (OMG) at the divisional level, cascading down to individual managers and to their employees in the VLS and the Communication Matrix. To drive the passion and accountability, daily department meetings which include 3 minute huddles for direct patient care, as well as monthly meetings, mentor groups, local roundtables, town hall meetings are held all focusing on the STAR. VLS Adjustments are done by managers developing action plans for any outliers from the goals on a periodic basis, which includes a continual cycle of developing, learning, recognition and celebration at all levels of the organization. SL personal actions reflect a commitment to the organizational values by personally reviewing every member of management demonstration of VV through the Best People Review (BPR) annually. Annual cluster meetings, part of the BPR, are conducted by all levels of management and provide an opportunity for personal growth and development and to ensure actions are reflecting the STAR and MVV. SL's and manager's ability to model the VV are evaluated as part of the annual employee satisfaction and engagement survey (EOS). SL personally promote an organizational environment that fosters, requires and results in legal and ethical behavior through the VLS which includes integrity. This value, along with caring and respect, are the core values established by the PG that and are deployed and exist at every level of the organization; all employees are evaluated through the BPR Process against their SSP and results based on the G&O's. Examples that promote integrity and promote the environment that supports legal and ethical behavior include:

- New Employee Orientation (NEO) delivery by SL
- Zero tolerance related to employees and medical staff that do not exhibit STAR values
- Annual Employee Opinion Survey (EOS) including questions on ethics with participation directly solicited by SL
- SL open door policy
- A SL chairs the ethics committee and all SLs review corporate compliance hotline call
- A SL acts as a liaison on each vendor contract

VH has a multi-step, systematic process (available on site) that is fully deployed and provides a pro-active and responsive approach to promote legal and ethical behavior. This process is reviewed tri-annually by Legal Counsel, Internal Audit and the Quality, Safety and Risk Management Group to ensure that it is up to date and meeting needs. More frequent revisions are accomplished based on changes in regulations or as advised by SL's, the Board Audit Committee and the three groups listed above.

CRITERIA QUESTIONS

In your response, include answers to the following questions:

a. VISION, VALUES, and MISSION

(1) Vision and Values How do senior leaders set your organization's vision and values? How do senior leaders deploy the vision and values through your leadership system, to the workforce, to key suppliers and partners, and to customers and other stakeholders, as appropriate? How do senior leaders' actions reflect a commitment to those values?

(2) Promoting Legal and Ethical Behavior How do senior leaders' actions demonstrate their commitment to legal and ethical behavior? How do they promote an organizational environment that requires it?

(3) Creating a Successful Organization How do senior leaders' actions build an organization which is successful now and in the future? How do they:

- create an environment for the achievement of your mission, improvement of organizational performance, performance leadership, and organizational learning, and learning for people in the workforce;
- create a workforce culture that delivers a consistently positive customer experience and fosters customer engagement;
- create an environment for innovation and intelligent risk taking, achievement of your strategic objectives, and organizational agility; and
- participate in succession planning and the development of future organizational leaders?

Notes:

1.1. Your organizational performance results should be reported in items 7.1–7.5. Results related to the effectiveness of leadership and the leadership system should be reported in item 7.4.

1.1a(1). Your organization's vision should set the context for the strategic objectives and action plans you describe in items 2.1 and 2.2.

1.1a(3). A successful organization is capable of addressing current business needs and, through agility and strategic management, is capable of preparing successfully for its future business, market, and operating environment. Achieving future success may require leading transformational changes in the organization's structure and culture. Both external and internal factors should be considered. Factors in your organization's sustainability might include workforce capability and capacity, resource availability, technology, knowledge, core competencies, work systems, facilities, and equipment. Success now and in the future might be affected by changes in the marketplace and customer preferences, in the financial markets, and in the legal and regulatory environment. In the context of ongoing success, the concept of innovation and taking intelligent risks includes both technological and organizational innovation to help the organization succeed in the future. A successful organization also ensures a safe and secure environment for its workforce and other key stakeholders. A successful organization is capable of addressing risks and opportunities arising from environmental considerations and climate change.

NIST (2015-2016) pp. 7 - 8

WORKSHEETS

1.1a(1) – Vision and Values

Set Organizational Vision and Values	Deploy Vision and Values through Leadership System to:	Verify that Vision and Values are deployed to:
	The Workforce:	The Workforce:
	Key Suppliers and Partners:	Key Suppliers and Partners:
	Customers and Other Stakeholders:	Customers and Other Stakeholders:

Note: Include how leader's personal actions systematically demonstrate a commitment to the organization's values and to a customer focus.

1.1a(2) – Promoting Legal and Ethical Behavior

How Senior Leaders' Actions Demonstrate Their Commitment To Legal Behavior	How Senior Leaders' Actions Demonstrate Their Commitment To Ethical Behavior	1.1a(1) - How Leaders Demonstrate Their Commitment To The Organization's Values

How Senior Leaders' Actions Promote An Organizational Environment That Requires Legal And Ethical Behavior

1.1a(3) – Creating A Successful Organization

How Do Senior Leaders Create (and ensure achieving) A Sustainable Organization in the following areas:[1]
Creating An Environment For Achievement Of Your Mission
Creating An Environment For Improvement Of Organizational Performance Leadership
Creating An Environment For Organizational And Learning For People In The Workforce
Create A Workforce Culture That Delivers A Consistently Positive Customer Experience
Create A Workforce Culture That Fosters Customer Engagement
Create An Environment For Innovation And Intelligent Risk Taking
Creates An Environment For The Achievement Of Your Strategic Objectives
Creates An Environment For The Achievement Of Organizational Agility
Participate In Succession Planning And The Development Of Future Organizational Leaders

1) Full Organizational sustainability may require consideration of a wide range of factors beyond those strategic factors described in the criteria. For example, the organization may wish to plan for both strategic and operational factors such as disaster recovery, ongoing operations and sustainability considering: money, data, people, critical skills, equipment, safety, facilities, Supply Chain and other factors.

ASSESSMENT

1	Senior Leaders have identified the key *stakeholders*, defined stakeholder *requirements*, and use those requirements to *set the direction* of the organization.	1	2	3	4	5	6	DK
2	Senior Leaders have set and role model the vision and values by consistently demonstrating, communicating, and reinforcing them on a daily basis.	1	2	3	4	5	6	DK
3	Senior Leaders are personally and visibly involved in creating an environment which promotes legal and ethical behavior.	1	2	3	4	5	6	DK
4	Senior Leaders are personally and visibly involved in creating an environment for organizational and personal learning, and the development of future leaders.	1	2	3	4	5	6	DK
5	Senior Leaders are personally and visibly involved in creating an environment for performance improvement, accomplishment of strategic objectives, innovation and organizational agility.	1	2	3	4	5	6	DK
6	Senior Leaders have defined the factors which will help to ensure sustainability and those factors are evaluated, planned, monitored, achieved, and improved.	1	2	3	4	5	6	DK

BLUEPRINT

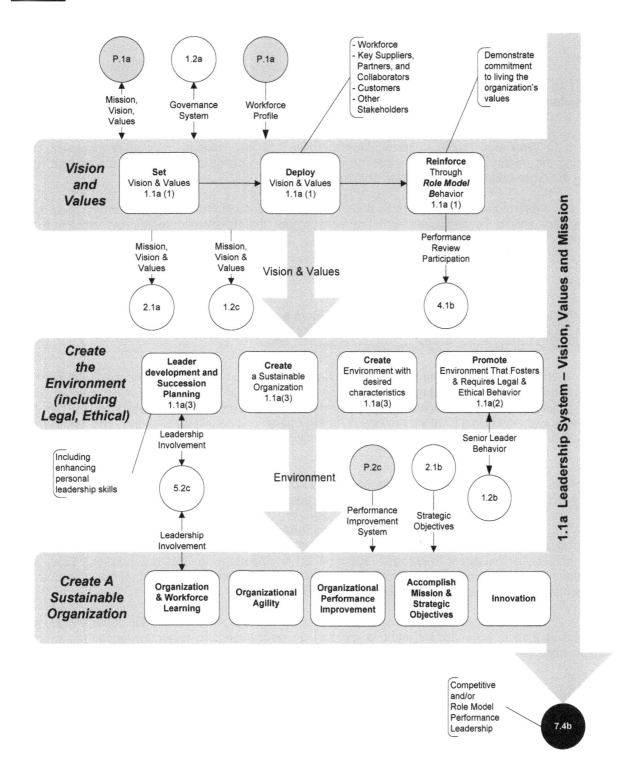

SYSTEM INTEGRATION

Context

P.1a > 1.1a Mission, Vision, Values - The "setting" of organizational values and direction including short and long-term expectations in 1.1a should be consistent with and include the purpose, mission, vision, and values described in the profile P.1a.

P.1a > 1.1a Workforce Profile - The workforce profile is a key input to developing, deploying, and reinforcing the mission, vision, and values. In addition, the workforce profile is also a key input when creating the organization environment for innovation, agility, etc.

P.2c > 1.1a Performance Improvement System - The performance improvement system described in the profile (P.2c) should be consistent with the environment that is created to support employee and organizational learning and performance improvement.

Systems

1.1a <> 1.2a Governance System - How well the leaders are doing setting, deploying, and reinforcing the mission, vision, values, and direction should be part of the Senior Leadership and Board Performance Review process described in 1.2a Governance System.

1.1a <> 1.2b Senior Leader Behavior - The activities and behaviors that senior leaders use to promote and environment that fosters and requires legal and ethical behavior should be consistent with the stated values, directions, and expectations are the ethical interactions of the employees described in 1.2b. Part of the issue with ensuring ethical interactions is having operational definitions of ethics. The definitions of ethics used in 1.2b should be consistent with and include the values of the organization as defined in 1.1a.

1.1a > 1.2c Mission, Vision, Values - The mission, vision, and values are all key inputs to determining areas of emphasis for community support and involvement described in 1.2c.

1.1a > 2.1a Mission, Vision, Values - The mission, vision, and values are key considerations when developing strategies described in 2.1a. This linkage, along with the performance review linkage, helps to create and send consistent messages about what is important to the organization. When the organization's strategy, values, and reviews are internally consistent, the probability of successful implementation throughout the organization is increased.

1.1a < 2.1b Strategic Objectives - The strategic objectives and the timetable for accomplishing them as described in 2.1b is an important input to creating an environment to foster the accomplishment of strategic objectives described in 1.1a.

1.1a > 4.1b Performance Review Participation - The values, direction, and expectations set by the leadership system should be consistent with and an input to the agenda for the organizational performance reviews described in 4.1b. In addition, the leaders' participation in the performance reviews is also important for reinforcing the direction and priorities. If the leadership team espouses certain priorities and expectations that are different from the metrics reviewed during periodic performance reviews, there is a mixed message to the employees, suppliers, partners, and so forth. Periodic reviews help hold people accountable and people will tend to emphasize those things the leaders are asking to review.

1.1a <> 5.2c Leadership Involvement - Succession planning shows up in two key places: 5.2c addresses the overall process to address succession planning for leadership and management positions and in 1.1a it asks how leaders personally participate in succession planning and the development of future leaders. The process and the leadership participation in that process should be designed as one integrated system. In addition, Leadership development should be based on the organization's leadership system, values, and vision.

Scorecard

1.1a/b > 7.4b Leadership System Performance focuses on transforming the organization to higher levels of performance. The leadership system is inextricably linked to the strategic management systems. These systems work together to improve performance. Performance that should be reported in 7.4b.

THOUGHTS FOR LEADERS

When people say the CPE process restricts the movement and improvement of an organization, it appears as though they do not understand (or have never used) the CPE framework. They simply do not understand the flexibility and competitive strength of what this business model provides. Not only does the framework focus on agility (even as one of the eleven core values), but it asks how leaders ensure the ongoing viability (sustainability) of the organization in a variety of ways. Most leaders who have used this model have even expanded their definition of the factors which must be used to ensure sustainability.

Using the CPE model requires a degree of understanding of the complexities of an organization. Some individuals want to use complexity as an excuse for not implementing a process. High performing organizations, however, clearly and simply define their leadership and business processes and define the decision criteria to be used in managing and improving those processes.

These process definitions and simplicity are critical to enable everyone in the organization to move quickly. With an understanding of their processes, an organization can move more quickly because they know how to employ and alter those processes. An individual leader may be quick to react to intuition, but it is difficult to repeat the same performance without a documented process. One well-known cartoon is of two little boys in a kitchen making a cake. The kitchen is a complete mess, and one little boy says to the other, "The problem with this is that if it comes out really good we'll never be able to make it again." Likewise, leadership successes need processes if they are to be repeated.

Smart, high performing organizations are using processes, leadership, and decision criteria to respond to rapidly changing market requirements. Employing these rather than using gut instinct alone, facilitates rapid and consistent movement of the organization in an ever-improving direction.

A Lighter Moment:

No one's a leader if there are no followers.

Malcolm Forbes

> *It is an immutable law in business that words are words,*
> *explanations are explanations, promises are promises*
> *but only performance is reality.*
>
> **Harold S. Geneen**

 FOUNDATION

In Area to Address 1.1a, the leaders established what is important in the organization, the organization's overall direction, and the culture which is focused on legal and ethical behavior and fostering high performance to ensure sustainability. In Area to Address 1.2a, leaders will establish an organizational governance structure. This is a culture which will turn governance from a plaque on the wall into a systematic process to ensure governance and the appropriate level of transparency in all organizational transactions.

This Area to Address, 1.1b, follows these foundations with a description of leaders' roles and responsibilities in institutionalizing the culture in the minds of all employees. Leaders must provide the organization and employees with the leadership, communication, empowerment, and motivation needed to drive organizational performance down to the action level. As with the earlier Area to Address 1.1a, 1.1b discusses the responsibilities that senior leaders cannot delegate.

Communication

This Area to Address asks how leaders communicate, and how they are involved in engaging the workforce. This includes frank two-way communication, communicating (and ensuring that the appropriate employees understand) the key decisions, and taking an active role in the reward and recognition programs in a manner which reinforces high performance, a customer focus and a business focus. The bottom line of Area to Address 1.1b is a leader's role in driving the high performance of the organization and of all employees.

Clarity of direction is the foundation for deploying the organization's direction from the top down to every employee. In fact, great leaders often see one of their most important roles as the clear and consistent communication of direction. Once the direction is set, leaders must ensure their performance expectations are clearly communicated throughout the organization - to every employee, supplier, partner, owner, stakeholder, and in some cases to the community as a whole. The Criteria for Performance Excellence (CPE) first focused on leadership's responsibility for two-way communication in 2003. Now, the CPE further asserts that an organization needs to understand the breadth and depth of their communications. Organizations need to understand: 1) which communication methods are two-way; 2) which methods are one-way; and 3) for the two–way communication, how (through measures or tangible validation) leadership ensures that the two-way communication process is effective.

It is implicit (in high performing organizations) that leaders create a culture where all information, including bad news, can quickly ascend to the ears of leadership. That does not mean every leader must take action themselves (the best people may already be working on the problem), but is does mean the organization communicates in an open and transparent manner. Problems are quickly communicated and addressed, and the "fix" to problems involves improving processes, not just blaming individuals.

Focus on Action

Leaders must drive action. To do this, the CPE ask how leaders review performance, how they use these reviews to assess where they are and how they decide what actions need to be taken on a short- and long-term basis. This organizational performance review itself is addressed in Area to Address 4.1b in the criteria. Leaders must ensure that the organizational-level objectives are translated down to every team (at a minimum) or, preferably, to every employee. Senior leaders must be able to understand what actions are needed, and ensure that those actions:

- Are linked to the higher-level goals or objectives;
- Flow-down the organization effectively to actions at the lowest level;
- Have sufficient resources allocated to them;
- Are tracked and appropriate changes are made based on actual performance (agility);
- And ultimately are achieved.

Additionally, during the process to establish the organization's objectives, leaders must understand the needs and expectations of all stakeholders. The goal is to develop generative solutions that create value for multiple stakeholders vs. simply reallocating resources among the stakeholders:

- Understand customer and stakeholder requirements
- Determine which requirements will be met (balance the overall value they will support)
- Plan the balance
- Resource the balance
- Deploy the balance
- Track the achievement of the balance
- Adjust to ensure the achievement of the balance based on actual performance
- Achieve the balance
- Assess the impact of achieving the balance on the customers and other stakeholders

New to the criteria this year is the term 'Intelligent Risk Taking.' A complete definition is included in the Glossary, but simply, this is the ability to ensure that the appropriate analysis has taken place so leaders can manage with data (the Core Values is Management-By-Fact). Additionally, an increased emphasis is placed on Innovation and driving discontinuous change at all levels of the organization.

EXAMPLES

PRO-TEC Coating Company (Baldrige Recipient 2007)

The PRO-TEC culture was established based on a self-directed empowered workforce and Ownership, Responsibility, Accountability (ORA). All leaders must be good listeners and communicators. This is pivotal to them aligning and integrating systems (and people) and achieving their goals. PRO-TEC systematically validates communication through a communication matrix.

This helps them verify that all Associates receive the business plan, performance, and technical information they need. Using this approach they validate the:

- Communication methods,
- Frequency,
- Message,
- One or two-way communication, and
- Method for validating two-way communication.

For example, the 2nd quarter communication meeting, called "Breakfast with Paul," is an informal breakfast meeting that allows opportunity for open dialogue between all Associates and the President. It is two-way communication on topics the Associates are interested in discussing. Also, part of fostering human potential is recognizing achievement, as shown in their Performance Management System Review Forums.

COMMUNICATION MATRIX												
Communication Event	Sender	Receiver	Forum	Frequency	P	S	T	V	ST	Message	Delivery Method	1/2 way
Management Committee Meeting	Leadership Team	Management Committee USS/Kobe Execs	Us and Japan	Three times per year	X	X	X	X	X	Plan/Results Governance	Verbal with visual resource	2 way
PRO-TEC Management Meeting	Managers Leaders internal auditors	Cross functional group of associates	PRO-TEC Training Room	Monthly	X	X	X	X	X	Plan/Results audits CARS/PARS	Verbal with visual resources	1 way
Significant Item Report	Direct Reports	Management committee USS/Kobe execs	Electronic Transmission	Monthly		X				Monthly Results	Written with charts and tables	1 way
Galvanews	President and other Contributors	All associates and Other Stakeholders	Published Newsletter	Quarterly	X	X	X	X		Information on Status of our Company. Personal interest articles	Written Glossy Paper Published	1 way
Weekly Safety Binder	President and Safety/ Environmental Leaders	All associates	Binders circulated to all associates	Weekly		X	X	X		Comments from President. Safety communication and procedure	Written	2 way

The "Types Of Communication" columns (P, S, T, V, ST) span across the middle of the table.

| COMMUNICATION MATRIX | | | | | | | | | | | | |
Communication Event	Sender	Receiver	Forum	Frequency	Types Of Communication					Message	Delivery Method	1/2 way
										review		
All associate communication meeting	President, VP Finance, Manager HR	All associates	Meeting Center	Quarterly	X	X	X	X	X	Forecast/results six key success factors	Written	2 way
Weekly safety meetings	Safety Leaders and subject matter presenters	All associates by team	Training rooms	Weekly	X	X	X	X		Review performance, incident and accidents at PRO-TEC and parent companies. Focused presentations	Verbal with visual resource	2 way
Daily Operations Meeting	Process Techs, Warehouse Leaders multifunction group	Multifunction group	Training Room CGL #2	7:15 Daily		X	X			Current safety, environmental, quality, customer operation issues	Verbal	2 way
Tactical Meeting	Leadership Team and other key associates	All associate representation with key associates	Main Conference Room	Mon, Wed, Fri	X	X	X	X		Current safety, environmental, quality, customer, operation issues	Verbal	2 way
PRO-TEC Monthly Update	Leadership Team	All associates	Intranet	Monthly	X	X				All results and forecast covering objectives for key success factors	Written with charts and tables	1 way
Galvavision	Leadership	All associates	Visual TV monitors	Continuous	X	X	X	X		General Comprehensive Job Postings/Awarded	Written/Charts	1 way
Intranet	Leadership Team	All associates	On-line	Continuous with weekly/monthly updates	X	X	X	X	X	Results of key success factors	Written words/charts	1 way
Work Instructions Bulletins	Quality Assurance Operations	Associates with specific responsibilities	Formal written communication	When necessary		X				Product process customer specific change or relevant info	Unique Form	1 way
1 to 1 Feedback Form	1 to 1 Leader	Affected Associates	Request form for feedback	After completion of PAR		X	X			Change communication request feedback to verity-buy-in of change	Form distribution and sign-off	2 way
Safety Leader Workshop	Leadership	President, All Safety and Operations Leaders	Discussion	Annual		X	X	X		OFI Themes for Safety	Meeting	2 way

By using this systematic approach to review the communication needed vs. the communication provided, PRO-TEC was able to identify areas where communication could be strengthened. This resulted in adding communication forums for middle management where the communication was effective at the other levels of the organization.

Charleston Area Medical Center (The Partnership For Excellence Recipient 2014)

The PRO-TEC culture was established based on a self-directed empowered workforce and Ownership, Responsibility, Accountability (ORA). All leaders must be good listeners and communicators. This is pivotal to them aligning and integrating systems (and people) and achieving their goals. PRO-TEC systematically validates communication through a communication matrix.

The Leadership System requires the ability to communicate as a prerequisite for becoming a leader (bottom of the center circle of the Leadership System - LS). SLs must communicate with and engage the entire WF, patients and other key customers, which includes a combination of face to face, electronic and print communication methods and social media (Figure 1.1-2). Specific methods are identified to encourage frank, two way communications that are continuously validated for effectiveness. To support frank communication, SL each participate in Crucial Conversations training with emphasis on creating a safe environment. Cycles of learning related to social media include content improvements and increased use of video.

Senior Leaders' ability to engage the WF [5.2a(1)] is monitored through annual surveys. As part of our ongoing commitment to engage our patients and families, SLs are integrating social media into processes to allow them to respond real time to patient concerns gathered via CAMC's social media sites. Key decisions are communicated through a systematic and cascading process from SL to managers to frontline workforce using the Leadership System's actions. The communication method (Figure 1.1-2) depends on the audience and how quickly the message needs to be delivered. Cycles of learning led to the CEO's "Inside the Boardroom" email sent to the workforce on BOT meeting day to provide transparency and timeliness of sharing meeting highlights.

To achieve the "Best Place to Work," SL take an active role in motivating the workforce including reward and recognition programs (LS) to reinforce high performance and a patient, other customer and health care focus. This approach involves formal and informal programs (Figure 5.2- 2) that are linked to the LS and are based on WF surveys (Figure 7.3-27). This approach ensures that reward and recognition programs are deployed to the workforce. As an example, the CEO recognizes Heart and Soul winners each month at CAMC Board Meetings. A cycle of learning led to recognizing departments with the most improvement in their overall HCAHPS score to reinforce high performance and a focus on patients and families.

Figure 1.1-2 Senior Leader Communication Model

Senior Leader Communication Methods (Figure 7.4-1)	Frequency	Key Decisions	Patients &	Workforce	Physicians	Partners &
*Board of Directors and Committees	Monthly	x		x	x	
*Senior Leader Staff Meetings	Weekly	x		x	x	x
*Associate Administrator and Corporate Director Staff Meetings	Weekly	x		x		
*Department Head Meetings	Monthly	x		x		
*Goal Cascade Meetings	Annually	x		x	x	x
*Huddles	Daily	x		x		
*Leadership Rounding	Daily		x	x	x	x
*MIMs	Quarterly	x		x	x	x
Safety Alerts	Real Time	x		x	x	x
*Manager Forums	Semi-Annually	x		x		
*Nursing Shared Governance Council	Monthly	x		x		
*Medical Staff Executive Committee	Bi-Monthly	x		x	x	
*Administrative Update for Medical Staff Department Meetings	Monthly	x			x	
*Physician Advisory Council	Monthly	x		x	x	
*Graduate Medical Education Committee	Bi-Monthly	x		x	x	
Inside the Boardroom	Monthly	x		x	x	
Employee Surveys	Annually			x	x	
*Intranet site (CAMnet)	Daily	x		x	x	
*Internet (CAMC.org)	Daily		x	x	x	x
CEN (closed circuit TV network)	Daily		x	x	x	x
Vital Signs	Monthly		x	x	x	x
Social Media (YouTube, Vine)	Daily	x	x	x	x	
*Social Media (CAMC Website, Facebook, Twitter, LinkedIn)	Daily		x	x	x	x
* Indicates two way communications validated for effectiveness.						

Pewaukee School District (Baldrige Recipient 2013)

Figure 1.1-3 identifies actions taken by SLs (Senior Leaders) to focus the organization to take action to accomplish our objectives. The SPP (Strategic Planning Process) is our key process to identify PSD (Pewaukee School District) objectives to be accomplished. Our SP Action Plans serve as our "do list," as we often say. SLs are systematic in how we drive our SPP to improve performance and attain our Mission and Vision, a PSD core competency. Figure 2.1-1 defines the system SLs used to make our SP actionable. In the 20+ years we have been creating a SP to drive improvement; we have become very systematic in deploying it. During our budget development process and our Administrative Retreat, SLs evaluate system effectiveness. SLs have deployed processes to balance value for students and other stakeholders by:

- Involving stakeholders in SPP/sharing SP with stakeholders

- Involving faculty/staff in Action Plan deployment
- Focusing our budget on key SP initiatives
- Involving students and stakeholders in the CRDP
- Involving partners in teams & committees
- Responding to VOC feedback
- Involving stakeholders in the hiring process
- Writing supplier contract specifications to meet SP goals

To determine stakeholder value, SLs evaluate the impact of any proposed improvement using four key questions asked in order: How does the proposed improvement positively impact student learning? How will we know? Does it do so in the most cost-effective manner so we are accountable to our taxpayers?

Figure 1.1-2 Communication Plan Process

Systematic Deployment Methods of MVV and SP	Deployment			Purpose				Target Group									Frequency					
	Two-Way	Upward	Downward	Engagement	Frank 2-way	Key Decision	Reward/Rec.	Employees	Students	Parents	Teachers	Community	Volunteers	Collaborators	Suppliers	Alumni	Yearly	Quarterly	Monthly	Weekly	Daily	Ongoing
Publishing/Sharing SP	•			•		•		•	•	•	•	•	•	•	•	•	•					
Branding of Mission		•	•			•		•	•	•	•	•	•	•	•	•						•
Administrative Retreat	•			•	•	•		AT									•					
Data Retreat	•			•	•	•	•	•									•	•			•	•
Satisfaction Survey Review		•		•				•	•	•		•					•	•				
New Employee Induction		•	•	•	•			•									•					
Welcome Back Breakfast	•			•	•	•		•									•					
Budget Planning Meetings	•			•	•	•		•							•							•
PES	•			•	•	•	•	•														•
1/2 Day Interviews	•			•	•	•	•	•									•					•
360° Feedback		•		•	•			•									•					
Annual Report		•	•	•		•						•					•					
Annual Meeting	•			•	•	•						•					•					
Volunteer Recognition	•			•			•						•				•					•
Perspective Newsletters	•			•		•		•			•	•				•	3x					
Meetings w/ PTO, BC	•			•								•	•					•				
SP Quarterly Updates	•			•	•	•		AT										•				
PAGs	•			•	•				•								2x					
BOC Minutes		•	•	•		•		•				•							•			•
School Newsletters	•			•	•	•	•		•	•									•			
AT / AC Meetings	•			•	•	•	•	AT			•											•
Curriculum Teams	•			•	•	•		•	•	•	•											•
PLC Meetings	•			•	•	•					•									•	•	
Faculty Bulletins & Curriculum Connection	•			•	•	•	•	•			•										•	
Learning Walks	•			•	•			•	•		•									•		
Thank You/Recognition Notes			•				•	•	•	•	•	•	•	•	•						•	
One-to-One Discussion	•			•	•	•	•	•	•	•	•	•	•	•						•	•	•
Faculty Meetings	•			•		•					•								•			
Web Site	•			•		•	•	•	•	•	•	•	•	•	•							•
Videos	•		•	•				•	•	•	•	•	•	•			•					
Facebook & Twitter Posts	•					•		•	•			•			•		•					
Supplier Review		•	•	•					•		•						•					
Spotlight on Teaching/Learning	•					•		•	•	•							•					
Kuhl Award, Chamber Award	•					•	•										•					
Honor Roll, Merit Award, Student of the Month, etc.			•			•		•	•								•	•				

Key: AT = Administrative Team, AC = Administrative Council, PR = Principal

141

CRITERIA QUESTIONS

In your response, include answers to the following questions:

b. Communication and Organizational Performance

(1) **Communication** How do senior leaders communicate with and engage the entire workforce and key customers? How do they:

- encourage frank, two-way communication, including effective use of social media when appropriate;
- communicate key decisions and needs for organizational change; and
- reinforce high performance and a customer and business focus by taking a direct role in motivating the workforce, including by participating in reward and recognition programs?

(2) **Focus on Action** How do senior leaders create a focus on action that will achieve the organization's mission? How do senior leaders:

- create a focus on action that will improve the organization's performance, achieve innovation and intelligent risk taking, and attain its vision;
- identify needed actions;
- in setting expectations for organizational performance, include a focus on creating and balancing value for customers and other stakeholders?

Notes:

1.1b(1). Use of social media may include delivering periodic messages through internal and external Web sites, tweets, blogging, and customer and workforce electronic forums, as well as monitoring external Web sites and blogs and responding, when appropriate.

1.1b(1). *Nonprofit organizations that rely on volunteers to accomplish their work should also discuss efforts to communicate with and engage the volunteer workforce.*

1.1b(2). Senior leaders' focus on action considers your strategy, workforce, work systems, and assets. It includes taking intelligent risks and implementing innovations and ongoing improvements in productivity that may be achieved by eliminating waste or reducing cycle time; improvement efforts might use techniques such as PDCA, Six Sigma, and Lean. Senior leaders focus on action also includes the actions needed to achieve your strategic objectives (see 2.2a[1]) and may involve establishing change management plans for major organizational change or responding rapidly to significant information from social media or other input.

NIST (2013-2014) p. 7

WORKSHEETS

1.1b(1) –Communication

Requirement	How Do Senior Leaders Do This For The Entire Workforce	How Do Senior Leaders Do This For The Key Customers
Communicate With		
Engage		
Encourage Frank, Two-way Communication (and Verify it is Two-Way)		
Ensure The Effective Use Of Social Media		
Communicate Key Decisions And Needs For Organizational Change		
Take An Active Role In Employee Reward and Recognition	To Reinforce High Performance:	To Reinforce A Customer and Business Focus:

1.1b(2) – Focus on Action

Requirement	How Do Senior Leaders Create A Focus On Action To:
Accomplish *The Organization's Mission*	
Improve the organization's performance	
Achieve Innovation And Intelligent Risk Taking	
Attain The Vision	

How Do Senior Leaders Identify Needed Actions?

How Senior Leaders Create A Focus On:	
***Creating and Balancing Value for Customers and Other Stakeholders*[1]**	

1) This should include how leaders determine, validate, plan, resource, deploy, and review the balance of value for customers and other stakeholders to ensure that the balance they intended was the balance they achieved.

ASSESSMENT

Rating Scale:

1 - **No Process** in place – We are not doing this
2 - **Reacting to Problems** – We use a basic (primarily reactive) process
3 - **Systematic Process** – We use a systematic process that has been improved
4 - **Aligned** – We use a process that aligns our activities from top to bottom
5 - **Integrated** – We use a process that is integrated with other processes across the organization
6 - **Benchmark** – We are the Benchmark in our industry or beyond!
DK - Don't Know

7	Senior Leaders clearly communicate the organizational direction, and each group's role in moving toward that direction, and engage the workforce through frank two-way communication.	1 2 3 4 5 6 DK
8	Senior Leaders use a systematic process to encourage two-way communication throughout the organization, and validate that the two-way communication is effective.	1 2 3 4 5 6 DK
9	Leaders take an active role in reward and recognition, which is aligned with reinforcing high performance.	1 2 3 4 5 6 DK
10	Leaders ensure performance analysis is performed to create a focus on action and intelligent risks to accomplish the organization's objectives and improve performance.	1 2 3 4 5 6 DK
11	The organizational performance expectations (as they are met) create the intended value for all stakeholders.	1 2 3 4 5 6 DK

BLUEPRINT

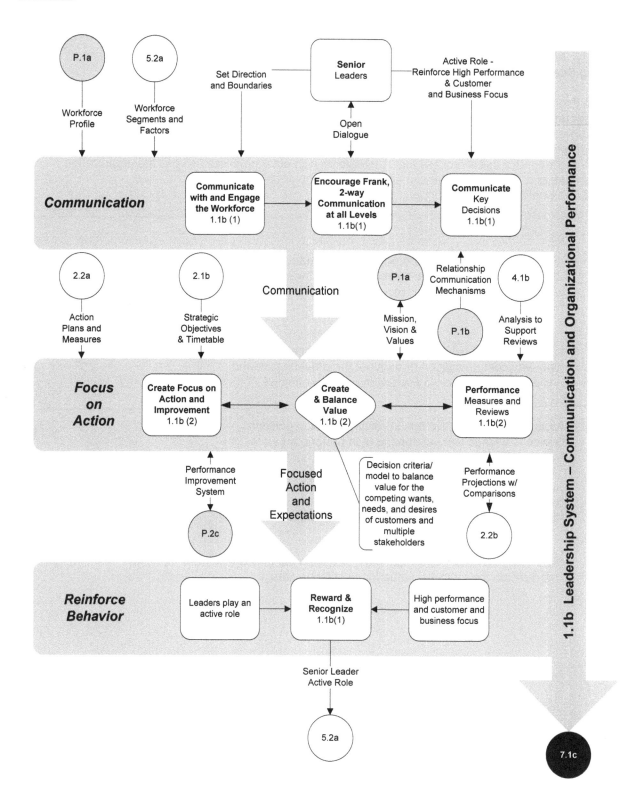

SYSTEM INTEGRATION

Context

P.1a > 1.1b Mission, Vision, Values - Creating a focus on action (performance and strategies) in 1.1b should be consistent with and support the mission, vision, and values of the organization described in P.1a.

P.1a > 1.1b Workforce Profile - The workforce profile is a key input to the design and selection of methods to communicate with and engage the workforce. First, employees are one of the stakeholders of the organization and as such their needs should be considered when setting expectations that create value and balanced the needs of customers and stakeholders. Second, the workforce profile is an input to setting the direction and empowerment and motivation of the workforce.

P.1b > 1.1b Relationship Communication Mechanisms - The creation and communication of the values, directions, and expectations to all employees, suppliers, and partners should include the communication mechanisms described in the profile (P.1b). In addition, the expectations should balance the needs of the customers and multiple stakeholders and those stakeholders are identified in P.1b.

P.2c > 1.1b Performance Improvement System - The performance improvement system described in the profile (P.2c) is a key enabler of the ability to focus on action to accomplish performance improvement, the organization's strategic objectives, and ultimately the vision.

Systems

1.1b < 2.1b Strategic Objectives and Timeline - The output of the strategy development process are strategic objectives and a timetable for accomplishing them as described in 2.1b. These objectives and the timetable are key considerations when creating a focus on action that will help in accomplishing the strategy.

1.1b < 2.2a Action Plans and Measures - In addition to the overall objectives and timeline, the specific action plans and measures described in 2.2a should drive the agenda for action in 1.1b. Creating a focus on action includes focusing on the right measures and their progress toward the strategic objectives to ensure they are on track and provide an opportunity to identify and address issues early before they are really big problems.

1.1b <> 2.2b Performance Projections and Comparisons - The performance projections, comparisons, and targets that are identified in 2.2b should also help drive the agenda for action in 1.1b. This allows the leaders to track the progress from the perspective of changes in the performance of the organization compared to targets and comparisons.

1.1b < 4.1b – Analysis to Support Reviews - Analysis to support reviews as described in 4.1b is an important input to the performance review process described in 1.1b.

1.1b < 5.2a Workforce Segments and Factors - Key factors for workforce engagement (by segment) are key inputs to the design and planning of leadership communication and engagement processes and practices in 1.1b.

1.1b > 5.2a Senior Leader Active Role - How senior leaders play an active role in rewarding and recognizing employees should be an integral and consistent part of the reinforcement processes described in 5.2a (compensation, recognition, rewards, and incentives).

Scorecard

1.1a/b > 7.1c Leadership System Performance focuses on transforming the organization to higher levels of performance. The leadership system is inextricably linked to the strategic management systems. These systems work together to improve performance. Performance that should be reported in 7.1c.

 THOUGHTS FOR LEADERS

Communication is critical to successful organizational performance. Leaders who suppress bad news may feel that they can change reality, but the circumstances, the problems, and the people reporting the bad news still exist. When bad news is suppressed, the only consequence is that the organization does not respond quickly enough to the facts that are reality.

Even if the situation is catastrophic, with effective communication the leader can prepare the organization for the bad news and begin damage control. In many cases, if bad news ascends quickly in an organization, leaders can actually take action to minimize the consequences. Unfortunately, what often happens is that leaders either consciously or unconsciously let it be known that no one should bring them bad news.

A great example is Lyndon Johnson during the Vietnam War. His staff could see that he was depressed by the public opinion of the war. They began to gradually shield him from the bad news until the only place he could find any touch of reality was television. Johnson kept three televisions in the Oval Office, one on each of the major television networks, so that he could stay informed about the war. His organization had isolated him for what they felt was 'the bosses' best interest.'

Leaders also have the responsibility to align what people are rewarded and recognized for with organizational performance. Often people will not act in accordance with how they are actually rewarded and recognized. They will act in accordance with how they *feel* they will be rewarded and recognized. If they do not believe the system is fair, all is lost. If they do not believe what the leaders tell them, then they will act in a manner which is counter to what the leaders say is important.

In taking intelligent risk, leaders must recognize that all risks, no matter how 'intelligent,' do not always have a favorable outcome. How the leader supports the risk which does not work out as planned can be a significant indicator for whether anybody in the organization will ever take another risk. If the risk takers are always punished, then no risks will be taken. If the risk which does not work out is assessed, and learning is gleaned, then the message will be sent that risks can be taken, but not haphazardly.

A Lighter Moment:

Be willing to make decisions.
That's the most important quality in a good leader.
Don't fall victim to what I call the ready-aim-aim-aim-aim syndrome.
You must be willing to fire.

T. Boone Pickens

> ***The best and noblest lives are those which are set toward high ideals.***
>
> **René Alemeras**

FOUNDATION

Governance System

Effective governance means it is not enough to have slogans on the wall or policies and procedures which that extol the importance of integrity, ethics, values, and governance. The actual behavior which demonstrates these qualities should be implemented down to each and every employee and each and every transaction. As with Item 1.1, governance has to be "role modeled" by every leader, every day. There are no "time outs" where when a leader can act in a manner not befitting a role model.

At one of the most recent *Quest for Excellence* conferences (where the new Baldrige Recipients tell their story for the first time), one of the Baldrige recipients was asked how they could ensure that "no employee ever did something wrong." The Baldrige recipient's answer was simple, "We Can't!" He went on to explain that leaders must establish a governance structure, metrics, training, systematic processes for governance, and monitoring for compliance, each of which can be consistently evaluated and improved. In the final analysis, however, individuals must execute the daily transactions every day. The system needs to be clear on the appropriate work instructions (so employees know how to do their job in an acceptable manner), clear on the rules, clear on the audits (both external and internal), and clear on the consequences of actions which do not fall within the acceptable guidelines.

Senior leaders must ensure that all employees (and particularly the leaders) are accountable for their actions, they are accountable for the strategic plans, that there is adequate fiscal accountability, that operations are transparent enough that they can be audited, and that all stakeholder and stockholder interests are effectively protected. To achieve these goals, the CPE ask how the organization ensures independence in external and internal audits. Finally, the succession planning for senior leaders must emphasize the values and behaviors endorsed by the organization.

This is impacted by the selection of governance board members and disclosure policies for them. Both internal and external audits must be independent and effective.

While an organization or its leaders cannot eliminate the possibility of someone doing something wrong, they can reduce the likelihood! Governance, like the all other parts of Categories 1 through 6, must be implemented through a systematic process. That is, a process that is defined, measured, stabilized, and improved.

Performance Evaluation

Finally, the criteria ask how the organization evaluates leadership performance, including the performance and compensation of the chief executive, the governance board, and the oversight board or board of directors. In this manner, the examiners can understand how the board reviews performance and how they evaluate the board and their personal effectiveness. These need to be tangible measures, tracking and audits, with tangible actions taken to follow-up on concerns or non-conformances.

These measures, reviews and results should be used to advance the development of senior leaders, to improve their personal leadership effectiveness, and that of their governance board and leadership board. As with other parts of the business model, these improvements need to be systematic. In addition to the evaluation and improvement of the leadership groups, which are at the top of the organization, performance improvement needs to be inculcated into every leader at every level. This needs to be systematically achieved through the leadership system.

 EXAMPLES

PRO-TEC Coating Company (Baldrige Recipient 2007)

Organizational governance is uniquely embedded into PRO-TEC's culture down to the responsibility of every Associate based on Ownership, Responsibility, Accountability (ORA) and the mission, vision, and values. Senior leaders are directly responsible for Associate safety, the company's actions, and the management systems that ensure the sustainability of the company. Figure 1.2-1 outlines the framework of PRO-TEC's organizational governance system, which embraces senior leader and Associate ORA along with open lines of two-way communication and oversight, which penetrates through all levels of the organization.

The governance system has been formed by: 1) External regulatory and community requirements (safety, environmental, legal, financial, etc.), 2) PRO-TEC formation agreements (partnership, substrate supply, and marketing agreements), 3) Customer and vendor requirements, and 4) Internal policies, procedures, and work instructions (Human Resources, departmental, ISO/QES).

Management Accountability: The Leadership Team is responsible for establishing policies and procedures and the direction of the organization through the strategic planning process. Each member of the Leadership Team is assigned responsibility for maintaining a specific key success factor (KSF) and for the ultimate deployment throughout the organization. At the monthly plant management meeting, each senior leader is responsible for reviewing performance for their assigned KSF and objectives through the balanced scorecard (BSC). The BSC is then presented at the Management Committee meeting held three times per year. Actions are taken at each review.

Fiscal Accountability: Through the BSC objectives and the monthly financial closing process, a detailed review of the financial performance is performed. Monthly detailed statements are prepared and presented to all department heads and both parent companies. The results are also presented as part of the monthly plant management meeting and summarized in the monthly detailed report to the Management Committee. Woven throughout the framework are the underlying policies and procedures that are continually being reviewed, evaluated, and communicated to address any changes in the regulatory and stakeholder requirements. When change is required, any Associate or stakeholder can initiate change by completing a preventive or corrective action request (PAR or CAR). These requests are monitored and reviewed on a routine basis through the Idea-to-Implementation (I-to-I) processes and at monthly plant management meetings.

Transparency in Operation: In order to validate the governance and all other management systems, independent internal and external auditors are used to routinely review the process requirements (Figure 1.2-1) (compliance and audit resources). Built into PRO-TEC's unique culture is the philosophy that internal and external input and audits are welcomed and necessary to ensure the sustainability of the system and the organization. Two of the three types of audits conducted are fully independent of the Leadership Team. The customer/vendor reports findings to the Leadership Team, and the external audits report findings directly to the Management Committee. These audits verify all actions are transparent up to the appropriate level.

Independence of Audits: To ensure the internal audits are robust and highlight all appropriate issues, the Management Committee initiates external audits on a pre-determined schedule. These independent external auditors can also be requested by the Leadership Team on a more frequent basis.

Protection of Stakeholder Interests: There is a direct focus of protecting stakeholder interests that is performed by linking the KSFs and objectives on the balanced scorecard to the stakeholders. An I-to-I team was assembled to enhance PRO-TEC's internal controls by establishing a formal competitive bidding procedure based on a USS audit recommendation. Through the implementation of this procedure, another layer to the internal control structure was added to protect all stakeholder interests.

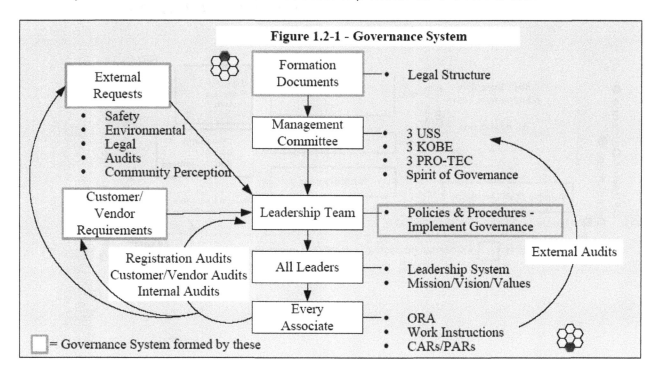

Figure 1.2-1 - Governance System

Source: PRO-TEC Coating Company

Methodist Healthcare System (San Antonio, Texas)

Methodist Healthcare System (MHS) consistently works to produce accurate, reliable, timely, secure and confidential information in line with the high expectations of our workforce, customers, stakeholders and partners. There is a systematic approach which demonstrates how data, information and knowledge is collected, validated, deployed, audited and maintained across MHS using a variety of safeguards and built-in security systems. For example, automated interfaces are continually validated through sophisticated monitors using an alert system. Accurate, real-time information is made available to appropriate individuals through a highly secure and user-friendly network, giving health care providers and clinical caregivers ability to deliver quality and safe patient care twenty-four hours a day, seven days a week.

MHS has several interlocking boards which provide a robust system of governance. The system is summarized in the figure below. The shaded boxes describe the Governance System. The governance flow includes two way guidance (1), deployment (2) and use (3). Validation with internal and external audits flows to the Board of Governors (BOG) (on the right) (4). The belief systems of both partners as well as the Clinical Groups (Medical Staff Executive and Nursing Executive) are also incorporated.

Accountability for management's actions and fiscal accountability flow through the chain-of-command to all associates. Appropriate Transparency (what should be seen) is ensured by the BOG using the partnership beliefs as guidance. This is validated by internal and external audits which are reported back to the BOG Audit Committee. The governance guidance flowing from the BOG ensures protection of stakeholder and stockholder interests through their responsibilities, audits and BOG, as well as Community Board Sub-Committees.

1.2 – Methodist Healthcare System (MHS) Condensed Governance System

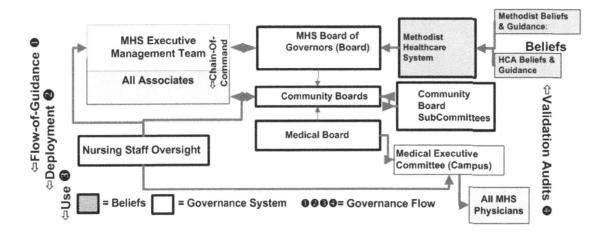

CRITERIA QUESTIONS

In your response, include answers to the following questions:

a. Organizational Governance

(1) Governance System How does your organization ensure responsible governance? How does your organization review and achieve the following key aspects of its governance system?

- Accountability for Senior Leaders' actions
- Accountability for strategic plans
- Fiscal accountability
- Transparency in operations
- Selection of governance board members, and disclosure policies for them, as appropriate
- Independence and effectiveness of internal and external audits
- Protection of stakeholder and stockholder interests, as appropriate
- Succession planning for senior leaders

(2) Performance Evaluation How do you evaluate the performance of your senior leaders, including the chief **executive, and your governance board**? How do you use these performance evaluations in determining executive compensation? How do your senior leaders and governance board use these performance evaluations to advance their development and improve both their own effectiveness as leaders and that of your board and leadership system, as appropriate?

Notes:

1.2. Societal responsibilities in areas critical to your ongoing marketplace success should also be addressed in **Strategy** Development (item 2.1) and Operations Focus (category 6). Key results should be reported as Leadership and Governance Results (item 7.4). Examples are results related to regulatory and legal requirements (including the results of mandated financial audits); reductions in environmental impacts through the use of "green" technology, resource-conserving activities, reduction of carbon footprint, or other means; or improvements in social impacts, such as the global use of enlightened labor practices.

1.2. The health and safety of your workforce are not addressed in this item; you should address these workforce factors in items 5.1 and 6.2.

1.2.a(1). The governance board's review of organizational performance and progress, if appropriate, is addressed in 4.1(b).

1.2a(1). Transparency in the operations of your governance system should include your internal controls on governance processes. For some privately held businesses and nonprofit organizations, an external advisory board may provide some or all governance board functions. For nonprofit organizations that serve as stewards of public funds, stewardship of those funds and transparency in operations are areas of emphasis.

1.2a(2). The evaluation of leaders' performance might be supported by peer reviews, formal performance management reviews, and formal or informal feedback from and surveys of the workforce and other stakeholders. For some privately held businesses and nonprofit and government organizations, external advisory boards might evaluate the performance of senior leaders and the governance board.

NIST (2015-2016) pp. 8-9

WORKSHEETS

1.2a(1) – Governance System
A framework for thinking about the governance process is as follows:

Who	What	Where	How	Why						Results
Group Responsible	Our Intent	Area to Address 1.2a(1)	Audits Performed (coded for internal & external)	Primary Stakeholder Impacted *						Area 7.4a(2) Figure Numbers
				C	S	CO	E	SH		
Board of Directors Senior Leaders All: • Employees • Suppliers • Partners	Comply with all: • International Laws & Regulations • National Laws & Regulations • Local Laws & Regulations • Local Ordinances	Accountability for Senior Leader's Actions								
		Accountability for Strategic Plans								
		Fiscal Accountability								
		Transparency in Operations, Selection & Disclosure Policies for Board Members								
		Audit Independence and Effectiveness • Internal Audits • External Audits								
		Protection of Stakeholder and Stockholder interests								
		Succession Planning For Senior Leaders								

* **Stakeholder Codes:**

Customers = C   Suppliers = S   Community = CO   Employees = E   Stockholder = SH

1.2a(2) – Performance Evaluation

	Group Being Evaluated:	
Requirement	Senior Leaders Including Chief Executive	Governance Board
How Do You Evaluate Performance?		
How Are The Performance Evaluations Used In Determining Executive Compensation?		
How Do They Use These Performance Evaluations To Advance Their Development And Improve Their Effectiveness As Leaders?		

How Do They Use These Performance Evaluations To Advance The Development And Improve The Effectiveness Of The Board?		
How Do They Use These Performance Evaluations To Advance The Development And Improve The Effectiveness Of The Leadership System?		

 ## ASSESSMENT

Rating Scale:

1 - **No Process** in place – We are not doing this
2 - **Reacting to Problems** – We use a basic (primarily reactive) process
3 - **Systematic Process** – We use a systematic process that has been improved
4 - **Aligned** – We use a process that aligns our activities from top to bottom
5 - **Integrated** – We use a process that is integrated with other processes across the organization
6 - **Benchmark** – We are the Benchmark in our industry or beyond!
DK - Don't Know

12	The governance processes are clearly defined, deployed, monitored, and improved.	1 2 3 4 5 6 DK
13	The governance processes are led by all of the Senior Leaders in the organization, and their performance evaluations include performance in governance.	1 2 3 4 5 6 DK
14	All employees are trained in the governance processes which impact them, and are clear on their personal responsibilities, and what are acceptable and non-acceptable actions or records.	1 2 3 4 5 6 DK
15	The organization has measures to track the governance for all employees and all transactions.	1 2 3 4 5 6 DK
16	Leadership performance reviews are used to improve the effectiveness of leaders, the governing board, and the leadership system, and are used in the succession planning process for Senior Leaders.	1 2 3 4 5 6 DK

BLUEPRINT

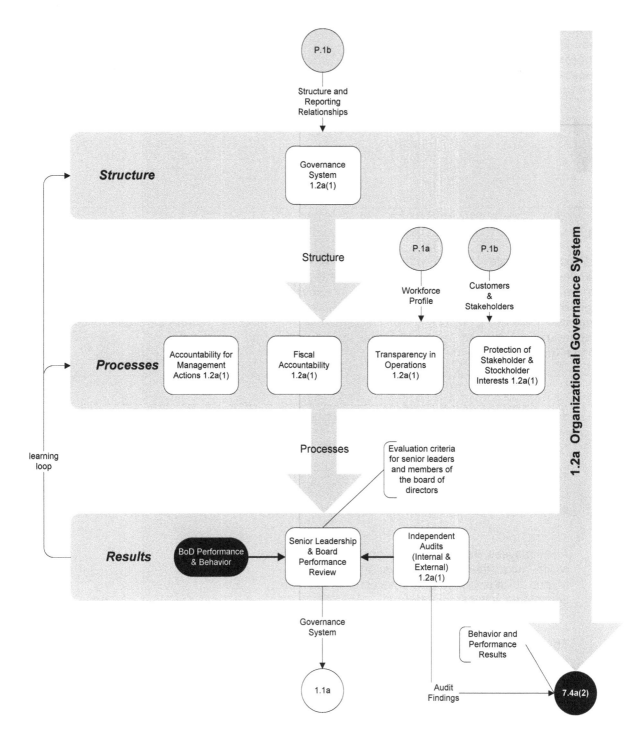

SYSTEM INTEGRATION

Context

P.1a > 1.2a Workforce Profile - The workforce profile (job types, employee education, etc.) are key inputs to the design and selection of organizational governance processes that protect the interests of stakeholders and stockholders.

P.1b > 1.2a Structure and Reporting Relationships - There are two key factors to consider when diagnosing or designing a governance system – first the structure and governance system and second the reporting relationships among the board of directors - both of which are described in the profile (P.1b). The approach to governance should be consistent with and appropriate for the specific situation described in P.1b. This can vary widely depending on the history of the organization, the ownership model, and the legal status of the organization (incorporated, 501c, etc.).

P.1b > 1.2a Customers and Stakeholders - The customers and stakeholders identified in P.1b should be addressed by the governance processes and practices identified in 1.2a for the protection of "stakeholder" and stockholder interests.

Systems

1.1a <> 1.2a Governance System - How well the leaders are doing setting, deploying, and reinforcing the mission, vision, values, and direction should be part of the Senior Leadership and Board Performance Review process described in 1.2a Governance System.

Scorecard

1.2a > 7.4a(2) Governance System Results - Employee behavior and accountability measures are included in 7.4a and should measure the effectiveness of the governance processes that address management accountability, fiscal accountability, and ultimately protect the interests of the stockholders and stakeholders. In addition, 7.4a includes the audit findings from both internal and external audits which also validate the effectiveness of the preventive approaches. As inputs these results are used to make governance decisions and also to evaluate and improve the governance structure, system, and processes.

THOUGHTS FOR LEADERS

Governance must impact all employees in all transactions they conduct for the organization. Thus, organizations must have a clear view of all legal and regulatory conditions and requirements, both current and in the future. These requirements must be translated into clear work instructions for the impacted employees. Organizations must train all employees in their personal responsibilities, and provide them with a very clear understanding of the consequences for the organization (and for them as employees) if they do not comply with every detail of the required governance processes.

Furthermore, organizations must establish processes which can ensure that mistakes can be discussed and effectively corrected. Where there are problems or clear violations they should be addressed quickly, legally, and ethically. If the culture hides them, however, they will not improve with time, and they will not be effectively corrected.

The Organizational-Level Governance processes must be structured to comply with all governmental, moral, and ethical requirements, as well as the best interests of the stakeholders. The general rule of thumb is that the organization needs to have proactive processes which prevent (to the degree that a process can prevent) activities or actions which the organization would not want to see on the front page of tomorrow's newspaper.

Finally, leadership must have a systematic approach to measure the performance of their senior leaders, including the chief executive and the governing board. This evaluation of performance needs to be in alignment with the leadership traits expected in all leaders (such as those described in the Leadership System), the values of the organization, as well as in alignment with the leader's personal goals.

> *Nobody grows old by merely living a number of years;*
> *people grow old only by deserting their ideals.*
>
> **Samuel Ullman**

> *In the arena of human life the honors and rewards fall*
> *To those who show their good qualities in action.*
>
> **Aristotle**

FOUNDATION

Governance (Item 1.2a) addresses the appropriate transparency and checks and balances. Similarly, legal and ethical behavior needs 100% compliance, and internal and external checks and balances.

Does the organization address public concerns, handle all transactions ethically, and support the key communities where it operates? In addition, does it ensure that all transactions of the organization meet the appropriate legal and ethical standards?

Legal and Regulatory Compliance

The first part of Area to Address 1.2b assesses whether or not the organization understands the "footprint" it leaves on the world it operates within. This section includes an organization understanding their impact on the public and society from:

- the **products** the organization produces;
- the **services** the organization renders and provides; and
- the organization's internal **operations**, including the processes and materials used.

In recent years, the Criteria for Performance Excellence (CPE) has turned its focus from merely meeting regulatory and legal requirements to anticipating and surpassing regulatory and legal requirements. This shift is most likely based on the belief that the regulatory and legal requirements will not diminish over time, but, quite possibly, will continue to become more stringent.

The CPE model challenges organizations to identify the key compliance processes, how these processes are measured, and how goals have been set. It recognizes how the organization understands these processes, measures, and goals and how it uses them to assess risk. Risks also need to be assessed for the organization's key products, services, and operations.

Moving from the current products, services, and operations to what could happen in the future, CPE wants an organization to understand the process used to anticipate what could happen. The specific question starts with "how do you anticipate public concerns?" The CPE model identifies how the organization anticipates concerns and what the organization is doing to prepare for those concerns if they should occur. Being proactive is more favorable than being behind the regulatory "power curve" and trying to catch up once public concerns drive new regulations.

Ethical Behavior

The CPE also focus on establishing an ethical foundation throughout the organization. This starts with understanding the organizational culture [requested in the Organizational Profile, [(P.1a(2)]. It is further discussed in Area to Address 1.1a(1), which asks how leaders set and deploy organizational values.

The CPE aim to ensure that ethical behavior is deployed throughout the entire organization at all times. The CPE focuses on establishing an ethical foundation which will ensure ethical behavior in all stakeholder transactions and interactions. As with other "how" questions, this area is looking for a specific systematic process. The CPE want to know how the processes are used, how well they are deployed, and how they are measured. Interestingly, the CPE do not ask for specific goals for ethical behavior. It may be assumed that any company would have a goal of no ethical violations. Nevertheless, actual ethical performance can be reported in Item 7.4 in the Results Category.

As with the governance structure discussed in Area to Address 1.2a, ethical behavior is to be monitored throughout the organization. It is also to be monitored with key partners, including suppliers, customers, community, and others. In simple terms, the CPE want to ensure that ethical behavior is everywhere all the time. Although this compliance is difficult for any company to guarantee, the CPE model is looking for processes, measures, and checks and balances to ensure that processes have been effectively implemented and are effectively enforced.

 EXAMPLES

Don Chalmers Ford (Baldrige Site Visited Company – Small Business 2008, 2012)

The figure below includes how potentially adverse impacts on society of Don Chalmer's Ford's services are addressed proactively. DCF has robust key compliance processes, measures, and goals for achieving and surpassing regulatory and legal requirements, and for addressing the possible risks associated with DCF's products, services, and operations. Additionally, they are able to show data which validates this achievement. A 2008 cycle of improvement innovation was the new DCF "Green Team" to analyze potential for recycling and waste reduction and implement strategies and action plans.

DCF promotes and ensures ethical business practices for all stakeholders annually in the "Driving Forward" report, in the Employee Handbook, the online manual, and employee pocket cards to focus on the core value of Individual and Organizational Integrity and Ethics. The Senior Leadership Team (SLT) evaluates and strengthens these deployment methods annually during the Strategic Planning Process (SPP), committing to model ethical business practices by example.

The SLT assesses all Stakeholder concerns and goes above and beyond in resolving the concern. DCF also communicates expectations of leading by example to all managers and expects them to perform their business transactions ethically.

In 2005, DCF's SLT upgraded the philosophy of ethical behavior to a core value, making all levels responsible for implementation. In key areas, like finance, video recordings allow third party audits that assess the process discipline, integrity and ethics of the transactions. Feedback is provided to ensure that continuous improvement takes place.

DCF's ethical behavior is promoted and ensured through a variety of methods. The SLT reviews Integrity and Ethics (I&E) at new employee orientation, the workforce has an I&E pocket card with a simple test, and can view the I&E test online.

A confidential employee hotline is available for employees to report any integrity, ethics or legal issues to a third party. Background checks and drug tests are performed on new employees, and random drug tests are run on existing employees. Immediate and serious consequences leading up to potential termination to discourage deviations from the organization's culture of integrity and ethics. When breaches are suspected or reported, the I&E Process is used to verify the concern, determine severity, and decide appropriate consequences.

Proactive Approach to Societal Impacts

Process to Address Adverse Impacts on Society of:	Process to Anticipate Public Concerns With Current & Future:	Proactive Preparation
Services: Emission control inspections; environmental regulation compliance	OSHA requirements are included in workforce processes	Concern Resolutions Process pocket card w/each employee
Operations: Outside lighting to respect neighbors; Public Relations processes to respond to customer feedback; Ford Bold Moves	Professional memberships in auto industry keep dealership current; lighting; no outside paging system	Open door policy; web site lists contact information for addressing customer concerns
Products: Compliance with Ford FSA recall process; hybrid vehicles; oil recycling	Flexible fuel vehicles accept alternative fuels; recall products & warranty: DCF honors customers wherever their vehicle was purchased & notify customers who haven't yet come in	Sales & F&I video

Source: Don Chalmers Ford (2008)

Virtua Health (Baldrige Site Visited Organization 2008)

Virtua believes that every associate must understand the desired behaviors to drive their culture or they cannot ensure that those behaviors are used in all transactions with all stakeholders. The basic approach can be summarized as teach, mentor, role model, inspect, and improve.

Virtua Health's approach to legal and ethical behavior is to ensure that the organization has world-class listening posts to track regulations and laws. What is learned from these listening posts, when combined with their beliefs (e.g. Mission, Vision, and Values) forms the baseline for how every associate should conduct themselves. These beliefs and requirements are translated into written standards, policies, procedures and work instructions, which go all the way up to the Board of Trustees (BOT) and the senior leadership, and all the way down to every associate.

The detailed behaviors are defined for every associate through the *STAR Standards of Performance.* These are clearly documented and are communicated to every level. They are even embedded in the hiring process, and are used to train every employee in their responsibilities to provide:

- Excellence Service
- Resource Stewardship
- Clinical Quality & Safety
- Caring Culture
- Best People

Once trained, associates must verify that they understand and agree to the behavior standards. These standards of behavior are also measured for all associates, and form the basis for all goals, strategies, actions and improvements.

Virtua Health Legal and Ethical Behavior System

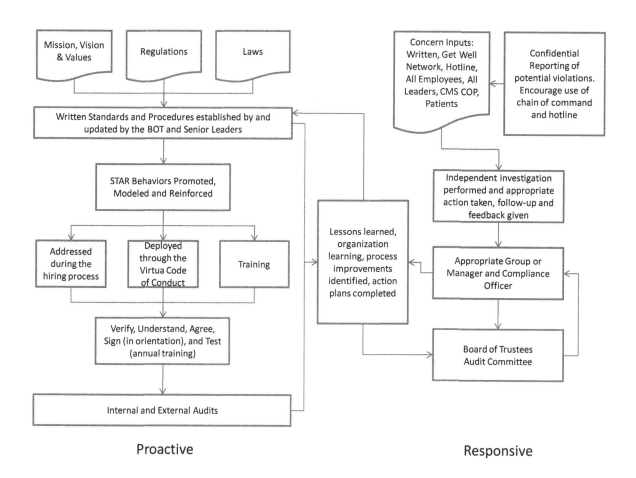

Proactive   Responsive

Up to this point in the process, all actions are PROACTIVE. Nothing is wrong, but the organization has taken many actions to ensure that nothing 'goes wrong.'

If a legal or ethical concern is raised, the organization has a defined process to investigate the issue, determine the appropriate actions, these are RESPONSIVE. The reports of the investigation findings go

162

all the way to the Board of Trustees and the senior leadership, and appropriate actions are taken on a timely basis.

Pewaukee School District (Baldrige Recipient 2013)

1.2b.(2) SLs (Senior Leaders) systematically deploy BOE (Board of Education) policies, regulations and training programs to promote ethical behavior (Figure 1.2-4). The HR Director monitors the deployment of ethical training and serves as the Complaint Officer to whom ethical violations are reported pursuant to BOE policy. Promotion of ethical behavior begins with hiring.

As part of the induction process, new employees receive training concerning PSD's high standards, requirements, and reporting processes. All employees receive BOE policies regarding ethical behavior, review them, and annually sign an affidavit of receipt. Processes are in place for all employees to learn of and respond to ethical breaches. Policies dictate when disclosures of ethical violations are called for, and employees are informed of the role of the Complaint Officer and means of reporting. The HR Director and Superintendent respond to breaches of ethical behavior as per contract and BOE policy.

Cycles of improvement are evident in how PSD (Pewaukee School District) enhances ethical responsibility. PSD is one of less than 2% of public schools in the nation to implement random student drug testing to reinforce our Athletics & Activities Code for students and promote legal and ethical behavior. PSD is nationally recognized as a forerunner in ethical use of this student drug prevention tool. Criminal background checks are used for all volunteers in addition to employees to identify, anticipate, minimize, and analyze regulatory, safety accreditation, and legal responsibilities and risks.

A complaint tracking system brings reports to the attention of the Superintendent and SAs for resolution. In a cycle of learning, this tracking system identified a parent concern regarding teacher use of Facebook, that resulted in a change of procedure for use of this social networking tool.

Figure 1.2-4 Systematic Processes for Measuring Ethical Responsibility				
Process Used	Requirements	Measurement Tool	SL & BOE Involve-ment	Results Found
Employees				
BOE Policy	BOE policies define ethical behavior & consequences; identify whom to contact	# policies / # breaches	BOE Supt	7.4-6
Hiring Process	Inform employees of requirements	% new employees receiving BOE polices	Supt., DHR	7.4-6
		% employees receiving handbook annually	DHR	7.4-6
Hiring Process	Hire employees with clean record	% checks conducted for new employees / # hired with felony convictions	DHR	7.4-6
Hiring Process	DPI fully licensed teachers, administrators & aides	% highly qualified	Supt., DHR	7.4-6
External Audit	Use district funds ethically	# significant findings	CFO	7.4-6
IRS Audits	Use district funds ethically	# IRS violations	CFO	7.4-6
BOE Policy	Workplace free of Harassment	# harassment complaints filed via BOE policy	Supt., DHR	7.4-6
Satisfaction Survey	Perception of a safe Workplace	% employees citing PSD is a safe place to work	AC, PIC	7.3-7
Standardized Test Management	Reliable & valid student test data submitted to State	# DPI violations	CA Principals	7.4-6
Personnel Process	Confidentiality for employ-ees and records	# sanctions due to HIPPA violations	DHR	7.4-6
Students				
Student Handbooks	Communicate BOE ethical standards, consequences	% handbooks given to students annually	Prin; BOE reviews	7.4-6
Merit Award	Positive Student Citizenship	increasing # per year	PHS Principal	7.4-6
Suspensions Expulsions	Positive Student Citizenship	decreasing #/% per year	Principals Supt.	7.4-6
Student Drug Testing	Positive Student Citizenship	% positive drug screens	PHS P/AP/ Dean	7.4-6
Acceptable Use Policy	Responsible Use of Technology	# students who had technology privileges suspended	DOT	7.4-6
Parents, Stakeholders, Vendors				
BOE Induction	Pledge of ethics in boardsmanship	% new BOE members citing ethics pledge	BOE	7.4-6
Volunteer Background Checks	Safe learning environment; Verify volunteers have clean criminal record	% criminal background checks completed / % volunteers with felony conviction working with students	DHR	7.4-6
				7.4-6
Vendor Contracts	Contracts awarded following BOE policies	% contracts found to be awarded inappropriately	CFO, Supt. BOE	7.4-6

CRITERIA QUESTIONS

In your response, include answers to the following questions:

b. Legal and Ethical Behavior

(1) **Legal and Regulatory Compliance** How do you anticipate and address public concerns with your products and operations? How do you:

- address any adverse impacts of your products and operations;
- anticipate public concerns with your current and future products and operations;
- prepare for these impacts and concerns proactively, including through conservation of natural resources and effective supply-chain management processes, as appropriate?

What are your key compliance processes, measures, and goals for meeting and surpassing regulatory and legal requirements, as appropriate? What are your key processes, measures, and goals for addressing risks associated with your products and operations?

(2) **Ethical Behavior** How do you promote and ensure ethical behavior in all interactions? What are your key processes and measures or indicators for enabling and monitoring ethical behavior in your governance structure, throughout your organization, and in interactions with your workforce, customers, partners, suppliers, and other stakeholders? How do you monitor and respond to breaches of ethical behavior?

Notes:

1.2b(1). Nonprofit organizations should report, as appropriate, how they meet and surpass the regulatory and legal requirements and standards that govern fundraising and lobbying.

1.2b(2). Measures or indicators of ethical behavior might include the percentage of independent board members, measures of relationships with stockholder and nonstockholder constituencies, instances of ethical conduct or compliance breaches and responses to them, survey results showing workforce perceptions of organizational ethics, ethics hotline use, and results of ethics reviews and audits. Measures or indicators of ethical behavior might also include evidence that policies, workforce training, and monitoring systems are in place for conflicts of interest; protection and use of sensitive data, information, and knowledge generated through synthesizing and correlating these data; and proper use of funds are in place.

NIST (2015-2016) pp. 8-9

WORKSHEETS

1.2b Legal and Ethical Behavior

1.2b(1) – Legal and Regulatory Compliance

Process to Address any Adverse Impacts On Society of:	Process to Proactively Anticipate Public Concerns With Current and Future:	Processes To Prepare For These Concerns In A Proactive Manner (including with the supply chain and conserving natural resources)	Compliance Processes, Measures and Goals For Meeting/ Surpassing Regulatory and Legal Requirements	Key Processes, Measures and Goals For Addressing Risks
Products:	Products:	Products:	Products:	Products:
Services: *	Services:	Services:	Services:	Services:
Operations:	Operations:	Operations:	Operations:	Operations:

* Note: The criteria does not require you to address Services, but if some of your Services have potential impacts on society, then they should be included.

1.2b(2) – Ethical Behavior

Source Of Ethical Requirements	Processes Used To Promote, Enable And Ensure Ethical Behavior	Measures Or Indicators Used In The Governance Structure And Throughout The Organization, And In Interactions With Workforce, Customers, Partners, Suppliers And Other Stakeholders	Results Figures (In Area 7.4a[4])
For Stakeholder_____			
For Stakeholder_____			
For Stakeholder_____			
For Stakeholder_____			
For Stakeholder_____			
Process Used To Monitor And Respond To Breaches Of Ethical Behavior:			

ASSESSMENT

Rating Scale:

1 - No Process in place – We are not doing this
2 - Reacting to Problems – We use a basic (primarily reactive) process
3 - Systematic Process – We use a systematic process that has been improved
4 - Aligned – We use a process that aligns our activities from top to bottom
5 - Integrated – We use a process that is integrated with other processes across the organization
6 - Benchmark – We are the Benchmark in our industry or beyond!
DK - Don't Know

17	There are measures and goals set and tracked to determine the impact on society of our products, services and operations.	1 2 3 4 5 6 DK
18	The organization anticipates the impact on society of our products, services and operations.	1 2 3 4 5 6 DK
19	The organization has clear ethical standards and guidelines.	1 2 3 4 5 6 DK
20	The ethical guidelines are communicated to and implemented through all employees using specific measures or indicators.	1 2 3 4 5 6 DK
21	The ethical behavior of our key partners is effectively communicated and monitored.	1 2 3 4 5 6 DK

BLUEPRINT

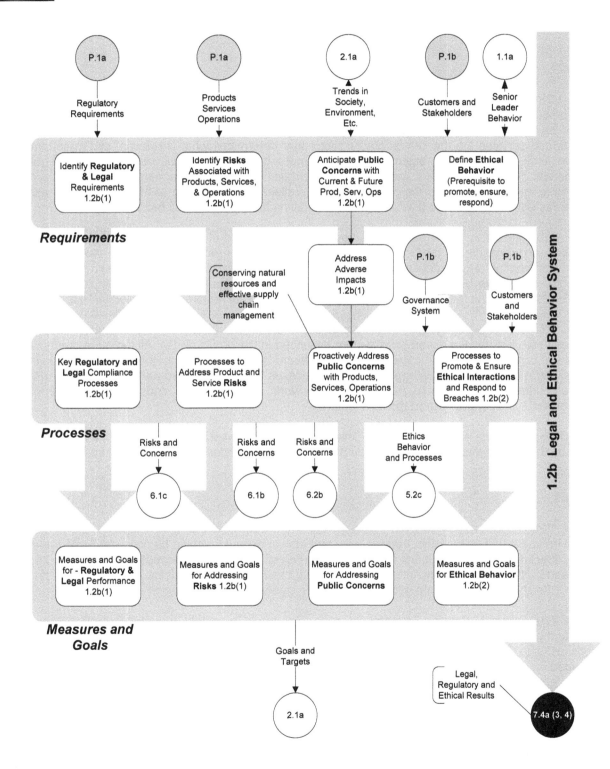

SYSTEM INTEGRATION

Context

P.1a > 1.2b Products and Services - The most important input to area 1.2b is the description and nature of the products, services and operations identified and described in the profile P.1a. Since this area is focused on the public concerns, risks, and regulatory and legal issues related to the firm, the type of products and services are the central driving factor that determines what is relevant and important. For example, if the products are eaten by the consumers then the FDA will be part of the regulatory environment. Some of the risks associated will be health risks to consumers, and there are public concerns to deal with, such as the case of Mad Cow disease. The design of the processes to address these areas will likely be different for a business consulting firm than they will be for an airline.

P.1a > 1.2b Regulatory Requirements - A key input to legal and ethical behavior (1.2b) requirements, processes, and measures is the description of the regulatory environment described in the profile (P.1a). This environment is largely driven by the nature of the products, services, and operations, but other factors can also drive this environment including the nature of the ownership, the employees, and so forth. This is a key input to the identification of regulatory and legal requirements called for in area 1.2b.

P.1b > 1.2b Governance System - The processes that ensure ethical interactions also need to be designed to work within the governance system described in the profile (P.1b). All too often organizations will create processes and structures that are different and distinct from the main systems of the organization. While this might be appropriate for processes that require "third party" status to be effective (e.g., ombudsman) they should be designed to work within and be consistent with the overall management systems and organizational structure.

P.1b > 1.2b Customers and Stakeholders - The customers and stakeholders identified in the profile (P.1b) should be the same groups addressed by the processes and practices to ensure ethical interactions.

Systems

1.1a <> 1.2b Senior Leader Behavior - The activities and behaviors that senior leaders use to promote and environment that fosters and requires legal and ethical behavior should be consistent with the stated values, directions, and expectations are the ethical interactions of the employees described in 1.2b. Part of the issue with ensuring ethical interactions is having clear definitions of ethics. The definitions of ethics used in 1.2b should be consistent with and include the values of the organization as defined in 1.1a.

1.2b <> 2.1a Trends in Society, Environment, etc. - The trends in society, the environment, etc., are key inputs to the strategy development process described in 2.1a. These trends should be consistent with the trends used to anticipate public concerns with current and future products, services, and operations described in 1.2b.

1.2b > 2.1a Goals and Targets - The goals for regulatory and legal performance along with the performance targets for risk, regulatory and legal, and public concerns are inputs to the analysis of financial, societal, ethical, regulatory and other risks addressed in 2.1a. These are then used as inputs to the strategy development process.

1.2b > 5.2c Ethics Behavior and Processes - The definitions and processes associated with the organizations ethics programs should also be incorporated into the workforce and leaders development needs assessment and offering design processes. Leaders need to know the organizations approaches and policies on ethics so they can implement and reinforce those policies. In addition, they also need to know how to be a role model for ethical behavior.

1.2b > 6.1b Risks and Concerns - The public concerns that are identified in the process described in 1.2b are direct inputs to the process requirements determination step described in 6.1b. Consequently, the output of 1.2b should be in a format that is useful for determining process requirements.

1.2b > 6.1c Risks and Concerns - The public concerns that are identified in the process described in 1.2b are direct inputs to the emergency readiness preparation requirements. The emergency readiness system should be designed in a way that inspires confidence and addresses the public concerns identified in 1.2b.

1.2b > 6.2b Risks and Concerns - The public concerns that are identified in the process described in 1.2a should be built into the process management practices and procedures. This helps ensure that the concerns are proactively addressed and problems prevented.

Scorecard

1.2b > 7.4a Regulatory and Legal - Regulatory and legal results found in 7.4a should reflect the same measures and goals described in 1.2b. The results in 7.4a confirm or deny the effectiveness of the approaches described in this area.

1.2b > 7.4a Risks and Concerns - The results in 7.4a should directly reflect the results and targets that determine the effectiveness of the processes and approaches to address the risks and public concerns associated with the products, services, and operations.

1.2b > 7.4a(3, 4) Ethical Behavior - Ethical behavior measures identified in 1.2b should be consistent with the results for ethical behavior presented in 7.4a.

THOUGHTS FOR LEADERS

Ethics, as with governance, must impact all employees in all transactions conducted on behalf of the organization. Organizations must have a clear view of all legal and regulatory conditions and requirements, both current and for the future. These regulations must then be translated into easy-to-understand directives, and all employees must be trained in the regulations and in their personal responsibilities. Even temporary and contract employees must be trained in their responsibilities in ethics, as they can appear to an outsider to represent the organization.

Beyond the basic beliefs and infrastructure for ethical behavior, systematic processes must be established to ensure that mistakes can be proactively prevented. If mistakes do occur, the processes and practices must ensure that they are not covered up, but are discussed and the root cause is assessed and corrected. In the instances where the mistakes result in clear violations, these infractions must be addressed in a straightforward manner quickly, legally, and ethically.

Some high performing organizations go as far as to screen all employees for values during the hiring process. Although this step is probably not foolproof, these organizations have seen the benefit and believe that this is a tangible way to ensure that the organization is established "from the ground up" on the ethics of every individual.

A CEO of one of these companies made the comment that he had 'gone against' the ethical screening four times. "Those were four of my mistakes," he readily admited.

> *To give away money is an easy matter, and in any man's power.*
> *But to decide to whom to give it, and how large and when, and*
> *for what purpose and how, is neither in every man's power –*
> *nor an easy matter. Hence it is that such excellence is rare,*
> *praiseworthy, and noble.*
>
> **Aristotle**

FOUNDATION

Over the last few years the Criteria for Performance Excellence (CPE) have evolved to include an increased emphasis on the three key dimensions of success now and in the future – economic, environmental, and societal or as Elkington, Emerson, and Beloe (2006) call it – the "triple bottom line." The intent of including these dimensions in the Leadership Category is so these concepts will permeate the organization's entire system including strategy, operations, scorecard and so forth.

Organizations of all types are facing increasing pressures from a variety of stakeholders including customers, employees, investors, and the public to operate in ways that not only make money but also are good for the environment and society as a whole (Grant 2007 and Latham 2008). Many customers are making purchase decisions based on the environmental performance of the products and services and on the environmental record of the company. Employees want to work for organizations that are "good citizens" and have a good environmental and societal record. Many investors now recognize the risks involved with companies that have poor environmental practices. For example, the profitability could change quickly for companies with a high carbon "footprint" if the government puts a price on carbon either through a carbon tax or a cap and trade system. To help investors assess the risk of companies, the Carbon Disclosure Project provides reports that describe the risks for each company, how well they are doing addressing those risks, and their plans to improve. For more information visit the CDProject website at: http://www.cdproject.net/. In addition, organizations are facing increasing pressures from a variety of influential organizations representing various stakeholder groups including the Intergovernmental Panel on Climate Change (IPCC) and the United Nations Framework Convention on Climate Change (UNFCCC). What seems clear is the "bar" is being raised once again and organizations are challenged with figuring out how to create value for multiple stakeholders.

Some have proposed that organizations simply cannot afford to do business in an environmentally sound way and still make money. This was the same argument that many proposed when U.S. companies were faced with competitors who were producing higher quality products and services and taking market share. Organizations eventually, however, discovered that high quality resulted in reduced cost and increased market share or as Phillip Crosby wrote in a book by the same title - *Quality is Free*! Many organizations that score high on the CPE maturity model have become quite good at "connecting the dots" or as FedEx called it - "people, service, profit" (AMA 1991). This same thinking used to improve the organization "system" to create value for employees, customers, and investors can be used to add additional stakeholders and requirements into the enterprise model and avoid the zero-sum game of reallocating resources from one stakeholder to another.

In support of key communities many organizations list all of the activities that they participate in and support. As impressive as these "laundry lists" may be, they miss the point of the CPE. The CPE are looking for a process and decision criteria within it, used by the organization to address societal needs. This is true anytime the CPE uses the word "how."

Societal Well-Being

When the CPE ask how the organization supports key communities, it is looking for a systematic set of steps that the organization follows to be proactive in their community support. This includes how the organization considers societal well-being and benefit as a part of the strategy, as well as how it is considered on a daily basis and as a part of daily operations. The CPE also emphasize how the organization considers the environmental, social, and economic benefit of this support. Many organizations, however, simply prioritize the vast list of requests they receive from their community for ongoing support. The CPE, in seeking a process, is asking companies to be more proactive and less reactive in aligning the community support with their organizational beliefs, needs, and interests.

Community Support

To establish the foundation for support of key communities, the criteria seek to understand how key communities are determined and how emphasis for organizational involvement is decided. Both of those questions require clear processes and decision criteria.

Most organizations identify key communities as the predominant communities in which they do business and in which their employees live. As simple as these decision criteria are, it does meet the criterion of being clear enough to support a process. Beyond deciding what the organization's key communities are, the criteria ask for the organization to list them, and then discuss how the organization decides to become involved. Simple logic for community support would include questions such as the following:

- How does the organization decide what they want to support?

- How does the organization decide whether or not a specific activity qualifies or is a match with what they want to support?

- How does the organization listen to what is going on in the community in order to be proactive in implementing the use of their decision criteria?

- How does the organization decide whether or not a specific activity warrants senior executive involvement?

Once the overall systematic process is described, the "laundry list" of community activities is no longer anecdotal examples but rather examples of deployment of the systematic approach. It can also show how the organization has used the process and decision criteria to support the community.

Area to Address 1.2c is a key area where an organization needs to demonstrate a systematic process. Many organizations do not answer 1.2c using processes, but only use examples of community support activities – but as we have shown – this is a mistake.

EXAMPLES

PRO-TEC Coating Company (Baldrige Recipient 2007)

The community is one of PRO-TEC's key stakeholders on the Balanced Scorecard (BSC). The primary communities in which the Associates work and live include Leipsic, Putnam County, and Findlay, Ohio. This is where the company outreach is focused. During the strategic planning meeting (Figure 1.2-3❶), they review opportunities or changes in the support criteria. The main areas of emphasis are students; learning, safety, sports, and music; community projects to improve quality of life; and local and national organizations impacting the people in the key communities.

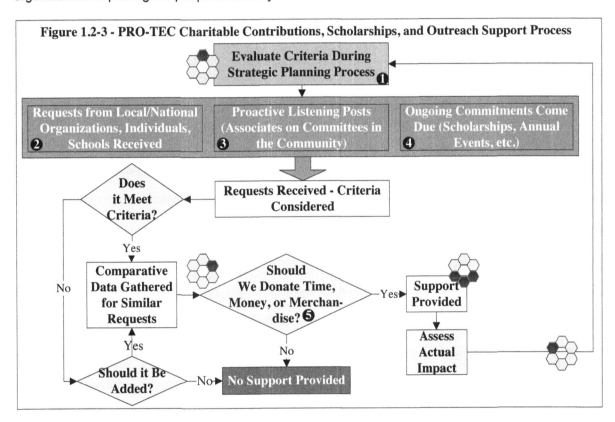

Figure 1.2-3 - PRO-TEC Charitable Contributions, Scholarships, and Outreach Support Process

PRO-TEC is committed to good citizenship providing financial and professional support to the key communities in a variety of methods. Figure 1.2-3❷,❸,❹ reflect the listening posts to develop future PRO-TEC Associates and create a positive environment for the Associates' families. This systematically supports the Key Success Factors (KSFs) of good citizenship and long-term viability.

PRO-TEC has defined the outreach support and commitments into three different categories. The **first** category (Figure 1.2-3❷) includes requests from many of the known local/national organizations such as the Boy Scouts, American Cancer Society-Relay for Life, YMCA, United Way, Putnam County Fair and 4-H, Leipsic, Ottawa, and Findlay Chambers of Commerce, and local hospitals. There are also many programs and events through the Leipsic and other Putnam County schools that directly impact the local youth either through learning, athletics, music, arts, or safety that meet the criteria for considering donations. Examples of these include supporting the athletic and music boosters and Right-to-Read.

There are also youth in the community that achieve individual goals and represent schools or local organizations in programs such as People-to-People or state competitions that they consider.

The **second** category (Figure 1.2-3❸), participation in community service by individual Associates, is also encouraged and celebrated, which enhances the contribution to the community. Associate outreach continues on a state, regional, and local basis with participation on numerous advisory boards which provides PRO-TEC with proactive listening posts in the community. Examples include participation of approximately twenty PRO-TEC Associates in the "School HOST/Mentors Programs," the Putnam County United Way Board, Eric Franks served as a council member and examiner for the Ohio Partnership for Excellence and is now a Baldrige examiner, and Rick Rupert on the Local Emergency Planning Committee. Shannon Shartell is on the Brookhill Industries Board and Putnam County Workforce Investment Act Board. Shaun Spainhower is a member of the West Central Ohio Safety Alliance. President Paul Worstell has volunteer, non-profit organization involvement focused on workforce development and youth in the following areas:

> ➢ Baldrige Outreach (MBNQA QFE, Ohio Partnership for Excellence, Quality New Mexico);
> ➢ Trustee for the Black Swamp Area Council Boy Scouts of America;
> ➢ Guest speaker on Leadership at the University of Findlay and Ohio Northern University;
> ➢ Board member, Ohio Manufacturer's Association;
> ➢ Executive Committee, Ohio Partnership for Excellence;
> ➢ Executive Committee, Greater Findlay Inc.; and
> ➢ Trustee, Blanchard Valley Regional Health Center.

All of the senior leaders are involved in community service organizations, associations, or events. Time allocated to community service by senior leaders is determined based on impact in the community, scope and impact of the project, senior leader availability, and interest of the leader. Senior leader time is directed to community service that requires their expertise and professional guidance. For example, the President is a trustee and an executive board member in many organizations in the community as listed above. Previous obligations on boards were transferred to other senior leaders in the organization so his time could be better utilized in the community.

The **third** category is ongoing commitments. Since the inception, PRO-TEC has annually presented a $20,000 scholarship (the highest of any local company, to the best of the knowledge) to a graduating Leipsic student (Figure 1.2-3❹). The recipient's only obligation is to return annually to their high school to share with younger students their college experiences and their perceptions of the need and value of a college education. Recipients are also offered internships along with other area engineering, technical, and business students. PRO-TEC also regularly participates with Ohio Northern University Accounting majors and the University of Findlay Environmental and Safety and Occupational Health majors in a win-win situation. The success of these programs is seen by the level of quality work PRO-TEC receives and the quality of the jobs the students receive after graduation.

PRO-TEC is also committed to offering employment to physical or mentally challenged individuals through Brookhill Industries. This offers the challenged individuals an opportunity for better quality of life. PRO-TEC currently has one person working part-time and has them contracted for janitorial services (Figure 1.2-3❹). These are Associates they are exceedingly proud of.

Requests and commitments (Figure 1.2-3❹,❸,❷) are considered, based on PRO-TEC's criteria, and then comparative data are gathered from similar requests. The basic question asked is, "Should they donate time, money, or merchandise?" If so, they determine whom, how much, or what they will donate (Figure 1.2-3❺). PRO-TEC is able to assess if the actual impact is what the company envisioned through many active listening posts throughout the community. This information, along with external information such as business needs and local or state economic concerns, is then evaluated at the strategic planning meeting or whenever needed (Figure 1.2-3)❶. If the information considered does not meet the criteria, it is considered whether it should be added, and if not, no support is provided.

Societal Responsibilities

Clarke American (Baldrige Recipient 2001)

Communities are one of the key stakeholder groups, and the Key Leadership Team (KLT) approaches the commitment to civic activities through a systematic approach. They provide support through both monetary contributions and involvement in volunteer activities. The KLT follows the process shown below to determine the investment of people and monetary resources. This approach to community involvement provides the greatest impact for the investment.

The current corporate support is focused in three key areas 1) overall community—United Way (UW) 2) education—Junior Achievement (JA); and 3) healthcare— Juvenile Diabetes Foundation (JDF). The United Way is the principal, nationwide charitable activity. Associates enjoy participating in UW fund raising and service projects in the communities where they have a manufacturing operation or contact center. Additionally, outside the corporate offices, plant or contact center managers identify two local causes to support in addition to UW. This enables the company to provide support where it is most needed.

Clarke American – Major Project Support & Cause-Related Checks Selection Process

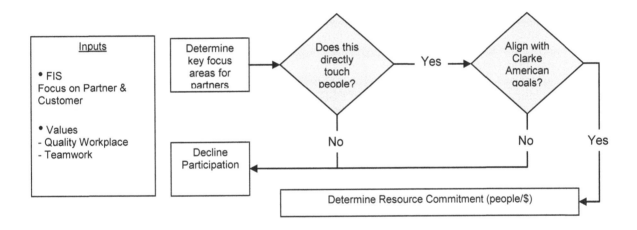

In 1998, corporate began working with the UW of San Antonio and Bexar County to help them adopt Clarke American's *FIS* process improvement methods. In addition to training, they provided additional hours consulting with UW leadership on incorporating *FIS* techniques into their processes. At the end of the training, a business review report similar to a Baldrige feedback report was provided to the UW leadership team. This effort received "rave" reviews from the Director of the local United Way.

Clarke American has taken a proactive approach to many societal concerns through the creation of "cause-related checking products" in partnership with a number of national organizations. They produce checks and related merchandise with designs for eight *causes* including Save the Children, National Breast Cancer Organization, Wildlife Preservation Trust, A Better Chance and others.

Source: Clarke (2002) pp. 9 - 10

Pewaukee School District (Baldrige Recipient 2013)

PSD (Pewaukee School District) views caring for society as part of its core value of citizenship; this propels us to model citizenship, be an environmental steward, and support our community Figures 1.2-5 & 1.2-6. Citizenship is systematically taught, role modeled, practiced, and proactively recognized by PSD SLs (Senior Leaders). A systematic program of study is deployed to teach and recognize student citizenship. Our elementary students learn citizenship in Guidance classes and receive BUG stickers when they are caught "Being Unusually Good."

Our middle and secondary students are recognized for their citizenship in school ceremonies and newsletters that publicly affirm this positive societal responsibility. It is part of our school culture. Our high school's Anti-Bullying Committee, comprised of students, is recognized statewide for its work. Evidence of innovation, in 2012 we began implementing a Digital Citizenship curriculum, designed to teach student responsible use of technology. Our commitment to the environment is made actionable in the current SP which has a strategic objective of operating more efficiently.

Our unique campus setting is our most powerful tool in environmental stewardship. By reducing the need to drive to meetings; facilitating campus-wide recycling efforts; and maximizing bus routes, technology networks and equipment sharing, our all-campus setting allows us to maximize efficiency while saving valuable resources. SLs have strategically deployed an energy management system integrated between the key work process areas of technology and facilities. PSD curriculum deploys and integrates energy conservation strategies that promote a healthier environment (Figure 1.2-5). We also recognize Energy Star classrooms. For deeper integration, we have also increased curricular opportunities for students to gain environmental awareness.

Extensive cycles of improvement are evident in PSD's deployment of environmental responsibility. While we have pursued Focus on Energy grants for some time, in 2009 SLs pursued larger projects to increase energy savings. A $600,000 investment was made to purchase new boilers and HVAC units which are increasing energy efficiency. 1.2c.(2) PSD prioritizes strong community partnerships as evidenced by one of the five SP Strategy Areas being Communication and Community Engagement. SLs personally serve the key communities identified as the City & Village of Pewaukee and Waukesha County (Figure 1.2-6). Key communities were identified when citizenship became a key PSD Value.

Stakeholders conveyed that students could best appreciate citizenship close to home, since it allows for more direct student involvement. Thus, SLs identified key communities as those within Pewaukee and Waukesha County. Subsequently, PSD support is given more frequently to local organizations rather than global causes. Support of the key communities is varied and rich (Figure 1.2-6) with some local agencies contacting us for assistance and with SLs determining avenues for service that match our Mission and values. Service is infused on our campus: SLs bring together students & faculty to support our local food pantry, blood drives, and walks for charitable causes, to name a few.

SLs are active participants in community and professional organizations where they provide leadership, volunteer support, and expertise. Additionally, all PSD SLs make annual donations to the Pewaukee Scholarship Fund (Figure 7.4-12). PSD provides facilities to the community free-of-charge or at a minimal cost. Many organizations are strengthened by this commitment including Pewaukee Parks and Recreation, Boy Scouts, Girl Scouts, and many youth sports clubs.

SAs regularly meet with civic leaders and with leaders in adjacent school districts to identify key issues and ascertain ways PSD could better communicate and serve the community. SLs also participate in and serve on the boards of many professional organizations and state task forces as a way to serve our profession and develop as leaders. Of late, our support of key communities is growing. PSD has been called upon to speak about our strategic planning, innovation, and systematic continuous improvement processes on the state, national and international level.

We are proud to share our core competencies and serve as role models to others on their continuous improvement journey; in doing so, we make our organization as well as other organizations stronger.

Support	Purpose	Senior Leader Involvement
Figure 1.2-6 Senior Leader Support of Key Communities		
Pewaukee		
Chamber of Commerce Positively Pewaukee	Provide volunteers, leadership, and event support	PIC, Supt. & AC on Committees; provide student & employee volunteers
City Strategic Planning	Provide SP expertise	Supt. serves as team member
Village & City Government	Work together to cut costs	Supt. & CFO meet 2xY
Pewaukee Rotary Club	Provide leadership, service	Supt. on Board; Served as President
Youth Sports Clubs, Boy Scouts & Girl Scouts	Provide leadership, service; make campus available for use	Many AT members volunteer; AAD provides facilities for use by Clubs
Pewaukee Library Board	Provide leadership	Supt. On Board; staff serve
Pewaukee Parks & Rec. Dept.	Make campus available for use	Supt., CFO, AAD provide facilities
Pewaukee Food Pantry	Provide support & service	Principals coordinate fundraising
Kiwanis	Provide support & service	AT membership; speak at meetings
Area Churches	Provide leadership, service	Many AT members volunteer
Waukesha County		
United Way	Provide financial support	AT participates; district participation
Pewaukee Scholarship Fund	Provide financial support	AT & BOE funds $1000 scholarships
County Superintendents	Provide leadership	Supt. facilitates meetings
Junior Achievement	Provide service & support	Supt. & CFO teach in program
Carroll, Cardinal Stritch, and Concordia Universities	Educate future leaders; Provide leadership	Supt. supervises Master's program on site; CAO, CFO, DOT, Principals teach
American Red Cross, Heart Association, Blood Center	Provide service (CC-C)	Principals organize fundraising efforts in each school
State & Nation		
CESA, ASQ/NQEC, WASB, NSBA, WFA, WASCD, WASBO , NSPRA	Role model; share best practices	Supt. Serves as Chair of SWSA & CESA#1 CFO & CAO serve on State organizations SLs & BOE speak at conferences

Advocate Good Samaritan Hospital (Baldrige Recipient 2010)

GSAM's systematic *Support of Key Communities* process is used to determine key communities and prioritize the areas of support. They revalidate their community selection during the Strategic Planning Process based on market information, listening posts, and a community needs assessment❶ and determine the aligned criteria that will be used to support their involvement❷. GSAM defines their key community as the 17 communities in their Primary Service Area.

Criteria aligned with community health needs and GSAM priorities is applied to needs and requests❸. Requests are solicited from their service line leaders to ensure that they identify what they want to support and evaluate additional unanticipated requests for support from the community❸ ❹.

All requests are screened against the established criteria with additional consideration given to ensure that they utilize their core competency of *building loyal relationships* with those who are critical to delivering care in our communities.

The impact of support is determined through the community benefit database , analysis of disbursements, and an annual process review . GSAM contributes to improving their communities by all ET members having multiple involvements on local boards; as well as the professional nursing staff, medical staff, and other members of the workforce actively participating in numerous professional and service organizations.

Advocate Good Sam Community Support Process

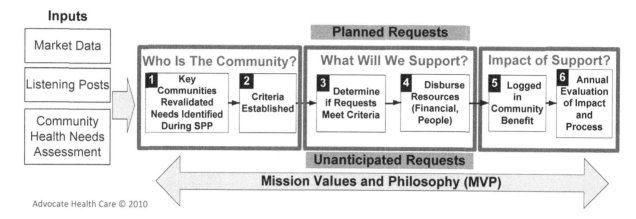

Advocate Health Care © 2010

 **CRITERIA QUESTIONS**

In your response, include answers to the following questions:

c. Societal Responsibilities

(1) **Societal Well-Being** How do you consider societal well-being and benefit as part of your strategy and daily operations? How do you contribute to the well-being of your environmental, social, and economic systems?

(2) **Community Support** How do you actively support and strengthen your key communities? What are your key communities? How do you identify them and determine areas for organizational involvement, including areas that leverage your core competencies? How do your senior leaders, in concert with your workforce, contribute to improving these communities?

Notes:

1.2c. Areas of societal contributions and community support might include your efforts to improve the environment (e.g., collaboration to conserve the environment or natural resources); strengthen local community services, education, health, and emergency preparedness; and improve the practices of trade, business, or professional associations.

1.2c. Some charitable organizations may contribute to society and support their key communities totally through mission-related activities. In such cases, it is appropriate to respond with any "extra efforts" through which you support these communities.

NIST (2013-2014) pp. 8-9

WORKSHEETS

1.2c Societal Responsibilities

1.2c (1) – Societal Well-Being

How You Consider Societal Well-being and Benefit As Part Of Your Strategy	

How You Consider Societal Well-being and Benefit As Part Of Your Daily Operations	

How You Consider Well-being Of Your Environmental Systems	

How You Consider Well-being Of Your Social Systems	

How You Consider Well-being Of Your Economic Systems	

1.2c (2) – Community Support

What Are Your Key Communities?	

How Do You identify Your Key Communities?	

How Do You Determine The Areas For Emphasis For Organizational Involvement and Support ?	

List Your Key Communities	Priorities/ Emphasis*	How This Leverages The Core Competency	Support Given*		Results Figures
			By Employees	By Senior Leaders	

* This should include the process and/or decision criteria used to determine the areas of emphasis or priorities, and to determine who should be involved.

ASSESSMENT

22	We use clear decision criteria to determine what communities or activities should be supported.	1 2 3 4 5 6 DK
23	There are clear guidelines for what level of the organization should be involved with a specific community group.	1 2 3 4 5 6 DK
24	Employees have the opportunity to contribute to community activities based on their interests and beliefs.	1 2 3 4 5 6 DK
25	The impact of our support of the community is tracked.	1 2 3 4 5 6 DK

BLUEPRINT

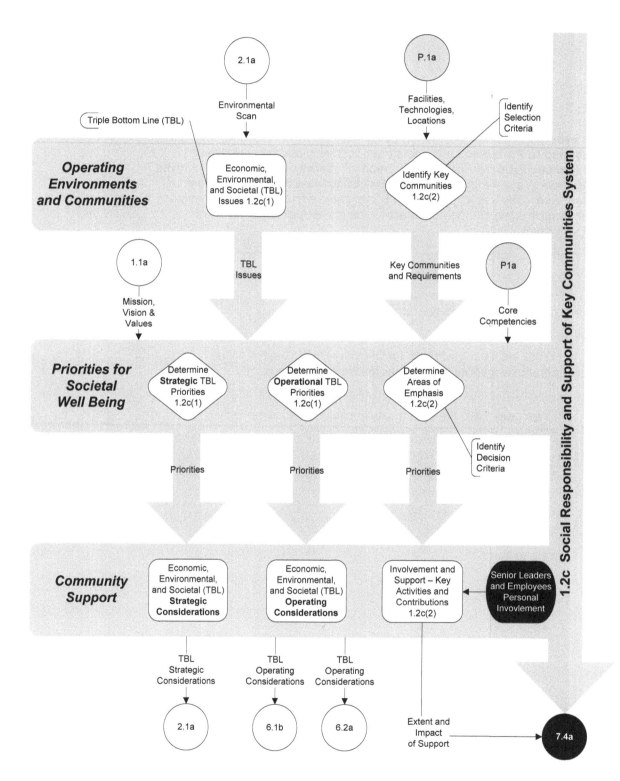

SYSTEM INTEGRATION

Context

P.1a > 1.2c Facilitates, Technologies, Locations - While the CPE do not specify that an organization has to be involved and support every community where they have an office, it does expect that the key communities will be determined from the major operating locations and possibly the locations where their products and services are used, which might be different from the production facilities. So, the communities that are considered by the processes that support key communities should include those identified in the profile (P.1a).

P.1a > 1.2c Core Competencies - The organizations core competencies are an important consideration when deciding on the areas of emphasis for supporting key communities. For example, an organization that designs and manufactures computers might support the local community center by providing computers and training for the local citizens.

Systems

1.1a > 1.2c Mission, Vision, Values - The mission, vision, and values are all key inputs to determining areas of emphasis for community support and involvement described in 1.2c.

1.2c < 2.1a Environmental Scan - The strategic planning environmental scan is a key input to identifying the economic, environmental, and societal issues associated with social responsibilities and community support in 1.2c.

1.2c > 2.1a TBL Strategic Considerations - The economic, environmental, and societal considerations identified in 1.2c are inputs to the strategic planning process described in 2.1a.

1.2c > 6.1b TBL Operating Considerations - The economic, environmental, and societal considerations identified in 1.2c are inputs to the identification of key work processes and their initial requirements.

1.2c > 6.2a TBL Operating Considerations - The economic, environmental, and societal considerations identified in 1.2c are inputs to the work process design process 6.2a.

Scorecard

1.2c > 7.4a Social Responsibility and Community Support - The results that indicate the extent and effectiveness of the social responsibility and community support system should be presented in 7.4a.

THOUGHTS FOR LEADERS

Leaders of high performing organizations have a bond with the communities in which they operate. These leaders understand the synergy between the well being of their community and the well being of their organization. As one leader stated: "We cannot be a healthy arm on a body which is dying." These leaders do not just view this as philanthropic support of the community, but feel it is good business. This gives meaning to the organization, and its employees, well beyond the normal organizational boundaries. It also can be a source of employee pride, training (e.g., leadership training as an employee leads a community activity) and rejuvenation.

As with everything else in the CPE business framework, these leaders need to use clear processes and well communicated decision criteria to help them decide which community activities to support. Unfortunately, there will always be more requests than resources. The key is how an organization decides which activities to support. Rather than choosing to support a cause based on personal preference, leaders should make the decisions based on a process that aligns the best interests of the organization with the needs of the community, and with the needs of the employees. Frequently employees of organizations involved in the community are proud of what their organization supports. The organization's community support actions are a tangible realization of the organization's values and beliefs.

A Lighter Moment:

Philanthropy (has become) simply the refuge of people who wish to annoy their fellow creatures.

Oscar Wilde

FOUNDATION

In Item 2.1 the organization officially establishes the strategy and begins to translate the direction set by the leaders in Item 1.1 into more specific goals and objectives. It is one of the few places in the Criteria for Performance Excellence (CPE) framework where a checklist of issues is provided that need to be addressed.

Strategic Planning Process

The criteria start by asking about the overall strategic planning process. Although all of these are not called for in the criteria, for this section, an organization's planning process should include a description of:

- the steps in the planning process;

- who is involved in these steps;

- **NOT** asked in the criteria, but details which will help you to explain you process:

    o   what happens in each step;

    o   the inputs for each step;

    o   the outputs for each step;

    o   the documents used or generated in each step;

    o   the reviews or decisions in each step; and

    o   the decision criteria used for the decisions made.

Additionally, the short- and longer-term time horizons should be clearly defined, including the rationale for choosing those time horizons. For example, the time horizons can be chosen to correspond to the organization's corporate planning cycles, customer planning cycles, or other logical (e.g., market-based) planning cycles. Market based reasons for choosing a planning cycle could include industry business cycles, technology cycles, or the time required to increase organizational capacity or capability. In addition, this section should establish how the organization is meeting the internal or external strategic needs in the way they have established their planning horizons.

New in the criteria this year, is understanding how the organization determines the need for transformational changes (defined in the Glossary at the back of this book), organizational agility, and operational flexibility.

Innovation

Throughout the previous 2013 – 2014 criteria there was an increased emphasis on innovation. It is mentioned in leadership, planning, and several other points (a count of innovation in the criteria shows it being mentioned approximately a dozen times). This emphasis has continued into the 2015 – 2016 criteria. Innovation is discontinuous improvement, and the implication of the criteria changes are clear – innovation is the responsibility of everyone, while being led/role modeled by the senior leadership. In Item 2.1 the criteria asks how leaders create an environment which supports innovation, and how they track strategic opportunities, and what are the strategic opportunities. Driving the decisions being made is the analysis being performed to ensure that the decisions are intelligent (intelligent risks). The criteria ask how the organization decides which strategic opportunities are intelligent risks for pursuing.

Strategy Considerations

When addressing each of the factors to be considered during the planning process, the organization should do so in a manner clear enough for someone reading the assessment document to understand. For example, it is not sufficient to discuss customer and market needs in general terms, there should be a specific point where these are addressed in the planning process in a very clear manner.

The basic belief surrounding the planning process is that several factors need to be assessed during planning. If one of these key factors is not effectively assessed (and the impact of the factor on the plan is not assessed during planning) the implementation of the plan might be hindered by the inability of the organization to understand and respond to one of the factors they should have assessed during planning.

These factors include:

- Your strategic challenges and strategic advantages

- Risks to your organization's future success

- Potential changes in your regulatory environment

- Potential blind spots in your strategic planning process and information

- Your ability to execute the strategic plan

One future success example within these strategy considerations could be if the organization assumes the workforce can support the new plan. If they do not formally assess workforce capability and capacity, however, they may not realize that training and development for the new skills are required and that this cannot be accomplished by the time the skills are needed. In this example, the development of those skills may not be a part of the overall plan, or may not be timely, and the plan implementation may fail.

Work Systems and Core Competencies

What are your Key Work Systems is a strategic decision, and the criteria now wants to know what are the key work systems, and how do you make key decisions, including:

- How do you make key work system decisions that facilitate the accomplishment of your strategic objectives?
- How do you decide which key processes will be accomplished by key suppliers and partners?
- How do your decisions consider your core competency (ies) and the core competency (ies) of potential suppliers and partners?
- How do you determine future core competencies?

Although not specifically asked for in the new criteria, any organization assessing themselves should show how their key work processes support the key work systems, and clearly identify the key work processes.

188

EXAMPLES

Tata Motors – Commercial Vehicle Business Unit (CVBU)

Strategic Planning Process

The Strategic Planning Process at CVBU has evolved over the last five years. The main objective of the process is to drive 'Profitable – Sustainable - Growth' for the business unit. It is also a means of developing and deploying short term and long term action plans to achieve ultimate business goals.

Tata Motors CVBU Strategic Planning Approach

APPROACH

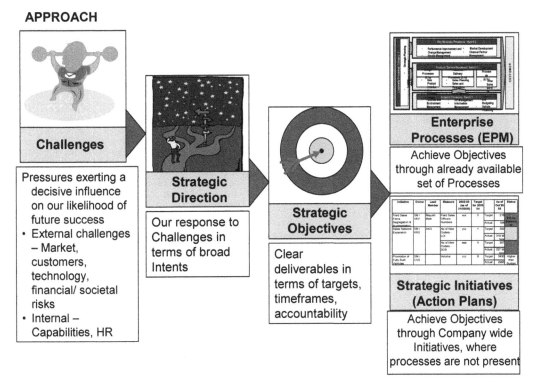

Evolution of the practice:

Five years back CVBU had a Strategic Planning Process (SPP) which was inadequate and organization-wide deployment was not strong. Taking a clue from a Baldrige-type assessment, CVBU received inputs from various Tata Group companies, their Company Quality Assessment Group and IBM and designed a new approach to the SPP.

From the beginning it was a ten step process which included deployment of a strategy down to the last working unit level in the organization. From year 2000-01 they created a Three Phase strategy based on this process and also started deploying a Balanced Scorecard as a deploying tool. In 2006, they revisited the process and removed the overlap between SPP and Leadership System and compressed the process to an eight step process. This process cannot only deploy goals, but it can effectively address sudden changes and changing business directions.

Framework of the planning system development:

Two business heads, President – Medium and Heavy Commercial Vehicles and President – Small and Light Commercial Vehicles are the owners of the process. The Head of Strategic Planning is the person who implements this process and runs it for all areas of operations.

CVBU used key people in the organization (up to and including the Managing Director - CEO) to drive the strategy down to all levels. With the business expanding at a much higher rate than in the past, CVBU introduced a Cross Functional Team (CFT) to drive the SPP. This group collects inputs from all areas of operations (i.e. from Steering Committee (SC) , Functional heads - HR, Sales and Marketing, Line of Business Heads, Market Research, Customer care, Manufacturing, etc.) and analyses it for further use.

Tata Motors CVBU Strategic Planning Process:

PHASES	THINK				DEVELOP			DEPLOY	REVIEW	
STEPS	**1** Environment Scanning	**2** Visioning	**3** Strategic Challenges	**4** Strategic direction setting	**5** Strategic Analysis	**6** Strategic Focus / Objectives	**7** Target setting & Resource Allocation	**8** BSC Deployment	**9** Review	**10** Evaluation & Improvement
ACTIVITIES	Study the foll.: • Global Auto Industry • Macro Economic trends • Impact on CVBU **Refer Fig 2.1-3**	Revisit Vision, Mission and Values	Identify Key challenges for Short term (upto 1 year) & Longer term (>1 year) **Refer OP2-4**	Determine Strategic Path- 3 Phase Strategy **Refer Fig MS-1**	Conduct Business environment analysis and Capability analysis based on **Inputs as mentioned in Fig 2.1-3**	Identify Strategic objectives to address key short & long term challenges **Refer Fig 2.1-4**	Finalise- • Operating Plans for: Product, Domestic & IB Marketing, Manufacturing, Sourcing, HR, CAPEX, Revenue Budgets • CVBU BSC: Goals Measures, timetable and Strategic initiatives **Refer Fig 2.1-4**	Develop next level BSCs & Initiatives for : • Plants/ Functions • Factories/ R.Os/ Divisions • CXs/ A.Os/ Department **Refer Fig 2.2-1**	Review (and update if required) BSCs and Initiatives monthly **Refer Fig 1.1-11,12** THINK	Evaluate the Strategic Planning process Incorporate improvements in next year's SPP **Refer Fig 2.2-5**
KEY PARTICIPANTS	Strategy planning, LOBs	Board, BRC	*CVBU* SC, MC, OC, BRC	*CVBU* SC, OC	Strategy Planning, IB & Domestic Sales & Marketing, NPI, Finance, HR, ERC, Manufacturing, Materials, Internal Audit, Auto Planning	*CVBU* SC	*CVBU* SC, MC, OC, Board	All SCs	All SCs	Strategy Planning
OUTPUTS	• Revisited Vision, Mission, Values • Key Challenges • Strategic Direction				• Business environment & Capability studies • Operating Plans- Product, Marketing, Manufacturing, HR, Sourcing • CAPEX, Revenue Budgets • CVBU BSC & Strategic Initiatives			• Cascaded BSCs	• Improvements to the SPP • SC committee reviews	
TIME LINE	3 years rolling- Annual review- Nov-Jan				Nov - Feb		Feb - Apr		Apr - Mar	

The strategy then gets cascaded, starting with the Town Hall communication meeting held by Managing Director and SC members. Every year the strategic objectives get converted into an organization-level Balanced Scorecard (BSC) which is cascaded down to Plant and Non-Plant locations and then to Lowest Working Unit level.

In the last 2 ½ years CVBU has integrated systematic inputs or competitor data and information on Suppliers & Channel Partners. The process has been validated by Senior Baldrige Examiners as consultants and by international benchmarking and balanced scorecard consultants. This year they have also used concepts addressed in recent issues of the Harvard Business Review.

Critical factors for success:

A number of factors were determined to be key to the success or the Strategic Planning Process:

- clear process ownership and responsibilities;

- all desired inputs collected, analyzed and used properly;

- involvement of people from all locations in the strategy making;

- role clarity in each step;

- success in deployment and regular reviews;

- strategy is everybody's job and people is the key to implement it;

- need for a good deployment tool for strategy, such as a balanced scorecard; and

- transparent cascade is a must for success.

Cross Functional Teams to drive the strategy is must to have both Top-down and Bottom-up focus.
Source: Tata Motors – CVBU

Tata Motors CVBU Strategy Review Process:

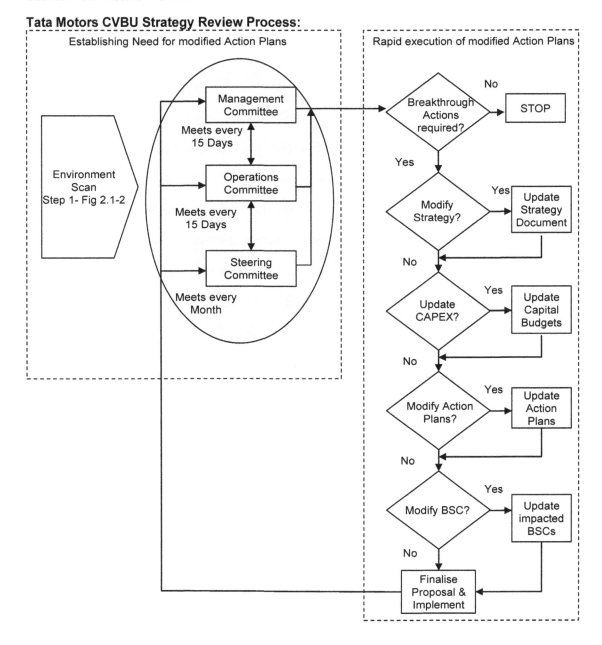

Charleston Area Medical Center (Charleston, West Virginia)

Senior Leaders at the Charleston Area Medical Center set organizational direction through the strategic planning process (Figure 2.1-2) using the 7 steps in the Leadership System. Our approach to strategic planning, plan deployment and performance review is aligned and integrated to drive performance improvement and innovation as described in 4.1c(3) through forcing functions at all levels: organizational, entity, work system, department and individual.

The CAMC Health System uses a four phase 16 step integrated strategic planning and deployment process (Figure below) to align the strategic plan with our vision pillars (Best Place to Receive Patient Centered Care; Best Place to Work; Best Place to Practice Medicine; Best Place to Learn; Best Place to Refer Patients).

The Strategic Planning Team (SPT) is responsible for the planning process and is comprised of all senior leaders (Executive Council), Associate Administrators, Clinical Directors, and key partners: WVU/ Charleston and Siemens. In addition, formal input is obtained from the Board Planning and Public Policy Committee, Medical Staff Officers, Physician Advisory Committee, CAMC Physician Group and Nursing Councils.

The SPP produces a rolling 4 year long range plan, an annual short term plan, and a continuous review component that allows for responsiveness and agility. These planning time horizons are a recent cycle of learning to align with health care reform legislation requirements (4 year) and our annual performance management process (1 year). A built-in agility to rapidly respond to opportunities or unexpected threats that may arise given the changing nature of the healthcare environment occurs through continuous review against the Environmental Analysis inputs.

Step ① begins in May when the Board Planning and Public Policy Committee reviews the MVV and CC to ensure relevance to our organizational sustainability. An improvement to this process for 2012 included the adoption of a systematic process for ongoing review and reassessment of our CC. Input about national issues ② occurs during May/June by national thought leaders at the annual Leadership Conference attended by BOT, MS leadership and EC. An ongoing annual Environmental Analysis (EA) ③ provides an extensive internal and external review and is available to the SPT via the intranet. Highlights or changes are reviewed in June and the ongoing review process is described in Figure 4.1-3. Also during June, changes to the SPP made as a result of the annual review of the process itself are outlined. The SPT then updates the SWOT, Strategic Advantages (SA) and Strategic Challenges (SC)④. During July and August each pillar owner reviews progress toward the 4 year strategic objective(s) ⑤ and provides: projected performance, best practice/ comparative data, industry knowledge, issues impacting the SO over the next 4 years, recommended changes for SO, goals, BIG DOTs, targets, how the SA/SC are addressed and the CC supported by the SO and proposed annual goals, capital, operating budget or workforce needs associated with the proposed SO, goals and BIG DOTs.

Input is obtained from the SPT and prior to SO and annual goals being finalized, a review is completed for gaps and blindspots ⑥ based on the EA strategy considerations. The SPP addresses key strategy elements and how these data inputs are collected and analyzed. Each of these strategy considerations are embedded in our SPP in Steps ② through ⑥ and ⑨. Ongoing assessment of our ability to execute the strategic plan through quarterly progress to plan review gives us the flexibility to adapt our strategy to changing healthcare service needs and direction ⑭ ⑮.

Figure 2.1-2 Strategic Planning and Deployment Process

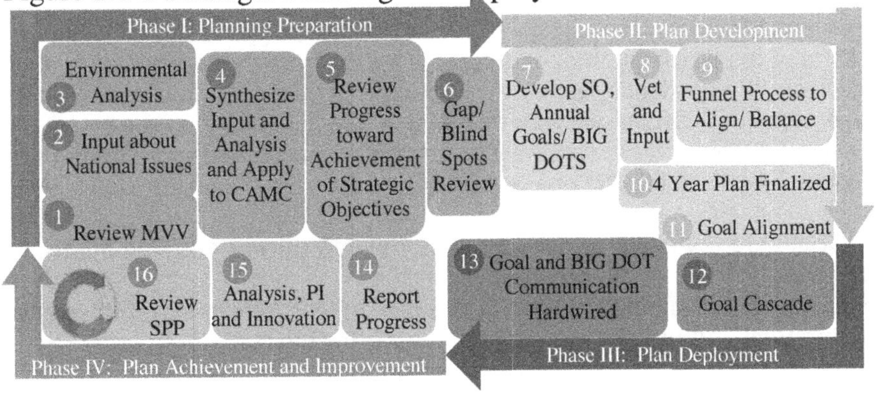

Pewaukee School District (Baldrige Recipient 2013)

Our strategic planning process (SPP) is a systematic process grounded in the use of PDSA (Plan, Do, Study, Act) and the Cook model of strategic planning (Figure 2.1-1). Implemented on a yearly cycle, PSD's (Pewaukee School District) 20 year commitment to SPP has created a culture of continuous improvement, one of our core competencies, as the process guides us in setting long-term direction supported by Action Plans that provide short-term direction to accomplish our SP Goals. PSD has deployed a SP since 1992, longer than most school districts in WI and the nation, and we are frequently called on to speak about our process at the state and national level. Our SPP is key to our continuous improvement, a core competency:

- **Relying on data to make decisions**
- **Anticipating and responding to student & stakeholder needs and market trends**
- **Measuring progress against plan**
- **Developing a broader ownership of Mission, Vision, Values**

PSD organizes this multi-step process using PDSA (Figure 2.1-1). The PLAN phase of the SPP clarifies purpose and direction. Participation from a wide representation of 45-55 stakeholders is proactively sought by SLs because it shapes a strategic direction responsive to stakeholder expectations and requirements. Annually, SP Teams include citizens without children in our schools, community leaders, parents representing multiple student segments, teachers, partners, collaborators, union representatives, BOE members, faculty, students, support staff representing multiple employee groups, and AT (Administrative Team) Members. The PLAN phase takes place over the course of 1-2 evenings and a full weekend day in spring prior to BOE budget approval; timing is vital so we can allocate resources in support of the SP in the budget for the upcoming school year. An external facilitator is used for this phase. Four activities are vital in this PLAN phase (Figure 2.1-1):

- **Review of work accomplished gives all SP Team Members, veteran or new, a framework for understanding operational performance and a clearer picture of what work is still to be completed. It is also a celebration of the accomplishments.**
- **MVV are reviewed for continued relevance and revised as needed.**
- **So the SP Team can better understand the broader evolving environment in which PSD operates and to better identify possible blind spots, a thorough Environmental Scan (ES) and SWOT Analysis is conducted The ES is conducted using information on market share, economic & societal trends, and competitive environment (Figure 2.1-3).**
- **Strategic challenges & advantages that impact the identified.**

Strategy Areas are identified and SP Goals for each identified Strategy Area (our Vision) is also reviewed. PSD's long history with SPP is of great benefit: through the repetition of this process year after year, profound patterns emerge which help us identify our core competencies. In a major cycle of refinement, the DO (Figure 2.1-1) phase of the SPP begins a phase of planning that is now performed by AT members rather than the entire SP Team. SL Action Plan ownership has increased accountability and SP Action Plan completion (Figure 7.1-14). In the DO phase:

- **Measures for SP Goals are reviewed and updated as needed during our Administrative Leadership Week.**
- **The budget planning process is integrated with the SPP so SP Action Plan initiatives are supported in the financial and human resource planning for the upcoming year PSD proactively budgets to make certain that necessary funds are available for realization of SP Action Plans.**
- **During this phase, capacity and intelligent risk in the name of innovation are weighed. The SL responsible for the work process drafts Action Plans in PDSA form.**
- **To deepen integration, the CAO works with Principals to develop School Improvement Plans (SIPs) for each Teaching & Learning Action Plan in the SP.**
- **Principals then work with their building leadership teams (BLTs) to complete these SIPs in support the Teaching & Learning SP strand to drill the work into each classroom.**
- **The BOE formally adopts the SP prior to the start of the school year in which it will be implemented.**
- **Once approved, a SP Communication/Deployment Plan is put in motion. This begins with the Superintendent reinforcing the Mission and conveying key elements of the SP in remarks at the Welcome Back Breakfast. Principals use initial school year faculty meetings to discuss SP Goals and begin work on SIPs. The SP is printed in the annual report distributed to all citizens and SP hard copies are given to all employees.**
- **The SP is then implemented throughout the academic school year with time allocated for SP work and corresponding professional development scheduled during staff development days and faculty, AT, and AC meetings.**

Employing multiple cycles of learning, the STUDY phase has become more robust with increased and more structured analysis of progress against plan (Figure 2.1-1). In a cycle of learning, the Board of Education now incorporates Board Goals, Learning Sessions and Spotlights on Learning into their meeting structure to further integrate the SPP in BOE work. In a further cycle of improvement, a system to strengthen internal accountability was put in place by Senior Advisors. Quarterly reporting of SP Action Plan progress is incorporated into AT meetings to heighten knowledge sharing and integration. The feedback loop begins in the ACT phase (Figure 2.1-1).

Action Plans not meeting timelines are evaluated to determine root cause. If needed, resources are reallocated. This analysis promotes agility and operational flexibility. We modify and re -assess on a quarterly basis; thus, we are not surprised at the end of a yearly cycle about what is and is not accomplished. On an annual basis the AT and BOE analyze the SPP and identify opportunities for improvement so that the process is made more effective and efficient. In this review, SLs have instigated multiple cycles of learning to improve the SPP: the publication of the SP in varying forms depending on user requirements, systematically embedding quarterly updates to better monitor SP Action Plan progress, increasing the number of stakeholders involved in the SPP as well as broadening segments and diverse voices in our SPP.

Figure 2.1-1 Strategic Planning Process Using PDSA

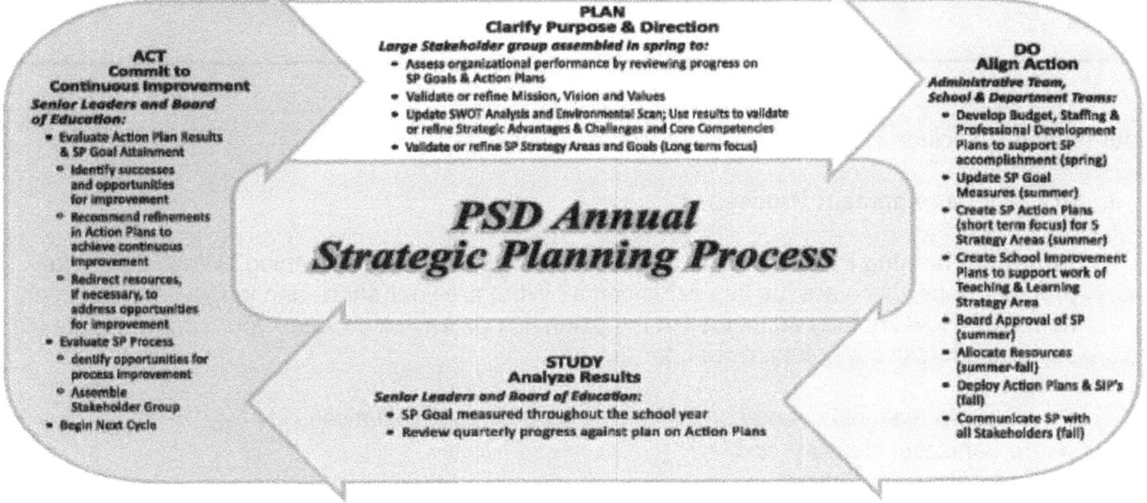

PLAN
Clarify Purpose & Direction
Large Stakeholder group assembled in spring to:
- Assess organizational performance by reviewing progress on SP Goals & Action Plans
- Validate or refine Mission, Vision and Values
- Update SWOT Analysis and Environmental Scan; Use results to validate or refine Strategic Advantages & Challenges and Core Competencies
- Validate or refine SP Strategy Areas and Goals (Long term focus)

ACT
Commit to
Continuous Improvement
Senior Leaders and Board of Education:
- Evaluate Action Plan Results & SP Goal Attainment
  - Identify successes and opportunities for improvement
  - Recommend refinements in Action Plans to achieve continuous improvement
  - Redirect resources, if necessary, to address opportunities for improvement
- Evaluate SP Process
  - Identify opportunities for process improvement
- Assemble Stakeholder Group
- Begin Next Cycle

DO
Align Action
Administrative Team, School & Department Teams:
- Develop Budget, Staffing & Professional Development Plans to support SP accomplishment (spring)
- Update SP Goal Measures (summer)
- Create SP Action Plans (short term focus) for 5 Strategy Areas (summer)
- Create School Improvement Plans to support work of Teaching & Learning Strategy Area
- Board Approval of SP (summer)
- Allocate Resources (summer-fall)
- Deploy Action Plans & SIP's (fall)
- Communicate SP with all Stakeholders (fall)

PSD Annual
Strategic Planning Process

STUDY
Analyze Results
Senior Leaders and Board of Education:
- SP Goal measured throughout the school year
- Review quarterly progress against plan on Action Plans

CRITERIA QUESTIONS

In your response, include answers to the following questions:

a. Strategy Development Process

(1) **Strategic Planning Process** How do you conduct your strategic planning? What are the key process steps? Who are the key participants? What are your short- and longer-term planning horizons? How are they addressed in the planning process? How does your strategic planning process address the potential need for:

- Transformational change and prioritization of change initiatives,
- organizational agility, and
- operational flexibility?

(2) **Innovation** How does your strategy development process stimulate and incorporate innovation? How do you identify strategic opportunities? How do you decide which strategic opportunities are intelligent risks for pursuing? What are your key strategic opportunities?

(3) Strategy **Considerations** How do you collect and analyze relevant data and develop information for your strategic planning process? In this collection and analysis, how do you include these key elements?

- Your strategic challenges and strategic advantages
- Risks to your organization's future success
- Potential blind spots in your strategic planning process and information
- Your ability to execute the strategic plan

(4) **Work Systems and Core Competencies** What are your key work systems? How do you make work system decisions that facilitate the accomplishment of your strategic objectives? How do you decide which key processes will be accomplished by external suppliers and partners? How do those decisions consider your core competencies and the core competencies of potential suppliers and partners? How do you determine future organizational core competencies and work systems?

Notes:

2.1. This item deals with your overall organizational strategy, which might include changes in product offerings and customer engagement processes. However, you should describe the product design and customer engagement strategies, respectively, in items 6.1 and 3.2, as appropriate.

2.1. "Strategy development" refers to your organization's approach to preparing for the future. In developing your strategy, you might use various types of forecasts, projections, options, scenarios, knowledge (see 4.2a for relevant organizational knowledge), analyses, or other approaches to envisioning the future in order to make decisions and allocate resources. Strategy development might involve key suppliers, distributors, partners, and customers. For some nonprofit organizations, strategy development might involve organizations providing similar services or drawing from the same donor population or volunteer workforce.

2.1. The term "strategy" should be interpreted broadly. Strategy might be built around or lead to any or all of the following: new products; redefinition of key customer groups or market segments; differentiation of your brand; new core competencies; revenue growth via various approaches, including acquisitions, grants, and endowments; divestitures; new partnerships and alliances; and new employee or volunteer relationships. Strategy might be directed toward becoming a preferred supplier, a local supplier in each of your major customers' or partners' markets, low-cost producer, market innovator, or a provider of a high-end or customized product or service. It might also be directed toward meeting a community or public need.

2.1a(2). Strategic opportunities arise from outside-the-box thinking, brainstorming, capitalizing on serendipity, research and innovation processes, nonlinear extrapolation of current conditions, and other approaches to imagining a different future. The generation of ideas that lead to strategic opportunities benefits from an environment that encourages nondirected, free thought. Choosing which strategic opportunities to pursue involves considering relative risk, financial and otherwise, and then making intelligent choices ("intelligent risks").

2.1a(3). Data and information may come from a variety of internal and external sources and in a variety of forms. Data are available in increasingly greater volumes and at greater speeds. The ability to capitalize on data ana information, including large datasets ("big data"), is based on the ability to analyze the data, draw conclusions, and pursue actions, including intelligent risks.

2.1a(3). Data and information might relate to customer and market requirements, expectations, and opportunities; your core competencies; the competitive environment and your performance now and in the future relative to competitors and comparable organizations; your product life cycle; technological and other key innovations or changes that might affect your products and services and the way you operate, as well as the rate of innovation; workforce and other resource needs; your ability to capitalize on diversity; opportunities to redirect resources to higher-priority products, services, or areas; financial, societal, ethical, regulatory, technological, security, and other potential risks and opportunities; your ability to prevent and respond to emergencies, including natural or other disasters; changes in the local, national, or global economy; requirements for and strengths and weaknesses of your partners and supply chain; changes in your parent organization; and other factors unique to your organization.

2.1a(3). Your strategic planning should address your ability to mobilize the necessary resources and knowledge to execute the strategic plan. It should also address your ability to execute contingency plans or, if circumstances require, a shift in plans and rapid execution of new or changed plans.

2.1a(4). Decisions about work systems are strategic. These decisions involve protecting intellectual property, capitalizing on core competencies, and mitigating risk. Decisions about your work systems affect organizational design and structure, size, locations, profitability, and ongoing success. In a generic view of an organization, for example, the organization might define three work systems: one that addresses production of the product or service, one that engages the customer, and one that comprises systems that support production and customer engagement.

NIST (2015-2016) pp. 10-11

WORKSHEETS

2.1a(1) – Strategic Planning Process

Planning Process Step (In The Proper Sequence)	Description Of What Happens In The Step (Including The Decision Criteria For Key Decisions)	Documents Used In This Step (Note Where The Documents Include Blind Spots)	Key Participants	Timing Of Step (Month)
1.				
2.				
3.				
n.				
Your Process To Address The Potential Need For Transformational Change:				
Your Process To Address The Potential Need For Prioritization Of Change Initiatives:				

Planning Horizons	Number Of Months Or Years	The Reason This Planning Horizon Was Chosen (Including Key Linkages With Other Groups Or Horizons)	How The Strategic Planning Process Addresses This Time Horizon	How The Planning Process Addresses The Need For Organizational Agility And Operational Flexibility
Short-Term				
Medium-Term				
Long-Term				

2.1a(2) – Innovation

How Does Your Strategy Development Process Stimulate and Incorporate Innovation?	

How You Identify Strategic Opportunities And Intelligent Risks For Pursuing?	

What Are Your Key Strategic Opportunities	1 -
	2 -
	3 -
	n -

2.1a(3) – Strategy Considerations

Key Factor To Be Addressed	Sources of Data	Data Collection Methods	Data Analysis Performed
Strategic Challenges			
Strategic Advantages			
Risks To Your Organization's Future Success [1]			
Potential Changes In Your Regulatory Environment			
Potential Blind Spots In Your Strategic Planning Process			
Potential Blind Spots In Your Strategic Planning Information			
Your Ability To Execute The Strategic Plan			

1) In previous editions of the Baldrige Criteria Future Success was called 'sustainability.' It was changed due to the multitude of definitions for sustainability.

199

2.1a(4) – Work Systems And Core Competencies

List Your Key Work Systems

How Do You Make Work System Decisions That Facilitate The Accomplishment Of Your Strategic Objectives?	

How Do You Decide Which Key Processes Will Be Accomplished By External Suppliers And Partners?	

How Do Your Work System and Outsourcing Decisions Consider Your Core Competencies And The Core Competencies Of Potential Suppliers And Partners?	

How Do You Determine Future Organizational Core Competencies?	

ASSESSMENT

Rating Scale:

1 - **No Process** in place – We are not doing this
2 - **Reacting to Problems** – We use a basic (primarily reactive) process
3 - **Systematic Process** – We use a systematic process that has been improved
4 - **Aligned** – We use a process that aligns our activities from top to bottom
5 - **Integrated** – We use a process that is integrated with other processes across the organization
6 - **Benchmark** – We are the Benchmark in our industry or beyond!
DK - Don't Know

26	There is a systematic process in place through which Senior Leaders develop a strategy to achieve an organizational competitive advantage.	1 2 3 4 5 6 DK
27	A variety of factors are considered in developing the strategy, these include: the organizational strategic challenges and advantages, sustainability factors, potential blind spots, and the ability to execute the plan (i.e., people, processes, and technology, etc.) will be available.	1 2 3 4 5 6 DK
28	The key work systems are clearly defined, with supporting processes. These drive the achievement of the core competency.	1 2 3 4 5 6 DK

BLUEPRINT

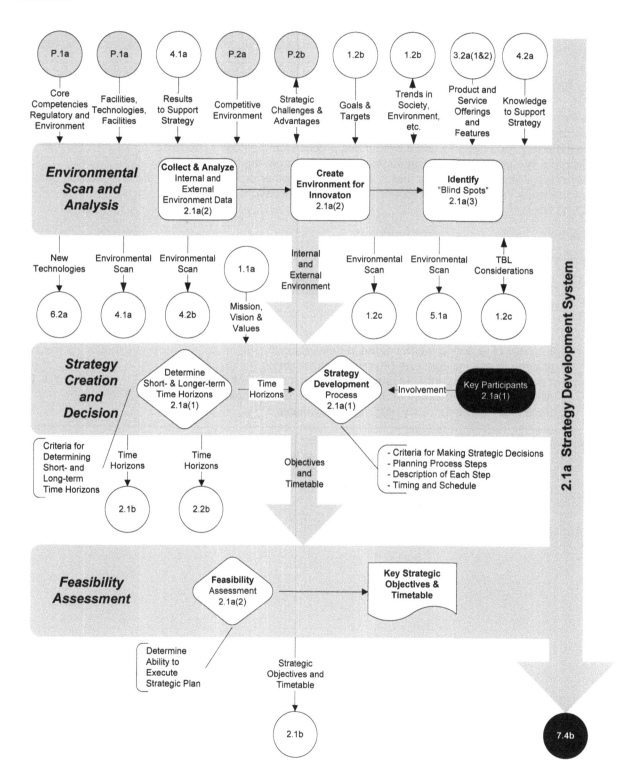

SYSTEM INTEGRATION

Context

P.1a > 2.1a Core Competencies - The organizations core competencies are a key input to strategy development. Core competencies is a strategic concept made popular by C. K. Prahalad and Gary Hamel in a 1990 *Harvard Business Review* article titled: The Core Competence of the Corporation. In this article they propose that core competencies provide the organization with a competitive advantage a key element in an effective strategy.

P.1a > 2.1a Regulatory Requirements - The regulatory environment described in the profile (P.1a) is a key input to strategy development and should be included in the SWOT analysis. The regulatory environment establishes parameters for the industry that can limit the strategic options that an organization can legally pursue.

P.1a > 2.1a Facilitates, Technologies, Locations - The analysis of facilities and locations along with technology changes and key innovations described in the profile are key inputs to strategy development. The SWOT analysis should be designed to include or address these issues and in particular the major technologies described in the profile (P.1a).

P.2a > 2.1a Competitive Environment - The competitive environment including the growth relative to competitors, size relative to competitors, and the number and type of competitors described in the profile (P.2a) are key inputs to strategy development and should be a central component of the SWOT analysis.

P.2b > 2.1a Strategic Challenges and Advantages - The strategic challenges and advantages identified in the profile (P.2b) are a direct input to the strategy development process and should be an integral part of the SWOT analysis. In addition, the strategic objectives that are developed as an output of this process should reflect and address these challenges and advantages.

Systems

1.1a > 2.1a Mission, Vision, Values - The mission, vision, and values are key considerations when developing strategies described in 2.1a. This linkage, along with the performance review linkage, helps to create and send consistent messages about what is important to the organization. When the organization's strategy, values, and reviews are internally consistent, the probability of successful implementation throughout the organization is increased.

1.2b <> 2.1a Trends in Society, Environment, etc. - The trends in society, the environment, etc., are key inputs to the strategy development process described in 2.1a. These trends should be consistent with the trends used to anticipate public concerns with current and future products, services, and operations described in 1.2b.

1.2b > 2.1a Goals and Targets - The goals for regulatory and legal performance along with the performance targets for risk, regulatory and legal, and public concerns are inputs to the analysis of financial, societal, ethical, regulatory and other risks addressed in 2.1a. These are then used as inputs to the strategy development process.

1.2c < 2.1a Environmental Scan - The strategic planning environmental scan is a key input to identifying the economic, environmental, and societal issues associated with social responsibilities and community support in 1.2c.

1.2c > 2.1a TBL (Triple Bottom Line) Strategic Considerations - The economic, environmental, and societal considerations identified in 1.2c are inputs to the strategic planning process described in 2.1a.

2.1a > 2.1b Time Horizons - The short- and long-term time horizons that are determined and used during strategy development (2.1a) are also used in 2.1b to evaluate whether the strategic goals balance short- and long-term challenges and opportunities.

2.1a > 2.1b Strategic Objectives and Timetable - The key outputs of the strategy development process are the strategic objectives and associated timetable. These objectives end up being the key input to the strategy deployment process described in 2.2a.

2.1a > 2.2b Time Horizons - The short- and long-term time horizons determined and used during strategy development (2.1a) are also used when determining short- and long-term performance projections in 2.2b.

2.1a < 3.2a(1&2) Product and Service Offerings and Features - The product and service offerings and associated features are inputs to the environmental scan and analysis process.

2.1a < 4.1a Results to Support Strategic Planning - The measures and associated results from 4.1a are direct inputs to the environmental scan and analysis process described in 2.1a.

2.1a > 4.1a Environmental Scan - The results of the environmental scan and analysis process is a key input to the performance measurement system and in particular the strategic management uses of the measures.

2.1a < 4.2a Knowledge to Support Strategy - Knowledge to support strategy development is in part derived from the information and knowledge contained in the system described in 4.2a.

2.1a > 4.2b Environmental Scan - The environmental scan and analysis results are key inputs to keeping the management information system current with changing business needs in 4.2b.

2.1a > 5.1a Environmental Scan - The environmental scan and analysis results are key inputs to forecasting the workforce capability and capacity needs in 5.1a.

2.1a > 6.2a New Technologies - The new technologies identified as part of the strategy development process (2.1a) are important inputs to the process design process in 6.1a. Design processes should consider the capabilities of the most recent technologies when designing processes.

Scorecard

2.1a > 7.1c Strategy Implementation Results - Progress toward achieving the strategies identified in the strategic planning process (2.1a) should be reported in 7.1c.

THOUGHTS FOR LEADERS

There is an old saying that "When you think your quality journey is over, you're right, it is." This means that when you quit trying to be better, you are finished as an organization.

A few days ago I watched a TV show with gifted children. It seemed like a brutal approach for kids, but of the 20+ contestants, they called out 5 names who had to leave right then! One young man, however, delivered a timeless message – "You can either get bitter or get better." And he went on to say he was going to get better and will be back. In my opinion, he has a role-model attitude at a young age.

We often ask the question – "Which organization is higher performing, the one that says they have many problems or one that does not have problems?"

An organization with many problems is *always* higher performing. The fact is - all organizations have problems, so now you can divide those organizations into two categories: those who know what their problems are, and those who do not. Organizations who do not know what their problems are will not do anything about them. Organizations who can identify and describe their problems are also the ones who will fix problems. It is against human nature to clearly articulate and identify a problem and then ignore it.

In short, organizations that identify their problems are going to perform better than organizations that do not. This organizational behavior, like everything else, is driven by leadership.

The process of identification and correction of problems must be embedded in an organization's planning at all levels. The planning cycle must be timed to use the research which is performed during the year, and the planning vision must consider all competitive threats. Actions planned and taken must address these threats.

Leaders do not have to generate all of the plans personally, but the senior leaders must ensure that plans take into consideration all of the appropriate research, that the correct people are involved, and that (once the plans are finalized) the direction is clear to all those who have a role in the implementation of the plan.

It is not unusual for many people to be involved in the gathering of planning data, only a few involved in establishing the overall strategy. Then virtually everybody is involved in the complete implementation of the plan.

Item 2.1 focuses on the development of the organizational strategy. This is easy, however, compared to the deployment of the strategy down to individual actions. This vertical alignment, however, is critical to competitiveness and even survival.

When the average *Baldrige Winning CEO* is interviewed one of my favorite questions is: "If you could go through your performance excellence journey again, what would you do differently?" The most common answer is "Align the organization top-to-bottom – from the strategy to actions. This is where the power is." This alignment, obviously, begins with ensuring that the strategy considers the right factors, and will keep the organization competitive.

A Lighter Moment:

You may not be interested in strategy, but strategy is interested in you.

Leon Trotsky

> *If you can't describe your strategy in twenty minutes, simply and in plain language, you haven't got a plan. 'But,' people may say, 'I've got a complex strategy. It can't be reduced to a page.' That's nonsense. That's not a complex strategy. It's a complex thought about the strategy.*
>
> **Larry Bossidy**

 FOUNDATION

This area of the Criteria for Performance Excellence (CPE) is straightforward. It asks for strategic objectives, and when those strategic objectives will be accomplished. It is the output of Area to Address 2.1a.

Key Strategic Objectives

Under the strategic objectives, the CPE ask for the goals the organization hopes to achieve for the strategic objectives, and the timeframe for achieving them.

Strategic Challenges and Advantages (P.2b)	Strategic Objectives (2.1b[1])	Long-Term Action Plans (2.2a[1])	Short-Term Action Plans (2.2a[1])
- Business - Operational - Human Resource	- Goals (2.1b(1)) - Measures (not required)	- Projected competitor performance (2.2b) - Timeframe (2.2b) - Organization performance versus competitor (2.2b) - Timetable (specific dates not required) - Changes in products and services (2.2a(3)) - Measures or indicators (2.2a(5)) - Goals (not required) - Projections (in timeframe (2.2b))	- Projected competitor performance (2.2b) - Timeframe (2.2b) - Organization performance versus competitor (2.2b) - Timetable (specific dates not required) - Changes in products and services (2.2a(3)) - Measures or indicators (2.2a(5)) - Goals (not required) - Projections (in timeframe (2.2b))

Additionally, the CPE ask the organization to link the strategic objectives back to the strategic challenges identified in P.2b in the Organizational Profile. The overall logic flow suggests that strategic challenges (external) should drive strategic objectives (internal), which should drive strategic goals.

The logic flow from the Organizational Profile to Item 2.1 to Item 2.2 is as follows:

⇨ **Strategic Challenges:** Understanding what is coming at us from the outside which we must address, but do not control

    ⇨ **Success Factors:** Understanding what anybody in our business needs to excel at if they wish to remain competitive today

        ⇨ **Strategic Advantages:** Understanding our organization's strengths vs. the competitors

            ⇨ **Strategic Opportunities:** Understanding what is happening in the marketplace (or internally) which is an opportunity the organization can leverage

                ⇨ **Strategic Objectives:** Understanding what we will be stronger in once our objectives are achieved

Organizations who clearly understand these linkages, have an advantage in developing plans which will keep them competitive.

Additionally, the criteria focus on how the organization addresses the opportunities for innovation in products, operations, and the business model should be addressed. This includes understanding how the organization capitalizes on the current core competency and addresses the potential need for new core competencies.

The CPE ask several difficult questions which relate to balancing the strategic objectives, the deployment of those objectives, short- and long-term timeframes, and balancing the needs of all stakeholders. Typically, organizations do not clearly address these issues. The most appropriate response is to describe how you ensure that the strategic objectives balance these factors using a systematic process. The systematic process used could include specific activities during particular timeframes or planning activities, as well as clear decision criteria for how the organization decides something and when they decide.

> Note: "balancing" does not mean equal attention, equal resources, or equal results. Balancing means that the balance the organization (and the leaders) **intended,** is the balance **planned,** is the balance **resourced,** is the balance **achieved.** For different organizations the balance could be significantly different. For example, one organization could be a "cash cow" and the balance of the stakeholder focus would be to give the owners a very high return. Another organization could be in a growth phase and the emphasis could be on building capacity and capability.

Finally, the criteria ask how the organization addresses the ability to adapt to sudden shifts in market conditions. This is similar to numerous other places where the criteria assess the organizational ability to adjust actions when results or conditions change.

EXAMPLES

Clarke American (Baldrige Recipient 2001)

Clarke American establishes high-level, long-term strategic objectives during development of the strategic vision. They define shorter-term objectives, linked to the vision, during goal deployment.

Clarke American Balanced Business Plan

	Balanced Business Plan Goals	Measures
Associates and Team	Develop, acquire, retain and motivate associates and teams to drive world class performance in core and emerging business	Retention of 2-year associates Implemented S.T.A.R. ideas Team huddles
Partner and Customer Value	Dramatically grow revenue through customer-preferred channels	Customer satisfaction e-Commerce revenue Customer contact center Revenue
Partner and Customer Value	Grow our business through partnership development and connectivity with partner service providers	Top 20 preferred service providers (PSP) Partner scorecards Branch loyalty
Partner and Customer Value	Retain partnerships	Partner retention
Process and Supplier Management	Company focus to reduce waste to achieve world class manufacturing and contract center performance.	Total order cycle time. Waste Reductions: Manufacturing Contact center Divisions/Processes
Process and Supplier Management	Manage and improve key supplier performance to deliver increased value, cost/waste elimination, and profit improvement.	Value management workshops conducted with key suppliers New products or services developed with suppliers
Shareholder and Community Value	Drive superior financial performance to increase shareholder value	Total revenue Operating profit Return on Invested Capital
Shareholder and Community Value	Accelerate the *FIS* journey to achieve world class performance and recognition	Compete for TQA Compete for MBNQA
Shareholder and Community Value	Be recognized as a responsible contributor committed to improving the communities where we live, work, and play.	% Participation and volunteers

Clarke American establishes a range of Balanced Business Plan Goals. These are linked to how they are tracked, and their associated measures. These are aligned around the company's key stakeholders. At a higher level, these stakeholders' requirements are aligned to the associated strategic challenges. The strategic challenges are translated into strategic objectives, which are then translated into shorter-term objectives and goals. At every level the plans and goals are linked to the level above it, and are linked to the measures which will be used to track performance.

Charleston Area Medical Center (The Partnership For Excellence Recipient 2014)

Our key strategic objectives (4 year) and annual goals and the timetable for accomplishing them are outlined in Figure 2.1-6. The full strategic plan is available on site. Key planned changes include implementation of Phase 2 TCT on all nursing units to increase capability in shared leadership, respect and collaboration, strategic engagement and stewardship to support the overall goals of the organization (operations); use of an automated phone callback system for patients post discharge to hardwire the identification of clnical and satisfaction issues needing follow-up (customers and products); and for the longer-term, implementation of new models for physician alignment and integration (markets and operations).

Figure 2.1-6 Alignment of Pillars, Strategic Challenges, Success Factors, Strategic Advantages, CC, and Strategic Objectives

Mission	CC	Pillars	2014 – 2017 Strategic Objectives (4-year long-term)	2014 Goals (1-year short-term) *Continued from Figure P.2-3*	Action Plans	BIG DOTs (4-year long-term) Results Figure #	1-Year Performance Targets	Short-Term Stretch Targets	4-Year Long-Term Targets and Projections	Innovation Examples
Striving to provide the best health care to every patient, every day. Improving the health and economics of our community		Best Place to Receive Patient Centered Care	• Improve HCAHPS patient experience results to top decile • Achieve top decile performance on clinical care outcomes	• Improve processes that support our customer service vision and impact our timeliness of responding to key customer needs. • Improve and deploy standardized processes for communication with patients and families, including communication of transition of care requirements. SOP(A,C,D) • Improve use of Soarian and workflows. SOP(B,D) • Improve coding and clinical documentation. SOP(B) • Improve Value Based Purchasing and reliability. • Improve effectiveness of transitions of care to reduce readmissions. SOP(A,C,D) • Deploy TCT Phase 1 to five ancillary departments and move 28 or more TCT Phase II departments to > 22 green. • Improve safety systems to reduce harm and improve the safety culture. SOP(B)	Cascaded aligned action plans and measures available in on-line planning system for each department (1 year short-term)	• HCAHPS Patient Experience Composite Score (7.2-11) • HCAHPS Discharge Information Composite (7.2-8) • O/E Mortality (7.1-1) • EBC Reliability (7.1-20, 7.1-21) • 30 Day O/E Readmission Rate (7.1-52) • TCT Phase 1 and Phase 2 Implementation (7.4-19) • Harm Composite (7.1-22)	70% 84% 0.70 90% 0.96 5 Anc. 28≥green 0.60	76% (QUEST Top Quartile) 89% (QUEST Top Decile) 0.64 (QUEST Top Decile) 95% 0.94 7 Anc. 30≥green 0.52	79% (QUEST Top Decile) 90% 0.63 96.28% (QUEST Top Quartile) 0.83 (QUEST Top Quartile) 8 Anc. 31≥green 0.00 (QUEST Top Quartile)	TCT Soarian Workflows
		Best Place to Work	• Improve employee satisfaction and engagement to "Employer of Choice"	• Identify at least one opportunity in each department from the 2013 Employee Survey and develop an action plan for improvement in department scores. • Identify and implement at least one opportunity in each department to reduce voluntary turnover.		• Employee Satisfaction Composite Score (7.3-19-7.3-20)	3.91	3.93	4.00	Best Place To Learn Education
		Best Place to Practice Medicine	• Ensure adequate medical resources to meet the needs of current and evolving service delivery and reimbursement models, and create the capability and capacity to respond agilely to healthcare reform	• Fill gaps in critical medical staff specialties. • Obtain Disease Specific Certifications. SOP (B) • Establish a process for quality measurement and reporting. SOP (B) • Enhance Medical Staff Development: SOP(B) 　a. Implement an onboarding process. 　b. Develop and implement a mentoring process. 　c. Identify Medical Staff leadership development needs and implement plan to address.		• Recruitment to Critical Specialties • HCAHPS Physician Communication Score (7.2-4)	6 of 11 80%	10 of 11 85% (HCAHPS Top Quartile)	11 of 11 88% (HCAHPS Top Decile)	Vascular Center of Excellence Model Workflows
		Best Place to Learn	• Ensure integrated education and research systems and academic partnerships that address workforce needs of our community and that promote organizational and individual learning, innovation and performance improvement	• Provide accredited programs and education affiliations to address workforce challenges and workforce capability needs for CAMC and the region. SOP(B) • Provide integrated learning systems and programs that address organizational sustainability and workforce challenges and that promote a culture of learning. • Establish research systems and partnerships that foster organizational learning and innovation and that promote recognition of CAMC as a teaching hospital and academic medical center. SOP(A) • Link academic education and research systems to patient safety, quality improvement, and goals, assuring a clinical learning environment that promotes a patient safety and learning culture. SOP(B)		• Environment for Learning and Safety Composite	Composite score of: Employee Survey "Comfortable discussing issues" 3.90 (60%) ACGME Resident Survey "Residents can raise concerns without fear and intimidation" 80 (20%) AHRQ Patient Safety Survey (Composite of 3 questions) 45 (20%)			Simulation Center QIPS
		Best Place to Refer Patients	• Grow market share in primary and secondary service areas • Establish competencies for success in the health care reform environment	• Recapture market share in orthopedics, cardiovascular, neurosciences, women's and pain service lines. SOP(A,B,C,D) • Ensure capacity and capability for patient access. SOP(A) • Achieve budgeted bottom-line. • Improve cost, efficiency and productivity. • Implement plan to improve the health of our communities. SOP(D)		• IP and OP Volume for Ortho, CV, Neurosciences and Women • MU Stage 2 • Operating Margin (7.5-1) • Expense/AA (7.5-2) • Excess of Revenue over Expense (7.5-9)	177,180 MU2 Req. Met 2.60% $13,377 $27.5M	180,689 2.65% $13,109 $28.0M	182,443 2.67% $12,976 $28.3M	Transfer Center Medical Neighborhood KCCHI

Our **strategic opportunities (SOP)** are: **SOP (A)** increasing affiliations with hospitals, other providers and payors, **SOP (B)** formalizing physician alignment, **SOP (C)** strengthening primary care, and **SOP (D)** population health. 1-year (short-term) goals that align with these SOPs are designated in the Goals column above.

Pewaukee School District (Baldrige Recipient 2013)

Strategic objectives, identified by PSD (Pewaukee School District) as SP Goals, are our most important goals and are developed as part of the PLAN Phase of the SPP (Strategic Planning Process).

SP Goals are determined to be in the five key areas that will help us accomplish our Mission. Our five SP Goals, identified in Figure 2.1-2, reflect our top priorities and are intended to be accomplished in 4-5 years. After determining the SP Goals, measures are created. We annually publish the results of our SP Goal measure results as they are received by the Board in the form of CIRs (Continuous Improvement Report).

Figure 2.1-2   2012-13 Strategic Plan using Plan-Do-Study-Act

Mission: Through our unique all campus setting, we will open the door to each child's future
Values: Our school community delivers an innovative and progressive education
We are: *Passionate about academic excellence   *Committed to fostering positive citizenship   *Dedicated to inspiring all students to flourish

PLAN

	Vision *Long term goals to be accomplished in 4-5 years*	Our Balanced Scorecard – Key Strategic Plan Goal Measures
T & L	PSD will provide a rigorous and relevant curriculum delivered by high quality educators who use innovative, research-based strategies to prepare students to compete in a global environment in the 21ˢᵗ century *(Addresses strategic challenges of teaching 21st century skills & increasing student achievement)*	*Action Plan Measure:* EPAS Scores 7-12 (Fig. 7.1-9 & 10), MAP Scores 2-6 (Fig. 7.1-3 & 4) *Key Measures:* Graduation Rate (Fig. 7.1-1), % Graduates Attending 2- or 4-year college (Fig. 7.1-2), ACT Composite Score (Fig. 7.1-9), AP Performance (Fig. 7.1-11)
WE & D	PSD will utilize best practices to hire, retain, engage, and develop a skilled and talented workforce that will enable the District to achieve its mission *(Addresses strategic challenge of developing our talented staff)*	*Action Plan Measure:* Professional Development Tracking (Fig. 7.3-17) *Key Measures:* TeacherInsight Scores (Fig. 7.3-5), Retention Rate (Fig. 7.3-14), Employee Satisfaction/Engagement Rate (Fig. 7.3-11 thru 13),% Teachers w/ Advanced Degrees (Fig. 7.3-16), Student/Staff Ratio (Fig. 7.3-1)
C & CE	PSD will communicate, engage, and develop partnerships with students, staff and citizens to help reach our Mission *(Addresses strategic challenge of growing partnerships)*	*Action Plan Measure:* Parent Satisfaction Rates (7.2-2), # of volunteers & partnerships (Fig. 7.2-12 & 13) *Key Measures:* Community Grading of Schools (Fig. 7.2-8), Stakeholder Sources of Information (Fig. 7.1-42 & 43), Overall Parent, Alumni & Student Satisfaction (Fig. 7.2-1 thru 7.2-7)
Technology	PSD will create classroom environments where students engage in collaborative, inquiry-based learning, facilitated by educators who are able to use technology to transform knowledge & skills into solutions, new information and products. *(Addresses strategic challenge of teaching 21ˢᵗ century skills & using technology to increase student and stakeholder engagement)*	*Action Plan Measure:* Student Technology Proficiency (Fig. 7.1-11 & 12) *Key Measures:* Teacher Technology Proficiency (Fig. 7.1-28), Growth of Computer Fleet (Fig. 7.1-25), Network Uptime (Fig. 7.1-39) and Ticket Resolution Rate (Fig. 7.1-26)
F & O	PSD will provide safe, healthy and efficiently operated schools to ensure the success of all students and accountability for our stakeholders *(Addresses strategic challenges of maintaining economic stability and operating with greater efficiency)*	*Action Plan Measure:* Energy Consumption (Fig. 7.1-31, Fig. 7.4-10), Camera/Fob Access Installation (Fig. 7.4-10), Facility Use (Fig. 7.4-11) *Key Measures:* Revenue Exceeds Expenses (Fig. 7.5-2), Bond Rating (7.5-1)

DO

Our Action Plans and Goals

T & L

#1: K-12 Literacy: By 2014, Increase percent of students who are College and Career Ready from 50% to 75% as measured by EPAS system in grades 7-12
    Action Plan Work: Implement Readers/Writers Workshop K-8; Literacy Learning Center Approach & Instructional Coaching at secondary level)
#2: K-12 Math: By 2014, Increase the percent of students who are College and Career Ready from 50% to 75% as measured by EPAS system in grades 7-12
    Action Plan Work: Enhance Math Expressions fidelity & differentiation strategies K-6; grow personalized learning model Pre-Algebra thru Algebra II)
#3: Grading for Learning: By June 2013, 100% of PSD teachers will be able to identify best practices for grading selected for implementation K-12
    Action Plan Work: Create task force; develop common understanding of standards-based grading throughout the District)
#4: Personalized Learning: By June 2015, 100% of PSD students will experience core curriculum delivered through a Personalized Learning Model
    Action Plan Work: Form task force; create Vision & Framework; Participate in CESA 1 Innovation Lab professional development to build capacity
#5: Response to Intervention: By 2015 develop and employ a comprehensive K-12 system of academic & behavioral interventions
    Action Plan Work: Draft RtI Handbook; determine universal screener and progress monitoring tools

WE & D

#1: Professional Development: By 2015, authentic and meaningful professional development by the teacher, paraprofessional, secretarial, custodial and food service workforce groups will increase to 100% a measured by the % of completion via online School Objects
    Action Plan Work: Develop tracking methodology; expand job embedded professional development; expand PD offerings for all workforce groups)
#2: Teacher Evaluation: By 2014-15 fully implement State Evaluation tools for teachers and administrators
    Action Plan Work: Teacher Effectiveness pilot of SLOs; Develop teaching compensation draft for implementation 2013-14

C & CE

#1: Web Training: By June 2015, parents will have 90% overall satisfaction with web/electronic communications as measured in the End of Year survey
    Action Plan Work: Update web for parent user-friendliness; hold parent learning sessions on use of website; place instructional videos on web
#2: Volunteer Program: By June 2014, increase the pool of non-student volunteers from 11,072 to 15,000 hours
    Action Plan Work: Hire Volunteer Coordinator; create Volunteer Handbook; implement system & place volunteers in classrooms; evaluate program
#3: Business Partnerships: By June 2014, connect businesses with at least 5 educators to begin sharing information & resources
    Action Plan Work: Form Chamber of Commerce Task Force to bring community connection to school; place partners in classrooms; create database

Tech

#1: Student Technology Proficiency: By June 2014, 100% of Grade 8 students will increase technology proficiency from 44 to 100% as measured by the Technology Proficiency Assessment
    Action Plan Work: Implement 1:1 in Horizon School; create Tech Plan for expansion at PLE; monitor implementation of Digital Citizenship curriculum

F & O

#1: Energy Management: By June 2015, reach & maintain a 30% cost avoidance savings in comparison to 2008 baseline data
    Action Plan Work: Reward Energy Star classrooms; create dashboard for energy monitoring; install digital control systems
#2: Security Camera/Door Access: By June 2014, fully implement safety plan pertaining to camera installation & fob access
    Action Plan Work: Install additional cameras; upgrade digital control capabilities
#3: Resource Conservation: By June 2015, reduce the cost of printing by 15%
    Action Plan Work: Create monitoring system with financial incentives for schools to use less paper; implement online registration and evaluate
#4: Facility Use Requests: By June 2015, 100% of all applications for facility use will be electronically submitted
    Action Plan Work: Monitor implementation; complete training for new users

STUDY

90-Day Action Plan Updates are conducted by the AT; Continuous Improvement Reports are submitted to the Board annually (available on site)

ACT

90-Day Action Plans are analyzed, and resources may be redirected, if needed; SP process is evaluated prior to implementation of the next PLAN phase

CRITERIA QUESTIONS

In your response, include answers to the following questions:

b. Strategic Objectives

(1) **Key Strategic Objectives** What are your organization's key strategic objectives and timetable for achieving them? What are your most important goals for these strategic objectives? What key changes, if any, are planned in your products, customers and markets, suppliers and partners, and operations?

(2) **Strategic Objective Considerations** How do your strategic objectives achieve appropriate balance among varying and potentially competing organization needs? How do your strategic objectives:

- address your strategic challenges and leverage your core competencies, strategic advantages, and strategic opportunities;
- balance short- and longer-term time horizons; and
- consider and balance the needs of all key stakeholders?

Notes:

2.1b(1). Strategic objectives might address rapid response, customization, co-location with major customers or partners, workforce capability and capacity, specific joint ventures, virtual manufacturing, rapid or market-changing innovation, ISO quality or environmental systems registration, societal responsibility actions or leadership, social media and Web-based supplier and customer relationship management, and product and service quality enhancements. Responses should focus on your specific challenges, advantages, and opportunities—those most important to your ongoing success and to strengthening your overall performance.

NIST (2015-2016) pp, 10-11

WORKSHEETS

2.1b Strategic Objectives

2.1b(1) – Key Strategic Objectives

Strategic Challenges* [2.1b(2)]	Key Strategic Objectives (Long-Term = L; Short-Term = S)	Timetable For Achieving The Objective	Most Important Goals For The Strategic Objective	Strategic Advantage Addressed [2.1b(2)]
Strategic Challenge 1	L1			
	S1			
Strategic Challenge 2	L2			
	S2			
Strategic Challenge n	Ln			
	Sn			

* = Strategic Challenges should be the same external Strategic Challenges identified in the Org. Profile (P.2b)

	Changes Planned In Your:
Products	
Customers	
Markets	
Suppliers	
Partners	
Operations	

2.1b(2) – *Strategic Objective Considerations*

Key Strategic Objectives (Should Be The Same As The List Above)	How Do Your Strategic Objectives:			
	Address Strategic Challenges	Leverage Your Core Competencies	Leverage Your Strategic Advantages	Leverage Your Strategic Opportunity
L1				
S1				
L2				
S2				
L3				
S3				
Ln				
Sn				

How You Ensure That Your Strategic Objectives Balance:	Short- and Longer-Term Time Horizons	The Needs Of All Key Stakeholders

Note: 'Balancing Stakeholder Needs' does not mean all needs (or responses to the needs) are 'equal.' *Balancing* **means the mix of needs** *planned,* **matches the needs** *resourced, and* **matches the needs** *achieved.*

ASSESSMENT

Rating Scale:

1 - **No Process** in place – We are not doing this
2 - **Reacting to Problems** – We use a basic (primarily reactive) process
3 - **Systematic Process** – We use a systematic process that has been improved
4 - **Aligned** – We use a process that aligns our activities from top to bottom
5 - **Integrated** – We use a process that is integrated with other processes across the organization
6 - **Benchmark** – We are the Benchmark in our industry or beyond!
DK - Don't Know

29	There are specific strategic objectives and goals for: 1) financial performance; 2) human resource development; 3) process improvement; and 4) customer results.	1	2	3	4	5	6	DK
30	Stretch goals are set to exceed external customer expectations, and the organization uses this approach to achieve a competitive advantage.	1	2	3	4	5	6	DK
31	We use comparisons and benchmarks for our key strategic objectives to ensure that the organization always stays ahead of the competitors and the industry.	1	2	3	4	5	6	DK
32	The strategic objectives are clearly linked to the organizational strategic challenges, strategic advantages, and core competency.	1	2	3	4	5	6	DK

BLUEPRINT

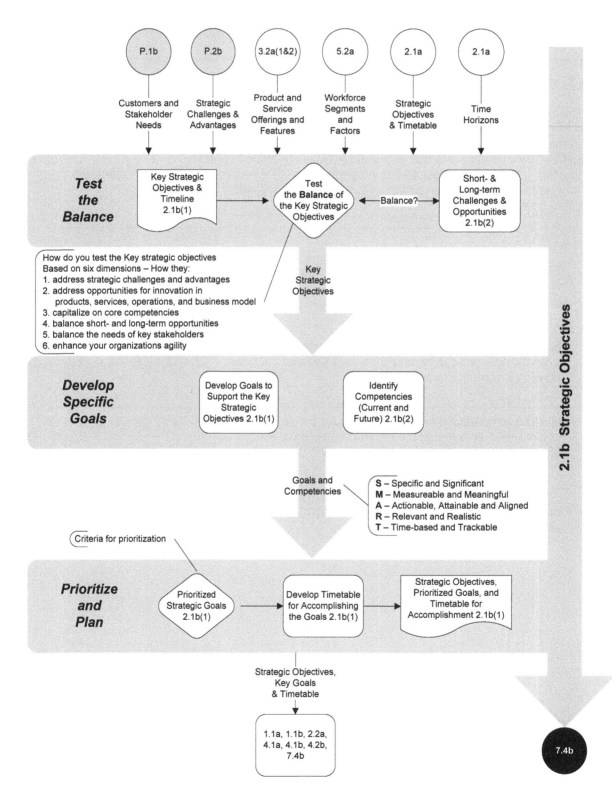

SYSTEM INTEGRATION

Context

P.1b > 2.1b Customers and Stakeholders - The test to determine whether the strategic objectives balance the needs of the key stakeholders is based in part on the customers and stakeholders and their needs identified in the profile (P.1b).

P.2b > 2.1b Strategic Challenges and Advantages - The criteria ask how the strategic objectives identified in 2.1b address the strategic challenges and advantages identified in the profile (P.2b). Consequently, there should be an explicit linkage and alignment between the challenges and advantages in P.2b and the objectives identified in 2.1b.

Systems

1.1a < 2.1b Strategic Objectives - The strategic objectives and the timetable for accomplishing them as described in 2.1b is an important input to creating an environment to foster the accomplishment of strategic objectives described in 1.1a.

1.1b < 2.1b Strategic Objectives and Timeline - The output of the strategy development process are strategic objectives and a timetable for accomplishing them as described in 2.1b. These objectives and the timetable are key considerations when creating a focus on action that will help in accomplishing the strategy.

2.1a > 2.1b Time Horizons - The short- and long-term time horizons that are determined and used during strategy development (2.1a) are also used in 2.1b to evaluate whether the strategic goals balance short- and long-term challenges and opportunities.

2.1a > 2.1b Strategic Objectives and Timetable - The key outputs of the strategy development process are the strategic objectives and associated timetable. These objectives end up being the key input to the strategy deployment process described in 2.2a.

2.1b > 2.2a Strategic Objectives and Timetable - The key outputs of the strategy development process are the strategic objectives and associated timetable. These objectives end up being the primary input to the strategy deployment process described in 2.2a.

2.1b < 3.2a(1&2) Product and Service Offerings and Features - The product and service offerings and associated features are inputs to the process of testing the balance of key strategic objectives. In particular, how the objectives address opportunities for innovation in products and services.

2.1b > 4.1a Strategic Objectives and Timetable - The objectives and their timetable for accomplishment drive the identification of performance and project measures to track the performance improvement. The identification of these measures should be part of the performance measurement process described in 4.1a.

2.1b > 4.1b Strategic Objectives and Timetable - The review process described in 4.1b asks the organization to assess the progress relative to strategic objectives and action plans. The objectives, goals, and timeline used should be the same as those developed in 2.1b.

2.1b > 4.2b Strategic Objectives and Timetable - The goals and timetable described in 2.1b are key inputs to the process of keeping the information systems current with changing business needs (4.2b).

2.1b < 5.2a Segments and Factors - The workforce segments and key factors for workforce engagement along with other key stakeholder requirements are key inputs to testing for balance of the key objectives.

Scorecard

2.1b > 7.4b Strategic Objectives, Timetable, and Progress - The results associated with the accomplishment of the organization's strategy and action plans should be reported in 7.1c.

 THOUGHTS FOR LEADERS

As stated earlier in this book "Your only sustainable competitive advantage is your rate of improvement."

The strategic objectives, once achieved, should propel (or keep) the organization ahead of the competition. The problem is, however, the competitors are not standing still – they are also improving. It is critical to understand the "rate of change" of your competitor, since you must improve at a greater rate. Something above normal continuous improvement may be required. Innovation starts with leadership. If a leader does not expect breakthroughs and include these in the planning or does not understand the nature of risk, an organization cannot innovate.

If leaders always have safe goals, the organization is not thinking about true breakthrough opportunities. If their goal is always "ten percent growth," they may achieve ten percent growth, but no more. When aiming for a ten percent change, organizations do not make behavioral changes. On the other hand, a forty percent change is dramatic and does require a behavioral change, a new order of things, or a new process.

A Lighter Moment:

Vision without action is a daydream.
Action with without vision is a nightmare.

Japanese proverb

> *The essence of strategy is choosing what not to do.*
>
> Michael E. Porter

 FOUNDATION

Item 2.1 developed the strategic plan. Item 2.2 asks "What do you do with the strategic plan?" Historically 2.2 has been worth more points than 2.1, since it is harder to deploy a plan than to develop a plan.

Action Plans

Specifically, the CPE ask "how" the organization develops action plans to achieve their strategic objectives. This typically involves the organization describing how they take the highest level strategy and deploy it through each organizational level down to individual goals, or (at a minimum) team goals for small teams throughout the organization. Later (in Area to Address 2.2b) the criteria will ask how you make changes in the action plans, based on changes in your performance or competitive position.

Action Plan Implementation

This ability to directly link the top strategies (plans) to the bottom actions has been described by many Baldrige recipients as the most important thing they have accomplished. In recent years, several Baldrige recipients were asked (if they could go through the journey again) what they would do differently. A predominance of these winners indicated they would align the organization (top to bottom as discussed in Item 2.2) more quickly. Frequently they will follow this view by stating "That is where the power is – to have everyone on the same page."

Resource Allocation

Any organization must effectively allocate resources if plans are to be realized. Although the CPE specifically mentions financial resources, the other resources which should be considered include data, people, critical skills, facilities, equipment, a safety environment, supply chain, and many others. This allocation should be in concert with the risk analysis performed by the organization to ensure that the risks associated with the plans are mitigated to ensure organizational sustainability.

In recent years, Baldrige has emphasized the ongoing sustainability of the organization. In Item 2.2 the sustainability of the actions taken is discussed. After the criteria address the deployment of the strategic objectives down to the action level, as well as the development of the action plans, it seeks to understand how the organization ensures the changes which result from these action plans can be sustained over the longer-term. Once again, a description of a process, rather than detailed activities and best intentions, is necessary.

Workforce Plans

In addition, this Area to Address seeks to understand how the key human resource plans support the overall strategy of the organization. While many organizations are reluctant to develop a human resource plan, it does not have to be overly complex. It should be a plan which considers factors, such as skills needed, turnover, development of technical skills, development of managerial and leadership skills, development of ethics and social value skills, and others. The human resource plan should describe how those skills are going to be trained and developed into the organization. These plans should be compatible with both the short- and longer-term strategic objectives and actions plans. Without the ability to develop people during the course of the year, the organization may be limited in its ability to achieve its strategic plan.

Performance Measures

All plans, goals and objectives should have measures or indicators for tracking the achievement and effectiveness of their plans. These measures should reinforce the alignment (up and down the organization). Additionally, they should address all key areas where the plans should be deployed.

Performance Projections

This is the only place in the CPE where an organization can get credit for something they have not yet achieved.

It asks for projections of performance which will be derived from the action plans, which are driven by the strategy (Note: these linkages should be clear and should start in the Organizational Profile with the external Strategic Challenges). Additionally, the CPE ask how the organization will know how its performance will compare to its competitors' during those same timeframes. This Area to Address requires the organization to project their own performance, project the performance of competitors, and assess the comparison between the two at some point in the future, presumably at least at the end of each planning time frame. Additionally, the basis for these projections needs to be described in enough detail that the projections are clearly plausible. This means the typical 'hockey stick' projections that says we are going to be the same in the near future, but 'soon' things will get dramaticlaly better. This is only possible if there are plans being implemented which can make things better.

Typically, organizations cannot provide direct competitive comparisons on a pure "apples-to-apples" basis. These comparisons, therefore, may have to come from industry knowledge or from common data points, which are infrequently gathered. It is important in 2.2b, however, to describe the process used to develop the projections and the assumptions that have been made in determining the organization's and the competitor's projections.

 EXAMPLES

Charleston Area Medical Center (Charleston, West Virginia)

The development of action plans starts at the system level. As shown in Figure 2.2-1, the system Strategic Objectives ❶ (with the associated metrics, or 4-year BIG DOTs) are translated into the system Short-Term Goals ❷ (with the associated metrics, or 1-year BIG DOTs, hereafter called BIG DOTs). BIG DOTs are sent to the entity level where they are translated into the entity's operational Action Plans ❸. Entity action plans are translated at the Department level to Individual Action Plans ❹ and the aligned Scorecards. This planning cascade is integrated across multiple years through the Strategic Objectives and the 4-year BIG DOTs, and is revisited and refined annually through the SPP. It is integrated top-to-bottom within the Health System through the Pillars, Strategic Objectives, Goals, and BIG DOTs, which are balanced based on needs. The short-and longer-term Action Plans and their relationship to the Strategic Objectives are shown in Figure 2.1-4.

Key planned changes include implementation of Phase 2 of TCT to increase capability in shared leadership, respect and collaboration, strategic engagement and stewardship to support the overall goals of the organizations; use of an automated phone callback system for patients post discharge to hardwire the identification of clinical and satisfaction issues physician alignment and integration.

The development and deployment of action plans is simultaneous. The goal cascade process promotes accountability and systematic deployment of the strategic plan [12]. Each VP holds half day goal cascade meetings with department manager groups during October and November to develop department goal priorities, action plans and targets that support the cascaded corporate goals. Department managers then enter their action plans into the online goal reporting system and Department Scorecards are developed.

The department managers then cascade department goals to individual employee performance planners. To hardwire communication of the goals and BIG DOTs [13], department goal wallmaps/TCT Top 5 Boards are provided for each department in December as a visual communication tool highlighting the alignment from top to bottom throughout the organization and to keep quarterly departmental progress to plan updated. By incorporating goals from our SP into our performance management system, we create strategy alignment from the entity to the employee level. Our PMS further sustains the key outcomes of action plans by continually aligning individual and organization goals. Deployment to MS occurs through the MS Officers and MS Executive Committee to MS departments, PAC and GME Council and through all project teams showing alignment of the team activity to the applicable goals. Key partners are involved in action plan development and deployment meetings to set goals and targets in the areas in which they support corporate goals and in meetings for review and improvement. For example, Crothall has goals and targets for HCAHPS cleanliness as part of their contract.

Our plan deployment process has also undergone many cycles of learning including the formalized goal cascade meetings, use of Individual Scorecards in addition to action plan reporting and ongoing improvements to the online goal reporting system. Changes from action plans are sustained by making changes in policies, procedures, or single-point lessons and through ongoing monitoring for control. Strategically the performance impact of the change is incorporated into the following year's SPP. Phase SL measure the effectiveness of the cascade deployment process each year through review of both organizational and individual goal achievement [14] and VOC tools. Senior Leaders review progress monthly with their direct reports.

The Board and Executive Council also conduct a quarterly review of progress towards goals and targets relative to the system and hospital measures [15]. Impact Leadership serves as the prioritization funnel for assignment of improvement teams if the need for course correction is identified. Changes are made and incorporated into the following year's SPP. The final step [16] occurs each January as the SPT does a formal review of the SPP and makes recommendations for improvement. The SPP is in its 10th cycle of learning. This final step closes the feedback loop in the SPP which includes a review of the process for organizational learning and ongoing cycles of learning.

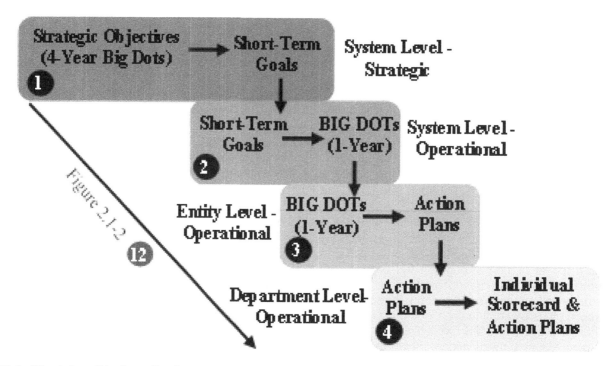

Tata Tinplate - Strategy Deployment

The Tinplate Company of India Limited (TCIL) has pioneered the production of tinplate in India way back in 1920 and is today the industry leader in India with a market share of over 35-40%. An associate company of Tata Steel, TCIL is engaged in providing packaging requirements for food through manufacturing and marketing of tinplate, an environment friendly packaging medium.

TCIL has revisited its Excellence Architecture and has redefined its Business purpose - "Provide cost effective metal packaging solutions for processed edibles". It has built a shared Vision and also revisited (earlier Strategy Architecture/Map) the Strategy alignment process to deploy the goals down the organization. This systematic deployment flows-down (with Criteria References) as follows:

Aligning this from top to bottom is difficult, and requires the organization to work to ensure that no goals or objectives 'disconnect' as they flow-down. This is affectionately called the called the *Mother Of All Charts* (MOAC) since it links many things together. MOAC is systematically used for development, alignment and deployment of Strategy at TCIL.

At TCIL MOAC outlines the Key stakeholders (Customer, Supplier, Employee, Community & Shareholder) and their requirements. Based on these Stakeholder requirements, the corresponding Strategic Challenges, which are External in nature, have been identified in line with the Vision. In order to address the Strategic Challenges, TCIL has outlined its Key Success factors, Strategic Objectives, Strategic measures and Goals which forms the integral part of MOAC.

In order to achieve and realize each of the Strategic objectives, a Long-Term (3 years) action plan and Short-Term (1 year) action plan with measures and targets are developed. The Long-Term and Short-Term action plans are included in MOAC. MOAC also includes competitor's projected performance and use of Benchmarks to compare Organizations performance Excellence.

In order to achieve these Strategic Objectives, LT and ST action plans and targets, MOAC measures are Cascaded to Corporate and Function level BSCs which is further cascaded to Individual Key Results Areas (KRAs) and Key Performance Indicators (KPIs)%> 2 of Employees. The Key Enterprise Processes help achieving these objectives. At TCIL, each Employee at various levels has been directly/indirectly involved in formulation of MOAC and can relate to this chart vis-à-vis their area of responsibility which has helped TCIL in achieving its Goals.

Stakeholder Requirements - Both Internal and External
⇓
    Strategic Challenges - External (P2b)
    ⇓
        Strategic Objectives – Internal (2.1b[1]) with the associated:
          o   Goals (2.1b[1])
          o   Timetable for Accomplishing the Strategic Objectives (2.1b[1])
          o   Measures (not required)
            ⇓
            Long-Term Action Plans - (2.2a[2]) with the associated:
              ■ Goals (not required)
              ■ Measures Or Indicators (2.2a[4])
              ■ Changes In Products/Services 2.2a[2]
              ■ Projections (and Timeframe For Projections) (2.2b)
                ⇓
                Short-Term Action Plans - (2.2a[2]) with the associated:
                  ■ Goals (not required)
                  ■ Measures Or Indicators (2.2a[4])
                  ■ Changes In Products/Services 2.2a[2])
                  ■ Projections (and Timeframe For Projections) (2.2b)
                    ⇓
                  Projected Performance for the period projected (2.2b)
                    ⇓
                    v. Comparisons With:
                      o   Key Benchmarks, Goals, or Past Performance (2.2b)
                      o   Competitor Projected Performance (2.2b)

The process ensures that the Objectives address all stakeholders and balance their needs. An illustrative example of MOAC used at TCIL for Customer as the Stakeholder being focused upon is given below:

Stake-holder	Strategic Challenge	Strategic Objective	Measures (UOM)	Goal 2009-10	Long-Term Action Plans	Measures (UOM) (2.2a(4))	Targets(2.2b)		
							2007-08	2008-09	2009-10
Customer	Threat of Substitutes	Develop role of providing enhanced value proposition(A1)	% of revenue generated from strategic downstream presence (beyond "bare" tin mill products sale)	Metal Packaging Solutions Provider 25% of revenue downstream.	Re- engineer the industry value thru either Growth of a Solution Center or acquisition or set up niche can making facilities (more comprehensive role of solution provider) but focusing on two key issues: consumer convenience and aesthetics / shelf appeal	Facilities enhancement	Coil and sheet cutting	Lug Caps & Closures	Easy Open Ends
						Start can making	3rd party conversions	Flattened Cans at Factory	Beverage Cans

Continuing to link long-term actions to short-term actions, the following chart would be a continuation from the right side of the chart above.

Short-Term Action Plans	Measures (UOM)	Target 2006-07	Competitors projected	Key Benchmarks
Develop Packaging Solutions	Number of solutions	Four per month	Competitors ABC and XYZ have no plans for downstream investments, presently	
Develop markets - spices and lubes	Sales in these markets	1500 MT for year		
Establish sustained operations of Solution Center	Q1 1-shift - Q4 3-shift	3 shift operation	Internationally, tinplate players have max 10% of revenues from downstream	

North Mississippi Medical Center (Baldrige Recipient as a hospital in 2006 and as a system in 2012)

North Mississippi Medical Center deploys their strategic plan through an Action Planning process that follows a standardized approach using a template. Included in this process is a venue for reporting progress on the Action Plans, which assists with accountability and ensuring that if there is not sufficient progress, the action plans are adjusted. The Action Planning Process is an integrated component of the Strategic Planning Process.

Figure 2.2-1	Sample 90 –day Action Plan • Women's & Children's Service Line (1/06-3/06)		
CSF	**Goal**	**Action Steps**	**90 Day Result Report**
People	Maintain FT Turnover rate	• Leader rounding x2 each day • Review rounding information at weekly manager meetings • Implement 90-day AP with direct reports.	• Turnover rate at <1.6% • One 90 day AP per unit
Service	Achieve 90th percentile on inpatient satisfaction	• Nurse rounding • Bi-weekly meeting with Women/Children's patient satisfaction team	• 90th percentile or higher in patient satisfaction
Quality	Reduce practice variation in DRG 372, 373 Pediatric asthma	• Physician champion identified • OM to perform CPA DRG 372-373 • PA to perform documentation analysis • Physician champion identified • Perform CPA on asthma DRG	• Decrease DRG 372 LOS • Assure appropriate DRG assignment • Decrease readmissions for pediatric asthma patients
Financial	Maintain expenses within budget	• Review OB/GYN financials with OB's • Nurse managers analyze & report OT needs to SLL	• BAR at or above 80 • Overtime below 3.0% • Expenses below budget
Growth	Develop a vision for pediatric services Implement Women/Children's Community Advisory Board	• Set up meeting with LeBonheur Children's Hospital to discuss increase in pediatric subspecialities • Develop cost benefit analysis with marketing for branding of pediatric services • Recruit Advisory Board members • Develop agenda for 1st meeting	• Present draft of vision by March SLOG • Pediatric branding identified and cost/benefit reported to SLOG w/in 30 days • First Advisory Board meeting on March, 2006

Action plans are developed through a systematic process by using a standard 90-day Action Plan content template The template components are selecting the Critical Success Factor that pertains to the issue, setting a goal, listing the action steps as well as the resources that are needed to carry out the changes and completing a 90-day Action Plan report. We initiate deployment of the strategic plan by communicating the Strategic Resource Plan and the Critical Success Factor -based goals to the Department Heads at their annual Operational Goals Retreat. These leaders provide their input into the planning process with their Strength-Weakness-Opportunities-Threats analysis and their Long Range Planning surveys and receive the integrated and prioritized summation of their collective efforts.

The Department Heads develop Critical Success Factor -based short-term goals and 90-day Action Plans that are aligned with the overall North Mississippi Medical Center Critical Success Factor-based short-term goals. Key partners and suppliers are frequently included in developing 90- day Action Plans as a delegated empowerment of the Department Heads. The Vice President of Finance and staff review these budget projections and reconcile them with each other. The Senior Leadership Team work with the Department Heads to create 90-day Action Plans that will achieve the Critical Success Factor -based goals and also meet the capital Strategic Resource Plan. This process ensures achievable, fully funded and sustainable action plans. The 90-day Action Plans are deployed once the budgets are finalized and approved.

Pewaukee School District (Baldrige Recipient 2013)

PSD (Pewaukee School District) is strategic in SP deployment using a structured process to optimize operational performance. Action Plans (Figure 2.1-1) are developed by the AT (Administrative Team) in the DO phase of the SPP. Where visionary LT SP Goals may be worked on for 4-5 years, SLs (Senior Leaders) design measurable Action Plans to be realized in 1-3 years. Upon determination of the SP Goals in the PLAN phase of the SPP, SLs work in AT Leadership Week to create SP Action Plans on a standardized template to best support the SP Goals. Once identified, Principals work with their building leadership teams (BLTs) to create School Improvement Plans (SIPs) to support the Teaching & Learning SP Goals.

2.2a.(2) To deploy the SP, in the DO phase of the SPP PSD develops Action Plans for each SP Goal (Figure 2.1-1). The AT drafts Action Plans to meet both ST and LT goals. Accountability is gained by publishing Action Plans in a gridded format that charts the steps to implement, delineation of responsibility, resource management, professional development needs and completion dates. Once the AT creates and grids these Action Plans, Principals work with their BLTs (Building Leadership Team) to design and deploy school-based Teaching & Learning Action Plans. Professional development time and PLC (Professional Learning Community) time throughout the school year is used to accomplish these plans. Similarly, the Non-Academic members of the AT work with their departments to deploy SP Action Plans. Deployment is monitored through AT quarterly review.

Figure 2.2-1 Key Planned Changes 2013-14 Impacting Workforce Capacity & Capability and Budget & Staffing	
SP Strategic Priority	**Key Changes**
Teaching & Learning	Science Curriculum Implementation (PD) Early Literacy & Personalized Math Expansion (Staff) Grading for Learning & RtI (PD)
Communication & Community Engagement	Orient parents to web site (Resource Time) Expand social media (PD) Increase partnerships & volunteers (Time)
Workforce Develop-ment & Engagement	Create Tool for Employee Compensation (PD) Track Professional Development (Time)
Technology	Technology Plan implementation in K-4; Google Expansion (Equipment Leasing)
Facilities & Operations	Energy Savings Plan (Resource Time/Equipment) Wellness Focus (PD)
Other Planned Changes	
Students	Growing resident enrollment
Market	Need to monitor OE #s Growing #s entering from private schools
Financial/Operational	Increase OE impacts budget; Implement heath & retirement benefit changes for cost effective-ness; Educator Effectiveness

CRITERIA QUESTIONS

In your response, include answers to the following questions:

a. Action Plan Development and Deployment

(1) **Action Plans** What are your key short- and longer-term action plans? What is their relationship to your strategic objectives? How do you develop your action plans?

(2) **Action Plan Implementation** How do you deploy your action plans? How do you deploy your action plans to your workforce and to key suppliers and partners, as appropriate, to ensure that you achieve your key strategic objectives? How do you ensure that you can sustain the key outcomes of your action plans?

(3) **Resource Allocation** How do you ensure that financial and other resources are available to support the achievement of your action plans while you meet current obligations? How do you allocate these resources to support the plans? How do you manage the risks associated with the plans to ensure your financial viability?

(4) **Workforce Plans** What are your key workforce plans to support your short- and longer-term strategic objectives and action plans? How do the plans address potential impacts on your workforce members and any potential changes in workforce capability and capacity needs?

(5) **Performance Measures** What key performance measures or indicators do you use to track the achievement and effectiveness of your action plans? How does your overall action plan measurement system reinforce organizational alignment?

(6) **Performance Projections** For these key performance measures or indicators, what are your performance projections for your short- and longer-term planning horizons? How does your projected performance on these measures or indicators compare with your projections of the performance of your competitors or comparable organizations and with key benchmarks, as appropriate? If there are gaps in performance against your competitors or comparable organizations, how do you address them?

Notes:

2.2. The development and deployment of your strategy and action plans are closely linked to other Criteria items. The following are examples of key linkages:
- Item 1.1: how your senior leaders set and communicate organizational direction
- Category 3: how you gather customer and market knowledge as input to your strategy and action plans and to use in deploying action plans
- Category 4: how you measure and analyze data and manage knowledge to support key information needs, support the development of strategy, provide an effective basis for performance measurements, and track progress on achieving strategic objectives and action plans
- Category 5: how you meet workforce capability and capacity needs, determine needs and design your workforce development and learning system, and implement workforce-related changes resulting from action plans
- Category 6: how you address changes to your work processes resulting from action plans
- Item 7.1: specific accomplishments relative to your organizational strategy and action plans

228

2.2a(2). Action plan implementation and deployment may require modifications in organizational structures and operating modes. Action plan success benefits from visible short-term wins as well as long-term actions.

2.2a(6). Measures and indicators of projected performance might include consideration of changes resulting from new ventures; organizational acquisitions or mergers; new value creation; market entry and shifts; new legislative mandates, legal requirements, or industry stands; and significant anticipated innovations in services and technology.

NIST (2015-2016) p. 12

WORKSHEETS

2.2a(1) - Action Plans

Key Strategic Objectives *	Related Action Plans		Stakeholder Impacted**	Progress Measures Area to Address 2.2a(5)	Process Used To Ensure The Action Plan Is Aligned Area to Address 2.2a(5)
	Long-Term	Short-Term			

*   See the Short- and Long-Term Strategic Objectives in 2.1b(1)
** Typical Stakeholder Codes: Customers = C; Suppliers = S; Community = CO; Employees = E;   Stockholder = SH

2.2a(2) Action Plan Implementation

Key Strategic Objectives *	Steps For Action Plan Development ** See Area To Address 2.2a(1)	Steps For Action Plan Deployment	Methods Or Steps To Sustain Key Changes From The Action Plans

*   See the Short- and Long-Term Strategic Objectives in Area To Address 2.1b(1)

* = If there are different approaches used for different levels of the organization, describe these differences. Also, describe any differences for the development of action plans at key suppliers or partners, as appropriate.

2.2a(3) Resource Allocation

Key Action Plans	Process To Assign Actual Resources Allocated To This Action Plan (People, Money, Time, Facilities, Etc.)	Process To Assess And Assign Financial And Other Risks To This Action Plan	Process To Ensure The Action Plan Has A Favorable Impact On The Financial Viability Of The Organization

2.2a(4) - Workforce Plans

Key Strategic Objectives*	Related Short- And Longer-Term Strategic Objectives And Action Plans*	Related Human Resource Plans	Related Impacts On Workforce Members And How They Are Addressed	How The Plans Address Changes In Workforce Needs For:	
				Capability	Capacity

* See the Short- and Long-Term Strategic Objectives in Area to Address 2.1b(1) or the Action Plans in Area to Address 2.2a(1)

2.2a(5) – Performance Measures

See Area to Address 2.2a(1) above for the measures and indicators and the objectives and plans they are aligned against.

How You Verify That The Action Plan Measurement System Reinforces Organizational Alignment	

2.2a(6) – Performance Projections

Performance Measures [From 2.2a(1) and 2.1a(5) Worksheets]	Short-Term Performance Projection	Long-Term Performance Projection	Comparison To Competitors Or Comparable Organizations	Comparison To Key Benchmarks, Goals, Or Past Performance

How The Short- and Longer-Term Performance Projections Were Determined:	

How You Will Ensure Progress So You Will Meet The Projections:	

How You Will Address Gaps In Performance vs. Competitors or Comparable Organizations:	

ASSESSMENT

Rating Scale:

1 - **No Process** in place – We are not doing this
2 - **Reacting to Problems** – We use a basic (primarily reactive) process
3 - **Systematic Process** – We use a systematic process that has been improved
4 - **Aligned** – We use a process that aligns our activities from top to bottom
5 - **Integrated** – We use a process that is integrated with other processes across the organization
6 - **Benchmark** – We are the Benchmark in our industry or beyond!
DK - Don't Know

33	The strategy is deployed down to actions at every level of the organization.	1 2 3 4 5 6 DK
34	Achievement of the action plans is tracked through goals and objectives which link from the organizational level all the way down to actions for every individual contributor.	1 2 3 4 5 6 DK
35	I know my role in achieving this year's organizational plan, and I have a way to track my progress at least monthly.	1 2 3 4 5 6 DK
36	We have a documented human resource plan which is derived from the short- and longer-term strategic objectives and action plans.	1 2 3 4 5 6 DK
37	Resources are systematically allocated to support the accomplishment of the action plans while meeting current obligations.	1 2 3 4 5 6 DK
38	In setting our long-term strategy, the competitors' performance is projected to ensure that we stay ahead of them in key performance measures.	1 2 3 4 5 6 DK
39	In setting our direction, key benchmarks, goals and past performance are analyzed and used.	1 2 3 4 5 6 DK
40	The strategy is used as a road map for the organization to guide decisions throughout the year.	1 2 3 4 5 6 DK

BLUEPRINT

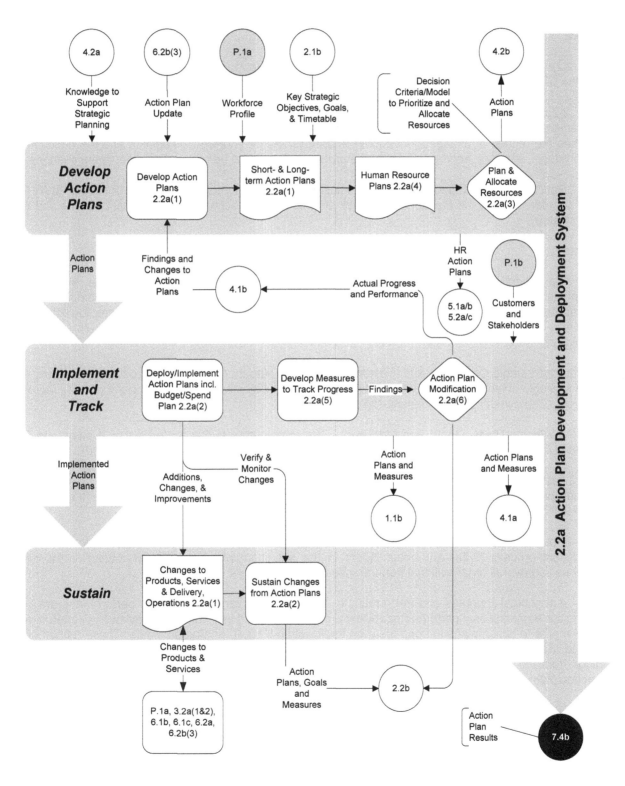

235

SYSTEM INTEGRATION

Context

P.1a > 2.2a Workforce Profile - The workforce profile is an important input to developing realistic action plans, the associated human resource plans, and deploying those action and human resource plans.

P.1a > 2.2a Change to Products and Services - Action plans often call for additions, changes, and improvement to products, services, and the processes that create them. In this case, the work system and processes are refined or changed to assist in accomplishing the strategic objectives and the description of the products, services, and operations in the profile (P.1a) should be refined to reflect these changes.

P.1b > 2.2a Customers and Stakeholders - The customers and stakeholders identified in the profile (P.1b) should be addressed by the measures that track progress toward accomplishing the action plans and the overall strategy.

Systems

1.1b < 2.2a Action Plans and Measures - In addition to the overall objectives and timeline, the specific action plans and measures described in 2.2a should drive the agenda for action in 1.1b. Creating a focus on action includes focusing on the right measures and their progress toward the strategic objectives to ensure they are on track and provide an opportunity to identify and address issues early before they are really big problems.

2.1b > 2.2a Strategic Objectives and Timetable - The key outputs of the strategy development process are the strategic objectives and associated timetable. These objectives end up being the primary input to the strategy deployment process described in 2.2a.

2.2a > 2.2b Action Plans, Goals, and Measures - The main output of this area are action plans and the associated measures which are used to determine performance projections described in 2.2b.

2.2a > 3.2a(1&2) Changes to Products and Services - The changes to products and services described in the action plans is an important input to the determination of product and service offerings and features described in 3.2a(1&2).

2.2a > 4.1a Action Plans and Measures - The action plans and measures determined in the action plan development process (2.2a) are direct inputs to the selection and alignment of measures for daily operations and overall organizational performance described in 4.1a.

2.2a <> 4.1b Actual Progress and Performance - Actual action plan progress and performance are key inputs to the organizational performance review process described in 4.1b. These reviews will often result in refinements to action plans to keep them on track, within budget, and on schedule. These refinements then find their way to the other plans including human resource plans as appropriate. In addition, the findings from the performance reviews described in 4.1b are key inputs to the revision or adjustment of the action plans described in 2.2a.

2.2a < 4.2a Knowledge to Support Strategic Planning - The knowledge transfer and availability system described in 4.2a should be designed to support the development of strategy and action plans described in 2.2a.

2.2a > 4.2b Action Plans - The action plans described in 2.2a will often contain improvements to the hardware and software systems described in 4.2b.

2.2a > 5.1a HR Action Plans - The Human Resource Plans are a key input to the recruitment of new employees with the right knowledge, skills, and abilities to support the new directions and specific changes detailed in the action plans. This helps to ensure that the hiring of new employees is focused on areas that are linked to the accomplishment of the overall strategy.

2.2a > 5.1b Action and HR Action Plans - The strategic action plans and associated human resource plans (2.2a) are a key input to the process of employee support and satisfaction (5.1b). These plans influence the segmentation of the workforce and the support services and benefits offered to employees along with the organization's policies.

2.2a > 5.2a HR Action Plans - The action plans and HR action plans developed in 2.2a are used by the employee performance management system to set expectations and provide feedback to employees on their contributions to the achievement of the action plans.

2.2a > 5.2c HR Action Plans - The strategy, action plans, and associated HR action plans also drive the workforce and leadership development efforts. The overall strategies are balanced with the needs of the individual to drive the development of both course content and the delivery methods.

2.2a > 6.1b Change to Products and Services - Action plans often call for additions, changes, and improvement to products and services, and the design of the key work processes that create them. In this case, the key work processes may need to be refined or redesigned to assist in accomplishing the strategic objectives.

2.2a > 6.1c Change to Products and Services - Action plans often include sustainability plans including those related to emergency readiness.

2.2a > 6.2a Change to Products and Services - The changes to products and services described in the action plans often require the work processes to be redesigned to support the changes.

2.2a > 6.2b(3) Changes to Products and Services - Action plans often drive the work process improvement agenda and help to focus the process improvement efforts 6.2b(3) on key issues important to achieving the overall organization strategy and action plans described in 2.2a.

2.2a < 6.2c Action Plan Update - Action plans described in 2.2a are updated based on the changes and results achieved through the work process improvement system described in 6.2c.

Scorecard

2.2a > 7.4b Action Plan Results - The results relating to progress toward achieving the action plans described in 2.2a and the associated changes in performance should be reported in 7.1c.

THOUGHTS FOR LEADERS

There is only one sustainable competitive advantage, and that is an organization's ability to learn and improve faster than its competitors.

Organizations which do not learn, do not survive. Some world-class companies that were top ten a hundred years ago quit improving, and they died. There is an old saying in the southern part of the United States, "If you're not rowing upstream, you're drifting down." There is no such thing as status quo — there is only improvement or deterioration.

Item 2.2 emphasizes this need for change and improvement. Not only do the strategic objectives need to be deployed down to detailed actions, but the actions need to keep the organization competitive.

After the actions are deployed, then the criteria essentially ask the question "If you implement these strategies and actions, how do you know you will still be competitive?" Answering this question requires leaders to understand the rate of change and improvement of their competitors and to ensure that their rate of improvement is greater than that of any competitor. Finally, actions need to be changed when the organizational performance or competitive position changes. This, typically, is during the year to maintain agility.

A Lighter Moment:

Though good may come of practice,
This primal truth endures,
The first time anything is done,
It is done by amateurs.

Art Buck

> *When you arrive at your future, will you blame your past?*
>
> **Robert Half**

 FOUNDATION

Action Plan Modification

Finally, this Area to Address asks how the organization aligns the overall action plans up to the strategic plan and how they are modified if circumstances require as shift in plans and rapid execution of new plans. Simply stated, the Criteria for Performance Excellence (CPE) are asking the organization to check the validity of the action plans and their ability to drive the achievement of the higher level organizational strategy, even if circumstances change.

In changing these action plans, everyone impacted must be included. This means suppliers, partners, collaborators, and others who's actions impact the organizational ability to meet their strategic objectives and action plans.

 EXAMPLES

PRO-TEC Coating Company (Baldrige Recipient 2007)

Past-to-future performance objectives for PRO-TEC are listed in Figure 2.1-3 for each action plan and a comparison or benchmark is provided on the corresponding result. "Best-in-class" benchmarks are established where appropriate to ensure continuous improvement is a core element of the strategic planning process. Their goals are linked to the Key Success Factors for the industry and the organizational Vision. This is linked to what the organization wants to Be, Have, and Do. The external Strategic Challenges are separated into Human Resource, Business, and Operational challenges. Finally, the action plans can be categorized as either short-term (Run the Business Short-Term – RST) or longer-term (Change the Business Long-Term – CLT). As can be seen from the example, some actions impact

both timeframes. Within the domestic steel industry, financial, operating, and quality performance are typically considered confidential and not shared. However, since the PRO-TEC quest is to be the unquestioned industry leader, PRO-TEC seeks appropriate best practices, comparisons, and benchmarks from the parent companies, industry data, Baldrige recipients, Baldrige/OPE (OPE - the quality award for Ohio) conferences, OPE recipients, and other industries to achieve breakthroughs.

Key Success Factor (KSF) Tied to Vision Statement		Strategic Challenges (P.2b) & Advantages (6.1a(1))	Action Plans ("Run the Business" Short Term [RST] & "Change-the-Business" Long Term [CLT])
KSF = Associate Quality of Life	**Vision:** a) Be – Totally committed to personal safety and wellness	**Human Resource Challenge:** Healthcare cost **Strategic Advantage:** Associates practicing ORA	**RST:** Improve recordable injury frequency (Figure 7.4a3-1)
			CLT: Achieve zero recordable injuries in year (10-year target)
			RST: Improve Wellness Program outreach
			RST/CLT: Implement Disease and Lifestyle Management Programs; in addition, continue to design and implement programs to control medical costs
	a) Have – A highly skilled, engaged workforce committed to ongoing performance excellence		**RST:** Improve Associate satisfaction survey results (Figure 7.4a1-1)
			RST: Conduct and support focused elective training for Associates
			CLT: Become a Malcolm Baldrige National Quality Award recipient (Figure 7.5a1.1)
KSF = Cust. Service	**Vision:** a) Do – Provide on-time delivery with world-class quality	**Operational Change:** Shift in auto. mfg. locations **Strategic Advantage:** Market leader in meeting/exceeding customer needs	**RST:** Manage supply chain mgmt. coated target inventory (Figure 7.1a1-10)
			RST/CLT: Achieve and maintain Automotive Group claim performance (Figure 7.2a1-5)
KSF = Techn. Innovation & Product Development	**Vision:** a) Be – Recognized as industry technology leader in both product and process	**Operational Challenge:** Changes in product mix **Strategic Advantage:** Innovative and reliable process and products	**RST:** Maintain overall internal diversion yield percentage (Figure 7.2a1-5)
			CLT: Increase value-added product development (Figures 7.1a1-2 & 7.1a1-5)
			CLT: Install $5.5 million induction preheater and continued review of heating and cooling constraints
			CLT: Not Available
KSF = System Reliability	**Vision:** a) Do – Develop/maintain world-class facility and business systems b) Have – Optimal utilization of production capacity and capability	**Operational Challenge:** 1) Sustaining world-class reliability 2) Information revolution **Strategic Advantage:** Innovative and reliable process and products	**RST:** Maintain operating ratio, CGL 1 & 2 (Figure 7.5a2-2)
			RST: Maintain internal finishing process efficiency (Figure 7.1a1-9)
			CLT: Installation of continuous shear capable of cutting AHSS
KSF = Good Citizenship	**Vision:** a) Do – Maintain high standard for community citizenship and service	– – –	**RST:** Utilize water recycling programs to maintain city water usage levels (Figure 7.5a1-8)
			CLT: Analyze, review, and if appropriate, make project recommendations to utilize raw water consumption
KSF = Long-Term Viability	**Vision:** a) Be – Consistently profitable b) Have – Valuable vendors/supplier relationship	**Business Challenge:** Competition/consolidation of steel industry	**RST:** Commit to repair and maintenance spending to ensure latest technology and reliability of facility (Figure 7.5a1-5)
			RST/CLT: Sustain return-on-assets ratio (ROA) (Figure 7.3a1-2)

PRO-TEC Targets

Measure	Measure Owner	Actual Performance FY 2006 YTD	Target FY 2007	Target FY 2009	Stakeholder
Recordable injuries/200K man-hours	S. Shartell	1.62	1.5	1.5	1,2,3,4,5,6
Health Risk Appraisal participation %	S. Shartell	50%	>=60%	>=75%	1,2,3,4
Programs implemented	B. Rosebrook/ S. Shartell	Selected Vendor	complete	ongoing	1,2,3
Average healthcare claim costs per Associate per month	B. Rosebrook/ S. Shartell	$477	$425	$450	1,2,3
Composite score	S. Shartell	3.15	3.05	3.20	1,2,3,4
Training man-hours	S. Shartell	2,069	1,840	2,320	1,2,3
Number of awards won	E. Franks	Site visit	1	1	1,2,3,4,5,6
% of inventory available on time	T. Smith	82%	>=90%	>=95%	1,2,3
Claims incurred (PPM parts/millions)	E. Franks	332 PPM	<750 PPM	<750 PPM	1,2,3
Internal diversion yield %	E. Franks	93.2%	94.0%	93.5%	1,2,3,4
Cumulative number of products developed	E. Franks	9	10	11	1,2,3,5
Equipment installation timeline	J. Stechschulte	Project approved	Complete	Ongoing review and monitoring	1,2,3
Project status	Project team	Project identified	Engineering & cost analysis	2010 to 2012 startup	1,2,3,4,5,6
Operation ratio%	J. Stechshulte	97.9% & 97.7%	97.5% & 97.5%	97.5% & 97.5%	1,2,3
Number of days to complete	P. Nuveman	5.2	<=4.5	<=4.5	1,2,3
Equipment installation timeline	J. Stechshulte	Project approved	Complete	Ongoing review and monitoring	1,2,3
Gallons of water/ton of steel	R. Rupert	64.73 gal./ton	<=65 gal./ton	<= 65 gal./ton	1,2,3,4,5,6
Project status	R. Rupter/ B. Rosebrook	Project identified	Planning study	Project complete	1,2,3,4,5,6
PP&S spending $/ton	B. Rosebrook	Not Available	Not Available	Not Available	1,2,3,4,5,6
Return-on-asset ratio%	B. Rosebrook	Not Available	Not Available	Not Available	1,2,3,4,5,6

STAKEHOLDER KEY: 1 – Customer, 2 = Owners, 3 = Associates, 4 = Suppliers, 5 = Community, 6 = Public

Bronson Methodist Hospital (Baldrige Recipient 2005)

Bronson Methodist Hospital uses a table / matrix format to show their strategic objectives, linked and aligned with their action plans, as do many other organizations. Their matrix includes the headings of Strategies & Strategic Challenges; Short Term Objectives; Long Term Goals; Key Tactics & Action Plans; Changes; Human Resource & Education Plans; Key Performance Measures; Past Performance Results; Performance Projections; and Projected Comparisons. The performance projections clearly link with the objectives, and are cross-referenced to the results in Category 7. Source – Bronson (2006) p. 8

Strategies & Strategic Challenges	ST Objectives	Lt Goals	Key Tactics & Action Plans	Changes	Hr & Education Plans	Key Performance Measures	Past Perf. 2004 Results
CE: Archive excellent patient outcomes 5C1 5C2	Medicare mortality at top 15%, Recognized by Leapfrog as safe environment, Exceed national standards for core indicators	Top 100 hospital, 5 stars for targeted areas, Third party recognition for patient safety	Decrease Ventilator Associated Pneumonia, Optimize Medicare Mortality & morbidity, Optimize core Indicator Performance, Build Computerized Physician Order Entry, Optimize Communication Among providers	Hospitalists admitting ortho patients. Medical management for adult patients w/ chronic diabetes & Heart Failure.	Situation-Background-Assessment-Recommend. education. Fill Computerized Physician Order Entry team positions.	Medicare morality	7.1-2
						Ventilator Associated Pneumonia	7.1-11
						Patient falls	7.1-12
						Skin ulcers	7.1-13
						Surgical Infection Prevention	7.1-10
						Core measures (AMI, HF, pneumonia)	7.1-7, 7.1-8, 7.1-9
						Hand washing	7.5-6
CASE: Enhance service excellence, staff competency, and leadership 5C3 5C4 5C5	Magnet status, Leader in MD satisfaction, Overall turnover & vacancy better than national best practice, Employee Opinion Survey diversity scores improve, Patient satisfaction scores improve from benchmark	Best practice customer & MD satisfaction, 100 Best Employer, Maintain Magnet status	Implement Respiratory care development program, Implement mentor program, Operationalize Diversity Council, Implement Employee Opinion Survey and Listening Post Monitoring System, Physical surroundings & discharge process recommendations	Gallup survey with national benchmarks. Campus expansion project moves some support services off campus.	Respiratory care development candidates. Mentor program education. Diversity education plan.	Vacancy	7.4-3
						Employee Opinion Survey diversity score	7.4-19
						MD satisfaction	7.5-12 to 7.5-14
						Patient satisfaction	7.2-1 to 7-2.12
						Pat. Sat. w/physical surroundings	7.2-7
						Pat. Sat. w/discharge	7.2-4
						Overall turnover RN turnover	7.4-1 7.4-2
CORE: Achieve efficiency, growth, financial and community benefit targets 5C6 5C7	Meet growth targets for targeted service lines, Profit margin	X marketshare in targeted services, Profit margin, Baldrige recipient	Implement long-term campus expansion plan, Implement short-term technology/facility plan, Recruit key physician specialists	MD ambulatory surgery and outpatient diagnostics centers. Expansion of adult medical unit capacity.	Realign campus project leadership. "Change management" training for move. Hire staff for new capacity. Train on new technology.	Service Line marketshare	7.3-14
						SL marketshare	7.3-14
						SL marketshare	7.3-16
						SL marketshare	7.3-14
						Profit margin	7.3-1

Legend: 5C1 – Application of evidence-based medicine, 5C2 – Meet needs of growing number of patients with complex conditions, 5C3 – Workforce shortage, 5C4 – Diversity, 5C5 – Customer Service, 5C6 – Capacity, 5C7 – Profitability, BP – best practice.

Chugach School District (CSD) (Baldrige Recipient 2001)

Chugach's key stretch goals and targets are based upon competitive comparisons, state standards and Baldrige Winners best practices. The indicators show key measure projections aligned to strategic objectives. Dues to innovative, visionary goals, it is difficult to make comparisons to other organizations. Changes resulting from Chugach Instructional Model (CIM) delivery, standards-based reporting, Carnegie waiver, Student Learning Profile (SLP), and other innovations have proven resoundingly successful for the students. CSD's Key Performance Indicators (KPIs) are, at times, solely established by CSD, thus creating a lack of benchmarking opportunities.

	2001	2002	2003	2004	2005	KPI
Longer-term Goal:	- Benchmark Continuous Improvement System	- PDER overlay Shared Action Plan Consistent Deployment Accurate Evaluation Proactive Refinement				7.1- 7.5
Basic Skills	- Increase reading comprehension - Math Training	- Refine reading & math - Refine writing targets	- Refine targets & assessments - Peer mentoring	- Web format for data collecting - Refine reporting documents	- Evaluate web format student performance	7.1
Transition Skills	- Refine transition program - Communication plan	- Mentor other districts in transition - Refine AH phases	- Create business certification for students	- Secure additional resources - Increase partnerships	- Follow-up longitudinal study - Communications system	7.2
Character Development	- Support local plans - Refine P/S/H	- Refine Plans Community meetings	- Provide teacher training - Update P/S/H	- Community/ parent training	- Refine P/S/H standards & assessments	7.4
Individual Needs	- SLP Training - Database Tracking	- Refine SLP & Diploma	- Benchmark testing waiver	- Refine ILP process	- Independent opportunities	7.1
Technology	- Wireless - Internet Access	- Increase bandwidth - Implement CASTS	- Web CASTS - Video conferencing	- Online training	- Web based learning tools implemented	7.5

Source: Chugach (2002) p. 90

CRITERIA QUESTIONS

In your response, include answers to the following questions:

b. Action Plan Modification

How do you establish and implement modified action plans if circumstances require a shift in plans and rapid execution of new plans?

Notes:

2.2b. Organizational agility requires the ability to adapt to changing circumstances, both internal and external.

NIST (2015-2016) p. 12

WORKSHEETS

2.2b - Action Plan Modification

Criteria To Determine An Action Plan Requires Modification	Steps For Action Plan Modification	Steps To Deploy Modified Action Plans	Methods Or Steps To Validate Effectiveness And To Sustain Changes
1	1	1	1
2	2	2	2
3	3	3	3
4	4	4	4
5	5	5	5
n	n	n	n

ASSESSMENT

Rating Scale:

1 - **No Process** in place – We are not doing this
2 - **Reacting to Problems** – We use a basic (primarily reactive) process
3 - **Systematic Process** – We use a systematic process that has been improved
4 - **Aligned** – We use a process that aligns our activities from top to bottom
5 - **Integrated** – We use a process that is integrated with other processes across the organization
6 - **Benchmark** – We are the Benchmark in our industry or beyond!
DK - Don't Know

41   Action plans are systematically modified if circumstances require a shift in plans and rapid execution of new plans.   1   2   3   4   5   6   DK

BLUEPRINT

2.2b Action Plan Modification

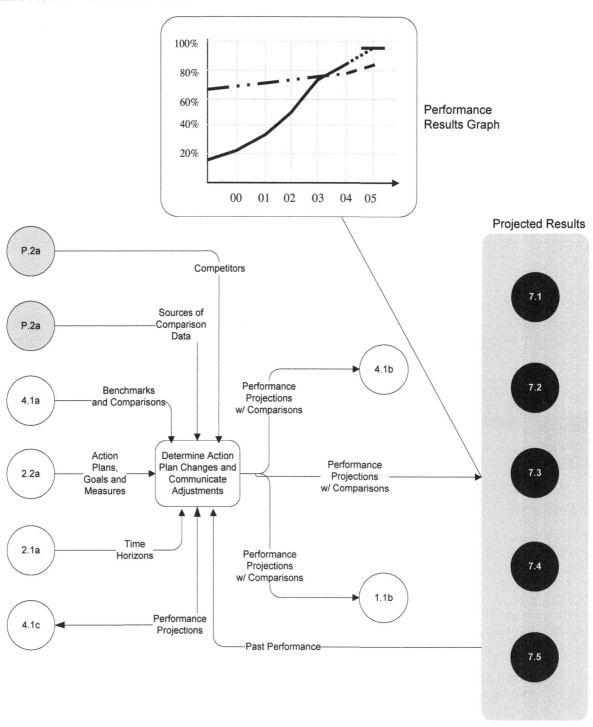

SYSTEM INTEGRATION

Context

P.2a > 2.2b Competitors - The competitors identified in the organizational profile (P.2a) are key inputs to determining the appropriate comparisons to include with the performance projections in 2.2b.

P.2a > 2.2b Sources of Comparative Data - The sources of comparison data described in the organizational profile (P.2a) will drive the types of comparisons that are available for inclusion with the performance projections described in 2.2b.

Systems

1.1b <> 2.2b Performance Projections and Comparisons - The performance projections, comparisons, and targets that are identified in 2.2b should also help drive the agenda for action in 1.1b. This allows the leaders to track the progress from the perspective of changes in the performance of the organization compared to targets and comparisons.

2.1a > 2.2b Time Horizons - The short- and long-term time horizons determined and used during strategy development (2.1a) are also used when determining short- and long-term performance projections in 2.2b.

2.2a > 2.2b Action Plans, Goals, and Measures - The main output of this area are action plans and the associated measures which are used to determine performance projections described in 2.2b.

2.2b < 4.1a Benchmarks and Comparisons - The benchmarks and comparisons used in 2.2b for projections should be consistent with those identified by the processes described in 4.1a.

2.2b > 4.1b Performance Projections with Comparisons - Part of the analysis provided by 4.1b to support strategic planning includes comparisons (e.g., competitive, benchmark, industry). The projections and comparisons determined in 2.2b are key inputs to the analysis described in 4.1b.

2.2b > 4.1c Performance Projections here in 2.2b and 4.1c Performance Improvement System inform and are inputs to each other.

Scorecard

2.2b > 7.1 thru 7.5 Performance Projections and Comparisons - The forecasted performance (projections) along with the projected comparison performance should be reflected in the results charts depicted in 7.1 through 7.5. While the CPE specifically ask for strategic plan accomplishments in Area to Address 7.1c, the ideal strategic plan will have projections for measures in all five results Items.

THOUGHTS FOR LEADERS

A CPE score may or may not be a good indicator of the organization's culture. For example, two 400-point companies may be quite different. One 400-point company may have a solid culture, an established framework, solid values, a customer focus, processes which are being developed and implemented, and a promising future. This company is a 400-point company that soon will be a 500-point company and beyond.

Another 400-point company may have gotten there by forcing processes onto people and by forcing the integration of the business to its customers. This company is never going to go much further beyond 400-points unless it can implement some fundamental changes and truly become process driven. It is always disappointing to see an organization reaching for performance excellence without having laid a proper foundation. These organizations cannot get much further and are stuck in-place year after year.

On the other hand, an organization with a CPE score of 650 points will to have a solid customer-focused and process driven culture! A 650-point organization has taken care of customers, employees, and processes, and their results are repeatable.

Key to this growth in excellence is the ability to plan, deploy the plan, and make modifications quickly as the circumstances change. High performing organizations can change action plans quickly and effectively. One of the best examples of this is the US Army. The Army has a saying "No battle plan survives contact with the enemy." This means you plan, plan, plan, and the minute reality hits you must adjust.

A Lighter Moment:

> *Never before has the future so rapidly become the past.*
>
> **Arnold Glasow**

> *You can't just ask customers what they want and then try to give that to them.*
> *By the time you get it built, they'll want something new.*
>
> **Steve Jobs**

 FOUNDATION

This Area to Address focuses on how the organization listens to customers to understand their needs, wants and desires to inform the development and improvement of products and services.

Listening to Current Customers

In the Organizational Profile (P.1b[2]) the Criteria for Performance Excellence (CPE) ask who the customer groups are and their requirements. These customer requirements should be segmented by customer group (how we group our customers based on their requirements – See 3.2a[3]), target customer segments (how we group our customers based on how we sell to them), or market segments (how the industry or marketplace groups customers or product offerings), as appropriate. Area to Address 3.2a asks how the organization systematically (through the process and criteria) determines the customer segments.

Within each of these segments, it is important to have an appropriate range of listening posts (both formal and informal). These need to be current enough to give the organization an understanding of what can cause marketplace damage in time to fix the problem before the damage actually occurs. In the 2011 – 2012 criteria the concept of use of social media and Web-based technologies was introduced to help to ensure that the information is easy for the customer to provide, and is timely. Throughout the 2013 – 2014 criteria the use of social media is strengthened.

These listening posts may vary for each of the customer groups, and across each stage of the customer life cycle, as a customer (or potential customer) moves through the following life cycle chain:

- Not knowing about the organization;
- Knowing about the organization;
- Trying the organization;
- Liking the organization;
- Being loyal to the organization; and
- Being an advocate for the organization.

Once this listening is gathered, the key is how quickly and effectively are the appropriate actions formulated, taken, verified, and improved.

Listening to Potential Customers

This same cycle of listening, planning and action needs to be taken for former customers, potential customers, and customers of competitors. In all cases the key is actionable information and the ability to measure the effectiveness of the actions taken.

Once the organization describes how information is gathered from the listening and learning techniques (Area to Address 3.1a) the question becomes "how is the information analyzed to determine, modify, or anticipate changes in customer needs for those product offerings." This includes analysis of data from current customers, potential customers, future customers, and customers of competitors.

As with other Areas to Address in Category 3, the organization should consider the customer needs during the life cycle of the customer. Although not stated, it is logical to assume that the organization also needs to understand the customer's needs during the product and service life cycles as well. This is particularly true for durable products. For example, our local coffee shop would not need to survey the customers to understand the customers' needs at the beginning, middle and end of drinking a cup of coffee. An automotive manufacturer, however, needs to understand the customer's needs (and maintenance and support requirements) during the various phases of a car's life.

From this analysis, how does the organization become more customer-focused (some organizations use the term customer-centric)? Simply stated, if the organization truly understands what drives customers' purchase behaviors, they can compete more effectively in the marketplace than if they do not have that understanding.

EXAMPLES

Don Chalmers Ford (Baldrige Site Visit 2008 and 2012)

DCF listens to current customer groups and market segments through established listening methods (Figure 3.1-1). The collection and analysis of feedback from these listening methods provides DCF with actionable information for determining customer satisfaction, making work system and work process improvements, creating marketing campaigns, and developing future business opportunities.

Both at the dealership and in the community, DCF engages current and potential customers to obtain information about their key requirements, expectations, and desires. It is through face-to-face communication that DCF's presence in the community is consistently reinforced as one of the key reasons people choose DCF over the competition. FMC's refusal of the government bailout is also a consistent topic of discussion and pride for DCF. Through e-mails, text messages, customer letters, and DCF websites, the dealership is able to gather actionable information from customers. DCF provides an opportunity in every e-mail sent for the customer to provide suggestions. Each piece of correspondence clearly states that the dealership values their feedback and thanks them for being a DCF customer. Also, a "Contact Us" option is available on each DCF website.

QuickTouch is a third-party follow-up service provided through FMC that DCF uses for NVS and M&R customers. Customers are contacted via e-mail for feedback. If they are not reached, QuickTouch contacts customers via phone to ensure the sales or service experience met the customer's expectations. NADA 24 is a third-party company that contacts Body Repair customers via phone to gain their feedback. The Customer Viewpoint (CVP) survey, administered through FMC via customer provided e-mail address or conventional mail, that collects NVS and M&R customer feedback. An internally generated postcard is mailed to UVS customers to gather their feedback after purchase. Through the use of consumer review sites such as DealerRater.com, DCF is able to gather additional actionable information from customers. This information is posted publicly, so potential customers and customers of competitors can use this information to influence their decisions for or against being a DCF patron.

DCF utilizes social media and web-based technologies to engage customers at all stages of the customer life cycle. Through such mediums as Facebook, Twitter, blogs, and donchalmersford.com, DCF encourages a two-way dialog with customers. DCF subscribes to the 4:1 Reciprocity Rule: providing content that customers feel is useful and beneficial four times before asking for anything in return. Example: DCF posts to Facebook and Twitter links on maintaining vehicle health, tips for improving gas mileage, ticket giveaways to upcoming community events, and the latest in vehicle technological advances before posting the latest service special. DCF uses social media dashboards such as HootSuite to monitor each of the social media platforms for customer interactions so they are best able to respond to customers in a timely manner. DCF also monitors the Internet via hashtags, such as Ford + Albuquerque and Don Chalmers Ford, for mentions of the organization so it can listen and respond to conversations happening outside the usual channels. Using the Work Process Design and Innovation and FORD (improvement) processes, the SLT discusses actionable information in the leadership and planning meetings, and other meetings. Listening methods are used to obtain actionable information throughout the customer life cycle.

DCF's sales and service follow-up processes and surveys also supply actionable information. Concerns voiced by customers provide opportunities to integrate improved services to meet customers' changing requirements and expectations. DCF's SLT and appropriate managers review the information for trends that indicate areas for improvement or to celebrate those areas that demonstrate good performance.

Two-way, face-to-face communication with customers provides critical information to align customers' purchasing and relationship needs. Example: with the increase in gas prices, customers have asked for better gas mileage vehicles. DCF has little influence over new vehicle availability, but can buy more used vehicles to meet this changing expectation.

DCF listens to former and potential customers and customers of competitors for feedback on products and services, customer support, and transactions mainly through social media and face-to-face conversations gleaned through community involvement (Figure 3.1-1). Example: a cycle of improvement for the service department was to add levels of oil change offerings. DCF had offered only one type of oil change, but after listening to the needs of the community, DCF decided to provide three different levels of oil change: Good, Better, Best – all still priced less than the competition and offering a greater value, but with differing options. DCF's "Best" level oil change offers the re-refined "green" oil, and the dealership is a close-looped provider recycling all of its oil using the Safety-Kleen service. In 2012, DCF has seen a 10% increase in oil changes per day.

DCF Listening Posts

Listening Method	Current Customers				Other Customer Types			Stakeholders			
	Sales		Service		F	P	C of C	WF	Co	FMC	S
	Market Segments										
	NVS	UVS	M&R	BR							
Face-to-face	X	X	X	X	X	X	X	X	X	X	X
Electronic (e-mail, web, text)	X	X	X	X	X			X	X	X	X
QuickTouch	X		X								
NADA 24				X							
CVP survey	X		X								
Postcard		X			X	X	X		X		
Consumer review sites	X	X	X		X						
Social media	X	X	X	X	X	X	X	X	X	X	X
Community events	X	X	X	X	X	X	X		X		
F = Former, P = Potential, C of C = Customers of Competitors											

Sharp Healthcare (Baldrige Recipient 2007)

The Sharp Experience's customer focus facilitates an infrastructure of training and mentoring Sharp's Leaders to use a wide range of methodically selected listening and learning tools. These tools empower employees to identify needs, expectations, and preferences of former, current, and potential customers/partners at the system, entity, department, and individual level. The resulting data drives strategic planning, organizational goal setting, product development, health care/business process redesign, technology selections, and consumer marketing.

Sharp Listening and Learning Tools

Listening and Learning Tools (Including Processes)	Frequency	Primary Users	Target Use
Former and Current Patients and Families			
Press Ganey Patient Satisfaction Surveys for inpatient, outpatient, emergency, urgent care, inpatient and outpatient rehab, home health, hospice, skilled nursing, inpatient and outpatient behavioral health, ambulatory surgery, outpatient oncology, and physician office visits. (7.2)	Real-time surveys sent monthly	Hospital and Medical Group, PFS, Managers, Staff	Process Improvement
Primary/Secondary Market Research. (Including focus groups, mystery shopping, predictive health care segmentation) Secondary data: OSHPD, Solucient, JCAHO. Primary data are collected by Sharp agents and employees via interviews (available for analysis at any time).	Annually, Quarterly, Ad Hoc	Strategic Planning and Business Development, System Marketing	Planning Services, Marketing
Encounter and Enrollment Data. Data from ambulatory, inpatient, and outpatient electronic records are uploaded to the CRM database. (7.2)	Monthly	Finance, IT, System Marketing, Business Dev	Business/Planning Services
Customer Contact Centers (82-Sharp, Sharp Nurse ConnectionÒ, Web Center). Call Center and Web Center data are uploaded monthly into the CRM database. Demographic are collected for target marketing and campaign effectiveness measurement. (7.5)	Monthly	Call Center, Web Center, System Marketing	Planning Services, Marketing
Rounding with Reason/Rounding Logs. Managers are trained and are accountable via performance standards, action plans, Accountability Grids, and Rounding Logs submitted to their supervisor. Information is shared at LDS and Employee Forums or Communication Expos.	Ongoing	Leaders	Process Improvement
Comment Cards and Interdepartmental Surveys. Data are aggregated by unit managers and shared at staff meetings.	Ongoing	Leaders, Staff	Process Improvement
Complaint System and Informal Feedback. Most complaints are responded to immediately at point-of-service with empowered staff performing service recovery. Information is shared at unit meetings. Data are rolled up across the system for trending and action. (7.2)	Ongoing	Leaders	Planning Services, Process Improvement
Selected Patient Follow-up Calls. Post-discharge and post-office visit telephone calls are made to assess outcomes and satisfaction.	Ongoing	Leaders, Staff	Process Improvement
SHP Member Surveys. Consumer Assessment Health Plan Surveys are mailed to a random sample of members to assess member satisfaction and needs. Brokers and employer groups are surveyed at varying intervals. (7.2)	Annually	Operations, Call and Operations Center, SHP Leaders, Quality/Risk Management, SHP Staff	Planning Services, Marketing, Process Improvement
Potential Patients and Future Markets			
Primary/Secondary Market Research (quantitative/qualitative/predictive health care segmentation). Sharp applies the Household View™ life-stage segmentation system and other research methods when planning marketing campaigns. Primary data are collected by Sharp employees and agents via interviews.	Annually and focused, Ongoing	System Marketing, Business Development, Sharp Leaders	Business/Planning Services

Listening and Learning Tools (Including Processes)	Frequency	Primary Users	Target Use
Customer Contact Centers (82-Sharp, Sharp Nurse Connection, Web Center). Data are uploaded monthly into the CRM database. (7.5)	Ongoing	Call/Web Center, System Marketing	Business/Planning Services
Brokers/Payors. Who contract with employers for employee health care coverage. (7.2)	Ongoing	SHP Leaders	Business/Planning Services

Sharp collaborates with health plans and brokers to determine key customer requirements. For example, Sharp worked with PacifiCare to develop the Secure Horizons Value Plan featuring benefits that was of greatest value to seniors from focus group research. Sharp also evaluates managed care membership retention/loss data to discover reasons patients disenroll from Sharp's medical groups and develop strategies to counter those issues. Employees are provided data, training, and tools to respond to customer/partner likes, needs, desires, and complaints with prescribed process improvement tools, service recovery methods, service experience mapping and design, and new product/service development. At LDS, leaders learn to analyze patient/customer satisfaction data, develop and implement process improvement initiatives, hardwire service and experience elements, and develop new product and service offerings. Additionally, innovative strategies to attract and retain customers are shared for implementation across the system. Sharp uses marketing methods tailored to the diverse needs of customer segments served by Sharp, including language, gender, age, race, and disease-specific needs. Sharp differentiates its services from competitors by responding to patient contact requirements, such as allowing patients to pay their bill online, requesting an appointment online, and providing same day and next day access.

Charleston Area Medical Center (The Partnership For Excellence Recipient 2014)

We listen to, interact with and observe (Figure 3.1-1) patients and other customers to obtain actionable information through a wide range of quantitative and qualitative listening posts (Figure 3.1-2 - the rows) that are distinct for all patient segments and other customer groups (Figure 3.1-2 - the columns). These are tailored to obtain feedback through all stages of the customer relationship (Figure 3.1-2 - Types of Patients and Figure 3.2-3). To ensure that data are actionable, each listening post (Figure 3.1- 2 - the rows) is assigned an owner who is responsible for the analysis (Figure 3.1-1). In a cycle of learning, we established the Service Excellence Team (SET) that is tasked to be the central repository for all VOC information and to systematically ensure actionable data for improvement (for each patient group/column).

The SET meets monthly to address key issues that affect customer service through (cultural and operational) action teams. Listening post owners conduct assessments of VOC data to identify the top issues that impact customer satisfaction and engagement which are further aggregated at the SET for development of patient experience improvement plans (Figure 3.1-1). Service improvement plans are cascaded to appropriate departments via our deployment process (Figure 2.2-2). VOC processes are also deployed through our key work processes (Figure 6.1- 1) at multiple touch points. Several listening posts ensure immediate action such as hourly rounding, leadership and executive rounding. We use social media and web-based technology to listen to and address customer concerns in real time. Our marketing team receives alerts via email and Smartphone apps when CAMC keywords are used in online venues. Compliments or complaints posted are reviewed at least hourly. When a posting requires follow-up, our marketing team responds by email or phone call to address the feedback.

Responses requiring multiple inputs are routed to the appropriate individual as part of the escalation process [3.2b(2)]. The effectiveness of social media campaigns are evaluated monthly and annually to ensure that information is accessible and messaging approaches are tailored to key customer requirements (Figure 3.1-1). Figure 3.2-3 and Figure 3.1-2 (Types of Patients) show how our listening post mechanisms vary across the stages of our customer relationships. To seek immediate and actionable feedback, we have multiple mechanisms (Figure 3.2-1) to proactively follow-up with patients and other customers on the quality of healthcare services, support and transactions including rounding, social media, post-discharge calls (Cipher Health) and a 24/7 Helpline.

In a cycle of learning, the SET developed a standardized approach to systematically evaluate the effectiveness of each listening post for capturing emerging and changing customer requirements (Figure 3.1-1). As a result of this process, we established a Customer Touchpoint Committee that integrates our VOC methods with our key work processes [preadmission/ admission, treatment, discharge and post discharge (Figure 6.1-1)] allowing us to further understand key patient and customer requirements at each of these key touch points. This enables us to enhance the overall experience and exceed patient and customer expectations. Our listening posts integrate operationally and strategically with our customer communication response process (Figure 3.1-1). If products or services require change (as described in 3.2a[1]), this is determined through the Analyze phase and is an input to Step and the SPP.

Listening to Potential Patients and Other Customers. Actionable information and feedback on healthcare services, support and transactions from former, potential and competitors' patients and other customers are obtained through formal and informal listening posts (Figure 3.1-2). The SET aggregates and analyzes data for improvement with the same approach and deployment process described in 3.1a(1). CAMC also conducts an annual Image and Awareness Survey to determine respondents' overall perception of CAMC and other competing area hospitals on a series of attributes including preferences for hospital choice, types of care (i.e. heart care) and top of mind awareness. Our participation in Hospital Consumer Assessment of Healthcare Providers and Systems (HCAHPS) enables us to benchmark against competitor hospitals on a broad spectrum of factors affecting the quality of services and support.

Figure 3.1-2 Patient/Stakeholder VOC Listening and Learning Posts

Key Work Processes	Listening & Learning Methods	Segments			Types of Patients				Stakeholders		
		IP	OP	ED	Current	Former	Potential	Patients of Competitors	Community	Physicians	Payors
PD	HCAHPS/CAHPS	x	x			x					
PD	Satisfaction Surveys		x	x		x				x	
A,T,D	Rounding	x	x	x	x		x		x	x	
A,T,D	Helpline	x	x	x	x	x			x		
P,PD	Health Fairs		x			x	x	x	x	x	
A,T	Quantros/Complaint	x	x	x	x	x		X		x	
P,PD	Physician Advisory Council						x	x	x	x	x
P,PD	KCCHI					x	x	x	x	x	x
P,PD	Image Awareness Survey				x	x	x	x	x	x	x
PD	Post -Discharge Calls/Cipher Health	x	x			x					
P,A,D,PD,T	CAMC Website, Social Media	x	x	x	x	x	x	x	x	x	x
P,PD	Partners in Health					x	x	x	x	x	x
P,A	Transfer Center	x	x	x	x		x	x		x	x
P,A	Community Liaisons				x	x	x	x	x	x	x
P,A,D,PD,T	Workforce	x	x	x	x	x	x	x			
Additional listening posts shown in Figure 3.2-3											
P=Preadmission, **A**=Admission, **T**=Treatment, **D**=Discharge, **PD**=Post-Discharge											

Pewaukee School District (Baldrige Recipient 2013)

As part of our Communication Plan (CP), PSD (Pewaukee School District) employs multiple stakeholder listening approaches to obtain actionable information to improve educational programs, offerings and services using a wide variety of direct, print, and technology tools depending on stakeholder segment (Figure 3.1-1). So data received becomes actionable, we utilize the PDSA (Plan, Do, Study, Act) process (Figure 3.1-2) and integrate findings to inform SP Action Plans. This key work is orchestrated by our Public Information Coordinator (PIC), a valued resource for a district our small size. Benchmarks indicate that only 5% of school districts have a dedicated communications specialist. SLs (Senior Leaders) have always valued strong engagement with our stakeholders and supported in in our SP. Because of this, SP Action Plans created this PSD position and the PIC guides its work.

While rich VOC information is sought & attained by direct communication and stakeholder participation in our SPP and conversation on campus, we deploy annual parent, employee, and student satisfaction surveys to obtain Voice of Customer (VOC) data. In place for over twelve years, these 20+ question surveys are our key tool to inform the SP and guide continuous improvement efforts. Survey questions obtain satisfaction and dissatisfaction data concerning engagement, service, safety, communication, and quality with segmented responses from end-of-year surveys analyzed annually by SLs and Data Review Teams.

District trends are determined and, if necessary, opportunities for improvement are integrated into SP Action Plans. Findings are presented annually to the BOE in CIRs as well as with all staff and parents. Cycles of learning are rich, incorporating form, content and deployment improvements including a move to technology deployment. Annually surveys are AC reviewed for question improvement. End-of-year surveys impact program & service improvement. As example, student survey responses prompted creation of SP Action Plans to address student respect; anti-bulling efforts that resulted have positively influenced school culture and integrated systematic reporting processes between schools. Focus groups and on-going meetings are also a vital approach to obtain VOC input.

Students' and parents' VOC input are gleaned directly in the curriculum renewal process. Parents were recently involved in updating our Human Growth & Development curriculum and students in creation of our Technology Plan. Additionally, Principals use PTO & Parent Advisory Groups to give them a pulse on parent perceptions of school operations. Segmented focus groups are also used to listen and learn from Title I, TAG, and Special Education parents. Key vendors also meet monthly with the CFO so we can respond with agility to issues or concerns. In addition to citizen input on each BOE meeting agenda, SLs meet regularly in community with the PTO, Booster Club, Chamber of Commerce, local government, and area school leaders. Principals and the Athletics/Activities Director meet regularly with student groups such as Student Council and Leadership Club to obtain student input, so students have a stronger voice in programming. Students and parents serve on interview committees for administrative hires. To add authentic voice, all teacher applicants teach a lesson and we obtain student feedback to inform our hiring decisions. When considering a major SP initiative, specialized VOC feedback is sought.

When considering the addition of Four Year Old Kindergarten (4K) program, a non-mandated program, we deployed a parent survey and learned that 88% of respondents expressed support of 4K. Thus, 4K planning was integrated in our SP and implemented the following year. In a cycle of learning, SP Communication Action Plans expanded to leverage social media, offering another vehicle to engage and listen to stakeholders. Customer engagement via social media now includes Facebook, Twitter, video sites, and blogs for online newspaper articles. In fall 2010, a successful referendum vote to renovate and add PSD facilities showed a spike in stakeholders accessing information via Facebook the day prior to the vote. Three referendum videos strategically placed on our web site, viewed through Vimeo, were viewed over 19,000 times.

The use of Google Alerts is valuable to monitor daily media and social commentary concerning PSD. A SP Action Plan prompted PSD to leverage the use of technology to obtain VOC input from identified segments. Multiple approaches now enhance our process:

258

- use of a web site suggestion box
- Survey Monkey, an online survey tool, to deploy stakeholder surveys
- Family Access integrating online technology to facilitate expedient, fact-based communication from parent to faculty regarding grades, absences, discipline or outstanding bills
- School Fusion accounts allow parents to track information on their child's homework, class assignments, and blogs

Predominantly, we learn from our students daily via our classroom assessments and instructional strategies. As we are data-driven, student behavioral and achievement data is used to guide teacher instruction and create interventions to assist students learn. In some classrooms we are using new student response systems designed to give teachers immediate feedback concerning a classes' understanding of content being learned. This tool prompts agility as the teacher can quickly assess the entire class to ascertain which students need more assistance to learn.

SLs conduct observations as part of our PES to obtain information on the quality of classroom instruction. Recently, goals were set regarding student and teacher use of technology based on classroom observations. Listening methods for students change depending on relationship stage. We listen to prospective students in a more individualized manner, often one-on-one or via informational school open houses. Current students on our campus daily are listened to using a wide variety of formal & informal listening methods, but when students become alumni we use primarily social media to obtain actionable information from this group.

Method	Stakeholder	Frequency	Internal Use of Data
Figure 3.1-1 Key Listening & Learning Methods			
Direct Communication			
Focus Group	S, P, C	O	SL, S, E, I
Classroom Obs.	S	O	SL, E, I
Parent Conferences	P	Q	SL, C
Strategic Plan Participation	All	A	SL, S, E, I
BOE Meetings	S, P, C, PC	2xM	C, I, S
PAGs	P	O	SL, S, E, C, I
Curriculum Comm.	S, P, C	O	SL, I
Hiring Committees	S, P, C	O	SL
Vendor Meetings	SU	M	S, E, I
Student Council, Leadership Club	S	O	SL, C
Open Houses	FS	A	S
Chamber Meetings	C	M	S, SL
Annual Meeting	C	A	S
Print			
Assessment/Tests	S	O	SL
Newsletters	C, PC	3xY	S, E, C
Correspondence	All	O	C
Higher Ed. Reports	P		SL
Technology			
Web site	All	O	S, C,
Surveys	S, A, P, C	A	SL, S, E, I
Suggestion Box	S, P, C, SU	O	C
Family Access/ School Fusion	P, S	O	SL, C
Facebook, Twitter	S, A, P, C	O	C
Telephone	All	O	SL, S, E, C
Registration	S, P	A	SL, E
E-mail	All	O	SL, S, E, C, I
Stakeholders: S=Student, P=Parent, C=Community, A=Alumni, PC=Partners/Collaborators, FS=Future Students **Frequency:** O=Ongoing, Q=Quarterly, A=Annually, M-Monthly, x=times, Y=Year **Use:** SL=Improve Student Learning, S=Improve Service, E=Improve Efficiency, C=Resolve Complaint or Individual Concern, I=Enhance Innovation			

CRITERIA QUESTIONS

In your response, include answers to the following questions:

a. Customer Listening

(1) **Current Customers** How do you listen to, interact with, and observe customers to obtain action-able information? How do your listening methods vary for different customers, customer groups, or market segments? How do you use social media and Web-based technologies to listen to customers, as appropriate? How do your listening methods vary across the customer life cycle? How do you seek immediate and actionable feedback from customers on the quality of products, customer support, and transactions?

(2) **Potential Customers** How do you listen potential customers to obtain actionable information? How do you listen to former customers, potential customers, and competitors' customers to obtain actionable information on your products, customer support, and transactions, as appropriate?

Notes:

3.1. The "voice of the customer" refers to your process for capturing customer-related information. Voice-of-the-customer processes are intended to be proactive and continuously innovative so that they capture stated, unstated, and anticipated customer requirements, expectations, and desires. The goal is customer engagement. In listening to the voice of the customer, you might gather and integrate various types of customer data, such as survey data, focus group findings, blog comments and data from other social media, warranty data, marketing and sales information, and complaint data that affect customers' purchasing and engagement decisions.

3.1. For additional considerations on the products and business of nonprofit organizations, see the notes to P.1a(1) and P.2b.

3.1a(1). Social media and Web-based technologies are a growing mode of gaining insight into how customers perceive all aspects of your involvement with them. Listening through social media may include monitoring comments on social media outlets you moderate on those you do not control, such as wikis, online forums, and blogs other than your own.

3.1a(1). The customer life cycle begins in the product concept or pre-sale period and continues through all stages of your involvement with the customer. These stages might include relationship building, the active business relationship, and an exit strategy, as appropriate.

NIST (2015-2016) p. 13

WORKSHEETS

3.1a(1) – Current Customers

Customer, Customer Group or Market Segment (Same As Shown In P1b[2])	Listening/Learning Method (Or Process) Used To Determine Key Customer Requirements, Needs, and Changing Expectations For Each Group (Including Product and Service Features)*	Analysis (Approach) Used To Ensure The Listening Results In Immediate And Actionable Information**	Approaches to Keep Listening/Learning Method Current

* Include the specific approaches to listening, including surveys, social media and Web-based technologies

** This could include feedback on the quality of products, customer support and transactions

Customer Life Cycle Stage (Such As Prospect, Current, Mature, Key, etc.)	Listening Methods Used During This Life Cycle Stage	Approaches to Using Information From Current and Former Customers*

* This Can Include Marketing and Sales Information, Customer Loyalty and Retention Data, Customer Referrals, Win/Loss Analysis, and Complaint Data For Purposes Of Planning As Shown In The Table Below.

3.1a(1) – Listening To Current Customers (Continued)

Process For Post Transaction Follow-Up For The Quality Of Products, Customer Support And Transactions				
Post Transaction Follow-up Process Step (In Sequence)*	Who Is Involved	How The Step Is Measured	Timing Of The Step	Immediate Actions Taken Based On The Feedback
1				
2				
n				

* This could include feedback on the quality of products, customer support and transactions

3.1a(2) – Listening To Potential Customers

List The Types Of Former Customers	• • • • • •
How You Determine The Requirements Of Former Customers	
How You Include Former Customers In Your Customer and Market Knowledge and Resulting Actions	

Note: The above processes should include feedback on your products, services, customer support, and transactions.

List The Types Of Potential Customers	• • • • • •

How You Determine The Requirements Of Potential Customers	

How You Include Potential Customers In Your Customer and Market Knowledge and Resulting Actions	

Note: The above processes should include feedback on your products, services, customer support, and transactions.

List The Types Of Customers of Competitors	• • • • • •

How You Determine The Requirements Of Customers of Competitors	

How You Include Customer of Competitors In Your Customer and Market Knowledge and Resulting Actions	

Note: The above processes should include feedback on your products, services, customer support, and transactions.

ASSESSMENT

42	There are systematic ways to listen to each customer group to obtain feedback on products, services and customer support. Where necessary these are tailored to the customer groups or market segments.	1　2　3　4　5　6　DK
43	There is a systematic method to follow-up with customers after they use our products or services. Their feedback can be used to drive the necessary improvements.	1　2　3　4　5　6　DK
44	There is a systematic approach to listen to former customers, potential customers, and customers of competitors to obtain actionable information.	1　2　3　4　5　6　DK

BLUEPRINT

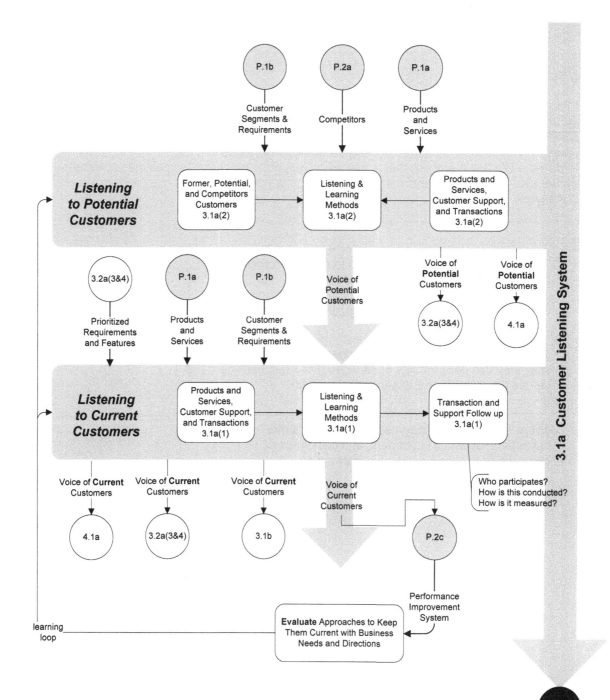

SYSTEM INTEGRATION

Context

P.1a > 3.1a Products and Services - Customer listening and learning methods should be designed to include specific feedback on the products and services described in the profile (P.1a).

P.1b > 3.1a Customers Segments and Requirements - The listening and learning methods described in 3.1a should address the customer segments, groups, etc. identified in the profile (P.1b).

P.2a > 3.1a Competitors - The customers of the competitors identified in the profile (P.2a) are an input to the listening and learning processes and practices described in 3.1a. The listening and learning processes not only address current customers but also those of the competitors identified in the profile (P.2a).

P.2c > 3.1a Performance Improvement System - The improvement activities to evaluate and keep the approaches to listening and learning and the aggregation and analysis of complaints current with changing business needs and directions should be consistent with and based on the performance improvement approaches described in the profile (P.2c).

Systems

3.1a > 3.1b Voice of the Customer - Listening to the customers' perceptions of their experiences using the products, services, transactions, key access mechanisms to seek information, conduct business, and complain, are key elements in the overall customer experience and should therefore be included in the customer satisfaction determination processes described in 3.1b.

3.1a < 3.2a(3&4) Prioritized Requirements and Features - Customer requirements and expectations by customer segment are often identified through the analysis of data as described in 3.2a(3&4). These requirements and expectations for each key customer and market segment are an important input to the design and implementation of the listening and learning methods described in 3.1a.

3.1a > 3.2a(3&4) Voice of the Customer - The voice of the current and potential customers derived from the listening and learning methods described in 3.1a are key inputs to the analysis of customer requirements and their relative importance to purchase decisions described in 3.2a(3&4).

3.1a > 4.1a Voice of Current and Potential Customers – Methods and Mechanisms to capture the voice of the customer are a key input to 4.1a(3) the selection and use of VOC data and information.

Scorecard

3.2a > 7.1a, 7.2 Aggregated Complaints - Complaints that are captured, aggregated and analyzed are part of customer dissatisfaction and should be included by segment in the results in area 7.2a.

THOUGHTS FOR LEADERS

One of the areas where the CPE uses approaches which can be both "formal and informal," is in external customer listening posts which include complaints. For example, formal complaints are received when a customer uses the formal complaint process. Informal complaints might be received by the organization in a different way, such as a customer walking by and mentioning a concern to an employee. Low performing organizations may ignore these types of informal complaints or may not have many complaints. They have either made it so diffiicult for the customer to complain that it is not worth it or they have ignored complaints for so long that customers know it is futile to complain. Either case is a failure of leadership. High-performing organizations accept customer input (complaints or compliments) in any way they can, both formal and informal. If anybody in the organization hears a comment from a customer, everybody in the organization has access to that information. Even informal complaints should be entered into the company database to be accessible to all appropriate employees.

When the CPE use the terms *formal* and *informal* (for areas such as complaints), some organizations may translate these terms to indicate what is documented or not documented. However, many high performing organizations feel that effectively translating some of the more informal characteristics of the business into organizational documentation will allow a company to become more competitive once the complaints are addressed.

A Lighter Moment:

Orthodox medicine has not found an answer to your complaint.
However, luckily for you, I happen to be a quack.

Richter cartoon caption

> *There is only one boss. The customer. And he can fire everybody in the company from the chairman on down, simply by spending his money somewhere else.*
>
> **Sam Walton**

 FOUNDATION

Once the organization has developed its overall relationship with the customer, segmented the customers and determined their needs and expectations, the CPE ask how the organization knows whether customers are satisfied, loyal and engaged. This means do the organization's customers value what the organization does enough to come back over and over, help the organization get better, and be an advocate for the organization and their products and services?

There is an understanding in the CPE community that satisfied customers may or may not return to buy products and services. Loyal customers, however, do return to repurchase products and services, hence the term *loyalty*. Finally, engaged customers have an investment in or commitment to the organization's brand and product and service offerings, and are willing to take their time to help.

In the final analysis, the CPE are trying to understand whether the organization can correlate its actions (through the organization's processes) to what the customer values, what the customer will pay for, and ultimately to the customers' behavior.

Satisfaction, Dissatisfaction, and Engagement

The CPE asks how the organization determines their customers' satisfaction, engagement (loyalty) and dissatisfaction. These determination methods can (and often should) vary for different customers and different customer groups. Organizations segment customers because they have different needs and requirements. The CPE ask how an organization knows if they are exceeding customer requirements (customer results data for this should be reported in Item 7.1) — another way to drive customer loyalty — and if they are able to "secure their future business" (customer engagement (loyalty) reported in Area to Address 7.2a[2]).

Another part of the CPE asks for a description of the organization's relationship with the customer after providing products, services, or transactions (Area to Address 3.2). The classic example of this type of relationship is one where an employee contacts the customer by phone after the product or service is delivered in order to understand the customer's satisfaction with the overall transaction as well as their initial satisfaction with the product or service. Today, social media is helping organizations accomplish this task.

Satisfaction Relative to Competitors

The CPE stretches the organization by asking how they obtain or use information about their customer satisfaction relative to the customer satisfaction of competitors or industry benchmarks. In some industries, this knowledge is difficult, if not impossible to gather. For example, in some governmental customer relationships (supplying to public sector customers), it is illegal to obtain and to have this information. In this instance there is no expectation that the organization would attempt to gather the information.

The CPE do not expect an organization to perform any action that is not 100% honest and ethical. Nevertheless, some organizations have not considered benchmarking sources that can help them compare their performance to other high performing groups. For example, organizations can ask customers how the organization ranks with their other suppliers. Even if the customers will not disclose which of their suppliers perform at which levels, they may still reveal where the organization in question ranks in the pack.

Finally, in the past the CPE asked how the organization kept the survey methods, contact methods, or customer satisfactions and dissatisfaction methods current. Although not as clearly stated in the current criteria, this is still a valid question. How do you know when the customer is tired of your surveys and how do you respond by updating your customer satisfaction processes?

Dissatisfaction

The CPE seek to understand how the organization determines customer dissatisfaction. This needs to be done early enough to capture actionable information which can prevent the loss of a customer. The actions taken should improve the organization's ability to meet or exceed the customer's current and future requirements.

It should be noted that low customer satisfaction is not the same as dissatisfaction. Dissatisfaction is an overt condition where the customer complains, or asks the organization to take action to correct a condition the customer does not feel should continue.

EXAMPLES

PRO-TEC Coating Company (Baldrige Recipient 2007)

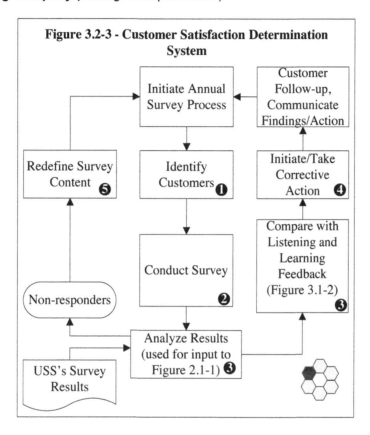

Figure 3.2-3 - Customer Satisfaction Determination System

Although customer satisfaction determination is among the direct responsibilities of the US Steel (USS) Marketing and Sales group, PRO-TEC elects to conduct its own customer satisfaction surveys as well. As Figure 3.2-3 illustrates, this annual survey process identifies the major customers accounting for over 90% of our customer base❶.

Surveys are conducted shortly after the close of the prior calendar year❷. Survey results from USS and PRO-TEC are analyzed by comparing customer responses to data collected through our listening and learning methods to identify new concerns❸. Based on the status of the concern, a formal corrective action may be initiated following the process described in Figure 3.2-3❹. The surveys' comments (or lack thereof) and the response rates are used as a means to determine whether the survey content should be redefined in order to enhance the value of the customer satisfaction survey process❺.

271

Sharp Healthcare (Baldrige Recipient 2007)

The Processes used to determine patient and other customer satisfaction and dissatisfaction are described in Figure 3.2-2. Generally, patient satisfaction surveys are mailed to patients one week after hospital discharge or physician visit. Several service-specific types of patient satisfaction surveys are used across Sharp and respondent comments are shared across the system.

Mean scores and percentile rankings are posted monthly on Sharp's "Patient Satisfaction" Intranet site and Press Ganey's Internet site. Sharp's Intranet site enables employees to view monthly survey results and trend data for the prior four years, and to conduct custom analyses by drilling down by key customer groups, age, gender, payor mix, and unit. Staff is trained through various mechanisms using consistent behaviors and practices to provide a quality experience for every patient, every time. Continuous measurement and report analysis allows the opportunity to revise education, process, and implementation.

A process flow for patient/customer satisfaction is available onsite. Patient comments are shared frequently at staff meetings and used as mechanisms for reward and recognition, as well as learning tools for improvement. Press Ganey's detailed quarterly reports feature key drivers of patient satisfaction through a correlation analysis. The resulting Priority Index identifies actionable areas that have a strong impact on overall satisfaction and areas that are low scoring. This index allows leaders and staff to know exactly where to focus improved service efforts. This priority index is commonly used in development of 90-day Action Plans, which are aligned by Pillar.

To further understand patient needs, Sharp employs focus groups and other tools. Corporate marketing staff conduct and analyze focus group findings on behalf of departments or entities. Marketing staff also employ mystery shopping (e.g., "first impressions audits" and "sensory assessments") to further identify areas for performance improvement. On a more personal and immediate basis, leaders frequently visit with staff, patients, and patient families through Rounding. Every fall, physician partners are surveyed to determine their needs, wants, and sensitivities, and to measure satisfaction with their experience at Sharp. Press Ganey conducts the physician satisfaction survey, and the results are compared with those of 290 other Press Ganey clients (7.2). Survey results are shared in a timely manner throughout the system.

Each manager is held accountable for reviewing department level survey results with his/her staff, developing an action plan based on the survey results, and improving scores. In addition to a robust patient/customer satisfaction and dissatisfaction assessment process, Sharp is dedicated to gaining learning from patients and staff at numerous touch points throughout the relationship continuum. All 1,300 Sharp leaders have received in-depth training on the practice of Rounding. This practice ensures that, on a daily basis, leaders are connecting both with patients and staff to exceed expectations. Sharp hospitals and facilities also employ the use of rapid feedback comment cards, post-discharge patient phone calls, Web site comments, patient interactions, telephone-based clinical outcomes tracking, and 1:1 consultation with risk management for difficult issues.

Through Press Ganey, Sharp compares its patient and physician satisfaction scores to almost 1,500 facilities nationwide and almost 290 medical practices. Sharp commissioned The Jackson Organization to conduct consumer awareness, perception and utilization research to learn about top-of-mind awareness, perception, and utilization of Sharp and other health care organizations in San Diego County. Additionally, the survey investigated consumers' provider preferences for health care delivery. Sharp obtains benchmark satisfaction data from other sources, such as the National HealthView Plus Survey, which focuses on health care attitudes, preferences, and how people make health care decisions. This study includes more than 22,000 households.

	Patients	Physicians	Employers, Brokers, Payors	Key Community Segments
Key Business Strategy	Increase overall market share across profitable service lines	Recruit and retain affiliated physicians	Increase referrals from brokers and retain employer clients	Increase overall market share and utilization across profitable service lines
Key Marketing Strategy	Increase physician-referral transactions	Achieve target physician satisfaction score	Maintain and enhance broker and employer relations	Sharp.com, 82-Sharp, Call Center, Sharp Nurse Connection®
Listening and Learning Methods	Press Ganey patient satisfaction survey, comment cards, mystery shopping and feedback from rounding logs, 82-Sharp calls, and email via Sharp.com	Press Ganey physician satisfaction survey and Annual All-Staff Assembly	Interactive meetings, issues/feedback, surveys, Sharp.com content survey and informal polling	Community-based interactions, focus groups, evaluations, community forums, and awareness, perception and utilization research
Satisfaction/Dissatisfaction Metrics	Press Ganey patient satisfaction mean score and percentile ranking, reduce dissatisfiers	Physician satisfaction mean score and percentile ranking, reduce dissatisfiers	Attendance at broker meetings, hits to Sharp.com, and payor feedback on written survey	Awareness, perception, and utilization scores, Press Ganey Survey and focus group results, and 82-Sharp usage.
How Deployed	Surveys mailed after service counters	Surveys mailed to physicians during the months of July and August each year	Broker reception, two small broker meetings, surveys, and 1:1 informal polling	Awareness, perception, and utilization research fielded by phone, Sharp leader reports on community activities

Patient and Other Customer Satisfaction and Loyalty Processes

Several methods are used to ensure Sharp's agility in determining customer/partner satisfaction:

- Patient satisfaction survey forms are evaluated internally at least annually to ensure content is appropriate, up-to-date, and useful. The Patient Satisfaction and Measurement Action Teams participate in this review process.
- Press Ganey conducts extensive factor analyses annually to assess reliability and validity of survey questions.
- Sharp benchmarks against other organizations, such as Press Ganey's national database and local competitors (assessed through awareness/perception/utilization research).
- Best practice research is used, including literature reviews, industry consultants, conferences, seminars, and onsite visits.
- Sharp uses HCAHPS, the CMS patient satisfaction survey, which was launched in California in 2006.

Sharp devotes an Intranet site entirely to patient satisfaction. Source: Sharp Healthcare

Charleston Area Medical Center (The Partnership For Excellence Recipient 2014)

We listen to, interact with and observe (Figure 3.1-1) patients and other customers to obtain actionable Patient and other customer satisfaction and engagement are systematically determined (Figure 3.1-3) using VOC inputs and the survey process. We identify our key customer segments and their requirements (shown in Figure P.1-4) to validate, through an analysis which aggregates the qualitative and quantitative data, if we are asking the most important questions in our surveys as well as to differentiate our determination methods for all customers. Each patient segment (Figure 3.1-2 - the columns) has customized survey instruments such as HCAHPS (the primary quantitative assessment for inpatients), outpatient and ED surveys. HCAHPS consists of nationally standardized survey questions.

Results are reported on a weekly basis via email to all leaders with composite and individual department scores for each hospital for analysis in comparison to organizational targets and national benchmarks . Understanding the top issues that are key drivers for satisfaction/dissatisfaction and aligning these requirements within our key work processes (each of which is owned, managed and improved) enables us to capture actionable information in order to exceed their expectations and secure their engagement with us for the long-term.

Results from our post discharge calls (Cipher Health) are aggregated through a dashboard (LINCs) that provides comparisons of post discharge surveys to HCAHPS results, trend analysis, control charts and action items. Nursing callbacks provide further analysis of problems identified for each patient experience and enable a targeted performance improvement approach and focus on areas with significant statistical correlations in driving positive change. Single point lessons (SPL) are utilized to standardize processes and help spread best practices throughout the organization. There are multiple tracking and monitoring systems at all levels of the organization to assess the effectiveness of practice improvements such as:

- Unit-specific action items posted on TCT inpatient unit Top 5 Boards for increased transparency and shared accountability.

- SET reviews results and progress on action plan deployment monthly.

- AAs and VPs conduct weekly rounding to sign-off on progress made on Action Item Lists.

- HCAHPS results are reviewed at the department level by managers during staff meetings.

- Individual performance assessments incorporate measures for achievement of customer satisfaction targets and standards of customer service behaviors.

- Improvements include refinements to the satisfaction and engagement determination process itself.

For example, we have made refinements to the Cipher Health post-discharge calls by revising a question to increase the degree of correlation with HCAHPS and changed our callback process to focus on respondents who gave us a "good" rating because our data analysis shows this as an area of opportunity. Satisfaction and engagement information integration occurs through use of BIG DOT measures as part of the SPP; with key work systems and process design (Figure 6.1-2) to help consistently exceed key customer requirements; providing input and feedback on products and services; and with the WF Learning Development System (Figure 5.2-3) to identify future training needs or refine existing course offerings to reinforce a service excellence culture.

Figure 3.1-3 Customer Satisfaction/Dissatisfaction and Engagement Determination System (Survey Process)

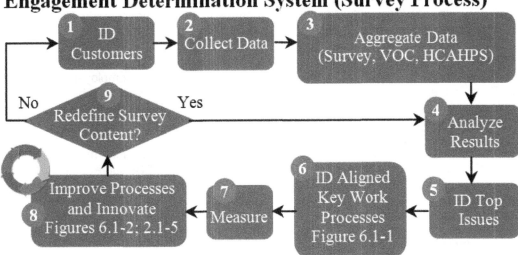

Monfort College of Business (Baldrige Recipient 2004)

3.2b(1) MCB uses several methods to gather information to determine student and stakeholder satisfaction, including the EBI Undergraduate Business Exit Study, the EBI Faculty Survey, the EBI Alumni Survey, the MCB student survey, the MCB employer survey, and MCB evaluations administered to students at the conclusion of each course. The EBI student instrument, administered to graduating seniors, provides a measure of overall satisfaction as well as other perceptual measures including quality of teaching, quality of teaching in major courses, accessibility of instructors, breadth of curriculum, global perspective, practitioner interaction, practical experiences, technology, classroom quality, and size of enrollment (Figures 7.2-1 to 7.2-12, 14, 17, 18).

While the EBI student survey is an assessment geared toward graduating seniors, the MCB student survey and course evaluations assess student attitudes at all levels. Student satisfaction with extracurricular activities (e.g., student clubs) is assessed through surveys, faculty advisors, and the SRC.

The EBI faculty satisfaction data are segmented by department and faculty rank. Alumni surveys are segmented by year graduated and by major. The data retrieved from these surveys constitute key inputs in the PDCA process used by the governance committees (Figure 6.1-1). Data are reviewed by the committees, which then make appropriate decisions and recommendations for improvement. Examples of recent decisions based on satisfaction data include the hiring of a director of technology because of decreasing satisfaction with some aspects of technology, and the FAC reviewing instructional evaluation procedures because of decreasing faculty satisfaction in that area.

CS conducts a survey of graduates to assess their employment and the extent to which the instructional program met their educational goals (Figure 7.5-6). High placement rates also provide some indication of employer satisfaction levels.

3.2b(2) One avenue for student feedback regarding programs, services, and offerings is through MCB's SRC. In addition to the SRC, ongoing surveys provide some measure of follow-up. Letters to parents encourage feedback, and MCB newsletters provide ongoing information. Any student complaints result in timely responses and feedback through the appropriate administrative channel.

3.2b(3) EBI surveys (student, faculty, and alumni) have benchmarks, with a national sample, as well as a group of peer schools selected by MCB. The College governance committees have access to trend and comparative data with which to work. AACSB salary surveys are also benchmarked to other institutions which are segmented in such a way for comparisons to be made to similar schools for similar faculty positions.

A PDCA review identified a need to obtain more information from the employer stakeholder group. Although EBI is in the process of developing such a survey, it is not yet available. As a result, MCB recently introduced its own employer survey to improve the quality of formal feedback until EBI's instrument becomes available.

3.2b(4) MCB uses both internal and external evaluation and improvement methods of keeping its satisfaction determination approaches current. Externally, the use of EBI surveys helps MCB maintain currency in surveying and benchmarking. EBI's guiding principle is continuous improvement, and its staff keeps current with national trends to determine what new aspects should be included in its surveys, while still providing MCB with the ability to do trend analyses. Internally, MCB assesses its needs for satisfaction data and determines how to address opportunities for improvement through the PDCA (Figure 6.1-1) processes used by the governance structure. The check step would evaluate the environment for changes and would also review any revisions of the strategic plan. This information helps to determine if changes in satisfaction determination methods are necessary. For example, MCB needed information from employers as an input in its processes. MCB is working with EBI to be a pilot school for an employer survey, but with the EBI timeline being uncertain, MCB has developed its own employer survey to use until EBI develops its instrument. Also, MCB has the ability to add customized questions to the EBI survey for internal use.

MCB also assesses the latest trends through faculty involvement in professional organizations and keeping current with research in the area. AACSB provides a means of keeping current through periodic workshops and seminars that are attended by the deans, as well as a number of faculty.

Source: Monfort (2005)

Pewaukee School District (Baldrige Recipient 2013)

PSD (Pewaukee School District) uses multiple approaches to determine student and stakeholder satisfaction through a process deployed to reach key market segments (Figure 3.1-3). Annual end-of year surveys referenced in 3.1a.(1) are a cornerstone of our data-driven approach to determine satisfaction. They provide insight to student and parent satisfaction of criteria determined by the AT (Administrative Team) and based on indicators of successful schools as identified by Gallup: communication, engagement, service, safety, and quality.

Survey results are available on site with key results presented in Figure 7.2-2 through 7.2-8. Surveying is also conducted for other strategic purposes: learning what new athletic/extracurricular programs students desire; curriculum review; food service; sport/coach satisfaction by parent & student. In a cycle of refinement, SLs (Senior Leaders) use Survey Monkey to efficiently tabulate data for analysis by the AT and Data Review Teams. In a further cycle of improvement, to increase participation these surveys are deployed via School Messenger to home emails with the survey link embedded.

State identified key indicators of student engagement (dropout rates, truancy rates, and attendance rate) are reported in our School Performance Report (SPR) and are benchmarked against county, State, and national comparables (Figures 7.2-9-11). Engagement is also measured by student and stakeholder volunteering (Figure 7.2-12-13) and partner donations (Figure 7.2–14). As part of a strategic effort to determine support for a possible referendum, the PSD community was surveyed 3 times from 2008 to 2010 to guide bond question design and project scope. Survey results prompted PSD to restructure the referendum ballot questions. On November 2, 2010, PSD posed the largest referendum on that day in our State, and it was widely approved. Strategic engagement was key in gaining community support and referenda passage. To thank our community, an open house was held in our new facilities in 2012 and over 1,500 community members attended.

Figure 3.1-3 Satisfaction Determination Process		
Segment	**Satisfaction Determination Approaches**	**Use of Data**
Students 4K-3	In-person	EE, SI, C
Students 4-6	In-person, survey	EE, SI, C
Students 7-8	In-person, survey, email,	EE, SI, C
Students 9-12	Email, in-person, survey	EE, SI, C
Parents	Email, phone, letter, in-person, survey	EE, IE, SI, C
Community	Email, phone, letter, in-person, survey, tax levy vote	EE, IE, SI, C
Alumni	Email, phone, letter, in-person, survey	EE, IE, SI, C
EE=Exceed student and stakeholder expectations, IE=initiate engagement, SI=system improvement; C=used to obtain comparative data		

CRITERIA QUESTIONS

In your response, include answers to the following questions:

b. Determination of Customer Satisfaction and Engagement

(1) **Satisfaction, Dissatisfaction, and Engagement** How do you determine customer satisfaction, dissatisfaction, and engagement? How do your determination methods differ among your customer groups and market segments, as appropriate? How do your measurements capture actionable information to use in exceeding your customers' expectations and securing your customers' engagement for the long term?

(2) **Satisfaction Relative to Competitors** How do you obtain information on your customers' satisfaction with your organization relative to other organizations? How do you obtain information on your customers' satisfaction:
- relative to their satisfaction with your competitors and
- relative to the satisfaction of customers of other organizations that provide similar products or to industry benchmarks, as appropriate?

Notes:

3.1b. You might use any or all of the following to determine customer satisfaction and dissatisfaction: surveys, formal and informal feedback, customer account histories, complaints, field reports, win/loss analysis, customer referral rates, and transaction completion rates. You might gather information on the Web, through personal contact or a third party, or by mail. Determining customer dissatisfaction should be seen as more than reviewing low customer satisfaction scores. Dissatisfaction should be independently determined to identify root causes and enable a systematic remedy to avoid future dissatisfaction.

3.1b(2). Information you obtain on relative customer satisfaction may involve comparisons with competitors, comparisons with other organizations that deliver similar products in a non-competitive marketplace, or comparisons obtained through trade or other organizations. Information obtained on relative customer satisfaction may also involve determining why customers chose your competitors over you.

NIST (2015-2016) pp. 13-14

WORKSHEETS

3.1b(1) – Satisfaction, Dissatisfaction, and Engagement

Customer Segment Or Group (Same As Above and in Area to Address P.1b[2])	How You Determine Satisfaction And Engagement	How You Determine The Importance Of Customer Requirements To The Customer's Purchasing Or Relationship Decisions	How You Measure Your Actions Toward Exceeding Customer Expectations And Securing Long-Term Customer Engagement

Note: This Can Include Marketing and Sales Information, Customer Loyalty and Retention Data, Customer Referrals, Win/Loss Analysis, and Complaint Data For Purposes Of Planning As Shown In The Table Below.

Customer Dissatisfaction		
Your Process Steps To Determine Customer Dissatisfaction	Measurements Used To Capture Actionable Information:	
	For Use In Meeting Customer Requirements (In The Future)	For Use In Exceeding Customer Expectations (In The Future)

3.1b(2) – Satisfaction Relative To Competitors

Customer Segment Or Group (Same As Above)	How You Obtain And Use Information On Your Customer's Satisfaction:	
	Relative To Their Satisfaction With Your Competitors	**Relative To The Satisfaction Levels Of Levels Of Organizations Providing Similar Products (Or Relative Industry Benchmarks)**

ASSESSMENT

Rating Scale:

1 - **No Process** in place – We are not doing this
2 - **Reacting to Problems** – We use a basic (primarily reactive) process
3 - **Systematic Process** – We use a systematic process that has been improved
4 - **Aligned** – We use a process that aligns our activities from top to bottom
5 - **Integrated** – We use a process that is integrated with other processes across the organization
6 - **Benchmark** – We are the Benchmark in our industry or beyond!
DK - Don't Know

45	There is a systematic process for determining the elements critical to customer satisfaction, and the information is used to exceed external customer expectations.	1	2	3	4	5	6	DK
46	There is a systematic process for assessing customer satisfaction, loyalty, and engagement.	1	2	3	4	5	6	DK
47	Customer satisfaction data are actionable and drive specific and clearly aligned actions to correct the source of customer complaints or dissatisfaction.	1	2	3	4	5	6	DK
48	The organization compares our customer's satisfaction/ dissatisfaction with leading organizations and our competitors.	1	2	3	4	5	6	DK

BLUEPRINT

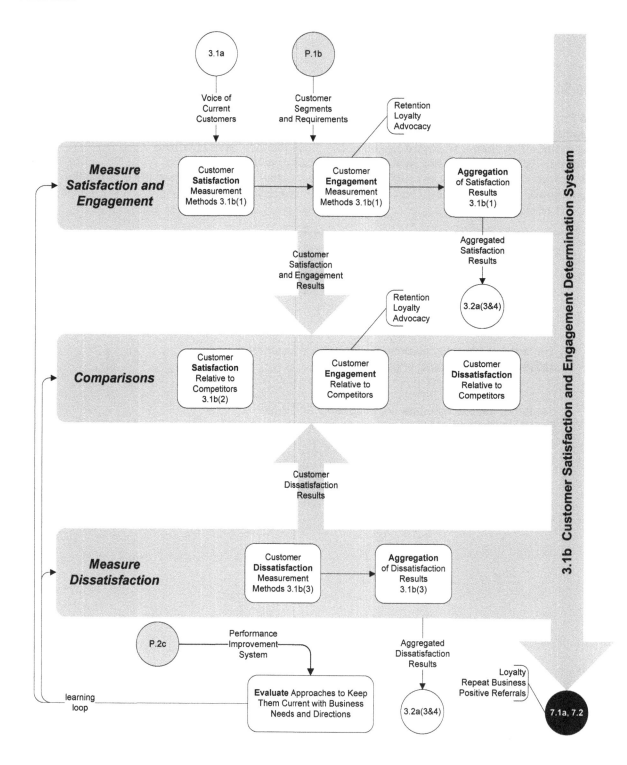

SYSTEM INTEGRATION

Context

P.1b > 3.1b Customers Segments and Requirements - The customer satisfaction determination processes should be designed to capture the satisfaction of the key customer and market segments and groups identified in the profile (P.1b). In addition, the mechanisms used to capture this information should also include the ability to capture the demographics of the segmentation scheme as described in P.1b and in 3.2a(3).

P.2c > 3.1b Performance Improvement System - The performance improvement system described in the profile (P.2c) should be a key input to the methods used to evaluate and keep the approaches to determining customer satisfaction and engagement current with changing business needs and directions.

Systems

3.1a > 3.1b Voice of the Customer - Listening to the customers' perceptions of their experiences using the products, services, transactions, key access mechanisms to seek information, conduct business, and complain, are key elements in the overall customer experience and should therefore be included in the customer satisfaction determination processes described in 3.1b.

3.1b > 3.2a(3&4) Aggregated Satisfaction Results - The measurement of customer satisfaction produces aggregated satisfaction results which are key inputs to the analysis and use of customer data to identify the customers' requirements and their relative importance to the purchase decision 3.2a(3&4).

3.1b > 3.2a(3&4) Aggregated Dissatisfaction Results - The measurement of customer dissatisfaction produces aggregated dissatisfaction results which are key inputs to the analysis and use of customer data to identify the customers' requirements and their relative importance to the purchase decision 3.2a(3&4).

Scorecard

3.1b > 7.1a, 7.2 Customer Satisfaction and Dissatisfaction Results - The customer satisfaction and dissatisfaction measurement methods identified in 3.1b will produce the satisfaction and dissatisfaction results that are displayed in 7.2a. In other words the results by segment as determined in 3.1b should be the same results (levels, trends, comparisons) that are displayed in 7.2a.

THOUGHTS FOR LEADERS

An important CPE message is that organizations need to understand what makes their customers successful. In simple terms, if the organization has a product or service that makes the customer successful, that organization should also be a success. Moreover, if your organization's products and services make the customer more successful than your competitors' products and services, then the organization should gain customer loyalty (assuming that customer make rational business decisions) and (if the organization is in a market environment) gain market share.

Great leaders know this equation and have a clear focus on what their organization does to drive the necessary products and services that make their customers successful.

Great leaders also have several means to determine if their customers are a success, as well as how the customers feel about the products and services they provide.

It is always interesting to see how much time the senior leaders spend with customers. In high performing organizations the leaders spend time with customers. That doesn't mean that they will use this personal contact knowledge instead of a customer satisfaction survey. It does mean, however, that this personal knowledge of the customer(s) will help them understand and interpret the customer satisfaction survey.

A Lighter Moment:

> *It is not the employer who pays the wages.*
> *Employers only handle the money.*
> *It is the customer who pays the wages.*
>
> **Henry Ford**

> *The purpose of a business is to create a customer.*
>
> Peter Drucker

 FOUNDATION

In the Organizational Profile (P.1b[2]) the Criteria for Performance Excellence (CPE) ask who the customer groups are and their requirements. Customer groups (*segments*) are determined based on the customers' requirements (like requirements are put into one customer group), as discussed in Area 3.2a(3). *Target* customer groups are based on how you sell to your customers.

In some instances you may need to group your product offerings the same way your industry groups theirs or you will not have comparison or benchmark data which is usable to evaluate your own performance.

Product Offerings

Within these groupings, the criteria ask how you identify the product offerings that will meet or exceed the needs and expectations of customers, and how you innovate those offerings. The CPE expect the organization to have a wide view of customers, including the consideration of customers of competitors, other potential customers, and previous customers of the organization.

Once you determine the customer and market needs, how do you identify and adapt your product offerings to meet the requirements and exceed expectations. Beyond this level of adaptation, how do you adapt the offerings to new markets, new customers, and to create new opportunities to expand relationships.

These product offerings (and the innovations) should be structured so they provide opportunities to expand the relationship with the existing customers.

In simple terms:

- How do you group your customers? (segmenting based on their requirements)
  - How do you sell to those requirements? (your customer targeting)
    - How do you deliver to those requirements? (your facilities)

Customer Support

In the overall relationship with the external customer, the CPE ask how the organization determines the key mechanisms needed to support the customer's use of the products and the access mechanisms for customers so that they can reach the organization whenever they need to seek information, conduct business, or complain. For example, many organizations provide 800 numbers, 24 x 7 hotlines, or, in the case of key customers, the home phone numbers of key customer contact employees. The first step in this process is to determine the key customers' contact requirements – how do they want to be contacted and how do they want to contact the organization.

The CPE recognize that each customer and customer group may have different contact requirements and different contact preferences. Some customers may wish to be contacted routinely, while others may wish to be left alone. How does the organization determine these customer preferences, and how do they ensure that all customer contact employees know these preferences? Quite frankly, this is a frequent shortcoming of many organizations. If you wish to have a relationship with a customer, you need to start with how they prefer to be contacted.

Another inherent part of Area to Address 3.2a is how to supply training to key customer contact employees. Although the criteria are not explicit on this training requirement, it is difficult for customer contact to be systematic or for customer contact employees to help "increase loyalty and repeat business and to gain positive referrals" if customer contact employees do not systematically (and consistently) receive the necessary training and knowledge reinforcement. In many organizations, however, some key customer contact groups are overlooked. For example, the executives and support staff may not be included in customer contact training even though they often have frequent contact with customers. Executives, by virtue of their position, often feel as though they already have the customer skills and knowledge required. Additionally, support staff members often spend a great deal of time in direct contact with customers even if they are not always viewed as critical to the customer response chain and may not be trained in customer contact.

In this item, the CPE attempt to assess whether the organization understands what drives their customers' purchase behaviors. Simply stated, if the organization truly understands what drives customers' purchase behaviors, they can compete more effectively in the marketplace than if they do not have that understanding.

Finally, Area to Address 3.2a seeks to understand how the organization uses the information and data from their listening and learning methods (and analysis performed) to identify when and how product offerings need to be updated or new products developed.

Customer Segmentation

In the Organizational Profile (P.1b[2]) the CPE ask who the customer groups are and their requirements. These customer requirements should be segmented by customer group, target customer segment, or market segment, as appropriate. Item 3.1 asks how the organization systematically listens to those segments and appropriate groupings to determine the drivers of customer satisfaction, customer loyalty and customer engagement. This listening must include obtaining feedback on your products, services and customer support. Listening may be different for each customer group and should be tailored for each group. There are certainly instances where tailoring the listening approach does not make sense, but typically there are many more instances where it does make sense. The listening methods need to be broader than the organization's current customers. For example, the organization can learn from listening to former customers, customers of competitors, and potential customers. Their requirements may expand the organization's view of what is needed, or what is possible.

EXAMPLES

Advocate Good Samaritan Hospital (GSAM) (Baldrige Recipient 2010)

Health care service offerings and programs to meet the requirements and exceed the expectations of GSAM patients, stakeholder groups, and market segments are identified through the *Program/Service Identification Process*. This process is integrated with the strategic planning process and once the need for a new process or service is identified it is integrated with the work system design approach. Listening post data❷and❸, an analysis of existing programs and services, and the Strategic Planning Process environmental scan are used to determine if patient/stakeholder requirements are being met, and to identify opportunities for new services/programs❹-❻. The use of both internal and external listening post data ensures that GSAM identifies offerings to attract new patient/stakeholders and opportunities to expand relationships with existing patients/stakeholders. Innovation of health care service offerings begins with GSAM's openness to any/all ideas followed by extensive benchmarking and engaging a diverse group of stakeholders in the design of the new programs/services❼. The process of identifying and innovating new programs and services is reviewed annually.

Product and Service Offerings

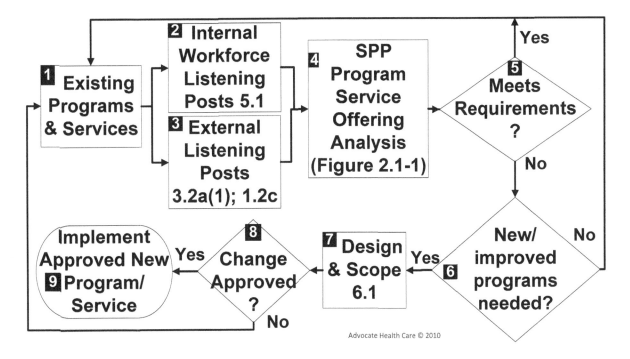

Advocate Health Care © 2010

Virtua Health (Baldrige Site Visit 2009**)**

VH systematically identifies and innovates health care services to meet the needs and requirements of customers and stakeholders using the Customer Segment and Healthcare Offering Process (CSHOP).

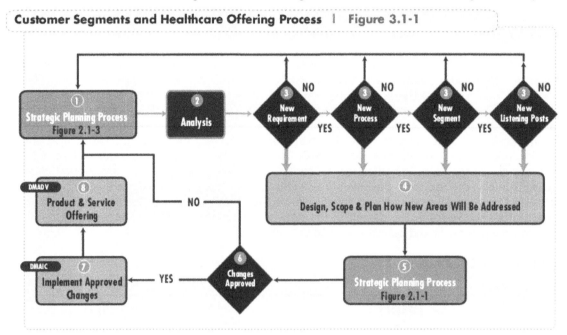

Customer Segments and Healthcare Offering Process | Figure 3.1-1

The process is initiated by SL and is integrated with the SPP and improvement process. They review and improve the process at the same time as the Strategic Planning Process (SPP). During the SPP they conduct an environmental scan, visioning and set direction using several inputs to identify any changes in existing healthcare offerings that enable them to continue to meet and exceed patient and stakeholder requirements and expectations. The SPP analysis is supplemented throughout the year using the voice of the customer and voice of the employee listening posts which are reviewed during facility/meetings, Friday morning briefings, the agility process, council meetings and during Six Sigma projects to identify ways to enrich the offerings.

If a new requirement, new process, new segment or new listening post is required they design, scope, and plan how new areas will be addressed. Market segments targeted for growth is primarily defined through Practices of Excellence (POE) leadership and planning. Patient and stakeholder needs are evaluated from a POE perspective with a comprehensive evaluation of the delivery service mechanisms and strategic need. This systematic approach provides a comprehensive evaluation to identify and innovate new services to attract new patients, expand relationships with current patients, partners and stakeholders, and provide services to differentiate VH from its competitors and enhance the OPE. They address the changes integrating them during the SPP develop phase and throughout the year as needed. For approved changes, they use DMAIC to improve and innovate current services and DMADV to develop new services.

Don Chalmers Ford (Baldrige Site Visit 2008 and 2012**)**

DCF enables customers to seek information and support through the key customer access mechanisms in Figure 3.2-2. These mechanisms are determined through analysis of data gathered from the listening methods (Figure 3.1-1). These requirements for customer support are communicated continually in department meetings and reinforced in focused skill training. DCF's sales force utilizes the specific sales training techniques modeled around DCF's unique sales process. M&R and BR employees are trained in the process of "under-promise and over-deliver."

Completely satisfying customers (CCS key strategic advantage) is essential to DCF's mission: Growth through Customer Loyalty. To reinforce thorough process deployment, the entire workforce is eligible for two annual bonuses of equal amounts if DCF wins the FMC President's Award and meets other critical results. Employees can receive up to $1,800 regardless of full or part-time status.

DCF uses customer, market, and product offering information in the SPP to identify current and anticipate future customer groups and market segments. This information is then aligned and integrated with FMC. Any person in need of any DCF product (Sales) and or service (Service) is a potential customer. The NVS market segment is for customers who prefer a new Ford vehicle. The UVS market segment is for those who prefer a pre-owned vehicle, and includes all makes and models. The M&R market segment includes customers that need scheduled maintenance, warranty repairs, or non-warrantable retail repairs. The BR market segment is customers who have vehicles requiring vehicle body repair.

DCF determines which customer, customer group, and market segments to pursue through strategic, annual, monthly, weekly, and daily planning. Examples of both formal and informal decisions are:
- Retail trade cycle (RTC) & lease expiration: a review of the customer buying cycle, and leases that may be expiring
- Inventory levels: daily reviews of aging used vehicle inventory for weekly advertising to a particular segment
- FMC Financial factory incentives: rebates, stair-step, and dealer cash to sell certain models to increase sales
- Market conditions: seasonal needs drive supply and demand of parts and servicing, and fluctuating fuel prices impact sales of fuel-efficient vehicles
- Extended service and maintenance plans: target customers who purchased extended service and maintenance plans and are more apt to return to DCF for repair work
- Target market: those who live closest to the dealership, using the DCF's primary market area (PMA) zip codes
- Insurance companies: provide opportunities when the dealership isn't already a "direct repair program" in BR
- Driving habits: used for pursuing another purchase or maintenance appointment, includes e-mails and postcards

Television, radio and newspaper advertisements, and word-of-mouth attract customers of competitors. The internet and e-mail are also mediums for advertising on sites such as donchalmersford.com. Direct marketing targets customers of competitors for defined geographic location, credit scores, and FMC provided lists. Both DCF's successful reputation of conducting business with a customer-focus and its prominent leadership in community philanthropy give customers added value compared to the competition.

DCF's has recently expanded its service base to include municipal fleet customers. Through subscriptions to municipal bid notification internet sites, DCF has won the service contracts of several municipalities' fleet vehicles. This newest customer group was identified through the SPP.

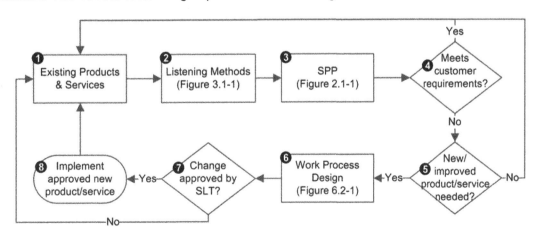

Jenks Public Schools (Baldrige Recipient 2005)

In order to determine students' and stakeholders' requirements and changing expectations, the District's Communications/Stakeholder Relations Process, which is established by senior leaders and implemented by both senior leaders and all site and department leaders, employs a variety of tools to listen and learn from the stakeholders in each segment. These tools include: periodic surveys, advisory boards, evaluations, regularly scheduled parent and teacher meetings, PTAG, PTO council, booster clubs, curriculum committees, CAPS (Career Action Planning), and electronic communication tools. Since 1995, district-wide surveys have been given in phases to patrons (parents/guardians), certified personnel, classified personnel, and students. The surveys are designed to ascertain how the District is meeting and/or exceeding the stakeholders' expectations. Jenks Public Schools utilizes the services of a management consultant in developing, administering, tracking, and reporting survey results.

Additionally, advisory boards comprised of teachers, administrators, parents, and community members with expertise or experience related to the segment provide valuable insight for JPS decision makers. Currently, advisory committees provide this essential guidance for the American Indian, economically disadvantaged, ELL, IEP, and gifted student segments. An example of one of the key methods for gleaning direction from stakeholders has been the Curriculum Development Process, which incorporates 50-60 stakeholders in a year-long process.

Stakeholder Segment	Key Communication and Satisfaction Determination Methods
Students (including Male, Female, Black, American Indian, Hispanic, Asian White. Economically Disadvantaged, ELL, IEP, and Gifted Segments	Board of Education meetings, CAPS conferences, classroom/site/district newsletters, classroom/site/district Web sites, classroom/site surveys, committees (i.e. Safe School, Healthy and Fit Kids, Student Council), course evaluations, online portal (7th-12th grade students), IEP meetings.
Staff (including certified and classified staff segments)	Advisory board membership, BOE meetings, classroom/site/district newsletters, classroom/site/district Web sites, committee membership, JCTA, staff meetings, surveys, visits by Superintendent, visits by BOE members.
Parents	Advisory boards, Back-To-School nights, BOE meetings, Booster Organization meetings, CAPS conferences, classroom/site/district newsletters, classroom/site/district Web sites, committee membership, online portal, IEP meetings, open houses, parent information meetings, PTAG meetings, parent/teacher conferences, PTO Council, placement need requests, surveys.
Community	Advisory boards, BOE meetings, classroom/site/district Web sites, district newsletters, committees (i.e. Bond Issue Task Force, Selected Committee on School Finance), community involvement by senior leaders, volunteer opportunities.

The District uses a variety of methods for communicating with students and Stakeholders.

Listening and learning to determine students' and stakeholders' requirements and expectations is a vital component of the District's CLEP (Comprehensive Local Education Plan). Each site leadership team utilizes a broad range of methods to gather information and input to develop the CLEP. These methods include: staff survey of needs, patron survey, group meetings to discuss needs and formulate goals, and evaluation of test data. Each CLEP includes PDSA processes, which directly correlate to stakeholder requirements and expectations.

Relevant information from current, former, and future students and stakeholders is used by senior leaders to plan educational offerings, expand educational programs, and develop services. It has become a practice in the District to conduct evaluations at the conclusion of professional development opportunities, district committee work, and community education courses to determine the stakeholders' level of satisfaction. Analysis of the data leads to improved processes and programs.

CRITERIA QUESTIONS

In your response, include answers to the following questions:

a. Product Offerings and Customer Support

(1) Product Offerings How do you determine product offerings? How do you:
- determine customer and market needs and requirements for product offerings and services;
- identify and adapt product offerings to meet the requirements and exceed the expectations of your customer groups and market segments; and
- identify and adapt product offerings to enter new markets, to attract new customers, and to create opportunities to expand relationships with current customers, as appropriate?

(2) Customer Support How do you enable customers to seek information and support? How do you enable them to conduct business with you?   What are your key means of customer support, including your key communication mechanisms? How do they vary for different customers, customer groups, or market segments? How do you:
- determine your customers' key support requirements and
- deploy these requirements to all people and processes involved in customer support?

(3) Customer Segmentation How do you determine your customer groups and market segments? How do you:
- use information on customers, markets, and product offerings to identify current and anticipate future customer groups and market segments;
- consider competitors' customers and other potential customers and markets in this segmentation; and
- determine which customers, customer groups, and market segments to emphasize and pursue for business growth?

Notes:

3.2. "Customer engagement" refers to your customers' investment in or commitment to your brand and product offerings. Characteristics of engaged customers include retention, brand loyalty, willingness to make an effort to do business—and increase their business—with you, and willingness to actively advocate for and recommend your brand and product offerings.

3.2a. "Product offerings" refer to the goods and services that you offer in the marketplace. In identifying product offerings, you should consider all the important characteristics of products and services and their performance throughout their full life cycle and the full consumption chain. The focus should be on features that affect customers' preference for and loyalty to you and your brand—for example, features that differentiate your products from competing offerings or other organizations' services. Those features might include price, reliability, value, delivery, timeliness, product customization, ease of use, requirements for the use and disposal of hazardous materials, customer or technical support, and the sales relationship. Key product features might also take into account how transactions occur and factors such as the privacy and security of customer data. Your results on performance relative to key product features should be reported in item 7.1, and those for customer perceptions and actions (outcomes) should be reported in item 7.2.

3.2a(2). The goal of customer support is to make your organization easy to do business with and responsive to your customers' expectations.

NIST (2015-2016) pp. 14-15

WORKSHEETS

3.2a(1) – Product Offerings

Note: Review Areas To Address 3.1a(1), 3.1a(2) as to how to determine the customer's requirements

Customer Segments [The Same As In Area To Address P1b(2)]	Requirements For Each Customer Or Market Segment [The Same As In Area To Address P1b(2)]	Methods Used To Determine Customer And Market Needs And Requirements For Product Offerings And Services	Methods Used To Identify And Adapt Product Offerings To Meet Requirements And Exceed Expectations Of Customer Groups And Market Segments

Process Step's Used To Identify New Product Offerings :	How This Step Is Used To Attract New Customers Or New Markets	How This Step Is Used To Expand Relationships With Current Customers
1.		
2.		
n.		

293

3.2a(2) – Customer Support

Your Key Means Of Customer Support:
Your Means Of Customer Support: (Include Differences For Different Customers, Customer Groups Or Market Segments)
Your Key Communication Mechanisms: (Include Differences For Different Customers, Customer Groups Or Market Segments)

Process Used To Determine Your Key Mechanisms To Enable Customers To:	How Your Determine Customer Support Requirements	How You Deploy These Requirements To All People And Processes Involved In Customer Support	How You Verify Deployment Of The Required Support And Communication
Use Your Products or Services			
Seek Information			
Conduct Their Business			
Provide Feedback On Products and Services			

3.2a(3) – Customer Segmentation

Customer Group (Same As Shown In P1b[2])	Method For Determining Whether Approach To Determining Customer Requirements Is Current	Method For Considering Customers of Competitors	Method For Considering Other Potential Customers	Method for Changing Approach Used For Customer Grouping	Potential New Customer Groups and Market Segments

Process Step's to Segment Customers Into The Customer Groups Or Market Segments Shown In Area To Address P1b(2)	Participants In The Segmentation	Decision Criteria Used To Segment Customer Groups or Market Segments
1.		
2.		
3.		
4.		
n.		

Use of Voice of the Customer Information for Future Requirements

Customers, Customer Groups or Market Segments [Same As Shown In P1b(2)]	Customer Requirements [Same As Shown In P1b(2)]	Products And Offerings Which Match The Current Requirements	Process To Determine The Projected Changes In Customer Requirements Or Expectations	How These Differ For Each Customer Group, Customer, Or Market Segment	Process To Determine How These Will Differ Across The Customer Life Cycle

ASSESSMENT

49	There is a systematic process for determining current and future customer needs/expectations for products and services.	1 2 3 4 5 6 DK
50	There is a systematic process for: 1) determining when to innovate product offerings to meet/exceed the requirements of customers; 2) innovating the product offerings; and to 3) implement/introduce the new product offerings.	1 2 3 4 5 6 DK
51	The approach to identifying and innovating product offerings (and for providing support) is systematically reviewed and improved to keep current with the customer's support needs.	1 2 3 4 5 6 DK
52	The organization has targeted specific customer segments to really understand the needs of the customers in each of those segments.	1 2 3 4 5 6 DK
53	The organization uses a systematic process to group (segment) customers based on their requirements.	1 2 3 4 5 6 DK
54	We understand and adjust to the different customer expectations across the customer life cycle.	1 2 3 4 5 6 DK
55	Analysis is performed which allows us to anticipate customer requirements. Our product offerings are adjusted to meet those requirements.	1 2 3 4 5 6 DK

BLUEPRINT 3.2a(1 & 2)

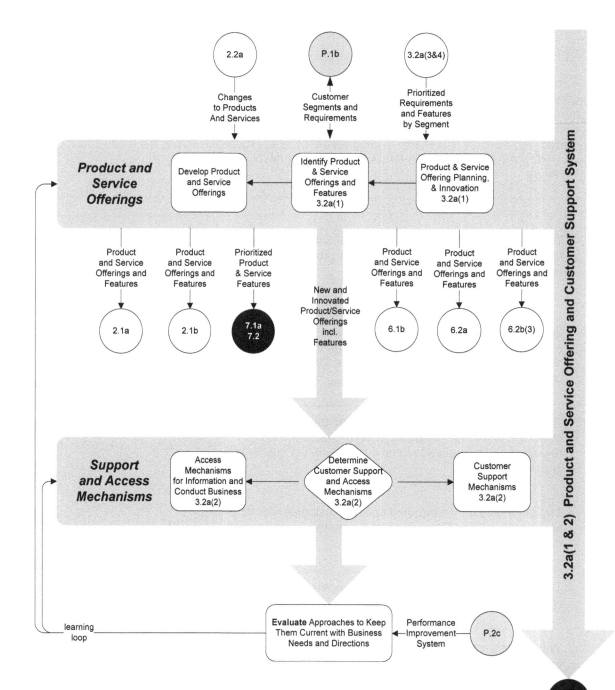

SYSTEM INTEGRATION 3.2a(1 & 2)

Context

P.1b <> 3.2a(1&2) Customers Segments and Requirements - The processes and practices described in 3.2a(1&2) to determine product and service offerings and features should be consistent with the customer segments and requirements described in the profile (P.1b).

P.2c > 3.2a(1&2) Performance Improvement System - The performance improvement system described in the profile (P.2c) should be a key input to the methods used to evaluate and keep the approaches to product and service offerings and customer support and access mechanisms current with changing business needs and directions.

Systems

2.1a < 3.2a(1&2) Product and Service Offerings and Features - The product and service offerings and associated features are inputs to the environmental scan and analysis process.

2.1b < 3.2a(1&2) Product and Service Offerings and Features - The product and service offerings and associated features are inputs to the process of testing the balance of key strategic objectives. In particular, how the objectives address opportunities for innovation in products and services.

2.2a > 3.2a(1&2) Changes to Products and Services - The changes to products and services described in the action plans is an important input to the determination of product and service offerings and features described in 3.2a(1&2).

3.2a(1 & 2) < 3.2a(3 & 4) Prioritized Requirements and Features by Segment - Customer requirements and expectations by customer segment are often identified through the analysis of customer data in 3.2c(3&4). These requirements and expectations for each key customer and market segments are an important input to the identification and development of product and service offerings described in 3.1a(1&2).

3.2a(1&2) > 6.1b Product and Service Offerings and Features - Ultimately, the prioritized product and service features are used to identify key work process requirements described in 6.1b.

3.2a(1&2) > 6.2a Product and Service Offerings and Features - The description of product and service offerings along with the features are key inputs to the deign of key work processes and the identification of key areas for process control to ensure the work processes produce the desired results.

3.2a(1&2) > 6.2b(3) Product and Service Offerings and Features - Changing product and service offerings and features is an important input to the continuous improvement of key work processes that produce and deliver those products and services.

Scorecard

3.2a(1&2) > 7.1a Prioritized Product and Service Features Results - The results for product outcomes reported in 7.1a should include "hard" measure results for each key product and service offering as well as the key features and their relative importance to purchasing decisions.

3.2a(1&2) > 7.1a, 7.2 Product and Service Offerings and Features Results - The customer focused results presented in 7.2a should include results for each key product and service offering as well as the key features and their relative importance to purchasing decisions. While it is very useful to survey customers and ask for their preferences it is even better to analyze their actual behavior and buying patterns along with their satisfaction results. This provides the organization with much better information for making adjustments to product and service offerings and the associated features.

BLUEPRINT 3.2a(3)

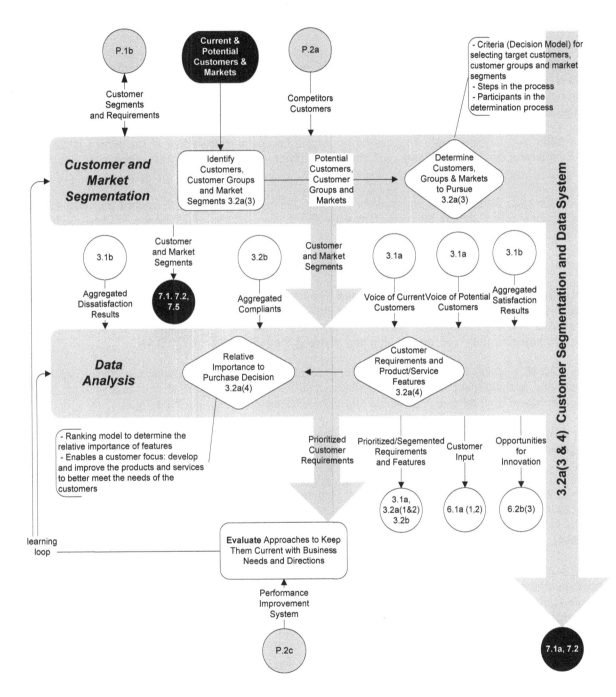

SYSTEM INTEGRATION 3.2a

Context

P.1b > 3.2a(3&4) Customers Segments and Requirements - The customer segments and requirements identified in the profile (P.1b) are key inputs to the customer segmentation and requirements determination processes and practices described in 3.2a. In addition, if this process modifies the customer and market segments then that should be reflected in an updated profile.

P.2a > 3.2a(3&4) Competitors - The customers of the competitors identified in the profile (P.2a) are an input to the process of identifying customers, customer groups, and market segments described in 3.2a(3&4).

P.2c > 3.2a(3&4) Performance Improvement System - The 3.2a(3&4) improvement activities based on customer satisfaction should be consistent with and based on the performance improvement system described in the profile (P.2c).

Systems

3.1a < 3.2a(3&4) Prioritized Requirements and Features - Customer requirements and expectations by customer segment are often identified through the analysis of data as described in 3.2a(3&4). These requirements and expectations for each key customer and market segment are an important input to the design and implementation of the listening and learning methods described in 3.1a.

3.1a > 3.2a(3&4) Voice of the Customer - The voice of the current and potential customers derived from the listening and learning methods described in 3.1a are key inputs to the analysis of customer requirements and their relative importance to purchase decisions described in 3.2a(3&4).

3.1b > 3.2a(3&4) Aggregated Satisfaction Results - The measurement of customer satisfaction produces aggregated satisfaction results which are key inputs to the analysis and use of customer data to identify the customers' requirements and their relative importance to the purchase decision 3.2a(3&4).

3.1b > 3.2a(3&4) Aggregated Dissatisfaction Results - The measurement of customer dissatisfaction produces aggregated dissatisfaction results which are key inputs to the analysis and use of customer data to identify the customers' requirements and their relative importance to the purchase decision 3.2a(3&4).

3.2a(1 & 2) < 3.2a(3 & 4) Prioritized Requirements and Features by Segment - Customer requirements and expectations by customer segment are often identified through the analysis of customer data in 3.2c(3&4). These requirements and expectations for each key customer and market segments are an important input to the identification and development of product and service offerings described in 3.1a(1&2).

3.2a(3&4) < 3.2b Aggregated Complaints - Complaint analysis is a key component of the analysis and use of customer data system described in 3.2a(3&4). The aggregated complaints from the customer listening and complaint system (3.2b) are key input to the identification of opportunities for improvement and innovation as described in 3.2a(3&4). Focusing improvement on areas that receive multiple complaints can help get to the root cause and redesign the processes to prevent future complaints.

3.2a(3&4) > 6.2a Customer Input - Ultimately, the prioritized product and service features 3.2a(3&4) are used to design key work processes so that they produce the desired results.

3.2a(3&4) > 6.2b(1&2) Customer Input - The prioritized product and service features 3.2a(3&4) are used to identify key work process control points and practices to ensure the processes produce products and services that produce the desired results and meet the requirements.

3.2a(3&4) > 6.2b(3) Opportunities for Innovation - The analysis of customers data is used in 3.2a(3&4) to identify opportunities for innovation that are important inputs to the work process improvement system described in 6.2b(3).

3.2b <> 3.2a(3&4) Requirements by Customer Segment - Customer requirements and expectations by customer segment are often identified through the analysis of customer data in 3.2a(3&4). These requirements and expectation for each key customer and market segments are an important input to building customer relationships (3.2b) that addresses the needs, wants, and desires of the various customer groups and segments.

Scorecard

3.2a(3&4) > 7.1a, 7.2 Customer and Market Segments - The segments and customer groups that are identified in 3.2a(3&4) should be the same segments and groups that are used for product and service results data presented in 7.1a. In other words, the results in 7.1a should include results requirements for each of the key customer and market segments and groups identified by the processes in 3.2a(3&4). In addition, results for the product and service features related to the prioritized requirements identified in 3.2a(3&4) should be included in the product and service results presented in 7.1a.

3.2a(3&4) > 7.1a, 7.2 Customer and Market Segments - The customer focused results presented in 7.2a should include results for each key customer or market segment and group identified in 3.2a(3&4). In addition, the results should include results on the key requirements and expectations for each segment and group. This area asks for how the organization determines key customer requirements and expectations and their relative importance to customers' purchasing decisions. While it is very useful to survey customers and ask for their preferences it is even better to analyze their actual behavior and buying patterns along with their satisfaction results. This provides the organization with insights for making adjustments to product and service offerings.

3.2a(3&4) > 7.5a Customer and Market Segments - Financial and in particular market results should be segmented using the same segmentation scheme as identified in 3.2a(3&4) and used in results areas 7.1a and 7.2a.

THOUGHTS FOR LEADERS

An organization cannot truly be competitive unless they are better than their competition at determining what the customer wants and providing those products and services. This concept is so basic that it seems overly rudimentary to include it in this book.

It's surprising, however, to see how many organizations *assume* they understand the customer's needs without asking them. In fact, it seems rare when a customer can provide an organization feedback and the organization is grateful. Many companies instill a long, cumbersome process for the customers to deliver feedback. Most customers will not bother with "writing a letter." The customer wants to give the organization feedback as a "gift," and the organization is making it difficult for the customer to give them the gift. Speaking as an individual, If they resist receiving feedback, I do not bother in the future! Clearly in those instances, I care more about the feedback (gift?) than they do.

Entire industries seem to have shut off their ability to learn from their customers. The imagination can run wild just thinking of what *could* happen if an organization in one of those industries developed a systematic closed-loop ability to determine customer requirements, and then delivered products and services which met those requirements!

Once the product and service offerings are determined, they must be effectively designed, implemented, measured and improved. This can only be optimized if the customer's voice is included in each step, and a closed-loop process exists to ensure that the new knowledge gained drives action.

A Lighter Moment:

Sham Harga had run a succesful eatery for many years by always smiling, never extending credit, and realizing that most of his customers wanted meals properly balanced between the four food groups: sugar, starch, grease, and burnt crunchy bits.

Terry Pratchett

> *The customer doesn't expect everything will go right all the time;*
> *the big test is what you do when things go wrong.*
>
> **Sir Colin Marshall**

FOUNDATION

One of the key responsibilities of senior leadership is to create a customer-focused culture. If customers are not important to the senior leaders, why should they be important to anybody else? Check the leader's calendar – do they spend time with customers?

Years ago I remember sitting in a senior leader's office and hearing him say "At my level, I don't meet with customers. The leaders who report to me meet with them." .... I held my breath for several reasons: 1) he certainly was not role-modeling building a customer-focused culture – if customers were not important to him, why should they be important to anybody else in his organization; 2) how did he know what the customer's really wanted (reading reports???????); 3) he was viewing the customer relationship as a spectator sport and not a contact sport; and 4) his corporate CEO (3 levels up from him) spent 25% of his time with customers!

A customer-focused culture is composed of several organizational competencies: 1) understanding what the customer wants and needs; 2) consistently delivering what the customers want; 3) engaging the customers to understand your performance now and what will happen in their environment in the future; 4) aligning the culture and individual performance with the customers' interests; and 4) systematically building relationships with customers.

Relationship Management

With these foundational processes in-place, the organization needs to be able to build and manage relationships with existing customers, to:

- acquire new customers;
- build market share;
- retain customers;
- meet their requirements;
- exceed their expectations; and
- increase their engagement with you.

This needs to be done systematically in each stage of the customer and product or service life cycle. Through these processes the organization should be able to increase customer satisfaction by meeting the customer's stated and unstated requirements, which should drive customer loyalty, which should drive customer engagement.

Complaint Management

The CPE ask how the organization uses the complaint system to drive customer engagement. A simple way to view complaints uses the following questions:

- Are all complaints (both formal and informal) captured?
- Once captured, is the complaint addressed?
- If the complaint is not addressed in a timely manner, is the complaint escalated within the organization?
- Is the complaint closed with the customer?
- Does the way the complaint is addressed and closed with the customer drive increased:
  - Customer Confidence?
  - Customer Satisfaction?
  - Customer Loyalty?
  - Customer Engagement?
- Are all parties (including suppliers, partners, collaborators, etc.) who contributed to the complaint aware of the complaint and responsible for correcting the root cause of the complaint? This should include:
  - Ensuring the responsible parties know about the complaint
  - Ensuring the responsible parties fix the root cause of the complaint
- Is the complaint data aggregated, analyzed, and used to drive improvement actions? For example, several small complaints, when added up, may constitute an overall concern that the company should address. Unless both formal and informal complaints are collected, aggregated, and analyzed, the smaller complaints may not reach the attention of the leaders who can initiate action.

EXAMPLES

PRO-TEC Coating Company (Baldrige Recipient 2007)

Due to the terms of the PRO-TEC joint venture agreement (the agreement which formed PRO-TEC as a joint venture between Kobe Steel of Japan and U. S. Steel from the United States), all direct customer contact (starting with the initial order placement) is with U. S. Steel (USS) acting as the exclusive agent and intermediary on behalf of PRO-TEC. Accordingly, PRO-TEC maintains a supporting role and, similar to the USS Automotive Sales Group organization, is organized by customer-specific teams and backups to ensure that all necessary activities and information are readily available to the USS customer contacts.

As illustrated in Figure 3.2-1, each year, USS establishes Customer Technical Service (CTS) business plan quality objectives by customer, some of which are established directly by the customer (such as the acceptable number of parts-per-million quality defects). These objectives are monitored as the data are updated throughout the year.

Data updates are provided through means such as customer visits, APEX (customer-focused) meetings, outside processor visits, satisfaction survey results, and claim activity. The data are summarized by customer and analyzed with their substrate steel suppliers and CTS engineers.

The outcome of the USS meetings and various types of feedback provides an effective means to make appropriate changes to the QES (quality standards) leading to continuous improvement in the customer relationship building process. In this way PRO-TEC assists USS in building customer relationships by meeting or exceeding expectations of current customers and USS. With a reputation of good product, cooperation, and responsiveness, PRO-TEC assists in acquiring new business and positive referrals.

Based on the joint venture status under the partnership agreement, their customers' first point of contact is a USS Sales or CTS liaison. USS Sales and CTS engineers can access us via e-mail, telephone, fax, and through cellular phones. USS can also access customer order status and inventory information via an internet-based SteelTrack application. This SteelTrack application also contains certain specific product information that their customers can access directly.

Key customer contact requirements for each mode of customer access are determined by USS using a systematic approach through their documented ISO/TS 16949 Quality Management System. These contacts extend into the corresponding PRO-TEC supporting role activities as part of a seamless communication network.

PRO-TEC Customer Relationship Building Process

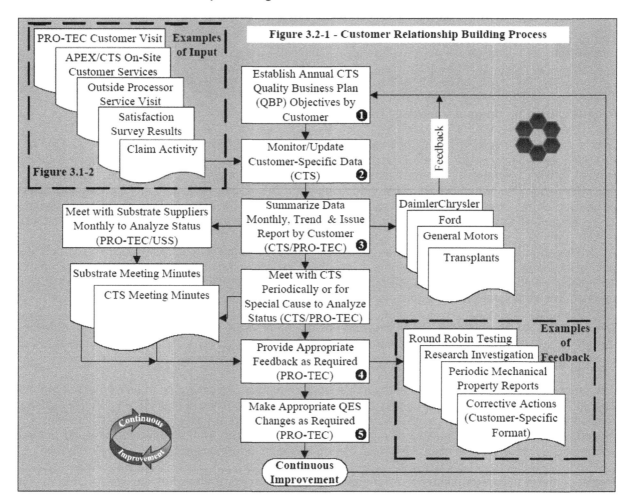

Figure 3.2-1 - Customer Relationship Building Process

Virtua Health (Baldrige Site Visit 2009)

Virtua's approach to building ongoing relationships with patients, partners and suppliers is critical to their growth and sustainability. The process takes prospective patients, patients and stakeholders from not knowing Virtua to advocating Virtua. For their key stakeholders they focus on the three steps of "trying Virtua", being satisfied with Virtua and being loyal to Virtua. The Chief Medical Officer (CMO) and President systematically build relationships with physicians. The approach is supported through numerous communication mechanisms. The medical staff committee structure, physician liaisons and physician satisfaction survey ensure that they hear and understand their needs and develop long lasting relationships with high admitters.

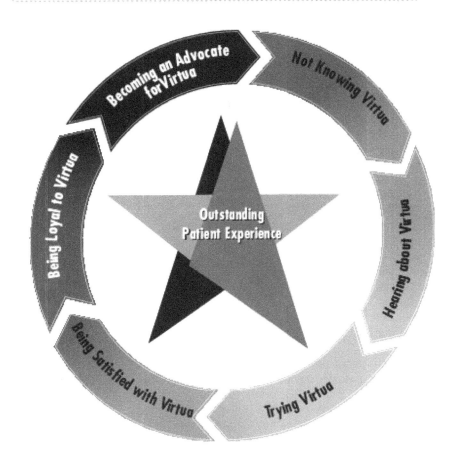

Customer Relationship Building | CAT 3 3.2a

Not Knowing Virtua

Hearing about Virtua

Trying Virtua

Being Satisfied with Virtua

Being Loyal to Virtua

Becoming an Advocate for Virtua

Outstanding Patient Experience

Approaches for keeping their patient and stakeholder relationship building and patient focused culture current include: monthly reviews of patient satisfaction data, voice of the customer information, and barriers to achieving the OPE at the Patient Satisfaction Steering Committee to develop improvements that are then presented to SL at the Patient Satisfaction Briefings. This ensures they are continually learning and improving their processes. Additionally, during the CSHOP (see the example in Area to Address 3.2a) they systematically review the need for new requirements, processes, segments and listening posts that impact both healthcare services and their relationship building.

Sharp Healthcare (Baldrige Recipient 2007)

Sharp is committed to creating long-term loyalty from its customers/partners across the continuum of care. In support of this strategy, Sharp provides extensive education and tools to its leaders and staff on the fundamentals of service excellence. All leaders and staff are held accountable to living and demonstrating the Behavior Standards, the Five "Must-Haves," the Five Fundamentals of Service, and service recovery. Sharp uses patient satisfaction survey data and accompanying Priority Indices to focus satisfaction and loyalty improvement efforts.

Key mechanisms for relationship building with customer/partners who are seeking information; receiving, providing, or supporting care; making complaints; or obtaining other services include:

- Branding Efforts,
- Broker/Payor Meetings,

309

- Community Events,
- Community Health Collaboratives and Programs,
- CRM Database,
- Customer Contact Centers,
- Multicultural Services,
- Sharp Experience Action Teams,
- Senior Resource and Information Centers, and
- Web Center.

Sharp Leaders determine key contact requirements for patient and customer access through the Strategic Planning Process. Key customer access mechanisms include:

- Face-to-Face contact
- Customer Contact Centers
- 82-SHARP
- Sharp.com (Web)
- SharpEnEspañol.com (Web)
- SRS Call Center (physician appointment scheduling)
- Sharp Nurse Connection® (offering 24-hour telephone medical triage)
- Health Fairs
- Community Events
- Written Materials
- Letter/Fax/Email
- Conferences
- Community Education Classes

Sharp stays abreast of customer needs through the use of listening and learning tools, trade journals, best practice research, and industry trends monitoring. Customer Contact Centers exist as the "answer place" for customers/partners. These Customer Contact Centers provide information by phone about 13,000 times per month and online over 275,000 times per month. Customer Contact Centers track customers by gender and age to determine how Sharp is serving its target segments. Sharp tracks online comment topics.

Sharp empowers its employees to resolve complaints at the point of service through resolution and service recovery programs and by monitoring unit-level patient satisfaction data. Sharp's comprehensive patient relationship system includes organizational beliefs and proactive input, and a feedback/complaint process (Fig. 3.2-1). Sharp believes in ongoing learning for continuous improvement, and uses a variety of proactive tools to solicit formal and informal feedback. The process includes aggregating feedback/complaints by type, analyzing the learning, and instituting process change if necessary. Learning is then integrated into the patient relationship system. Key outputs from this process include creating same-day/next-day appointment availability and creating an online physician appointment request feature for Sharp medical groups.

Employees are trained to use a four-step service recovery process immediately upon identifying a service gap to ensure the customer service issue does not happen again: Apologize, Correct the situation, Track, and Take action (ACTT).

Charleston Area Medical Center (The Partnership For Excellence Recipient 2014)

Relationships with patients and other customers are systematically built and managed through the Customer Relationship Model (Figure 3.2-2). focus on acquiring new patients; enable us to retain our patients/other customer relationships, meet their requirements and exceed their expectations; and provides us with opportunities to increase their engagement. Figure 3.2-3 details the strategies to build relationships with patients at each stage of the relationship cycle through the use of tools and practices designed to move our customers from one relationship stage to the next. The effectiveness of our relationship building strategies is established through key measures at each stage. Deployment of the customer relationship strategies permeates our entire organizational structure beginning with new hire orientation, Service Plus, job instructional training (JIT) for competency validation, and single point lessons (SPL) to reinforce standards of behavior.

We leverage social media to enhance patient and other customer engagement and relationship with our organization by responding to postings that enable us to connect with patients, families and the community; promote services and events; monitor online conversations; disseminate pertinent health information, and process feedback. The real time interactive and multi-directional touchpoint provided by social media enables us to increase our responsiveness to customers and provide additional opportunity for service recovery. Our Marketing and Public Affairs Department systematically evaluates all of our communications including social media for newsworthiness, immediacy, value to the audience and broad appeal to help drive improvements in our customer relationship building strategies. In a cycle of improvement we have partnered with Krames Staywell health content to provide a branded resource that features a symptom checker and current health information on thousands of topics. This allows us to establish our social media sites as a trusted resource for online health information. Increased participation by our CAMC-affiliated physicians and other health experts by integrating videos and tips by our own providers further elevates our social media presence and expands our reach to current and potential patients.

Figure 3.2-2 Customer Relationship Model

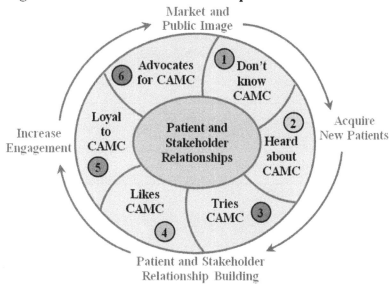

Figure 3.2-3 Strategies for Customer Relationship Building at Each Stage

Stage	Tools/Practices to Move Relationship to the Next Level	Measure/Figure #	How Level is Determined
1. Don't know CAMC	• Billboards • Newspaper Articles • TV Ads • Social Media* • CAMC Website*	• # of Calls to Community Liaisons (7.1-51) • # of Calls to Transfer Center (AOS) • Social Media (7.2-33) • Image Awareness Survey Results (7.2-26 - 7.2-28)	• Increases in each measure
2. Heard about CAMC	• "Stories" of CAMC • Healthfest* • FRC Classes • Trauma Outreach Program • CME for Physicians • ImagineU & Civic Affairs Council	All of the above plus: • Community Benefit Programs and Services • # of Participants in Health Fairs &Screening • # of Participants in Educational Programs • # of CAMC Sponsored Community Events (7.4-13) (full report AOS) • Imagine U participants (7.3-3)	• Increases in each measure
3. Tries CAMC	• Efficiency Improvements • Transfer Center* • Central Scheduling for OP • Pre-registration Services • AIDET • Patient Whiteboards	• # of Calls to the Transfer Center (AOS) • # of Referrals (7.1-45) • Average Time to Next Available Appointment (7.1-46) • Operational Efficiency Measures (7.1-45 – 7.1-52)	• Volume growth • Increase in patient satisfaction
4. Likes CAMC	• Hourly and Leadership Rounding* • Service Recovery (Take the HEAT) • CPOE • Multi-disciplinary Rounds • Discharge Information • Discharge Call-backs/Cipher Health* • Service Plus	• Satisfaction Survey (7.2-1 – 7.2-25) • Market Share (7.5-19 – 7.5-27) • Best Attributes (7.2-26 – 7.2-27) • WF Engagement (7.3-12 – 7.3-16) • Resident Overall Perception (7.3-21)	• Increases in each measure
5. Loyal to CAMC	• Series Appointments • Specialty Clinics • Center of Excellence • "Blue Distinction" Services	• "Definitely Recommend" (7.2-29 - 7.2-31) • Physician Using CPOE (7.3-22 – 7.3-23) • Top Choice Hospital (7.2-26)	• Increases in each measure
6. Advocates for CAMC	• Donors/Fundraising • Foundation Gala • Roundtables/Presentations • Professional Recognition • Support to Care for Patients	• Community Benefit Programs and Services (7.4-13) • # of Donors (AOS) • # of Employees with 30+ Years of Service (AOS) • Awards and Recognition (7.4-11)	• Increases in each measure

*Also Listening Posts (Figure 3.1-2)

Pewaukee School District (Baldrige Recipient 2013)

PSD (Pewaukee School District) uses multiple approaches housed in our CP (Communication Plan) to create a student/stakeholder focused culture in support of our Mission. This involves systematically listening to and engaging with key stakeholder groups to improve customer satisfaction while prompting improvement and innovation (Figure 3.1-1). We employ multiple approaches to market, build, and manage relationships with stakeholders.

Most relationships begin with in-person contact at our schools. To retain our customer base, we make it a priority to exceed expectations in the high quality personal relationships we develop with our stakeholders. Our CP strategically deploys relationship management strategies designed for segmented stakeholder groups yet recognizes that quality relationships are built with individualized two way communication.

Figure 3.2-3 Building Relationships with Students, Parents & Other Customers	
Relationship Building Method	**Purpose**
Individual School Open Houses	Provide general information about school to prospective students
Student Orientation	Assist students in smooth transition to a new school
Parent Web Accounts	Give parent access to teacher/class/assignment info via School Fusion
Parent Family Access	Provides electronic information on student grades, fee payment, discipline
Parent Workshops	Offer families learning opportunities (e.g. Internet safety, new curriculum)
Parent Advisory Groups	Gives voice to parent concerns; gives principals pulse of parent perception
Summer School	Offer remediation & enrichment to resident students & build relationship with non-resident students and families
Open Enrollment Marketing Tours	Offer prospective families school information to make informed decisions
Conflict Mediation Programs	Anti-Bullying Clubs teach students mediation techniques
Business & Community Partnership Committee	Pewaukee Chamber of Commerce members provide internships and speakers; PSD strengthens community relationships
Community Volunteer Program	Community members without children tutor in reading and math
Social Media	Facebook and Twitter used for all workshops, events, productions, etc.
Alumni Surveys	Alumni surveyed within a year of graduation to
Board of Education Meetings	Students & teachers featured in Spotlights; Citizen address the Board

CRITERIA QUESTIONS

In your response, include answers to the following questions:

b. Customer Relationships

(1) **Relationship Management** How do you build and manage customer relationships? How do you market, build, and manage relationships with customers to:

- acquire customers and build market share;
- manage and enhance your brand image;
- retain customers, meet their requirements, and exceed their expectations in each stage of the customer life cycle; and
- increase their engagement with you?

How do you leverage social media to enhance customer engagement and relationships with your organization?

(2) **Complaint Management** How do you manage customer complaints? How do you resolve complaints promptly and effectively? How does your management of customer **complaints** enable you to recover your customers' confidence, enhance their satisfaction and engagement, and avoid similar complaints in the future?

Notes:

3.2b. Building customer relationships might include developing partnerships or alliances with customers.

3.2b(1). Brand management is generally associated with marketing to improve the perceived value of your product or brand. Successful brand management builds customer loyalty and positive associations, and it protects your brand and intellectual property.

NIST (2015-2016) pp. 14-15

WORKSHEETS

3.2b(1) – Relationship Management

Build Customer Relationships Through How You:	To Achieve The Following:				
	Acquire Customers	Build Market Share	Manage And Enhance Your Brand Image	Retain Customers, Meet Their Requirements, And Exceed Their Expectations In Each Stage Of The Customer Life Cycle	Increase Their Engagement With You
Market					
Build					
Manage Relationships					

Steps Used For Customer Relationship Building	Social Media Used In This Step	How This Is Used To Manger Your Brand	How This Is Used To Enhance Customer Engagement	How This Is Used To Enhance Customer Relationships
1				
2				
3				
n				

3.2b(2) - Complaint Management

Complaint Process Steps (In Sequence)	How The Step Is Managed And Measured	How You Ensure The Step Helps To Resolve The Complaint Promptly And Effectively	How The Step Helps To Ensure That Similar Complaints Are Avoided In The Future

Complaint Management Process		
Your Process To Ensure That The Complaint Management Recovers Customer Confidence	Your Process To Ensure That The Complaint Management Enhances Customer Satisfaction	Your Process To Ensure That The Complaint Management Enhances Customer Engagement

ASSESSMENT

56	There is a systematic process for creating a customer-focused culture.	1 2 3 4 5 6 DK
57	The organization has a process which has defined the levels of desired customer relationships and assists us to systematically improve the customer relationship with all customer groups.	1 2 3 4 5 6 DK
58	There is a systematic process to ensure that the customer requirements and expectations are always met.	1 2 3 4 5 6 DK
59	There is a systematic process to determine when the customer engagement processes need to be improved to keep current with the customer's business needs.	1 2 3 4 5 6 DK
60	There is a systematic complaint resolution process in place which ensures rapid and effective handling of all customer complaints and problems.	1 2 3 4 5 6 DK
61	The complaint resolution process ensures aggregation and analysis of all complaint data to identify and eliminate the root causes of problems.	1 2 3 4 5 6 DK

BLUEPRINT

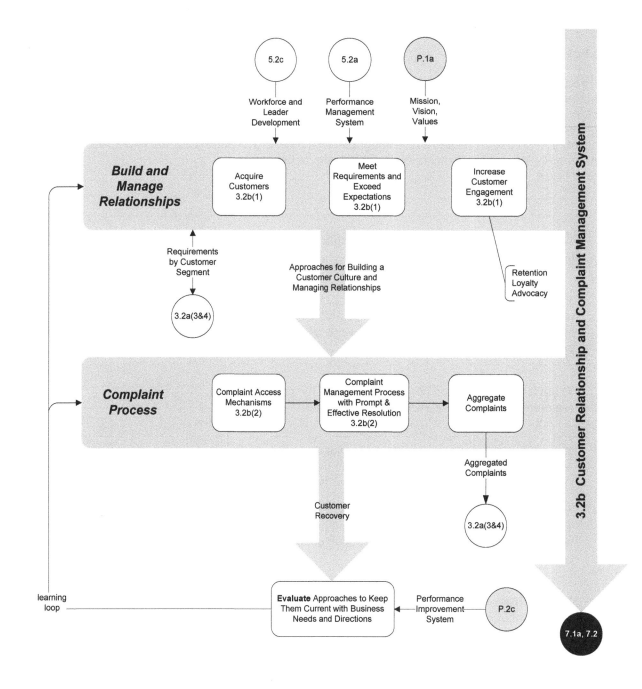

SYSTEM INTEGRATION

Context

P.1a > 3.2b Mission, Vision, Values - Creating a customer focused culture in 3.2b should be consistent with the overall organization mission, vision, and values described in P.1a. One issue that organizations often run into when developing a customer-focused culture is the tendency to sacrifice other stakeholders and their needs in order to serve the customers. While this can be a useful strategy in the short-term, it is seldom a sustainable strategy for the longer-term.

P.2c > 3.2b Performance Improvement System - The performance improvement system described in the profile (P.2c) should be a key input to the methods used to evaluate and keep the approaches to the customer focused culture and the building and management of relationships current with changing business needs and directions.

Systems

3.2b <> 3.2a(3&4) Requirements by Customer Segment - Customer requirements and expectations by customer segment are often identified through the analysis of customer data in 3.2a(3&4). These requirements and expectation for each key customer and market segments are an important input to building a customer culture (3.2b) that addresses the needs, wants, and desires of the various customer groups and segments.

3.2b < 5.2a Performance Management System - The performance management system described in 5.2a should be designed to support the building of a customer culture. The expectations, performance evaluation, and feedback should include the behaviors and practices that are consistent with a customer focused culture.

3.2b < 5.2c Workforce and Leader Development - The workforce and leader development system should be designed to include the necessary knowledge, skills, and abilities to support a customer focused culture.

3.2a(3&4) < 3.2b Aggregated Complaints - Complaint analysis is a key component of the analysis and use of customer data system described in 3.2a(3&4). The aggregated complaints from the customer listening and complaint system (3.2b) are key input to the identification of opportunities for improvement and innovation as described in 3.2a(3&4). Focusing improvement on areas that receive multiple complaints can help get to the root cause and redesign the processes to prevent future complaints.

Scorecard

3.2b > 7.1a, 7.2 Customer Relationship and Complaint Management Results - The customer focused results presented in 7.2a should include results on the extent and effectiveness of the organization's customer relationship and complaint management systems.

THOUGHTS FOR LEADERS

It is always interesting to look at where a leader spends their time, and from that time allocation decides what is important. If customers are important, the leaders spend time with them. If they do not spend time with customers, then there is very little a leader can say to convince the rest of the organization that customers are really important.

Leaders must also drive a customer-focused culture which ensures that the customer has a consistently favorable experience. This can only be accomplished through customer-facing processes that have be carefully designed, **measured**, stabilized and improved. Through the **measurements** the leaders need to assess the level of customer engagement and understand what product offerings and service levels are driving and improving that level of engagement.

A key message which can be sent down the organization is to make it clear that no leader can be assessed as 'top talent' if they do achieve their customer satisfaction and engagement goals.

The level of engagement must be robust enough that it will help the organization attract new customers and address all stages of the customer life cycle. This last concept is new to the CPE, and (taking the thought process further) it could be assumed that the organization should be able to address the customer's requirements during all phases of the product or service life cycle as well.

Finally, the leaders must drive continuous improvement in these processes. The improvements must go far beyond what "feels good" and encompass changes which the customer values.

A Very Serious Moment:

If you are out there, you have fans.
You have a champion.
Organize these champions.
You probably know who your best customers are.
Make them a star on your site.
Make those people your superheroes.

Jamison Stafford

> *A strong conviction that something must be done*
> *is the parent of many bad measures.*
>
> **Daniel Webster**

FOUNDATION

In many ways measurement and information are the "bloodstream" that flows within the performance excellence model of any organization. Although Categories 1 – 6 focus on several hundred 'hows' which require processes, these processes cannot be effective without performance measures. These measures must include both in-process and outcome (end-of-process) measures.

Performance Measures

Performance measurement begins with establishing the criteria that will be used to select performance measures and data. Many organizations have not consciously thought about this decision. Consequently, much of the data they collect and use evolves informally or is established on a case by case basis without clear decision criteria. The Criteria for Performance Excellence (CPE) model challenges the organization to take a more systematic approach, one that includes a repeatable selection process and explicit criteria for selection. The most basic *data selection decision* criteria include the following:

- **Required data** – Data may be required by regulatory agencies, governmental groups, higher level authority (internal or external to the organization), the organization's policies, industry standards, or others. Simply stated, if an organization is required to collect specific data, then it should collect those data.

- **Actionable data** – Using this data, an organization can understand what actions need to be taken.

Other more complex data selection criteria can include the two criteria above plus:

- data can be collected with integrity;

- data are easy to collect;

- data are meaningful to the owner of the data or the organization;

- data are understood by the users of the data; and

- data are available at the source of the data or area to be monitored.

Although data selection criteria are not specifically requested by the CPE (the criteria question is 'how do you select…'), answering this question allows an organization to more easily understand why they are collecting data and integrate their data collection process with how they actually use the data.

Comparative Data

Another approach addressed in Area to Address 4.1a is how the organization collects, selects, and uses key comparative data. Most organizations are attempting to drive a comparative mindset throughout the organization. They use comparisons not only at the highest level to make organization-wide decisions, but they also used comparisons (or benchmarks) to make decisions at all levels.

Sometimes inexperienced examiners will write feedback to the organization that indicates that there should be a benchmark for virtually everything. This is usually impracticable. Some comparisons are simply not available. The most important things to benchmark are the areas the organization must be successful at – as described in P.2a and P.2b in the Organizational Profile. If these are the factors which drive organizational success, then this is what the organization should fully understand through benchmarking.

Baldrige Award applications frequently discuss the organization's "benchmarking" processes. Few applications, however, describe the following components in their comparison selection and use process:

1. When the organization determines that the performance (or some other characteristic) is not what they wish.

2. How the organization decides a comparison is needed.

3. How the organization decides what data need to be compared.

4. How the organization decides what other groups or organizations to compare against.

5. The process the organization uses to collect comparative data (this is frequently called the *benchmarking process*).

6. How comparative data are analyzed once they are gathered.

7. How the analysis is turned into an action plan.

8. How the action plan is implemented.

9. How performance metrics are monitored to ensure that desired changes are achieved.

10. How corrective actions are taken if performance levels do not improve.

The fundamental question in the above sequence is whether the data drive meaningful action.

Customer Data

The customer-focused organization starts with the senior leaders, in Item 1.1. If they don't set a customer agenda, then it doesn't exist. Several places in Category 3 discuss the collection and use of customer-focused data. This part of the CPE asks how you select and ensure the effective use of the customer-focused data that you collect (including complaints). This includes how the data are used in strategic and operational decision making and innovation.

Measurement Agility

Once data have been gathered, analyzed and have driven improvement, the CPE ask how the performance measurement system is kept current with changing business needs. Once again, this systematic process needs to ensure that the organization's data collection, tracking, and decision processes can move at least as quickly as the external changes influencing the organization. This includes responding to unexpected organizational or external changes and changing the measures accordingly. The key thought is that high performing organizations use data, analysis, performance reviews, and course corrections to respond to rapidly changing organizational needs. This ability makes the organization more competitive. Once data are selected, collected, aligned, and integrated, leaders and employees throughout the organization need to use the data and information to support decisions. The CPE core value of *management by fact* is a key concept underlying Category 4.

EXAMPLES

Don Chalmers Ford (Baldrige Site Visit 2008 and 2012)

The Data Selection, Collection, Alignment & Integration System DCF uses correlates to the SPP and stakeholder/regulatory requirements. Data and information collection sources (Step 1) come from FMC and include Fordstar training certification, VOC, Sales rebates, incentives, and results. Service, Parts, and Body Shop information for Field Service Action Recalls (FSAs) and current promotions are available. The integrated computer system (UCS) provides reports from all program systems including accounting, finance, sales, customer satisfaction, and sales prospect control. 20 Group comparisons for financials, productivity, and customer satisfaction data are received monthly.

v-Auto is an innovative tool added in 2009 as a cycle of improvement for used vehicle inventory management, stocking in inventory for pricing, stocking and marketing. v-Auto provides "make-buy" information on vehicles the dealership is considering adding to the inventory and comparison data for similar vehicles, historical market pricing.

NADA 24 customer follow-up calls for the Body shop provide satisfaction results, and serve as learning tools to improve customer retention and satisfaction.

Selection and alignment of data and information (Step 2 & 3) are deployed in conjunction with Strategic and Annual Planning processes short- and longer-term goals and action plans. The overriding principles are effectiveness in measuring performance, action-oriented, ease of acquisition and maintenance. A key decision is made: Is this the key data and information needed to assess progress toward the strategic objectives and action plans?

The outcome is daily and weekly integration reports (Step 4) including the UCS generated Daily Operating Control (DOC), daily sales from local Ford division dealers, VOC from FMC and NADA 24, and the General Manager's daily forecast.

To engage the workforce, Monthly integration (Step 5) includes the monthly financial statement providing monthly and year-to-date information after the month closes in all business areas. The Driving Forward Report is provided monthly to each employee as a communication tool with each employee's department's BPR (stoplight colors assess progress to the forecast). Also included is "What's Important Now" (WIN) information like VOC results, community events, monthly employees' hire date anniversaries, and a foundational element of the month.

The DCF 20 Group Meeting is the epicenter of organizational reviews. Performance down the organization is reported and compared to the 20 Group data of FMC's highest performing dealers nationwide and the two local competitors. This review addresses volume, gross, VOC, market share, productivity, continuous improvement projects, employee satisfaction/issues, market share, training, employee retention, Top 100, President's Award and a wide range of other measures. DCF targets dealers with similar business models in the 20 Group book to meet or beat their performance in key areas of productivity. Each Department Manager then presents their departmental BP with progress for the previous month, status to their action plans, and SMART goals, with action plans and key measurable drivers based upon the annual plan. Results are color coded; green if meeting or exceeding the monthly and year to date plans; yellow if within 10% and red if below 10%. Actions from this meeting range from simple adjustments to get back on track, to broad-sweeping organization-wide decisions. This cycle of improvement in 2011 assists the managers in keeping their goals in front of them and staying focused on the actions to meet their annual plan.

A BPR example:

Butler						Business Plan Review (BPR)					
Key Success Drivers:		**Meet Annual Plan**				**Improve Productivity**	**Improve Consumer Experience**	**Continuous Learning (Training)**	**Improve Employee Satisfaction & Engagement**	**Community Project**	**Process Improvement**
		Month		YTD		Percentage of training schedule milestones accomplished	President's Award	Sessions of Covey Inspiring Trust completed & Compliance to I &E reqmts.	Employee Survey scores	Rotary, MOW & BBBS	Completed red book process, Baldrige application, and the FORD improvement process
		Plan	Actual	Plan	Actual						
Measure of Progress (quantifiable)	Rev	$ 500	$ 500	$ 28,500	$ 23,969						
	Expenses	$ 600	$ 160	$ 7,200	$ 2,753						
	Net	$ (100)	$ 340	$ 21,400	$ 21,216						

Color Coding: Green: meeting the strategic objective / Yellow: Making Progress

		SMART Goals to meet the Strategic Objectives									
Tactical (SMART) Goals to meet the Key success Drivers (ex: Improve employee satisfaction from 3.9 to 4.2 on question #20)	1	Goals are above				Meet 90% or better delivery of the training plan for 2012 by 12/12	Achieve President's Award in 2012	Meet 100% completion in the monthly leadership meetings held on the 4th Tuesday by 10/12	Improve the Employee survey satisfaction score from 4.02 to 4.1 and engagement from 3.87 to 4.0 by 12/12	Continue Rotary Membership and being Jacob's big brother	Implement Red Book (Taska) process at DCF, by 6/12
	2						Segment Used vehicle satisfaction by location	Improve I&E Compliance from 90% to 95% Annual (I & E) Certification Training		Do 9 Meals on Wheels routes with another employee	Submit Baldrige application on 5/24 (Option)
	3										Implement the FORD improvement process by 6/2012
	4										

		Action Plans for meeting the Goals									
Actions to meet the goals (ex: put in steps in your one improvement sheet)	1	1. Continue to work with Westside and Womens on their Zias and determine how I fit in at Kirtland now. (3/12)				1. Determine key processes for sales and service (1/12) 2. Determine process experts (including employees?) to train key processes implement into weekly/monthly training training (2/12) 3. Determine the annual schedule for key process training, who is responsible and last to measure learning (3/12)	1. Determine benefits & requirements implement any necessary process changes (3/2012) 2. Develop and submit proposed bonus plan changes to replace Blue Oval and areas of focus (3/2012) 4. Measure performance monthly on VOC and others key measures as identified. (monthly beg. 4/12)	1. Get certified (1/2012) 2. Hold training monthly in Leadership training sessions 3. Evaluate effectiveness with a before and after assessment. 4. Offer the class as a lunch and learn for all employees(9/12) 5. Start weekly class (10/12)	1. Use the tools we get from OEM and see how we can use them to improve and compare our results	Attend weekly meetings and support Foundation	1. Meet with Don to determine his expectations (1/2012) 2. Develop course guidelines and who is responsible for training content or where the material is located (started, complete 2/12) 3. Write the new/existing salesperson training process and recertification process including electronic tests (4/12) 4. Communicate plans, key measures of effectiveness and start training (5/12) **Launched 7/12**
	2						Work with Marketing to use coding to evaluate and track satisfaction by location (1Q12), track results the balance of the year and provide feedback to Brad and the managers(on-going)	1. Establish the key elements, schedule, trainer and audit schedule for Integrity and Ethics Certification (Use on-line process manual as much as possible) Includes AXZD plans, Red flags and customer privacy(12/11) 2. Conduct certification training 3. Audit per schedule, use red cards and green cards. (1/12)		Have Margie put me on the schedule and do the route with Brad or Brandon	Update Results for decision (1/12) , if yes 1. Submit eligibility form (1/12) 2. Coordinate writing teams (1/12) 3. Initial draft 3/12 4. Have Marlene come and visit again to review processes and results (3/12) 5. Update based on review (4/12) 6. Submit to ASQ (5/12) All complete
	3										1. Design the solutions board and implement into the driving forward on the back page (6/12) 2. Finish layout and implement into BPR per Don's direction (6/12). Develop training materials (6/12) 4. Train and implement (6 & 7/12) All complete

Clarke American (Baldrige Recipient 2001)

Clarke American's systematic process for selecting, gathering, analyzing and deploying information is linked from strategic planning to daily operations. They gather and integrate data and information through a system of organizational performance metrics to continually set goals, analyze performance and achieve deployment to the individual associate. This process helps them reflect the company values of Knowledge Sharing, Measurement, and Integrity and Mutual Respect. Performance metrics are defined for both change the business and run the business perspectives.

Change the business. In 1999, they incorporated the balanced stakeholder approach into the Balanced Business Plan (BBP) and Balanced Scorecard (BSC). They refined these tools with emphasis on changing the business.

Clarke American Leading and Lagging Indicators

Change the Business	Run the Business

Predictive Indicators (Leading)

▪ Customer Satisfaction ▪ Branch Loyalty ▪ Value Management workshops/symposiums ▪ Implemented S.T.A.R. ideas ▪ Total order cycle time	▪ Plant cycle time ▪ 24-hour service ▪ Utilization of Avenue ▪ Partner reporting satisfaction/on-time ▪ Associates hired in 60 days ▪ 401k participation ▪ % APS units ▪ % spend co-sourced

Diagnostic Indicators (Lagging)

▪ Revenue growth ▪ Customer contact center total revenue ▪ Total contact center revenue ▪ Revenue per call ▪ E-Commerce revenue ▪ Retention of 2-year associates ▪ Operating profit growth	▪ Branch telephone survey ▪ Waste (voids and spoilage) ▪ Total errors ▪ Credits/reprints ▪ PSPs integrated ▪ ROIC ▪ Cash flow ▪ Revenue per associate ▪ Total profit improvement and contribution

Run the business. The Key Process Indicators (KPIs) reflect the process view of the business and are used to constantly track the efficiency and effectiveness of the processes relative to the customer requirements, based upon their targets. A Key Leadership Team (KLT) member owns each metric. The leader is responsible for formally and systematically ensuring the relevance of the metric, as well as evaluating and improving the processes for gathering and reporting the information. These metrics are defined and deployed through all levels of the organization, providing for consistent and reliable analysis and decision making. The KLT reviews key metrics for continued relevance and integrity during goal deployment. Targets are established to achieve increasing performance levels. Metrics are further reviewed for *change the business* and *run the business* items. Using both predictive and diagnostic indicators provides the continual ability to test and understand the correlation between the various metrics.

Clarke American Performance Measurement Selection Process and Criteria

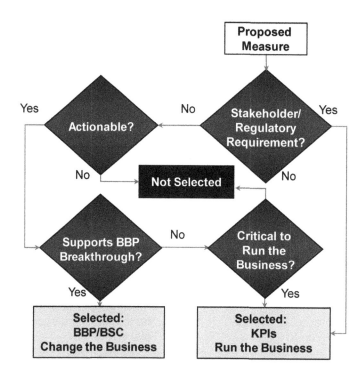

Selection and alignment of balanced organizational measures and indicators begins with and is driven through the strategic goal deployment process. This integrated approach ensures that metrics are systematically chosen, deployed and aligned with all company objectives. Metrics are evaluated for alignment with daily operations, as well as overall organizational performance and needs, based on a leadership review.

Change the business: The KLT agrees on appropriate measures, targets and impacts for each strategic goal within the four quadrants of the BBP as part of goal deployment. BBP measures are the primary tools used by the KLT to evaluate organizational performance and support attainment of change the business breakthrough goals. Measures are used to support division BBP and BSC objectives. Run the business: KPIs are the measures they associate with running the business "day-to-day." Each KPI is championed by a KLT member and reviewed at least monthly at the KLT level. Each division and process also defines KPIs, directly aligned with the company KPIs, to assess ongoing performance. These KPIs include measures of accuracy, responsiveness and timeliness for deliverables to internal or external customers.

Clarke American's drive to achieve world class manufacturing and servicing processes leads them to select and effectively use a variety of comparative data to assess relative performance and establish targets. During annual goal deployment, they determine the type of comparative information needed (what they compare). This is based on three factors: 1) strategic importance, 2) degree of improvement, and 3) new measure definition. The gap analysis process identifies key areas requiring breakthrough improvement, and they often set performance measures with comparative indicators when establishing appropriate targets. The Process Champion identifies the appropriate comparative measure, both within and outside the industry, and is responsible for the effective use of that information.

Clarke American seeks competitive comparisons from various sources (with whom they compare). Benchmarking has played a key role in improvement at Clarke American for many years. The CEO and other KLT members have been personally involved in "study tours" from which numerous best practices have been adopted. A cycle of improvement is a move to a more systematic 10-step approach to process benchmarking.

Clarke American's performance measurement system is kept current with business needs and directions through a variety of reviews and processes, including the Business Excellence Assessment and the "evaluate and improve" step in Goal Deployment. The measurement process has undergone numerous cycles of improvement. Each year during Goal Deployment, the KLT assesses business risks and identifies key measures for the upcoming year. Each KPI is owned by a KLT member who leads the formal assessment of the KPI through the review of its value and its match with business requirements. The BBP and BSC are reviewed at this same time. A recent improvement added an "impact" element to the BBP to better understand the implications of goal achievement. The number of measures included on the BSC and tracked as company KPIs has been reduced over time to ensure focus on the critical few. Measurement systems in each division and process are evaluated during the Business Excellence Assessment. They use the strengths and opportunities identified in the assessment to create action plans for improving the measurement system. A wide range of incremental improvements to the performance measurement system also come from Suggestions, Teams, Actions, Results (S.T.A.R.) ideas submitted by associates or teams.

Source: Clarke (2002) pp. 15 – 17

Poudre Valley Health System (Baldrige Recipient 2008)

Through the Balanced Scorecard (BSC), Poudre Valley Health System (PVHS) has established a process for selecting, collecting, aligning, and integrating data to track organizational performance, including progress relative to the strategic plan. As described in the organization's formal BSC Policy, the annual process begins with Strategic Development and Deployment Process (SDD), when the Senior Management Groups (SMG) identifies: 1) strategic goals and plans in support of each Strategic Objective (SO); and 2) key performance measures indicating progress toward the strategic plan. These key performance measures, including short- and longer-term financial measures, populate the system BSC. Next, BSC measures go to the multidisciplinary Knowledge Management Team, where each measure is assigned to a point person with relevant expertise for standards review (Figure 4.1-1).

Each point person sets performance goals and ranges (Figure 4.1-2) to drive innovation and performance improvement, based on comparative data for the top 10 percent of U.S. organizations or an internal stretch goal determined by trending historical data.

SMG gives final BSC approval, and the system BSC is created in PVHS' innovative electronic BSC system. From the system BSC, individual SMG members create BSCs with division specific measures and goals that support the system BSC. Directors then create department BSCs with service area-specific measures and goals that support the division and system BSCs. Each month, managers of data related to HR, patient satisfaction, financials, market share, and key clinical process/outcome measures globally populate the electronic BSCs. SMG and directors populate additional key measures on their respective BSCs.

At a glance, system BSC users can gauge organizational progress relative to the strategic plan. If key performance measures are blue or green, PVHS is on track to accomplish the corresponding strategic plan items; if key performance measures are yellow or red, the organization is not on track to accomplish these items. On the system BSC, if a measure is red for one month or yellow for three months, the point person for that measure determines why the measure is not on track and develops a BSC improvement/ action plan, which is approved and monitored by the appropriate SMG member and hyperlinked to the electronic BSC. The result is continual performance improvement and progress toward the organization's strategic plan.

When a measure is proposed a systematic checklist is used:

Definition Sheet 2009

Strategic Objective

Name of Measure:
Manager Submitting Measure: Phone number:
Which entity is this measure for? PVH ☐   MCR ☐   PVHS ☐
What cost centers does this definition sheet apply?
Person(s) responsible for obtaining and entering the data:
Define the measure:
Purpose of the measure:
Why was this measure chosen?
How was this measure chosen?
List the industry benchmark resource(s) for comparing the result of the measure - (if benchmark should not be used, see last question):
How often should this item be measured? ☐ Monthly ☐ Quarterly ☐ Other:
Measure range format: ☐ Whole Number ☐ Percentage ☐ Timeline ☐ Other:
Record goal ranges below:
Name of Measure:

	* World Class or Stretch Goal (blue)	Meets Goal (green)	Requires Monitoring (yellow)	Below Goal (red)
All BSCs for cost centers mentioned above				
Dept/Cost Center Specific				

Check all of the following that apply to the *BLUE* range listed above.

External to PVHS AND a World Class Goal	*External to PVHS but NOT a World Class goal*	*External stretch goal*	*Internal stretch goal*
☐ Top 10% of a national data base ☐ 90th percentile of a national data base	☐ Top 25% of a national data base	☐ A National Norm ☐ A National Mean	☐ Based on historical data trends

Would the range and definition be the same for all levels of the organization?
☐ Yes ☐ No   ☐ N/A
If no, what would be the exception(s)?
If a benchmark should not be used, explain why.
Other factors for consideration:

In addition to using the BSC to track organizational performance and drive innovation and performance improvement, PVHS also analyzes data for information to make fact-based decisions at both strategic and operational levels. One critical tool across the organization is the monthly Key Performance Indicator (KPI) reports that go to each Director. These cost center reports let Directors monitor departmental revenue and expenses and perform drill down analysis.

The KPI reports roll up from department to division to facility to system. The resulting system Monthly Financial Results report goes to all Directors, SMG, and the BOD.

Figure 4.1-1: BSC Standards Review

1. What is the purpose of the measure?
2. Why was the measure chosen?
3. Ho was the measure chosen?
4. How should the measure be defined?
5. How often should this item be measured?
6. What is the format of the measure?
7. What are the acceptable and unacceptable values for this measure?
8. Are the definition and range acceptable for all levels of the organization?
9. What sources were consulted for possible industry benchmarks?
10. Is there an industry benchmark?
11. Are there a data source and benchmark for this measure?
12. If a benchmark is not appropriate, why not?
13. Are there other factors to consider?

	Figure 4.1-2: BSC Performance Goals & Ranges
BLUE	The best practice or world –class [P.1a(2)] stretch goal
GREEN	An indicator of acceptable performance
YELLOW	An indicator that performance is in transition and warrants monitoring
RED	An indicator that performance falls outside the acceptable range and warrants immediate action

Since this process also includes the selection of benchmarks, PVHS uses the following flow diagram to explain the hierarchy and definition of world call within their organization.

Vision of PVHS:
To provide world-class health care

World-class is defined as:
Striving for results in the 90th percentile or top 10% of available national comparative databases

National Comparative Databases used by PVHS:
Gallup Physician Engagement   MSA Employee Engagement
Reuter Care Discovery   Avatar Patient Satisfaction   NDNQI Nursing Quality
CMS Core Measures   National Patient Safety Goals

Presentation of performance improvement for reporting results from databases is in two formats:
Dashboards and Balanced Scorecards (BSC)

Scheduled analysis of results on Dashboards and BSCs is by:
CQIC   MEC   MSQC   Board Quality Committee   SMG   Directors
Credentials Committee   Customer Service Committee   Human Resources
QR Dept.   Patient Safety Committee   Resource Services Dept.

Quality results not performing to 90th percentile or top 10% are prioritized for improvement

Source: Poudre Valley Health System

Monfort College of Business (Baldrige Recipient 2004)

MCB's mission, values, and strategic plan serve as the framework for establishing its key performance indicators (KPIs). MCB has established KPIs as its performance measures for tracking overall organizational performance and guiding the College's daily operations. KPIs measure achievement, satisfaction, and quality across MCB's key stakeholder groups. Each KPI has stated one- and five-year measurable goals that are reviewed annually to assess progress and opportunities for improvement.

4.1a (1) KPIs are selected and aligned to measure performance in meeting the College's mission, vision, and values. The KPIs are also aligned with the University's mission and the College's AACSB accreditation requirements.

MCB's shared governance structure (i.e., its faculty, student committees, and senior leaders) establishes and implements action plans in pursuit of the mission of the College. These groups also are responsible for selecting the KPIs and other indicators including the review of data from the ETS and EBI reports and student surveys. The Student Affairs Committee (SAC) recommends measures for student performance, satisfaction, admission, and continuation. The Faculty Affairs Committee (FAC) recommends measures for faculty composition, performance, satisfaction, evaluation, and retention. The Technology Committee (TC) recommends measures for technology capacity, investment, and performance. The Curriculum Committee (CC) recommends measures for curriculum content, student learning, and satisfaction. The Administrative Council (ADMC) oversees the final selection of KPIs and other measures.

Internal and external review groups for establishing the College's measures include UNC administration, the Dean's Leadership Council (DLC), and MCB faculty committees. Annual surveys are used for formal alumni and employer input, and the MCB Student Representative Council (SRC) serves as the primary student review agent.

The MCB Dean's Office coordinates data collection and management activities. The MCB Advising Center, EBI, and ETS, as well as UNC's Institutional Research and Planning (IRP), Admissions, Career Services (CS), Budget, and Foundation offices provide data for the KPIs at regular intervals. The MCB Advising Center provides data on student admissions, retention, graduation and academic performance. MCB's EBI benchmarking coordinator administers and reports annual EBI benchmarking results. UNC's IRP, Admissions, and Budget offices provide data on expenditures and salaries, student admissions, retention, graduation, and other performance and satisfaction measures. ETS provides data on graduating student learning performance in multiple areas. CS provides the College with a range of placement data on its graduates. In addition, CS annual surveys, AACSB corporate reports, biannual meetings with the DLC, and annual alumni surveys provide information from individuals outside higher education.

Alignment and integration of data with the mission, values, and KPIs are formally reviewed annually, with adjustments made as additional information becomes available and analysis warrants. The committees review and revise the mission and values and subsequently revise the KPIs to assure selected performance measures are linked to meeting the College's mission and accomplishing its strategic objectives.

KPIs are useful in recognizing areas that need attention and in identifying cause and effect. For example, students had been demonstrating steady progress in MCB's overall learning results as determined by ETS test results (Figures 7.1-1, 3). A dip in 2001-02 results led the ADMC to seek the cause for the decline. No curriculum defects were identified in course work or grades earned. However, after analyzing student performance by class section and follow-up with students, it was determined that two faculty members had discounted the importance of doing one's best on the test. Follow-up discussion occurred between the deans and appropriate faculty. Further, a dean now meets with each of the testing classes, and students are educated on the importance of accurate test results to the students, and MCB. Student performance improved immediately.

Performance data are used to make decisions for student admission, retention and graduation requirements, curriculum revisions, faculty and staff performance evaluation, and technology assessment.

To provide data and information that supports organizational decision-making and innovation, MCB's shared governance structure, DLC, and external constituencies evaluate the KPIs, other indicators, and comparative data annually as part of the PDCA process (Figure 6.1-1). Should the measures fall below the one-year goal, the unit responsible for the indicator performs an analysis and makes recommendations to the administration for improvement, as outlined in the PDCA process. UNC recognition of MCB's assessment, decision, and action efforts is exhibited in Figure 4.1-1.

4.1a (2) MCB selects and ensures the effective use of key comparative data by selecting measures that determine how well the College is achieving its mission, provide comparative benchmarks against peer institutions, and allow the College to evaluate performance over an extended period of time.

MCB incorporates best practices in business administration education into its strategic planning process. Several best practices are defined through the accreditation process, while others are defined through comparative analysis. For example, MCB recently purchased the AACSB report "Effective Practices: Undergraduate Career Services and Placement Offices" to assist in evaluating and improving the student placement function. Several members of MCB's leadership recently toured the facilities of a key competitor to meet with its leadership and attempt to identify process refinements that can help MCB improve. Leaders also visited other programs outside the College's normal peer set in order to extend their own views on practices and norms for success. This spring, for example, the dean is completing a pattern of visits to each member of the DLC at their place of business to learn more about how their organizations operate and compete. Leaders also recently visited the Colorado School of Mines, which houses the state's premier engineering education program. MCB representatives participate in professional association conferences that offer additional opportunities to learn of peer successes and failures and the implementation of various programs and initiatives.

Figure 4.1-2 Primary Key Performance Indicators (KPIs) of Organizational Performance			
KPI	**Strategic Categories**	**Source**	**Results**
Quality of incoming freshmen students (avg. ACT)	Recruits	UNC	7.3-6; 7.5-1, 2
Quality of transfer students (avg. GPA)	Recruits	UNC	7.5-3
Student retention rates	Students	UNC	7.2-20
Business major counts	Students	UNC	7.3
MCB current student satisfaction (% recommending)	Students	MCB	7.2-16
Student learning in business (avg. overall ETS)	Curriculum	ETS	7.1-1
High-touch curriculum (avg. class size)	Curriculum	MCB	7.5-11, 13
Quality of faculty (% academic or professional qualification)	Faculty	UNC	7.4-1
Quality of professional faculty (% professional qualification)	Faculty	UNC	7.4-2
Quality of academic faculty (assessment by exiting students)	Faculty	EBI	7.2-4,5
Faculty program satisfaction (avg. overall)	Faculty	EBI	7.4-7
Student satisfaction—facilities/computing resources	Facilities/technology	EBI	7.2-8
Faculty satisfaction—computing resources	Facilities/technology	EBI	7.4-10
Total available state funds (annual)	Financial resources	UNC	7.3-1
Total available private funds (annual)	Financial resources	UNC	7.3-3
Placement of graduates (% employed full-time)	Grads/alums	UNC	7.5-6
Exiting student satisfaction (avg. overall)	Grads/alums	EBI	7.2-1
Alumni satisfaction (avg. overall)	Grads/alums	EBI	7.2-2
Employer satisfaction (avg. overall)	Employers	MCB	7.2-3
MCB press coverage (media coverage generated)	Program reputation	MCB	7.5-9, 10

Many data sources used by the College are externally derived. EBI benchmark data (182 U.S. business schools in 2003) provide comparative and long-term performance and satisfaction measures for faculty, student and alumni, as well as administrative measures, such as faculty FTE and program expenditures. ETS exit examination data (359 U.S. business schools in 2003) provide information on student performance. The EBI and ETS measures are considered highly reliable and externally valid measures of performance and satisfaction. These data sources reflect the best practices in business administration education.

MCB has established a formal review schedule for the College's processes. This is separate from the review of comparative data and key indicators. MCB senior leaders and the appropriate faculty groups annually review processes to determine if they are effective in improving quality and to identify where improvement opportunities exist. The schedule for process review is published on SEDONA. Also, the individual review groups have established methods for process review, also described on SEDONA. Such processes aid in the selection and revision of KPIs and other measures. Recommendations to revise MCB processes are made to the ADMC and reflect the PDCA appropriate for an existing system.

4.1a (3) To ensure MCB's performance measures are current and sensitive to change with educational needs and directions, the College mission, values, and KPIs are: (1) aligned with the current AACSB accreditation standards, (2) reviewed annually by senior corporate managers (including the DLC), alumni and academic personnel, and (3) measured against data from external agencies (e.g., EBI, ETS) that invest in developing reliable, valid, and timely measures for business administration education. These three criteria provide a standard of currency and quality for MCB's KPIs and other indicators. To ensure that performance measure systems are sensitive to rapid or unexpected organizational or external changes, the College annually reviews its indicators and incorporates external reviews of the indicators by the DLC. Further, MCB, ETS, AACSB, and EBI incorporate changes in their performance and satisfaction instruments to assure currency in the data.

Source: Monfort (2005)

CRITERIA QUESTIONS

In your response, include answers to the following questions:

a. Performance Measurement

(1) **Performance Measures** How do you use data and information to track daily operations and overall organizational performance? How do you:
- select, collect, align, and integrate data and information to use in tracking daily operations and overall organizational performance; and
- track progress on achieving strategic objectives and action plans?

What are your key organizational performance measures, including key short-term and longer-term financial measures? How frequently do you track these measures?

(2) **Comparative Data** How do you select and effectively use comparative data and information to support operational decision making?

(3) **Customer Data** How do you use voice-of-the-customer and market data and information? How do you:
- select and effectively use voice-of-the-customer and market data and information (including aggregated data on complaints) to build a more customer-focused culture and to support operational decision making, and
- use data and information gathered through social media, as appropriate?

(4) **Measurement Agility** How do you ensure that your performance measurement system can respond to rapid or unexpected organizational or external changes?

Notes:

4.1. The results of organizational performance analysis and review should inform the strategy development and implementation you describe in category 2.

4.1. Your organizational performance results should be reported in items 7.1–7.5.

4.1a. Data and information from performance measurement should be used to support fact-based decisions that set and align organizational directions and resource use at the work unit, key process, department, and organization levels.

4.1a(2). Comparative data and information are obtained by benchmarking and by seeking competitive comparisons. Benchmarking is identifying processes and results that represent best practices and performance for similar activities, inside or outside your industry. Competitive comparisons relate your performance to that of competitors and other organizations providing similar products and services. One source of this information might be social media or the Web.

NIST (2015-2016) pp. 16 - 17

WORKSHEETS

4.1a(1) – Performance Measures

Use Of Data and Information	Processes Used To:			
	*Select Data and Information**	*Collect Data and Information*	*Align Data and Information*	*Integrate Data and Information*
Track Daily Operations				
Track Overall Organizational Performance				
Track Progress Relative To Strategic Objectives				
Track Progress Relative To Action Plans				

* *This should include the use of clearly defined data selection criteria which can be used at all levels of the organization.*

Key Organizational Performance Measures:	Short-Term Financial Measures	Longer-Term Financial Measures	The Process To Determine How Frequently To Determine These Measures	How Frequently You Track These Measures
1				
2				
3				
4				
5				
6				
7				
8				
9				
N				

4.1a(2) – Comparative Data

The Steps In Your Process To Determine The Need For and To Gather Benchmarks and Comparative Data
1
2
3
4
5
n

Uses Of Data:	Processes Used To:	
	Select Key Comparative Data	Ensure The Effective Use Of Key Comparative Data
Operational Decision Making		

4.1a(3) – Customer Data

Uses Of Data:	Voice-Of-The-Customer Data (Including Aggregated Data On Complaints) – How Do You:	
	Select Data	Ensure The Effective Use Of Data
Build A more customer-focused culture		
Support Operational Decision Making		
Social Media Gathered Data		

4.1a(4) – Measurement Agility

How You Ensure That Your Performance Measurement System Can Respond To Rapid Or Unexpected Organizational (Internal) Or External Changes:	

ASSESSMENT

Rating Scale:

1 - **No Process** in place - We are not doing this
2 - **Reacting to Problems** – We use a basic (primarily reactive) process
3 - **Systematic Process** – We use a systematic process that has been improved
4 - **Aligned** – We use a process that aligns our activities from top to bottom
5 - **Integrated** – We use a process that is integrated with other processes across the organization
6 - **Benchmark** – We are the Benchmark in our industry or beyond!
DK - Don't Know

---

62   The criteria for data selection are clearly defined and have been deployed to each organizational level so they can collect the data they need.   1   2   3   4   5   6   DK

63   The organization has a systematic process through which data and information are gathered and integrated to support daily operations and short- and longer-term organizational decision-making.   1   2   3   4   5   6   DK

64   The functional data and information which are collected and reviewed are linked to overall organization plans, goals, and directions.   1   2   3   4   5   6   DK

65   The organization has a process to: 1) select, 2) collect, and 3) use benchmark data or comparisons as a way of regularly improving our own internal processes and performance.   1   2   3   4   5   6   DK

66   The performance measurement system is systematically kept current with the needs of the organization.   1   2   3   4   5   6   DK

BLUEPRINT

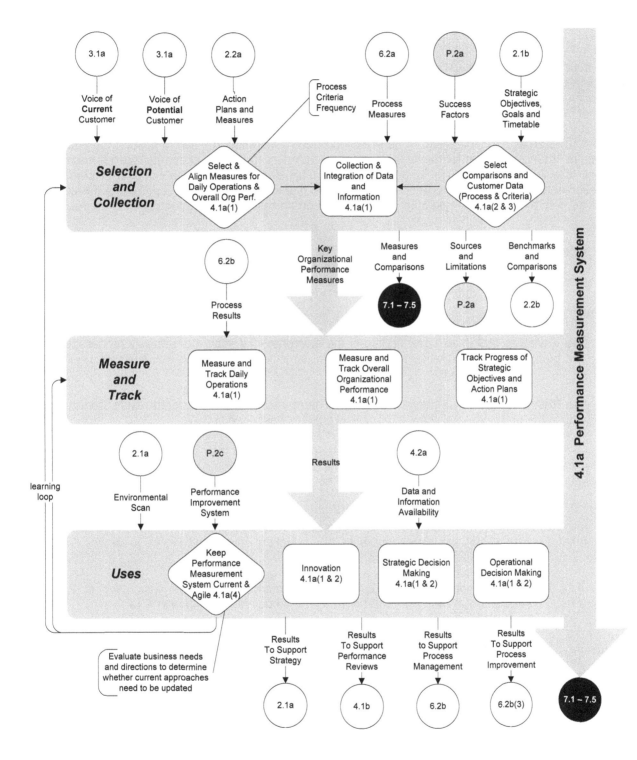

SYSTEM INTEGRATION

Context

P.2a > 4.1a Success Factors - The key success factors for the key markets and competitive environments along with the competitors described in the profile (P.2a) are key inputs to the selection of comparison information measures and sources described in 4.1a. This is particularly important in areas that are linked to market performance.

P.2a < 4.1a Sources and Limitations - The selection of comparison information to support the analysis of all facets of organizational performance is limited due to barriers to sharing of competitive information and the cost of collecting comparison information. The profile describes both the sources of comparison information and the limitations to collecting comparisons that the organization faces. Both of these should be derived from the processes and criteria used by the organization to select comparisons as describe in 4.1a.

P.2c > 4.1a Performance Improvement System - The process that the organization uses to evaluate, improve, and keep current the performance measurement system should be consistent with and based on the improvement approaches described in the profile (P.2c).

Systems

2.1a > 4.1a Environmental Scan - The results of the environmental scan and analysis process is a key input to the performance measurement system and in particular the strategic management uses of the measures.

2.1a < 4.1a Results to Support Strategic Planning - The measures and associated results from 4.1a are direct inputs to the environmental scan and analysis process described in 2.1a.

2.1b > 4.1a Strategic Objectives and Timetable - The objectives and their timetable for accomplishment drive the identification of performance and project measures to track the performance improvement. The identification of these measures should be part of the performance measurement process described in 4.1a.

2.2a > 4.1a Action Plans and Measures - The action plans and measures determined in the action plan development process (2.2a) are direct inputs to the selection and alignment of measures for daily operations and overall organizational performance described in 4.1a.

2.2b < 4.1a Benchmarks and Comparisons - The benchmarks and comparisons used in 2.2b for projections should be consistent with those identified by the processes described in 4.1a.

3.1a > 4.1a Voice of Current and Potential Customers – Methods and Mechanisms to capture the voice of the customer are a key input to 4.1a(3) the selection and use of VOC data and information.

4.1a > 4.1b Results to Support Performance Reviews - The measures and associated results from 4.1a are direct inputs to the periodic performance reviews described in 4.1b.

4.1a < 4.2a Data and Information Availability - Data and information availability (4.2a) including quality (accurate, reliable, timely, etc.) is an important input to the process of collecting data for tracking and analyzing operations, overall organization performance, and progress relative to strategic objectives.

4.1a < 6.2a Process Measures - The selection and alignment of key performance measures for daily operations and process management (4.1a) is driven by the key process requirements and the in-process control requirements identified in the work process design process described in 6.2a.

4.1a > 6.2b Results to Support Process Management - The key performance measures identified in 4.1a for operational decision making and process management are important inputs to the process management practices described in 6.2b.

4.1a < 6.2b Process Results - The results that are derived from the measurement and control of processes as described in 6.2b are direct inputs to the measurement methods described in 4.1a.

4.1a > 6.2b(3) Results to Support Process Improvement - The key performance measures identified in 4.1a to support process improvement are important inputs to the process improvement practices described in 6.2b(3).

Scorecard

4.1a > 7.1 through 7.5 Comparisons - The comparisons selected using the processes described in 4.1a should be the same comparisons that are presented in all the results areas 7.1 through 7.5.

4.1a > 7.1 through 7.5 Measures – The results produced by the measures identified in 4.1a should be the same results presented in all the results areas 7.1 through 7.5.

THOUGHTS FOR LEADERS

Performance measurement is key to the success of any organization. Nevertheless, organizations frequently select their metrics or balanced scorecard measures without linking them to what is important to the success of the organization. To link the organization from the highest levels of planning down to metrics tracked, the following logic sequence should be followed:

- Strategic Challenges (External Influences)

- Success Factors (What Anybody In This Industry Needs To Be Good At)

- Strategic Advantages (What This Organization Is Good At)

- Strategic Opportunities (Where We Can Leverage An Opportunity)

- Strategic Objectives (Internal Actions)

- Long-Term Action Plans And Measures

- Short-Term Action Plans And Measures

- Balanced Scorecard Measures

- Team Goals And Measures

- Individual Goals And Measures

- Other Metrics

Frequently, however, the linkages between these levels of external influences and the internal actions, plans, and metrics cannot be seen. Without this linkage, the organization's higher-level objectives are wishes and good intentions, but will not systematically become a reality. Conversely, when performance is tracked up the organization, the lower-level actions can drive the achievement of the higher-level strategic objectives.

This flow-down of goals should be described in Item 2.2. The concurrent selection of measures should be addressed in Area 4.1a (this Area to Address). The "flow-up" of performance reviews and the use of data should be described in Area 4.1b.

A Lighter Moment:

Data is not information,
Information is not knowledge,
Knowledge is not understanding,
Understanding is not wisdom.

Cliff Stoll & Gary Schubert

> *"Management" means, in the last analysis, the substitution of thought for brawn and muscle, of knowledge for folklore and superstition, and of cooperation for force.*
>
> **Peter Drucker**

 FOUNDATION

Once performance measurement and data selection (as described in 4.1a) are completed, analysis is used as the tool to translate raw data into actions. The Criteria for Performance Excellence (CPE) address this analysis at the most senior level of the organization because senior leaders review organizational performance and take actions that can impact the achievement of the organization's strategic plans. Nevertheless, high performing organizations also have the ability to perform similar analysis at every organizational level.

While the CPE focus on the highest levels of the organization, they do ask how the results of those analyses are deployed to the work group and functional levels within the organization so that every level of the organization can effectively support the decisions made at higher levels. Performance analysis is the key tool to translate data into usable or actionable information. The organization needs to then use this information to help drive actions to improve.

Once performance is measured and the results are analyzed, the criteria ask how organizational performance is reviewed and how senior leaders participate and how do they use the reviews to

- assess:
    o organizational success,
    o competitive performance,
    o progress on achieving strategic objectives and action plans; and
- respond rapidly to
    o organizational needs,
    o challenges in your operating environment
    o need for transformational change in organizational structure and work systems

In high performing organizations, however, the senior leaders spend the majority of their time on *changing the business* and not *running the business*. Sure those senior leaders review performance and make course corrections. They are intimately familiar with the current performance of the organization, and may spend one or two days a week reviewing the past performance. That is not, however, where they spend the majority of their time. The *change the business* activities may absorb up to eighty percent of a senior leader's time in a high performing organization.

EXAMPLES

PRO-TEC Coating Company (2007 Baldrige Recipient)

The systems for review of both performance and capabilities are highly integrated into the PRO-TEC model shown for "Organizational Performance Model" and "Organizational Decision-Making Matrix" shown in the Figures.

Figure 4.1-1 shows references to the "Goal Flow-Down Tools" described and how they are evaluated in the "Organizational Decision-Making Matrix." Senior leadership is present and participates in review of performance meetings outlined in Figure 4.1-2❶,❷,❸ on the next page.

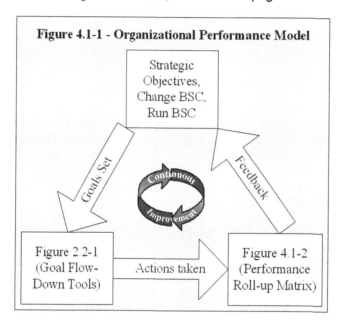

Analysis done to validate the results of decisions made at each level are both business, as measured by our Accounting and Finance and Business Planning departments, and technical, as done by the Operations, QA, and IS departments. Accounting and Business Planning primarily analyze inventories, orders booked, and proceeds against the strategic objectives and the "run the business BSC" metrics. Operations analyzes data collected by process sensors for the purpose of verifying expected results as well as support or track the impact of innovations. The QA department, in addition to tracking standard quality assurance measures for steel, also supports innovation by analyzing what process conditions support optimal conditions for product quality. The IS department looks at process data and does statistical analysis in support of updating process models and tables. Detailed explanations of analysis are available on site. The results of these analyses are used to drive departmental and organizational decision-making.

They measure organizational success and competitive performance relative to strategic objectives by the use of the BSC and by use of benchmarks against competitors when available. The ability to address rapid changes in organizational needs and challenges is facilitated by the structure of the organization, which supports appropriate decision-making authority at all levels.

PRO-TEC's decision-making matrix is designed for agility. Figure 4.1-2❶,❷ represents meetings that occur either daily or three times weekly where senior management is present to assess current status of either operational or business conditions. Priorities are set, and continuous improvement and breakthrough performance activities are identified at these meetings, or at departmental meetings described in Figure 4.1-2❸. Continuous improvement is identified, planned for, and implemented at all levels of the organization, a reflection of Associates practicing Ownership, Responsibility, and Accountability (ORA). Breakthrough improvement is accomplished many times by lower levels coming up with the ideas for breakthrough improvement but requiring management approval coming at meetings described in Figure 4.1-2❷,❺. Through the "Goal Flow-Down Tools" described in Category 2, the opportunities for innovation are communicated through the organization. Much of the innovation that occurs happens at the meetings described in Figure 4.1-2❸, since departments use their subject matter experts to provide solutions possibly not conceived by the originator of the improvement.

Figure 4.1-2 – Organization Decision-Making Matrix					
	Operational 1	Tactical 2	Departmental 3	Monthly 4	Others 5
Who	Value creation processes	Value creation processes, support processes	Each department personnel	Leadership team and stakeholders	PRO-TEC Board, Leadership team (strategic planning), Departmental planning
When	Daily	3 times weekly	1-2 month	Monthly	3 times a year, annual
What	Run Balanced Scorecard (BSC) – Quality, volume, uptime	Run BSC – Inter-departmental cooperative efforts, corrective actions; Change BSC – Current issues driving change	Run BSC – Review projects, departmental issues, plan versus actual; Change BSC – support of tactical and strategic planning	Run BSC – Review departmental performance, action items	Run BSC – Review company performance; Change BSC – Develop change strategy for long term viability (update Change BSC)
Analysis	Trending, process logs	Review of operations, pareto, correlation, statistical	Statistical, uptime metrics, correlation, pareto	Statistical, uptime metrics, correlation, pareto	Roll-up of measures done at lower levels
Decisions made	Production, operational, equipment	Safety, business direction, operational	Innovation	Resourcing	Strategic planning, Change BSC items
Improvement methodology	I-to-I processes	I-to-I processes	I-to-I processes	I-to-I processes	Roll-up of processes done at lower levels

PRO-TEC (2007) Application Summary

Saint Luke's Hospital of Kansas City (Baldrige recipient, 2002)

Saint Luke's Hospital of Kansas City uses a Balanced Scorecard methodology for Performance Analysis, Review, and Improvement. The scorecard is linked with the strategic planning process. Saint Luke's Hospital conducts a number of analyses to support the quarterly Balanced Scorecard (BSC) review. The results of these efforts are published in a BSC report, which is provided to senior leaders and available for more widespread distribution. The report includes the overall scorecard, with quarterly performance highlighted in color coded boxes indicating performance above (blue), or at goal (green), moderate risk (yellow), and at risk (red). This permits senior leaders to quickly determine where performance is relative to the goals established by the strategic plan.

To obtain the BSC information, performance data are gathered and analyzed from across the hospital. These data are plotted on run charts so trends can be identified, and in key clinical outcome and operational performance measures, control limits are established to allow determination of process stability. This information is available for drill-down analysis during the BSC reviews and is included in the BSC report. Comparative or benchmark data are also included. Saint Luke's Hospital annually acquires Medicare data from Solucient in order to measure health care outcome performance and works closely with Mercer/Solucient to turn Diagnosis Related Group (DRG) hospital based information into index scores for reporting purposes. Medicare data that are released include Medicare discharge volumes, DRG severity index, average length of stay index, mortality index, and DRG Resource index per market analysis. With this information, Saint Luke's Hospital can measure its performance against local/regional competitors.

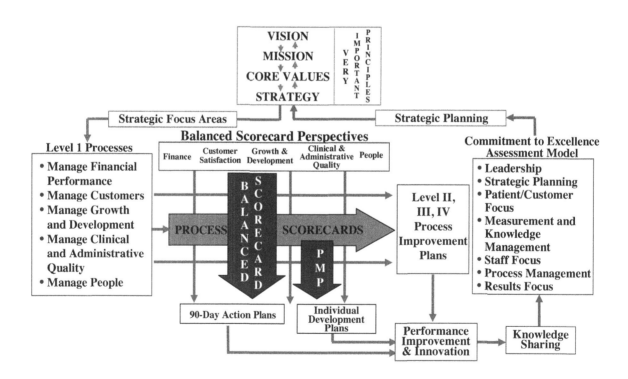

When determining market-related performance, Saint Luke's Hospital calculates a **Market Value Index (MVI)**. This computation is based on inpatient market share as determined by the Kansas City Business Journal, the NRC Perception Rating, and the "Would Recommend" ratings obtained from the Press

Ganey survey. The MVI indicates the perceived value Saint Luke's Hospital has in its market area in relation to its competitors. In addition, SLH tracks and trends eligible and profitable market share.

Human resource performance is analyzed by trending data and obtaining comparisons from the Saratoga Institute. Financial performance is analyzed by tracking variance to budget on a monthly basis, including an analysis of volume indicators, revenues, and expenses for personnel, supplies, and other operational areas. These are analyzed by month, year-to-date, and compared to the previous year's results.

Saint Luke's Hospital Scorecard
3rd Quarter 2003

	Key Measure	3rd Qtr 2003 Performance	Target 10	Stretch 9	Stretch 8	Goal 7	Moderate 6	Moderate 5	Moderate 4	Risk 3	Risk 2	Risk 1	Raw Score
Financial	Total Margin	8.5%	14.0%	12.5%	11.1%	8.1%	6.7%	5.2%	2.3%	-0.6%	-2.1%	-3.6%	7
	Operating Margin	6.2%	12.0%	10.5%	9.0%	6.1%	4.6%	3.1%	0.2%	-2.6%	-4.2%	-5.7%	7
	Days Cash on Hand	355.5	350.4	338.6	326.7	303.0	291.1	279.2	255.5	231.7	219.8	208.0	10
	Cost per CMI Adjusted Discharge	$7,938	$7,557	$7,707	$7,858	$8.158	$8,308	$8,458	$8,759	$9.059	$9,210	$9,360	7
CUSTOMER SATISFACTION	Longer Than Expected Wait Time (IP, OP, ED)	9.3%	10.1%	10.4%	10.7%	11.0%	13.2%	15.3%	17.5%	19.6%	23.9%	28.2%	10
	Overall Satisfaction (IP, Op, ED)	94.0%	96.3%	94.1%	93.1%	92.1%	90.8%	89.7%	88.6%	87.5%	85.2%	83.0%	8
	Responsiveness to Complaints	89.7%	98.1%	95.8%	93.5%	91.2%	90.0%	88.8%	87.7%	86.5%	84.2%	81.9%	5
	Outcome of Care	92.5%	97.0%	95.6%	94.2%	92.8%	92.1%	91.3%	90.6%	89.9%	88.5%	87.0%	6
	Active Admitting Physician Ratio	40.6%	42.8%	41.3%	39.7%	38.2%	37.5%	36.7%	35.9%	35.1%	33.6%	32.1%	8
GROWTH & DEVELOPMENT	**Community Market Share	9.1%	9.9%	9.6%	9.4%	9.1%	9.0%	8.8%	8.7%	8.6%	8.3%	8.1%	7
	Eligible Market Share	8.2%	9.1%	8.9%	8.6%	8.4%	8.3%	8.2%	8.1%	7.9%	7.7%	7.4%	5
	Contributing DRGs Profitable Market Share	8.7%	9.9%	9.6%	9.3%	9.0%	8.9%	8.7%	8.6%	8.4%	8.0%	7.7%	5
	PCP Referral – Draw Service Area	29.3%	34.5%	32.8%	31.1%	29.4%	28.6%	27.7%	26.9%	26.0%	24.3%	22.6%	6
CLINICAL ADMINISTRATIVE QUALITY	***Maryland Quality Indicator Index	10	10	9	8	7	6	5	4	3	2	1	10
	Patient Safety Index***	4	10	9	8	7	6	5	4	3	2	1	4
	Infection Control Index***	8	10	9	8	7	6	5	4	3	2	1	8
	***Medical Staff Clinical Indicator Index	5	10	9	8	7	6	5	4	3	2	1	5
	***Pneumococcal Screening and/or Vaccination	59.4	83.1	77.0	70.9	58.7	52.6	46.5	34.3	22.1	16.0	9.9	7
	CHF ALOS	5.0	4.1	4.3	4.4	4.8	5.0	5.2	5.5	5.9	6.1	6.2	6
	CHF Readmission Rate	8.8	2.2	3.0	3.8	5.4	6.2	7.0	8.6	10.2	11.1	11.9	3
	Net Days in Accounts Receivable (IP/OP)	37.9	32.5	33.4	34.3	35.2	38.7	42.2	49.2	56.1	59.6	63.1	7
PEOPLE	Human Capital Value Added	$77,252	$72,682	$69,867	$67,081	$61.510	$58,724	$55,939	$50,368	$44,797	$42,011	$39,226	10
	Retention	89.9%	86.9%	86.0%	85.1%	83.3%	82.4%	81.5%	79.7%	77.8%	76.9%	76.0%	10
	Diversity	9.5%	11.5%	11.0%	10.4%	9.2%	8.6%	8.0%	6.9%	5.7%	5.15	4.5%	7
	Job Coverage Ratio	10	10	9	8	7	6	5	4	3	2	1	10
	**Competency	99.0%	99.0%	98.8%	98.7%	98.6%	98.3%	97.9%	97.6%	97.2%	97.0%	96.9%	10
	**Employee Satisfaction	89.4%	96.8^	94.3%	91.9%	89.4%	88.2%	86.9%	85.7%	84.5%	82.0%	79.5%	10

** Indicates annual measure.   ***Detail in Appendix B

Overall score: 7

Exceeding Goal	2003	1 Qtr	2 Qtr	3 Qtr	4 Qtr	Goal 7
Goal						
Moderate	Overall Score	7	7	7		Stretch 10
Risk						

In addition, Saint Luke's Hospital produces both weekly and quarterly patient satisfaction reports for inpatient, outpatient, and emergency areas as part of its **Customer Satisfaction Research Program.**

To support Saint Luke's Hospital's strategic planning; the Environmental Assessment (EA) is produced, containing four sections: market assessment, internal assessment, medical education/research, and emerging market trends. For this report, numerous internal and external data sources are used and linked to analyze and report information by market, product line, payor, etc.

Source: Saint Luke's Hospital of Kansas City (2003) Quest for Excellence Presentation

Charleston Area Medical Center (The Partnership For Excellence Recipient 2014)

Figure 4.1-3 shows our systematic organizational performance and capabilities review process that includes analyses that we perform to support the validity of these reviews and ensure that conclusions are valid. The organization and SL use these reviews to assess organizational success, competitive performance, financial health and progress relative to strategic objectives, goals and action plans to support decisions made as a result of these reviews. Organizational performance reviews occur by clinical areas, nursing, physicians, support services and by SL. The frequency of our review process (Figure 4.1-3) and our built-in agility to quickly deploy action plans as described in 2.2a(6), enables us to respond rapidly to changing organizational needs and challenges in our operating environment. We also have forcing functions (Figure 2.2-1) that ensure alignment and integration of our organizational performance. Executive Council conducts quarterly reviews of organizational performance and progress on strategic objectives and action plans relative to the system and hospital measures (Figure 2.1-2). The Board reviews the BIG DOT Scorecard quarterly.

Figure 4.1-3 Organizational Performance and Capabilities Review (Full Table AOS)

PILLAR PERFORMANCE DATA — WHEN	CA	N/P	SS	SL	ANALYSIS	DECISIONS MADE
DAILY					• Variance (Daily vs. Budget) • Trending • Review of Quantros • Social Media monitored by Marketing and issues communicated	• Operational • Business development • Service recovery • Safety/Regulatory • Resource Pool/Call-offs • Physician notification • Additional results
Census/Volume	x		x	x		
Staffing	x	x				
Admissions/Referrals	x	x				
Productivity	x					
Revenue				x		
Safety (Patient/Employee)	x	x	x	x		
Social Media	x	x	x	x		
WEEKLY					• Trending/Variances • Patient complaints reviewed • Change in process standardization • Root cause	• Safety/Regulatory • Staffing/Recruitment • Recognition • Reinforce Action Plans • Service recovery • Operational changes
Census/Volume	x			x		
Rounding	x					
Productivity	x			x		
Patient Satisfaction	x	x	x	x		
QI/PI Projects (SPL, A3)	x	x	x	x		
MONTHLY					• Budget vs. Actual • Statistical comparison • Action Plan evaluation • National benchmark or DRG	• Modify Action Plans/PI • Resource allocation/New teams
WEEKLY DATA PLUS:						
Clinical Outcomes	x	x		x		
Rounding	x	x	x	x		
Scorecards	x	x	x	x		
TCT Project Status				x		
QUARTERLY					• Budget/Target vs. Actual • Statistical comparison • Action Plan evaluation • Aggregation of Social Media data	• Safety/Regulatory • Modify Action Plans • Resource allocation • Operational changes
WEEKLY & MONTHLY DATA PLUS:						
Patient Satisfaction	x	x		x		
BIG DOTs/Goals/Action Plans				x		
Social Media Trending				x		
ANNUAL/BIANNUAL					• Budget vs. Actual • Gap analysis • Action Plan evaluation • Actual vs. Benchmark	• Safety/Regulatory • Recognition • Unit/Hospital Action Plans • Opportunities for improvement/innovation
WEEKLY, MONTHLY, QUARTERLY PLUS:						
Workforce Performance Reviews	x	x	x	x		
Employee Satisfaction	x	x	x	x		
Physician Satisfaction	x	x		x		
Patient Safety Culture	x	x	x	x		
CONTINUOUS					Shifts in technology, market, services, competition, economy, regulatory environment	Change in strategic objectives to adapt to shifts in market conditions
Environmental Analysis				x		

Legend: **CA** Clinical Areas, **N/P** Clinical Nursing and Physicians, **SS** Support Services, **SL** Senior Leadership

Monfort College of Business (Baldrige Recipient 2004)

To perform an organizational review of the College, Key Performance Indicators (KPIs) and Supporting Performance Indicators (SPIs) are reviewed to assess MCB's effectiveness in meeting its strategic plan, mission, and values. These indicators encompass the following strategic categories: recruits, students, curriculum, faculty, facilities/ technology, financial resources, alumni, employers, and program reputation. The KPIs and SPIs are aligned with the Student Focused Process Framework.

Mapping the Scorecard to the Enterprise Framework - Student Centered Process Framework

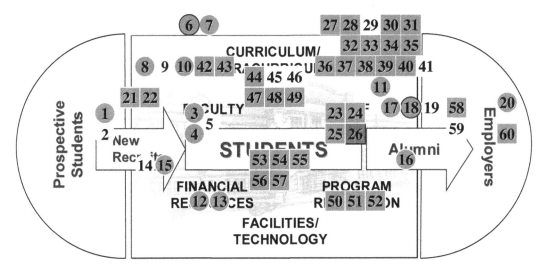

Key Performance Indicators

\#   Supporting Performance Indicators

MCB uses a variety of analysis tools in support of senior leaders' review of organizational performance. Tools or techniques such as trend analysis are used to assess progress in the areas of student learning, retention, quality, and satisfaction, as well as faculty productivity and satisfaction. Benchmark comparisons are used to determine the level of progress as measured against the College's peer set in areas such as learning environment, faculty qualifications, and quality of technology. Correlation analysis is used to assess the relationship between user satisfaction with technology and the addition of a technology director's position. MCB also performs correlation analyses to examine relationships between variables, such as incoming student quality and exiting student performance. Root cause analysis is used in situations where a problem is identified without a clear indication of what led to the substandard performance.

The results of annual organizational-level analyses are communicated to faculty and staff via reports, meetings, and other venues including the MCB and SEDONA Web sites. These venues house the KPI documents and other committee information (e.g., College and departmental committee minutes) under a faculty section on each. The College publishes eight monthly reports through which it communicates results and decisions related to organizational performance and deliberations. The reports also are available on the MCB Web site.

While MCB holds college-wide faculty meetings each semester, the majority of analysis-based results are communicated through regular meetings of the academic departments and functionally-based committees within the shared governance structure. Given that each academic department has a representative on the ADMC, the quantity and quality of inter-organizational communications between groups is enhanced.

Senior Leader Organizational Performance Review:

MCB senior leaders use KPIs (Figure 2.2-1) to help gauge capacities and performance results. A review and analysis of these indicators represents the College's best methods for gauging organizational success. For example, each semester the ADMC reviews the utilization of instructional resources and establishes enrollment targets that match MCB's resources. The review includes comparing course enrollments to capacities to determine a precise number of class offerings to meet discipline standards and student demand. The resulting in-process measure KPI of student majors is based on maximum class sizes (as recommended by the CC) and resource availability, so an average class size consistent with the College's instructional values is maintained.

The key tools used to evaluate and improve organizational performance are the EBI surveys and the Educational Testing Service (ETS) Field Achievement Test in business. Each is recognized as the national standard for benchmarking by undergraduate business programs. As examples, the EBI Student Satisfaction Survey allowed comparison to 182 U.S. business programs in 2003, and the ETS test in business provided a comparison pool of 359 peers. MCB participates in four EBI studies: graduating students, faculty, alumni, and program administration. The EBI instruments provide relevant benchmarks against a range of comparable universities across the U.S. MCB can track trends on its performance, as well as compare its results to trends at other institutions. MCB has developed target points (e.g., top 10%) within specified KPIs (Figure 2.2-2, 4.1-2). With these goals, the committees begin their performance evaluation processes.

The ETS Major Field Exam is given to all MCB seniors prior to graduation to help assess student learning outcomes relative to national norms. Over time, ETS exam results indicate to senior leaders and members of the faculty how well students are mastering core business knowledge. Trends and national benchmarks offer a basis for determining the level of program performance and any areas that need additional attention (Figures 7.1-1 – 7.1-3).

Each MCB committee evaluates these data. In particular, the committees spend significant time studying the results and then recommending program improvements to help MCB best serve its students and other stakeholders. In addition, the AACSB accreditation process is an important input in reviewing organizational performance and holding management accountable for organizational results.

The EBI and ETS results offer an indication of quality and, in combination, provide a comprehensive view of the overall quality of MCB's programs. The results of these measures undergo a systematic review by leadership, as well as by appropriate College committees, and the faculty-at-large. Upon analysis, determination is then made whether or not to take corrective action.

KPI results (Figure 2.2-2, 4.1-2) are regularly reviewed by faculty committees, ADMC, and the dean as part of the strategic planning process. For example, reviewing the results of the ETS exam is an important part of the curriculum review process by the CC. In a recent instance where performance on the economics portion of the exam was below target, meetings were initiated with that department's chair (economics is administered outside MCB) to devise a plan for assuring improved area coverage. Economics performance has since improved. Graduating seniors and alumni also complete satisfaction surveys which provide faculty and leaders with important trend information to be used in making adjustments to MCB's programs. Other statistical information, including reports on enrollment and budget issues, is provided by UNC administration. Results from these tools indicate significant improvements in recent years (Figures 7.1-1 to 7.1-3, 7.2-1 to 7.2-20).

Annually, the ADMC reviews current performance results and works with the dean to identify priorities for program improvement. Priorities are shared with the faculty committees through a schedule of prioritized tasks for each committee during the upcoming fall term. Each group is charged with reviewing the various results and developing program changes or program additions that will improve overall performance. Committees are encouraged to be innovative in their approaches and strive to provide new high quality learning experiences within the classroom. Through the SEDONA database system and other reports, all faculty and staff have access to information needed for identifying improvement opportunities to be forwarded to senior leaders. Academic departments also use this data to evaluate and select courses of action for improvement. The dean shares findings from such reviews with key groups (e.g., the Dean's Leadership Council (DLC)), to solicit external input for helping to improve College programs. Data are also shared with the UNC president, provost, and SRC.

The College also provides the UNC Admissions Office with up-to-date information regarding its changing programs to assist in recruiting qualified students. MCB seeks to maintain a current stream of information through its Web site and other communication channels to encourage prospective student interest, relay important news to current students, and promote ongoing contact with alumni and friends of the College. Through all of these interactions, the College is able to generate new ideas to align programs and improve performance.

The University has a formal evaluation process that includes annual performance reviews of all senior leaders, faculty members, and staff. The provost evaluates the dean's performance on an annual basis, and faculty members and chairs complete a triennial survey on the dean that includes a variety of inputs, in addition to written comments. The results of this annual review and triennial survey help the provost and dean determine the dean's managerial and leadership effectiveness, as well as areas for continuous improvement. The annual evaluation of department chairs begins with a report prepared by the chair that is then shared with the department's faculty members and the dean. The department faculty meet with the dean to discuss chair performance and opportunities for improvement. The dean then meets with the department chair to review the report, communicate feedback, and form conclusions. The dean annually evaluates the performance of the assistant and associate deans. Since these positions are part-time administrative, each is also evaluated as a faculty member by his department chair.

Results of the annual EBI Faculty Satisfaction Survey also contain information about administration and leadership issues. As a unit within the University, MCB does not directly evaluate the Board of Trustees, other than to communicate its ideas through the provost.

The information resulting from the various performance review processes is shared immediately with the dean, assistant and associate deans, and department chairs to help improve performance. When corrective measures are needed, follow-up sessions are initiated to assure that each senior leader is given every opportunity and available assistance to improve performance. Further, the dean meets monthly with the University provost and bi-weekly with the Dean's Council (i.e., deans of each college and the provost), which offers additional avenues for insight into College and leadership performance.

Overall organizational performance is also measured via recognition earned from external organizations (e.g., AACSB, CCHE Program of Excellence, national and regional media) regarding the quality of College programs and faculty. Prestigious business publications and area radio and television news outlets are now seeking MCB professors for opinions and quotes on current financial and other business topics and producing favorable stories on the unique MCB educational programs (e.g., SAFF, Applied Networking) (Fig 7.5-9, 10).

Source: Monfort (2005)

CRITERIA QUESTIONS

In your response, include answers to the following questions:

b. Performance Analysis and Review

How do you review organizational performance and capabilities? How do you use your key organizational performance measures, as well as comparative and customer data, in these reviews? What analyses do you perform to support these reviews and ensure that conclusions are valid? How do your organization and its senior leaders use these reviews to

- assess organizational success, competitive performance, financial health, and progress on achieving your strategic objectives and action plans; and
- respond rapidly to changing organizational needs and challenges in your operating environment, including any need for transformational change in organizational structure and work systems?

How does your governance board review the organization's performance and its progress on strategic objectives and action plans, if appropriate?

Notes:

4.1b. Organizational performance reviews should be informed by organizational performance measurement and by performance measures reported throughout your Criteria item responses, and they should be guided by the strategic objectives and action plans you identify in Category 2. The reviews might also be informed by internal or external Baldrige assessments.

4.1b. Performance analysis includes examining performance trends; organizational, industry, and technology projections; and comparisons, cause-effect relationships, and correlations. This analysis should support your performance reviews, help determine root causes, and help set priorities for resource use. Accordingly, such analysis draws on all types of data: product performance, customer-related, financial and market, operational, and competitive. The analysis should also draw on publicly mandated measures, when appropriate.

NIST (2015-2016) pp. 16-17

WORKSHEETS

4.1b Performance Analysis and Review

Process To Review Organizational Performance and Capabilities	Process To Use Key Organizational Performance Measures In These Reviews	Process To Perform Analysis To Support Reviews (Include The Types Of Analysis and How You Ensure The Conclusions Are Valid)
1		
2		
3		
n		

Types Of Organizational Performance Reviews	How Reviews Are Used To Assess Organizational Success	How Reviews Are Used To Assess Competitive Performance	How Reviews Are Used To Assess Financial Health	How Reviews Are Used To Assess Progress Relative To Strategic Objectives and Action Plans
1				
2				
3				
n				

Types Of Organizational Performance Reviews (Same As Above)	How Does The Organization And Senior Leaders Use These Reviews To Respond Rapidly To Changing Organizational Needs In Your Operating Environment	How Does The Organization And Senior Leaders Use These Reviews To Respond Any Need For Transformational Change In The Organizational Structure	How Does The Organization And Senior Leaders Use These Reviews To Respond Any Need For Transformational Change In Work Systems
1			
2			
3			
N			

How Does The Governance Board Review The Organization's Performance And Progress On:	
Strategic Objectives:	Action Plans:

ASSESSMENT

Rating Scale:

1 - No Process in place - We are not doing this
2 - Reacting to Problems – We use a basic (primarily reactive) process
3 - Systematic Process – We use a systematic process that has been improved
4 - Aligned – We use a process that aligns our activities from top to bottom
5 - Integrated – We use a process that is integrated with other processes across the organization
6 - Benchmark – We are the Benchmark in our industry or beyond!
DK - Don't Know

67	Each organizational level periodically reviews their performance, compares the performance to expectations, and makes adjustments appropriate to their level.	1	2	3	4	5	6	DK
68	Information is integrated, aggregated and analyzed to get an overall picture of the organization's performance.	1	2	3	4	5	6	DK
69	Decisions made by leaders are made based on information and analysis of data, rather than on personal preferences or "gut feel."	1	2	3	4	5	6	DK
70	Leaders review organizational performance at all levels in a systematic manner, and use these reviews to make course corrections which allow the organization to respond rapidly to the changing organizational needs.	1	2	3	4	5	6	DK

Performance Analysis and Review– 4.1b

BLUEPRINT

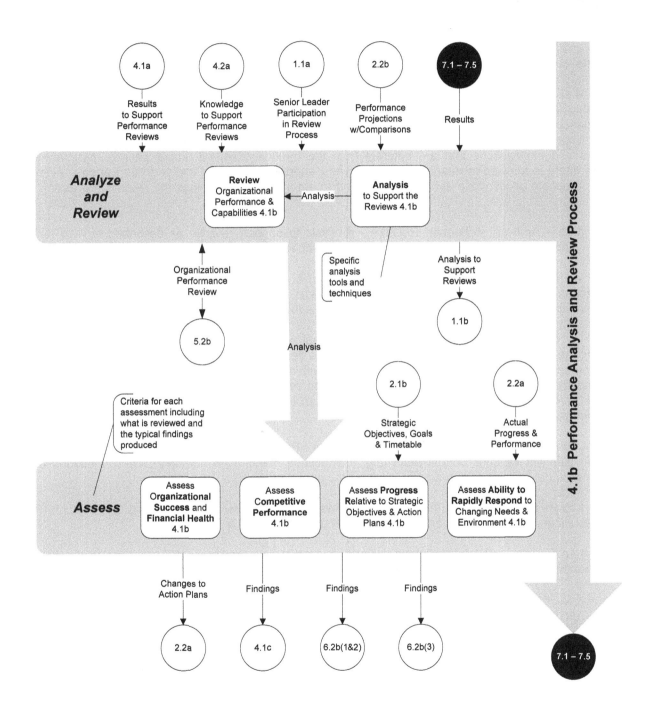

355

SYSTEM INTEGRATION

Systems

1.1a > 4.1b Performance Review Participation - The values, direction, and expectations set by the leadership system should be consistent with and an input to the agenda for the organizational performance reviews described in 4.1b. In addition, the leaders' participation in the performance reviews is also important for reinforcing the direction and priorities. If the leadership team espouses certain priorities and expectations that are different from the metrics reviewed during periodic performance reviews, there is a mixed message to the employees, suppliers, partners, and so forth. Periodic reviews help hold people accountable and people will tend to emphasize those things the leaders are asking to review.

1.1b < 4.1b – Analysis to Support Reviews - Analysis to support reviews as described in 4.1b is an important input to the performance review process described in 1.1b.

2.1b > 4.1b Strategic Objectives and Timetable - The review process described in 4.1b asks the organization to assess the progress relative to strategic objectives and action plans. The objectives, goals, and timeline used should be the same as those developed in 2.1b.

2.2a <> 4.1b Actual Progress and Performance - Actual action plan progress and performance are key inputs to the organizational performance review process described in 4.1b. These reviews will often result in refinements to action plans to keep them on track, within budget, and on schedule. These refinements then find their way to the other plans including human resource plans as appropriate. In addition, the findings from the performance reviews described in 4.1b are key inputs to the revision or adjustment of the action plans described in 2.2a.

2.2b > 4.1b Performance Projections with Comparisons - Part of the analysis provided by 4.1b to support strategic planning includes comparisons (e.g., competitive, benchmark, industry). The projections and comparisons determined in 2.2b are key inputs to the analysis described in 4.1b.

4.1a > 4.1b Results to Support Performance Reviews - The measures and associated results from 4.1a are direct inputs to the periodic performance reviews described in 4.1b.

4.1b > 4.1c Findings - The findings from the performance review process (4.1b) are direct inputs to the performance improvement prioritization process (4.1c).

4.1b < 4.2a Knowledge to Support Performance Reviews - Knowledge to support the performance reviews (4.1b) also comes from the knowledge management system described in 4.2a. This knowledge can help those reviewing performance understand how the changes in performance for individual measures and components impacts the larger system. This understanding can help the reviewers identify the "leverage points" and develop improvement plans.

4.1b <> 5.2b Organizational Performance Review - The performance reviews (4.1b) often identify areas for improvement that involve workforce engagement, satisfaction and performance (5.2b). And, the assessments of workforce are often inputs to the overall organization performance review.

4.1b > 6.2b(1&2) Findings - The findings from the performance analysis described in 4.1b directly supports work process management and control 6.2b(1&2).

4.1b > 6.2b(3) Findings - The findings from the performance analysis described in 4.1b directly supports work process improvement by identifying opportunities for improvement.

Scorecard

4.1b < 7.1 through 7.5 Results - All results displayed as part of the results areas 7.1 through 7.5 are potential inputs to the organizational performance review system (4.1b).

4.1b > 7.1 through 7.5 Findings - The explanation of performance levels, trends and comparisons should be included in the applicable results areas (7.1 thorough 7.5).

THOUGHTS FOR LEADERS

High performing organizations always have a strong ability to perform analysis and make fact-based decisions. In simple terms, they have the ability to turn data into information and turn information into action. This ability, however, requires that the organization have standards to define when the results (the data tracked) require analysis. These organizations also use a range of standard analytical tools to analyze the data to develop an understanding of what the data means.

These organizations also have standards as to when comparisons or benchmarks are required and from what types of organizations these comparisons or benchmarks are sought. The overall Data-To-Action logic flow can be as follows:

- Standards that document what level of performance deviation (from the plan or expected performance) must be analyzed;
- Tools to perform the analysis;
- Leaders who review the results of the analysis;
- Standards that document when comparisons or benchmarks are needed;
- Standards that document where comparisons or benchmarks are sought;
- Processes to analyze the comparisons or benchmarks to determine the potential actions that should be considered;
- Processes to propose actions and the expected impact;
- Decision criteria or processes to chose the course of action;
- Processes to ensure the effective implementation of the actions;
- Processes to track the performance impact of the actions;
- Processes to reevaluate the actions if the desired results are not achieved; and
- Processes to change the actions and monitor the new performance.

Although this list of steps is long and cumbersome, high performing organizations complete this cycle quickly and simply through constant practice. Additionally, if the cycle is not embedded in the way the organization operates, the Data-To-Action flow will not survive.

A Lighter Moment:

*Analysis and synthesis ordinarily clarify matters for us about as much
As taking a Swiss watch apart and dumping its wheels, springs, hands,
threads, pivots, screws and gears into a layman's hands for reassembling,
clarifies a watch to a layman.*

Author unknown

> *Become addicted to constant and never-ending self improvement.*
>
> Anthony J. D'Angelo

FOUNDATION

Once the performance measures are identified, data collected and analyzed and reviewed, the next question is how does this process help improve the organization. The CPE focus on three aspects of improvement: best practice sharing, future performance and continuous improvement and innovation.

Best Practices

Sharing best practices within the organization leverages lessons learned in one part of the organization to improve the entire organization. This means if one group improves, they also have the systematic ability to share it with others who can benefit from the improvement. This ability to share can be initiated during performance reviews when one group performs better than others. It simply is not acceptable to outperform your peers and not do something to help them systematically get better using the techniques you found to be helpful.

Ideally, the performance review process and improvement projects include a step that requires they share the gain.

Future Performance

Along with the performance reviews should be the ability to project future results. Some high performing organizations report the current results, but also project the performance (for each key metric) at the end of the evaluation period. This helps them to understand the cyclicality of the business, and what actions need to be taken to achieve the final results desired. It can help keep focused during a high performing period, and ensure that the organization does not become complacent if a down cycle is predictable. In both cases, the organization's progress toward a goal may not be linear, and the cycles incurred need to be understood and adjusted for with appropriate plans and actions.

Continuous Improvement and Innovation

The CPE also ask how the organization translates the performance review findings into priorities for continuous (ongoing) and breakthrough improvements. This process to translate the reviews into improvement actions should be visible in the senior leadership meeting notes. Do they ask for analysis? Do they ask for action to be taken? Do they understand the level to which breakthroughs have to be supported? Do they drive continuous improvement to all levels of the organization?

The criteria also ask how the leaders foster innovation and the alignment of these reviews and the related actions and course corrections with suppliers and partners. This, as with all other aspects of the organizational focus, needs to be done through a systematic process. This process should, typically, start externally with the customer listening and learning posts, which should tell the organization how much innovation is expected, wanted, or needed.

EXAMPLES

PRO-TEC Coating Company (Baldrige Recipient 2007)

The overall approach to continuous improvement methods is illustrated in Figure P.2-2, with methods contingent on the complexity and scope of an opportunity. The cornerstone of improvement at PRO-TEC is "I-to-I" or *Initiation-to-Implementation*.

Associate Responsibility is fostered by teaching Associates to fix problems as they are identified and empowering them to do so. Organizational learning and sharing starts with the initial Associate selection process and continues through new employee orientation, assigned mentors, cross-training, cultural (Ownership, Responsibility, and Authority – ORA – personal empowerment) training, management system training, and through team interactions that serve to develop Associate responsibility.

Technical Resources or subject matter experts have been developed and designated to support opportunity definition and resolution. These resources are essential to support a 24x7 operation with self-directed work teams to ensure process and product reliability as well as Associate safety. Associates can ask for technical help at any time, based on their own assessment of the need.

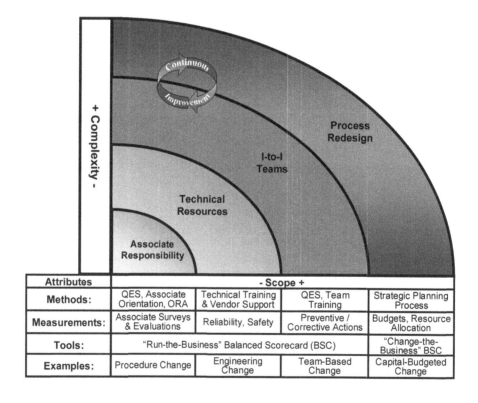

The **Initiation-to-Implementation** (I-to-I) process for continuous improvement of team-based changes provides the means and methods for organizational learning and sharing, with its resource committee meeting twice a month to monitor, allocate resources as required, evaluate, and improve the process.

The activities of these cross-functional teams are posted on bulletin boards and on the intranet, and typically at least one team activity is presented at each monthly plant management review meeting.

The **Process Redesign** corresponds to strategic planning changes requiring capital budget funding and significant project management requirements. The supporting activities are monitored and tracked on the recently developed "Change the Business" balanced scorecard.

This improvement cycle begins with each employee's ORA level of authority. In simple terms, if they see a problem "we just fix it." If they need help they can access the necessary technical resources. If the scope and complexity is even greater, they can initiate an "I-to-I" or *Initiation-to-Implementation* team who conducts a systematic assessment of the issue using defined problem solving techniques. If the scope and complexity is even greater then it is referred to the leadership team who has the ability to approve the capital (if required) or to integrate it into the short- or longer-term plans.

Each level of improvement uses specific methods to ensure that the approach used is consistent across the organization. Each level also has measurements and can be tracked through the two balanced scorecards. The 'Change the Business' Scorecard is fully integrated with the 'Run the Business' Scorecard and with lower-level individual and team goals and objectives.

North Mississippi Medical Center (Baldrige Recipient as a hospital in 2006 and as a system in 2012)

North Mississippi Medical Center describes their cycles of learning and improvement related to their performance improvement system, and also notes that they have already been identified as a role model for their current process, not only within their state award program, but also nationally. Further, they point to their results to show the maturity of their performance excellence journey.

In 1983, NMMC implemented Quality Circles, which were succeeded by Quality Improvement Teams and the implementation of the PLAN-DO-CHECK-ACT (PDCA) model as the overall approach to improvement efforts. In 1992, NMMC developed the Clinical Practice Analysis (CPA) process, which provided physicians with individualized performance profiles of their care management and outcomes that were compared to local and national benchmarks. Sharing comparative data engaged physicians in performance improvement, and set the stage for the development of the Care-Based Cost Management (CBCM) approach. CBCM links health care quality and cost containment by looking beyond traditional cost drivers (people, equipment, supplies) to the care issues that have a much greater impact on the actual cost of care, namely: practice variation, complications, and social issues. The CBCM approach has produced significant results (7.1), has been featured in numerous national forums and has resulted in national recognition and awards, including the 2003, 2004 and 2005 Solucient's 100 Top Hospital Performance Improvement Leaders and first prize in the 2005 American Hospital Association McKesson Quest for Quality Prize. In 1996, NMMC began using Baldrige Criteria to identify Opportunities for Improvement (OFIs). The state of Mississippi Baldrige program awarded NMMC the Excellence Award in 1997 and the Governor's Award in 2000. NMMC continues to use Baldrige criteria to critically examine its approaches and processes.

NMMC's systematic evaluation and improvement of key processes have evolved from our Baldrige-based performance analysis. Senior Leadership teams meet monthly and use Performance Score Cards (PSCs) to assess performance. Each team's PSC is organized by the Critical Success Factors, and each key process indicator has a target and a benchmark and is tracked (monthly in most cases). In addition, each SL and department produces a monthly Budget Accountability Report (BAR) that incorporates the unit's revenues, expenses and productivity into an overall measure. If the measure is below the established threshold, then an Action Plan (AP) is required. NMMC also uses the PSC system for organizational learning by routinely sharing these results and the lessons from them with the staff and Board of Directors.

Source: NMMC (2007) p. vi

CRITERIA QUESTIONS

In your response, include answers to the following questions:

c. Performance Improvement

(1) **Best Practices** how do you share best practices in your organization? How do you identify organizational units or operations that are high performing? How do you identify their best practices for sharing and implement them across the organization, as appropriate?

(2) **Future Performance** How do you project your organization's future performance? How do you use findings from performance reviews (addressed in 4.1b) and key comparative and competitive data in projecting future performance? How do you reconcile any differences between these projections of future performance and performance projections developed for your key action plans (addressed in 2.2a[6])?

(3) **Continuous Improvement and Innovation** How do you use findings from performance reviews (addressed in 4.1b) to develop priorities for continuous improvement and opportunities for innovation? How do you deploy these priorities and opportunities
   - to work group and functional-level operations and
   - when appropriate, to your suppliers, partners, and collaborators to ensure organizational alignment?

NIST (2015-2016) pp. 16-17

WORKSHEETS

4.1c(1) Best-Practice Sharing

Types Of Organizational Performance Review Findings	Determining Priorities and Opportunities:*			
	How Do You Identify Organizational Units Or Operations That Are High Performing	How Do You Identify Their Best Practices	How Do You Share Their Best Practices	How Do You Measure And Track The Impact Of The Sharing
1				
2				
3				
n				

* = Refer to the process improvements (and approach) shown in Area to Address 6.1b(3).

4.1c(2) Future Performance

Future Performance Projected In Area To Address 2.2a(6)	How You Use Findings From Performance Reviews (Addressed In 4.1b) In Projecting Future Performance:	
	How These Projections Are Impacted By Key Comparative Data	How These Projections Are Impacted By Key Competitive Data
1		
2		
3		
n		

How You Reconcile Differences Between Projections Of Future Performance	

And Performance Projections Developed For Your Key Action Plans	

4.1c(3) Continuous Improvement and Innovation

Types Of Organizational Performance Review Findings (From Area 4.1b)	Determining Priorities And Opportunities:*		
	The Process Used To Translate Findings Into Priorities For Continuous Improvement	The Process Used To Translate Findings Into Priorities For Breakthrough Improvement	The Process Used To Translate Findings Into Opportunities For Innovation

* Note: Refer to the process improvements (and approach) shown in Area to Address 6.1b(3).

Priorities and Opportunities (From Chart Above)	Approaches To Ensure Organizational Alignment		
	The Process Used To Deploy These Priorities and Opportunities To Work Groups	The Process Used To Deploy These Priorities and Opportunities To Functional Level Operations	The Process Used To Deploy These Priorities and Opportunities To Suppliers, Partners and Collaborators

ASSESSMENT

Rating Scale:

1 - **No Process** in place - We are not doing this
2 - **Reacting to Problems** – We use a basic (primarily reactive) process
3 - **Systematic Process** – We use a systematic process that has been improved
4 - **Aligned** – We use a process that aligns our activities from top to bottom
5 - **Integrated** – We use a process that is integrated with other processes across the organization
6 - **Benchmark** – We are the Benchmark in our industry or beyond!
DK - Don't Know

---

71   A systematic set of tools have been developed which are used for improvement throughout the organization.   1   2   3   4   5   6   DK

72   Most employees have been taught the improvement tools and use them regularly to improve organizational performance.   1   2   3   4   5   6   DK

BLUEPRINT

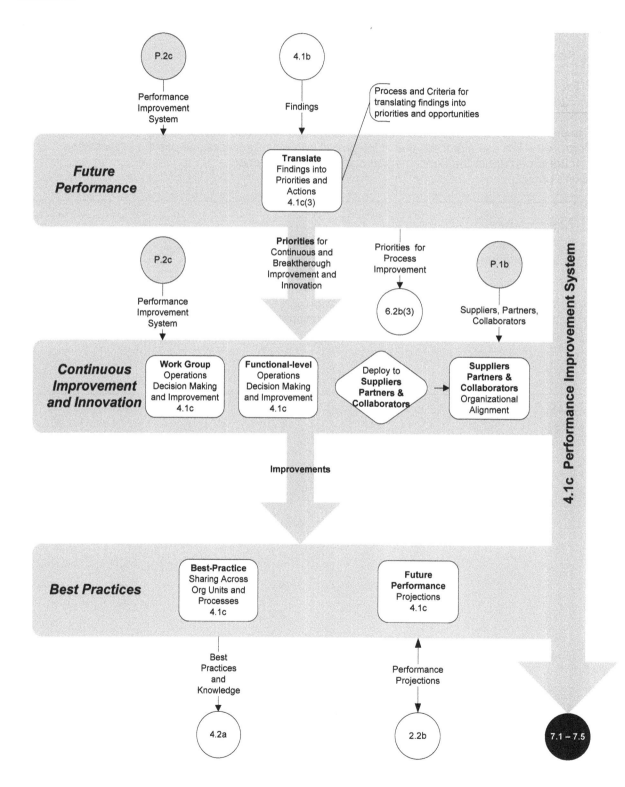

SYSTEM INTEGRATION

Context

P.1b > 4.1c Suppliers, Partners, Collaborators - Suppliers, partners, and collaborators identified in the profile (P.1b) should be addressed when determining the appropriate or most effective methods to deploy the organization's priorities for continuous and breakthrough improvement and opportunities for innovation.

P.2c > 4.1c Performance Improvement System - The improvement activities described in 4.1c should be consistent with and based on the performance improvement system described in the profile (P.2c).

Systems

4.1b > 4.1c Findings - The findings from the performance review process (4.1b) are direct inputs to the performance improvement prioritization process (4.1c).

2.2b > 4.1c Performance Projections here in 2.2b and 4.1c Performance Improvement System inform and are inputs to each other.

4.1c > 4.2a Best Practices and knowledge gained during the use of the Performance Improvement System is captured by the knowledge management system described in 4.2a.

4.1c > 6.2b(3) Priorities for Process Improvement - The priorities for improvement and actions identified in 4.1c directly support work process improvement described in 6.2b(3).

Scorecard

4.1c > 7.1 through 7.5 Improvement Results - Performance improvement that results from the actions identified in 4.1c should be reflected in the trends in all results areas (7.1 through 7.5).

THOUGHTS FOR LEADERS

High performing organizations always have a strong ability to improve at a rate greater than their competitors. This means most (all?) employees have been taught the organizational improvement approach, and use it on an ongoing basis.

What is common, however, is for organizations to have many improvement approaches. This is not a problem if it is clear when an approach is to be used and why. It is problematic is when it is unclear when to improve, what tools to use, or why improvement is necessary. Earlier we discussed turning data into information and turning information into action. This ability, however, requires that the organization have standards to define when the results (the data tracked) require analysis, and improvement action.

In many high performing organizations the improvement tools are simple enough for every employee to understand and use them. Additionally, every employee uses the tools weekly or daily. Some organizations even have a minimum number of suggestions which every employee must submit or participate in annually.

Whatever the approach, a few continuous improvement basics are key:

- The current performance level (or status quo) must be categorically unacceptable - continuous improvement must be required and relentless.

- The improvement approach must be simple enough for everybody to use.

- The improvement approach must be taught to most (or all) employees.

- The approach must be used by most (or all) employees or the knowledge of how to use the approach will be forgotten.

- The impact of the improvements must be tracked.

A Lighter Moment:

It requires a very unusual mind to undertake the analysis of the obvious.

Alfred North Whitehead

> *Everybody gets so much information all day long*
> *that they lose their common sense.*
>
> **Gertrude Stein**

FOUNDATION

This area to address focuses on the data, information and knowledge management system to support the analysis and review of performance to improve organization performance and then share those improvements throughout the organization.

Knowledge Management

Managing organizational knowledge includes systems, collection of data, analysis, knowledge management, sharing of best practices, and decisions based on the data. These, however, cannot be effective if the data cannot be relied upon. This Area to Address focuses on being able to rely on the data. After several Baldrige recipients demonstrated an ability to leverage organizational knowledge for competitive advantage, knowledge management was officially added to the criteria. In its ultimate form knowledge management means anything that is known to one person in the organization should be usable by all people in the organization. Within that framework, the CPE ask how an organization collects and transfers employee knowledge. As with other parts of the CPE, a process with clear steps and decision criteria needs to be employed. The two components of this process - collection and transfer - are handled separately by most organizations.

Some organizations have an excellent ability to collect data and develop world-class databases. In some cases, however, their ability to transfer it to the employees who need the data is insufficient. Clearly, the effective use of organizational knowledge to accomplish increased performance requires both collection and the use of knowledge.

The CPE also ask how the organization transfers relevant knowledge from customers, suppliers, and partners. This process is certainly more difficult across organizational, and often contractual, lines. As with any process, the examiners will be looking for the process steps, the decision criteria, and the metrics to know the process is a success. Most organizations collect best practices in some form. The CPE require not only the identification of best practices, but effective sharing as well. Some high performing companies have the ability to measure the impact of this sharing of best practices.

Organizational Learning

When an individual 'learns' it is something the CPE calls it Personal Learning. Organizational learning is achieved through research and development, evaluation and improvement cycles, workforce and stakeholder ideas and input, best-practice sharing, and benchmarking. Personal learning is achieved through education, training, and developmental opportunities that further individual growth.

To be effective, learning should be embedded in the way an organization operates. Learning contributes to a competitive advantage and sustainability for the organization and its workforce.

 EXAMPLES

PRO-TEC Coating Company (Baldrige Recipient 2007)

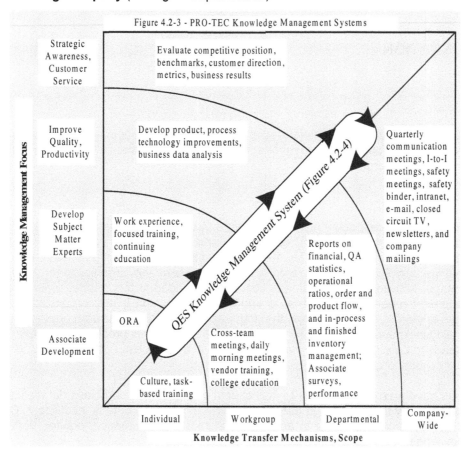

Figure 4.2-3 illustrates both the knowledge management focus as well as knowledge transfer mechanisms within the organization. Central to Figure 4.2-3 is the Quality and Environmental Management System (QES) process for data management. These processes allow for rapid identification, sharing, and implementation of best practices.

Inova Fair Oaks Hospital (Fairfax, Virginia)

Organizational knowledge at Inova Fair Oaks Hospital (IFOH) is collected, shared/transferred, used and evaluated through the systematic methodology shown in the figure below. The methods are tailored to each workforce and stakeholder group. Knowledge is collected from the workforce, patients, suppliers, partners, collaborators and other stakeholders through systematic practices in column A. Relevant knowledge is transferred through the mechanisms in column B and implemented through the mechanisms in column C to ensure their use. Effectiveness of the knowledge is evaluated through the approaches in column D.

Examples of Knowledge Management Mechanisms

Knowledge Used By	A - How Knowledge is Collected	B - Transfer Mechanisms	C - Forces Us of knowledge	D - Evaluation Measures
Workforce	Rounding Satisfaction Surveys Policies/ procedures Shared Governance	Orientation Department meetings Nursing huddles	Shared Beliefs Standards of Behavior Performance reviews	Regulatory compliance Workforce Engagement
Patients	VOC listening posts Rounding White Boards GWN	Rounding White boards	Customer Satisfaction Discharge phone calls	Regulatory audits Department dashboards
Physicians	Rounding Physician Liaisons Satisfaction Survey	Dashboards Strategic Reports Issue communication/Resolution System	Re-Engineering System Modifications/Enhancements	Physician Satisfaction Survey Participation in hospital activities
Suppliers Partners Collaborators	Contracts	Vendor User Groups Vendor to HIS Leadership Meetings/Updates	System Modifications/Enhancements Process Redesign	Contracts, performance evaluations, on site reviews
Stakeholders	Community Survey Volunteers	Dashboards Strategic Reports Issue Communication/Resolution Systems	Process Redesign System Re-Engineering	Market assessments, press releases
Rapid identification and Sharing of Best Practices	To meet organizational needs: IAMS Awards, ILI meetings To meet patient needs: Web site Patient education	Strategic Presentations Blogs Intranet Dashboards Knowledge Databases	System Modifications/Enhancements Process Redesign	Core Measures Strategic Metric Measures
Use in Strategic Planning	Environmental Scan Data and Literature reviews (internal and external)	SWOTTS	Strategic Planning Process	Changes in Service line offerings

Rapid identification, sharing and implementation of best practices and innovations occur through sharing at an awards gathering where specific practices are discussed and recognized. Best practices are presented at leadership meetings implemented by cascaded through the organization though shared governance, department meetings and huddles. A Step of our Strategic Planning Process includes the review of data against our past strategic plan to ensure that best practices and innovations are considered in our next planning cycle. We systematically compile, analyze and trend data through our reviews and scorecards throughout the year and share our progress against plan via the approaches discussed in Item 1.1. We track and trend both clinical and financial data to provide insights into the quality of our services and processes. Detailed clinical data is placed into a clinical data repository and allows for the in-depth review of patient outcomes based on any number of factors. This system allows for the development of best practices against not only national benchmarks but among Inova physicians, providing "scorecards" of quality care among peers, physicians and patient populations. IFOH has multiple mechanisms in place to pinpoint enhancements and workflow re-engineering efforts. Key metrics are identified and monitored to re-evaluate and provide a mechanism for continuous improvement.

Charleston Area Medical Center (The Partnership For Excellence Recipient 2014)

Figure 4.2-1 details the mechanisms that we use to systematically accomplish knowledge management (KM). We feel KM must be a seamless part of how we run the organization and cannot be a separate system superimposed on the existing infrastructure.

To accomplish this, the domains we primarily focus on (where sharing is most critical) include workforce, patients, suppliers, partners, collaborators and other customers.

As shown in Figure 4.2-1, for each of these groups we have specific techniques to collect knowledge , transfer knowledge to those who can use it , and force the use of the knowledge . For each stakeholder group we have measures which can be used to track and improve the use and impact techniques to share and implement best practices . Many of the tools used help us to assemble and transfer relevant knowledge for use in innovation and in the strategic planning process .

Figure 4.2-1 Knowledge Management (Full Table AOS)

Knowledge Used By (1)	How Knowledge is Collected (2)	Transfer Mechanisms/ Sharing Forums (3)	Forced Use of Knowledge (4)	Evaluation / Measures (5)
Workforce	•Rounding/Forums •Email/Surveys •Performance Management •Top 5 Boards •Goal Wall Maps •Organization performance and capability reviews •Staff Meetings	•Best Practice Sharing •Inservices/Meetings/Huddles •EduTrack/SPL/JIT/Skills Lab •CAMC University •Professional Nursing Programs •Simulation Center •Order Sets; Protocols •Council Structure •Collaborative Practice	•Performance Reviews •Annual Competencies •Action Plans •PI Teams •TCT	•Scorecard 7.4-19 •Regulatory/Compliance Audits 7.4-8; 7.4-10 •Engagement Survey 7.3-13 •Performance Reviews 7.3-26 •Survey Results 7.3-27
Patients	•Rounding Figure 3.1-1 •Shift to Shift Handoffs •IPOC •Cipher Health	•White Boards/IPOC/Survey •IP/OP Visits •Print, Radio, TV, Education on Demand •Rounding, CEN	•Shift to Shift Handoffs •Care Provider Communication •Discharge Instructions •Teach-back	•Scorecard/Quality Indicators 7.2-9-7.2-10 •Satisfaction/Engagement Survey 7.2-26 - 7.2-31 •Market Share 7.5-19-7.5-27 •Cipher Health 7.2-32
Suppliers, Partners, Collaborators	•Contracts •Meetings •Strategic Alliances •Quarterly Operational Reviews	•Communication Methods •Community Forum •Vendor Credentialing •Conferences	•Contracts •Programs/ Innovations	•Contract Performance 7.1-55 •Length of Relationship 7.1-58
Other Customers	•Regulatory Agencies •Referring Medical Staff •KCCHI Survey	•Communication Methods •Marketing/Meetings/Outreach •Transfer Center	•Outreach Programs •Facility Changes •New Program Development	•Market Awareness Measures 7.2-27 •Referral Volumes 7.1-45
Sharing and Implementing Best Practices (6)	•Shared Governance •QIC/PIC •Communication Methods	•RCAs; Collaborative Practice •Safety Alerts, Huddles, Email •Education (SPL, JIT, EduTrack), Nursing Councils TCT Manager Meetings	•Key Work Processes and Enabling Systems •TCT	•Process Outcomes 7.1-45-7.1-52 •Adoption of Best Practices 7.1-17; 7.1-34 •EduTrack Training (AOS) •PIC Scorecards (AOS)
Use in Innovation and Strategic Planning (7)	•Environmental Analysis •Internal And External Data Review •Pillar Review	•SPP/Individual Performance Planner •TCT/Top 5 Board •Best Practices Sharing •Goal Cascade; Wallmaps	•Strategic Objectives •Goals/Action Plans •Scorecards •Process Management •Pillar Reviews	•Scorecard/Goal Evaluations 7.4-19 •Individual Performance Planners 7.3-26

CRITERIA QUESTIONS

In your response, include answers to the following questions:

a. Organizational Knowledge

(1) Knowledge Management How do you manage organizational knowledge? How do you:

- collect and transfer workforce knowledge;
- blend and correlate data from different sources to build new knowledge;
- transfer relevant knowledge from and to customers, suppliers, partners, and collaborators;
- assemble and transfer relevant knowledge for use in your innovation and strategic planning processes?

(2) Organizational Learning How do you use your knowledge and resources to embed learning in the way your organization operates?

Notes:

4.2a(1). Blending and correlating data from different sources may involve handling big data sets and disparate types of data and information, such as data tables, video, and text. Furthermore, organizational knowledge constructed from these data may be speculative and may reveal sensitive information about organizations or individuals that must be protected from use for any other purposes.

NIST (2015-2016) p. 18

WORKSHEETS

4.2a(1) – Knowledge Management

Sources Of Knowledge	Process To Collect Knowledge	Process To Transfer Knowledge (To Or From The Source)	Process to manage knowledge
Workforce Knowledge			
Customer Knowledge			
Supplier Knowledge			
Partner Knowledge			
Collaborator Knowledge			
Assemble And Transfer Relevant Knowledge For Use In The Innovation And Strategic Planning Processes			

How Do You Blend And Correlate Data From Different Sources To Build New Knowledge: *	

* Blending and correlating data from different sources may involve handling big data sets and disparate types of data and information, such as data tables, video, and text. Furthermore, organizational knowledge constructed from these data may be speculative and may reveal sensitive information about organizations or individuals that must be protected from use for any other purposes.

4.2a(2) Organizational Learning

Processes and Examples:	How You Use These To Embed Learning In The Way Your Organization Operates:	
	Knowledge	Resources
Process Used:		
Example:		
Example:		
Example:		

ASSESSMENT

Rating Scale:

1 - **No Process** in place - We are not doing this
2 - **Reacting to Problems** – We use a basic (primarily reactive) process
3 - **Systematic Process** – We use a systematic process that has been improved
4 - **Aligned** – We use a process that aligns our activities from top to bottom
5 - **Integrated** – We use a process that is integrated with other processes across the organization
6 - **Benchmark** – We are the Benchmark in our industry or beyond!
DK - Don't Know

---

73   A systematic process is in place to manage the rapid identification, collection, and transfer of relevant knowledge from and to employees, customers, suppliers and partners so they can use the knowledge.   1   2   3   4   5   6   DK

74   Knowledge and resources are used to embed learning in the way we operate.   1   2   3   4   5   6   DK

BLUEPRINT

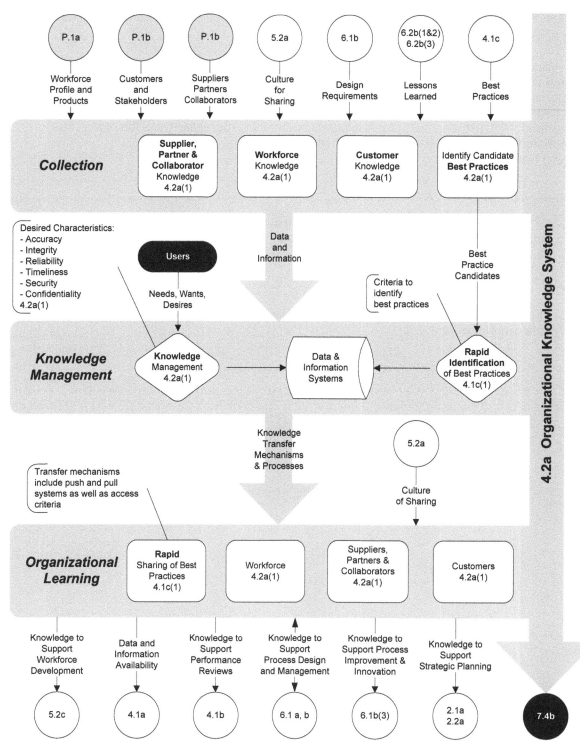

SYSTEM INTEGRATION

Context

P.1a > 4.2a Workforce Profile - The number, type, and nature of the workforce described in the workforce profile (P.1a) is a critical input to the design of the data and information processes and systems that makes the right data available to the right employees. The goal is to design the system to ensure that the appropriate information is available for all employee groups.

P.1a > 4.2a Products and Services - The types and nature of the products, services, and operations are key inputs to the information system characteristics and the types of data and information needed by the workforce, suppliers and partners, customers, etc.

P.1b > 4.2a Customers and Stakeholders - The number, type, and nature of the customers, groups, segments and stakeholders described in the profile are critical inputs to the design of the data and information processes and systems that makes the right data available to the right customers and stakeholders.

P.1b > 4.2a Suppliers, Partners, Collaborators - The number, type, and nature of the suppliers, partners, and collaborators as described in the profile (P.1b) are critical inputs to the design of the data and information processes and systems that makes the right data available to the right suppliers, partners, and collaborators.

Systems

2.1a < 4.2a Knowledge to Support Strategy - Knowledge to support strategy development is in part derived from the information and knowledge contained in the system described in 4.2a.

2.2a < 4.2a Knowledge to Support Strategic Planning - The knowledge transfer and availability system described in 4.2a should be designed to support the development of strategy and action plans described in 2.2a.

4.1a < 4.2a Data and Information Availability - Data and information availability (4.2a) including quality (accurate, reliable, timely, etc.) is an important input to the process of collecting data for tracking and analyzing operations, overall organization performance, and progress relative to strategic objectives.

4.1b < 4.2a Knowledge to Support Performance Reviews - Knowledge to support the performance reviews (4.1b) also comes from the knowledge management system described in 4.2a. This knowledge can help those reviewing performance understand how the changes in performance for individual measures and components impacts the larger system. This understanding can help the reviewers identify the "leverage points" and develop improvement plans.

4.1c > 4.2a Best Practices and knowledge gained during the use of the Performance Improvement System is captured by the knowledge management system described in 4.2a.

4.2a < 5.2a Culture for Sharing - The organizational knowledge area 4.2a calls for the sharing of information and knowledge. There is no process in the world that can make sharing happen if the overall culture and environment do not encourage and reward sharing. The cooperative environment promoted by the organization and management of work as described in 5.2a has a big impact on the degree to which the employees share information and knowledge.

4.2a > 5.2c Knowledge to Support Workforce Development - The knowledge that the organization creates and manages (4.2a) should be leveraged and used to inform the design of the workforce development offerings (5.2c). This is just one way the organization's knowledge can be disseminated throughout the workforce.

4.2a < 6.1a Design Requirements - The work process design requirements identified during the processes described in 6.1b are inputs to the knowledge system for use throughout the organization.

4.2a <> 6.1a Knowledge to Support Process Design - Organizational knowledge from the knowledge management systems described in 4.2a is an important input to the design of processes (6.2a). This connection allows the organization to take advantage of and leverage knowledge throughout the organization. In addition, lessons learned during the design and development of processes should be captured as part of the knowledge management system.

4.2a > 6.1b Knowledge to Support Process Management - Organizational knowledge from the knowledge management systems described in 4.2a is an important input to the management of work processes (6.2b). This connection allows the organization to take advantage of and leverage knowledge through out the organization.

4.2a < 6.1b(1&2) Lessons Learned - The lessons learned from work process management efforts and experiences in 6.2b(1&2) are an important input to the process of identifying best practices for inclusion into the organization's knowledge base.

4.2a < 6.1b(3) Lessons Learned - The lessons learned from work process improvement efforts and experiences in 6.2b(3) are important inputs to the process of identifying best practices for inclusion into the organization's knowledge base (4.2a).

4.2a > 6.1b(3) Knowledge to Support Process Improvement - The knowledge management system (4.2a) ideally contains many best practices and lessons learned to support the improvement of processes of all type throughout the organization.

Scorecard

4.2a > 7.4b Knowledge Management Results - Results that address the effectiveness of the management of data, information, and knowledge should be included in the results presented in 7.1b.

THOUGHTS FOR LEADERS

Having the right data and information available is key to high performance and improvement. One of these enabling tools is data and information. Leaders need to ensure that employees at all levels have the data needed to run the business, and the data needed to analyze performance to determine what is needed to change the business.

One of the widely held misconceptions is that the organization must wait for the IT department to provide them the information they need to manage the business. High performing organizations, however, expect employees at all levels to track some of the data they need on their own. If tracking is pervasive, over time it may require a formal system. Prior to that, however, employees are expected to understand what data can be acted upon and track those data. Many times, simple tools are used to track performance at the working level, and data are displayed to describe a range of topics, such as safety, goals, attendance, performance, improvement efforts, and comparisons.

Organizations have been struggling with the concept and reality of knowledge management. In theory, knowledge management is simple, but the implementation needs to be significantly greater than establishing a database where employees can seek information. The highest performing organizations in this area have established knowledge sharing as a key value or belief, and they embed this thinking in many aspects of the business. Examples of this practice are as follows:

- Improvement teams are responsible for sharing their improvements.

- Councils or committees are responsible for ensuring the sharing of approaches, information, or processes across locations or groups.

- Leaders and leadership teams are responsible for ensuring the sharing across locations and groups.

- The leadership system and approaches emphasize the sharing of knowledge.

- Employees are judged on their ability to use the knowledge of others and helping others use their knowledge.

This list could go on, but the key is the last bullet. If knowledge is power, knowledge management will not work. If employees are not motivated to use the knowledge of others and to share their knowledge with others, the concept of knowledge management will not survive. From a leadership perspective, knowledge management surfaces as an essential business issue. Leaders should be willing to pay the price to learn a practice or fix a problem *once* and not be willing to pay for every employee, location, or group to learn the same lesson. Knowledge management is the key to the transfer of lessons learned.

Knowledge management requires a number of components:

- A process (and clear decision criteria) as to what knowledge could be valuable to others.

- A process to capture the knowledge (typically in an automated data base).

- A process (and clear decision criteria) as to what knowledge is needed by an employee.

- A process to connect the database with the employee who needs the knowledge.

- A process to track the reliability and VALUE of the knowledge used or flowed-through the knowledge management system.

If even one of these characteristics missing, leaders cannot use data to make decisions. Each of these characteristics should be ensured by using a systematic process to validate that the desired properties of the data are achieved on a repeatable basis.

A Lighter Moment:

If knowledge can create problems,
it is not through ignorance that we can solve them.

Isaac Asimov

> *Technology is dominated by two types of people:*
> *those who understand what they do not manage, and*
> *those who manage what they do not understand.*
>
> **Putts Law**

 FOUNDATION

Most of Area to Address 4.2b needs to be viewed from the "user of data" point of view rather than from the IT department's point of view. The beginning of 'user's needs' should start (obviously) with the users. This, however, is not always the case. The IT department may feel they know what the users want/need and that the users have what they need. The proof is whether or not the users have the right data at the right time, which can only be assessed by the users.

Data and Information Quality

Area to Address 4.2b(1) asks how an organization ensures the following properties of their data, information, and organizational knowledge: accuracy, validity, integrity, reliability and currency.

To effectively address these characteristics, all solutions (practices and methods) must be designed to address the individual requirements. While some methods or practices may impact more than one characteristic, the details of how each is addressed should be explicit and clear. Unfortunately, organizations will often attempt to answer this part of the criteria with a vague over-arching statement that does not specifically address the processes, methods and technology used to achieve each characteristic. Additionally, when answering this question, the differences between organizational data and information should be addressed.

Data and Information Security

This reviews how the organization manages electronic and other data and information to ensure that it is secure, confidential, and only the appropriate people have access. This includes all aspects of ensuring cybersecurity.

Data and Information Availability

A critical part of the CPE is how the organization makes the needed data and information available to those who are involved with the organization. This should be addressed from the point of view of the user of data. Do they have what they need and how do you give them the access required? Making data available to the users of the data includes also making it available to suppliers, partners, collaborators, and customers, although they may need less data than internal employees need.

Data and information availability is the ability of the organization to put data and information in the hands of individuals who need it to "run the business" as well as those who are working to "change the business" (the focus on the latter should increase as you go up in the organization). Ensuring data and information availability can include both automated and mechanical means so everyone has the data and information they need when they need it.

Hardware and Software Properties

Although IT may drive the processes to ensure that hardware and software have the characteristics of reliability, security, and being user-friendly, the ultimate judge of whether the organization is achieving their hardware and software availability and friendliness goal is the user's opinion. As such, this process needs to start with the user (requirements) and end with the user (satisfaction).

Emergency Availability

How does the organization ensure that hardware and software will be available to those who are running the business (and to the appropriate suppliers and partners) in the event of an emergency? Simply stated, are our data and systems backed-up in case something happens? Some organizations can answer this for their large systems, but do not have effective back-up for other types of data which are manual or on portable computers. Both of these media can have critical data which would hurt the organization if lost.

Finally, how does the organization keep the data and information availability mechanisms current? This does not mean new equipment as much as it means you should focus on the user's needs and systematically meet those needs.

 EXAMPLES

Inova Fair Oaks Hospital (Fairfax, Virginia)

The approach to **organizational data, information and knowledge** is shown in the figure below.

The specific interventions and evaluation methods used to address the objectives for accuracy, integrity, reliability, timeliness, security and confidentiality form a framework to achieve a solid foundation for patient care decision making, improved patient safety and positive financial returns. The approaches and safeguards applied to column A ensure that the information and knowledge in columns B and C possess the same properties.

Data and Information Availability. Inova Fair Oaks Hospital (IFOH) focuses on providing the right information and the right tools for our workforce, suppliers, partners, collaborators, patients, and stakeholders. IT systematically collaborates and seeks VOC data from the appropriate users to define requirements, evaluate, select, and implement systems that meet their needs. Once a system is live, IT continues to meet with users to determine if new or additional functionality is needed to ensure data availability.

We provide access to needed data and information through the traditional PC workstation, as well as laptops, wireless carts, tablets, and smartphones. Our portable approaches ensure access to right tools to enhance and support the workflows. Remote access is also provided via an Internet-delivered Citrix solution, giving users access to required information from home or office. Secure key identification overlays the inherent Citrix security to provide the highest levels of protection and confidentiality. Remote access is available 24 hours a day, seven days a week with redundancy mechanisms in place to ensure continuity.

Quality Data, Information and Knowledge Assurance Approaches

Property*	Process to Ensure This Property Is Achieved and Maintained:		
	A. Organizational Data	B. Organizational Information	C. Organizational Knowledge
Accuracy	•Data Standards/ Edits	• Evidenced based data	•Expert rules, decision support
Integrity	•Screen design, logic controls, field edits	•Diminished data entry redundancy •IT Change control practices	•IT Change control practices •Code validation
Reliability	•System backup standards •Critical system redundancy	•Network surveillance •Standardized Contracting	•Database redundancy/ •Clinical/ Financial Analytic Tools
Timeliness	•Real time data / system processing	•Interface transmission •Response monitoring	•Currency of application versioning
Security	•Robust password controls •External access controls	•Duplicate login prevention •Audit standards for access expiration	•Multifactor identify validation
Confidentiality	•Employee compliance standards/ code of ethics	•HIPAA compliance standards training	•Release of Information Proc/ Policy

PRO-TEC Coating Company (Baldrige Recipient 2007)

System reliability is addressed at all three computing levels (Embedded and PLC controller, Supervisory process control, and Mainframe and business systems) utilizing scheduled outages as shown in Figure 4.2-2, with warm hardware backups for critical systems. System security is controlled using login IDs and passwords for authorized users. User-friendliness is addressed using a design review process where users are systematically involved for all software changes that involve a change to the user interface. These reviews involve both users and IS personnel.

Figure 4.2-2 – Planned System Outages	
Mainframe Business Systems, (Level III)	Twice a Month
Plant Process Control, (Level II)	Every Third Week
Production Line Control, (Level I)	Every Third Week

Figure 4.2-3 shows a table which describes how PRO-TEC ensures the accuracy, integrity, reliability, timeliness, security, and confidentiality of our data, information, and organizational knowledge. For the purposes of this table, "Data" are considered raw data from either production data collection systems or business systems. "Information" is what is being sent to databases. "Organizational Knowledge" is information that has been evaluated by the criteria of the "QES Knowledge Management Process."

Figure 4.2-3 - Data Quality Matrix			
	Data	**Information**	**Organizational Knowledge**
Accuracy	Audit, 2nd method of verification	Process experts evaluate	QES audits/review
Integrity	Computer Systems protocols	Evaluation actual vs. expected results-range checking	Computer Systems protocols
Reliability	Redundancy on critical systems	Disaster recovery plans, backups, uninterruptible power supplies, generators	Same as "Information"
Timeliness	Real-time processing on most data	Real-time processing, batch processing	Scheduled updates
Security	Login ID, password	Login ID, password	Login ID, password
Confidentiality	Application access rights	Application access rights	All Associates have access

SSM Healthcare (Baldrige Recipient 2002)

SSMHC's **Information Management Council (IMC)** determines the data and information needed by entity, network and system staff, suppliers/partners, stakeholders, and patients/customers through an **information management planning process** that is part of the overall Strategic, Financial and HR Planning Process (SFPP). The IMC is a multi-disciplinary subcommittee of System Management that represents the system, networks and entities. The IMC consists of approximately 20 System Management members, entity presidents, physicians and representatives from operations, finance, nursing, planning, and information systems. The information management (IC) plan is developed by the IMC and implemented by the SSM Information Center.

Common information systems platforms are deployed in each entity via SSMHC's network. Key clinical, financial, operational, customer and market performance data for all entities and SSMHC as a whole are provided in automated information systems that allow for significant reporting capability. Based on best practices at several entities, the ePMI (Exceptional Performance Management Initiative) Team in 2002 recommended a systemwide model for redesigning the Financial and Decision Support services within SSMHC. The new model enables improved monitoring of performance, additional decision support for executive leaders, and more rapid response to strategic opportunities.

Based on the needs of the organization, the IMC follows established criteria to classify its information systems into three categories: Required (standardized across the system and must be implemented at each facility); Standard (standardized systems that entities implement according to their needs); and Non-

Standard (not standardized across the system and entities may implement according to their needs). There is a focus on standardizing information systems to ensure that standard data and information will be available for reporting at a regional and system level. The SSMIC works collaboratively with key functional areas (e.g., corporate finance) to ensure its systems meet common data definitions as, for example, with the system-wide Performance Indicator Reporting process. The required and standard information systems are deployed throughout the system by the SSMIC. The SSMIC has also implemented a sophisticated technical infrastructure that allows the physician partners to access data and information needed for their practice from any location at any time from multiple devices, including PCs, PDAs, pagers, and fax.

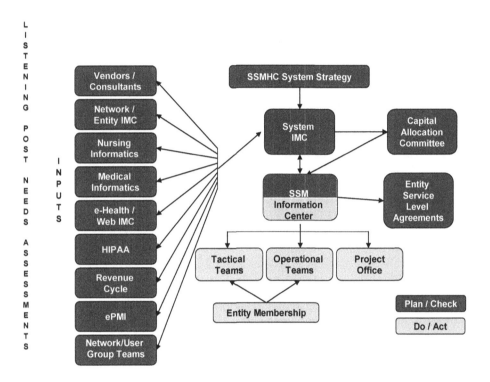

The SSMIC has a technology management function that monitors its information systems to ensure high availability and access of data and information. This is accomplished through the Operations Center and the use of system monitoring tools such as Spectrum and ITO. A variety of file servers are monitored for disk and CPU utilization and system uptimes. Data are used for forecasting and planning server upgrades. Additionally, network performance is monitored to ensure access to the application systems. As appropriate, the SSMIC has implemented redundancy for specific systems and within its network infrastructure for high availability.

The SSMIC's Compliance Administration Group (CAG) has developed **Security Policies and Procedures** that document the system's intentions and staff responsibilities regarding information confidentiality, privacy, and security. The policies and procedures cover all employees of SSMHC and physicians who use SSMHC information or information processing services during the course of their work. They also cover all consultants, payors, contractors, contract and resident physicians, external service providers, volunteers, and suppliers/vendors who use SSMHC information or information processing services.

To ensure data and information security and confidentiality, the SSMIC has established a department for Compliance Administration and Security, which is responsible for ensuring appropriate authorized access to its computer systems. A formal Computer Authorization process for granting access to systems and a process of routinely requiring passwords to be changed have been implemented. The department leader also is working with the project manager for HIPAA compliance and heads up the HIPAA Technical Security team to ensure that the confidentiality of electronic patient records is in compliance with federal standards.

Data integrity, reliability and accuracy is addressed through a multidimensional approach. The SSMIC's Decision Support department works with entity customers to audit the data and information loaded into its databases for accuracy. For electronic business partners, such as payors, the SSMIC has established checks and balances in the control process to validate the timely receipt and integrity of submissions for payroll direct deposit and electronic claims submissions. The SSMIC uses the **Catholic Healthcare Audit Network (CHAN)** to perform audits of information systems and processes for integrity, reliability, accuracy, timeliness, security and confidentiality. Hospitals also complete the MHA Conformance Assessment Surveys to check the accuracy and validity of clinical data and improve data reporting.

SSMHC keeps its data and information systems current through the SFPP and IS Planning & Management Process. Technology needs are assessed through the internal and external assessment step of the SFPP. The external emerging technologies analysis addresses the current situation in the industry and marketplace. The internal physical plant/technology analysis assesses the technology needs of SSMHC's entities and networks to support achievement of goals and action plans. The IMC uses the information collected through an SSMIC-sponsored IMC Education Day, and the SFPP and its own listening posts and learning tools to develop the information management (IC) plan, which incorporates network and entity information systems needs. Following approval by the IMC, the IC plan is incorporated into the system's SFP. The SSMIC communicates its goals and objectives to each entity and network through a Service Letter Agreement that details the products and services the SSMIC will provide to that entity and network during the year. A measurement system for evaluating the SSMIC's performance is a key component of the agreement.

The SSMIC also contracts with and participates in external industry research and educational groups, including the Gartner Group, Meta Group, Washington University's CAIT program, HIMSS/CHIME, and INSIGHT (participation by individual and board membership) as a way of keeping current with health care service needs and directions.

Source: SSM (2003) pp. 22 - 23

CRITERIA QUESTIONS

In your response, include answers to the following questions:

b. Data, Information, and Information Technology

(1) **Data and Information Quality** How do you verify and ensure the quality of organizational data and information? How do you manage electronic and other data and information to ensure their accuracy and validity, integrity and reliability, and currency?

(2) **Data and Information Security** How do you ensure the security of sensitive or privileged data and information? How do you manage electronic and other data and information to ensure confidentiality and only appropriate access? How do you oversee the cybersecurity of your information systems?

(3) **Data and Information Availability** how do you ensure the availability of organizational data and information? How do you make needed data and information available in a user-friendly format and timely manner to your workforce, suppliers, partners, collaborators, and customers, as appropriate?

(4) **Hardware and Software Properties** How do you ensure that hardware and software are reliable, secure, and user-friendly?

(5) **Emergency Availability** In the event of an emergency, how do you ensure that hardware and software systems and data and information continue to be available to effectively serve customers and business needs?

Note:

4.2b(2). Managing cybersecurity (the security of electronic data) includes, for example, protecting against the loss of sensitive information about employees, customers, and organizations; protecting assets stored in the cloud or outside your organization's control; protecting intellectual property; and protecting against the financial, legal, and reputational aspects of data breaches.

NIST (2015-2016) p . 18

WORKSHEETS

4.2b(1) Data and Information Properties

Property Of Your Organizational Data, Information, and Knowledge:	Process to Ensure This Property Is Achieved and Maintained:
Accuracy	
Validity	
Integrity	
Reliability	
Currency	

Note: Each of these should be answered separately.

4.2b(2) - Data and Information Security

Key Data Characteristic:	Process To Ensure The Quality Of Organizational Data And Information:
Confidentiality	
Electronic Data Protected	
Other Data And Information Protected	
Only Appropriate Access	
Cybersecurity Of Information Systems	

4.2b(3) - Data and Information Availability

Key Group:	Process To Make Needed Data Available To The Key Group:	Process To Make Needed Information Available To The Key Group:	Process To Ensure (And Verify) That The Needed Data And Information Are User-Friendly:
Workforce			
Suppliers			
Partners			
Collaborators			
Customers			

4.2b(4) - Hardware and Software Properties

Attribute	Process Used* To Ensure That This Attribute Is Achieved For:
Reliable	Hardware:
	Software:
Secure	Hardware:
	Software:
User Friendly	Hardware:
	Software:

* These processes should have a primary focus on the user's requirements and not on the Information Technology Department's requirements.

4.2b(4) – Emergency Availability

Processes Used To Ensure The Continued Availability Of Data and Information To Effectively Serve Customers In The Event Of An Emergency
For Hardware:
For Software:
For Data And Information:

ASSESSMENT

75	Organization-wide hardware and software are reliable, secure and user friendly (in the eyes of the users).	1 2 3 4 5 6 DK
76	In the event of an emergency, the organization has the systematic ability to ensure the continued availability of hardware and software systems.	1 2 3 4 5 6 DK
77	The organization has systematic processes to ensure that we evaluate and improve software and hardware systems as the user's business needs and directions require.	1 2 3 4 5 6 DK
78	The organization has systematic processes in place to ensure data integrity, reliability, timeliness, security, accuracy and confidentiality.	1 2 3 4 5 6 DK

BLUEPRINT

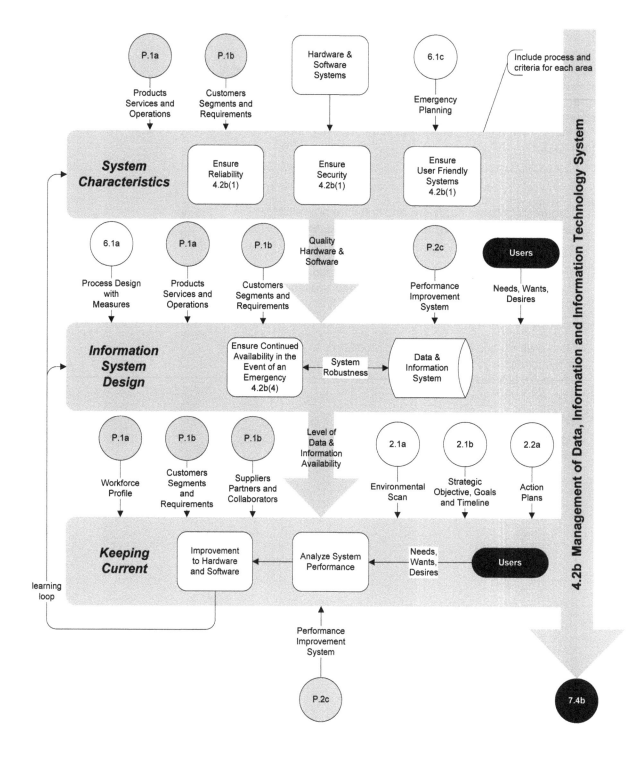

SYSTEM INTEGRATION

Context

P.1a > 4.2b Products and Services - The nature of the products and services can be an important consideration in the information systems characteristics (e.g., reliability, security, user friendliness). For example, a government customer with high technology products might require an unusually high degree of security to ensure the protection of classified documents, etc.

P.1a > 4.2b Workforce Profile - The number, type, and nature of the workforce described in the workforce profile is a critical input to keeping the data and information processes and systems current with the changing needs of the workforce.

P.1b > 4.2b Customers Segments and Requirements - The number, type, and nature of the customers, groups, and segments described in the profile are critical inputs to the design of the data and information processes and systems that makes the right data available to the right customers. There should be processes to ensure the appropriate information system is reliable, secure, and user friendly for all customer segments and groups.

P.1b > 4.2b Suppliers, Partners, Collaborators - The number, type, and nature of the suppliers, partners, and collaborators as described in the profile (P.1b) are critical inputs to the design of the data and information systems (reliability, security, user friendliness).

P.2c > 4.2b Performance Improvement System - The processes for keeping the data and information availability processes and systems current with changing business needs and directions should be based on the overall performance improvement system described in the profile (P.2c).

Systems

2.1a > 4.2b Environmental Scan - The environmental scan and analysis results are key inputs to keeping the management information system current with changing business needs in 4.2b.

2.1b > 4.2b Strategic Objectives and Timetable - The goals and timetable described in 2.1b are key inputs to the process of keeping the information systems current with changing business needs (4.2b).

2.2a > 4.2b Action Plans - The action plans described in 2.2a will often contain improvements to the hardware and software systems described in 4.2b.

4.2b < 6.2c Emergency Planning - The continuity of operations planning process (6.1c) should include plans to ensure the information resources and technology system (4.2b) is included and protected to ensure the necessary information to support operations.

4.2b < 6.2a Process Designs with Measures - The work processes designs resulting from the methods described in 6.2a are important inputs to the design of the information system that supports those processes.

Scorecard

4.2b > 7.1b, 7.4b Information System Results - Results addressing the extent and effectiveness of the management of information resources and technology system should be presented in 7.1b.

THOUGHTS FOR LEADERS

Leaders certainly have the responsibility to ensure that the organization is sustainable. No organization is operationally OR strategically sustainable, however, unless they have the data needed to run the business and to change (improve) the business. This means that leaders must ensure that the hardware, software, data and information are:

- Reliable (in the eyes of the users);

- Secure;

- User Friendly (in the eyes of the users);

- Available in the event of an emergency; and

- Kept current (in the eyes of the users).

Without these characteristics of hardware, software, data and information, the organization will not thrive, and the leaders may not understand why!

This also means that the need for data must start and end with the users. The users should be a key input to the IT Roadmap, and should be involved in both the operation of the existing systems (through their calls to the help desk), and the development of new systems (through their approvals at every phase).

A Lighter Moment:

It is a very sad thing that nowadays there is so little useless information.

Oscar Wilde

> *An employee will give their all, as long as they feel valued and respected.*
>
> **Amy Armstrong**

FOUNDATION

Capability and Capacity

This area to address begins with identifying the capabilities (skills) the organization needs and how much of each capability is required (capacity = the numbers of employees with the appropriate skill). The capability assessment can include the skills and competencies needed, and the capacity assessment can include the staffing ratios or levels. Key questions are: How does the organization assess their current workforce capability and capacity? How does the organization know what they are going to need in the future regarding workforce capability and capacity?

New Workforce Members

How does the organization find the right people and ensure they are brought on board? Once the organization determines what is required, how does it hire, develop, and keep the new employees? This can include new employee orientation and what some organizations call "on-boarding". Additionally, how do you ensure that your recruiting represents the same mix of ideas, cultures, and thinking of your hiring community? This view of diversity can be market-focused. For example, if your customer base has a wide range of backgrounds, experiences, needs, and expectations, you may need to have an employee base with that same diversity to be able to effectively serve your customer.

Work Accomplishment

How do you get the work done which is required? Once you have identified the needs and have the right employees on board, the CPE ask for a description of the process to manage and organize work to capitalize on the organization's core competencies. In simple terms, how do we put the right person and team doing the right work?

These individual competencies, and how they are applied to the work, should be managed in a way that drives a competitive advantage. Additionally, the CPE ask how the organization reinforces a customer and business focus (presumably at all levels of the organization) to exceed the performance expectations (and goals) at each level.

Finally, the CPE address how the organization integrates its strategic challenges (externally at the highest level) all the way down to detailed action plans, particularly as business needs change.

Workforce Change Management

How do you make changes as necessary, and prepare your workforce? As changes occur in organizational needs, particularly as they impact workforce capacity and capability, the organization needs to have a systematic process that addresses those needs and their impact on the workforce. Where the workforce size has to be changed (increased or decreased) there should be a process that can ramp up if capability and capacity needs to be increased, or minimize the impact of workforce reductions if the overall workload decreases. For example, many organizations use temporary employees to minimize the impact of a downturn. If the downturn occurs, they reduce the use of temporary employees to protect the jobs of their permanent workforce.

 EXAMPLES

Sharp Healthcare (Baldrige Recipient 2007)

Workforce capability and capacity are assessed through a systematic workforce planning and development process depicted in Figure 5.2-1. In direct response to business need, the workforce characteristics and skills required to meet those needs are analyzed and clearly identified through the development of competency-based job descriptions maintained through a Web-based job library. Workforce capacity is assessed through the development of specific staffing plans with timelines considering expected and contingency demand levels and determining the need for supplemental staff, such as SRN's per-diem employees, to fill immediate or unexpected demand on a temporary basis. Positions are posted and candidates are sourced internally and externally through a skills match and referral process.

Candidate clinical and behavioral profiles are developed and questions are crafted for use in conducting structured job interviews to assess prior work experiences, skills, technical strengths, values, and perceptions. Candidates are hired or promoted from within, skills and performance are evaluated within the first 90 days, and if successful, employees are moved into regular positions. As employees acquire new skills through job performance and formal training and development, they are sourced to fill future position openings.

Recruitment, hiring, placement, and retention of new staff are part of Sharp's Workforce Capability and Capacity. The recruitment phase consists of applicant sourcing, screening, referencing, search, and selection. Strategically aligned multimedia sourcing plans identify diverse workforce groups and segments to guide the scope of each recruitment effort and identify the specific solicitation strategies such as referrals, job fairs, conferences, and open houses.

Once candidates are identified, behavioral-based selection and peer interviewing techniques guide the selection and placement process. Periodically, workforce diversity is compared to community diversity demographics. To ensure that the workforce represents the diverse cultures of the community, Sharp has implemented specific, long-term, workforce development strategies that extend across gender, age group, cultures, and local communities to:

- Partner with local schools and universities to create future applicant pools and improve public perception of health care professions,
- Sponsor clinical affiliations at local colleges and universities and establish a presence of Sharp Leaders,
- Mentor new nursing graduates through a progression of learning covering technical, critical thinking, and relationship skills, and
Affiliate with OU to sponsor a local nursing program to develop future applicant pools.

Sharp Figure 5.2-1: Workforce Planning and Development Process

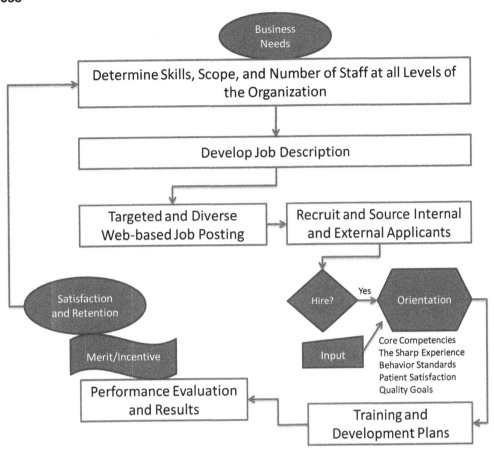

Sharp's workforce is managed and organized through an entity-based operational structure segment by the key workforce groups, and aligned with the overall work systems for patient care delivery and a centralized organizational structure for support services across the system. The centralized support services structure provides consistent, high-quality services across the system while realizing economies of scale and the ability to capitalize on and implement best practices in every entity with precision and agility. Senior Leaders provide system oversight and strategic direction via the Leadership System. The entity-based structure leverages The Sharp Experience for point-of-service patient care customized to patient need. Entity leaders serve as catalysts for the planning and delivery of health care and achievement of action plans via the Leadership System. Work groups organized in cross-functional or multidisciplinary teams deliver care with the patient as the primary focus.

Workforce environment (Figure 5.2-2) is addressed through workforce capability and capacity process. Sharp staffing plans provide the opportunity to ensure continuity through using supplemental staff including SRN per-diem's, contracted labor, or incentive programs such as BidShift to minimize the impact of reductions in workforce. To ensure and improve the health, safety, and security of the workplace, Sharp uses a proactive, comprehensive and multi-faceted process that begins with developing and maintaining management plans. The plans define key goals, objectives, processes, responsibilities, process improvement plans, and performance measures at the system and entity levels.

Sharp Figure 5.2-2: Workforce Environment

Workforce Planning
(Fig. 5.2-1)
Identify Key Positions and
Establish Criteria

Workforce & Leadership
Development
(Fig. 5.1-2)
Mentoring, Education and
Training, Skills Enrichment

Lean
Six Sigma

Workforce Development
(Fig. 5.2-1)
Applicant Sourcing & Identity
Potential Candidates

Performance Management
(Fig. 5.2-1)
Career Development & Progression
Plans, Growth Opportunities,
Career Ladders

Evaluation of the plans, objectives, and goals occur annually for effectiveness, and goals and objectives are assessed to determine future strategies. Safety training related to the plans occurs annually and includes such factors as disaster preparedness and evacuation plans. Annual results are reported at the system and entity safety committees and quality councils. The plan environments include access control (e.g., hospital, clinic, home health) or business setting, occupation (e.g., nursing, lab, radiology, rehab,) or function. Involvement spans from Senior Leaders to staff, and targets patients, visitors, volunteers, employees, and physicians. Entity Safety Officers and unit-based Safety Associates assist in identifying and addressing safety concerns, meeting injury prevention goals, and disseminating safety information.

Employee participation includes involvement in policies, equipment, work method processes, injury prevention, and work hazards using the WISH reports. Ergonomic assessments and training are proactively initiated to prevent employee injury. Findings from injury prevention initiatives, safety improvement processes, and Ergonomic evaluations are analyzed and used to determine process improvements. A safety Intranet site provides information on employee safety including a self-guided computer ergonomics tutorial.

SSM Healthcare (Baldrige Recipient 2002)

Employee retention is critical in any organization. It is even more critical for organizations like SSM who are facing nationwide shortages in nurses over the next decade. To combat this condition, SSM instituted a Nursing Recruitment and Retention Steering Team which goes beyond merely educating, measuring, and compensating nurses, as was done in 2000.

SSMHC uses a wide variety of recruitment methods. The recruitment efforts focus on SSMHC's commitment to quality and culture of teamwork to interest candidates who have the potential to be valued

400

employees. SSMHC screens advertising outlets and sources of job candidates based on the SSMHC valued employee profile. The system also recruits electronically, both on its external Web site and from all SSMHC intranet pages. Openings are also posted on wall bulletin boards at the entities. During 2001, SSMHC recruited 2,459 employees via the web. An online application is available. Information about all applicants, including online applicants, is tracked electronically. This tracking program helps HR staff to better focus their recruiting efforts. SSMHC has addressed the industry's critical nursing shortage by bringing together nurse and human resources executives to develop innovative recruitment and retention strategies. System Management is taking the following actions based upon the recommendations of the five system wide nursing recruitment and retention teams: (1) implementing nursing shared accountability models at the entities, (2) improving nursing education and orientation programs offered within the system, (3) improving nursing access to technology, (4) developing programs to foster collaborative relationships between nurses and physicians, (5) offering a variety of benefits such as improved tuition reimbursement and bonuses for employees who recruit a peer.

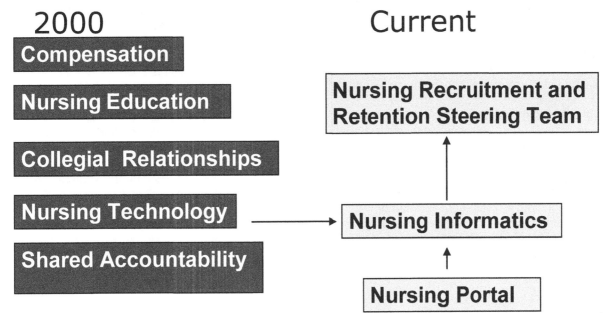

Other recruiting strategies are student nurse internships and post-graduate clinical teaching site experiences. These programs are designed to give student nurses and postgraduate nurses an opportunity to work side-by-side with experienced nurses. As an example, in 2001, 84 percent of the student nurses stayed on as SSMHC St. Louis employees. SSMHC's entities celebrate their diversity in many ways, including events that feature ethnic foods, observances of ethnic holidays and other events celebrating racial, ethnic, and religious significance.

Source: SSM (2003) pp. 25 - 26

Pewaukee School District (Baldrige Recipient 2013)

PSD (Pewaukee School District) recognizes that building and maintaining a talented workforce is crucial to reach our Mission; Workforce Development is integrated in our SPP because of this. We utilize a systematic workforce allocation process integrated in our budgeting process. (Figure 5.1-1) The Budget & Staffing Plan is annually updated and presented to the BOE for approval. As we are in a service-providing business, close to 80% of our annual budget is invested in staff salary & benefit costs. Consequently, led by the CFO, the AT (Administrative Team) carefully assesses capability and capacity needs as the Budget & Staffing Plan is developed each year using a tightly flowcharted process (Figure 5.1-1).

The AT systematically assesses capability by determining what new knowledge & skills will need to be learned by staff. Capacity is determined by our determining how many staff members are needed to deliver our programs & services. To conduct this assessment we use a systematic review of school & class enrollment projections based upon the following criteria: SP initiatives; CRDP(Curriculum Review & Design Process) revision; resignations & retirements; student learning needs; enrollment; available funds; class size models; changes in instructional delivery, licensure, skill sets; performance evaluations and department/ school needs. Figures 7.3-1 & 7.3-2 illustrate the consistent staffing levels maintained by the District successfully using this criteria.

Our campus setting enhances flexibility in capability and capacity needs by fostering the sharing of staff between buildings and among most workforce segments (Figure P-3). While enrollment and optimal class size greatly determine staffing levels, the SPP is heavily integrated with planned changes (Figure 2.1-3). A HR Plan is developed and reviewed to determine additional workforce capacity and capability needs. As example, in 2012 a new Readers Writers Workshop curriculum was implemented in accord with the SPP, and extensive training was provided for faculty prior to and during the 2012-13 school year (impacting capability), and a Literacy Coach was hired to provide ongoing support (impacting capacity). Identified needs for increased staff capability is met by implementation of our Professional Development Plan so our staff is equipped with necessary knowledge. Completion of Professional Development is tracked by the HR Department for all workforce groups using an online tool. This ensures that all identified staff members receive the necessary PD for their positions.

Prior to posting positions, workforce capability is further assessed; job descriptions are reviewed to identify current required knowledge, skills and abilities (KSAs) as well as certifications and/ or licenses. The HR Department uses a defined tracking process to ensure that candidates for teaching, administration and support positions have current required certifications and/or licenses. In a cycle of learning, HR presents the Hiring & Retention Report to the AT and opportunities for improvement in the hiring process are identified. Volunteers are also a part of our workforce and in a cycle of improvement, the District hired a Volunteer Coordinator in 2012 to recruit and coordinate the selection, placement and training of volunteers for classroom tutoring. These volunteers work directly with students under the direction of teachers to provide extra assistance to students. Our volunteer workforce represents a diverse cross section of our community including parents, senior citizens and other community residents.

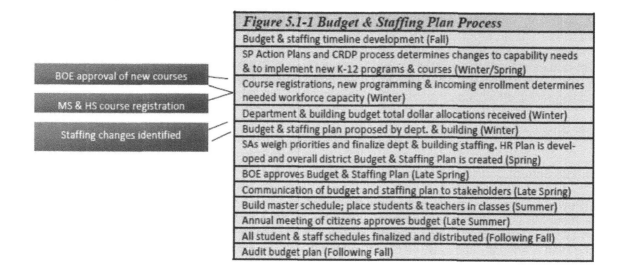

Figure 5.1-1 Budget & Staffing Plan Process
Budget & staffing timeline development (Fall)
SP Action Plans and CRDP process determines changes to capability needs & to implement new K-12 programs & courses (Winter/Spring)
Course registrations, new programming & incoming enrollment determines needed workforce capacity (Winter)
Department & building budget total dollar allocations received (Winter)
Budget & staffing plan proposed by dept. & building (Winter)
SAs weigh priorities and finalize dept & building staffing. HR Plan is developed and overall district Budget & Staffing Plan is created (Spring)
BOE approves Budget & Staffing Plan (Late Spring)
Communication of budget and staffing plan to stakeholders (Late Spring)
Build master schedule; place students & teachers in classes (Summer)
Annual meeting of citizens approves budget (Late Summer)
All student & staff schedules finalized and distributed (Following Fall)
Audit budget plan (Following Fall)

BOE approval of new courses

MS & HS course registration

Staffing changes identified

CRITERIA QUESTIONS

In your response, include answers to the following questions:

a. **Workforce Capability and Capacity**

(1) **Capability and Capacity** How do you assess your workforce capability and capacity needs? How do you assess the skills, competencies, certifications, and staffing levels you need?

(2) **New Workforce Members** How do you recruit, hire, place, and retain new workforce members? How do you ensure that your workforce represents the diverse ideas, cultures, and thinking of your hiring and customer community?

(3) **Work Accomplishment** How do you organize and manage your workforce? How do you: organize and manage your workforce to
- accomplish your organization's work,
- capitalize on your organization's core competencies,
- reinforce a customer and business focus, and
- exceed performance expectations?

(4) **Workforce Change Management** How do you prepare your workforce for changing capability and capacity needs? How do you:
- Manage your workforce, its needs, and your organization's needs to ensure continuity, prevent workforce reductions, and minimize the impact of such reductions, if they become necessary;
- Prepare for and manage periods of workforce growth; and
- Prepare your workforce for changes in organizational structure and work systems, when needed?

Notes:

5.1. "Workforce" refers to the people actively involved in accomplishing your organization's work. It includes permanent, temporary, and part-time personnel, as well as any contract employees you supervise. It includes team leaders, supervisors, and managers at all levels. People supervised by a contractor should be addressed in categories 2 and 6 as part of your larger work system strategy and your internal work processes. For organizations that also rely on volunteers, "workforce" includes these volunteers.

5.1a. "Workforce capability" refers to your organization's ability to carry out its work processes through its people's knowledge, skills, abilities, and competencies. Capability may include the ability to build and sustain relationships with customers; innovate and transition to new technologies; develop new products, services, and work processes; and meet changing business, market, and regulatory demands.

"Workforce capacity" refers to your organization's ability to ensure sufficient staffing levels to carry out its work processes and successfully deliver products to customers, including the ability to meet seasonal or varying demand levels.

5.1a. Your assessment of workforce capability and capacity needs should consider not only current needs but also future requirements based on the strategic objectives and action plans you identify in Category 2 and the performance projections you discuss in 4.1c(2).

5.1a(2). This requirement refers only to new workforce members. The retention of existing workforce members is considered in item 5.2, Workforce Engagement.

5.1a(3), 5.1a(4). Organizing and managing your workforce may involve organizing the workforce for change as you address changes in your external environment, culture, technology, or strategic objectives.

5.1a(4). Preparing your workforce for changing capability and capacity needs might include training, education, frequent communication, consideration of workforce employment and employability, career counseling, and outplacement and other services.

NIST (2015-2016) pp. 19 - 20

WORKSHEETS

5.1a(1) – Capability and Capacity

Area Assessed	Process Used To Assess:	
	Capability	Capacity
Skills		
Competencies		
Certifications		
Staffing Levels		

5.1a(2) – New Workforce Members

Process Used For New Employees:	Process To Ensure Employees Represent The Diversity Of The Community In:		
	Diverse Ideas	Diverse Cultures	Diverse Thinking
To Recruit:			
To Hire:			
To Place:			
To Retain:			

5.1a(3) – Work Accomplishment

Areas To Capitalize On:	Process Used To: Organize and Manage The Workforce To Accomplish The Work Of The Organization
The Accomplishment Of The Organizations' Work	
The Organization's Core Competencies	
Reinforcing A Customer Focus	
Reinforcing A Business Focus	
Exceeding Performance Expectations	

5.1a(4) – Workforce Change Management

Area Managed:	Processes Used To Prepare The Workforce For Changing Needs In:	
	Capability	Capacity
Ensuring Continuity		
Organizational Need To Ensure Continuity		
Organizational Need To Prevent Workforce Reductions		
Organizational Need To Minimize The Impact Of Workforce Reductions		
Prepare For and Manage Periods Of Workforce Growth		
Prepare For Changes In Organizational Structure		
Prepare For Changes In Work Systems		

ASSESSMENT

Rating Scale:

1 - **No Process** in place - We are not doing this
2 - **Reacting to Problems** – We use a basic (primarily reactive) process
3 - **Systematic Process** – We use a systematic process that has been improved
4 - **Aligned** – We use a process that aligns our activities from top to bottom
5 - **Integrated** – We use a process that is integrated with other processes across the organization
6 - **Benchmark** – We are the Benchmark in our industry or beyond!
DK - Don't Know

79	There is a systematic process used to identify the characteristics and skills (capability) needed by existing and potential employees.	1	2	3	4	5	6	DK
80	There is a systematic process uses to identify the numbers of (capacity) each skill needed by the organization.	1	2	3	4	5	6	DK
81	A systematic process is used to recruit, hire, and retain new employees.	1	2	3	4	5	6	DK
82	There is a systematic process used to organize and manage the workforce to ensure the: 1) work of the organization is accomplished; 2) work links to the organization's core competency; 3) work reinforces a customer and business focus; 4) workforce exceeds their performance expectations to; 5) achieve action plans and address external strategic challenges.	1	2	3	4	5	6	DK
83	The organization systematically prepares for and addresses changing workforce capability and capacity needs. This includes planning for minimizing the impact of workforce reductions or managing periods of growth.	1	2	3	4	5	6	DK

BLUEPRINT

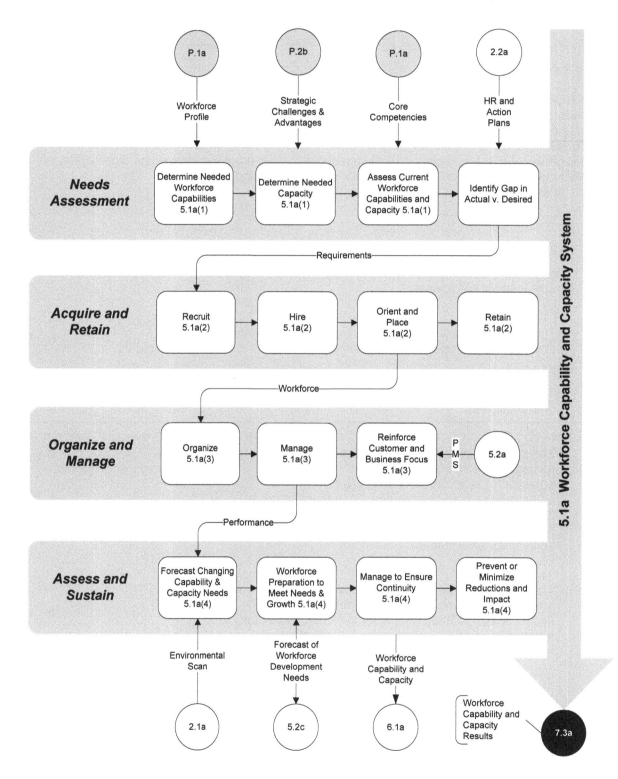

SYSTEM INTEGRATION

Context

P.1a > 5.1a Workforce Profile - The workforce segments identified in the profile together with the organization's requirements will determine the gaps that need to be filled with new employees. These can be gaps in technical skills, diversity, education and so forth. In addition, the employee profile describes the current available labor pool.

P.1a > 5.1a Core Competencies - The assessment of the workforce capability and capacity should include their capability and capacity related to the core competencies. Not only does the workforce need to continually develop the knowledge skills and abilities related to the core competencies, ensuring that the organization attracts, retains, and manages the workforce to ensure it has sufficient capability and capacity associated with the core competencies.

P.2b > 5.1a Strategic Challenges and Advantages - The strategic challenges and advantages described in the profile (P.2b) are important inputs to the workforce needs assessment process. Both challenges and advantages are important considerations when determining the gaps in the actual v. the desired workforce capability and capacity to overcome the challenges and to sustain or enhance the advantages.

Systems

2.1a > 5.1a Environmental Scan - The environmental scan and analysis results are key inputs to forecasting the workforce capability and capacity needs in 5.1a.

2.2a > 5.1a HR Action Plans - The Human Resource Plans are a key input to the recruitment of new employees with the right knowledge, skills, and abilities to support the new directions and specific changes detailed in the action plans. This helps to ensure that the hiring of new employees is focused on areas that are linked to the accomplishment of the overall strategy.

5.2a > 5.1a Performance Management System - The performance management system (5.2a) is a key part of the overall management of the capability and capacity of the workforce as described in 5.1a.

5.2c > 5.1a Forecast of Workforce Development Needs - The forecast of workforce capability and capacity needs identified as part of the assessment and sustain phase of the workforce capability and capacity system (5.1a) are important considerations when designing the development offerings and delivery methods (5.2c).

5.1a > 6.1a Workforce Capability and Capacity - The capability and capacity of the workforce (5.1a) is a key input to the work placement strategy (6.1a).

Scorecard

5.1a > 7.3a Workforce Capability and Capacity Results - The results related to workforce capability and capacity (e.g., turnover, qualifications, etc.) should be reported in 7.3a.

THOUGHTS FOR LEADERS

This portion of the CPE focuses on the capability and capacity of the workforce. Leaders have the responsibility to ensure that the workforce capability and capacity are properly and rationally planned. When changes are necessary, it is key to plan these carefully and to let the organization know what factors are considered in that planning. This is particularly true if the organization is downsizing. Obviously if this is not done properly, the wrong people can be lost. Everyone in the organization is quick to sympathize with the downsized person. The real casualty, however, can be the organization itself. If everyone sees that the leaders are not walking the talk (and are not keeping the right employees), then motivation takes a dive, and those employees who are still on the payroll are not the most capable.

Additionally, nothing can send a stronger message throughout an organization than the message sent by those who get promoted. Their promotion communicates to the rest of the employees what company leaders truly value, regardless of what they espouse.

We have heard organizations talk about engaged employees, empowerment, and teams, and spend significant amounts of money on training in these areas. From all outward appearances, these organizations are "walking the talk."

The truth, however, comes out when these organizations promote someone. If leaders promote an old-school autocratic leader, they have put themselves years behind in employee trust. The employees now know what is actually valued in the organization and in the future they will act based on how they perceive they will be rewarded, not on what leadership says will be rewarded.

To truly engage the workforce, trust needs to be the glue that holds the workforce team together. Leaders must not only earn that trust, but they must "re-earn" it every day. One mistake can erase many years of goodwill and trust, and can take a long time to recover. As discussed in Item 1.1, leaders cannot delegate being a role model. This includes how they act, who they trust, and who they promote.

A Lighter Moment:

> *We judge ourselves by what we feel capable of doing,*
> *while others judge us by what we have already done.*
>
> **Henry Wadsworth Longfellow**

> *The superior man, when resting in safety, does not forget that danger may come.*
> *When in a state of security he does not forget the possibility of ruin.*
> *When all is orderly, he does not forget that disorder may come.*
> *Thus his person is not endangered,*
> *and his States and all their clans are preserved.*
>
> **Confucius**

FOUNDATION

Area to Address 5.1b focuses on the work environment an organization creates for its employees. Is the environment safe and secure and is the organization prepared for short- and long-term emergencies or disasters?

Workplace Environment

Baldrige applications frequently discuss the tracking of health, safety and security issues on a reactive basis rather than taking proactive steps to prevent the safety issues. Proactive steps can include safety or ergonomics audits, security audits, health assessments, and tracking near misses. Near misses are incidents in which no one was hurt, but someone might get hurt if the same circumstance occurred again. In other words, they were lucky. This is typically a leading indicator of accidents which could happen in the future.

Another aspect of work environment protection is how employees participate in improving the work environment and how the organization measures their performance. Additionally, the CPE ask for performance measures and the levels or targets the organization is attempting to achieve.

Paraphrased, this portion of the criteria asks how you design, implement, audit, and keep the workplace safe.

Workforce Policies and Benefits

In the Organizational Profile, an employee profile is requested. Differences in employee group needs should be addressed in this area. For example, if one group of employees is required to drive to customer locations and another group is not, the first group may have vastly different work place environment needs. Those differences should be described in 5.1b(2). This tailoring to the needs of a diverse work force and different work groups and segments is critical. We must understand their needs before we can effectively address them.

To accomplish this, high performing organizations have listening posts to understand what policies and benefits are common or needed, a systematic process to determine whether a proposed policy or benefit is desirable from the organizational viewpoint, and finally, whether the policy of benefit is a good business decision.

411

EXAMPLES

Don Chalmers Ford (Baldrige Site 2008 and 2012)

Don Chalmers Ford (DCF) ensures and improves workplace health, safety, and security by assessing the current state and listening to employees and third parties. Focusing on awareness, available to employees and their families is an on-site health and wellness clinic staffed with a certified nurse practitioner. Health and Wellness and Safety Awareness training are provided in the monthly safety meetings.

DCF's health insurance provider is active in promoting wellness with employees through an annual health fair and completion of a personal health assessment. DCF has replaced some vending machine options to supply healthier food with healthier items priced lower. The building is non-smoking with designated smoking areas outside (21% down from 29%). DCF pays for assistance medication and a $1,000 bonus if an employee quits smoking.

In alignment with the core value of Family Values, DCF is not open on Sundays. A very unusual move for a car dealership. To ensure a safe workplace, new employees receive safety training at orientation and all employees receive periodic updates based on guidelines and materials supplied by Sentry Insurance, DCF's commercial insurance provider. DCF has a safety committee that performs periodic inspections (at least semi-annually) to review the safety conditions and report any findings to the SLT and the responsible manager. Periodically, Sentry Insurance participates and provides written feedback for improvement. On-going training, monthly Sales and Shop meetings, and reinforcement is the approach to meeting the expectations for safety, with quarterly meetings for those who miss the other meetings.

Security processes are generated from the National Automotive Dealers Association (NADA) industry guidelines and input from the workforce. Proactive methods used to provide security include 24-hour camera surveillance and electronic keys that identify the employee's name when entering the dealership. Fingerprint entry secures the salesroom, accessed only by authorized employees. To ensure safety in the Service and Body Shop areas, eye wash areas and safety goggles are available. Lift locks on vehicle hoists and safety jack stands are used when under-body work is performed. Hazardous materials are left in sealed containers. Cleaning individual work areas and driving 5 MPH while on the lot protect all employees' safety. To promote safety on a daily basis, employees play "Safety Bingo" for cash prizes for every accident-and-injury-free workday, or all games start over.

Improvement comes from listening to employees in the annual workforce survey (for example, this resulted in an exhaust system in service bays) and to the certified nurse practitioner (moving the smoking area). Don Chalmers' personal vision of improving quality-of-life and concern for employees promotes improvement.

DCF offers an on-site health and wellness facility with a Certified Nurse Practitioner with no co-pay for employees and their families for medical attention. DCF is proud to offer this unique benefit to employees' families. According to Ardent Healthcare Systems, DCF's health insurance provider in New Mexico, Oklahoma, and Tennessee, DCF is the only employer they support who offers an on-site wellness clinic, an innovative best practice. Health fairs are held at the dealership, and employees and spouses can have key health indicators measured, and fill out a health risk assessment. A third-party supplies a report back to the employee and spouse.

Performance measures include the number of smoking cessation bonuses awarded (1 employee/year), percent of smokers (< than the previous year), health fair participation (increased by 10% per year), lost work days (EMR Rate < 1.0), stolen vehicles logged claims (< previous year), and logged claims for workman's comp (< industry average).

DCF supports the workforce through policies, services, and benefits to provide above-average benefits. Green highlighted benefits can be tailored to employees' needs, and align to the core values of Outstanding Employee Satisfaction, Family Values, and Community Partnerships. Due to the Monday-Friday schedule of key insurance company suppliers for collision work, the Body Shop is closed on Saturdays, while the Service and maintenance departments remain open. Feedback to the SPP includes employee input.

In order to establish that DCF's benefits program exceeds those offered in the auto industry at large, comparisons are made with the surveys of competing dealerships (by a third party). Interviewees and new hire employees are asked about the benefits at their previous jobs. In 2007, the employee survey indicated a need to review employee benefits. In 2008, DCF provided a choice to employees for health coverage providers due to a 27% increase in the most recent provider's premiums. A comparison of the plans was presented to the employees and their families. The Health & Wellness Clinic was part of either option. The employees voted to replace the existing provider.

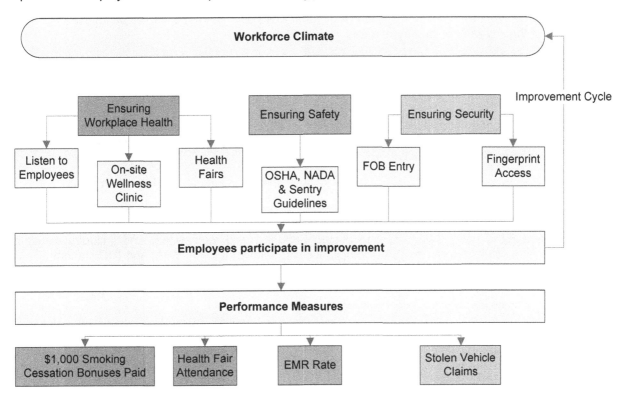

Workforce services include a free, on-site health and wellness clinic including acute care, wellness programs, immunization services, prescription services, and blood and drug screening services. Other workforce services include family vehicle discounts based on Ford's "D-plan" pricing to immediate family members, parts and service discounts, educational financial assistance, and internal career opportunities.

The Community Relations Director matches employees to the community service and agency that supports their passion with paid leave for participation. An anonymous hotline is available for the workforce to voice concerns.

DCF provides $50,000 of term life insurance to all employees based on IRS guidelines. Employees can acquire additional coverage for themselves and/or spouses if desired.

413

Based on months of service during the plan year, for the performance bonuses tied to Ford's President's Award and Blue Oval certification, all employees receive the same fixed dollar bonus because all employees contribute equally in completely satisfying the customer.

Employee policies are in the Employee Handbook and follow recommendation from NADA and benefit providers. The categories covered are General Information, Employment, General Policies, Pay and Performance, Leave Policies, and Benefits. The handbook is available in hard copy (every new employee receives a copy), the employee page on the web site, and the on-line process manual.

Source: Don Chalmers Ford

Advocate Good Samaritan Hospital (Baldrige Recipient 2010)

The table provides the wide variety of strategies that GSAM uses to ensure and improve workforce health, safety and security. Their Employee Health function provides a resource for staff on work-related health issues. New staff and volunteers are screened for proper vaccinations. Annually, mandatory TB tests and voluntary, free flu vaccinations are offered to all staff, volunteers, and physicians. GSAM has a 13-step *Workforce Work Environment System* (AOS) that ensures systematic identification, tracking, and improvement of the key work environment areas.

In **Step 2** of the process, the ENVIRONMENTAL CARE COMMITTEE (EOC) conducts an annual assessment of their risks based on a wide spectrum of inputs. The EOC rates and prioritizes these risks, and a defined rating threshold is set, above which action plans are required.

These plans address and mitigate risks and sets milestones for review of progress in **Steps 3-6**. Plans are presented to the seven (7) safety committees who determine performance goals/indicators and review/ implement the plans.

Activities and events associated with the plans are tracked and deviations are addressed in **Steps 7-9.**

Steps 10-13 monitor the work environment to ensure it remains safe utilizing systematic drills, and environment tours (audits). As issues arise, they are sent to the EOC for remediation; quarterly reporting to Directors and ET occurs. Safety training occurs annually, and as needed, and includes disaster preparedness. The safety program ensures compliance with relevant OSHA, EPA, and TJC standards.

Figure 5.2-2 Workplace Health, Safety, & Security

Area	Strategies (unique workforce environment)	Key Measure	Result
Health	• Pre-employment physicals • Fitness for duty testing • Flu shots • Titers (blood tests) * • Annual safety modules	• % physicals • % TB testing	7.4-24 7.4-24
Safety	• Infection control procedures • Hazardous materials procedures • Environmental tours • Ergonomic assessments + • Annual safety fair • Annual safety modules • Chemical inventory process • RASMAS recall system • Blood borne pathogen incident review	• Fire drills • Hand hygiene • % chemical inventories	7.5-11 7.1-28 7.4-25
Security	• 24-hour campus security ** • Associate/vendor ID badges • Escorts and car assistance** • Code grey: combative help • Card readers for access • Surveillance cameras	• Associate satisfaction question *'My working conditions are safe.'*	7.6-8
	* Direct care givers ** Night shift + Non-clinicians		

Advocate Health Care © 2010

414

CRITERIA QUESTIONS

In your response, include answers to the following questions:

b. Workforce Climate

(1) **Workplace Environment** How do you ensure workplace health, security, and accessibility for the workforce? What are your performance measures and improvement goals for your workplace environmental factors? For your different workplace environments, what significant differences are there in these factors and their performance measures or targets?

(2) **Workforce Benefits and Policies** How do you support your workforce via services, benefits, and policies? How do you tailor these to the needs of a diverse workforce and different workforce groups and segments? What key benefits do you offer your workforce?

Note:

5.1b(1). Workplace accessibility maximizes productivity by eliminating barriers that can prevent people with disabilities from working to their potential. A fully inclusive workplace is physically, technologically, and attitudinally accessible.

NIST (2015-2016) p. 19 -20

WORKSHEETS

5.1b(1) –Workplace Environment

Processes Used To Ensure The Workplace Has :	Processes Used To Improve The Workplace For :	Performance Measures For Each Of The Processes	Improvement Goals
Accessibility	*Accessibility*	*Accessibility*	*Accessibility*
Health	*Health*	*Health*	*Health*
Security	*Security*	*Security*	*Security*

Significant Differences In Above Processes Based On Different Workplace Environments, Differences In These Factors Or Their Performance Measures Or Targets

5.1b(2) – Workforce Benefits and Policies

Factors Assessed:	Process Focuses		
	Processes Used To Support The Workforce:	Processes Used To Tailor The Factors To The Needs Of A Diverse Workforce:	Processes Used To Tailor The Factors Based On The Needs Of Different Work Groups and Segments
Services			
Benefits			
Policies			

Key Benefits Offered The Workforce

ASSESSMENT

Rating Scale:

1 - **No Process** in place - We are not doing this
2 - **Reacting to Problems** – We use a basic (primarily reactive) process
3 - **Systematic Process** – We use a systematic process that has been improved
4 - **Aligned** – We use a process that aligns our activities from top to bottom
5 - **Integrated** – We use a process that is integrated with other processes across the organization
6 - **Benchmark** – We are the Benchmark in our industry or beyond!
DK - Don't Know

84	The organization cares for the safety, well-being and morale of all employees by proactively addressing workplace environmental factors such as security, safety and health.	1	2	3	4	5	6	DK
85	Workplace security, safety and health have performance measures and improvement goals.	1	2	3	4	5	6	DK
86	The organization ensures that the policies, services and benefits offered match the employee needs for each of the diverse work groups.	1	2	3	4	5	6	DK

BLUEPRINT

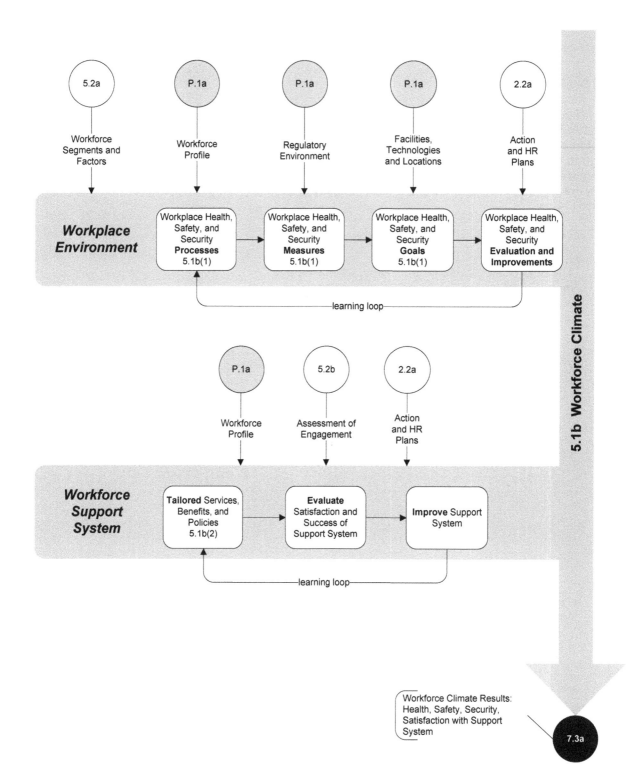

SYSTEM INTEGRATION

Context

P.1a > 5.1b Workforce Profile - The workforce profile is a key input to the nature of employee segments, groups, work units, and work environments which, in turn, influence the design of the processes, measures, and goals to create the desired work environment. In addition, the workforce profile (groups and needs) is a key input to the design of the services, benefits, and policies (support system) tailored to the various segments' and groups' needs, wants, and desires.

P.1a > 5.1b Regulatory Requirements - The regulatory environment is a key consideration when determining the requirements, practices, processes, and measures for workplace health, safety, security, and ergonomics.

P.1a > 5.1b Facilitates, Technologies, Locations - The location and type of facilities and the nature of the technology used in the facilities is a direct input to the safety and security approaches. In other words, the safety and security threats differ depending on location and the nature of the technologies used. In addition, the facilities and industry impact the workplace health and ergonomics requirements, practices, processes and measures.

Systems

2.2a > 5.1b Action and HR Action Plans - The strategic action plans and associated human resource plans (2.2a) are a key input to the process of employee support and satisfaction (5.1b). These plans influence the segmentation of the workforce and the support services and benefits offered to employees along with the organization's policies.

5.2b > 5.1b Assessment of Engagement - Workforce engagement and satisfaction (5.2b) are key inputs to the development of tailored services, benefits, and policies (5.1b).

Scorecard

5.2b > 7.3a Workforce Climate Results - Results on the workforce climate (e.g., safety, health, security, etc.) should be reported in 7.3a.

THOUGHTS FOR LEADERS

A safe work environment is now addressed in Area 6.2c(3), but the workplace environment which sets up the ability to have safety is address in this area.

Although workplace environment is clearly one of the most important aspects of any organization, leaders often fail to communicate this primary focus to employees. Ask factory employees what their leaders most frequently discuss, and the answers may disappoint you. The topics range all over the place (profit, customers, costs, image) and many times the leaders do not make it clear that they value employees.

In a heavy industrial environment, there can only be one #1 topic - SAFETY! In other (fundamentally safer) environments leaders must still make it known that employees are very important. This can be achieved a number of ways, including spending time with them, education, and a range of other ways to let them know how important they are.

One example was a plant manager and great leader who spoke passionately on this topic. He began his thoughts with this question: "What is the greatest crime we can commit against our employees and their families?" His answer was "to hurt them!" Without adequate workplace safety, no company can be a good place to work. When leaders talk with employees, employee safety and well-being need to be primary themes.

In taking care of employees, benefits are also important. The smartest organizations are those who let the employees tailor the benefits to their own need, and do not spend money on benefits that the employees do not value.

A Lighter Moment:

There is no safety in numbers, or in anything else.

James Thurber

> ***The secret of joy in work is contained in one word - excellence.***
> ***To know how to do something well is to enjoy it.***
>
> **Pearl Buck**

FOUNDATION

As Category 3 evaluated the customer segments, determined the requirements for each segment, and determined how the internal processes of the organization could be aligned to meet those requirements, Category 5 does many of the same tasks for the workforce.

Organizational Culture

Once the organization has determined the key factors in workforce engagement, the Criteria for Performance Excellence (CPE) go on to ask how the organization establishes a culture which will effectively address those factors. Those factors should be aligned to drive high performance and a motivated workforce. These factors include workforce and workplace benefits from the:

- ability to benefit from the diverse ideas, cultures, and thinking of the workforce (the CPE proposes that customers, partners, and collaborators have a wide range of experiences, needs, and expectations. Unless an organization has a workforce with this same breadth and depth, the organization may not be able to understand customer requirements or be able to meet their needs in a way which will drive long-term performance or loyalty.).

Once the above processes have been established to understand what drives workforce engagement, and to align the workplace to address those factors, the CPE ask how the organization empowers the workforce.

Elements of Engagement

The logic flow of workforce engagement begins in Area 5.2a which asks how the organization systematically determines the key factors that will encourage workforce engagement. Although workforce loyalty is not specifically discussed in the CPE, loyalty should be assumed to be included as a step along the way to engagement. The results for workforce loyalty factors, such as absenteeism and voluntary turnover, are reported in Item 7.3 – Workforce-Focused Results.

Area 5.2a asks what process the organization uses to determine the different needs, requirements and satisfaction and engagement factors for the various workforce groups or segments which were reported in the Organizational Profile.

Assessment of Engagement

This assessment of engagement can be a combination of both formal and informal assessment methods. Regardless of whether they are formal or informal, the organization should work toward developing as objective and quantifiable methods as is possible and practical. If these assessment methods differ across workforce groups and segments, the process to define what these differences should be clearly described. It is acceptable for one process to be used for all workforce groups or different processes to be used for each workforce group. In either case, the CPE ask why that decision was made and the process steps for making the decision.

Where there are other indicators such as workforce retention, absenteeism, grievances, safety, and productivity, which give the organization insights into the workforce engagement, the processes to collect and use these indicators should also be described.

Performance Management

The workforce performance management system needs to be a systematic process that focuses on enabling and driving high performance work and workforce engagement. The process may be different for different workforce segments and different levels in the organization, but all workforce segments should: (a) understand what is required of them; (b) understand their own goals; (c) understand their performance against those goals; (d) understand course correction and adjustments as they are made and the impact of these on their goals and actions; and (e) understand the linkage of their performance to compensation, reward, recognition, and incentives. Finally, the workforce performance management system should systematically reinforce a customer and business focus as it aligns action plans with the overall organizational goals and objectives.

The CPE specifically seek to understand how the organization's Performance Management System supports:

- high performance work;

- workforce engagement;

- workforce compensation, reward (note: this does not have to be only monetary), recognition, and incentive practices;

- intelligent risk taking to achieve innovation;

- a customer focus;

- a business focus; and

- the achievement of action plans.

Not only does the performance management system need to be linked to the organization's goals (as discussed in Item 2.2) but it also should be linked to the overall development and growth of employees. Once employees clearly understand their goals and objectives, have the tools to perform, and have the leadership support, the performance management system should link and align compensation, recognition, and related rewards and incentive practices to the individual's and the team's performance.

Reward and recognition is an area in which most organizations have a tremendous opportunity for improvement. Even high performing organizations can still improve further by more effectively aligning reward and recognition with the performance of the individual and aligning the performance of the individual with the objectives, goals, and direction of the organization.

Most organizations have some form of non-monetary reward and recognition, but this too, is typically, an area of significant opportunity for improvement. As organizations increase the alignment of their reward and recognition of employees, including increases in non-monetary reward and recognition, the impact can be significant in its favorable effect on overall organizational performance. In the end, the goal is to align every employee's efforts with the efforts of the overall company. The performance management system is one of the major tools used to achieve that alignment.

EXAMPLES

PRO-TEC Coating Company (Baldrige Recipient 2007)

The PRO-TEC Culture Process (Figure 5.1-1) ensures their Associates will succeed. Associates perform meaningful work with ORA. Their culture was created based on industry experience and best practices.

Their Associate Survey process validates this culture internally. They closely monitor their Associate engagement and satisfaction relative to key business results. The Associate satisfaction survey results are reviewed by a group of managers once the results are tabulated. The items are reviewed using a structured process at an off-site, half-day meeting. The same data are then reviewed by an Associate focus group. Action items from both groups are combined, prioritized, and assigned to specific managers or continuous improvement (CI) teams. The results of the survey, the summary of action items that resulted, and the status of the action items are communicated to the Associates during 3rd quarter communication meetings.

Culture Process

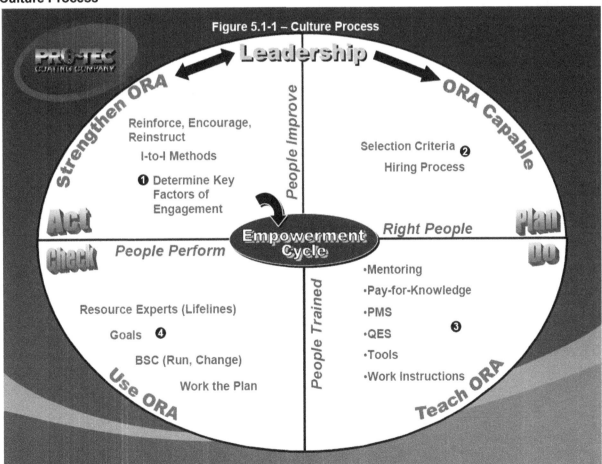

Figure 5.1-1 – Culture Process

Source: PRO-TEC Coating Company

PRO-TEC determines the key factors that engage their workforce (Figure 5.1-1). As mentioned above, the annual Associate Survey process is one method. The results of the survey help them determine what is important to their Associates to keep them engaged and to strengthen their ORA culture.

Every year their survey questions are reviewed to ensure they are gathering data that is meaningful. Other indicators that they monitor to determine workforce engagement are safety statistics, leading/lagging safety indicators, their retention rate, and the Associate referral program.

They also recognize that there are different engagement factors for the different work groups. The survey data are analyzed with this in mind. It also helps them determine key factors that affect workforce satisfaction (survey results are available on-site). Other methods of determining satisfaction are participation in safety and wellness initiatives, CI teams, personal development, and flexible work schedule options.

To support high performance work, everyone has goals. Goals are reviewed as part of the Performance Management System (PMS). High performers have an opportunity for ongoing development and improvements that may be discussed through the PMS. Performance is expected to meet expectations as shown in the figure ❺. This aligns performance to organizational and individual goals leading to rewards and recognition.

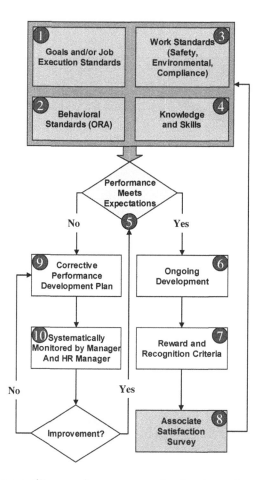

Individually, all Associates receive a written performance evaluation based upon selected measurements and goals. This influences their annual merit increase or salary progression increase. The salary progression system is designed to review performance in three areas to ensure expectations are understood: Job Execution Standards❶, Behavioral Standards❷, and Work Standards❸. Thirty one individual non-exempt positions have defined Job Execution Standards for their position which include specific expectations for that job. Goals are included with specific alignment to balanced scorecard measurables. The behavioral standards are the same for all jobs and include teamwork, communication, problem solving, and leadership (ORA). The work standards include expectations of Safety, Environmental, Attendance, and Policies and Procedures (including QES requirements).

The salary progression system was designed to reward performance that meets expectations. Expectations are set high, so meeting expectations should not be construed as 'just average' performance❺. The PMS process also provides the opportunity for discussion; high performing Associates can receive verbal recognition along with better promotional opportunities❻. Associates that are not meeting expectations receive a corrective performance development plan❾. This is typically a three- or six-month development plan with specific measurables. The HR Manager and the appropriate department manager monitor this plan❿.

Team performance is recognized formally, with participation in a company profit-sharing plan. All Associates participate on an equal percentage basis. Individual and team achievements are recognized informally in a variety of ways including off-site celebrations with spouses/guests, verbal recognition, special catered meals, recognition in company publications, and helmet stickers. Educational achievements are recognized in the quarterly newsletter, "The Galvanews," and a closed-circuit TV network, "Galvavision." Safety recognition is defined in a company policy. For every 500,000 man hours without a lost-time accident, everyone in the plant receives some form of incentive/recognition❼.

The Associate satisfaction survey is designed to collect feedback in all areas of our business❽. One area is the performance management system. Feedback from the survey is reviewed, and actions are assigned. If changes to the plan are needed, they are implemented during the next annual review process.

Poudre Valley Health System (Baldrige Recipient 2008))

Figure5.1-1: Rewards & Recognitions					
REWARDS & RECOGNITIONS	STAFF	PHYSICIANS	VOLUNTEERS	GIVEN BY	FREQUENCY
Hospital Week & Nurses Week Celebrations	•	•	•	SMG	Yearly
Summer Picnic & Holiday Parties/Gifts	•	•	•	SMG	Yearly
Founders Day	•	•	•	SMG	Yearly
Employees of the Year	•			Workforce	Yearly
Volunteer Week Celebration			•	Management	Yearly
Physician Thank You Dinner		•		SMG	Yearly
Spotlight Volunteers & Traveling Thank You Cart			•	Directors	Ongoing
Special Meals in Physician Lounge		•		Management	Ongoing
Service Awards	•		•	Management	Ongoing
Theme Days	•	•	•	SMG	Ongoing
Birthday Certificates	•		•	Management	Ongoing
Peer-to-Peer Coupons	•	•	•	Workforce	Ongoing
R&R Certificates ($5-$500)	•			Workforce	Ongoing
Thank You Notes	•	•	•	All	Ongoing
Retail & Entertainment Discounts	•	•	•	All	Ongoing

Reward and recognition is integrated into the Poudre Valley Health system culture and support high performance. There are multiple forms of reward and recognition for staff, physicians and volunteers that are awarded by the SMG, management, directors and among peers. Managers may request an R&R Certificate for staff who demonstrate: 1) high performance, innovation, and patient/customer focus toward achievement of the SOs; or 2) Behavior Standards and values. The certificates are redeemable for $10 to $500 at a diverse list of area businesses that support the PVHS Foundation. Peer-to-peer coupons, redeemable for $3, allow staff, volunteers, and physicians to reward each other for actions supporting Behavior Standards and values.

Another example is the Employees of the Year award where members of the workforce nominate staff for consistently supporting SOs and V/M/V. PVHS uses numerous other informal and individualized rewards. However, federal law limits rewards hospitals can give independent physicians thus, PVHS cannot extend many of its reward programs to physicians.

The quality of a person's life is in direct proportion to their commitment to excellence, regardless of their chosen field of endeavor.

Vince Lombardi

Don Chalmers Ford (Baldrige Site Visit 2008 and 2012)

DCF supports the workforce through policies, services, and benefits to provide above-average benefits, with employee input included in the SPP. Green highlighted benefits can be tailored to employees' needs, and align to the core values of Outstanding Employee Satisfaction, Family Values, and Community Partnerships. Due to the Monday-Friday schedule of key insurance company suppliers for collision work, the Body Shop is closed on Saturdays, while the Service and Maintenance departments remain open.

In order to establish that DCF's benefits program exceeds those offered in the auto industry at large, comparisons are made with the surveys of competing dealerships (by a third party).

Interviewees and new hire employees are asked about the benefits at their previous jobs. 2007 employee survey feedback indicated a need to review employee benefits. In 2008, DCF provided a choice to employees for health coverage providers due to a 27% increase in the most recent provider's premiums. A comparison of the plans was presented to the employees and their families. The Health & Wellness Clinic was part of either option. The employees voted to replace the existing provider. This recurred again in 2010 and 2011 as premiums continued to rise, options were added for higher deductibles and employees could ask questions and determine the plan best for them.

In a 2011 cycle of improvement, a Health Reimbursement Account was added to offset increases.

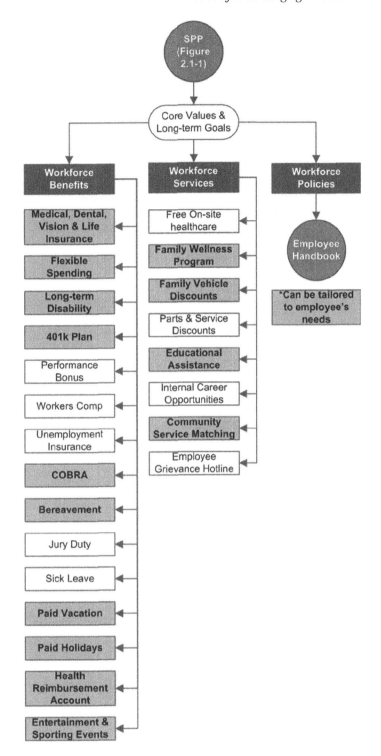

Figure 5.1-4 Workforce Benefits

Workforce services include a free, on-site health and wellness clinic (including acute care, wellness programs, immunization services, prescription services, and blood and drug screening services), family vehicle discounts based on FMC's "D-plan" pricing to immediate family members, parts and service discounts, educational financial assistance, and internal career opportunities. The Community Relations Director matches employees to the community service and agency that supports their passion with paid leave for participation. An anonymous hotline is available for the workforce to voice concerns.

Workforce benefits include standard items like medical, dental and life insurance and legal items like COBRA unemployment insurance. The unique benefits DCF provides are a performance bonus (based on months of service during the plan year) for the performance tied to FMC's President's Award and customer satisfaction. Every employee receives the same fixed dollar bonus because all employees contribute equally in completely satisfying the customer. Employees and their families also have access to a night at the Albuquerque Isotopes games (AAA baseball affiliate of the Los Angeles Dodgers), University of New Mexico Athletic events, the NM Mustangs (junior hockey) and the NM Stars (arena football team). Entertainment events are available in the DCF suite at the local Santa Ana Star Center.

Employee policies are in the Employee Handbook and follow recommendations from NADA and benefit providers. The categories covered are General Information, Employment, General Policies, Pay and Performance, Leave Policies, and Benefits. The handbook is available in hard copy (every new employee receives a copy), the employee page on the web site, and the on-line process manual.

Reinforcement of the customer, business, and family focus methods are included in the figure below.

Title	Who Is Eligible	How It Is Paid	Focus C	B	F
FMC's President's Award	Workforce	Up to a $900 bonus	X	X	
Consumer Experience	Workforce	Up to a $900 bonus	X	X	
Sell to previous customer	Sales staff	Bonus $100	X	X	
Quarterly sales	Sales staff	Airline ticket vouchers		X	
March Forward	Workforce	% of objective/ money/trips		X	
Christmas party/ Summer picnic	Workforce	Social event with prizes		X	X
Productivity/bonus sheet	Sales & Service staff	Bonus for reaching goal		X	
Master Technician certification	Technicians	Bonus	X	X	
Employee Excellence (FMC)	Sales & Service staff	Spins, trips & gifts	X	X	
Safety bingo	Workforce	Cash ($500 max)	X	X	
Stop smoking	Workforce	Bonus $1,000	X	X	X
Isotopes baseball suite/ entertainment	Workforce by dept.	Free tickets & catered food		X	X
On-site health care & wellness	Workforce & family	Free		X	X
D-Plan	Workforce & family	Lowest price on new vehicles		X	X

Figure 5.2-3 Workforce Rewards, Recognition & Incentives

Branch-Smith Printing (Baldrige Recipient 2002)

Satisfaction Assessment Methods

The primary formal method of determining employee satisfaction is through the employee satisfaction survey. The survey addresses communication, management, customer focus, quality, job responsibility and training, procedures and processes, teamwork, and overall satisfaction. Employees rate their agreement with 50 statements in these categories as Strongly Agree, Agree, Disagree, or Strongly Disagree. Statement ratings of less than 60% agreement are given particular focus for improvement. Results are broken out by department to provide feedback to specific supervisors and to senior management for their performance. This provides upward feedback to leaders in conjunction with their normal performance evaluation. The data is shared with all employees in department and Division meetings.

Demographic information is gathered as part of the survey to determine well-being and satisfaction among the diverse workforce and to ensure no major gaps between ethnic, age, gender, or tenure groups exist. Employees also rate the importance of each issue to determine level of concerns. Focus groups, which allow employees to express concerns, ask questions, or make suggestions, provide more specific responses about problem areas. Results are used to create QIPs and as input into the SPP.

The second major approach to determine employee satisfaction is voluntary employee turnover. Reducing turnover is a Division goal and is measured for each department. The established goal is reducing voluntary turnover to 10%, which is below the average of the Fortune 100 Best Places to Work for in America. Employees that leave voluntarily are given exit interviews to provide feedback in job satisfaction and dissatisfaction.

Monthly Division meetings are an open forum to express specific concerns as well as the "open door" style of management. Concerns that affect all employees are reviewed in the monthly CLT meeting. Concerns that affect the Division are reviewed in the monthly PLT. QIPs are used to review and follow up on areas as necessary.

Assessment Finding Relative to Business Results

Through analysis of cause and affect of the relationship between customer satisfaction, employee satisfaction, and business results, they determine key priorities for improvement as part of the SPP. Positive results from the customer survey reveal quality products and services from employees, indicative of a highly satisfied and well trained, empowered employee base. Customer satisfaction results show that commitment to employee satisfaction and training affects customer satisfaction directly. Employee survey results continue to indicate that employees know who their customers are and understand goals for meeting their needs.

A training plan is developed for each employee to improve skills and grow within the company. This plan, along with reduced turnover and increased satisfaction, is related to the positive growth in Value Added Sales, etc.

Several important QIP improvements have impacted the bottom line. Due to low scores in communication on the 1999 employee survey, a QIP implemented a solution that involved better department schedules, monthly department meetings, and bulletin boards tracking performance and goals. Better communication has helped reduce PONC and brought satisfaction to employees by connecting them personally to the goals. QIP teams continue to enhance the quality focus and improve the processes, hence creating the business results desired.

The most compelling evidence of effectiveness of the HR approach is the impact of the appraisal and training method on employee satisfaction and productivity. In early 2001, the full system of roll-up reviews was implemented, linking individual employee performance goals to the goals for their work group, department, and the Division. The employee establishes performance goals in his/her annual review activity along with required training for the year. Performance to those goals is reviewed weekly and adjustments are made to the training plan. Aggregate results are reviewed quarterly as a department. Roll-ups continue through the organization on these measures. Results of satisfaction scores in many areas reflect the improved satisfaction of employees with their work as a result of the improved communication with supervisors, and satisfaction with training and the performance review. These improvements correlate closely with the accelerated improvements in 2001 results for individual process effectiveness. Source: Branch-Smith (2003) pp. 24 – 26

Poudre Valley Health System (Baldrige Recipient 2008)

PVHS has been systematically building a culture of workforce satisfaction and engagement for the past decade. In 1997, based on a best practice from Baldrige recipient Wainwright Industries, PVHS surveyed employees as customers and asked: 1) What makes you want to jump out of bed and come to work? and 2) How do we build a culture that supports that? In 1999, to further understand drivers of staff satisfaction and engagement, PVHS collaborated with the Industrial and Organizational Psychology Department at Colorado State University (CSU) to survey and interview staff from all disciplines and shifts and identify key staff requirements (shown in the OP in Figure P.1-5). These requirements — or culture dimensions — are universal to all staff segments and remain the framework for the semi-annual Employee Culture Survey, which drives improvement efforts in the organization, based on their established segmentation. The Workforce Focus Team, a multidisciplinary staff team including representatives from HR, education, employee health/safety, and clinical/nonclinical areas — collaborates with CSU in evaluating and improving the survey tool. In 2003, PVHS initiated an annual physician survey to assist in determining key factors that affect physician satisfaction and engagement. Volunteer Services also performs an annual volunteer survey. A listing of the types of surveys, the methods and segmentation is as follows:

Figure 5.1-5: Assessing Workforce Satisfaction & Engagement		
WORKFORCE GROUP	METHOD	SEGMENTATION
Staff	Employee Culture Survey, MSA survey, Magnet designation, leadership rounding, voluntary turnover, stay/exit interviews, safety indicators	Demographics, job family, tenure, position, shift, department
Physicians	Physician survey, size of Medical Staff, leadership rounding	Demographics, tenure, specialty
Volunteers	Volunteer survey, leadership rounding	Adult, student, teen

The annual Employee Culture Survey results are used to drive improvement. Annually, SMG identifies opportunities for improvement, prioritizes them, chooses one for action plan development, and monitors progress through a measure on the system BSC. Individual departments also engage staff to develop an action plan that addresses department-specific survey results. The organization uses other indicators of workforce satisfaction and engagement to validate survey results, monitor action plans and prompt additional just in time adjustments.

Pearl River School District (Baldrige Recipient 2001)

The figure below portrays how managers evaluate staff. All individual goals stem from district short-term goals and projects. In addition to the formal evaluation process based upon clearly defined goals, administrators provide support through their daily management practices – in feedback following class visitations, at staff and department meetings, during employee conferences, in memos and notes, and through daily management by walking around. The leader visits each building every week where he meets with the principal and visits classrooms. He also meets with the director of operations and director of facilities weekly. The focus on continuous improvement and high performance aligned with district goals is constant. They conduct formal reviews quarterly. The BOE ultimately holds the AC accountable for high performance results based upon positive faculty and staff performance.

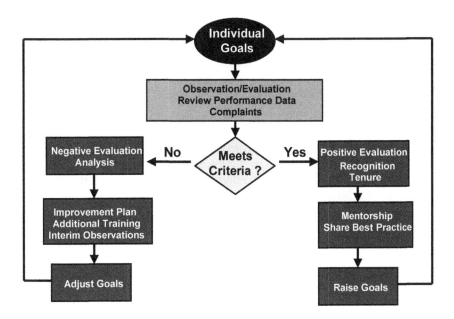

Pearl River School District gives each person the ability to know how they are performing compared to the expectations for them. This starts with individual goals, and cycles through a review of performance, and development of improvement plans. Where performance meets the criteria, the organization has developed the ability to help the person improve further based on sharing best practices and/or providing a mentor to help the person learn from the experience of others. Source: PRSD (2002) pp. 152 – 153

CRITERIA QUESTIONS

In your response, include answers to the following questions:

a. Workforce Engagement and Performance

Workforce Engagement and Performance

(1) **Organizational Culture** How do you foster an organizational culture that is characterized by open communication, high performance, and an engaged workforce? How do you ensure that your organizational culture benefits from the diverse ideas, cultures, and thinking of your workforce? How do you empower your workforce?

(2) **Drivers of Engagement** How do you determine the key drivers of workforce engagement? How do you determine these drivers for different workforce groups and segments?

(3) **Assessment of Engagement** How do you assess workforce engagement? What formal and information assessment methods and measures do you use to determine workforce engagement, including satisfaction? How do these methods and measures differ across workforce groups, and segments? How do you also use other indicators, such as workforce retention, absenteeism, grievances, safety, and productivity, to assess and improve workforce engagement?

(4) **Performance Management** How does your workforce performance management system support high performance and workforce engagement? How does it consider workforce compensation, reward, **recognition**, and incentive practices? How does it:
- reinforce intelligent risk taking to achieve innovation,
- a customer and business focus, and
- achievement of your action plans?

Notes:

5.2. Understanding the characteristics of high-performance work environments, in which people do their utmost for their customers' benefit and the organization's success, is key to understanding and building an engaged workforce. These characteristics are described in detail in the definition of high-performance work (page 49).

5.2a(2) Drivers of workforce engagement (identified in P.1a[3') refer to the drivers of workforce members' commitment, both emotional and intellectual, to accomplishing the organizations work, mission, and vision.

5.2a(4). Compensation, recognition, and related reward and incentive practices include promotions and bonuses that might be based on performance, skills acquired, and other factors. Recognition can include monetary and nonmonetary, formal and informal, and individual and group mechanisms. In some government organizations, compensation systems are set by law or regulation; therefore, reward and recognition systems must use other options.

NIST (2015-2016) pp. 21-22

WORKSHEETS

5.2a(1) – Organizational Culture

Performance Factor To Be Used	Process To Use The Performance Factors To Foster An Organizational Culture Conducive to:		
	Open Communication	High-Performance Work	An Engaged Workforce
Ability To Benefit From Diverse Ideas			
Ability To Benefit From Diverse Cultures			
Ability To Benefit From Diverse Thinking			

How Do You Empower Your Workforce:

5.2a(2) – Drivers Of Engagement

Workforce Group Or Segment (Same As P1a[3])	Process Used To Determine The Key Factors That Affect Workforce Satisfaction	Process Used To Determine The Key Factors That Affect Workforce Engagement	Process Used To Validate The Drivers Of Satisfaction and Engagement

5.2a(3) – Assessment of Engagement

Employee Segment/Group (Same as P1a[3])	Processes To Assess Workforce Engagement and Satisfaction		Measures Or Indicators Tracked To Verify Workforce Engagement*
	Formal	Informal	

*Note: Measures can include factors such as workforce satisfaction, retention, absenteeism, grievances, safety, and productivity.

5.2a(4) – Performance Management

Factor Which The Performance Management System Supports or Reinforces	Performance Management System Process Used To Achieve This Factor:
High Performance Work	
Workforce Engagement	
Consideration Of Workforce Compensation, Reward, Recognition, and Incentive Practices	
Intelligent Risk Taking to achieve innovation	
A Customer Focus	
A Business Focus	
Achievement Of Action Plans	

ASSESSMENT

Rating Scale:

1 - **No Process** in place - We are not doing this
2 - **Reacting to Problems** – We use a basic (primarily reactive) process
3 - **Systematic Process** – We use a systematic process that has been improved
4 - **Aligned** – We use a process that aligns our activities from top to bottom
5 - **Integrated** – We use a process that is integrated with other processes across the organization
6 - **Benchmark** – We are the Benchmark in our industry or beyond!
DK - Don't Know

87	The organization has a systematic approach to determine what factors will engage and motivate each workforce group or segment.	1 2 3 4 5 6 DK
88	The processes used to design the work culture consider all factors which will drive workforce motivation, high performance and engagement for each workforce group or segment.	1 2 3 4 5 6 DK
89	The workforce performance management system (or systems) applies to all employees and drives high performance, including the reinforcement of a business focus and achievement of action plans.	1 2 3 4 5 6 DK
90	Employees are formally and informally rewarded and recognized for demonstrating the desired behaviors (such as a business and customer focus) and for achieving their goals.	1 2 3 4 5 6 DK
91	There is a systematic process used to evaluate the level of workforce satisfaction, loyalty and engagement.	1 2 3 4 5 6 DK
92	The organization assesses the key factors which adversely affect workforce engagement, satisfaction and motivation. These assessment methods and measures differ across workforce groups and segments.	1 2 3 4 5 6 DK
93	Other indicators (such as retention, absenteeism, grievances, safety and productivity) are used to assess and improve workforce engagement.	1 2 3 4 5 6 DK

436

94 | The organization systematically links the workforce engagement data to business results, and uses these correlations to identify opportunities to improve engagement and business results. | 1   2   3   4   5   6   DK

95 | Appropriate action is taken to improve workforce engagement. | 1   2   3   4   5   6   DK

BLUEPRINT

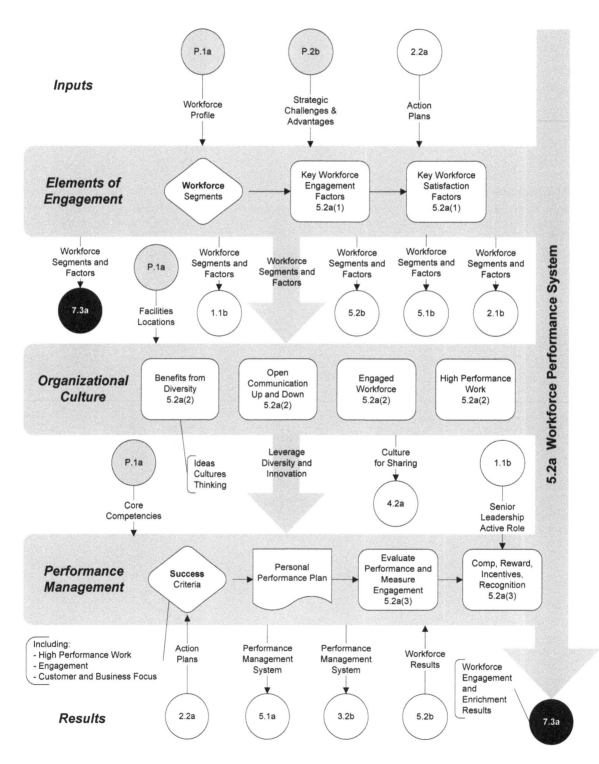

SYSTEM INTEGRATION

Context

P.1a > 5.2a Workforce Profile - The workforce profile is an important input to the determination of the workforce segments. The profile provides demographics that can be useful in determining the segments that differ in their requirements for satisfaction and engagement.

P.1a > 5.2a Core Competencies - The organization's core competencies are key inputs to the performance management system. Core competencies are a key part of the "success criteria" and the subsequent planning, evaluation, and reinforcement of the knowledge, skills, and behaviors that result in the workforce achieving the success criteria.

P.1a > 5.2a Facilitates, Technologies, Locations - The location of the facilities as described in the profile determines the nature and make up of the local communities. The demographic profile of the local communities influences the approaches to capitalize on the diverse ideas, cultures, and thinking of the local communities.

P.2b > 5.2a Strategic Challenges and Advantages - The strategic challenges and advantages described in the profile (P.2b) are key inputs to the overall workforce enrichment and engagement system including: (a) the identification of key factors; (b) the creation of a high performance culture; and (c) the performance management system. The challenges and advantages should be addressed by each of these processes and practices.

Systems

1.1b < 5.2a Workforce Segments and Factors - Key factors for workforce engagement (by segment) are key inputs to the design and planning of leadership communication and engagement processes and practices in 1.1b.

1.1b > 5.2a Senior Leader Active Role - How senior leaders play an active role in rewarding and recognizing employees should be an integral and consistent part of the reinforcement processes described in 5.2a (compensation, recognition, rewards, and incentives).

2.1b < 5.2a Segments and Factors - The workforce segments and key factors for workforce engagement along with other key stakeholder requirements are key inputs to testing for balance of the key objectives.

2.2a > 5.2a HR Action Plans - The action plans and HR action plans developed in 2.2a are used by the employee performance management system to set expectations and provide feedback to employees on their contributions to the achievement of the action plans.

3.2b < 5.2a Performance Management System - The performance management system described in 5.2a should be designed to support the building of a customer culture. The expectations, performance evaluation, and feedback should include the behaviors and practices that are consistent with a customer focused culture.

4.2a < 5.2a Culture for Sharing - The organizational knowledge area 4.2a calls for the sharing of information and knowledge. There is no process in the world that can make sharing happen if the overall culture and environment do not encourage and reward sharing. The cooperative environment promoted by the organization and management of work as described in 5.2a has a big impact on the degree to which the employees share information and knowledge.

5.2a > 5.1a Performance Management System - The performance management system (5.2a) is a key part of the overall management of the capability and capacity of the workforce as described in 5.1a.

5.2a > 5.1b Workforce Segments and Factors - Workforce segments and engagement and satisfaction factors (5.2a) are key inputs to the development of a workplace climate that is safe, healthy, and secure (5.1b). In addition, these segments and factors are key inputs to the development of a support systems with tailored services, benefits, and policies (5.1b).

5.2a > 5.2b Workforce Segments and Factors - Workforce segments and the factors (5.2a) that impact satisfaction and engagement are key inputs to the methods to assess workforce engagement and satisfaction (5.2b). The assessment methods should assess the various factors and produce results that can be segmented by workforce segment.

5.2a < 5.2b Workforce Results - The assessment methods to measure engagement (5.2b) are also an input to the evaluation phase of the performance management system (5.2a).

Scorecard

5.2a > 7.3a Workforce Engagement and Enrichment Results - Workforce engagement and enrichment results are reported in 7.3a.

5.2a > 7.3a Workforce Segments and Factors - The workforce segments and factors identified in 5.2a are key inputs to the segmentation and types of measures that should be included in 7.3a.

BLUEPRINT

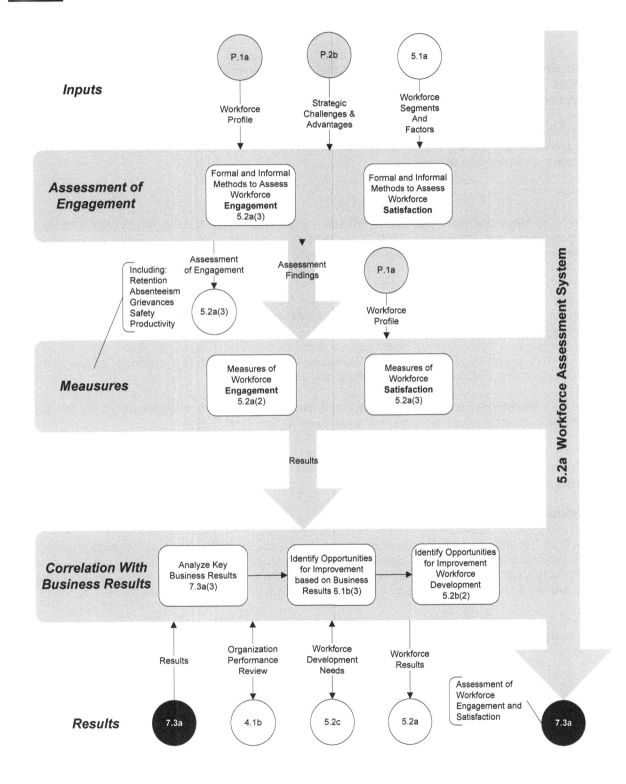

SYSTEM INTEGRATION

Context

P.1a > 5.2b Workforce Profile - The workforce profile identifies the number, type, and characteristics of key employee segments. The description of the employees in the profile should correspond to the segments used to determine key factors, processes, and measures for workforce satisfaction and engagement.

P.2b > 5.2b Strategic Challenges and Advantages - The strategic challenges and advantages described in the profile (P.2b) are key inputs to the identification of key issues and factors to measure regarding workforce satisfaction and engagement.

Systems

4.1b <> 5.2b Organizational Performance Review - The performance reviews (4.1b) often identify areas for improvement that involve workforce engagement, satisfaction and performance (5.2b). And, the assessments of workforce are often inputs to the overall organization performance review.

5.1a > 5.2b Workforce Segments and Factors - Workforce segments and the factors (5.1a) that impact satisfaction and engagement are key inputs to the methods to assess workforce engagement and satisfaction (5.2b). The assessment methods should assess the various factors and produce results that can be segmented by workforce segment.

5.2b > 5.1b Assessment of Engagement - Workforce engagement and satisfaction (5.2b) are key inputs to the development of tailored services, benefits, and policies (5.1b).

5.2a < 5.2b Workforce Results - The assessment methods to measure engagement (5.2b) are also an input to the evaluation phase of the performance management system (5.2a).

5.2c <> 5.2b Workforce Development Needs - Opportunities for improvement are often identified as part of the assessment of workforce engagement described in 5.2b. These opportunities should be an input to the needs assessment process in 5.2c.

Scorecard

5.2b < 7.3a Results - Human resource results (levels, trends, and comparisons) influence the employee satisfaction and engagement approaches in two ways. First, they can be analyzed and used to determine the key factors by segment that affect well-being, satisfaction, and motivation. Second, human resource results are used to evaluate and improve employee services, benefits, and policies.

5.2b > 7.3a Workforce Engagement and Satisfaction Results - The results from the assessment and measurement of workforce engagement and satisfaction identified in 5.2b should be reported in 7.3a.

THOUGHTS FOR LEADERS

Leaders need to clearly understand the relationship between the work environment, workforce engagement, workforce motivation, and business results. These begin with understanding what is expected from the workforce, and being able to effectively integrate these factors into a high performance work culture. The way this is addressed for each workforce group may, in fact, be different. Each group may respond to a different set of motivational factors, and may respond differently to different survey instruments.

In assessing leadership engagement, senior leaders often ask, "How do I ensure that people will listen to my coaching, follow my guidance, and take my coaching to heart?" When in a coaching session, leaders should ask what is truly important. The typical leader reveals that the clarity and accurateness of their direction, as well as actionable and correct coaching, is most important. These things are important, but most important is that the employee feels the leader cares about them and their personal growth and development.

If employees know in their hearts that their leaders care about them, those leaders can be open with feedback. Employees will still listen and try to make changes. On the other hand, if employees have even a small doubt about the leader's intentions, employees can be thin-skinned.

If people do not think leaders care about them, why would they follow those leaders?

Among several other responsibilities, senior leaders must make the work environment emotionally safe. For example, we have all seen instances where a *high risk, high probability of failure project* needs to be staffed. Clearly, an organization will want one of their best people to run this project. The superstar is chosen. If the high risk, high probability of failure project does fail, however, despite a fine effort from one of the company's best people (the person you chose to lead the project), organizations either fire that person or leave them isolated, but still inside. Leaving the person inside the company can be worse because everybody knows the person failed, which, given the stigma that can be involved, can be worse than being fired. The result - When another *high risk, high probability of failure project* comes along and leaders ask for candidates to run the project, no one volunteers. Strangely, the leaders are often surprised.

In order to be successful, organizations must truly understand both successes and failures. Why did the project succeed? Why did the project not succeed? If the failure was not a personal shortcoming of the project leader, the senior leaders need to ensure that the individual can return to a safe environment and use the learning which the organization recently paid for in the cost of the failure. On the other hand, if the failure was the result of a performance issue, leaders must address this situation honestly and fairly. When poor performance is ignored <u>or</u> high performance is under-valued, high performers are demoralized.

Additionally, no leader can delegate being involved in leading people or the review of performance. If the leader does not care about organizational and personal performance, why should anybody else care? Once performance is understood, leaders need to make course corrections that will keep the organization motivated to meet new objectives.

A key part of this motivation is reward and recognition. Reward and recognition, however, remains an opportunity for improvement - or "low-hanging fruit" - for many organizations, leaving employees ultimately unfulfilled. By increasing reward and recognition, and aligning it with high performance (including a significant amount of non-monetary recognition), leaders can align employee efforts with the desired organizational performance. However, the reward and recognition must be tied to performance-related events and not life events, such as anniversaries and birthdays. Life events can still be celebrated, but in high performing organizations, they are not celebrated as enthusiastically as performance-related events.

A Lighter Moment:

The follies which a man regrets most in his life,
are those which he didn't commit when he had the opportunity.

Helen Rowland

A Lighter Moment:

The sad truth is that excellence makes people nervous.

Shana Alexander

A little learning is a dangerous thing,
but a lot of ignorance is just as bad.

Bob Edwards

 FOUNDATION

The concept of a performance management system (PMS) was discussed in Area to Address 5.2a. The PMS identifies areas for employee development that are inputs to the workforce and leader development system. The workforce and leader development system addresses how individuals improve, assesses their improvement, and integrates their improvement with their career progression.

Learning and Development System

The manner in which the workforce learning and development aligns to core competencies, strategic challenges, and goals and objectives should be deployed all the way down to the short- and longer-term action plans. Additionally, workforce development should consider:

- Organizational core competencies, strategic cahllenges and achievement of:
  - Short-term plans,
  - Long-term plans,
- organizational performance improvement,
- organizational change,
- innovation,
- ethics and ethical business practices,
- customer focus,
- the transfer of knowledge from departing or retiring workforce members,
- the reinforcement of new knowledge and skills on the job.

In the past the CPE went on to ask about the breadth of development opportunities for the workforce, including education, training, coaching, mentoring, and work-related experiences. Each of these could play a role in the overall development of employees. One of the above questions asks how knowledge is transferred from departing or retiring workers. As with other aspects of the criteria, this should be achieved through the use of a systematic process.

Leader development follows many of the same basic tenets of workforce development such as identifying core competencies, tying development to organizational performance, and ensuring that breadth and

445

depth of development needed is achieved. In addition, leadership development should align with other parts of an organization, such as the leadership system discussed in Item 1.1. First, each of the characteristics in the leadership system must be a part of the leadership development process and the characteristics expected in leaders should be a part of the leadership evaluations. If not, leaders will not know how to lead in a consistent way and will not think that the leadership attributes described in the leadership system are expectations of their personal leadership style. Secondly, leaders must be taught to develop people and taught to develop the processes (organizational learning) within their span of control. Finally, leaders must be role models at all levels. If the leader is not a role model, then those individuals who look up to that leader will not feel they are expected to act in a role model manner either.

Learning and Development Effectiveness

Once the training of the workforce and leadership is accomplished, the organization has a responsibility to evaluate the effectiveness of the development and learning systems. This can be not only the impact on the individuals trained, but can also be the impact on the organizational performance. That linkage and impact are quantified in some high performing organizations. Typically organizations will at a minimum ask for the reactions and feedback of those who attended the training. Some organizations actually assess the learning that took place through tests and examinations. It is one thing to have knowledge and another to be able to apply that knowledge on the job. Consequently, some organizations assess the impact of training to performance on the job. Finally, the most advanced organizations link the impact to performance on the job with overall enterprise performance measures associated with the overall strategy. The cost in both time and money increases as the organization implements more advanced assessment methods. Consequently, some organizations use the more expensive methods for only a few key or expensive training events. For more on the four levels of assessment search on the key words "Kirkpatrick Model."

Career Progression

Finally, the organization has a responsibility to help employees manage their career progression. This does *not* mean that every employee should have an explicit career path mapped out including their next three positions. Most organizations have found that to be a low value-added activity. This is however, common in some technical paths, such as the steps of a nursing ladder as nurses develop in tenure and skill. However, what it does mean is that for the highest levels of the organization succession plans should be in place, with the associated development plans for each of the leaders on the succession plan. At all levels, employees should have the following knowledge of their job, their performance, and their potential:

- an understanding of their current job requirements;

- an understanding of their current performance versus their job requirements (and the gap);

- an ability to receive the education, training, or experience to close the gap;

- an understanding of the difference between their current job performance and the job they desire (and the gap);

- an ability to receive the education, training, or experience to close the gap; and

- an understanding and belief that once they receive the training, education, or experience required for the job they desire that the job selection process will be fair.

Employee education, training, and development should link to the organization's strategic plan. The impact of people and employee capabilities were considered in the early stages of developing the strategic plan (Item 2.1). The human resource plan was considered during the deployment of the strategy into action plans (Item 2.2), leaving this portion of the CPE to address the specific development and training of leaders and the workforce to implement those plans. This plan begins with aggregating the training requirements at the highest levels in the organization so that the organization can directly link education and training to the achievement of action plans. The overall macro training and development plans must be deployed throughout the organization to link and align individual actions with short- and long-term organizational objectives.

The beginning of an employee's education and training starts with new employee orientation – while no longer specifically required by the CPE, it is necessary if new employees are to systematically learn the culture and necessary tools. This orientation should typically address the culture of the organization, the values and beliefs, and what employees have to do to grow into productive members of the organization. New employees should understand the same skills and tools that all other employees understand so that the new employee can use those skills and tools productively to solve problems or to progress within the culture, as well as to improve organizational performance.

Motivation and career development starts with the needs and expectations of the leaders and the employees and focuses on how the organization helps them achieve their development objectives through both formal and informal techniques. In the past few years, the CPE have asked about succession planning at all levels of the organization. Very few organizations truly plan for the succession of anyone except top leaders. The criteria now ask for how the organization accomplishes effective succession planning for leadership and management positions. Nevertheless, the organization has the responsibility to ensure all employees have the opportunity to progress in their careers. The CPE now ask how an organization manages effective career progression for all employees throughout the organization. The organization should post all job openings so that eligible candidates have the opportunity to apply for all positions for which they are qualified and for which they have an interest.

 EXAMPLES

Ritz-Carlton (Baldrige Recipient 1999 and 1992)

Education and training is designed to keep individuals up to date with business needs. The Corporate Director of Training and Development and the Hotel Directors of Training and Development have the responsibility to make sure that training stays current with business needs. To do this, they work with Human Resource and Quality Executives who input organization and job performance training requirements or revise existing ones. The flow of this process is shown on the next page. Key development training needs are addressed through a core of courses that all employees receive. All employees (regardless of their level in the company) receive the same mandatory two day orientation process, which includes classroom type training on The Gold Standards and their GreenBook of improvement tools.

As shown in the figure above, they use input from employees and their supervisors in determining education needs primarily via a review and analysis of performance appraisal documents. The Hotel Director of Training and Development and the Quality Trainers also receive and consider direct feedback from Ritz-Carlton personnel. When training is designed, it is piloted and approved in a fashion similar to the new product and service development process described in Category 3. Participants in the pilot provide direct, candid feedback to the designers and instructors.

Although job induction training is classroom delivered by the Director of Training and Development and the General Manager, most training delivery is on-the-job. This consists of: (1) daily line-up (2) self-study documents (3) developmental assignment and (4) training certification. Most training is evaluated through examinations, while other methods include audits, performance reviews and appraisals.

Approximately 80% of the training received by The Ritz-Carlton Ladies and Gentlemen is from in-house sources which allows Ritz-Carlton to have direct control over the method of training delivery and evaluation. To gain real-life developmental experiences, they make extensive use of developmental assignments in which people choose to expand their knowledge and experience through requesting new assignments within and across hotels and functions. Since most executives came up the ranks this way, this is a widely accepted and expected process for people who would like to be promoted.

Ritz-Carlton Course Development Process

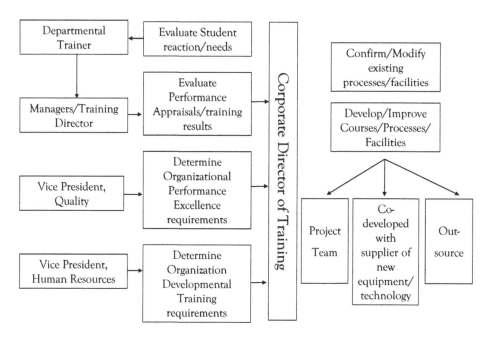

Source: Ritz-Carlton (2000) pp. 14 – 15

North Mississippi Medical Center (Baldrige recipient, 2006 as a Hospital, and 2012 as a System)

North Mississippi Medical Center terms their workforce and leader development process "EXCEL." This process includes the annual performance evaluation, as well as the Leadership Development Institute coursework. Both of these processes are aligned with the organizational mission, vision, and values as well as the critical success factors key to the internal career development process framework.

Because the key to success is to give each employee the opportunity to "EXCEL," the EXCEL process was designed by North Mississippi Medical Center to create a partnership between the employee and supervisor, which enables each employee to become an empowered expert. EXCEL is behaviorally driven and describes not only what must be done, but also how the job is done. EXCEL is a cyclical process of planning, coaching, reviewing and rewarding/ recognizing performance. EXCEL begins each year with the individual employee submitting their Performance Plan (aligned with the Critical Success Factors and strategic goals) to their supervisor for review and approval. The Performance Plan has specific actions under each Critical Success Factor, and measurable results and/or observable behaviors. Employees record their Performance Plan on "Keys to Success Cards," a copy of their performance plan kept on their person. Each employee (all areas, not just direct patient care) includes a patient satisfaction goal as a personal goal to strengthen our emphasis on Patient Centered Care. As part of an ongoing EXCEL process, performance is formally reviewed after the first 90 days of employment and then biannually.

448

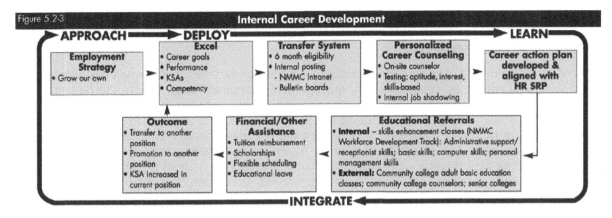

Figure 5.2-3 Internal Career Development

Leaders model desired behaviors daily through their interactions with employees and customers. During the mid-cycle and annual review process, feedback is solicited from at least six of each employee's customers and/or co-workers to produce a 360° evaluation profile on each of the Critical Success Factors. Employees are rewarded with merit increases based on performance.

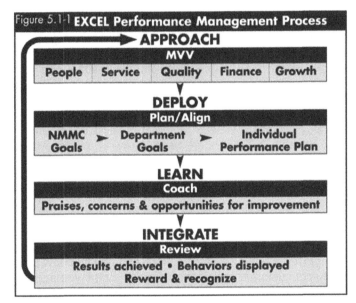

Figure 5.1-1 EXCEL Performance Management Process

In addition to EXCEL, leaders (including physician leaders) and managers participate in a leadership development process, called Servant Leadership, that includes a 360-degree profiles on eight servant leader attributes followed by aggregation of results and development of an action plan. Servant Leadership is one component of the Leadership Development Institute.

The Leadership Development Institute is designed to develop knowledge and skills for new and tenured leaders. Leadership development is systematically deployed and includes: 1) leader assessment (360-degree profiles on eight servant leader attributes);

2) leader development planning with leader/mentor; 3) Leadership Development courses; 4) performance evaluation (EXCEL); and 5) succession planning. New physicians receive initial orientation, continuing medical education and leadership training. During orientation, physicians learn about the Mission, Vision, and Values, the Resource Center, committee structures, services and resources. The Continuing Medical Education offerings are aligned with annually targeted clinical outcomes goals. Source: NMMC (2007) pg 29-31

Figure 5.1-4 Leadership Development Institute

People: NEO, Servant Leadership, Employee Engagement/ Satisfaction/ Rounding, Employee Relations, Employee Selection/ Behavioral Interviewing, Excel, 7 Habits for Leaders, 7 Habits of Highly Effective People, Coaching Beyond the Basics, 4 Roles of Leadership

Service: Customer Service for Leaders, Analysis of PGA Data, Presentation Advantage, Writing Advantage

Quality: Mgt Orientation, Execution of a Plan, Patient Safety, Focus (Time Mgt), Meeting Advantage

Financial: Budget/Financial Mgt, Financial Mgt for Non-Financial Managers

Growth: EPP, Analysis of Market Share Data

Branch-Smith Printing (Baldrige Recipient 2002)

Satisfaction Assessment Methods

The primary formal method of determining employee satisfaction is through the employee satisfaction survey. The survey addresses communication, management, customer focus, quality, job responsibility and training, procedures and processes, teamwork, and overall satisfaction. Employees rate their agreement with 50 statements in these categories as Strongly Agree, Agree, Disagree, or Strongly Disagree. Statement ratings of less than 60% agreement are given particular focus for improvement. Results are broken out by department to provide feedback to specific supervisors and to senior management for their performance. This provides upward feedback to leaders in conjunction with their normal performance evaluation. The data is shared with all employees in department and Division meetings.

Demographic information is gathered as part of the survey to determine well-being and satisfaction among the diverse workforce and to ensure no major gaps between ethnic, age, gender, or tenure groups exist. Employees also rate the importance of each issue to determine level of concerns. Focus groups, which allow employees to express concerns, ask questions, or make suggestions, provide more specific responses about problem areas. Results are used to create QIPs and as input into the SPP.

The second major approach to determine employee satisfaction is voluntary employee turnover. Reducing turnover is a Division goal and is measured for each department. The established goal is reducing voluntary turnover to 10%, which is below the average of the Fortune 100 Best Places to Work for in America. Employees that leave voluntarily are given exit interviews to provide feedback in job satisfaction and dissatisfaction.

Monthly Division meetings are an open forum to express specific concerns as well as the "open door" style of management. Concerns that affect all employees are reviewed in the monthly CLT meeting. Concerns that affect the Division are reviewed in the monthly PLT. QIPs are used to review and follow up on areas as necessary.

Assessment Finding Relative to Business Results

Through analysis of cause and affect of the relationship between customer satisfaction, employee satisfaction, and business results, they determine key priorities for improvement as part of the SPP. Positive results from the customer survey reveal quality products and services from employees, indicative of a highly satisfied and well trained, empowered employee base. Customer satisfaction results show that commitment to employee satisfaction and training affects customer satisfaction directly. Employee survey results continue to indicate that employees know who their customers are and understand goals for meeting their needs.

A training plan is developed for each employee to improve skills and grow within the company. This plan, along with reduced turnover and increased satisfaction, is related to the positive growth in Value Added Sales, etc.

Several important QIP improvements have impacted the bottom line. Due to low scores in communication on the 1999 employee survey, a QIP implemented a solution that involved better department schedules, monthly department meetings, and bulletin boards tracking performance and goals. Better communication has helped reduce PONC and brought satisfaction to employees by connecting them personally to the goals. QIP teams continue to enhance the quality focus and improve the processes, hence creating the business results desired.

The most compelling evidence of effectiveness of the HR approach is the impact of the appraisal and training method on employee satisfaction and productivity. In early 2001, the full system of roll-up reviews was implemented, linking individual employee performance goals to the goals for their work group, department, and the Division. The employee establishes performance goals in his/her annual review activity along with required training for the year. Performance to those goals is reviewed weekly and adjustments are made to the training plan. Aggregate results are reviewed quarterly as a department. Roll-ups continue through the organization on these measures. Results of satisfaction scores in many areas reflect the improved satisfaction of employees with their work as a result of the improved communication with supervisors, and satisfaction with training and the performance review. These improvements correlate closely with the accelerated improvements in 2001 results for individual process effectiveness. Source: Branch-Smith (2003) pp. 24 – 26

Poudre Valley Health System (Baldrige Recipient 2008)

PVHS has been systematically building a culture of workforce satisfaction and engagement for the past decade. In 1997, based on a best practice from Baldrige recipient Wainwright Industries, PVHS surveyed employees as customers and asked: 1) What makes you want to jump out of bed and come to work? and 2) How do we build a culture that supports that? In 1999, to further understand drivers of staff satisfaction and engagement, PVHS collaborated with the Industrial and Organizational Psychology Department at Colorado State University (CSU) to survey and interview staff from all disciplines and shifts and identify key staff requirements (shown in the OP in Figure P.1-5).These requirements — or culture dimensions — are universal to all staff segments and remain the framework for the semi-annual Employee Culture Survey, which drives improvement efforts in the organization, based on their established segmentation. The Workforce Focus Team, a multidisciplinary staff team including representatives from HR, education, employee health/safety, and clinical/nonclinical areas — collaborates with CSU in evaluating and improving the survey tool. In 2003, PVHS initiated an annual physician survey to assist in determining key factors that affect physician satisfaction and engagement. Volunteer Services also performs an annual volunteer survey. A listing of the types of surveys, the methods and segmentation is as follows:

Figure 5.1-5: Assessing Workforce Satisfaction & Engagement		
WORKFORCE GROUP	METHOD	SEGMENTATION
Staff	Employee Culture Survey, MSA survey, Magnet designation, leadership rounding, voluntary turnover, stay/exit interviews, safety indicators	Demographics, job family, tenure, position, shift, department
Physicians	Physician survey, size of Medical Staff, leadership rounding	Demographics, tenure, specialty
Volunteers	Volunteer survey, leadership rounding	Adult, student, teen

The annual Employee Culture Survey results are used to drive improvement. Annually, SMG identifies opportunities for improvement, prioritizes them, chooses one for action plan development, and monitors progress through a measure on the system BSC. Individual departments also engage staff to develop an action plan that addresses department-specific survey results. The organization uses other indicators of workforce satisfaction and engagement to validate survey results, monitor action plans and prompt additional just in time adjustments.

CRITERIA QUESTIONS

In your response, include answers to the following questions:

b. Workforce and Leader Development

(1) **Learning and Development System** How does your learning and development system support the organization's needs and the personal development of your workforce members, managers, and leaders? How does the system:
- address your organization's core competencies, strategic challenges, and achievement of short- and long-term actions plans;
- support organizational performance improvement, organizational change, and innovation;
- support ethics and ethical business practices;
- improve customer focus;
- ensure the transfer of knowledge from departing or retiring workforce members; and
- ensure the reinforcement of new knowledge and skills on the job?

(2) **Learning and Development Effectiveness** How do you evaluate the effectiveness and efficiency of your learning and development system? How do you:
- correlate learning and development outcomes with findings from your assessment of workforce engagement and with key business results reported in category 7, and
- use these correlations to identify opportunities for improvement in both workforce engagement and learning and development offerings?

(3) **Career Progression** How do you manage career progression for your organization? How do you manage career development for your workforce? How do you carry out succession planning for management and leadership positions?

Notes:

5.2b. Your response should include how you address any unique considerations for workforce development, learning and career progression that stem from your organization. Your response should also consider the breadth of development opportunities you might offer, including education, training, coaching, mentoring, and work-related experiences.

NIST (2015-2016) pp. 21 – 22

WORKSHEETS

5.2b(1) – Learning and Development System

Workforce and Leader Development Factors	Process Used To Address This Factor In The Workforce and Leader Development and Learning System: *
Organizational Core Competencies	
Organizational Strategic Challenges	
Achievement Of Action Plans (Both Short- And Long-Term)	
Organizational Performance Improvement And Innovation	
Ethics And Ethical Business Practices	
Improve Customer Focus	
Ensure The Transfer Of Knowledge From Departing Or Retiring Workforce Members	
Ensure The Reinforcement Of New Knowledge And Skills On The Job	

* This can include education, training, coaching, mentoring, and work-related experiences

5.2b(2) Learning and Development Effectiveness

Employee Segment/Group (Same as P1a[3])	Process To Link Workforce Assessment Findings To Key Business Results (Reference The Figure Number Or Data From Category 7)	Process To Identify Opportunities In:	
		Workforce Engagement	Learning And Development Offerings

5.2b(3) - Career Progression

Employee Group	Process Used To Manage:	
	Succession Planning	Effective Career Progression
*Senior Leaders and Other Key Leadership Positions**		
Professional Staff		
Workforce (If Addressed Differently From Professional Staff)		
Other Groups Or Unique Considerations		

* Succession Planning is typically only performed for a few top leaders, and a few other key hard to replace positions

ASSESSMENT

96	The organization has a systematic process for: 1) identifying need for, 2) delivering, and 3) evaluating the effectiveness of training.	1	2	3	4	5	6	DK
97	Leadership training is linked to the characteristics of the Leadership System.	1	2	3	4	5	6	DK
98	Learning and development links to the organization's core competency and the achievement of action plans.	1	2	3	4	5	6	DK
99	Learning and development includes ethics and ethical business practices, safety, and a customer focus.	1	2	3	4	5	6	DK
100	Employees and leaders have the ability to provide input on their education and training needs.	1	2	3	4	5	6	DK
101	New knowledge and skills are systematically reinforced on the job.	1	2	3	4	5	6	DK
102	The effectiveness of workforce and leader development and learning systems are systematically evaluated.	1	2	3	4	5	6	DK
103	Career progression is managed for the entire workforce. The workforce knows what is expected, knows how they are doing, and knows what is necessary for advancement.	1	2	3	4	5	6	DK

BLUEPRINT

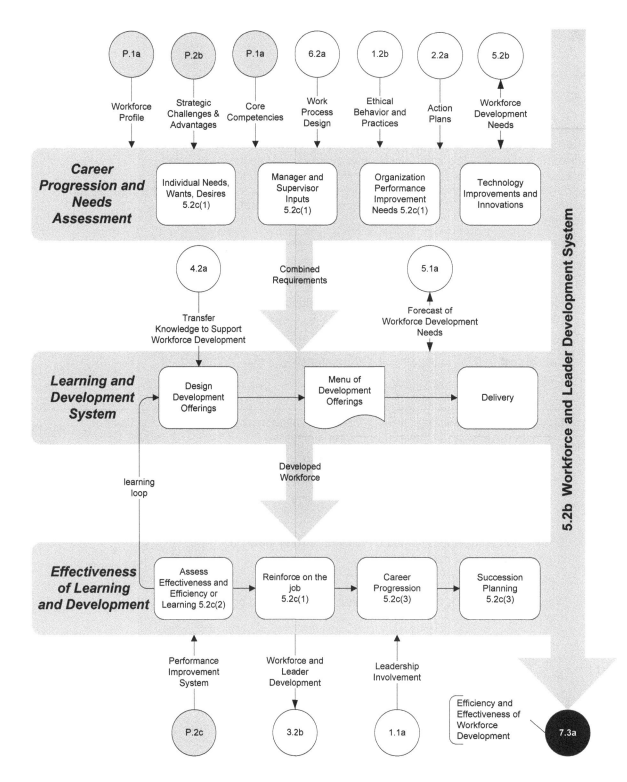

SYSTEM INTEGRATION

Context

P.1a > 5.2c Workforce Profile - The workforce profile is an important input to the workforce development needs assessment process. The needs will often vary depending on the type of employees, their education level, etc. For example, employees handling hazardous cargo will have additional development needs vs. those working in the office. In addition, the workforce profile – is an important input to the leadership development needs assessment process. The type of leadership development that is needed at each level can vary depending on the make up of the existing workforce.

P.1a > 5.2c Core Competencies - The workforce has to continuously develop and improve their knowledge, skills, and abilities related to the organization's core competencies. Consequently, the core competencies should be part of the needs assessment process that drives the workforce and leader development system described in 5.2c.

P.2b > 5.2c Strategic Challenges and Advantages - The strategic challenges and advantages described in the profile (P.2b) are in important part of the workforce development needs assessment process (5.2c). Both the challenges and advantages are important considerations when deciding what areas to emphasize in workforce and leader development to overcome the challenges and to sustain or enhance the advantages.

P.2c > 5.2c Performance Improvement System - The processes for evaluating and improving the workforce and leader development programs and keeping them current with changing business needs and directions should be based on the overall performance improvement system described in the profile (P.2c).

Systems

1.1a <> 5.2c Leadership Involvement - Succession planning shows up in two key places: 5.2c addresses the overall process to address succession planning for leadership and management positions and in 1.1a it asks how leaders personally participate in succession planning and the development of future leaders. The process and the leadership participation in that process should be designed as one integrated system. In addition, Leadership development should be based on the organization's leadership system, values, and vision.

1.2b > 5.2c Ethics Behavior and Processes - The definitions and processes associated with the organizations ethics programs should also be incorporated into the workforce and leaders development needs assessment and offering design processes. Leaders need to know the organizations approaches and policies on ethics so they can implement and reinforce those policies. In addition, they also need to know how to be a role model for ethical behavior.

2.2a > 5.2c HR Action Plans - The strategy, action plans, and associated HR action plans also drive the workforce and leadership development efforts. The overall strategies are balanced with the needs of the individual to drive the development of both course content and the delivery methods.

3.2b < 5.2c Workforce and Leader Development - The workforce and leader development system should be designed to include the necessary knowledge, skills, and abilities to support a customer focused culture.

4.2a > 5.2c Knowledge to Support Workforce Development - The knowledge that the organization creates and manages (4.2a) should be leveraged and used to inform the design of the workforce development offerings (5.2c). This is just one way the organization's knowledge can be disseminated throughout the workforce.

5.2c > 5.2b Workforce Development Needs - Opportunities for improvement are often identified as part of the assessment of workforce engagement described in 5.2b. These opportunities should be an input to the needs assessment process in 5.2c.

5.2c <> 5.1a Forecast of Workforce Development Needs - The forecast of workforce capability and capacity needs identified as part of the assessment and sustain phase of the workforce capability and capacity system (5.1a) are important considerations when designing the development offerings and delivery methods (5.2c).

5.2c < 6.2a Process Designs - The design of work processes is an important input to the workforce development needs assessment. In addition, new designs or redesigned work processes are also key inputs to the needs assessment process.

Scorecard

5.2c > 7.3a Workforce Development Results - The results from the evaluation of the extent and effectiveness of training and education should be part of the human resources results presented in 7.3a.

THOUGHTS FOR LEADERS

An organization cannot move any faster than its leaders can learn and improve. Some leaders believe that they do not need to learn, that they can always follow their "gut," but an organization will never be great as long as it is lead by somebody who does not learn. Some of the greatest leaders we have ever known are lifelong learners. The office of N.R. Narayana Murthy, the retired Chairman & CEO of InfoSys, is lined with books, and he has probably read them all. Another great lifelong learner is Charles Korbell, the CEO of Clarke American when they won Baldrige in 2001.

Leaders have three responsibilities related to learning:

- **First**, they have responsibility for their **own** learning. If leaders are not learning, not stretching their capabilities, not pressing themselves, why should anyone else in the organization learn or think that learning is important?

- **Second**, leaders have a responsibility to ensure that **everyone** in the organization is willing to stretch their capabilities through learning and that they have the opportunity to do so. If the leader does not budget for learning, if they do not require learning, then few employees, if any, will take the time to learn.

- **Lastly,** leaders have a responsibility to make sure the **processes** in the organization learn. In CPE terms this is "organizational learning." It is tragic to go through several years or cycles of a process and find that the process does not get any better, or that the organization tries to prove that they are getting better but they have not changed, updated, or improved the processes.

Leaders must model everything they want the organization to do. If the organization is not learning, it points back to the fact that the leaders are not learning.

Leaders must reward what they expect. Approximately ten years ago, a large aerospace company CEO went out to a remote location and held a management club meeting of 1,500 managers. He was passionate about his beliefs as he spoke for an hour and a half on every leader's responsibility to support innovation and the innovators.

The example he used in his speech was of Thomas Edison. Edison completed 4,500 experiments before he found Tungsten as the filament for the light bulb. A lady asked him, "Mr. Edison, don't you feel like a failure? I mean, you had 4,500 failures." Edison replied, "No ma'am, you do not understand. I had 4,500 successful experiments, and each one proved what would not work for the filament of a light bulb."

The speaker's whole point was for the leaders to support the innovators. The company made spacecraft, so they had to have innovators.

What happened the next day, however, was dramatic. In one of the director's offices, someone poked his head in the door and asked, "What did you think of the boss's speech last night?" The director replied, "Not in this company. C.Y.A., be very safe." Clearly, the CEO was attempting to set a new direction, but the processes and measurements were not genuine in the minds of the leaders at other levels of the organization.

People do not behave in the manner in which they *will* be incentivized; rather, they behave based on the manner in which they *believe* they are going to be incentivized. The two must be the same, or the organization's behavior and incentives are not aligned. In large organizations, it may take a couple of years for people to truly understand that a measurement evaluation system has changed. They have to believe that this change has occurred, or their behavior will not change.

A Lighter Moment:

To be proud of learning is the greatest ignorance.

Bishop Taylor

> *Change is the process by which the future invades our lives.*
>
> **Alvin Toffler**

FOUNDATION

This area to address focuses on how the organization designs their products and key work processes, including key design concepts and product and process requirements.

The term 'work process' refers to how the work of your organization is accomplished. Work processes support the work systems discussed in Item 2.1 – Strategy Development. These involve your workforce, your key suppliers and partners, your contractors, your collaborators, and other components of the supply chain needed to produce and deliver your products and your business and support processes.

For example, a health care organization may have inpatient and outpatient *work systems*. Each of these *work systems* could be supported by the underlying work processes of:

       1) Welcome the patient;
       2) register them;
       3) diagnose their illness;
       4) treat them;
       5) educate them;
       6) discharge them; and …
       7) follow-up after discharge.

Work processes coordinate the internal work processes and the external resources necessary for you to develop, produce, and deliver your products to your customers and to succeed in your marketplace. Decisions about work systems are strategic (Item 2.1 Strategy Development). These decisions involve protecting and capitalizing on organizational core competency and deciding what should be procured or produced outside your organization in order to be efficient and sustainable in your marketplace.

> **Note:** It is helpful to understand the definitions of systems and processes, and understand the difference prior to addressing the Category 6 Areas to Address. These can be found in the Glossary.

> Additional definitions critical to this understanding which are provided by the author, and not supported by the CPE include: Systematic Process, Enterprise Systems Model, Guidance Systems, and Support Systems.

Over the years, the CPE have used several different approaches to describe the process management category. This description has included terms such as core processes, product and services processes, supplier processes, business processes, value creation processes, support processes, and others. In the 2011 – 2012 criteria, Category 6 discusses two types of processes:

- **Key Work Processes** – these are the key processes in the creation of products or services consumed by your external customers or those processes that are most critical to achieving your intended outcome.

- **Work Processes** – All processes. A subset of these is all other processes in the organization beyond the Key Work Processes. Sometimes the using organizations' or, as some call them, the internal customers refer to these processes as the "enabling processes." These processes support (or enable) other processes that produce the products and services for external customers.

Area to address 6.1a asks how the organization designs their key work processes including design concepts and how they identify the work process requirements.

Product and Process Requirements

Processes are a step where something occurs. Processes have: 1) inputs; 2) outputs; 3) requirements; and 4) resources.

The overall work process requirements can start with inputs from the work systems, as well as customers, suppliers, partners, collaborators, and possibly others. The output of the process must meet what is expected by the customer of the process (the downstream process and the higher-level system). If it is a key work process, the customer (typically) will be external. If it is a support process (typically), the customer will be internal (see Area to address 6.1b[2]). In both cases, however, the customer requirements must be systematically determined and the process must be designed to meet those requirements.

At the highest level, a clear understanding or "picture" of an enterprise system (key systems and their relationships) facilitates the identification of key work system requirements and the lower work process requirements. The key to clarity in this case is simplicity. In too many cases, the organization describes itself in terms so complex that the reader cannot understand and, in fact, the employees in the organization cannot clearly agree on the key systems and processes, the inputs, outputs, requirements and resources.

To describe the organization simply, the authors recommend that an organization develop a one-page graphical description of their business (an Enterprise Systems Model or 'stadium chart'). This works for all sectors, including business, health care, and even government or not-for profit. This model can also be the basis for the organization's approach to process management. For example, the one page description (or "stadium chart" because it describes the entire business as one view above the stadium) shows many of the key components of the business that can be broken-down further into the various levels of processes. These high-level systems can be broken down to the lower-level processes (typically broken down two or three more levels). This "stadium" chart concept was originally described in Section P.1a of this book and an example of the Stadium Chart for PRO-TEC Coating Company is shown below.

Design Concepts

This part of the CPE assumes that the overall work systems have been designed and the work processes within that system need to be designed. This is the level where actual work is performed. Additionally, the CPE want the organization to understand how these processes contribute to delivering customer value. This presupposes that the customer value requested from the organization is aligned with the key work processes which are aligned to the core competencies. To achieve the work necessary, every core competency should be addressed by one or more key work process to drive that core competency throughout the organization. Once the alignment of processes to delivering customer value is established, the processes must also drive profitability and sustainability as well as overall organizational success. For more on a design framework and process see the chapter on Organization Design in Part 5 – Path to Performance Excellence.

The first part of this area to address focuses on the product and work process design and key considerations. Work process design typically includes an analysis of the overall work system being supported, and the role of the process in that system.

The first key consideration is how to design the products and work processes to help achieve and/or leverage the organization's core competencies. This was identified in the context section (Organization Profile). Core competency (ies) refer to the organization's area (s) of greatest expertise. These are those competencies that are strategically important and provide a sustainable competitive advantage in the market place or service environment.

These core competencies should have some alignment to the principal factors that determine the organization's success relative to its competitors (success factors). These principal factors were discussed in the Organizational Profile in Item P2. The core competencies should also be linked to the organization's mission (e.g., this is what we have to be good at to achieve our mission), competitive environment (e.g., this is how you achieve a competitive advantage), and action plans (e.g., this is specifically what you will do to achieve the competitive advantage). Anyone evaluating the organization would expect to see significant investments in improving or maintaining the capabilities within each of the core competencies.

EXAMPLES

PRO-TEC Coating Company (2007 Baldrige Recipient)

A small business centrally located to the American automotive industry in northwest Ohio, PRO-TEC Coating Company (PRO-TEC) provides world-class coated sheet steel products and services primarily to the quality-critical automotive market.

It was established as a 50/50 joint venture partnership in 1990 by two global leaders in steel technology – U.S. Steel Corporation (USS) and KOBE Steel (KOBE) of Japan. The partnership agreement was designed to ensure organizational sustainability with an assured substrate (raw material) supply from USS as well as 'shared services' type of external support services (see the support blocks on the left in Figure P.1-1). Finally, USS provides the interface to the final customer (supported by PRO-TEC, particularly where there is a processing or technical issue). The basis for sales/marketing of the product was legally established as illustrated in Figure P.1-1.

This model has allowed all participants to leverage their strengths. For example, KOBE is a world leader in advanced steel technology and processing requirements, USS is a product and technology leader within the United States, and has a marketing presence throughout North America, and PRO-TEC is a leader in process control, and innovative approaches to bringing new products to market. In many ways, this partnership is viewed as a global alliance which is a model for many future organizations.

PRO-TEC feels its core competency is being *An Innovation Leader in Coated Steel.* This would be a "high level slogan" if the organization had not thought-through the enabling processes and capabilities which drive this core competency. This is driven by the ability to provide break-through processes to meet the customers' needs, and the ability to utilize expertise in coated steels. Through highly flexible, innovative teams, PRO-TEC demonstrates the agility to develop solutions delivering high-quality, reliable products that meet the customer's demands.

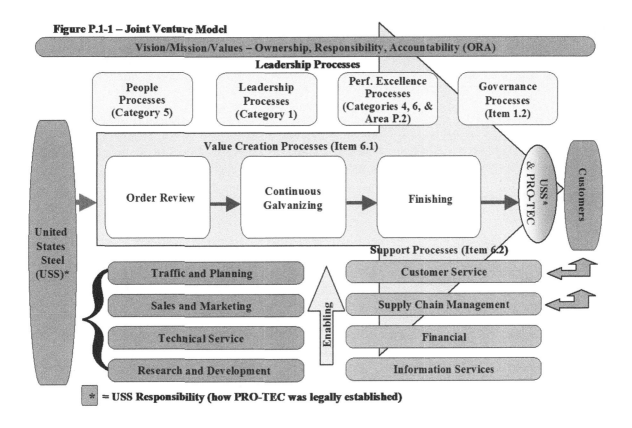

Figure P.1-1 – Joint Venture Model

The enabling Strategic Themes (areas of particular emphasis) inside the organization include:

- innovative people, process, and products;
- advance High-Strength Steel;
- value-Added Coated Steel Products;
- meet the needs of the customer – first choice of the customer;
- market Leadership;
- self-directed work-teams focused on performance excellence;
- process systems perspective – managing through process; and
- ongoing personal and organizational learning.

PRO-TEC's strategic position as an "Innovation Leader in Coated Steel" is what sets the company apart from other suppliers (its core competency). At the core of these themes are people, processes, and advanced products. PRO-TEC encourages and capitalizes on the innovativeness, knowledge, flexibility, and dedication of the Associates of the organization. PRO-TEC Associates work in self-directed work teams, practice Ownership, Responsibility, and Accountability (ORA), and utilize continuous improvement teams to improve processes and products. In addition, PRO-TEC along with its parent companies are market leaders in the supply of advanced high strength steels in the industry. This leadership in the market has given the joint venture a favorable position with its customers and a competitive advantage in the industry.

Advocate Good Samaritan Hospital (Baldrige Recipient 2010)

GSAM"s Enterprise Systems Model [Figure 6.1-1]shows the integration of our guiding organizational systems ❶, key work systems❷, key work processes ❸, key support systems ❹, and our core competency ❼.

Voice of the customer (VOC) inputs ❺, are utilized to determine work system and process requirements. VOC input also drives the design and improvement of our key work systems and key work processes. All elements are integrated and result in the achievement of our vision, the living out of our mission ❻, and contribute to accomplishing our core competency of Building Loyal Relationships ❼.

GSAM Figure 6.1-1 Enterprise Model

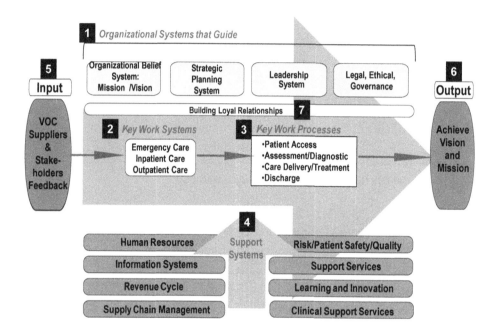

The *Work System Design Approach*, is a 6-gate process utilized to design and innovate GSAM"s work systems. Each gate requires specific data inputs, the use of performance improvement (PI) tools, completion of activities, and tangible outcomes. The process to determine and justify the need for a new system/service is accomplished in Gates 1-3. A multi-disciplinary team is convened in 4 to determine the processes in the new system. The design and deployment of those processes within the new work system are completed in 5 and 6.

We evaluate which processes will be internal or external to the organization using specific criteria in step 5 of the Work Process Design Approach [Figure 6.2-1]. The ET also annually reviews the need for external resources during step 4 of the SPP utilizing criteria that includes cost/ benefit analysis, internal availability of the expertise (capacity and capability), availability of external expertise with the quality we require, and the potential opportunity to build loyal relationships.

Poudre Valley Health System (Baldrige Recipient 2008))

Poudre Valley Health System's SMG and BOD first identified PVHS core competencies at a retreat a decade ago as part of a strategy for providing a lifetime of care. The organization has continued to strengthen these core competencies and verifies them through a systematic process involving senior leaders and interdisciplinary teams. Most recently, in 2007, the performance excellence teams identified unique PVHS strengths and performed an affinity sort that verified the core competencies. SMG independently performed the same process for further verification. Driven by the organization's strategic challenges these core competencies give PVHS strategic advantages that enable it to achieve its strategic plan and ultimately its mission and vision. Figure 6.1-1 below shows these linkages.

Figure 6.1-1: Core Competencies, Competitive Environment, & Strategic Context				
STRATEGIC CHALLENGES (Figure P.2-2)	**CORE COMPETENCIES** [P.2a(2)]	**STRATEGIC ADVANTAGES** (Figure P.2-2)	**STRATEGIC OBJECTIVES** (Figure P.1-1)	**RESULTS (7.0)**
• Labor shortages • Growth/reimbursement • Clinical outcomes	Engaging the Workforce	• Low turnover/vacancy • Strong referral base • High-quality, low-cost care	1,5,6	• Turnover (7.4-11,12) • Vacancy (7.4-13) • National certifications (7.4-14) • Workforce satisfaction (7.4-1-6)
• Labor shortages • Growth/reimbursement • Market share • Partnerships • Clinical outcomes	Partnering	• Strong referral base • No service duplication • Innovation • High-quality, low-cost care	2,4,5	• Joint venture equity earnings (7.5-1) • Clinical outcomes (7.1) • Community (7.6)
• Labor shortages • Growth/reimbursement • Market share • Partnerships • Clinical outcomes	Driving Innovation	• Low turnover/vacancy • Innovation • High-quality, low-cost care • Performance excellence	1-6	• Medical staff size (7.4-6) • Market share (7.3-8,9) • Turnover (7.4-11) • Performance excellence (7.5)
• Growth/reimbursement • Market share • Partnerships	Ensuring Financial Stability	• Innovation • Focus on future • Community benefits	1,3,6	• Profit per discharge (7.3-1) • Financial flexibility (7.3-2) • Community benefits (7.6-8)

Pewaukee School District (Baldrige Recipient 2013)

PSD (Pewaukee School District) organizes our work into two large systems, each with multiple key processes supporting each system. We have four Academic work processes encompassing all our learning centered work processes. Our Support processes embody six key support work processes (Figures 6.1-1) that manage the operations of the school district. For integration, PSD links our key work systems & processes with our SP Strategy Areas and identifies key work process owners (Figure 2.1-2 & 6.1-1). Processes are organized into vertical work systems that are reflected in a departmental structure. Integration is attained with direct reporting to either the CAO or CFO. The PDSA approach (Figure 6.2-1) is used to systematically innovate our Academic and Support work processes.

In Step 1 (PLAN) SLs (Senior Leaders) identify the need to design a new or innovate an existing work process.

In Step 2 (PLAN), inputs & requirements (Figure 6.1-1) are used to determine which key work processes are to be accomplished, how they can be integrated into existing processes or systems, organizational knowledge to be utilized, work process tools to be used, new reporting relationships, opportunities for improvement, and best practice innovations. In Step 2 SLs elicit input from key stakeholders, as appropriate, on needs to be met in a revised work process including the opportunities for the incorporation of new technologies.

During Step 3 (PLAN), work process design improvements are developed. In this step PSD explores the opportunity to outsource a key work process. The determination to outsource is based a strategic review using SA identified criteria: strategic contribution of the key work process to our Mission, strength of SP link, cost-benefit, risk analyses, and viability of managing the outsourced service. PSD has elected not to outsource learning-centered processes because they are Mission-critical, yet does outsource food service management and transportation because the PDSA confirms it is cost-effective, efficient, and less learning focused.

In Step 4 (DO), the final work system design innovation is implemented.

In Step 5 (STUDY), PSD monitors how well the work system is performing by regular collection of data and AT & departmental review of dashboard results. For example, SLs and BLTs review student performance data during the Annual Data Review. Analysis triggers the inception of subsequent PDSA cycles and possibly new Action Plans.

In Step 6 (ACT) standardization of the design innovation in other work systems is conducted. Quarterly review of SP Action Plans allows for agility in modifying plans when new opportunities are presented. In a recent cycle of improvement, SAs used PDSA to innovate our Technology Management area by restructuring our leadership & reporting system.

Key requirements for the Academic and Support process areas are presented in Figure 6.1-1. In a recent summer leadership retreat SLs worked with Bob Ewy, ASQ author & process management consultant from Baldrige winning Community Consolidated School District 15 in Palatine, IL, to help the AT identify our key work processes and requirements. The process for determining Academic and Support work process requirements is informed greatly by DPI regulations but also by the ES in our SPP, and through the systematic CRDP which integrates the key work processes in the Academic work system. In the CRDP (Curriculum Review & Design Process), inputs reviewed include Federal, WI SS, DPI standards and regulatory requirements, BOE policy, and student and stakeholder expectations/requirements. Teacher involvement and student and parent focus groups used in the CRDP give voice to user requirements. Requirements for the Support Process areas are determined by reviewing regulations and with input.

Figure 6.1-1 Key Academic & Support Work Processes, Requirements and Performance Measures

Work Process	SP Link	Key Process Tools	Key Requirements	Key Performance Measures	Contribution Delivered By Work Process
Key Academic Processes					
Curriculum Mgmt.	TL	Curriculum Renewal Process	Meet WSS, DPI curriculum content standards and BOE requirements; increasing rigor	**Leading:** % of PSD curriculum BOE approved in advance of implementation year *(Fig. 7.1-16)*, % of curriculum entered on BYOC *(Fig. 7.1-16)* **Lagging:** Compliance with DPI Reporting *(Fig. 7.4-6)*, # of AP Classes *(Fig. 7.1-17)*, PLTW Cert. *(Fig. 7.1-16)*	**SLS/OS:** Design rigorous and relevant curriculum & assessments to enhance student learning; ensure accountability to content/learning standards
Instruction Mgmt.	TL	Professional Development Plan Performance Evaluation System	Meet DPI standard for days/hrs of instruction; Meet NCLB standard of highly qualified teachers	**Leading:** Hiring new employees who are highly qualified *(Fig. 7.4-6)*, % PES goal setting completed on time *(Fig. 7.4-6)* **Lagging:** % compliance with instruction meeting days/hrs of instruction *(Fig. 7.4-6)*, % of PSD Teachers deemed "Highly Qualified" via NCLB *(Fig. 7.4-6)*, 100% of PES evaluations submitted on time *(Fig. 7.1-30)*	**SLS/OS:** Deploy instructional methods that reflect diverse learning needs and best practices
Assessment Mgmt.	TL	Curriculum Renewal Process Annual Data Review	Valid, fair, equitable testing; Academic proficiency that meets NCLB and State regulatory requirements	**Leading:** % of students meeting or exceeding RIT target growth on MAP *(Fig. 7.1-3 & 7.1-4)* **Lagging:** Meeting AYP by district, school and all sub-groups *(Fig. 7.1-16)* ; # DPI violations for WKCE test security *(Fig. 7.4-6)*	**SLS/OS:** Evaluate learning progress and proficiency against standards using formative/summative assessment methods
Student Services Mgmt.	TL	Response to Intervention Professional Learning Communities	Compliance with regulatory requirements set by state and federal law	**Leading:** # students referred for SPED *(Fig. 7.1-19)* **Lagging:** # students placed in SPED *(Fig. 7.1-19)*, % SPED students receiving a diploma *(Fig. 7.1-20)*, % students dismissed from Reading Recovery *(Fig. 7.1-22)*, Compliance with IDEA via DPI Reporting *(Fig. 7.4-6)*	**SLS/OS:** Evaluate & support student learning needs; create improved capabilities to learn
Key Support Processes					
Financial Mgmt.	FO	Budget Planning Cycle Budget & Staffing Plan	Effective fiscal management; Efficient fiscal reporting; Meet regulatory requirements	**Leading:** BOE meeting minutes reflect approval of check register and revenue & expense report *(Fig. 7.4-6)* **Lagging:** Revenue exceeds expenses *(Fig. 7.5-2)*, # DPI reports submitted on time *(Fig. 7.4-6)*, Sustained bond rating *(Fig. 7.5-1)*	**SLS/OS/SU:** Ensure accountability in use of District finances; employ budget planning methods for sustainability of District
Human Resource Mgmt.	WE	Performance Evaluation System Recruitment & Retention	Meet regulatory requirements	**Leading:** AESOP Fill Rate *(Fig. 7.3-3)*; Filling vacancies *(Fig. 7.3-Narrative & Fig. 7.4-6)* **Lagging:** Performance Appraisal Submission *(Fig. 7.1-31)*, Teachers deemed "Highly Qualified" *(Fig. 7.4-6)*, Employee Retention *(Fig. 7.3-14)*	**OS/SU:** Hire, develop, engage & retain talented employees; administer performance evaluation system to all employees
Technology Mgmt.	T	Technology Plan	Systems availability; Compliance with Internet child protection regulation	**Leading:** Cycle time for work order completion *(Fig. 7.1-27)*, Core server up-time *(Fig. 7.1-39)*, customer satisfaction *(Fig. 7.1-28)* **Lagging:** Growth of fleet *(Fig. 7.1-26)*, Technology breaches acted upon *(Fig. 7.4-6)*	**SLS/SSV/OS:** Enhance student learning; Manage IT infrastructure to support decision-making, efficiency & learning
Facilities Mgmt.	FO	-5 Year Capital Projects Plan -10 Year Campus Plan -Crisis Plan	Meet federal, state, and county req. for workplace health, safety and security; Cost-effective; Efficient	**Leading:** Cycle time for work order completion *(Fig. 7.1-33)*, energy consumption *(Fig. 7.1-32)* **Lagging:** Facility use by school & community *(Fig. 7.4-11)*, Evacuation data *(Fig. 7.1-37)*; # MSDS violations *(Fig. 7.1-24)*	**SSV/FR/SU:** Manage safe & healthy plant operations
Communication Mgmt.	C	Comm. Plan	Clear & timely information about district activities; Meet state/federal requirements	**Leading:** # Newsletters sent on time to community per year *(Fig. 7.1-24)*, # uses of School Messenger /Zoomerang *(Fig. 7.1-24)*, # press releases sent *(Fig. 7.1-24)* **Lagging:** Community reliance on district sources of information *(Fig. 7.1-33,* Customer grading of PSD *(Fig. 7.2-8)*	**SSV/OS/SU:** Ensure accessibility of information and transparency; Engage stakeholders and obtain input
Contracted Service Mgmt.	F&O	Contracts with Key Vendors	Meet federal/state regulatory requirements	**Leading:** Transportation timeliness *(Fig. 7.1-38;* food service participation *(Fig. 7.1-35)* **Lagging:** food service profitability *(Fig. 7.1-35)*	**SSV/FR/SU:** Provide nutritious and cost-effective meals; Provide safe and efficient transportation

Key. SP Link. TL–Teaching & Learning, F&O–Facilities & Operations, WED–Workforce Engagement & Development, C–Communications & Community Engagement, T=Technology

Contribution: SLS=student learning & success; SSV = student/stakeholder value; FR = financial return; OS = organizational success; SU = sustainability

CRITERIA QUESTIONS

In your response, include answers to the following questions:

a. Product and Process Design

(1) **Product and Process Requirements** How do you determine key product and work process requirements? What are your organization's key work processes? What are the key requirements for these work processes?

(2) **Design Concepts** How do you design your products and work processes to meet requirements? How do you incorporate new technology, organizational knowledge, product excellence, and the potential need for agility into these products and processes?

Notes:

6.1. The results of improvements in product and process performance should be reported in item 7.1.

6.1a(1). Your key work processes are your most important internal value-creation processes. They might include product design and delivery, customer support, and business processes. Your key work processes are those that involve the majority of your workforce and produce customer, stakeholder, and stockholder value. Projects are unique work processes intended to produce an outcome and then go out of existence.

6.1a(2). The potential need for agility could include changes in work processes as a result of overall work system changes, such as bringing a supply-chain process in-house to avoid disruptions in supply due to increasing external events triggered by climate change or other unpredictable factors.

NIST (2015-2016) p. 23

WORKSHEETS

6.1a Product and Process Design

6.1a(1) Product And Process Requirements

List Key Products	Process Used To Determine Key Product Requirements	List Key Work Processes	Process Used To Determine Key Work Process Requirements
1			
2			
3			
n			

6.1a(2) Design Concepts

Steps In The Process Used To Design And Products And Work Processes	
Product Design Steps	**Work Systems Design Steps**
1	1
2	2
3	3
n	n
How You Validate That All Key Requirements Are Met:	*How You Validate That All Key Requirements Are Met:*

How You Incorporate Into Your Products And Processes:			
New Technology	Organizational Knowledge	Product Excellence	Potential Need For Agility

ASSESSMENT

104	The core competency (ies) for the organization has been defined, and it is clear how this is aligned with what makes the organization a success.	1	2	3	4	5	6	DK
105	The organizational-level systems have been clearly defined and drive the achievement of the core competency.	1	2	3	4	5	6	DK
106	There is an established process to determine key work system (and process) requirements incorporating input from the workforce, customers, suppliers, partners, and collaborators.	1	2	3	4	5	6	DK

BLUEPRINT

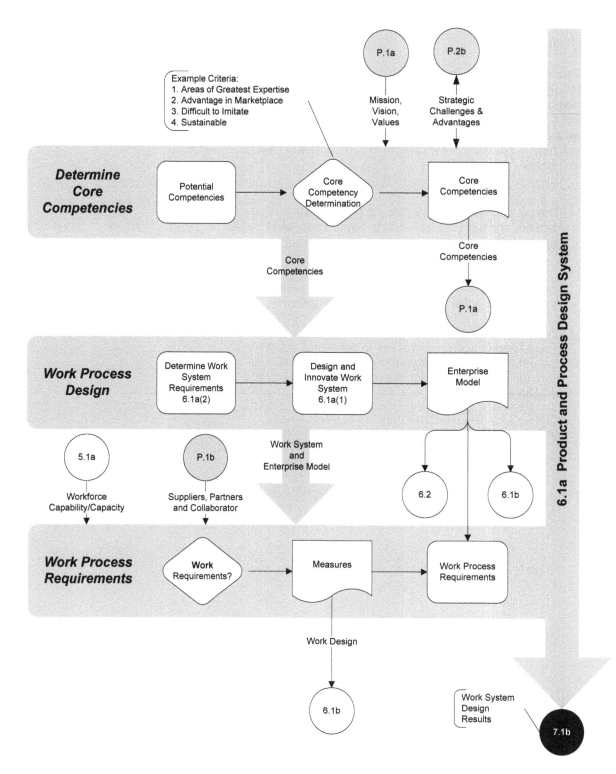

SYSTEM INTEGRATION

Context

P.1a > 6.1a Mission, Vision, Values - The mission, vision, and values of the organization set the parameters of organization operations and products and services. This is an important input to the identification of core competencies which should be consistent with the mission, vision, values of the organization. If the core competencies are not consistent with the mission, the organization has two choices - adjust the mission or the core competencies.

P.1a < 6.1a Core Competencies - The core competencies described in the profile (P.1a) are determined using the process described in 6.1a. The core competencies are also a critical input to the work placement strategy. It is difficult to maintain a competency and the associated competitive advantage if the organization outsources activities associated with the core competency.

P.1b > 6.1a Suppliers, Partners, Collaborators - The suppliers, partners, and collaborators identified in the profile (P.1b) are key inputs to the work placement strategy (6.1a). Core competencies constitute strategic advantage and as such would not be candidates for outsourcing. Where to place work (inside or outside the organization) is directly influenced by the nature of the work, if it is part of a core competency, and the capability and capacity of the suppliers, partners, and collaborators identified in the profile (P.1b).

P.2b > 6.1a Strategic Challenges and Advantages - The identification of core competencies is directly influenced by the strategic challenges and advantages described in the profile (P.2b). By definition, "the organization's core competencies are those strategically important capabilities that provide an advantage in your marketplace or service environment. Core competencies frequently are challenging for competitors or suppliers and partners to imitate, and they provide a sustainable competitive advantage" (NIST 2007 p. 66).

Systems

5.1a > 6.1a Workforce Capability and Capacity - The capability and capacity of the workforce (5.1a) is a key input to the work placement strategy (6.1a).

6.1a > 6.1b Enterprise Model – The enterprise model which depicts key activities and relationships is a key input to the identification of key work processes and their requirements and subsequent design.

6.1a > 6.1b Work Placement Strategy – The work placement strategy (in source v. out source) is a key input to the identification of key work processes and their requirements and subsequent design.

6.1a > 6.2a Enterprise Model – The enterprise model which depicts key activities and relationships is a key input to the design of key work processes and their requirements.

Scorecard

6.1a > 7.1b Work System Design Results - Results that indicate the performance of the organization in areas related to the core competencies and the overall work system design should be reported in 7.1b.

THOUGHTS FOR LEADERS

Product and process design must begin with the customer of the process. It is amazing how many people consider themselves 'process owners' who have never formally met with the process users (or process customers) and asked them what they need from the process.

Even when organizations have documented hundreds of processes they do not attempt to be world-class in all processes.

A small number of those processes may actually drive the organization's overall competitiveness. These directly feed what the CPE call the core competencies. These processes might impact the organization either externally or internally. They may interface with the external customer or drive the delivery of the products and services that influence the external customer's future behavior. For example, only a few processes may interface with the organization's external customers, but these processes need to be world-class. In fact, some organizations sit down with their customers every year and redefine the key customer-facing processes, and assess the current effectiveness of those processes. They feel that process excellence and process improvements must be driven by what the customer cares about.

Customer-focused processes may even need to be re-certified each year. This procedure ensures that the process in question is capable of delivering the desired output and is in-control because the customer says the organization needs to "be really good at" these processes. Internally, organizations assess which processes drive their quality, schedule, and/or cost, and they will improve these processes first.

A Lighter Moment:

> *Life was simple before World War II.*
> *After that, we had systems.*
>
> G. Hopper

> *Real success is finding your lifework in the work that you love.*
>
> **David McCullough**

FOUNDATION

This part of the CPE assumes that the key work systems have been identified (2.1a) and have been designed (6.1a), and those work process have been focused on the core competencies of the organization. The question is asked in 6.1b is "How are the work systems managed and improved?"

Process Implementation

The Stadium Chart (See the *Foundation* section in Area 6.1a – an example from PRO-TEC, or the Sharp HealthCare example, below) should show the systems, how they relate to each other, how they leverage the core competencies and how they delivery customer value. This presupposes that the creation and delivery or customer value is aligned with the key work systems which drive the achievement of the core competencies. Once the alignment of systems to delivering customer value is established, the systems must also drive profitability and sustainability as well as overall organizational success.

How do you ensure that the work systems are managed and improved to deliver customer value and organizational success as defined by the multiple stakeholders? Organizational success implies that the organization is sustainable – economic, societal and environmental. A high performing organization must be high performing in all three areas.

Support Processes

The Stadium Chart (See the *Foundation* section in Area 6.1a, or the definition for the Enterprise Systems Model – ESM – in the Glossary) should show the systems, how they relate to each other, how they leverage the core competencies and how they deliver customer value.

The systems which drive customer value are work systems (or key work systems), but these must be supported by at least two other types of systems. Systems that Guide (Guidance Systems – in the Glossary) and systems that Support (Support Systems – in the Glossary). These are not described by the Criteria for Performance Excellence (CPE), but are key to understanding the organization and an enterprise-wide view of the interrelationship of all systems. All systems are supported by lower-level processes. The support systems are supported by support processes, which the CPE does ask about.

The CPE ask how you 1) determine your key support processes, what are they, 2) their requirements, and 3) how you ensure that you meet their requirements on a daily basis. This is achieved by 1), and 2) working with the customer of the system to define the requirements, measures and deliverables, and 3) by tracking the metrics to ensure that they are being achieved (output measures) and that the processes are in-control (in-process measures).

Product and Process Improvement

In the Organizational Profile (P2c) a question was asked: "What are the key elements of the organization's performance improvement system, including the evaluation and learning process?" This question feeds directly into Area to Address 6.1b(3), which asks how you improve your work processes to improve your work processes to improve products and performance and reduce variation. Better performance can include both continuous improvement and breakthroughs (see Area 6.2d) and can be improvement in any aspect of the organization. Typical areas for improvement include cost, cycle time, variation, schedule, and quality.

The improvements in the processes, however, should be improvements that the customer or the stakeholders of the process (internal and external) value. As discussed earlier, all processes should have Process Owners – somebody who is responsible for the caretaking and improvement of the process. Also, the Process Owners should have the responsibility to define, measure, stabilize and improve the process. In improving the work processes, specific tools should be used. This does not mean that the organization must use only one improvement tool. Where several tools are used, however, it should be clear where and why each tool is used.

To drive these improvements, there should be input from the users of the output from the process. Where conditions change, or where the user wants a change in the output, the process improvement should be responsive to those differences and keep the process current with the changing needs. Finally, where improvements are achieved, there should be a systematic process to understand who could learn from this improvement, and to ensure that the improvement is understood by those individuals or groups. Some high-performing organizations also track the value of the improvements made in this manner.

 EXAMPLES

Don Chalmers Ford (Baldrige Site Visit 2008 and 2012)

At DCF it's real simple: the key work systems are sales and service. Management is accomplished by documentation of the key work processes that are aligned (Figure 6.2-1) and found on-line in the Process manual for deployment to the workforce. These are segmented by Customer groups for easy access. Improvement inputs take place from constant review of stakeholder input from customer listening methods (Figure 3.1-1) and the performance analysis reviews (Figure 4.1-4) to deliver customer value (VOC), achieve organizational success (key success drivers) and sustainability (cycles of improvement).

The FORD Process (Figure P.2-4) is used to guide improvements as necessary.
6.1b(2) Cost Control Requirements for key work systems are determined by listening to employees, suppliers, partners, collaborators, and customers who utilize and benefit from the system outcomes. These requirements are reviewed by the process owner for possible cost and integration into the process design, then analyzed for their relationship to the key success drivers and cost impact to implement or improve the system. If the need is critical, a cost benefit analysis is performed and the decision is made from the analysis.

DCF has processes in sales and service for preventing and minimizing defects, service errors and rework and minimizing warranty costs (Figure 6.1-3). Minimizing the costs of inspections, tests and process or performance audits is accomplished by using members of the DCF workforce. Example: the safety committee provides a proactive approach to fire prevention through walk-arounds of the facilities to assess possible safety issues or violations. Fire inspections are performed at a minimum annually by the

478

Rio Rancho Fire Department, and the Delivery Manager is a retired Battalion Fire Chief. Audits for protecting the privacy of customer information are done by the DPE at least monthly. The GM audits D-plans to ensure proper documentation is in the deal. In areas like finance and insurance, process discipline 3rd party audits are preferred to ensure objectivity and the cost is value added.

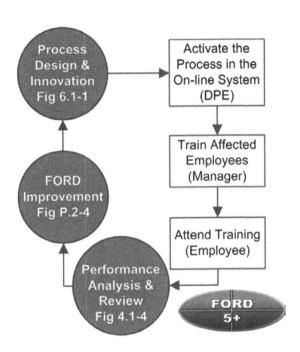

Sharp Healthcare (Baldrige Recipient 2007)

Workforce capability and capacity are assessed through a systematic workforce planning and Sharp's core competency is transforming the health care experience through The Sharp Experience, which drives the activities of the organization from strategic planning down to individual goal-setting along the Six Pillars. The core competency is determined and critically evaluated through the SWOT analysis during the Strategic Planning Process. Directly related to Sharp's Vision, the core competency is the enabling strategy for Sharp to be the best place to work, practice medicine, and receive care. It is this cultural transformation that has delivered success across the Pillars and differentiated Sharp from its competitors. It also has driven the gains in market share Sharp has enjoyed for the past three years.

Sharp designs and innovates its work systems through the Value Creation Process (Figure 6.1-1). Sharp's work systems connect the health care services delivered and the management and support processes, providing the resources, supplies, and support to enable successful health care delivery. The design process begins with the identification of a health care service need, business opportunity, or support process need, through the Strategic Planning Process using listening and learning tools. With a need identified, customer/stakeholder requirements are solicited, outputs determined, a work system is mapped, inputs identified, and suppliers/partners and resources determined.

Evidence of this systematic work system design is seen in joint venture initiatives, new clinical program, such as Bariatric care, and other examples available onsite. Work systems link to key work processes as shown in Figure 6.1-2. Each work system contains all of the key work processes. Performance of the sub-processes for these key work processes is measured.

Key work processes that are central to Sharp's core competency are determined and re-evaluated during the Strategic Planning Process. The decision-making regarding the use of internal systems versus external resources is made through the Strategic Planning Process using the Outsource Decision Process.

Value Creation Process 6.1-1

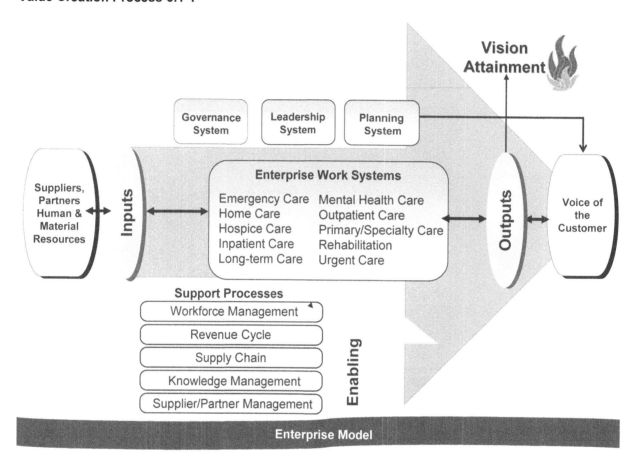

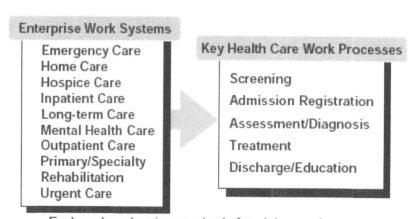

Each work system is comprised of each key work process.

Figure 6.1-2 Work System/Process Linkage

Source: Sharp Healthcare

480

Richland College (Baldrige Recipient 2005)

Richland College (RLC) has learning-centered processes that directly interface with students and accomplish their Mission and Purpose. RLC has identified three key student-learning processes and 7 well-defined student service processes; a list appears in *Figure 6.1A shown below*. Defining and focusing on these key processes enables the prioritization of resources for use in areas of greatest impact.

These processes create value for the college because RLC 1) focuses them on performance in areas important to student and organizational success and 2) aligns them to KPIs.

These processes create value for students and other stakeholders because they enable RLC to meet and exceed requirements and expectations. For example, a key student, regulatory, and community requirement is that education be accessible. To create strong value for these stakeholders, RLC has a convenient location, affordable course offerings, effective advising, and appropriate developmental education. Expectations exceed the requirements by making quality education available to the diverse community through off-peak hours; self-paced options; and a variety of courses and delivery methods, including classroom instruction, learning labs, learning communities, service learning, academic enrichment, study abroad, distance learning, fast-track scheduling, and transferability. To accommodate students' diverse lifestyles, RLC offers services, such as eConnect, *eCampus*, and Internet access, which even further maximize student success.

A wide spectrum of listening and learning methods are used to determine student educational needs addressed through the learning centered processes. Varying needs are balanced during strategic planning. RLC designs processes to incorporate requirements into programs by directly linking program elements to specific program requirements. Curriculum committees annually review new and revised programs to ensure they are educationally sound and comply with applicable district, state, and accreditation guidelines. Upon completion of program development, the Vice President for Student Learning/CEO validate that the program meets all student and operational requirements.

Key Processes	Process Requirements	Key Measures
Student Learning		
Curriculum design approach - separate processed for Credit or Tech-Occ and CE programs	– Appropriate use of learning techniques and technology – Meeting student/stakeholder requirements – Inclusion of regulatory requirements	– Student success for all student groups in credit/CE/Workforce courses (E) – Compliance to requirements (I) – Compliance to requirements (I)
Education delivery to curriculum design	– Meet requirements outlined in curriculum design	– Student success for all student grps (E) – Stakeholder satisfaction (E)
Education effectiveness evaluation and improvement (QEP process)	– Continuously improve success of students – Assess student-learning outcomes	– Student success for all student grps (E) – Stakeholder satisfaction (E)
Student Services		
Advising and	– Correct course placement	– Point of service survey (I) - # transfers (E)

481

Assessment	– Formal articulation agreements – ADA Compliance	– # articulation agrmts (E) – CCSSE and NLSSI results (I)
Financial Aid Application and Awarding	– Government Regulations – High ethical standards & confidentiality – Control measures	– Annual $ disbursed & # serviced (E) – Sources, e.g. PELL (E) – CCSSE and NLSI results (I)
Career Placement	– Accurate career information – Career counseling & exploration – Placement	– Demographics of users (E) – Point of service surveys (I) – NLSSI and CCCSSE results (I)
Admissions and Student Records	– Effective data mgmt system – High ethical standards – Accuracy & timely access – Compliance with guidelines & policies	– FERPA requirements (E) – Comprehensive college catalog (E) – # Degree plan (I) – CCSSE, NLSSI and CQS results (I)
Connecting learners with knowledge	– Timely information access – Responsiveness – Infrastructure currency – Operational efficiency	– # items circulated (E) – # new collections developed (E) – Survey results for, NLSSI, CQS, CCSSE, Point of Service (I)
Safety and Security	– Safe environment – Responsive & Helpful Police Force and Facilities Staff	– CQS and NLSSI results (I) – # campus crimes (E) – # requests for assistance (I)
Student Health Services	– Prompt, friendly basic health services	– CQS and NLSSI results(I) – Point of Service Survey (I) – Number of Students Service (E)

(I) = in –process measure, (E) = end-process measure

Source: Richland College Application Summary

CRITERIA QUESTIONS

In your response, include answers to the following questions:

b. Process Management

(1) **Process Implementation** How does your day-to-day operation of work processes ensure that they meet key process requirements? What key performance measures or indicators and in-process measures do you use to control and improve your work processes? How do these measures relate to end-product quality and performance?

(2) **Support Processes** How do you determine your key support processes? What are your key support processes? How does your day-to-day operation of these processes ensure that they meet key business support requirements?

(3) **Product and Process Improvement** How do you improve your work processes to improve products and performance and reduce variability?

Notes:

6.1b(2). Your key support processes should support your value-creation processes. They might support leaders and other workforce members engaged in product design and delivery, customer interactions, and business and enterprise management.

6.1b(3). To improve process performance and reduce variability, you might implement approaches such as a Lean Enterprise System, Six Sigma methodology, ISO quality system standards, PDCA methodology, decision sciences, or other process improvement tools. These approaches might be part of the performance improvement system you describe in P.2c in the Organizational Profile.

NIST (2015-2016) p. 23

WORKSHEETS

6.1b(1) - Process Implementation

Key Work Systems (Including Key Work Systems In 2.1a[4])	Related Key Work Processes	How Do Your Day-To-Day Operation Of These Processes Ensure That They Meet Key Process Requirements	Key Performance Measures Or Indicators	In-Process Measures	How Do These Measures Relate To End-Product Quality & Performance
1					
2					
n					

6.1b(2) Support Processes

How Do You Determine Your Key Support Processes:

Key Support Processes	How Do Your Day-To-Day Operation Of These Processes Ensure That They Meet Key Business Support Requirements
1	
2	
n	

6.1b(3) - Product and Process Improvement

Key Work Processes	Processes Used To Improve Products and Work Processes			
	To Improve Work Processes	To Improve Products	To Improve Performance	To Reduce Variability

ASSESSMENT

107	Key work processes are implemented to ensure they meet key work system requirements, which come from the work system customer.	1 2 3 4 5 6 DK
108	Support processes are implemented to ensure they meet key process requirements, which come from the support process customer.	1 2 3 4 5 6 DK
109	Key work processes are improved to deliver customer value and to achieve organizational success and sustainability.	1 2 3 4 5 6 DK
110	Work processes are controlled to prevent defects, service errors and rework and to minimize warranty costs or customer productivity losses.	1 2 3 4 5 6 DK

BLUEPRINT

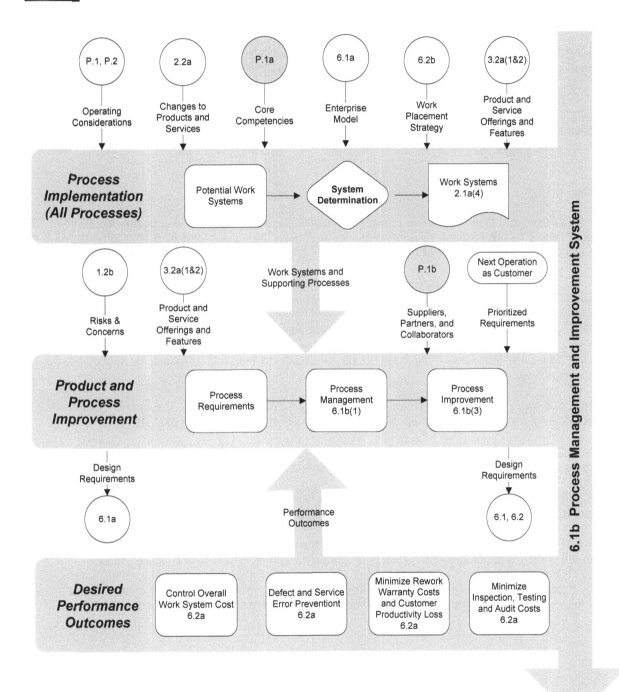

SYSTEM INTEGRATION

Context

P.1a > 2.1 Core Competencies - The organization's core competencies are also an important input to the identification of the key work processes.

P.1b > 6.2b Suppliers, Partners, Collaborators - The suppliers, partners, and collaborators identified in the profile (P.1b) are key inputs to both the requirements determination process a key input into the design of the processes (6.1b). In addition, the suppliers', partners', and collaborators' capabilities and needs should be part of the requirements process to ensure that the supply chain works as an integrated system.

Systems

1.2b > 6.2a Risks and Concerns - The public concerns that are identified in the process described in 1.2b are direct inputs to the process requirements determination step described in 6.1b. Consequently, the output of 1.2b should be in a format that is useful for determining process requirements.

1.2c > P.1, P.2 Operating Considerations - The economic, environmental, and societal considerations identified in 1.2c are inputs to the identification of key work processes and their initial requirements.

2.2a > 6.1a Change to Products and Services - Action plans often call for additions, changes, and improvement to products and services, and the design of the key work processes that create them. In this case, the key work processes may need to be refined or redesigned to assist in accomplishing the strategic objectives.

3.2a(1&2) > 6.1a(2) Product and Service Offerings and Features - Ultimately, the prioritized product and service features are used to identify key work process requirements described in 6.1b.

4.2a < 6.1b Design Requirements - The work process design requirements identified during the processes described in 6.1b are inputs to the knowledge system for use throughout the organization.

6.1a > 6.1b Enterprise Model - The enterprise model which depicts key activities and relationships is a key input to the identification of key work processes and their requirements and subsequent design.

6.1a > 6.1b Work Placement Strategy - The work placement strategy (in source v. out source) is a key input to the identification of key work processes and their requirements and subsequent design.

6.1b > 6.2a Design Requirements - The key requirements determined by the work process and requirements process (6.1b) are key inputs to the design of work processes described in 6.2a.

Scorecard

6.1b > 7.1b Key End of Process Results - The results related to the key process requirements (levels, trends, comparisons) should be presented in area 7.1a. These measures include those characteristics most important to the customers' buying decisions or in other words the "proxies" for customer purchase and satisfaction. The measure included here are often characteristics such as timeliness, quality (defects), reliability, etc.

6.1b > 7.1b Key In Process Results - In addition to the outputs the efficiency and effectiveness of the process is determined through in-process measures. The results (levels, trends, comparisons) for key in-process and control measures should be included in the results displayed in area 7.1b. Just as the product and service results are predictors of customer satisfaction, the operational including in-process results are predictors of the product and service results.

THOUGHTS FOR LEADERS

Every leader who wants repeatable results should drive process management in their organization. Without a clear process which is defined, measured, stabilized, and improved, the organization is at the mercy of each employee's desire and talent, rather than being able to systematically drive consistency and drive out variation. If you only have one defect per million, what do you say to that *millionth customer?*

Area 6.1a discussed the design. This Area discusses the implementation of those processes within each of the systems. Both have to be defined, measured, stabilized, and improved.

In both instances the requirements must come from the customers of those systems and processes and in both cases they need to be managed for improvement. In both cases they should be aligned to the organizational core competencies. That is the only way leaders can be certain that the work being performed in the organization is helping the organizational performance in the eyes of the customer.

Finally, improvement! High performing organizations are tough on themselves and ~~strive~~ drive to be better. Organizations who 'do not have problems' are in very deep trouble. They have problems, but they do not know what they are and are not systematically fixing them.

A Lighter Moment:

Hard work never killed anybody, but why take a chance?

Edgar Bergen

> *Great leaders make it safe for others to innovate.*
>
> **Jorge Barba**

 FOUNDATION

The criteria itself (not including the notes and other portions of the criteria booklet) mentions innovation 11 times as follows:

Organizational Profile
    P.1b(3) Suppliers and Partners
    P2a(2) Competitiveness Changes

Category 1 - Leadership
    1.1a(3) Creating a Successful Organization
    1.1b(2) Focus on Action

Category 2 – Strategic Planning
    2.1a(2) Innovation

Category 4 – Measurement, Analysis, and Knowledge Management
    4.1c(3) Continuous Improvement and Innovation
    4.2a(1) Knowledge Management

Category 5 – Workforce Focus
    5.2a(4) Performance Management
    5.2b(1) Learning and Development System

Category 6 – Operations Focus
    6.1c Innovation Management ----------------------→ **This Area To Address**

Category 7 - Results
    7.1b(1) Process Effectiveness and Efficiency

Few, if any other topics are addressed so frequently in the Criteria for Performance Excellence (CPE). When discussed with the Baldrige Office, they have stated that **innovation is both a process and a culture**. This dichotomy is clearly reflected in the criteria. This Area to Address (6.2d) describes innovation as a culture (What is your process to <u>manage</u> innovation), and other parts of the CPE address it as a process (Area 4.2a[1] – where it states *'assemble and transfer relevant knowledge for use in your innovation and strategic planning processes?'*).

The CPE asks how you manage innovation and how do they come from the strategic opportunities, which are analyzed to determine the appropriate risks (called intelligent risks). Once a potential innovation is identified, the CPE asks how you make the appropriate resources available.

All innovations, strategic opportunities, and risks need to be effectively vetted to ensure that they are reasonable.

 EXAMPLES

Generic Example – Innovation At All Levels

Leaders at all levels need to be aware of:

- Internal customer's requirements of their group
- External customer's requirements of their group
- Their role/impact on the strategic planning process
- Knowledge they need or can share
- Industry best practices and benchmarks
- Functional best practices and benchmarks

They then need to determine (for their function, department, or span of influence):

- The level of change needed
- The rate of change the organization can accept
- The previous blind spots which, if unaddressed, can hurt them or the organization
- The level of innovation needed
- The level of agility needed
- The checks, balances, measures, practices, which should be introduced
- The plan for introduction

Once they have determined and planned the changes needed, if the changes are within their cost and action level of authority, they can design and implement the changes. If they are not within their cost and action level of authority, they can submit the innovations into the next year's planning cycle for consideration and/or approval.

A graphical depiction of this cycle is as follows:

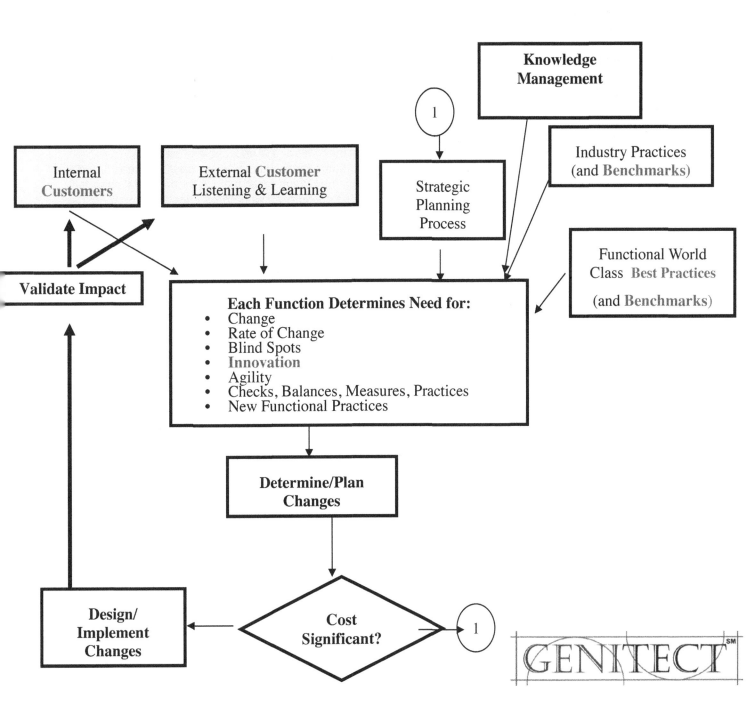

Generic Example – Based on The Baldrige Definition of Innovation

Definition:

> **Innovation**: Making meaningful change to improve products, processes, or organizational effectiveness and create new value for stakeholders. Innovation involves adopting an idea, process, technology, product, or business model that is either new or new to its proposed application. The outcome of innovation is a discontinuous or breakthrough change in results, products, or processes. Innovation benefits from a supportive environment, a process for identifying strategic opportunities, and a willingness to pursue intelligent risks.
>
> Successful organizational innovation is a multistep process of **development** and **knowledge sharing**, a **decision to implement**, **implementation**, **evaluation**, and **learning**. Although innovation is often associated with technological innovation, it is applicable to all key organizational processes that can benefit from change through innovation, whether breakthrough improvement or a change in approach or outputs. Innovation could include fundamental changes in an organization's structure or business model to accomplish work more effectively.

This indicates that the process for innovation should have the following steps:

1. Development
2. Knowledge Sharing
3. Decision to Implement
4. Implementation
5. Evaluation
6. Learning

Charleston Area Medical Center (The Partnership For Excellence Recipient 2014)

Our Innovation System and Environment to Support Innovation describe our process for determining if we have a gap in our services or a strategic opportunity. Using our gap decision criteria, we determine if our Process improvement (PI) process will address the gap or if a discontinuous or breakthrough change is needed.

We use the DMAIC process to review and manage both PI and innovations. We pursue the strategic opportunities we determine are intelligent risks through the 5 steps in Figure 6.2-2. We review financial and other resource needs in and resource in . Following implementation, we monitor results against the gap decision criteria and outcome targets.

If targets are not met, DMAIC is used for improvement and if improvement is not achieved the innovation is reviewed to determine if it should be discontinued to enhance support for a higher priority opportunity.

Figure 6.2-2 Innovation Management

WHO	Based on organizational level decision making group (Figure 2.1-4)				
WHAT	❶ Decision to Innovate vs. PI	❷ Validate need Determine approach Approval for innovation	❸ Figure 2.1-5 (8) Test Strategic Opportunity based on Intelligent Risk Criteria Resource	❹ Approval for pilot or fully deploy	❺ 1. Stable/Scale Up 2. Improve 3. Discontinue if not meeting gap decision criteria (Figure 2.1-5 (5))
HOW	Figure 2.1-5 (6)(7b)	Intelligent risk assessment Align with Enterprise System (Figure 6.1-1)	Develop detailed plan with outcome targets and resource needs identified.	Roll out plan and resource	Knowledge sharing – successes or improvement to process

CRITERIA QUESTIONS

In your response, include answers to the following questions:

c. Innovation Management

How do you manage for innovation? How do you pursue the strategic opportunities that you determine are intelligent risks? How do you make financial and other resources available to pursue these opportunities? How do you discontinue pursuing opportunities the appropriate time to enhance support for higher priority opportunities.

Notes:

6.1c. Your innovation management process should capitalize on strategic opportunities identified in 2.1a(2).

NIST (2015-2016) p. 23

WORKSHEETS

6.1c – Innovation Management

How You Manage Innovation:

How You Pursue The Strategic Opportunities That You Determine Are Intelligent Risks: *

* - This should include your criteria or process for identifying and assessing intelligent risks.

How You Make Financial And Other Resources Available To Pursue These Opportunities:

How You Discontinue Pursuing Opportunities At The Appropriate Time To Enhance Support For Higher Priorities:

ASSESSMENT

111	We have a process / methodology through which we ensure that innovation is guided and used.	1	2	3	4	5	6	DK
112	Process owners must ensure that their processes have both incremental and breakthrough improvement.	1	2	3	4	5	6	DK
113	The methodology to achieve breakthroughs is clearly defined and is taught to the appropriate employees.	1	2	3	4	5	6	DK
114	Improvements are systematically shared with all individuals and organizations that can learn from the process improvement.	1	2	3	4	5	6	DK

BLUEPRINT – 6.2d

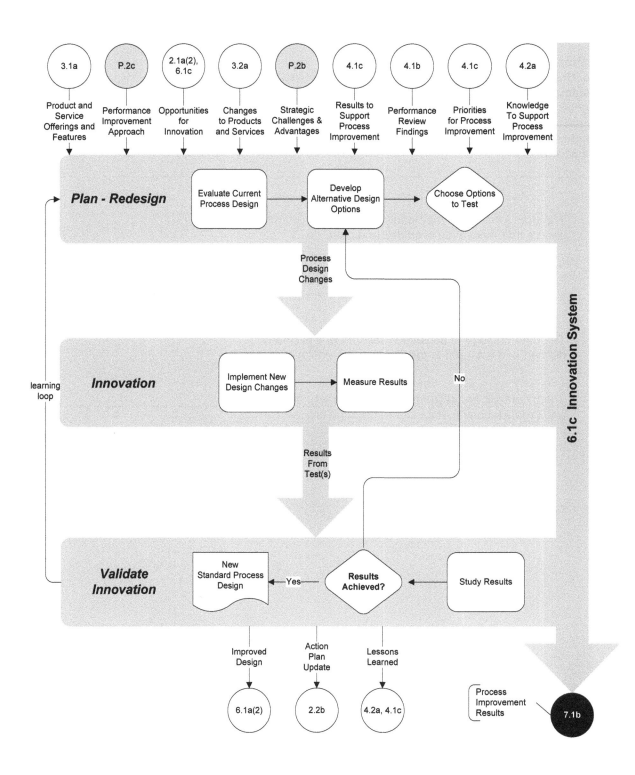

498

SYSTEM INTEGRATION – 6.2d

Context

P.2b > 6.1b(3) Strategic Challenges and Advantages - Most organizations have more opportunities for improvement than they have the resources (time and money) to work on at any given time. Consequently, the priorities for process improvement 6.1b(3) should be influenced by the strategic challenges and advantages identified in the profile P.2b.

P.2c > 6.1b(3) Performance Improvement System - Process improvement methods and approaches described in 6.1b(3) should be consistent with the overall approach to performance improvement described in the profile P.2c.

Systems

2.2a > 6.1b(3) Changes to Products and Services - Action plans often drive the work process improvement agenda and help to focus the process improvement efforts 6.1b(3) on key issues important to achieving the overall organization strategy and action plans described in 2.2a.

2.2a < 6.1b(3) Action Plan Update - Action plans described in 2.2a are updated based on the changes and results achieved through the work process improvement system described in 6.1b(3).

3.2a(1&2) > 6.1b(3) Product and Service Offerings and Features - Changing product and service offerings and features is an important input to the continuous improvement of key work processes that produce and deliver those products and services.

3.2a(3&4) > 6.1b(3) Opportunities for Innovation - The analysis of customers data is used in 3.2a(3&4) to identify opportunities for innovation that are important inputs to the work process improvement system described in 6.1b.

4.1a > 6.1b(3) Results to Support Process Improvement - The key performance measures identified in 4.1a to support process improvement are important inputs to the process improvement practices described in 6.1b(3).

4.1b > 6.1b(3) Findings - The findings from the performance analysis described in 4.1b directly supports work process improvement by identifying opportunities for improvement.

4.1c > 6.1b(3) Priorities for Process Improvement - The priorities for improvement and actions identified in 4.1c directly support work process improvement described in 6.1b(3).

4.2a > 6.1b(3) Knowledge to Support Process Improvement - The knowledge management system 4.2a ideally contains many best practices and lessons learned to support the improvement of processes of all type throughout the organization.

4.2a < 6.1b(3) Lessons Learned - The lessons learned from work process improvement efforts and experiences in 6.1b(3) are important inputs to the process of identifying best practices for inclusion into the organization's knowledge base 4.2a.

6.1b(3) < 6.1b(3) Improved Design - New and improved process designs are the output of the process improvement methods described in 6.1b(3). The improved processes are implemented, managed, and measured using the methods described in 6.2b(1&2).

Scorecard

6.2b > 7.1b(1) Process Improvement Results - Work process improvements that result in the improvement of the products and services should be reported in 7.1a.

6.2b > 7.1b(1) Process Improvement Results - Process improvement results including cost reductions should be included in the results presented in 7.1b. These support process cost reductions are often in important part of the contribution to profit and are often viewed together with process, product, and service quality to gain a system perspective.

Note: The results determine the difference between process change and process improvement.

 # THOUGHTS FOR LEADERS

There is a significant difference between human error, at risk behavior, and reckless behavior.

- **Human error** may never be preventable in all instances, even though we can try to mistake-proof our activities.

- **At risk behavior** can be corrected by helping the person understand the consequences, and redirecting their focus toward the steps and discipline of doing it *the right way* (or using the approved methods) on a consistent basis.

- **Reckless behavior** can be an individual who knows the right way to do something, and ignores the discipline of doing it right by choice.

Leading innovation means you must recognize that all types of behaviors exist, and as a leader you must role-model the need to innovate, and protect those who take reasonable risks. This also means you teach what are/are not reasonable risks. If someone repeatedly choses to exhibit reckless behavior and will not accept the practices necessary to reduce the risk, then a leader must determine if they still fit in the organization.

Although the 2013 – 2014 CPE calls out innovation 14 times (as noted above), it basically boils down to a few organizational perspectives:
- **Is status quo acceptable?**
  - If it is, people will not be motivated to innovate.
- **Do you have a process or analytical capability to determine what is an acceptable (or well thought out) risk?**
  - If it is not, people will not analyze the risks they take in sufficient detail to ensure that they are taking intelligent risk.
- **Is taking acceptable (or well thought out) risk safe?**
  - If it is not, people will not be foolish enough to innovate. A subset of this is:
    - Do people know what approach to use to change?
    - Can we move quickly to change?
    - Can we quickly prototype changes?
    - Can we learn from mistakes?
    - Can we share successes and the learning from mistakes?
- **Are goals tough?**
  - If they are not, people will not feel they have to innovate to meet their goals.
- **Are goals serious?**
  - If they are not, people will not be motivated to innovate to advance their career.
- **Is there a culture and process used to innovate?**
  - If there is not, people may not know what to do

> ***Opportunity is missed by most people***
> ***because it is dressed in overalls and looks like work.***
>
> **Thomas Edison**

FOUNDATION

Although the criteria focuses heavily on work processes, all systems and processes must be effectively designed, managed (kept under control) and improved. Each of these phases must consider the overall control and outputs, both initially, and long-run.

Cost Control

The work systems, work processes, and the other types of systems and processes (such as those used for Guidance and Support – see the Glossary for definitions) need to be designed to achieve what the customers and the stakeholders of those systems and processes require. This design must include controls on factors such as cycle time, productivity, and other efficiency and effectiveness factors. The overall focus can be described as cost, schedule, and quality. To do this the design and operation of the systems and processes must prevent defects, service errors, and rework.

To minimize warranty costs, customer's productivity losses, inspection/test costs, and process/performance audits, processes and systems need to have in-process measures. Through the tracking of these measures the systems and processes need to be kept in-control.

The Criteria for Performance Excellence (CPE) is non-prescriptive and will never require a specific technique such as Statistical Process Control (SPC), but having short-interval in-process measures are critical to not having to 'inspect-in-quality' after a product or service are provided.

The essence of this portion of the criteria is 'control' not artificially reducing the number of inspectors or audits without a methodology of ensuring the appropriate characteristics are maintained upstream of the outcome measures for the systems or processes.

Furthermore, incorporating cycle time, productivity, cost control and other efficiency and effectiveness factors into the design of the processes, the organization should have the ability to link those characteristics back to the customer listening and learning posts (as described in Item 3.1) to ensure that these flexibility and productivity factors meet customer and/or marketplace requirements.

EXAMPLES

PRO-TEC Coating Company (Baldrige Recipient 2007)

The planning phase of process management utilizes the data and information collected from the market, customers, and competitors. PRO-TEC and its parent companies are closely engaged with customers through programs such as Early Vendor Involvement, Automotive Task Force and the Automotive Technical Center for the development of new products (see Figure 6.1-1).

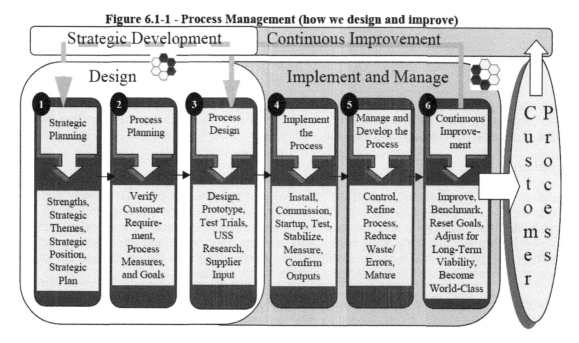

Figure 6.1-1 - Process Management (how we design and improve)

To support new product launches, the product requirements are translated to process requirements. Combining the customer and product requirements along with knowledge and technical experience gained from equipment suppliers, raw material suppliers, and engineering and technical resources from the parent company organizations, the necessary resources are summarized in a requirements document.

Sharp Healthcare (Baldrige Recipient 2007)

The design of Sharp's health care processes stem from customer/partner requirements identified via listening and learning tools. Requirements are communicated to cross-functional teams for review and compliance per:

- Available/new technology,
- Regulatory issues,
- Patient safety,
- Equipment needs,
- Reimbursement,
- Accreditation, and
- Payor restrictions.

A process pilot is launched and measured against standards and process metrics. Feedback is solicited from customer/ partners and incorporated in final implementation. Throughout the design, customer/partner requirements are communicated to and examined by service line providers to ensure quality and compliance outcomes. The health care design process, including the use of multi-disciplinary, cross-functional teams for designing, deploying, evaluating, and improving a process, is applied across the system for any new service line and technology. Validation and transfer are conducted by system cross-functional committees to advance organizational learning across entities (e.g., Diabetes Data Mart).

Source: Sharp Healthcare

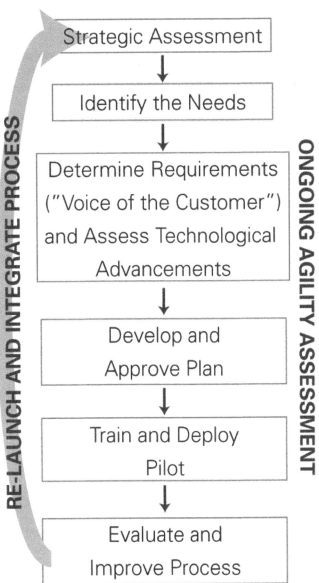

Pewaukee School District (Baldrige Recipient 2013)

Pewaukee School District uses both in-process (leading) and resulting (lagging) measures for our Academic and Support processes to monitor how we are meeting our identified requirements (Figure 6.1-1). Our key work process tools that are implemented on a daily basis are the systematic approach we use to implement our work processes.

We have flowcharted these key work process tools as a way to improve work processes integration and understanding. Student learning is enhanced by the four key Academic work processes. There is strong integration between these four key processes as they are linked by four powerful questions that guide our work in the name of meeting our Mission (Figure P-2):

- Curriculum: What do students need to know and be able to do?
- Instruction: How will students learn what they need to know & be able to do?
- Assessment: How will students demonstrate what they know and can do?
- Intervention/Student Services: How will we respond if students don't learn or if they already know it?

The Teaching & Learning Strategy Area of our SP is our key strategy tool for implementing and innovating our Academic work system in tandem with our Curriculum Review & Design Process (CRDP). Via our CRDP, the Academic value chain begins with the development of curriculum and assessments that meets Wisconsin State Statutes, BOE, and identified stakeholder requirements. The Academic work system delivers value to students and stakeholders by maximizing student learning potential that, in turn, delivers on our Mission while meeting and exceeding regulatory requirements.

There is proof this implementation is working: we have raised ACT scores by a full two points in the past ten years. While we wish that having a high quality curriculum and instruction helps all students learn, we know that students learn at different rates and in differing ways. That is why we have a Student Services process area. This process area is key to making certain that all students' learning needs are supported. Response to Intervention (Rt) is our key work process tool for this. PSD uses evidence-based methods to anticipate and prepare for individual differences in learning, capabilities, rates and styles. Our comprehensive system, best shown in a pyramid proactively and systematically addresses the diverse needs of students. This RtI pyramid (Figure 6.1-2) ensures resources and services are made available for students needing learning assistance. Modifications to student interventions intensify for students not making targeted progress.

During PLC time students in need of assistance are identified by classroom teachers, counselors, and/or administration. Identified students then receive additional and more focused resources and interventions to address specific needs with increasing frequency and intensity in order to see learning results. While interventions may begin with classroom innovations, moving up the pyramid it may include such things as individualized reading tutoring. We seek to exhaust interventions prior to pursuing a special education designation at the upper end of the pyramid. Progress is monitored through tools such as the Individualized Education Plan (IEP) and Differentiated Education Plan (DEP). We view high student achievement evidence of product excellence. To proactively foster excellence in student achievement, SLs and teachers collaborate in a systematic review of student performance data in ongoing PLCs and annual Data Reviews. During teacher PLC time, curriculum, instruction and assessment work processes are modified to meet the needs of students.

As part of our Annual Data Review, teams of teachers and administrators analyze student achievement and stakeholder satisfaction by student segments identified in Figure P-3. This segment analysis has greatly informed SP initiatives and work processes in the District. Programmatic changes, staffing additions and transfers, and professional development are adjusted as a result of this segment analysis. Due to the size of the District, however, it is equally common to analyze the performance of individual students, not just groups of students.

PSD's small size allows us to drill down to a more personalized level. PSD is proactive in using leading data to guide instruction (Figure 6.1-1). MAP results, s which are taken and turned around within a few days/hours, allow classroom instruction to be differentiated more quickly to address specific student needs. Elementary data walls track student reading performance in a visual and powerful way. Processes are reviewed for these measures on AT agendas. Regular performance review meetings are held with contracted service providers to ensure high quality performance.

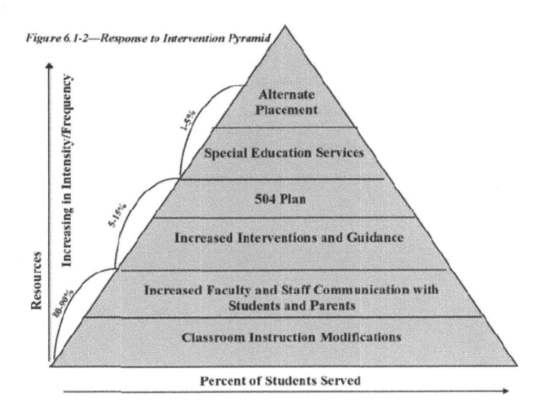

Figure 6.1-2—Response to Intervention Pyramid

CRITERIA QUESTIONS

In your response, include answers to the following questions:

a. Process Efficiency and Effectiveness

How do you control the overall costs of your operations? How do you:
- incorporate cycle time, productivity, and other efficiency and effectiveness factors into your work processes;
- prevent defects, service errors, and rework;
- minimize warranty costs or customers' productivity losses, as appropriate;
- minimize the costs of inspections, tests, and process or performance audits, as appropriate;
- balance the need for cost control with the needs of your customers?

NIST (2015-2016) p. 24

WORKSHEETS

6.2a – Process Efficiency and Effectiveness

Work Processes (Same As Above)	In-Process Measures*	How Do You Incorporate:*			
		Cycle Time	Productivity	Efficiency Factors	Effectiveness Factors

* = These should describe how you use these characteristics to minimize the costs of inspections, tests, and process or performance audits, as appropriate.

Work Processes (Same As Above)	In-Process* Measures	How Do You Prevent:*				
		Defects	Service Errors	Rework	Warranty Costs	Customers' Productivity Losses

* = These should describe how you use these characteristics to minimize the costs of inspections, tests, and process or performance audits, as appropriate.

How You Balance The Need For Cost Control With The Needs Of Your Customers:

507

ASSESSMENT

Rating Scale:

1 - **No Process** in place - We are not doing this
2 - **Reacting to Problems** – We use a basic (primarily reactive) process
3 - **Systematic Process** – We use a systematic process that has been improved
4 - **Aligned** – We use a process that aligns our activities from top to bottom
5 - **Integrated** – We use a process that is integrated with other processes across the organization
6 - **Benchmark** – We are the Benchmark in our industry or beyond!
DK - Don't Know

115	Cycle time, productivity, and other efficiency and effectiveness factors are incorporated in the design and operation of work and other processes.	1 2 3 4 5 6 DK
116	Work and other process defects, service errors, and rework are minimized through the use of effective in-process controls.	1 2 3 4 5 6 DK
117	Costs of inspections, tests, and process performance audits are minimized through the use of effective in-process controls.	1 2 3 4 5 6 DK

BLUEPRINT

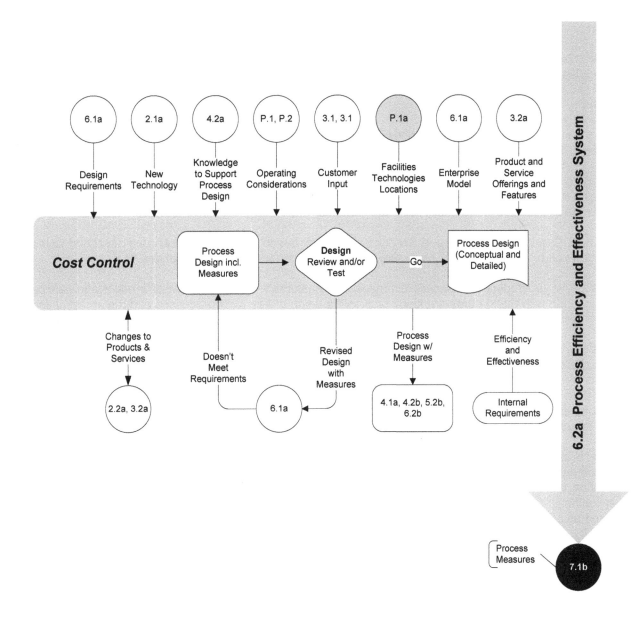

SYSTEM INTEGRATION

Context

P.1a > 6.2a Facilitates, Technologies, Locations - The facilities (type, layout, etc.) along with the technologies and locations are key inputs to the design of the work processes.

Systems

1.2c > 6.2a TBL Operating Considerations - The economic, environmental, and societal considerations identified in 1.2c are inputs to the work process design process 6.2a.

2.1a > 6.2a New Technologies - The new technologies identified as part of the strategy development process (2.1a) are important inputs to the process design process in 6.2a. Design processes should consider the capabilities of the most recent technologies when designing processes.

2.2a > 6.2a Change to Products and Services - The changes to products and services described in the action plans often require the work processes to be redesigned to support the changes.

3.2a(1&2) > 6.2a Product and Service Offerings and Features - The description of product and service offerings along with the features are key inputs to the deign of key work processes and the identification of key areas for process control to ensure the work processes produce the desired results.

3.2a(3&4) > 6.2a Customer Input - Ultimately, the prioritized product and service features 3.2a(3&4) are used to design key work processes so that they produce the desired results.

4.1a < 6.2a Process Measures - The selection and alignment of key performance measures for daily operations and process management (4.1a) is driven by the key process requirements and the in-process control requirements identified in the work process design process described in 6.2a.

4.2a <> 6.2a Knowledge to Support Process Design - Organizational knowledge from the knowledge management systems described in 4.2a is an important input to the design of processes (6.2a). This connection allows the organization to take advantage of and leverage knowledge throughout the organization. In addition, lessons learned during the design and development of processes should be captured as part of the knowledge management system.

4.2b < 6.2a Process Designs with Measures - The work processes designs resulting from the methods described in 6.2a are important inputs to the design of the information system that supports those processes.

5.2c < 6.2a Process Designs - The design of work processes is an important input to the workforce development needs assessment. In addition, new designs or redesigned work processes are also key inputs to the needs assessment process.

6.1a > 6.2a Enterprise Model – The enterprise model which depicts key activities and relationships is a key input to the design of key work processes and their requirements.

6.1b > 6.2a Design Requirements - The key requirements determined by the work process and requirements process (6.1b) are key inputs to the design of work processes described in 6.2a.

510

6.2a > 6.2b Revised Design with Measures - The main output of the design process (6.2a) includes redesigned processes with the associated measures and management controls. These are key inputs to the management of processes described in 6.2b.

6.2a < 6.2b Doesn't Meet Requirements - Once the process is deployed (6.2b) if it doesn't meet the requirements identified in the design it is sent back to the design process (6.2a) for modifications.

6.2a > 6.2b Process Design with Measures - The design of the processes along with the associated measures (6.2a) are key inputs to the implementation, management, and measurement of the key work processes (6.2b).

Scorecard

6.2a > 7.1a Process Output Measures - The quality of the process design is determined primarily by the quality of the outputs. The output or key final products and services results (levels, trends, comparisons) should be presented in area 7.1a. These measures include those characteristics most important to the customers' buying decisions or in other words the "proxies" for customer purchase and satisfaction. The measure included here are often characteristics such as timeliness, quality (defects), reliability, etc.

6.2a > 7.1b Process Measures - In addition to the outputs the efficiency and effectiveness of the process is determined through in-process measures. The results (levels, trends, comparisons) for key in-process and control measures should be included in the results displayed in area 7.1b. Just as the product and service results are predictors of customer satisfaction, the operational including in-process results are predictors of the product and service results (7.1a).

THOUGHTS FOR LEADERS

Every process should have the requirements for the process defined by the customer of that process. Some of these customers are external and some are internal. When leaders meet with process owners they should ask questions such as:

- How did you establish the requirements for your process? (they should have met with the process user)
- How did you establish the performance levels for the process? (they should have met with the process user)
- How and how often do you track the process performance?
  - Who's scorecard has these measures?
- How and how often do you meet with the process user to review the performance?
- What improvements have you made?
  - Show me the quantitative results of your improvements.
  - What improvements are you currently working on? (it should be unacceptable to not have ongoing improvements)
  - What is a process breakthrough you need that you have not been able to achieve?
- Who have you learned from? (knowledge management)
  - Show me the quantitative impact of what you have learned.
- Who learns from you? (knowledge management)
  - Show me the quantitative impact of what they have learned from you.

The answers to these types of questions can give a leader a very quick assessment of whether the process management is being used, and whether the process being discussed is being effectively defined, measured, stabilized and/or improved.

The processes, if effectively managed, should meet the customer of the processes' requirements. Short-term this means meet their initial requirements. Longer-term it means controlling and improving factors such as cycle time, productivity, and other efficiency and effectiveness factors.

> *A Lighter Moment:*
>
> ### *I used to work in a fire hydrant factory.*
> ### *You couldn't park anywhere near the place.*
>
> **Steven Wright**

> *To the degree one company integrates its supply chain better, and continuously improves it more rapidly than its competitors. . . It creates a competitive advantage for itself and the entire chain.*
>
> **Mike Katzorke**

 FOUNDATION

This area asks how the organization manages and improves work processes including the supply chain. The way the supply chain processes are planned, managed and improved should be as rigorous as if they were internal.

Once the internal and external processes are designed and aligned to the work systems, the question is, how does the organization implement the processes to ensure that all key customer and stakeholder requirements are met? How does the organization ensure that the work processes are stable? This refers to minimizing costs associated with inspection - if the processes are in-control then they do not have to be inspected as often. In addition, to keep the processes current the processes should be able to incorporate new technology, new organizational knowledge (through knowledge management), and the level of agility or innovation required by the customers or by the marketplace.

As with the controls in Item 6.1, they need to be extended to the supply base. Although some organizations do not rely on suppliers to a significant degree, most organizations cannot thrive without a healthy supply chain feeding them.

As one leader stated: "You no longer compete *company-to-company*, you compete *supply chain-to-supply chain*."

Supply-Chain Management

The CPE asks how you manage your supply chain. This is an area that over the years has gone in and out and in and out of the criteria over the years. For some organizations the supply chain is pivotal to even short-term sustainability. For other organizations it is not as significant and does not need to be as robustly addressed. Where a robust supply chain is critical to an organization the following questions should be answered:

- How do you appropriately include your supply-chain in your strategic planning process?
  - This is key since plans must be supported by the suppliers.
- How you determine when to buy and when to make?
- How you qualify the supplier and determine who to buy from?
- How do you track supplier performance?
- How you help suppliers improve their performance?
- What do you do if a supplier is performing poorly?

EXAMPLES

Tata - Commercial Vehicle Business Unit

The Tata Motor's Commercial Vehicle Business Unit (CVBU) approach to enterprise process management (EPM) was initiated five years ago. The idea was to map all 19 key level one (i.e. business level) processes in the organization and to flow-down the mapping to the lower-level processes. Additionally, systematic process management manual was developed. The EPM process manual was designed to help the process owners establish the processes and driving the use of process management.

After using process management for one more than a year, CVBU improved the business processes based on benchmarks and external assessment feedback. In 2002-03, they decided to map down to the level two processes. This time they assigned all of CVBU's external (Baldrige-type) assessors to work with each process owner for mapping the 90+ level two processes. This proved to be great success. It brought clarity in process management. In the same year they aligned and integrated the third level of processes.

Now there is a standard practice that every year (mostly in the November – January timeframe) a Process Owner revisits their process based on: 1) the key performance indicators performance (KPIs); 2) key performance measures (KPMs) performance; 3) business needs; and 4) requirements of Process Users. This best practice helps to focus on 'running the organization on processes' and minimize the 'influence of individual employees' in running the operations. In other words, this helps to make the organization 'process-centric.' Another important aspect was that through documenting the processes a lot of clarity emerged in terms of roles and responsibilities of the process owners, inputs & outputs, in-process & end-process measures, and in process-user interfaces. This approach to EPM has also helped in picking up the right measures.

Integration of all levels of processes and procedures, and BSC / SQDCM (Safety/Quality/Delivery/ Cost/Morale) measures creates a 'birds-eye-view' picture of the process driven organization. EPM is a graphical representation of the entire business on one page. This was linked to the existing procedures and work instructions (in all departments) by recognizing that process management was being driven 'top-down' and the lower-level procedures were supportive of each of the processes. An Organizational Process Pyramid was crafted which conceptually described the overall Process Management approach from the strategic (process levels 1, 2, 3) down to the operating level (detailed work instructions, policies and procedures.

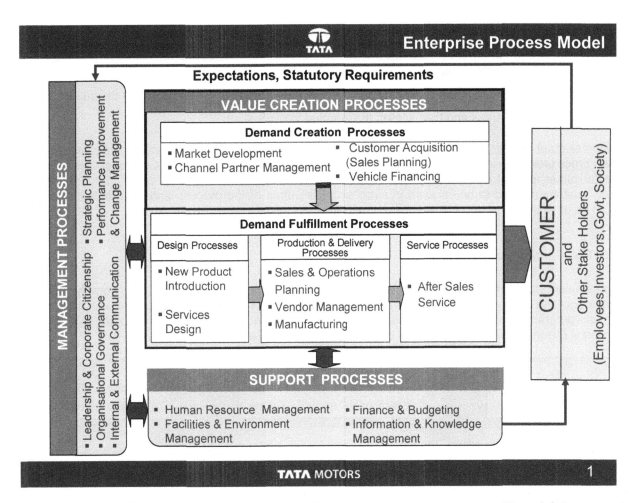

Being a multi-location organization, engaged in the design, manufacture and selling of full range of commercial vehicles in domestic and International markets, process management has very significant relevance. They have always been process-driven in the manufacturing and in the recent past of four years have become process driven through out all business processes.

The Enterprise Process Model (EPM) is the framework used to identify and show the interconnections of the organization's top-level processes. The level 1 EPM consists of 19 business processes and level 2 has 90+ processes. With the EPM established, the key value-creation processes and support processes were determined to be different process families. The criteria for this determination include: 1) which processes have external customers; 2) which processes contribute most directly to the products and services required by external customers.

EPM helps to ensure that the organization addresses all aspects of the business. As you break each process box of EPM down to more details (to levels 2 or 3), you deploy the ownership of process design, management and improvement down the organization. EPM has also helped to fully integrate process management at highest level in the organization. As the EPM level 1 is deployed down to level 2 and 3, the EPM process ensures full alignment (i.e. by being linked to the processes above and below it in the EPM model). When the process owners flow their process from the 'suppliers' to the process to the 'customers' of the process, the organization is integrating the process users across CVBU at each level.

The lessons learned, which can be helpful to others include:

- The need to map the organizational processes in a document so that the whole organization understands.

- Establish an easy and simple system which a layman understands.

- Use standard formats.
- Start at the top level processes first. They are not only critical, but difficult to map. They cut across the organization.
- Use Operating managers for mapping the processes and involve them to get the buy-in.

First pilot it out in few areas and then spread the learning to other place.

Customer input is critical for both the initial design of processes, and for the ongoing improvement of those processes. The initial input on what product or service needs to come out of the process (this is true for either internal or external processes) needs to include customer participation. On an ongoing basis, customers need to be involved in assessing the output of the process and what output changes would be of value.

PRO-TEC Coating Company (Baldrige Recipient 2007)

The planning phase of process management utilizes the data and information collected from the market, customers, and competitors. PRO-TEC and its parent companies are closely engaged with customers through programs such as Early Vendor Involvement, Automotive Task Force and the Automotive Technical Center for the development of new products (see Figure 6.1-2).

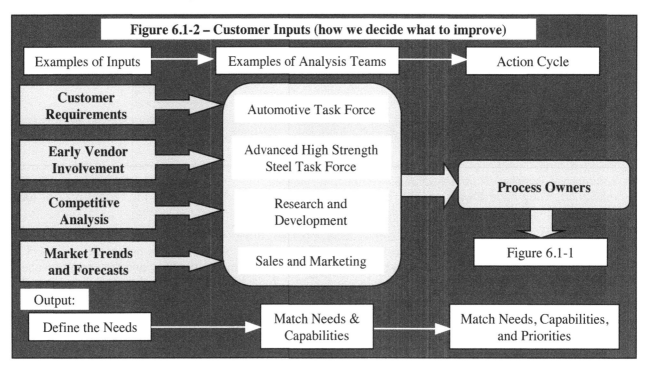

To support new product launches, the product requirements are translated to process requirements. Combining the customer and product requirements along with knowledge and technical experience gained from equipment suppliers, raw material suppliers, and engineering and technical resources from the parent company organizations, the necessary resources are summarized in a requirements document.

Advocate Good Samaritan Hospital (Baldrige Recipient 2010)

Key work processes requirements are determined during the SWOT analysis conducted in Step 3 of the Strategic Planning Process. Data from key listening posts are aggregated by the listening post owners and are utilized by service line leaders and the Executive Team to ensure that appropriate measures are selected and reviewed to support the achievement of plan and manage day-to-day business. These requirements are reviewed in the *Work Process Design Approach. K*ey patient and stakeholder requirements are defined and regulatory requirements and impacts are researched during Steps ❶ and❸. The key process requirements include high quality, safety, timeliness, effectiveness, and efficiency.

Figure 6.1-3 Process Measures

Key Work Process	Process Requirement	Process Measurement	I/O	Results
Patient Access	Timely	Patient satisfaction with wait time in registration	O	7.2-6
	Timely	Patient satisfaction with wait time to noticed arrival	O	7.2-10
	Timely/Safe	ED arrival to triage	I	7.5-13
	Timely/Safe	Patient Satisfaction with Wait time to see MD	O	7.2-10
	Efficiency	Length of Stay	O	7.5-7
	Timely	Central Scheduling abandoned calls	I	7.5-12
Assessment Diagnostic	Effective	Blood cultures prior to antibiotics	I	7.1-18
	High Quality Safe	Code Blue outside CCU/RRT volumes	O	7.1-23
	Effective	MD satisfaction with scheduling diagnostic tests	O	7.5-14
	Safe	OSA screenings to identify high-risk patients	I	7.5-15
	Timely, High Quality, Safe	Average Door to Balloon times	I	7.5-16
Care Delivery / Treatment	High Quality Safe	Risk adjusted mortality, Complications, 30 day Medicare readmissions	O	7.1-6, 10, 15
	Timely	Timeliness of antibiotics <6 hrs for PN patients	I	7.5-18
	Safe	CPOE orders	I	7.5-20
	High Quality	Core Measure Bundles	I	7.1-17
	Timely	Timeliness of VTE prophylaxis in surgical patients	I	7.5-4
	Effective	Cardiac patients 6 a.m. glucose	I	7.5-4
	Effective	Discontinuation of antibiotics within 24 hrs	I	7.5-4
	Effective	PN appropriate antibiotic selection	I	7.5-1
	Efficient	Uptime of electronic medical record	I	7.5-26
	Timely	H&P transcribed within 4 hours	I	7.5-28
	Safe	3rd and 4th degree lacerations	I	7.1-19
	High Quality/ Safe	VAPs , Decubitus Ulcers, Deep Vein Thrombosis, Falls, Bloodstream Infections	O	7.1-22,24, 25,26,27,
	Safe	Overall Hand hygiene	I	7.1-28
	Effective	Patient Sat: Staff worked together to provide care	O	7.2-6
	High Quality	Assoc Sat: Staff provides quality/compassionate care	O	7.4-11
	Safe	Patient Safety Event reporting	I	7.1-21
Discharge	Effective Safe	IP- CHF discharge instructions	I	7.5-22
	Efficient	IP-social worker dc screens with 24 hours of admission	I	7.5-21
	Efficient	Length of Stay vs CMI	O	7.1-14

I = in-process measure; O = outcome measure

Monfort College of Business (Baldrige Recipient 2004)

MCB identifies and manages its key processes for creating student and stakeholder value and maximizing student learning and success using a variety of methods, each grounded in the principle of academic freedom.

MCB's learning-centered processes are determined through its mission, vision, and its shared governance structure. The College's key learning-centered activities include processes for the areas of curriculum, technology, and faculty evaluation. These processes offer the greatest potential for creating student and stakeholder value and impact the delivery of MCB's educational programs. The CC the primary responsibility for managing curriculum processes uses ETS data. The director of technology uses technology survey data to work with the TC to manage the College's technology processes. The ADMC and FAC manage the faculty and staff evaluation processes. Each governance committee uses the Plan-Do-Check-Act (PDCA) process shown in Figure 6.1-1 to plan, control, and improve processes in its respective areas of responsibility. When designing a new process, the plan step is the first step of the cycle. When assessing existing processes, the check step is the beginning point.

Using the CC as an example, in the plan step the CC develops and/or reviews the key process requirements listed in the curriculum process. In the do step, the CC implements new processes and programs such as requiring graduating seniors to take the ETS exam and to complete the EBI surveys. In the check step, the CC reviews ETS and EBI results. In the act step, the CC recommends improvements such as specific curriculum changes (i.e., requiring a second statistics course for all business majors) to better prepare students. The key learning-centered processes, their key requirements, in-process requirements, and assessment measures for each process are shown in Figure 6.1-2.

The curriculum learning-centered processes are managed by the CC using the PDCA process shown in Figure 6.1-1.

In addition, department- and course-level processes (Figure 1.1-2) also provide evaluation and control of the curriculum processes. For example, meeting of curriculum objectives is facilitated through development of course syllabi by faculty. Syllabi are reviewed and updated annually (spring) by department chairs and faculty. These syllabi reinforce the curriculum objectives developed by the CC by specifying how ethical, global, technology, and communication issues are to be covered.

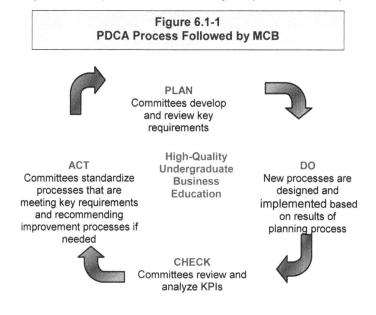

**Figure 6.1-1
PDCA Process Followed by MCB**

PLAN
Committees develop and review key requirements

DO
New processes are designed and implemented based on results of planning process

CHECK
Committees review and analyze KPIs

ACT
Committees standardize processes that are meeting key requirements and recommending improvement processes if needed

High-Quality Undergraduate Business Education

The CC follows an extensive review process for the College's curriculum, in addition to University-mandated program reviews and AACSB evaluation cycles. Reviews range from annual for some CC processes and AACSB progress reports to a five- year cycle for the major AACSB program review.

The evaluation process is managed by the dean, the ADMC, and the FAC, and ensuring that faculty are instructionally current and appropriately qualified to teach the classes they teach. The faculty evaluation process for determining instructional currency and academic or professional qualification is aligned with AACSB guidelines and is consistent with MCB's undergraduate mission. The annual staff evaluation process seeks to assess employee performance levels that align with customer service excellence in knowledge, interpersonal skills, and technical competence. The ADMC is responsible for implementing evaluation processes and for evaluating and improving the staff evaluation process. The FAC is responsible for periodic reviews of the faculty evaluation process and for recommending steps toward improvement. For example, recent EBI Faculty Satisfaction Surveys have indicated a slight decline in faculty satisfaction regarding teaching evaluations. One major 2004 FAC task has been to evaluate the data and make recommendations to improve the teaching evaluation process per the PDCA process.

Figure 6.1-2 Key Learning-Centered Processes, Requirements & Measures			
Learning-Centered Processes	**Key Process Requirements**	**In-Process Measures**	**Measures**
Curriculum	Introduce students to contemporary business knowledge and practice.	• Review of course syllabi	• ETS exam results (7.1-1)
	Provide students a broad understanding of the functional areas of business.	• Review of course syllabi	• ETS exam results (7.1-2)
	Prepare students to recognize ethical dilemmas and make ethical business decisions.	• Minutes of coverage in core by ethical topic • Review of course syllabi by each department	• EBI UG Business Exit Study (7.6-1) • ETS exam results (7.1-2)
	Prepare students to address the unique issues of competing in a global business environment.	• Minutes of coverage in core by global topic • Review of course syllabi by each department	• EBI UG Business Exit Study (7.2-7) • ETS exam results (7.1-2)
	Prepare students to use oral/written communication skills in a business environment.	• Amount & types of oral communication in core • Review of course syllabi by each department	• EBI UG Business Exit Study (7.1-6)
	Provide students with the knowledge of business technology and the opportunity for application.	• Amount & types of technology usage in core • Review of course syllabi by each department	• EBI UG Business Exit Study (7.2-8) • EBI Alumni Survey (7.1-9)
	Introduce students to business information resources and their application.	• Amount & types of info. resources usage in core • Review of course syllabi by each department	• EBI UG Business Exit Study (7.2-9)
	Prepare students to work in a demographically diverse business environment.	• Amount/type of diversity coverage in core • Review of course syllabi by each department	• ETS exam results (7.1-2)
Technology	Provide students with access to a broad array of existing and emerging business technologies.	• Upgrade/replacement schedule in student labs, classrooms, and offices	• EBI UG Business Exit Study (7.2-8, 10, 11) • EBI Faculty Survey (7.4-10)
Faculty Evaluation	Ensure faculty are academically and/or professionally qualified.	• Amount and types of intellectual contributions (i.e., refereed works)	• % academically or professionally. qualified (7.4-1, 2, 5)

Technology is interwoven throughout MCB's curriculum and is a part of its wide-tech strategy. The purpose of the TC is to manage MCB's technology plan and to serve as an intra-college communications network to disseminate information regarding technology. A primary goal of the committee is to anticipate the technology environment MCB graduates are likely to experience on the job. The TC develops the MCB technology plan and reviews the effectiveness of current technology per the PDCA process. As new technological innovations emerge, the TC recommends to the dean and ADMC the innovations MCB should incorporate into its curriculum and learning facilities.

MCB uses educational delivery processes appropriate to the type and level of the class. Many courses, especially at the higher level, are designed to provide hands-on learning in a small class environment with enhanced opportunities for faculty/student interaction. Examples of these classes include the Student and Foundation Fund (SAFF) class (i.e., students manage a UNC Foundation portfolio of over $1 million), small business counseling (students serve as consultants for actual businesses), marketing research (students conduct primary research for businesses like State Farm and Union Colony Bank), and direct marketing (students develop a ready-to-implement strategy each year for a national client such as the New York Times or Toyota as part of a Direct Marketing Educational Foundation program). MCB courses taught on special topics and delivered through its executive professor program are designed to capitalize on an instructional specialty, capability, or a timely topic of interest.

The process also supports additional hands-on educational opportunities such as internships, independent studies, and exchange programs. Last year, the College used distance technology to bring two notable guest speakers into MCB classrooms—Harvey Pitt (one week prior to his stepping down as chair of the Securities & Exchange Commission) and U.S. Representative Michael Oxley (co-sponsor of the Sarbanes-Oxley Act on corporate accountability). Both of these events were made possible through personal contacts by current MCB executive professors.

These processes create value for MCB, its students, and other key stakeholders in the following ways: (1) providing current knowledge and skills to students, (2) enhancing the reputation of MCB, as it receives recognition for its programs and well-prepared graduates, (3) providing increased opportunities for student/faculty interaction, and (4) providing well-qualified business professionals to the Colorado marketplace (more than 80 percent of MCB graduates remain in-state as employees).

These processes aid student educational, developmental, and well-being needs and maximize the potential for student success, based on graduates being well-prepared to enter the business world with the necessary skill sets (i.e., those identified by MCB and its external stakeholders as necessary for success). In addition to business knowledge and skills, students complete a well-rounded educational program with a foundation in general education and the liberal arts—a balanced approach designed to better prepare graduates for future success and promotional opportunities. The curriculum process ensures that students are well prepared to continue their education through graduate programs as well—though graduates are generally encouraged to build a work experience portfolio prior to entering a graduate program. Business student organizations offer individuals the opportunity to participate in extracurricular activities (e.g., visiting speakers, visits to businesses, and regional/national student conferences) that supplement their classroom experiences. Many students serve in leadership positions within these student organizations, providing them with valuable leadership experience. MEPP offers students the ability to work with and learn from experienced executives who have managed organizations of significant size. Executive professors also utilize their personal contacts in the business world to assist students who are initiating their job searches.

Source: Monfort (2005)

CRITERIA QUESTIONS

In your response, include answers to the following questions:

b. Supply-Chain Management

How do you manage your supply chain? How do you:
- select suppliers and ensure that they are qualified and positioned to not only meet operational needs but also enhance your performance and your customers' satisfaction;
- measure and evaluate your suppliers' performance;
- provide feedback to your suppliers to help them improve, and
- deal with poorly performing suppliers?

Note:

6.2b. Feedback to suppliers should involve two-way communication, allowing suppliers to express what they need from you.

NIST (2015-2016) p. 24

WORKSHEETS

6.2b Supply Chain Management

How You Select Suppliers:

Key Suppliers	Process Steps To Manage Key Suppliers	How You Evaluate That They:	
		Are Qualified	Are Positioned To Enhance Your Performance and Customer Satisfaction
•	1		
	2		
	3		
•	4		
	5		
	6		
•	7		
	8		
	n		

How Do You Measure And Evaluate Your Suppliers' Performance:

How Do You Provide Feedback To Suppliers To Help Them Improve:

How Do You Deal With Poorly Performing Suppliers
(including assessment, diagnosis, corrective plan, and termination):

ASSESSMENT

118	We have an effective methodology to use suppliers in the planning process and then deploy plans down to the suppliers.	1	2	3	4	5	6	DK
119	We have an effective methodology to select suppliers and manage their performance to ensure they remain competitive.	1	2	3	4	5	6	DK
120	Poorly performing suppliers are given help to improve, and if they are unable to improve, they are no longer our suppliers.	1	2	3	4	5	6	DK

BLUEPRINT – 6.2b

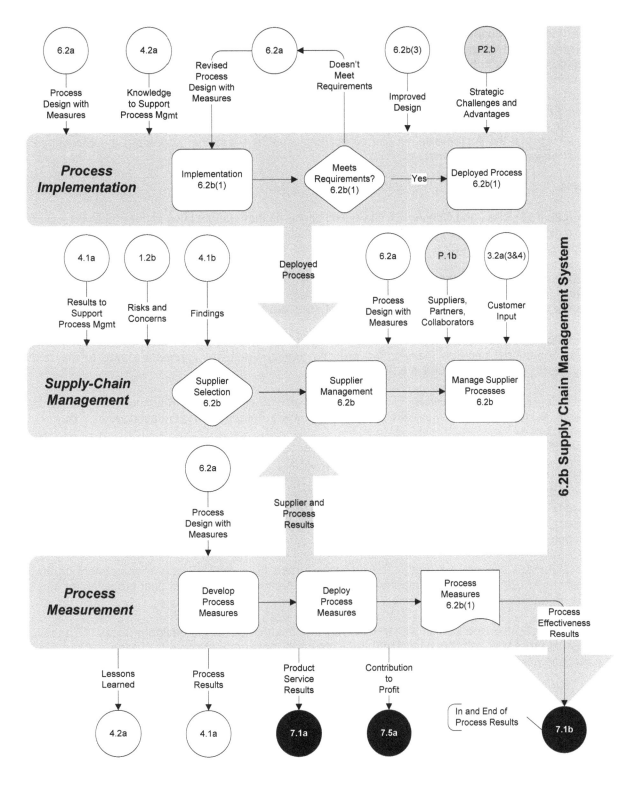

SYSTEM INTEGRATION – 6.2b(1&2)

Context

P.1b > 6.2b(1&2) Suppliers, Partners, Collaborators - Suppliers, partners, and collaborators are often engaged in and an integral part of the work processes. In addition, suppliers, partners, and collaborators are often key inputs to the work process management activities. In fact, they often work side-by-side or even accomplish key tasks by themselves.

P.2b > 6.2b(1&2) Strategic Challenges and Advantages - The strategic challenges and advantages described in the profile P.2b should be considered during process implementation and management 6.2b(1&2) so that the implementation can be accomplished in a way that addresses the challenges and potentially leverages the advantages.

Systems

1.2b > 6.2b(1&2) Risks and Concerns - The public concerns that are identified in the process described in 1.2a should be built into the process management practices and procedures. This helps ensure that the concerns are proactively addressed and problems prevented.

3.2a(3&4) > 6.2b(1&2) Customer Input - The prioritized product and service features 3.2a(3&4) are used to identify key work process control points and practices to ensure the processes produce products and services that produce the desired results and meet the requirements.

4.1a > 6.2b(1&2) Results to Support Process Management - The key performance measures identified in 4.1a for operational decision making and process management are important inputs to the process management practices described in 6.2b(1&2).

4.1a < 6.2b(1&2) Process Results - The results that are derived from the measurement and control of processes as described in 6.2b are direct inputs to the measurement methods described in 4.1a.

4.1b > 6.2b(1&2) Findings - The findings from the performance analysis described in 4.1b directly supports work process management and control 6.2b(1&2).

4.2a > 6.2b(1&2) Knowledge to Support Process Management - Organizational knowledge from the knowledge management systems described in 4.2a is an important input to the management of work processes 6.2b(1&2). This connection allows the organization to take advantage of and leverage knowledge through out the organization.

4.2a < 6.2b(1&2) Lessons Learned - The lessons learned from work process management efforts and experiences in 6.2b(1&2) are an important input to the process of identifying best practices for inclusion into the organization's knowledge base.

6.2a > 6.2b(1&2) Revised Design with Measures - The main output of the design process (6.2a) includes redesigned processes with the associated measures and management controls. These are key inputs to the management of processes described in 6.2b(1&2).

6.2a < 6.2b(1&2) Doesn't Meet Requirements - Once the process is deployed 6.2b(1&2) if it doesn't meet the requirements identified in the design it is sent back to the design process 6.2a for modifications.

6.2a > 6.2b(1&2) Process Design with Measures - The design of the processes along with the associated measures 6.2a are key inputs to the implementation, management, and measurement of the key work processes 6.2b(1&2).

6.2b(1&2) < 6.2b(3) Improved Design - New and improved process designs are the output of the process improvement methods described in 6.2b(3). The improved processes are implemented, managed, and measured using the methods described in 6.2b(1&2).

Scorecard

6.2b > 7.1a Product and Service Results - Ultimately, the test of the effectiveness of process management is the quality of the output. For those processes that produce final products and services that go to the customers the results are reported in 7.1a.

6.2b > 7.1b In and End of Process Results - For processes that produce products and services for internal customers the results should be presented in area 7.1b. These measures include those characteristics most important to the internal customers or in other words the "proxies" for internal customer satisfaction and overall value chain performance. The measures included in 7.1b are often process characteristics such as timeliness, quality (defects), reliability, etc. In addition, the results for key in-process and control measures should be included in the results displayed in area 7.1b. Just as the product and service results are predictors of internal customer satisfaction, the operational including in-process results are predictors of the product and service results.

6.2b > 7.5a Contribution to Profit - The contribution to profit of the key work processes should be reported in 7.5a.

THOUGHTS FOR LEADERS

Leaders who drive their entire business to be competitive also drive the supply chain to be as capable as the internal value creation and support processes. Thus, any internal process owner can rely on their suppliers to improve as all other (internal and external) process owners.

It is typically a sign of organizational maturity when the level of process management for all processes (and suppliers) is at or near the same level of development and capability. In the earlier stages of an organization's journey, supplier processes are often not as well developed as the internal value creation and support processes.

Some leaders do not hold supply chain process owners responsible for the performance of their processes. Additionally, when the supply chain does not deliver, they do not see it as their responsibility to help the supplier improve. If process management is to work, and to benefit the organization, it is critical that process ownership be viewed as a serious responsibility for suppliers as well as for internal process owners. This means that the supplier process owners should be responsible for defining, measuring, stabilizing and improving their processes. If they do not, the organization will not be able to rely on the products and services supplied.

A Lighter Moment:

It is impossible to enjoy idling thoroughly unless one has plenty of work to do.

Jerome K. Jerome

> **Action springs not from thought, but from a readiness for responsibility.**
>
> G. M. Trevelyan

 FOUNDATION

Safety

The CPE wants to ensure that the workplace is safe, secure, and ergonomic. Specifically, they ask how you provide a safe operating environment, including prevention, inspection root-cause analysis, and recovery.

The CPE ask how the organization ensures that its work systems and workplace preparedness is adequate to survive and operate during disasters or emergencies. This includes prevention, management, and continuity of operations and/or recovery. To ensure the overall operational (short-term) sustainability of the organization, the organization will require:

- People
- Critical Skills
- Facilities
- Equipment
- Data
- Money
- Adequate Supply Chain Availability
- Distribution Channels

Emergency Preparedness

Without any one of these factors, the organization will not be able to either respond to an emergency and/or ensure ongoing sustainability. An organization needs to assess:

- Prevention of disasters or emergencies
- Management of disasters or emergencies
- Continuity of operations when a of disasters or emergency occurs
- Recovery from a disasters or emergency

More strategically, the factors noted in 1.1a(3) address the longer-term sustainability issues. Although the criteria do not cover all of these factors, it can serve an organization well to take an integrated view of Emergency Readiness and Preparedness. This will ensure that the organization does not look at one aspect of Emergency Readiness. For example, most organizations have a comprehensive IT Disaster Plan. Although this may help the organization protect their data, the organization can still be crippled if a critical aspect of the Supply Chain cannot deliver crucial products or services. The key issue is protecting the stakeholders. For example, protecting the customers so they will receive the products or services from the organization, and protecting the employees so they will have ongoing employment.

 EXAMPLES

Indian Hotels Company Limited (Taj Hotels) - India

At Indian Hotels Company Limited (Taj) sustainability is an integrated process involving the entire leadership team. In our dramatic growth, this integrated approach to sustainability has been a significant strength. Sustainability is viewed as ongoing operations, disaster preparedness, disaster recovery as well as impact on triple-bottom line as shown in Fig 1.1-3. The following factors are considered:

i) **Money** – Financial forecasting, allocation of resources, fiduciary evaluations, contingency planning for a systematic part of every strategic objective, plan, initiative and project.

ii) **Data** – IT recovery plan, data integrity process, implementation plan for technology brand standards is a key element of existing operations and growth

iii) **People, Critical Skills** - Manpower and skill requirements to meet current operational and future growth plans. Strong process orientation is emphasized by the organization to reinforce standardized approaches and consistent results. Certification processes such as ISO 22000, ISO 14001 & OHSAS 18001 help to ensure continuous process improvements.

iv) **Facilities, Equipment** - Integrated in existing plans for ongoing operations and in plans for new initiatives and projects.

v) **Supply Chain** - Building supplier capability to meet growing demand, identification of new supplier sources for operational needs and new projects

vi) **Strategy** - The process to ensure that the strategy is sustainable includes the following steps:
   • approach to the geography (from 1 year to 5 years) – map, identify and plan to open the geographical region
   • approach to a hotel (from 1 to 2 years) - identify, assess, choose (M&A) / design (new build) Hotel –
   • acquire and refurbish or build hotel (from 2 years to 5 years)
   • run the hotel (from 1 year to more than 100 years)

   All of the above steps have built-in checks and balances to ensure that Taj can execute and accelerate the strategy in a dynamic environment.

vii) **Leadership** – the quality of our leadership including the Managing Director and the senior leadership team is formally reviewed annually using the following processes – Leadership Appreciation Centre, Performance Management System (PMS) review process, 360-degree feedback. Each leader also receives feedback on his / her personal leadership style through his / her Employee Survey Q12 scorecard. Using this Q12 scorecard each leader can create an action plan to build engagement levels of associates and address factors leading to disengagement.

Action plans to address Opportunities for Improvement (OFIs) emerging from the Surveillance Audits, TBEM (Baldrige) Critical Systems Reviews, Mystery Shopper Audits, surveys and assessments ensures that the processes remain on a trajectory of continual improvement (as validated in the Business Results reported). Leaders ensure a sustainable environment by tracking the organization's performance on certain critical parameters such as capital expenditures, ROI, compliance to growth plan, HR performance and changes in macro and micro economic factors and taking proactive actions. Taj's Strategic Planning Process ensures that the organizational objectives and the initiatives needed to realize the objectives remain current with the changing business needs and Stakeholders' expectations through regular analysis of prevalent business scenario.

Taj Hotels - India

		Operational Sustainability Factors							Strategic Sustainability	
		Money	Data	People	Critical Skills	Facilities	Equipment	Supply Chain	Strategy	Leadership
Reference Text		i	ii	iii	iii	IV	IV	V	VI	VII
Who is Involved?		ED Finance	CIO & Sr VP IT	Sr VP HR + Dir Grp Security	VP – L&D	COO's + Dir Grp Security	ED Hotel Ops + COO's	VP – Materials	Ex Com + VP – Dev & Projects	MD + ManCom
Sustainability	Ongoing Operations	√	√	√	√	√	√	√	√	√
	Disaster Preparedness	√	√	√	√	√	√	√	√	√
	Disaster Recovery	√	√	v		√	√	√	√	√
Triple Bottom-Line	Economic Value Addition	√	√			√	√	√	√	√
	Environmental Factors	√		√		√	√	√	√	√
	Building Social Capital	√		√	√ + Sr VP HR			√	√	√

Figure 1.1-3 Operational & Strategic Sustainability vs. Triple Bottom Line – Primary Relationship Matrix

Bronson Methodist Hospital (Baldrige Recipient 2005)

The disaster management plan (DMP) ensures workplace preparedness for disasters or emergencies. Using findings from the annual hazard vulnerability analysis, the emergency preparedness committee creates the annual priorities for safety training, drills, emergency preparedness activities, and ensures alignment with the Clinical Excellence Strategic Oversight Team patient safety action plans. Drills and emergency preparedness activities are held quarterly to test staff learning and knowledge gained through the safety education programs. Written objectives for all types of disasters are evaluated at each drill, using a criteria measurement of 1 to 5. Any scores under "3" require action plans and follow up using the Plan-Do-Check-Act model. The departmental safety champions serve a vital role in preparedness training, education and assessment. A select group of organizational leaders is specifically trained to be incident commanders in the hospital's state-of-the-art, best practice hospital emergency incident command system (HEICS). This system provides the necessary leadership structure, advanced communication technology, policies and procedures to manage any emergency situation.

The *Hospital Emergency Incident Command System,* modeled after the FIRESCOPE management system, was first tested by six hospitals in Orange County, California. HEICS features a flexible management organizational chart which allows for a customized hospital response to the crisis at hand. Confusion and chaos are common characteristics of any disaster. However, these negative effects can be minimized if with a quickly implemented, structured and focused direction of activities. The Hospital Emergency Incident Command System (HEICS) is an emergency management system which employs a logical management structure, defined responsibilities, clear reporting channels, and a common nomenclature to help unify hospitals with other emergency responders, resulting in an organized division of tasks and a realistic span of control for each manager. The plan has been used in single hospital emergencies and in many disaster exercises. From these repeated uses of the HEICS program, much insight has been gained.

Many hospitals are transitioning to a Hospital Incident Command Systems (HICS). HICS is an incident management system specific for hospitals, and based on the traditional Incident Command System (ICS). This assists hospitals in improving their emergency management planning, response, and recovery capabilities for unplanned and planned events. HICS is consistent with the National Incident Management System (NIMS) principles. HICS will strengthen hospital disaster preparedness activities in conjunction with community response agencies and allow hospitals to understand and assist in implementing the 17 Elements of the hospital-based NIMS guidelines. Additional information about these systems, and the associated organizational structures, job action sheets, and training manuals can be found at numerous internet sites by conducting a search of the acronyms. Source: Bronson (2006) p. 23

 CRITERIA QUESTIONS

In your response, include answers to the following questions:

   c. Safety and Emergency Readiness

   1) **Safety** – How do you provide a safe working environment? How does your safety system address accident prevention, inspection, root-cause analysis of failures, and recovery?

   2) **Emergency Preparedness** – How do you ensure that your organization is prepared for disasters or emergencies? How does your disaster and emergency preparedness system consider prevention, continuity of operations, and recovery? How does your disaster and emergency preparedness system take your reliance on suppliers and partners into account?

Notes:

   6.2c(2) Disasters and emergencies might be related to weather, utilities, or a local or national emergency. The extent to which you prepare for disasters or emergencies will depend on your organization's environment and its sensitivity to disruptions of operations. Acceptable levels of risk will vary depending on the nature of your products, services, supply chain, and stakeholder needs and expectations. The impacts of climate change could include a greater frequency of disruptions. Emergency considerations related to information technology should be addressed in item 4.2.

NIST (2015-2016) p. 24

WORKSHEETS

6.2c(1) – Safety

How You Provide A Safe Operating Environment:

How Your Safety System Addresses:			
Accident Prevention :	Inspection:	Root-Cause Analysis Of Failures	Recovery From Problems Or Accidents

6.2c(2) – Emergency Preparedness

Processes To Ensure Preparedness For:		Process Used To Incorporate These Factors Into The Readiness Of Key Work Systems and Workplace:		
Disasters	Emergencies	Prevention	Continuity Of Operations	Recovery

Note: Emergency Readiness can consider a wide range of other factors. For example, for an organization to remain *operationally* successful, the organization must ensure an adequate supply of:

- **Money**
- **People**
- **Critical Skills**
- **Facilities**
- **Equipment**
- **Data**
- **Products and Services From Suppliers**

For an organization to remain *strategically* successful will require the above factors, and will be dependent upon the quality of the:

- **Environment For The Achievement Of Your Mission**
- **Environment For Improvement Of Organizational And Personal Learning**
- **Consistent Customer Experience**
- **Innovation**
- **Intelligent Risk Taking**
- **Leadership**
- **Succession Planning**
- **Strategy**
- **Improvement**

ASSESSMENT

Rating Scale:

1 - **No Process** in place - We are not doing this
2 - **Reacting to Problems** – We use a basic (primarily reactive) process
3 - **Systematic Process** – We use a systematic process that has been improved
4 - **Aligned** – We use a process that aligns our activities from top to bottom
5 - **Integrated** – We use a process that is integrated with other processes across the organization
6 - **Benchmark** – We are the Benchmark in our industry or beyond!
DK - Don't Know

121   The organization has a systematic methodology to ensure that disasters or emergencies will have a minimal impact on ongoing operations (protecting People, Critical Skills, Facilities, Equipment, Data, Money and Adequate Supply Chain Availability) to ensure that the products or services provided customers will continue.   1   2   3   4   5   6   DK

122   Both disaster and emergency plans are prepared and consider prevention, problem management, continuity of operations, and recovery.   1   2   3   4   5   6   DK

BLUEPRINT

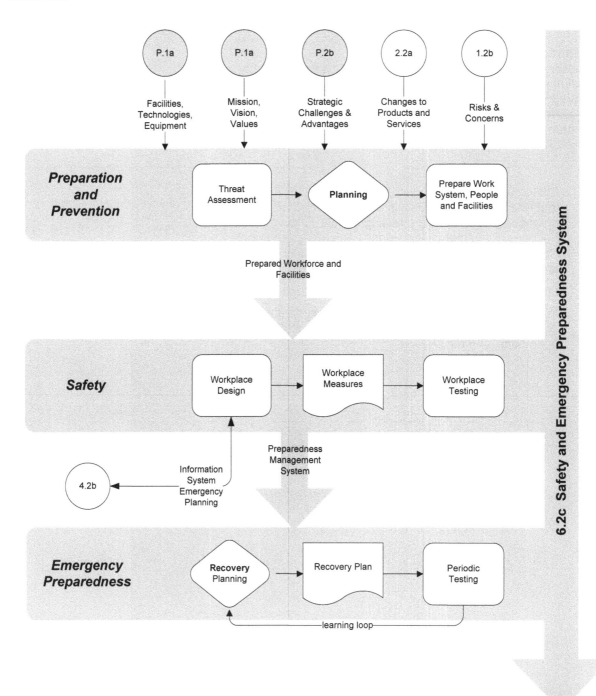

SYSTEM INTEGRATION

Context

P.1a > 6.1c Mission, Vision, Values - The nature of the mission also is an important consideration when determining the requirements for the emergency readiness system. Some organizations can shut their doors for a week or even a month without much impact on their customers. However, some organizations such as hospitals need to be able to conduct business and provide critical services during emergencies.

P.1a > 6.1c Facilitates, Technologies, Locations - The types of facilities, technologies, equipment, and locations will make a big difference in the threat assessment and the identification of requirements for the emergency readiness system. For example, organizations that handle hazardous materials have different emergency preparation and COOP requirements than do organizations that provide internet services. In addition, location will drive the type of environmental threat (weather, earthquakes, etc.) that an organization should prepare for.

P.2b > 6.1c Strategic Challenges and Advantages - The strategic challenges and advantages described in the profile (P.2b) are important considerations when determining the threats and the requirements for the emergency readiness system. In some cases, the ability to operate during emergencies might be a competitive advantage.

Systems

1.2b > 6.1c Risks and Concerns - The public concerns that are identified in the process described in 1.2b are direct inputs to the emergency readiness preparation requirements. The emergency readiness system should be designed in a way that inspires confidence and addresses the public concerns identified in 1.2b.

2.2a > 6.1c Change to Products and Services - Action plans often include sustainability plans including those related to emergency readiness.

4.2b <> 6.1c Emergency Planning - The continuity of operations planning process (6.1c) should include plans to ensure the information resources and technology system (4.2b) is included and protected to ensure the necessary information to support operations.

Scorecard

6.1c > 7.1b Emergency Readiness System Results - The results that indicate the effectiveness of the emergency readiness system should be presented in 7.1b.

THOUGHTS FOR LEADERS

Emergency and disaster preparedness is sketchy in many organizations. It is normal for the IT Department to have robust disaster, recovery, and backup plans, but these plans for other critical parts of the business are often not as complete. It is important that organizational leadership ensures that the following (emergency and disaster) factors are addressed by the appropriate departments:

Factor	Typical Department
People	Human Resources
Critical Skills	Human Resources with input from each department
Facilities	Facilities Management
Equipment	Operations/ each department
Data	IT
Money	Finance
Adequate Supply Chain Availability	Supply Chain Management

Establishing an integrated emergency and disaster preparedness plan through these organizations working together can not only help cross-training between the groups, but can ensure that the organization has done as much as possible to prepare.

If needed, the execution of these plans can help the organization keep their commitments to their stakeholders.

A Lighter Moment:

This isn't the sort of thing you can leave to chance. You never know when you might find yourself in some sort of cake emergency.

**Takayuki Ikkaku, Arisa Hosaka and
Toshihiro Kawabata**

The results presented in CPE Category 7 allow the organization to understand how well the processes described in CPE Categories 1 through 6 are performing. Instead of focusing on processes, the results areas focus on the actual results including levels, trends and comparisons. The seven CPE areas to address include: products and services; operations; strategy implementation; customers; workforce; leadership, governance and corporate citizenship; and financial performance.

Nearly half (450 of 1000) of the total points available in the CPE model are awarded based on the levels, trends, comparison and maturity of the results.

Organization Scorecard

High performing organizations have figured out how to improve key leverage points in their system to improve results in all seven areas and create sustainable value for multiple stakeholders. Performance measurement is the foundation for fact-based management and organizational learning. The organization scorecard provides organizations with a framework for a performance measurement system that supports the strategic management system (development and deployment of strategy) and the execution of processes of all types.

This framework helps organizations:

- clarify and translate vision and strategy;
- link the external forces (strategic challenges) to the internal strengths and objectives
- communicate and link strategic objectives and measures;
- plan, set targets, and align strategic initiatives; and
- enhance strategic feedback and learning (Kaplan and Norton, 1996, p.10).

The notion here is that organizations concentrating solely on one area, such as financials, do not have all the data they need to understand how the organization performs as a system and continuously improve that system.

In short, any one measure (or category of measures) by itself is a bad measure.

Sustainable performance is only achieved by understanding how the various components of the organization work together to form a coherent and congruent system. The organization scorecard addresses several types of results, including:

- product and service quality (proxies for customer satisfaction);

- operations effectiveness and efficiency (productivity, cycle time, disaster preparedness, etc.);

- strategy implementation (cost, quality, schedule and performance improvements);

- customer satisfaction, dissatisfaction, and loyalty (hard and soft measures including surveys, complaints, repeat purchases, referrals, etc.);

- workforce performance (engagement, development, capability, capacity, and climate including health, safety, and security;

- leadership performance (governance, accountability, regulatory and legal compliance, ethics, societal responsibilities);

- financial performance (revenue, profitability, cost reductions, etc.); and

- market share (including trends and projections compared to key competitors).

Developing an Organization Scorecard

There are many ways to develop an enterprise scorecard. The following nine steps provide a systematic method starting from the outside of the organization and working in:

1. Determine the outcome measures expected by the owners or guidance group (parent organization). These are often expressed using financial measures.

2. Determine the customer satisfaction measures soft (surveys and complaints) and hard (sales and repeat purchases).

3. Determine the "proxies" for customer satisfaction (key product and service quality measures that drive purchase decisions).

4. Determine the in-process measures that will "predict" the product and service quality measures in step 3.

5. Determine the key supplier and partner measures that "predict" in-process performance (Step 4) and product and service quality (Step 3).

6. Determine the people measures that will "predict" in-process performance (Step 4), product and service quality (Step 4), and customer relationship satisfaction (Step 2).

7. Determine additional financial measures that indicate the overall health of the organization including expenses, income, etc.

8. Determine the governance, social responsibility and environmental measures.

9. Determine the measures that leaders feel are critical to drive action in the organization toward the strategic objectives.

Once the top level enterprise scorecard is developed the next step is to translate and deploy the measures down through the organization. Many high performing companies drive their measurement groupings down to every employee. It is hard work, but most who have achieved this feel the work was well worth every employee being aligned to the organization's focus. Many of these companies display key performance data in the workplace for each team or workgroup.

Displaying the Results

An ideal results graph displays the performance level, trend, and comparisons all in one view. Comprehensive charts like the one below often take several years to fully develop. People always ask: "Shat is the silver bullet in the performance excellence journey?" While there are not 'silver bullets' in the journey, any data or results which are prominently displayed – tend to get better!

Ideal Results Graph

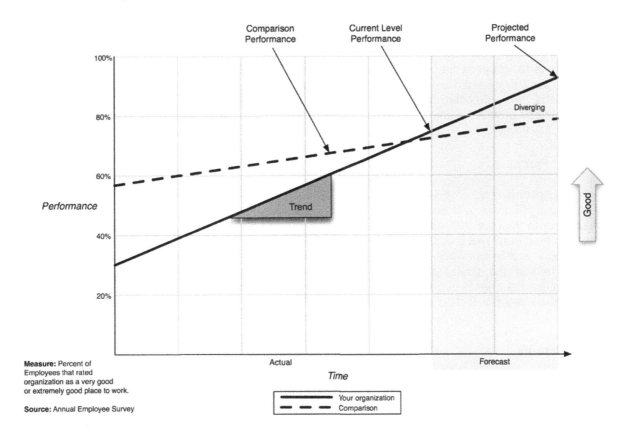

Key chart characteristics:

1. The current levels of performance with actual percentages for both company and the comparison to determine how large a gap exists today.

2. Trend of performance and comparisons (e.g., Industry Benchmark, Best Competitor, etc.) to analyze the changing gap between organization and relevant comparison to assess if: (a) the organization is closing in on the competition; (b) the competition is closing in on the organization; (c) the competition is leaving the organization behind; or (d) the organization is leaving the competition behind.

3. Target for future performance based on organization action plans. Forecast or projection of organization and comparison performance based on successful action plan completion or progress.

4. Clear label with source(s) of data identified.

5. Arrow indicating which direction is favorable.

Ideal Chart Enhancements

One technique that can be used to enhance this chart even further would be to add the completion dates for significant improvement initiatives. Even though there may be a lag between the completion dates and the contributions to the trend line, over time it does provide an impressive visual of the impact of the efforts.

541

Another enhancement might be additional trend lines that show **different employee segments** and locations. "Overall" trends are useful but can cover up problem areas. It is possible to have the trend line above and still have an entire location (e.g. plant, facility, etc.) or demographic segment (customer service, engineering, etc.) that is dissatisfied.

It is one thing to influence the results of one performance measure or indicator in isolation. It is quite another to positively influence the results of all or most of the key performance indicators. The ideal results charts are combined into a comprehensive picture that illuminates the cause-and-effect relationships and provides a comprehensive picture of organization performance.

Long-term Perspective

How do organizations develop sustained trends like those in the example? Typically, an organization will have multiple initiatives over several years. In this case, the initiatives might have been: (a) leadership development to improve the relationship between management and employees; (b) policy and process changes to help employees do their job better and improve their ability to take pride in their work; and (c) initiatives to improve teamwork and camaraderie. These initiatives "play out" over time and their effects often lag behind the actual execution by several months. Long-term trends in overall employee satisfaction like the ones presented in this chart clearly show that what ever this organization is doing to influence employee satisfaction, it is working.

Results Maturity

The results maturity model also includes four dimensions LTCI: levels, trends, comparisons, and integration or importance (a.k.a. linkages and gaps). Results areas call for data showing performance levels, relevant comparative data, and improvement trends for key measures and indicators of organizational performance. Results Items also call for data on the breadth of performance improvements. This is directly related to the "deployment" and "learning" dimensions; if improvement processes are widely deployed, there should be corresponding results. A score for a Results Item is thus a composite based upon overall performance, taking into account the rate and breadth of improvements and their importance.

In evaluating the data presented in CPE Category 7, consider several factors:

- Are the data aligned to the approaches described in the Process Categories 1 - 6?

- What is the current **level** of the performance?

- What is the historical **trends** and how long have the performance levels and improvement trends been sustained?

- How do the performance levels, trends, and projections **compare** to relevant comparisons? There are several types of comparisons that are useful including:
    - competitor performance (this is often difficult to acquire but can be very important to strategy development);
    - industry performance (this can be very useful especially if the organization's specific competitors are not very high performing);
    - best-in-class (this can be inside or outside the particular industry – e.g., the best warehousing performance may or may not be found inside the organization's particular industry);
    - organizations recognized as having role model performance (e.g., Baldrige winners); and

- internal company comparisons (this comparison typically has less useful than the other options).

- Are dips in performance explained? This section is the one time in Category 7 where a detailed explanation of the data is appropriate. This explanation should describe: 1) what happened, 2) how the organization recovered or is in the process of recovering, and 3) what checks have been put in place to ensure the dip in performance will not reoccur.

When is a Benchmark or Improvement Trend Not Necessary?

It should be noted that an improvement trend may not be a reasonable expectation when a particular measure is already at an exceptionally high level of performance. This issue is often "hotly" debated among examiners. Novice examiners may approach the evaluation as more of an *audit* where every metric can or should be improving. Some metrics, however, may have an upper *reasonable* limit. The following are examples where the improvement trend might be flat:

- 100% Environmental Compliance,

- 0 Ethical violations,

- 97+% Employee or Customer Satisfaction over an extended period of time, and

- 30 - 50% Market Share where several large customers control the demand for the products or services.

In these instances, the upper limit of performance may have already been reached or the next level might not be worth the required effort. The organization may not be able to justify the additional cost to achieve a small improvement in performance. I remember a young examiner writing an Opportunity for Improvement (OFI) because the applicant's salt was .3% less 'salty' than the competitions. The problem was, however, that the salt was 2% higher than a human can taste! This was a meaningless 'audit' OFI. Nobody would be foolish enough to tell the CEO that he should invest millions of dollars making their salt more 'salty.'

Category 7 *Introductions* are different than those used for Categories 1 through 6. They are not a description of the meaning or impact of the area to address because this impact is obvious. Instead, it is a listing of the types of data that should be shown in the Item.

Levels

According to NIST (2013 - 2014), "the term 'levels' refers to numerical information that places or positions an organization's results and performance on a meaningful measurement scale. Performance levels permit evaluation relative to past performance, projections, goals, and appropriate comparisons" (p. 47).

Key questions:

- How is the process doing today?

- Current level of performance (e.g., 95%).

- By itself the current level tells us little about the performance of the process in question.

Trends

According to NIST (2013 - 2014), "The term "trends" refers to numerical information that shows the direction and rate of change for an organization's results or the consistency of its performance overtime. Trends provide a time sequence of organizational performance" (p. 50).

Key questions:

- How has the process been doing?

- Trends of actual performance are used to analyze the impact of improvement efforts over time.

- Rate (e.g., slope of the trend line)?

- Breadth (e.g., how widely deployed and shared are the performance improvements?

Comparisons

As previously noted there are several types of comparisons including: competitors, industry, best in class, role model organizations, and internal organization units. When comparing performance levels and trends with other organizations, there are four distinct situations. These four situations are based on two variables: which organization is currently on "top" and are the trend lines diverging or converging.

Four Comparison Situations

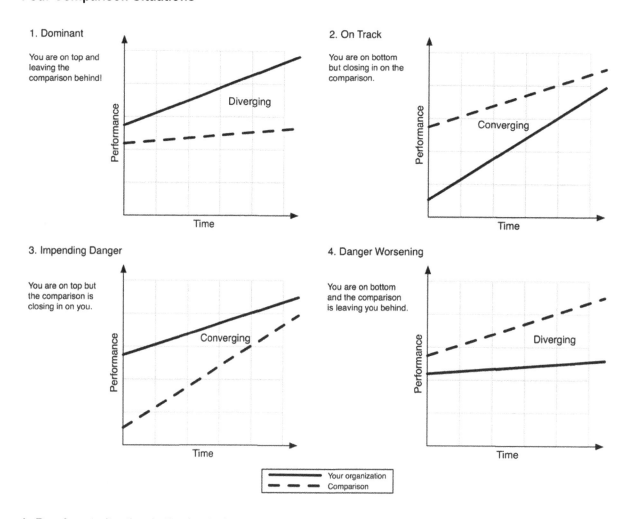

1. Dominant situation is the best place to be. The dominant position is when the organization is on top and improving at a faster pace than the comparison. Life is good and getting better. The danger with this situation is arrogance. Some organizations in this situation find that they do not continue to improve at the same rate they did when they were behind the competition. Consequently this dominant situation can quickly become and impending danger situation and if not addressed, eventually a "danger worsening" situation.

2. On Track is the second best place to be. In this situation the organization is on bottom but it is improving at a faster rate than the comparison which means that it will soon overtake the comparison. This is one of the easier situations to maintain. The motivation is high for two reasons: the organization is still behind the competition and what ever they are doing to improve is working. An organization that stays on this path may eventually find itself in the dominant situation.

3. Impending Danger is not a good place to be but there is still time. In this situation the organization is currently performing better than the comparison but the comparison is improving at a faster rate than the organization and consequently will soon be overtaken if it does not change the approach to improvement. If this is caught in time and addressed aggressively it is possible to turn this around and back to a dominant situation.

4. Danger Worsening is the least attractive place to be. In this situation things are bad and they are getting worse. The organization's performance is not as good as the comparison and they are improving at a faster rate. In this situation, if something does not change quickly and dramatically, the situation will continue to get worse. Organizations that cannot turn this around sometimes find themselves in a situation where they have to make tough choices to continue or get out of particular businesses, product lines, etc.

Integration or Importance

"Integration refers to the extent to which your results measures (often through segmentation) address **important** customer, product, market, process, and action plan performance requirements identified in your Organizational Profile and in Process Items" (2013 – 2014, p. 47).

Key questions:

- How comprehensive is the scorecard?

- Are the areas important to the specific perspective (e.g., 7.2a Customer-Focused Results) included?

- Is there linkage of the results measures (often through segmentation) to important customer, product and service, market, process, and action plan performance requirements identified in the organizational profile and process items?

Keep in mind, a Results Item score of 50 percent represents a clear indication of improvement trends and/or good levels of performance in the principal results areas covered in the Item. Higher scores reflect better improvement rates and/or levels of performance, better comparative performance, and broader coverage and integration with business requirements. In summary, the results areas are interested in four things – the level of current performance, the trend of performance, the comparisons, and the importance of the results. As the organization continues to develop the scorecard and assess the organization's performance keep these four dimensions in mind.

Caution!
More often than not, when applying for an award, the score for the five Category 7 Items is inversely proportional to the number of words used. Too many words and not enough data frequently results in a lower results maturity score. Where words are essential, however, is when an adverse trend needs to be explained. This should be done in a manner that relates to the processes described in Categories 1 through 6.

Results Maturity Model (a.k.a. Results Scoring Guidelines)

Points	Levels	Trends	Comparisons	Integration
Level 6 90%, 95%, or 100%	**Excellent** organizational performance levels are reported that are **fully responsive** to the **multiple requirements** of the item.	**Beneficial trends** have been **sustained over time** in **all areas** of importance to the accomplishment of your organization's mission.	**Industry and benchmark leadership** is demonstrated in **many** areas.	Organizational performance results and projections are reported for **most key customer, market, process, and action plan requirements**.
Level 5 70%, 75%, 80% or 85%	**Good to excellent** organizational performance levels are reported, responsive to the **multiple requirements** of the item.	**Beneficial trends** have been **sustained over time** in **most areas** of importance to the accomplishment of your organization's mission.	**Many to most trends** and current performance levels have been **evaluated against relevant comparisons** and/or benchmarks and show areas of leadership and very good relative performance.	Organizational performance **results are reported for most key customer, market, process, and action plan requirements**.
Level 4 50%, 55%, 60%, or 65%	**Good** organizational performance levels are reported, responsive to the **overall requirements** of the item.	**Beneficial trends** are evident in areas of importance to the accomplishment of your organization's mission.	**Some current performance levels** have been **evaluated against relevant comparisons** and/or benchmarks and show areas of good relative performance.	Organizational performance **results are reported for most key customer, market, and process requirements**.
Level 3 30%, 35%, 40%, or 45%	**Good** organizational performance levels are reported, responsive to the **basic requirements** of the item.	**Some trend data** are reported, and **most** of the trends presented are **beneficial.**	**Early stages** of obtaining **comparative information** are evident.	**Results** are **reported for many areas of importance** to the accomplishment of your organization's mission.
Level 2 10%, 15%, 20%, or 25%	A **few** organizational performance **results** are reported, responsive to the **basic requirements** of the item, and **early good performance** levels are evident.	**Some trend data** are reported, with **some adverse** trends evident.	**Little or no** comparative information is reported.	**Results** are **reported for a few areas of importance** to the accomplishment of your organization's mission.
Level 1 0% or 5%	There are **no** organizational performance results or the **results reported are poor.**	Trend data either are **not reported or** show mainly **adverse trends**.	Comparative information is **not reported.**	**Results** are **not reported** for any **areas of importance** to the accomplishment of your organization's mission.

Source: NIST (2015 - 2016), p. 35)

> ***It is quality rather than quantity that matters.***
>
> **Seneca (5 BC - 65 AD)**

FOUNDATION

These results measure how the organization performs against the external customer's requirements (as reported in Area P1b[2] in the Organizational Profile). Product and service results are the "proxies" for customer satisfaction, and if they are understood should correlate to customer satisfaction, loyalty, and engagement. Because customer satisfaction measures are often lagging, these product and service measures provide timely feedback to help manage internal processes. Considering the requirements identified in the Customer Focused Items (3.1 and 3.2), what product and service characteristics, if done well, will result in a satisfied customer? For example, the customer might define quality and on-time delivery with no defects as an important service characteristic. This customer request might translate into percentage delivered on-time, average variance of delivery times, and number of defects per product found during final inspection, all measurable by the organization. The product and service results should directly correlate with the customer's satisfaction results.

Customer satisfaction and purchase behavior are the ultimate measures of product and service quality, however, customer satisfaction (reported in 7.2a) often lags behind the actual delivery of the products and services (7.1a). Consequently, customer satisfaction is often not timely enough to be used to control the quality of the products and services. An organization needs early warning "proxies" for customer satisfaction. These proxies come in the form of tracking the organizational performance against the characteristics of the products and services that determine customer behavior. The process to determine these requirements are reported in Item 3.1, and the requirements themselves are reported in the Organizational Profile in P1a(1). Data reported here should align to what was listed in the Organizational Profile for each customer requirement within each customer segment.

Health Care Criteria

In addition to the Item 7.1 requirements noted above, the CPE Health Care criteria also asks "What are your current levels and trends in key measures or indicators of health care outcomes ....."

Unfortunately, we have seen some health care applicants ONLY provide health care outcomes and not the internal measures which respond to the Customer's (Patient's) Requirements shown in Area P1b[2] in the Organizational Profile. While these clinical outcomes are critical for any health care organization, they do not answer the full breadth and depth of what Area to Address 7.1a asks.

The answer to P1b[2] gives an organization the ability to understand how they are meeting/not meeting what is important to customers (patients) which should correlate to satisfaction, loyalty, and engagement. If it does not correlate, the organization does not fully understand the customer's requirements. Clinical outcomes alone cannot create this alignment.

EXAMPLES

Pewaukee School District (Baldrige Award Recipient 2013)

- Student Academic Achievement & Growth
- Student On-Track & Postsecondary Readiness
- Advanced Placement Exam Pass Rate
- Student Technology Proficiency
- Student Engagement Participation in Extra-curricular Activities

Source: Pewaukee School District (2013) p. 33-35 – 60

Advocate Good Samaritan Hospital (Baldrige Recipient 2010)

- Risk Adjusted Mortality
- Length of Stay (LOS)
- Unplanned Readmissions within 30 Days
- Decreased Code Blue Events outside of the Critical Care Unit

Source: Advocate Good Samaritan Hospital (2010) pp. 31-34

PRO-TEC (Baldrige Recipient 2007)

- System Reliability Percentages
- Impact of Value-Added Product on Fleet Life-Cycle Fuel Savings
- Improved Customer Service Experience

Source: PRO-TEC (2007) pp. 38 – 40

Monfort College of Business (2004 Baldrige Recipient)

- ETS Field Achievement Test in Business
    - Overall percentile
    - Percentile for each business area (e.g., Accounting)
    - Percentage of MCB students in the top percentiles
- Employer Survey Evaluation of Student Learning
- Parent Survey Evaluation of Student Learning
- EBI Undergraduate Exit Study abilities and Skills Development
- EBI Alumni Survey on Learning

Source: Monfort (2005) pp. 37 – 38

CRITERIA QUESTIONS

Provide data and information to answer the following questions:

a. Customer-Focused Product and Process Results

What are your results for your products and your customer service processes? What are your current levels and trends in key measures or indicators of the performance of products and services that are important to and directly serve your customers? How do these results compare with the performance of your competitors and other organizations with similar offerings? How do these results differ by process types, as appropriate?

Notes:

7.1. Results should provide key information for analyzing and reviewing your organizational performance (item 4.1), demonstrate use of organizational knowledge (item 4.2), and provide the operational basis for customer-focused results (item 7.2) and financial and market results (item 7.5). There is not a one-to-one correspondence between results items and Criteria categories 1–6. Results should be considered systemically, with contributions to individual results items frequently stemming from processes in more than one Criteria category.

7.1a. Results for your products and customer service processes should relate to the key customer requirements and expectations you identify in P.1b(2), which are based on information gathered through processes you describe in Category 3. The measures or indicators should address factors that affect customer preference, such as those listed in the notes to P.1b(2) and 3.2a.

7.1a. For some nonprofit organizations, funding sources might mandate product or service performance measures. These measures should be identified and reported here.

NIST (2015-2016) p. 25

WORKSHEETS

7.1a Customer-Focused Product and Service Results

Customer Segment (From P.1b[2])	Requirements (Both Product and Service)	Measure	Performance Level*	Trend (Favorable, Flat or Unfavorable)	Comparison To Competitor's Performance**
	1				
	2				
	3				
	4				
	1				
	2				
	3				
	4				
	1				
	2				
	3				
	4				
	1				
	2				
	3				
	4				
	1				
	2				
	3				
	4				
	1				
	2				
	3				
	4				

* Attaching the appropriate data charts can be of benefit, but at a minimum the above data needs to be included.
** If it is not possible to obtain the competitor's performance, explain why. Use the best comparative data available.

Note: For Health Care Organizations, the key clinical results should also be included in this Area To Address. These should include core measures, Value Based Purchasing measures, and other measures reported to CMS or other regulatory agencies.

ASSESSMENT

123	The organization has measures of product and service performance.	1	2	3	4	5	6	DK
124	The product and service performance factors which are measured were determined from customer requirements.	1	2	3	4	5	6	DK
125	The product and service performance factors which are measured are segmented for each key customer segment or group.	1	2	3	4	5	6	DK
126	The product and service performance factors which are measured are benchmarked against competitors or other organizations with similar offerings.	1	2	3	4	5	6	DK

BLUEPRINT

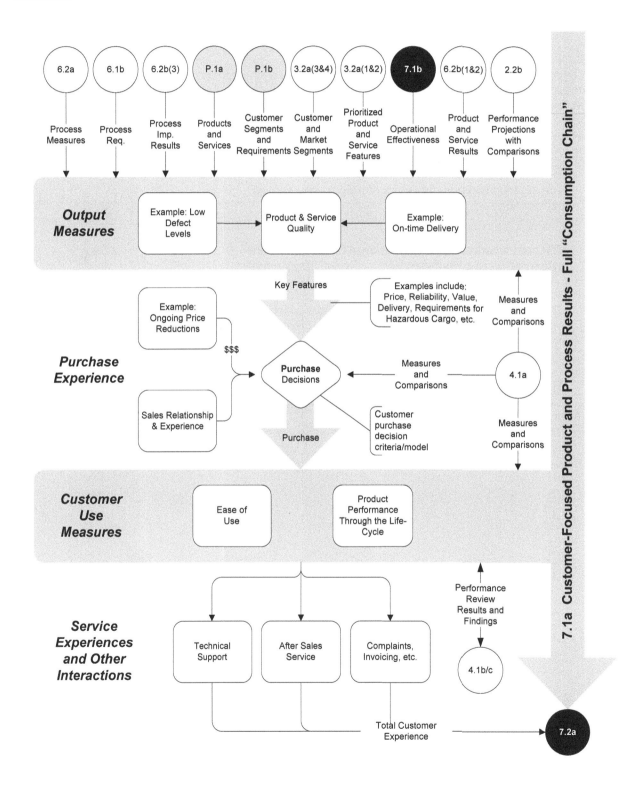

SYSTEM INTEGRATION

Context

P.1a > 7.1a Products and Services - The results presented here should be those associated with the products and services identified in the profile P.1a.

P.1b > 7.1a Customers Segments and Requirements - Customer segments and the associated requirements as described in the profile (P.1b) are key inputs to determining and segmenting the key product and service results that are "proxies" for customer satisfaction (7.1a).

Systems

2.2b > 7.1 thru 7.5 Performance Projections and Comparisons - The forecasted performance (projections) along with the projected comparison performance should be reflected in the results charts depicted in 7.1 through 7.5. While the CPE specifically ask for strategic plan accomplishments in Area to Address 7.1c, the ideal strategic plan will have projections for measures in all five results Items.

3.2a(1&2) > 7.1a Prioritized Product and Service Features Results - The results for product outcomes reported in 7.1a should include "hard" measure results for each key product and service offering as well as the key features and their relative importance to purchasing decisions.

3.2a(3&4) > 7.1a Customer and Market Segments - The segments and customer groups that are identified in 3.2a(3&4) should be the same segments and groups that are used for product and service results data presented in 7.1a. In other words, the results in 7.1a should include results requirements for each of the key customer and market segments and groups identified by the processes in 3.2a(3&4). In addition, results for the product and service features related to the prioritized requirements identified in 3.2a(3&4) should be included in the product and service results presented in 7.1a.

4.1a > 7.1 through 7.5 Comparisons - The comparisons selected using the processes described in 4.1a should be the same comparisons that are presented in all the results areas 7.1 through 7.5.

4.1a > 7.1 through 7.5 Measures – The results produced by the measures identified in 4.1a should be the same results presented in all the results areas 7.1 through 7.5.

4.1b < 7.1 through 7.5 Results - All results displayed as part of the results areas 7.1 through 7.5 are potential inputs to the organizational performance review system 4.1b.

4.1b > 7.1 through 7.5 Findings - The explanation of performance levels, trends and comparisons should be included in the applicable results areas (7.1 thorough 7.5).

6.1b > 7.1a Key End of Process Results - The results related to the key process requirements (levels, trends, comparisons) should be presented in area 7.1a. These measures include those characteristics most important to the customers' buying decisions or in other words the "proxies" for customer purchase and satisfaction. The measure included here are often characteristics such as timeliness, quality (defects), reliability, etc.

6.2a > 7.1a Process Output Measures - The quality of the process design is determined primarily by the quality of the outputs. The output or key final products and services results (levels, trends, comparisons) should be presented in area 7.1a. These measures include those characteristics most important to the customers' buying decisions or in other words the "proxies" for customer purchase and satisfaction. The measure included here are often characteristics such as timeliness, quality (defects), reliability, etc.

6.2b(1&2) > 7.1a Product and Service Results - Ultimately, the test of the effectiveness of process management is the quality of the output. For those processes that produce final products and services that go to the customers the results are reported in 7.1a.

6.2b(3) > 7.1a Process Improvement Results - Work process improvements that result in the improvement of the products and services should be reported in 7.1a.

Scorecard

7.1a > 7.2a Product and Service Outcomes - The product and service results included in 7.1a should be "proxies" for customer satisfaction (7.2a). Consequently, the customer satisfaction results in 7.2a should correlate with the results presented in 7.1a. The analysis of this correlation will help to validate and refine the product and service measures selected for inclusion in 7.1a.

7.1a < 7.1b Operational Effectiveness - The level of operational effectiveness as presented in 7.1b should have a direct impact on the performance levels and trends presented in 7.1a. Results presented in 7.1a are the end-of-process or output results that should be a direct result of the operations that are measured in 7.1b. The analysis of this correlation will help to validate and refine the operations (in-process) measures selected for inclusion in 7.1b.

 THOUGHTS FOR LEADERS

Organizations who understand what their customers truly want and which characteristics will drive their purchase behavior, will win in the marketplace over organizations that are unclear about these issues. Most organizations feel they do understand customer requirements, but in many cases they have not systematically determined those requirements.

Item 7.1 is the first look at how an organization is performing against customer requirements. These results must be aligned against the following logic flow:

- Customer **segments** (Baldrige Criteria P.1a[2])
- Customer **requirements** by segment (Baldrige Criteria P.1a[2])
- Organizational **performance** against customer requirements by segment (Baldrige Criteria 7.1a) – *This Item*
- Customer **satisfaction** by segment (Baldrige Criteria 7.2a[1])
- Customer-perceived value, including customer **loyalty**, by segment (Baldrige Criteria 7.2a[2])

If these data are clearly aligned, an organization can hold a strong competitive advantage. This alignment allows the organization to know how the customer feels about the company's performance long before the customer can complete a Customer Satisfaction Survey.

Clearly aligning these data is one of the most important roles a leader performs!

A Lighter Moment:

Those who speak most of progress measure it by quantity and not by quality.

George Santayana

> *Change is the constant, the signal for rebirth, the egg of the phoenix.*
>
> **Christina Baldwin**

FOUNDATION

Once an organization has identified what the customers want, the next question requires identification of the necessary internal support products, services, and processes needed to enable the key outcomes. High performing organizations have a strong ability to identify the internal indicators used to control and improve the key product and service processes. These internal process performance indicators are important to the organization, but very often the customer could not care less about them. For example, if it is completion time for the foundation or the frame of a home a customer has purchased, the customer does not care if the foundation is finished on time. They only want high quality and the house ready to move into when predicted. The builder, however, knows that the probability of the house being ready to move into on time is dramatically increased by finishing the foundation on time. Thus, completing the foundation on time would be an in-process measure that the builder might use to ensure they meet the end-of-process measures that are important to the customer.

Process Effectiveness and Efficiency

The products and services provided to external customers by an organization are outputs of the organization's system of processes, including the outputs of both the key work processes and all other processes. This Area to Address focuses on the predictors of product and service quality reported in 7.1a. Results reported should include the key measures for performance of the work systems, including productivity, cycle time, and other measures of process efficiency (in-process measures), effectiveness (end-of-process measures) and innovation (if valued by the customer of the process).

It also is key to report key output measures of internal processes that enable (or support) the processes that provide the products and services provided to external customers as well as output measures of the Key Work processes. These measures, as well as others, should be used to proactively manage the organization's processes and to evaluate their overall performance.

Emergency Preparedness

Results reported against emergency preparedness should include the key indicators and measures for the achievement of the planning and mitigation of workplace preparedness for disasters or emergencies. This should show the factors addressed as important in 6.1b(2) – Emergency Preparedness.

EXAMPLES

Pewaukee School District (Baldrige Award Recipient 2013)

- % of Teachers Deemed "Highly Qualified"
- Advanced Placement Offerings
- Professional Development Mediums
- Students with Disabilities Referrals & placements
- English Language Learners
- Student to PC Ratio
- Number of School Messengers Sent
- Reading Recovery Dismissal Rate
- Compliance with Tornado, Fire, and Lockdown Drills

Source: Pewaukee School District (2013) pp. 35 - 37

Advocate Good Samaritan Hospital (Baldrige Recipient 2010)

- Average Inpatient Length of Stay
- Medicare Cardiac Readmissions within 30 Days
- Medicare Readmissions within 30 Days
- Emergency Department % of Blood Cultures prior to Antibiotics
- Patient Safety Event Reporting
- Hospital Acquired Deep Vein Thrombosis
- Hand Hygiene
- Fall Prevention

Source: Advocate Good Samaritan Hospital (2007) pp. 31 - 34

PRO-TEC (Baldrige Recipient 2007)

Example Measures
- Prime Production Hours
- Value-Added Product Development
- Days Elapsed in Finishing Process
- Average Days for Order Review
- Fuel Savings

Source – PRO-TEC (2007)

Monfort College of Business (Baldrige Recipient 2004)

- Student Quality – Proportion of Entering Freshmen with > or = 24 ACT
- Student Quality – Average ACTs for Entering Freshman
- Student Quality – Transferring Student GPAs
- Number of Graduates Produced
- MCB Press Coverage – Number of Stories in the Media
- Comparison with Peers – Value: Class Size v. Tuition

- Average Starting Salaries for MCB Graduates
- Comparison with Peers – Average Class Size v. Percent Classes Taught by Doctorally Qualified Faculty
- Ratio of Students to Lab Computers

Source; Monfort (2005) pp. 46 – 49

CRITERIA QUESTIONS

Provide data and information to answer the following questions:

b. Work Process Effectiveness Results

(1) **Process Effectiveness and Efficiency** What are your process effectiveness and efficiency results? What are your current levels and trends in key measures or indicators of the operational performance of your key work and support processes, including productivity, cycle time, and other appropriate measures of process effectiveness, efficiency, and innovation? How do these results compare with the performance of your competitors and other organizations with similar processes? How do these results differ by process types, as appropriate?

(2) **Emergency Preparedness** What are your emergency preparedness results? What are your current levels and trends in key measures or indicators of the effectiveness of your organization's preparedness for disasters or emergencies? How do these results differ by location or process type, as appropriate?

Notes:

7.1b. Results should address the key operational requirements you identify in the Organizational Profile and in Category 6.

7.1b. Appropriate measures and indicators of work process effectiveness might include defect rates; rates and results of product, service, and work system innovation; results for simplification of internal jobs and job classifications; waste reduction; work layout improvements; changes in supervisory ratios; Occupational Health and Safety Administration (OSHA)-reportable incidents; response times for emergency drills or exercises; and results for work relocation or contingency exercises.

NIST (2015-2016) p. 25

WORKSHEETS

7.1b(1) – Process Effectiveness And Efficiency

Measurement Category**	Key Measure Or Indicator ** (Listings Below Are Only Examples)	Perf. Level*	Trend	Comparison
Operational Performance Of Key Work And Support Processes	Productivity Measures			
	Cycle Time Measures			
	Process Efficiency Measures			
	Process Effectiveness Measures			
	Innovation Measures			
	Work Layout Improvements			
	Changing Supervisory Ratios			

*Attaching The Appropriate Data Charts Can Be Of Benefit, and These Can Include Other Factors Such As Productivity, Cycle Time Improvement, Lead-Times and Set-Up Times, Time To Market, Time To Profit, and Other Process Effectiveness, Efficiency and Innovation Measures.

7.1b(2) - Emergency Preparedness

Key Measure Or Indicator (Listings Below Are Only Examples)	Perf. Level*	Trend	Comparison
Work System Preparedness For Disaster Or Emergency			
Workplace Preparedness for Disaster Or Emergency			
Audit Results In Emergency or Disaster Preparedness			
Just-In-Time Delivery Results In Emergency or Disaster Preparedness			
External Product, Service, or Process Acceptance Results			
Supplier Or Partner Performance In Emergency or Disaster Preparedness			
Product, Service, and Work System Innovation Rates			
Results From (Or Impact Of) Innovation In Emergency or Disaster Preparedness			

ASSESSMENT

Rating Scale:

1 - **No Business Results** – We do not have these data
2 - **Few Business Results** – We have some data, but are early in improving
3 - **Improvements And/Or Good Results Reported** – We have data but in the early stages of trends
4 - **Good Trends In Most Areas** – No adverse trends and some comparisons
5 - **Good To Excellent In Most Areas** – Most trends are sustained and most have comparisons
6 - **Excellent Performance In Most Important Areas** –We are the Benchmark in our industry or beyond!
DK - Don't Know

127 The organization tracks the key measures or indicators of the performance of key work (value creation) processes.   1   2   3   4   5   6   DK

128 The organization tracks trends in key measures in work system performance.   1   2   3   4   5   6   DK

129 The organization tracks the operational performance of key support processes and systems.   1   2   3   4   5   6   DK

130 The organization measures workplace preparedness for disasters or emergencies and the results are favorable.   1   2   3   4   5   6   DK

BLUEPRINT

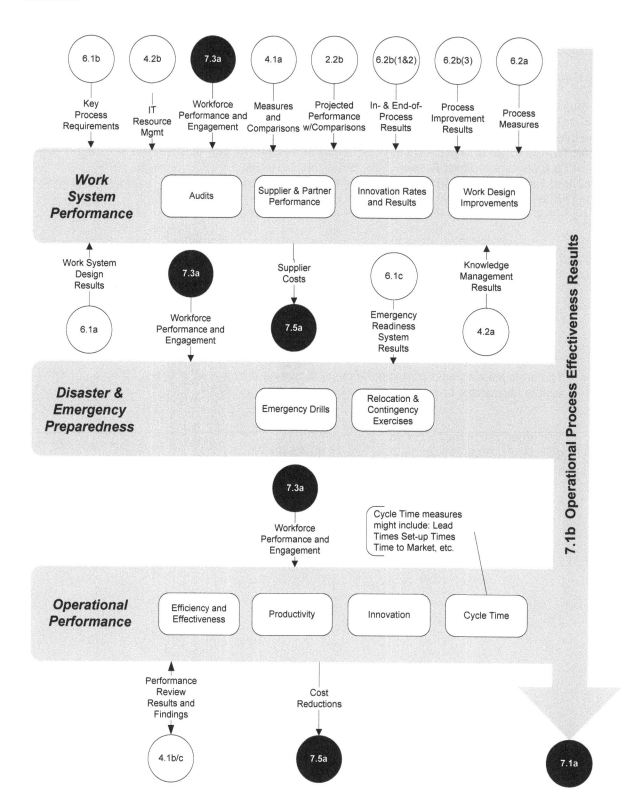

SYSTEM INTEGRATION

Systems

2.2b > 7.1 thru 7.5 Performance Projections and Comparisons - The forecasted performance (projections) along with the projected comparison performance should be reflected in the results charts depicted in 7.1 through 7.5. While the CPE specifically ask for strategic plan accomplishments in 7.1c, the ideal strategic plan will have projections for measures in all five results Items.

4.1a > 7.1 through 7.5 Comparisons - The comparisons selected using the processes described in 4.1a should be the same comparisons that are presented in all the results areas 7.1 through 7.5.

4.1a > 7.1 through 7.5 Measures – The results produced by the measures identified in 4.1a should be the same results presented in all the results areas 7.1 through 7.5.

4.1b < 7.1 through 7.5 Results - All results displayed as part of the results areas 7.1 through 7.5 are potential inputs to the organizational performance review system (4.1b).

4.1b > 7.1 through 7.5 Findings - The explanation of performance levels, trends and comparisons should be included in the applicable results areas (7.1 thorough 7.5).

4.2a > 7.1b Knowledge Management Results - Results that address the effectiveness of the management of data, information, and knowledge should be included in the results presented in 7.1b.

6.1a > 7.1b Work System Design Results - Results that indicate the performance of the organization in areas related to the core competencies and the overall work system design should be reported in 7.1b.

6.1b > 7.1b Key In Process Results - In addition to the outputs the efficiency and effectiveness of the process is determined through in-process measures. The results (levels, trends, comparisons) for key in-process and control measures should be included in the results displayed in area 7.1b. Just as the product and service results are predictors of customer satisfaction, the operational including in-process results are predictors of the product and service results.

6.1c > 7.1b Emergency Readiness System Results - The results that indicate the effectiveness of the emergency readiness system should be presented in 7.1b.

6.2a > 7.1b Process Measures - In addition to the outputs the efficiency and effectiveness of the process is determined through in-process measures. The results (levels, trends, comparisons) for key in-process and control measures should be included in the results displayed in area 7.1b. Just as the product and service results are predictors of customer satisfaction, the operational including in-process results are predictors of the product and service results 7.1a.

6.2b(1&2) > 7.1b In and End of Process Results - For processes that produce products and services for internal customers the results should be presented in area 7.1b. These measures include those characteristics most important to the internal customers or in other words the "proxies" for internal customer satisfaction and overall value chain performance. The measures included in 7.1b are often process characteristics such as timeliness, quality (defects), reliability, etc. In addition, the results for key in-process and control measures should be included in the results displayed in area 7.1b. Just as the product and service results are predictors of internal customer satisfaction, the operational including in-process results are predictors of the product and service results.

6.2b(3) > 7.1b Process Improvement Results - Process improvement results including cost reductions should be included in the results presented in 7.1b. These support process cost reductions are often in important part of the contribution to profit and are often viewed together with process, product, and service quality to gain a system perspective.

Scorecard

7.1a < 7.1b Operational Effectiveness - The level of operational effectiveness as presented in 7.1b should have a direct impact on the performance levels and trends presented in 7.1a. Results presented in 7.1a are the end-of-process or output results that should be a direct result of the operations that are measured in 7.1b. The analysis of this correlation will help to validate and refine the operations (in-process) measures selected for inclusion in 7.1b.

7.5a < 7.1b Cost Reductions - The value creation and support process cost reduction results depicted in 7.5a are a direct input to the profitability of the organization and the financial results in 7.5a.

7.5a < 7.1b Supplier Costs - The supplier costs are a component of the overall expenses and are a direct input to the profitability of the organization. For some organizations the cost of supplies is a significant amount of money.

7.3a > 7.1b High Performing and Engaged Workforce - The high performing workforce that is a result of improvements in well-being, satisfaction, learning, development, and work system performance directly impact the performance in the operational results presented in 7.1b.

THOUGHTS FOR LEADERS

A leader has a natural tendency to look at the "bottom line," which is only a few metrics, when reviewing results. However, this type of review is rarely successful in the longer-term. Leaders must understand a range of metrics, as well as the *cause and effect* relationships within the organization and between the operations of the organization. A leader can learn much about an organization and how the people within the organization perform their jobs, by asking how the organization knows that their processes are in-control, efficient (working well internally) and effective (doing the right things and getting the right outputs).

The questions are simple, but the answers — along with a few simple follow-up questions — can reveal the following:

- Whether they even have processes.

- Whether they understand process management and how it differs from functional management or project management.

- How the processes are measured.

- Whether the person being asked knows what the process control approaches are.

- Whether action is taken when the process goes out-of-control.

- Whether there are both end-of-process and in-process measures used.

Leaders need to drive process management, and insist that all activities of the organization are defined as a process, each process has an owner, and each process owner:

1) defines;
2) measures;
3) stabilizes; and
4) improves their process.

Process owners should not be allowed to be caretakers. They should be required to improve their processes, and to share those improvements with others who can benefit.

Additionally, leaders have a responsibility to ensure that the organization is prepared for emergencies. This is not only to protect life and property, but is also to protect the supply to the customers and to ensure that employees still have a safe and secure place to work. Therefore emergency preparedness needs to ensure protection in case of both emergencies and disasters, and should include plans to ensure ongoing operations.

> *There is only one sustainable competitive advantage ......*
> *the rate of your improvement.*
>
> **John Vinyard**

> *Amateurs discuss tactics, professionals discuss logistics.*
>
> **Napoleon**

FOUNDATION

Once an organization has identified what the customers want, the next question requires identification of the necessary internal AND EXTERNAL support products, services, and processes needed to enable the key outcomes. High performing organizations have a strong ability to identify the suppliers they need, and to integrate those suppliers into the full supply chain. Without this ability, many organizations may be ignoring over 50% of their total cost.

This means the suppliers must be effectively rationalized into the entire value chain, and become a seamless part of planning, deployment, management, and improvement.

Unless an organization truly understands the impact of suppliers, they may put their business at risk in a manner which is difficult to recover. For example, a strong trend in the US has been to offshore many products and services. Studies have shown, however, that some of these 'outsourcing' decisions have ignored factors which contribute as much as 20% of the total cost. Clearly these decisions can put 'at risk' some of the key factors which drove the decision to outsource, and may even put the competitiveness of the organization at risk.

EXAMPLES

Advocate Good Samaritan Hospital (Baldrige Recipient 2010)

Suppliers, Partners & Collaborators: GSAM depends on strong, synergistic relationships with suppliers, partners, and collaborators. Their roles in GSAM's key work systems, health care offerings, and support services, affect the quality of care and the effectiveness of care delivery. An established systematic mechanism for communicating and managing relationships with these key groups contributes to GSAM exceeding customer requirements. These roles and mechanisms are outlined in the figure below. Advocate Health Care (AHC) Supply Chain requirements include on-time delivery, electronic communication, savings for the organization, and accuracy.

P.1-9 Key Types of Partners, Suppliers & Collaborators

	Key Strategic Partners (E.g. Cerner, ACL Lab)	Suppliers (E.g. AHC Supply Chain, vendors)	Collaborators (E.g. Schools, key consultant groups)
Role in Work Systems	• Care delivery • Process improvement • Information management	• Delivery of products and supplies	• Care delivery • Process improvement • Facility design
Role in Innovation	• Early adopters of cutting-edge technology & practices	• New products & services	• Brings expertise
Mechanisms to Manage Relationships and Communicate	• Transparency of data • Meetings • Shared goals • Shared risk	• Contracting Meetings & business reviews • Email, phone, web • Vendor guidelines	• Participation in task forces / committees • Progress reports • Scorecards

CRITERIA QUESTIONS

Provide data and information to answer the following questions:

c. Supply-Chain Management Results

What are your supply-chain management results? What are your results for key measures or indicators of the performance of your supply chain, including its contribution to enhancing your performance?

Notes:

7.1c This requirement does not ask for levels and trends. The reason is that some significant supply-chain results may be either qualitative or not amendable to trending over time. Examples for suppliers could be training hours on new products or processes, knowledge-sharing activities, audit hours that vary by supplier experience or specification complexity, or joint process and product development. When appropriate, however, you should report levels and trends for results that are numeric and trendable.

7.1c. Appropriate measures and indicators of supply-chain performance might include supplier and partner audits, just-in-time delivery, and acceptance results for externally provided products, services, and processes. Measures and indicators of contributions to enhancing your performance might include those for improvements in subassembly performance and in downstream supplier services to customers.

NIST (2015-2016) pp. 25 - 26

WORKSHEETS

7.1c - Supply-Chain Management Results

Category	Measure	Perf. Level*	Trend	Comparison With Competitors
Supply Chain Measures	**Plans For Disaster Or Emergencies**			
	Supplier Audit Results			
	Just-In-Time Delivery Results			
	Just-In-Time Acceptance Results			
	Training For Disasters Or Emergencies			

ASSESSMENT

131	The supplier results are tracked and show that the suppliers are high performing.	1 2 3 4 5 6 DK
132	The supplier performance levels are linked to our organizational performance, and help to increase the overall organization excellence.	1 2 3 4 5 6 DK

BLUEPRINT

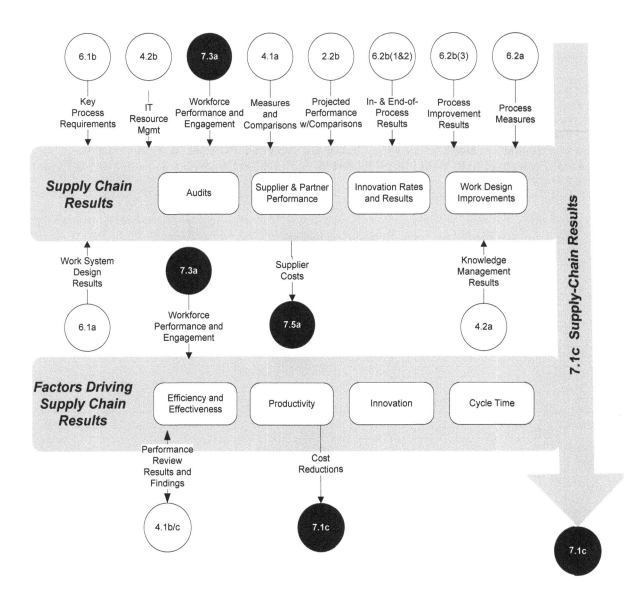

SYSTEM INTEGRATION

Systems

2.2b > 7.1 thru 7.5 Performance Projections and Comparisons - The forecasted performance (projections) along with the projected comparison performance should be reflected in the results charts depicted in 7.1 through 7.5. While the CPE specifically ask for strategic plan accomplishments in 7.1c, the ideal strategic plan will have projections for measures in all five results Items.

4.1a > 7.1 through 7.5 Comparisons - The comparisons selected using the processes described in 4.1a should be the same comparisons that are presented in all the results areas 7.1 through 7.5.

4.1a > 7.1 through 7.5 Measures – The results produced by the measures identified in 4.1a should be the same results presented in all the results areas 7.1 through 7.5.

4.1b < 7.1 through 7.5 Results - All results displayed as part of the results areas 7.1 through 7.5 are potential inputs to the organizational performance review system (4.1b).

4.1b > 7.1 through 7.5 Findings - The explanation of performance levels, trends and comparisons should be included in the applicable results areas (7.1 thorough 7.5).

4.2a > 7.1b Knowledge Management Results - Results that address the effectiveness of the management of data, information, and knowledge should be included in the results presented in 7.1b.

6.1a > 7.1b Work System Design Results - Results that indicate the performance of the organization in areas related to the core competencies and the overall work system design should be reported in 7.1b.

6.1b > 7.1b Key In Process Results - In addition to the outputs the efficiency and effectiveness of the process is determined through in-process measures. The results (levels, trends, comparisons) for key in-process and control measures should be included in the results displayed in area 7.1b. Just as the product and service results are predictors of customer satisfaction, the operational including in-process results are predictors of the product and service results.

6.2a > 7.1b Process Measures - In addition to the outputs the efficiency and effectiveness of the process is determined through in-process measures. The results (levels, trends, comparisons) for key in-process and control measures should be included in the results displayed in area 7.1b. Just as the product and service results are predictors of customer satisfaction, the operational including in-process results are predictors of the product and service results 7.1a.

6.2b(3) > 7.1b Process Improvement Results - Process improvement results including cost reductions should be included in the results presented in 7.1b. These support process cost reductions are often in important part of the contribution to profit and are often viewed together with process, product, and service quality to gain a system perspective.

Scorecard

7.1a < 7.1c Operational Effectiveness - The level of operational effectiveness as presented in 7.1b should have a direct impact on the performance levels and trends presented in 7.1a and the supplier performance in 7.1c.

THOUGHTS FOR LEADERS

Organizations must meet their strategic objectives and achieve the supporting action plans or, over time, they normally wither. As such, the organization must have metrics which show that they are achieving the strategic objectives and detailed actions. These detailed actions, typically, include the performance of the supply chain.

It's amazing how many organizations have a significant amount of controllable cost (not to mention the overall performance of their product) in the hands of suppliers. Many of these organizations, however, delegate the management of suppliers down the organization, and do not view supplier performance as a key strategic issue, competitive advantage, threat, or vulnerability.

All suppliers know where to send the inferior product. Many years ago I was the head of manufacturing in a sports products company. We rejected significant amounts of material on a routine basis. As we worked with the supplier to get their processes in-control (so they could deliver to our standards routinely), we asked them "What do you do with all this rejected material?" They replied "Oh, its no problem, we just send it to your competitor!"

It's great to see leaders who are 'customer focused.' They must also understand, however, how the value is created to meet the customers' requirements. This typically includes a significant supply chain. Leaders cannot just take a position which says "we have a principal-to-principal relationship with our suppliers.... any problems are their problem, not ours." Effective leaders pick the right suppliers, and then help to strengthen them.

> *However beautiful the strategy, you should occasionally look at the results.*
>
> **Winston Churchill**

FOUNDATION

How satisfied are the customers? Are they more satisfied today than they were yesterday? How satisfied are the competitors' customers? These three questions are the validation questions for how well an organization is creating and delivering products and services that meet and exceed customer expectations, as well as how that performance is viewed by the customer. Immediate customer feedback, however, is often impractical. Thus, formal and informal tools are needed to assess the customers' level of satisfaction and the resulting loyalty.

Customer Satisfaction

The customer-focused results reported here in 7.2a, validate the performance of the organization from the perspective of the customer and sometimes from the perspective of the customer's customer. Regardless of whether the organization collects revenue for their services, provides the service free of charge, or uses tax dollars, the primary beneficiaries of the key work processes are, for the purposes of this area, the customers that are external to the organization.

Why measure the customers' perceptions and purchase behaviors? One reason is to validate the product and service measures (reported in 7.1a) used to determine the quality of the output of the key work processes. An organization determines customer requirements, translates those requirements into product and service features, then measures how well the products and services meet those requirements. An organization knows that they have truly understood the customer's requirements only after they have measured the satisfaction, dissatisfaction and behavior of the customer (reported here in 7.2a). As with most results, these should be compared to the performance levels of your competitors and of other organizations providing similar products or services.

Customer Engagement

The ultimate objective is not just customer satisfaction as a stand-alone measure. Customer satisfaction at a high level should lead to customer loyalty. If it does not, then the organization does not understand the customer's requirements (reported in 7.1a). An organization does not want happy customers who leave, they want happy customers who stay (known as loyal customers) and will be advocates for the organization's products and services (known as engaged customers). The data presented here should be reflective of the customer relationship building processes described in Area to Address 3.2b. As with most results, these should be compared to the performance levels of your competitors and of other organizations providing similar products or services.

EXAMPLES

Pewaukee School District (Baldrige Award Recipient 2013)

Example Measures:

- Parent Satisfaction
- Alumni Satisfaction: Curriculum Preparation
- Student Satisfaction: Communication
- Community Satisfaction

Source: Pewaukee School District (2013) pp. 41 – 42

PRO-TEC (Baldrige Recipient 2007)

Example Measures:

- Overall Customer Satisfaction
- Customer Claim (warranty) Performance Satisfaction
- Appliance Customer Survey – Customer Service
- Honda – Competitive On-Time Delivery Benchmark
- Growth of Honda Business – Customer service
- General Motors – Supplier of the Year
- KTH Steel Supplier of the Year Award

Source: PRO-TEC (2007) pp. 40 - 42

Advocate Good Samaritan Hospital (Baldrige Recipient 2010)

- Inpatient Satisfaction
- Outpatient Satisfaction
- Emergency Department Satisfaction
- Sensitivity to Needs – Outpatient Satisfaction
- Prompt Response to Call – Inpatient Satisfaction
- Wait time to Noticed Arrival – Emergency Department Satisfaction
- Likelihood to Recommend – Patient Loyalty

Source: Advocate Good Samaritan Hospital (2010) pp. 34 – 37

Monfort College of Business (Baldrige recipient, 2004)

Example Measures:

- Student Satisfaction EBI Exit Study
  - Overall Satisfaction
  - Satisfaction with Quality of Faculty and Instruction

- o Satisfaction with Quality of Teaching in Business Courses v. non-Business Course on Campus
  - o Satisfaction with Accessibility of Major Course Instructors Outside of Class
  - o Satisfaction with Breadth of Curriculum: Global Perspective, Interaction w/ Practitioners, Instructors presenting tech. issues, Practical experiences, and Overall
  - o Satisfaction with Facilities and Computing Resources
  - o Satisfaction with Quality of Classrooms
  - o Comparing Expense and Quality of Education Rate the "Value" of Your Investment
- Alumni Satisfaction – EBI Survey
- MCB Employer Survey
  - o Value
  - o Recommend MCB
- MCB Student Survey
  - o MCB Emphasizes High Quality Teaching
  - o Would you recommend MCB to other family members?
  - o How inclined to recommend MCB to a close friend?
- MCB Parent Survey
  - o Value of MCB investment
  - o Recommend to a close friend
- Student Retention

Source: Monfort (2005) pp. 39 – 4

CRITERIA QUESTIONS

Provide data and information to answer the following questions:

a. Customer-Focused Results

(1) **Customer Satisfaction** What are your customer satisfaction and dissatisfaction results? What are your current levels and trends in key measures or indicators of customer satisfaction and dissatisfaction? How do these results compare with those of your competitors and other organizations providing similar products? How do these results differ by product offerings, customer groups, and market segments, as appropriate?

(2) **Customer Engagement** What are your customer engagement results? What are your current levels and trends in key measures or indicators of customer engagement, including those for building customer relationships? How do these results compare over the course of your customer life cycle, as appropriate? How do these results differ by product offerings, customer groups, and market segments, as appropriate?

Notes:

7.2. Results for customer satisfaction, dissatisfaction, engagement, and relationship building should relate to the customer groups and market segments you identify in P.1b(2) and to the listening and determination methods you report in item 3.1.

7.2a(1). For customers' satisfaction with your products relative to satisfaction with those of competitors and comparable organizations, measures and indicators might include information and data from your customers, from competitors' customers, and from independent organizations.

NIST (2015-2016) p. 26

WORKSHEETS

7.2a(1) Customer Satisfaction, and 7.2a(2) Customer Engagement

Category	Measure	Results for Each Customer Segment (From P.1b[2])			Perf. Level*	Trend	Comparison With Competitors
		A	B	n			
Customer Satisfaction (7.2a[1])	**Survey – Overall Satisfaction**						
Customer Dissatisfaction (7.2a[1])	**Complaints**						
Customer Engagement - *Customer Relationships (7.2a[2])*	**Survey–Satisfaction with Relationship**						
	Survey – Perceived Value						
Customer Engagement - *Customer Loyalty (7.2a[2])*	**Repeat Business (sales)**						
Customer Engagement - *Customer Retention (7.2a[2])*	**Referred Business (sales)**						
Customer Engagement - *Customer Positive Referral (7.2a[2])*	***Referred Business (sales)***						

* Attaching the appropriate data charts can be of benefit, but at a minimum the above data needs to be included. Additionally, the customer measures should be shown which can track over the customer life cycle, as appropriate.

ASSESSMENT

Rating Scale:

1 - **No Business Results** – We do not have these data
2 - **Few Business Results** – We have some data, but are early in improving
3 - **Improvements And/Or Good Results Reported** – We have data but in the early stages of trends
4 - **Good Trends In Most Areas** – No adverse trends and some comparisons
5 - **Good To Excellent In Most Areas** – Most trends are sustained and most have comparisons
6 - **Excellent Performance In Most Important Areas** – We are the Benchmark in our industry or beyond!
DK - Don't Know

133	Customer satisfaction, loyalty and engagement compare favorably to the results of competitors or other organizations providing similar products or services.	1	2	3	4	5	6	DK
134	The organization has quantitative results measures for customer dissatisfaction for each of the customer segments or groups.	1	2	3	4	5	6	DK
135	Customer dissatisfaction compares favorably to the results of competitors or other organizations providing similar products or services.	1	2	3	4	5	6	DK
136	The organization has quantitative results measures for customer loyalty, retention and engagement for each of the customer segments or groups.	1	2	3	4	5	6	DK

BLUEPRINT

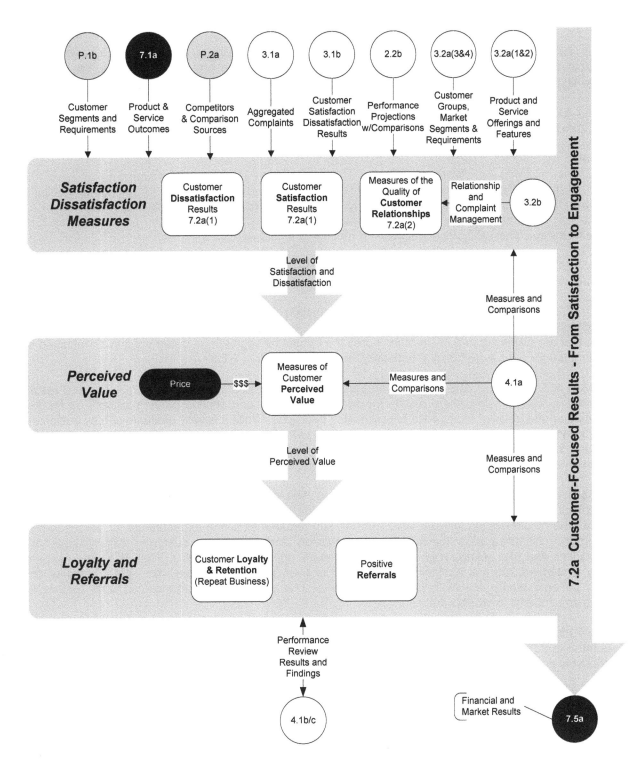

SYSTEM INTEGRATION

Context

P.1b > 7.2a Customers Segments and Requirements - Customers, customer groups, and market segments along with the associated requirements described in the profile (P.1b) are a key input to determining and segmenting the customer focused results presented in 7.2a.

P.2a > 7.2a Competitors and Comparisons - The comparisons presented in the customer-focused results (7.2a) should be consistent with the competitors and comparison sources identified in the profile (P.2a).

Systems

2.2b > 7.1 thru 7.5 Performance Projections and Comparisons - The forecasted performance (projections) along with the projected comparison performance should be reflected in the results charts depicted in 7.1 through 7.5. While the CPE specifically ask for strategic plan accomplishments in Area to Address 7.1c, the ideal strategic plan will have projections for measures in all five results Items.

3.1a > 7.2a Aggregated Complaints - Complaints that are captured, aggregated and analyzed are part of customer dissatisfaction and should be included by segment in the results in area 7.2a.

3.1b > 7.2a Customer Satisfaction and Dissatisfaction Results - The customer satisfaction and dissatisfaction measurement methods identified in 3.1b will produce the satisfaction and dissatisfaction results that are displayed in 7.2a. In other words the results by segment as determined in 3.1b should be the same results (levels, trends, comparisons) that are displayed in 7.2a.

3.2a(1&2) > 7.2a Product and Service Offerings and Features Results - The customer focused results presented in 7.2a should include results for each key product and service offering as well as the key features and their relative importance to purchasing decisions. While it is very useful to survey customers and ask for their preferences it is even better to analyze their actual behavior and buying patterns along with their satisfaction results. This provides the organization with much better information for making adjustments to product and service offerings and the associated features.

3.2a(3&4) > 7.2a Customer and Market Segments - The customer focused results presented in 7.2a should include results for each key customer or market segment and group identified in 3.2a(3&4). In addition, the results should include results on the key requirements and expectations for each segment and group. This area asks for how the organization determines key customer requirements and expectations and their relative importance to customers' purchasing decisions. While it is very useful to survey customers and ask for their preferences it is even better to analyze their actual behavior and buying patterns along with their satisfaction results. This provides the organization with insights for making adjustments to product and service offerings.

3.2b > 7.2a Customer Relationship and Complaint Management Results - The customer focused results presented in 7.2a should include results on the extent and effectiveness of the organization's customer relationship and complaint management systems.

4.1a > 7.1 through 7.5 Comparisons - The comparisons selected using the processes described in 4.1a should be the same comparisons that are presented in all the results areas 7.1 through 7.5.

4.1a > 7.1 through 7.5 Measures – The results produced by the measures identified in 4.1a should be the same results presented in all the results areas 7.1 through 7.5.

4.1b/c < 7.1a through 7.5 Results - All results displayed as part of the results Items 7.1 through 7.5 are potential inputs to the organizational performance review system 4.1b/c.

4.1b/c > 7.1 through 7.5 Findings - The explanation of performance levels, trends and comparisons should be included in the applicable results Items (7.1 thorough 7.5).

Scorecard

7.1a > 7.2a Product and Service Outcomes - The product and service results included in 7.1a should be "proxies" for customer satisfaction (7.2a). Consequently, the customer satisfaction results in 7.2a should correlate with the results presented in 7.1a. The analysis of this correlation will help to validate and refine the product and service measures selected for inclusion in 7.1a.

7.2a > 7.5a Customer Results - The revenue results depicted in 7.5a should correlate to the customer satisfaction results presented in 7.2a. The notion here is that if customer satisfaction is high compared to competitors the customer will come back (repeat business) and tell their friends (referral business) which should result in growth in revenue.

THOUGHTS FOR LEADERS

High performing organizations MUST understand what drives their customer's behavior. In the Thoughts for Leaders in Item 7.1, the following logic flow was presented:

- Customer segments (Baldrige Criteria P.1a[2])
- Customer requirements by segment (Baldrige Criteria P.1a[2])
- Organizational performance against customer requirements by segment (Baldrige Criteria 7.1a)
- Customer satisfaction by segment (Baldrige Criteria 7.2a[1])
- Customer-perceived value, including customer loyalty, by segment (Baldrige Criteria 7.2a[2])

If an organization is able to correlate their performance against the customer requirements (Area to Address 7.1a) v. the customer's behavior (Area to Address 7.2a[2]), they know that they truly understand the customer's requirements. If these two data points do not correlate and show a linkage between an improvement in meeting the customer's requirements and an improvement in customer loyalty (or customer perceived value) then the organization does not understand the customer's requirements. The customer requirements they are working toward are not the true "complete" set of customer requirements and need to be revised.

A Lighter Moment:

A dog owns nothing, yet is seldom dissatisfied.

Irish proverb

> *Your most precious possession is not your financial assets.*
> *Your most precious possession is the people you have*
> *Working there, and what they carry around in their heads,*
> *and their ability to work together.*
>
> **Robert Reich**

FOUNDATION

Process performance is important but seldom occurs without an engaged workforce. People measures are an important input and predictor of process performance and in some situations, customer satisfaction. Included in this area might be indicators of employee satisfaction, learning, and performance. Are the employee results good? Are they getting better? How does this organization's employee results compare to its competitors or organizations in the same business? Are their employees more or less satisfied? Who is getting better faster?

Are to address 7.3a measures the multiple aspects of the people component of the organization. Product and service quality measures are not the only "proxies" of customer satisfaction. Heskett, Sasser, and Schlesinger (1997) link key people measures, such as capability, satisfaction, and loyalty, with productivity and services quality, which is linked to customer satisfaction and, in turn, revenue growth. Others, including Becker, Huselid, and Ulrich (2001), have proposed a Human Resources scorecard aligned with and supporting the overall organizational strategy.

Workforce Capability and Capacity

The organization needs to have a process to determine the skills required (capability) and the numbers of people required (capacity). The measures for these should reflect the results tracked from the process described in Figure 5.1a(1).

Workforce Climate

The culture described in the Organizational Profile (P.1a) and reflected in the Workforce Climate (5.1b) should be tracked in the results reported here. At a minimum, this should include the current levels and trends in key measures or indicators of health, safety, security, and services and benefits.

Workforce Engagement

The *people* results should be comprehensive enough to provide a clear picture of the overall status of the workforce and should also provide insight into the various segments of the workforce. As with the other measures discussed in this book, the human resource measures should include both leading and lagging measures. Measures should include how the organization knows the workforce is engaged and satisfied.

Workforce Development

The development of the workforce and the leaders should be reported. At a minimum, this includes leading and lagging measures of development. Measures should include how the organization knows the workforce is developing, increasing capability and capacity.

 EXAMPLES

Pewaukee School District (Baldrige Recipient 2013)

- Student to Staff Ratio
- Students in Enrollment & Staffing Levels
- Teacher Applications Received
- New Hire Teacherinsight Assessments
- Staff Perceptions of Safety
- Worker's Compensation Claims
- Staff Exercise Habits
- Wage & Benefit Satisfaction
- Involvement & Engagement
- Length of Service
- Teachers with Advanced Degrees
- Professional Development Attendance

Source: Pewaukee School District (2013) pp. 42-44 – 56

Advocate Good Samaritan Hospital (Baldrige Recipient 2010)

- Associate Satisfaction
- Overall Physician Satisfaction
- Efficiency of Operations
- Safe & Error-Free care
- Training Hours per Full Time Employee
- Satisfaction with Career Development
- Voluntary Associate Turnover
- Impact of leader Development Hours on Action Plan Readiness Scores
- Associate Satisfaction with Benefits
- Associate Indicators Workplace Safety (Security)

Source: Advocate Good Samaritan Hospital (2013) pp. 40 – 43

Monfort College of Business (Baldrige recipient, 2004)

- Faculty Qualifications – Proportion of Classes Taught by Academically and/or Professionally Qualified Faculty
- Faculty Qualifications – Number of Executive Professors
- Faculty Survey
   o Satisfaction with Salary, Promotion, Tenure Process Rating
   o Degree to which Senior Faculty Mentor Junior Faculty
   o Faculty Well-being and Support

- Number of Faculty Intellectual Contributions (Number of Refereed Publications Last 5 Years)
- Staff Technology Certifications
- Faculty Satisfaction Survey – EBI
  - Overall Satisfaction
  - Overall Evaluation of Undergraduate Program
  - Faculty Sharing a Common Vision for the School
  - Faculty Satisfaction with Computer Support

Source: Monfort (2005) pp. 44 – 46

 ## CRITERIA QUESTIONS

Provide data and information to answer the following questions:

a. Workforce Results

(1) **Workforce Capability and Capacity** What are your workforce capability and capacity results? What are your current levels and trends in key measures of workforce capability and capacity, including appropriate skills and staffing levels? How do these results differ by the diversity of your workforce and by your workforce groups and segments, as appropriate?

(2) **Workforce Climate** What are your workforce climate results? What are your current levels and trends in key measures or indicators of your workforce climate, including those for workforce health, safety, and security and workforce services and benefits, as appropriate? How do these results differ by the diversity of your workforce and by your workforce groups and segments, as appropriate?

(3) **Workforce Engagement** What are your workforce engagement results? What are your current levels and trends in key measures or indicators of workforce engagement and workforce satisfaction? How do these results differ by the diversity of your workforce and by your workforce groups and segments, as appropriate?

(4) **Workforce Development** What are your workforce and leader development results? What are your current levels and trends in key measures or indicators of workforce and leader development? How do these results differ by the diversity of your workforce and by your workforce groups and segments, as appropriate?

Notes:

7.3. Results reported in this item should relate to the processes you report in category 5. Your results should also respond to the key work process needs you report in category 6 and to the action plans and workforce plans you report in item 2.2.

7.3. Organizations that rely on volunteers should report results for their volunteer workforce, as appropriate.

7.3a(3). Responses should include results for the measures and indicators you identify in 5.2a(3).

NIST (2015-2016) p. 27

WORKSHEETS

7.3a(1) Workforce Capability and Capacity

Category	Measure	Perf. Level	Trend	Comparison With Competitors
Workforce Capacity and Capability	Staffing Levels			
	Retention			
	Appropriate Skills			
	Differences Between Diverse Groups			
	Differences Between Workforce Groups			

7.3a(2) Workforce Climate

Category	Measure	Perf. Level	Trend	Comparison With Competitors
Workforce Climate	Health			
	Safety			
	Security			
	Workforce Services			
	Workforce Benefits			
	Voluntary Turnover			
	Turnover Of Key Work Groups (i.e., Nursing For Health Care)			
	Absenteeism			
	Complaints (Grievances)			
	Sick Days			
	Accidents (Number And Severity)			

7.3a(3) Workforce Engagement

Category	Measure	Perf. Level*	Trend	Comparison With Competitors
Workforce Engagement	Workforce Satisfaction Levels*			
	Workforce Loyalty Levels*			
	Workforce Engagement Levels*			

These should be shown for the entire workforce, as well as for critical workforce groups.

7.3a(4) Workforce Development

Category	Measure **	Perf. Level*	Trend	Comparison With Competitors
Workforce Development	Hours Trained Per Employee			
	Percent Promoted From Within Or From Succession Plan			
	Skill Improvement			
	High-Potential Employees Promoted			
	Retention Of Top Talent			
	Leadership Training Per Leader			
	Effectiveness of Training			
	Impact of Training			

* Attaching the appropriate data charts can be of benefit, but at a minimum the above data needs to be included.

** Measures should be segmented into employee groups, as appropriate.

ASSESSMENT

Rating Scale:

1 - No Business Results – We do not have these data
2 - Few Business Results – We have some data, but are early in improving
3 - Improvements And/Or Good Results Reported – We have data but in the early stages of trends
4 - Good Trends In Most Areas – No adverse trends and some comparisons
5 - Good To Excellent In Most Areas – Most trends are sustained and most have comparisons
6 - Excellent Performance In Most Important Areas – We are the Benchmark in our industry or beyond!
DK - Don't Know

---

137   The organization effectively plans for the skills and staffing levels needed in the future, and can validate their availability with data.   1   2   3   4   5   6   DK

138   The organization validates, through measures and tracking, that the workplace is secure, safe, and healthy.   1   2   3   4   5   6   DK

139   The organization tracks trends in key measures in employee well-being, satisfaction, and engagement, and can show a favorable result.   1   2   3   4   5   6   DK

140   The organization tracks trends in key measures of employee development, and can show a favorable result.   1   2   3   4   5   6   DK

BLUEPRINT

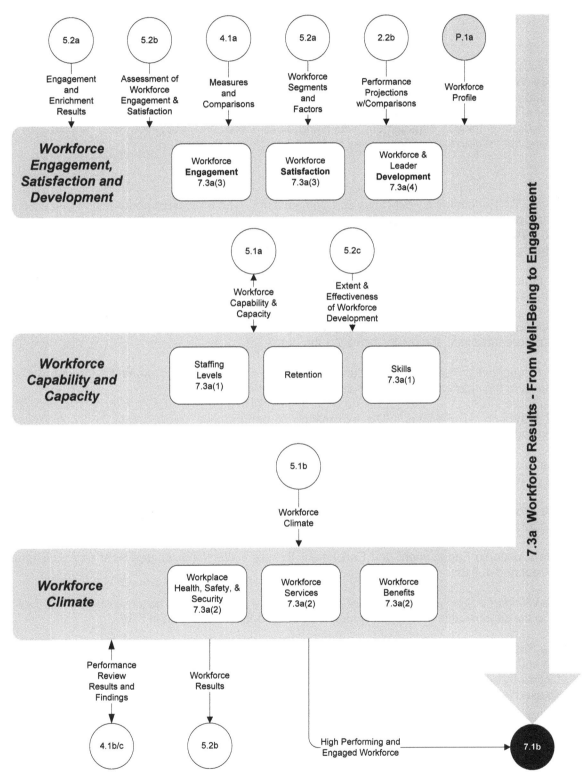

SYSTEM INTEGRATION

Context

P.1a > 7.3a Workforce Profile - The workforce profile is a key input to determining the workforce segments that are appropriate for the various workforce results including engagement, satisfaction, well-being, dissatisfaction, learning, etc. In addition, the employee profile is a key input to the identification of the key factors for employee engagement, well-being, satisfaction, and motivation which should also be measured and the results reported for the key factors by employee segment.

Systems

2.2b > 7.1 thru 7.5 Performance Projections and Comparisons - The forecasted performance (projections) along with the projected comparison performance should be reflected in the results charts depicted in 7.1 through 7.5. While the CPE specifically ask for strategic plan accomplishments in Area to Address 7.1c, the ideal strategic plan will have projections for measures in all five results Items.

4.1a > 7.1 through 7.5 Comparisons - The comparisons selected using the processes described in 4.1a should be the same comparisons that are presented in all the results Items 7.1 through 7.5.

4.1a > 7.1 through 7.5 Measures – The results produced by the measures identified in 4.1a should be the same results presented in all the results Items 7.1 through 7.5.

4.1b/c < 7.1 through 7.5 Results - All results displayed as part of the results areas 7.1 through 7.5 are potential inputs to the organizational performance review system (4.1b).

4.1b/c > 7.1 through 7.5 Findings - The explanation of performance levels, trends and comparisons should be included in the applicable results areas (7.1a thorough 7.5).

5.1a > 7.3a Workforce Capability and Capacity Results - The results related to workforce capability and capacity (e.g., turnover, qualifications, etc.) should be reported in 7.3a.

5.1b > 7.3a Workforce Climate Results - Results on the workforce climate (e.g., safety, health, security, etc.) should be reported in 7.3a.

5.2a > 7.3a Workforce Engagement and Enrichment Results - Workforce engagement and enrichment results are reported in 7.3a.

5.2a > 7.3a Workforce Segments and Factors - The workforce segments and factors identified in 5.2a are key inputs to the segmentation and types of measures that should be included in 7.3a.

5.2b < 7.3a Results - Human resource results (levels, trends, and comparisons) influence the employee satisfaction and engagement approaches in two ways. First, they can be analyzed and used to determine the key factors by segment that affect well-being, satisfaction, and motivation. Second, human resource results are used to evaluate and improve employee services, benefits, and policies.

5.2b > 7.3a Workforce Engagement and Satisfaction Results - The results from the assessment and measurement of workforce engagement and satisfaction identified in 5.2b should be reported in 7.3a.

5.2c > 7.3a Workforce Development Results - The results from the evaluation of the extent and effectiveness of training and education should be part of the human resources results presented in 7.3a.

Scorecard

7.3a > 7.1b High Performing and Engaged Workforce - The high performing workforce that is a result of improvements in well-being, satisfaction, learning, development, and work system performance directly impact the performance in the operational results presented in 7.1b.

THOUGHTS FOR LEADERS

How leaders measure their human resource performance may be an indicator of the leader's belief in their people as the enablers of all progress. Using the CPE model, leaders tend to change what they measure and try to move from *lagging* "people" measures which track what has already happened to *leading* measures which can help them predict how employees will react in the future.

For example, after studying their safety performance, one organization was only able to correlate safety to one other characteristic. That characteristic, fortunately, could be used as a leading indicator to predict, and try to influence, future safety performance. In their case, employee safety correlated to the amount of time employees spent with their immediate supervisors. This indicator may not fit for all other organizations, however, in this particular organization, the more time an employee spent with his or her supervisor, the more safely the employee performed the job. Obviously, the organization took action to improve the time employees spent with their supervisor.

Additionally, leaders using the CPE model start to understand the relationships between the human resource measures and the bottom-line organizational measures better. Understanding these enabling relationships allows them to determine what actions need to be taken to drive overall organizational performance.

> *One of the most important ways to manifest integrity is to be loyal to those who are not present. In doing so, we build the trust of those who are present.*
>
> **Stephen Covey**

> *Leadership is based on inspiration, not domination;*
> *on cooperation, not intimidation.*
>
> **William Arthur Wood**

 FOUNDATION

While it is critically important to satisfy customers and empower the workforce, these measures are incomplete. Performance excellence is only sustainable if the organization is operating in a way that is consistent and in the interests of the communities in which it operates as well as the public at large. Consider the company that pollutes the town's water supply. Eventually, the reaction from the local community will make it difficult for the business to profitably operate in that community. If the executives act unethically, trust with the employees, customers, partners, and investors will be destroyed. Without trust and support from these key stakeholders, the processes, no matter how fancy, will fail to produce sustainable results. This area focuses on how well the organization achieves a range of results. These aspects include:

- *Leadership:*
  - Communication,
  - Engagement,
  - Deployment of Vision and Values,
  - Communication,
  - Action focus.
- *Governance:*
  - Governance,
  - Fiscal Accountability,
  - Internal and external measures.
- *Law and Regulation:*
  - Surpassing legal requirements,
  - Surpassing regulatory requirements.
- *Ethics:*
  - Ethical behavior,
  - Stakeholder trust in senior leaders,
  - Stakeholder trust in governance,
  - Key indicators of breaches in ethical behavior.
- *Society:*
  - Fulfillment of societal responsibilities,
  - Support of the community,
  - Contributions to community health (for the Health Care Criteria).

EXAMPLES

PRO-TEC (Baldrige Recipient 2007)

- Compliance Audit Outcomes
- Associate Contributions to the United Way
- Company Key Community Contributions
- Good Citizenship
- Long Term Viability

Source: PRO-TEC (2007) pp. 49 - 50

Pewaukee School District (Baldrige Recipient 2013)

- District Commitment to Education
- Employee Work Contributions
- Number of policies on ethics
- Minutes Show Monthly Board of Education Approval of OE Seats & Class Size
- Percent of Teachers Highly Qualified
- Number of students who had technology privileges suspended due to improper use of technology on campus
- Kohl Fellowship Awards

Source: Pewaukee School District (2013) pp. 45 - 46

Advocate Good Samaritan Hospital (Baldrige Recipient 2010)

- Health Professionals Education
- Charity Care
- Business Conduct Hotline Calls
- Associate perception of ethical behavior
- Compliance in Signing Conflict of Interest Statements
- Success of the Good to Great Journey

Source: Advocate Good Samaritan Hospital (2010) pp. 43 - 47

Monfort College of Business (Baldrige Recipient 2004)

- Student Satisfaction with Curriculum Presenting Social Responsibility Issues
- Student Satisfaction with Curriculum Presenting Ethical Issues
- Audit Results - Violations ,etc.
- Number and Type of Legal Violations
- Number and Type of Ethical Violations
- Faculty and Staff Community Involvement – Extent and Type

Source: Monfort (2005) p. 50

CRITERIA QUESTIONS

Provide data and information to answer the following questions:

a. Leadership, Governance, and Societal Responsibility Results

(1) **Leadership** What are your results for senior leaders' communication and engagement with the workforce and customers? What are your results for key measures or indicators of senior leaders' communication and engagement with the workforce and customers to deploy your vision and values, encourage two-way communication, and create a focus on action? How do these results differ by organizational units and customer groups, as appropriate?

(2) **Governance** What are your results for governance accountability? What are your key current findings and trends in key measures or indicators of governance and internal and external fiscal accountability, as appropriate?

(3) **Law and Regulation** What are your legal and regulatory results? What are your results for key measures or indicators of meeting and surpassing regulatory and legal requirements? How do these results differ by organizational units, as appropriate?

(4**) Ethics** What are your results for ethical behavior? What are your results for key measures or indicators of ethical behavior and of stakeholder trust in your senior leaders and governance? How do these results differ by organizational units, as appropriate?

(5) **Society** What are your results for societal responsibilities and support of your key communities? What are your results for key measures or indicators of your fulfillment of your societal responsibilities and support of your key communities?

Notes:

7.4. Most of the requirements in this item do not ask for levels and trends. The reason is that some significant results may be either qualitative in nature or not amenable to trending over time. Examples could be results of intelligent risk taking and governance accountability. For such results, qualitative explanation may be more meaningful than current levels and trends. When appropriate, however, you should report levels and trends for results that are numeric and trendable.

7.4a(1). Responses should relate to the communication processes you identify in item 1.1.

7.4a(2). Responses might include financial statement issues and risks, important internal and external auditor recommendations, and management's responses to these matters. Some nonprofit organizations might also report results of IRS 990 audits.

7.4a(3). Legal and regulatory results should relate to the requirements you report in 1.2b. Workforce-related occupational health and safety results (e.g., OSHA-reportable incidents) should be reported in 7.1b(1) and 7.3a(2).

7.4a(4). For examples of measures of ethical behavior and stakeholder trust, see the note to 1.2b(2).

7.4a(5). Responses should relate to the societal responsibilities you report in 1.2b(1) and 1.2c(1), as well as the support of the key communities you report in 1.2c(2). Measures of contributions to societal well-being might include those for reduced energy consumption, the use of renewable energy resources and recycled water, reduction of carbon footprint, waste reduction and utilization, alternative approaches to conserving resources (e.g., increased audio and video conferencing), and the global use of enlightened labor practices.

NIST (2015-2016) p. 28

WORKSHEETS

7.4a(1) Leadership

Category	Measure Or Indicator	Perf. Level	Trend	Comparison
Leadership	Communication Levels			
	Communication Impact			
	Engagement Levels			
	Engagement Impact			
	Deployment of Vision and Values			
	Validation of Two-Way Communication			
	Validation of a Focus On Action			

7.4a(2) Governance

Category	Measure Or Indicator	Perf. Level	Trend	Comparison
Governance	Governance			
	Fiscal Accountability			
	Internal Audit Results (Major Findings And Actions)			
	External Audit Results (Major Findings And Actions)			
	Fines Or Sanctions			

7.4a(3) Law and Regulation

Category	Measure Or Indicator	Perf. Level	Trend	Comparison
Law and Regulation	Meeting Or Exceeding Regulatory Requirements (Several Measures)			
	Meeting Or Exceeding Legal Requirements (Several Measures)			
	Internal Audits (Major Findings And Actions)			
	External Audits (Major Findings And Actions)			
	Certification Results			

7.4a(4) Ethics

Category	Measure Or Indicator	Perf. Level	Trend	Comparison
Ethics	Ethical Requirements (several measures)			
	Internal Audits			
	External Audits			
	Findings and Violations			

7.4a(5) Society

Category	Measure Or Indicator	Perf. Level	Trend	Comparison
Society	Level of Support			
	Impact of Support			
	Sustainability of Support			
	Society Validation of Organizational Support			

ASSESSMENT

Rating Scale:

1 - No Business Results – We do not have these data
2 - Few Business Results – We have some data, but are early in improving
3 - Improvements And/Or Good Results Reported – We have data but in the early stages of trends
4 - Good Trends In Most Areas – No adverse trends and some comparisons
5 - Good To Excellent In Most Areas – Most trends are sustained and most have comparisons
6 - Excellent Performance In Most Important Areas – We are the Benchmark in our industry or beyond!
DK - Don't Know

141	Key measures are used which show that the Senior Leaders effectively communicate with and engage the workforce to deploy the vision and values.	1	2	3	4	5	6	DK
142	Key measures are used which show that the Senior Leaders effectively communicate with and engage the workforce to create a focus on action.	1	2	3	4	5	6	DK
143	Key measures are tracked and show ethical behavior and stakeholder trust in the organizational governance.	1	2	3	4	5	6	DK
144	Key measures are tracked and show high regulatory and legal compliance.	1	2	3	4	5	6	DK
145	Key measures are tracked and show strong ethics and fiscal accountability including the results of internal and external audits.	1	2	3	4	5	6	DK
146	Key measures are tracked and show strong organizational citizenship in support of the key communities.	1	2	3	4	5	6	DK

BLUEPRINT

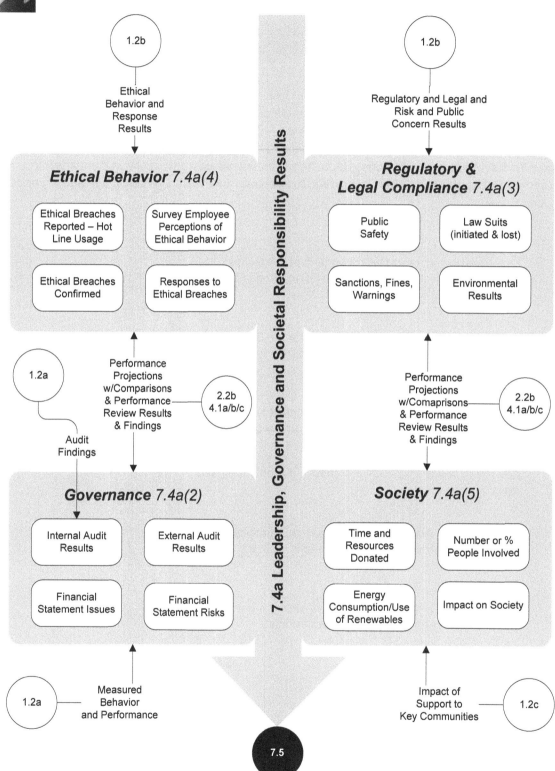

SYSTEM INTEGRATION

Systems

1.2a > 7.4a Governance System Results - Employee behavior and accountability measures are included in 7.4a and should measure the effectiveness of the governance processes that address management accountability, fiscal accountability, and ultimately protect the interests of the stockholders and stakeholders. In addition, 7.4a includes the audit findings from both internal and external audits which also validate the effectiveness of the preventive approaches. As inputs these results are used to make governance decisions and also to evaluate and improve the governance structure, system, and processes.

1.2b > 7.4a Regulatory and Legal - Regulatory and legal results found in 7.4a should reflect the same measures and goals described in 1.2b. The results in 7.4a confirm or deny the effectiveness of the approaches described in this area.

1.2b > 7.4a Risks and Concerns - The results in 7.4a should directly reflect the results and targets that determine the effectiveness of the processes and approaches to address the risks and public concerns associated with the products, services, and operations.

1.2b > 7.4a Ethical Behavior - Ethical behavior measures identified in 1.2b should be consistent with the results for ethical behavior presented in 7.4a.

1.2c > 7.4a Social Responsibility and Community Support - The results that indicate the extent and effectiveness of the social responsibility and community support system should be presented in 7.4a.

2.2b > 7.1 thru 7.5 Performance Projections and Comparisons - The forecasted performance (projections) along with the projected comparison performance should be reflected in the results charts depicted in 7.1 through 7.5.

4.1a > 7.1 through 7.5 Comparisons - The comparisons selected using the processes described in 4.1a should be the same comparisons that are presented in all the results areas 7.1 through 7.5.

4.1a > 7.1 through 7.5 Measures – The results produced by the measures identified in 4.1a should be the same results presented in all the results areas 7.1 through 7.5.

4.1b/c < 7.1 through 7.5 Results - All results displayed as part of the results areas 7.1 through 7.5 are potential inputs to the organizational performance review system (4.1b).

4.1b/c > 7.1 through 7.5 Findings - The explanation of performance levels, trends and comparisons should be included in the applicable results areas (7.1 thorough 7.5).

THOUGHTS FOR LEADERS

Organizations must meet their strategic objectives and achieve the supporting action plans or, over time, they normally wither. As such, the organization must have metrics which show that they are achieving the strategic objectives and detailed actions.

On another front, organizations must also have measures which validate (or question?) the ethics of the organization. Favorable results on these measures can be key in driving stakeholder trust in the leadership. If there are caution signs, or in-process measures which indicate that the organization's stakeholders have concerns, the action taken must be timely, direct and result in correcting the root cause of the concern.

Another measure which can drive stakeholder trust is the validation that the organization is fiscally responsible. This typically comes from a robust network of internal and external audits, checks, and balances. This same approach using a network of internal and external audits, checks, and balances is key for all regulatory and compliance issues as well.

Finally, an organization can only be great if it is a good steward of the community trust, the community well-being, natural resources, and the laws around them. This starts and ends with leadership, as described in Category 1. Leadership must model the behaviors that they want all others to follow, and model the behaviors they want the organization to endorse.

Item 7.4 does not attempt to measure whether an organization is great, but unfavorable results presented here can indicate that an organization has not yet reached greatness.

A Lighter Moment:

People ask the difference between a leader and a boss.
The leader leads, and the boss drives.

Theodore Roosevelt

FOUNDATION

This area to address focuses on the results achieved from the implementation of your actions plans identified in Area to Address 2.2a. While improving results are reported in the trends throughout the results Items 7.1 through 7.5, this area asks for results specific to the effectiveness of the action plans. These results include the projections provided in Area to Address 2.2b.

While one would expect the improvement trends related to strategy to be found in all results area, this area focuses on how well the organization achieves the results related to the implementation of the action plans identified in 2.2a and the related projections identified in 2.2b. These results include key measures or indicators of:

- the accomplishment of the organizational strategic goals and objectives – 2.1a;

- the accomplishment of the organizational action plans (this should be focused at the organizational level, or for key plans) – 2.2a and related performance projections – 2.2b; and

- the building and strengthening of the organization's core competencies.

The metrics shown can be a combination of both leading and lagging indicators. While these results are not the central purpose of the organization, they are essential aspects that determine overall success. An organization cannot succeed merely by performing well on these metrics. To perform poorly on one or more of these metrics, however, may spell disaster.

EXAMPLES

Sharp Healthcare (Baldrige Recipient 2007)

- Earnings Before Interest, Taxes, Depreciation, and Amortization (EBITDA)
- Outpatient to Total Revenue
- Capital Spending Ration

CRITERIA QUESTIONS

Provide data and information to the following questions:

b. Strategy Implementation Results

What are your results for the achievement of your organizational strategy and action plans? What are your results for key measures or indicators of the achievement of your organizational strategy and action plans? What are your results for building and strengthening core competencies? What are your results for taking intelligent risks?

Notes:

7.4b. Measures or indicators of strategy and action plan achievement should relate to the strategic objectives and goals you report in 2.1b(1) and the action plan performance measures and projected performance you report in 2.2a(5) and 2.2a(6), respectively.

NIST (2015-2016) p. 28

Worksheets

7.4b – Strategy Implementation Results

Category	Measure Or Indicator	Perf.* Level	Trend	Comparison	Link To Taking Intelligent Risks	Link To Strengthening Core Competencies
Organizational Strategy						
Action Plans						

* This should be a measure showing the ability of the organization to meet the intent of their strategy repeatedly.

ASSESSMENT

Rating Scale:

1 - **No Business Results** – We do not have these data
2 - **Few Business Results** – We have some data, but are early in improving
3 - **Improvements And/Or Good Results Reported** – We have data but in the early stages of trends
4 - **Good Trends In Most Areas** – No adverse trends and some comparisons
5 - **Good To Excellent In Most Areas** – Most trends are sustained and most have comparisons
6 - **Excellent Performance In Most Important Areas** – We are the Benchmark in our industry or beyond!
DK - Don't Know

147   Key measures are tracked to show the accomplishment of the organizational strategy.   1   2   3   4   5   6   DK

148   Key measures are tracked to show the accomplishment of the action plans and the strengthening of the achievement of the core competency.   1   2   3   4   5   6   DK

BLUEPRINT

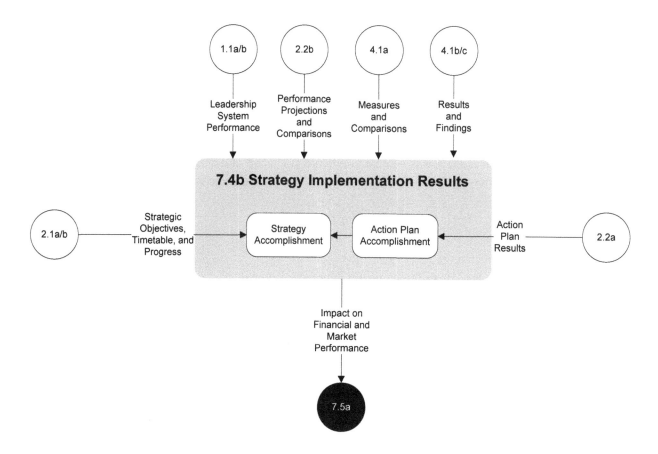

SYSTEM INTEGRATION

Systems

1.1a/b > 7.4b Leadership System Performance focuses on transforming the organization to higher levels of performance. The leadership system is inextricably linked to the strategic management systems. These systems work together to improve performance. Performance that should be reported in 7.1c.

2.1a/b > 7.4b Strategic Objectives, Timetable, and Progress - The results associated with the accomplishment of the organization's strategy and action plans should be reported in 7.1c.

2.2a > 7.4b Action Plan Results - The results relating to progress toward achieving the action plans described in 2.2a and the associated changes in performance should be reported in 7.1c.

2.2b > 7.1 thru 7.5 Performance Projections and Comparisons - The forecasted performance (projections) along with the projected comparison performance should be reflected in the results charts depicted in 7.1 through 7.5. While the CPE specifically ask for strategic plan accomplishments in Area to Address 7.1c, the ideal strategic plan will have projections for measures in all six results areas.

4.1a > 7.1 through 7.5 Comparisons - The comparisons selected using the processes described in 4.1a should be the same comparisons that are presented in all the results areas 7.1 through 7.5.

4.1a > 7.1 through 7.5 Measures – The results produced by the measures identified in 4.1a should be the same results presented in all the results areas 7.1 through 7.5.

4.1b/c < 7.1 through 7.5 Results - All results displayed as part of the results areas 7.1 through 7.5 are potential inputs to the organizational performance review system (4.1b).

4.1b/c > 7.1 through 7.5 Findings - The explanation of performance levels, trends and comparisons should be included in the applicable results areas (7.1 thorough 7.5).

Scorecard

7.5a < 7.4b Strategy Accomplishment - The results presented in 7.1c include results on the accomplishment of the organization's strategy. Successful accomplishment of the strategy should have a direct impact on the financial results of the organization including market share, revenue, and expenses (7.5a).

THOUGHTS FOR LEADERS

Organizations must meet their strategic objectives and achieve the supporting action plans or, over time, they normally wither. As such, the organization must have metrics which show that they are achieving the strategic objectives and detailed actions.

On another front, organizations must also have measures which validate (or question?) the ethics of the organization. Favorable results on these measures can be key in driving stakeholder trust in the leadership. If there are caution signs, or in-process measures which indicate that the organization's stakeholders have concerns, the action taken must be timely, direct and result in correcting the root cause of the concern.

Another measure which can drive stakeholder trust is the validation that the organization is fiscally responsible. This typically comes from a robust network of internal and external audits, checks, and balances. This same approach using a network of internal and external audits, checks, and balances is key for all regulatory and compliance issues as well.

Finally, an organization can only be great if it is a good steward of the community trust, the community well-being, natural resources, and the laws around them. This starts and ends with leadership, as described in Category 1. Leadership must model the behaviors that they want all others to follow, and model the behaviors they want the organization to endorse.

Item 7.6 does not attempt to measure whether an organization is great, but unfavorable results presented here can indicate that an organization has not yet reached greatness.

> **A Lighter Moment:**
>
> *In real life, strategy is actually very straightforward.*
> *You pick a general direction and implement like hell.*
>
> **Jack Welch**

> *Poor is the man who does not know his own intrinsic worth and tends to measure everything by relative value. A man of financial wealth who values himself by his financial net worth is poorer than a poor man who values himself by his intrinsic self worth.*
>
> **Sidney Madwed**

 FOUNDATION

Financial and market results measure the outcome of how well the organization produces products, delivers services, and creates a positive customer experience by measuring the customers' purchase behavior through revenues and growth. This area also shows how well the organization can control their costs and thus their overall profit. The financial and market results, when considered over the long-term, provide a reasonably good overall indication of the organization's performance - at least for commercial for-profit organizations. These results include levels, trends, and comparisons for financial performance, including aggregate measures of financial return and economic value. For marketplace performance, these results also include market share or position, business growth, and new markets entered, as appropriate. The financials combine the effectiveness of the value creation processes (revenue) with the efficiency of the processes (expenses). Together, they provide useful insight into the workings of the organization system.

Financial Performance

By measuring expenses, financial measures also determine how efficient the organization is at creating and delivering products and services. Financial measures are the ultimate validation of both process effectiveness and efficiency. Like customer satisfaction, however, they are lagging measures and are often not so useful for managing the processes and people to ensure future organizational performance.

Marketplace Performance

This Item also looks at marketplace performance. Is the market share growing or shrinking? Market share trends are rarely a stand-alone number. For example, if the organization has a dominate market share, they may be world-class in all that they do but still not be able to hold their market share if enough competitors enter, and/or if competitors take irrational actions (such as dumping their products on the marketplace below their cost).

EXAMPLES

Pewaukee School District (Baldrige Recipient 2013)

- Moody's Bond Rating of WI School Districts
- Fund Balance
- Net Assets
- Instructional Expenditures per Pupil
- Grant & Gift Contributions
- Student Fees
- Public School Market Share

Source: Pewaukee School District, 2013, pp. 49 – 50

Advocate Good Samaritan Hospital (Baldrige recipient, 2010)

- Operating Profit Margin vs. Benchmark "AA" Rated Hospitals
- Operating Income – Actual vs. Budget
- Malpractice Costs – Total Insurance Expense
- Gross Days in Accounts Receivable
- Medical Records Charts Delinquency
- GSAM Market Share – Overall
- Unbilled Accounts Receivable Days
- Credit Balance Days

Source – Advocate Good Samaritan Hospital (2010)

PRO-TEC (Baldrige Recipient 2007)

- Net Profit –Long Term Viability
- Debt-to-Equity Ratio
- Operating at Full Capacity
- Total Revenue per Associate
- PRO-TEC Share of U.S. HDG Market by Customer Group
- Aged Inventory (> 180 days) as a % of Finished Inventory

Source: PRO-TEC (2007) pp. 42 – 43

Monfort College of Business (Baldrige recipient, 2004)

- MCB State Budget Growth Relative to Inflation
- MCB Direct Costs v. Inflation
- MCB Growth in Non-State Budget (excludes scholarship funds)
- MCB v. Peers Annual Tuition and Fees for a Full-Time, In-State Student
- MCB Student Scholarships – Number and Dollar Amount
- MCB Share of WUE Scholars at UNC
- MCB Freshman Admits and Enrollees

Source: Monfort (2005) pp. 42 - 44

CRITERIA QUESTIONS

Provide data and information to answer the following questions:

a. **Financial and Market Results**

(1) **Financial Performance**

What are your financial performance results? What are your current levels and trends in key measures or indicators of financial performance, including aggregate measures of financial return, financial viability, and budgetary performance, as appropriate? How do these results differ by market segments and customer groups, as appropriate?

(2) **Marketplace Performance**

What are your marketplace performance results? What are your current levels and trends in key measures or indicators of marketplace performance, including market share or position, market and market share growth, and new markets entered, as appropriate? How do these results differ by market segments and customer groups, as appropriate?

Notes:

7.5a(1) Aggregate measures of financial return might include those for return on investment (ROI), operating margins, profitability, or profitability by market segment or customer group. Measures of financial viability might include those for liquidity, debt-to-equity ratio, days cash on hand, asset utilization, and cash flow. Measures should relate to the financial measures you report in 4.1a(1) and the financial management approaches you report in item 2.2. For nonprofit organizations, additional measures might include performance to budget, reserve funds, cost avoidance or savings, administrative expenditures as a percentage of budget, and the cost of fundraising versus funds raised.

7.5a(2) For nonprofit organizations, responses might include measures of charitable donations or grants and the number of new programs or services offered.

NIST (2015-2016) p. 29

WORKSHEETS

7.5a Financial and Market Results

Category	Measure	Results For Each Customer (or other appropriate) Segment			Perf. Level*	Trend	Comparison With Competitors
		A	B	C			
Financial Performance	Revenue						
	Profit						
	Return on Investment						
	Earnings per share (ROI)						
	Return on Net Assets (RONA)						
	Financial Viability						
	Budgetary Performance						
	Cash-to-cash Cycle Time						
	Growth						
Marketplace Performance	Change in Market Share						
	New Markets Entered						
	New Products and Services						
	Market Share (Including Growth)						

* Attaching the appropriate data charts can be of benefit, but at a minimum the above data needs to be included.

ASSESSMENT

Rating Scale:

1 - **No Business Results** – We do not have these data
2 - **Few Business Results** – We have some data, but are early in improving
3 - **Improvements And/Or Good Results Reported** – We have data but in the early stages of trends
4 - **Good Trends In Most Areas** – No adverse trends and some comparisons
5 - **Good To Excellent In Most Areas** – Most trends are sustained and most have comparisons
6 - **Excellent Performance In Most Important Areas** – We are the Benchmark in our industry or beyond!
DK - Don't Know

149	The organization tracks a full range of financial measures which show strong performance.	1	2	3	4	5	6	DK
150	The measures of aggregate financial return show favorable results.	1	2	3	4	5	6	DK
151	The organization tracks the market share for each key market segment, and this shows favorable results.	1	2	3	4	5	6	DK
152	There are measures of the new markets entered, which show favorable results.	1	2	3	4	5	6	DK

BLUEPRINT

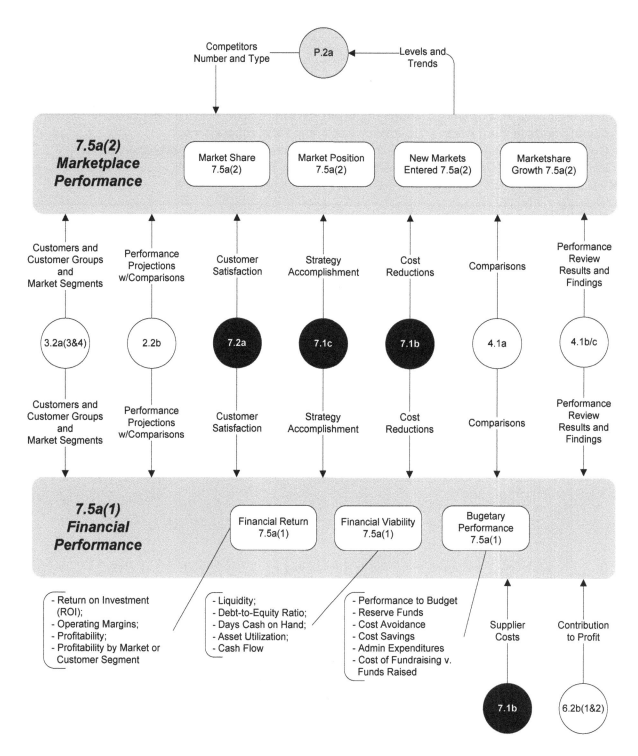

SYSTEM INTEGRATION

Context

P.2a > 7.5a Competitive Environment - The competitors (number and type) are key inputs to the results in 7.5a Financial and Market Results. The actual results should include the level of performance or size of the organization relative to competitors and the trends in the results indicating the growth relative to competitors.

P.2a < 7.5a Levels and Trends - The levels and trends in the growth and market share are an input to the competitive position described in the profile (P.2a).

Systems

2.2b > 7.1 thru 7.5 Performance Projections and Comparisons - The forecasted performance (projections) along with the projected comparison performance should be reflected in the results charts depicted in 7.1 through 7.5. While the CPE specifically ask for strategic plan accomplishments in Area to Address 7.1c, the ideal strategic plan will have projections for measures in all five results Items.

3.2a(3&4) > 7.5a Customer and Market Segments - The market results presented in 7.5a should include results for each key market segment identified in 3.2a(3&4). In addition, the results should include results on the key requirements and expectations for each segment. This area asks for how the organization determines key customer requirements and expectations and their relative importance to customers' purchasing decisions. While it is very useful to survey customers and ask for their preferences it is even better to analyze their actual behavior and buying patterns along with their satisfaction results. This provides the organization with insights for making adjustments to product and service offerings.

4.1a > 7.1 through 7.5 Comparisons - The comparisons selected using the processes described in 4.1a should be the same comparisons that are presented in all the results areas 7.1 through 7.5.

4.1a > 7.1 through 7.5 Measures – The results produced by the measures identified in 4.1a should be the same results presented in all the results areas 7.1 through 7.5.

4.1b/c < 7.1 through 7.5 Results - All results displayed as part of the results areas 7.1 through 7.5 are potential inputs to the organizational performance review system (4.1b).

4.1b/c > 7.1 through 7.5 Findings - The explanation of performance levels, trends and comparisons should be included in the applicable results areas (7.1 thorough 7.5).

6.2b(1&2) > 7.5a Contribution to Profit - The contribution to profit of the key work processes should be reported in 7.5a.

Scorecard

7.2a > 7.5a Customer Results - The revenue results depicted in 7.5a should correlate to the customer satisfaction results presented in 7.2a. The notion here is that if customer satisfaction is high compared to competitors the customer will come back (repeat business) and tell their friends (referral business) which should result in growth in revenue.

7.5a < 7.1b Cost Reductions - The value creation and support process cost reduction results depicted in 7.1b are a direct input to the profitability of the organization and the financial results in 7.5a.

7.5a < 7.1b Supplier Costs - The supplier costs are a component of the overall expenses and are a direct input to the profitability of the organization. For some organizations the cost of supplies is a significant amount of money.

7.5a < 7.1c Strategy Accomplishment - The results presented in 7.1c include results on the accomplishment of the organization's strategy. Successful accomplishment of the strategy should have a direct impact on the financial results of the organization including market share, revenue, and expenses (7.5a).

 ## THOUGHTS FOR LEADERS

It is common for leaders who have not used or explored the CPE model to feel that it is not sufficiently focused on results. Nothing could be further from the truth. It is a comprehensive model, is heavily weighted toward results, and requires good results across a wide range of factors.

First, 45% of the total score of a CPE assessment is based on results.

Second, the results are across all aspects of performance, constituting (as in Category 7) a robust balanced scorecard.

Third, and perhaps most essential, the organizations that use the CPE model are keenly focused on bottom-line performance. They understand the alignment between their approach (systematic processes), deployment (where the processes are used), and the results (those processes drive). They also clearly understand that without bottom-line performance, the organization will not even survive!

Leaders who truly understand the power of the model in helping an organization to become more competitive feel they have a significant competitive advantage as long as their competitors are not using the model. If their competitors ARE using the model, its use becomes even more imperative to maintain their competitiveness.

Many times we have told organizations that the only reason for using the model in a for-profit environment is to be more competitive in the marketplace and to make more money.

In a not-for-profit environment, organizations understand that *not-for-profit is a tax status, not a business model*. This means that these organizations must still be effective stewards of the resources given to them, and the CPE model helps them to drive overall organizational performance.

> ### A Lighter Moment:
>
> ### Spare no expense to save money on this one.
>
> ### Samuel Goldwyn

FOUNDATION

Before any organization undertakes an assessment they should think about their strengths. These can be expressed as what an outside examiner will remember about an organization after the entire assessment is over.

These are called Themes, and can have several sources:

- The Organizational Profile
- What the organization says is really important (success factors)
- What the organization is good at (strategic advantages)
- Where they have a strength which can be leveraged over the short-term (short-term differentiation)
- What is mentioned throughout the application repeatedly, and addresses many aspects of organizational performance
- What is changing in the marketplace or on the competitive landscape which needs to be taken advantage of (leveraged) by the organization (these are sometimes called strategic opportunities), and need to be leveraged before the competitors can leverage them
- What is a key factor to integrate the organization
- Other factors

WORKSHEETS

Cross-Cutting Themes Based On:		
	Strengths	**Core Values**
Practices		
Processes		
Linkages		
Knowledge		
Systems/Data		
Other Categories		

According to Niccolo Machiavelli, "there is nothing more difficult to take in hand, more perilous to conduct, or more uncertain in its success, than to take the lead in the introduction of a new order of things" (*The Prince*, 1532, ch. 6). The path to performance excellence consists of developing three key organization competencies: strategic leadership, execution excellence and organizational learning.

Path to Performance Excellence

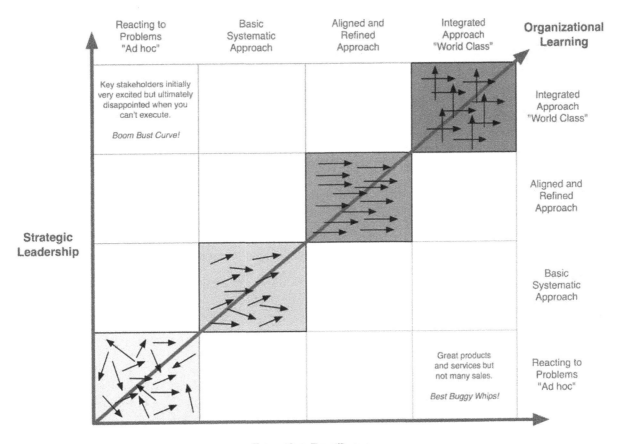

Execution Excellence

Adapted from: Tang, V. & Bauer, R. (1995). *Competitive Dominance: Beyond Strategic Advantage and Total Quality Management*, p. 9.

According to Tang and Bauer, an organization needs to develop strategic maturity and execution maturity to achieve and sustain performance excellence or, in their terms, "competitive dominance."

This means that the organization should chart a path to develop both of these competencies in parallel.

Execution and learning, however, should follow a sound strategy. The above concept builds on this notion and adds the competency of organizational learning as an enabler for the development of both strategic leadership and execution excellence. The three competencies address all CPE areas. In addition, the maturity models presented here are based on the CPE scoring scales.

While some organizations have developed strengths in one or two competencies, the path to performance excellence requires competency in all three in order for the organization to achieve and sustain excellence. For example, if the organization is great at developing strategies and new product offerings but is not good at executing, they will experience the boom then bust curve. The consumers will get excited about the new offerings but then become disappointed once the company fails to deliver a quality product and service. If the organization is great at executing but not so good at strategy, they will become what some call the best buggy whip manufacturer. In other words, the products and services are high quality but no one wants to buy them. When posed with the question: "Which buggy whip manufacturer went out of business last?" The answer is: "The best one." But they all still went out of business.

The path to performance excellence is one of continuous learning and improvement. This is true for both the organization and every individual in the organization. Ford and Evans (2001) and Latham (1997) found that the Criteria for Performance Excellence (CPE) self-assessment and improvement cycle is essentially an organizational learning cycle. In addition, although they are key players in the process, the learning cannot be delegated to the quality or performance excellence department, consultants, or middle management. Senior leaders must learn and lead the learning in order for the organization to achieve and sustain performance excellence. The good news is that a repeatable learning process facilitates the journey. The journey is a continuous process or cycle of learning and consists of three main components - diagnosis, design, and transformation:

1. **diagnosis,** including questions from the criteria, answers or responses for each question from the award application, and evaluation based on the responses or examiner feedback;

2. **design/redesign** of the processes and systems to improve performance; and

3. **transformation,** the implementation of the new designs to transform the organization.

Diagnosis, Design and Transformation

The process begins with an understanding of the organization and their environment. Responding to the questions in the organizational profile (see Part 2 Organization Context) helps an organization understand who they are, where they are headed, what their challenges are, what they have to do well, and how they improve. These areas of the organization are often called the key context factors. Responding to the questions in Categories 1 through 6 (Part 3 Organization Systems) helps the organization define their management systems and processes. Responding to the results asked for in Category 7 (Part 4 Organization Scorecard) helps the organization document their level of success and how it compares with relevant comparison organizations. Responding to the CPE questions results in a documented description of the organization's current context or key factors, current "as is" processes, and the associated results. In an award process, this documented description is summarized in the award application document. These descriptions are assessed, and a feedback report is provided that details the diagnosis. In an award process, the feedback report is developed by a team of external award examiners. The diagnosis is then used to set improvement priorities and drive the creative redesign the processes to increase performance.

The design or redesign of the leadership and management systems often follows the diagnosis phase. However, the design framework and process can be used at anytime including prior to a full-blown organization assessment. If the organization already has an explicitly defined process along with a diagnosis then the redesign process can begin with the current design and assessment. However, if the organization doesn't have explicitly defined processes they may want to begin with a design process and develop and implement the key organization systems described in Part 3. Then they will be in a better position to get the full value from an organization assessment.

620

The implementation of the new processes contributes to the overall transformation of the organization, which will evolve over several years. During this transformation leaders will face numerous challenges that will test their ability to lead large-scale organization change. Researchers at the Monfort Institute have developed a framework for leading sustainable transformation. This framework consists of five key components: leader behaviors, leader approaches, leader characteristics, force of change and culture change. In addition, these five components include 35 sub-elements. This learning cycle of diagnosis, design and transformation is repeated over and over again and is the essence of the journey.

The Reinforcing Loop

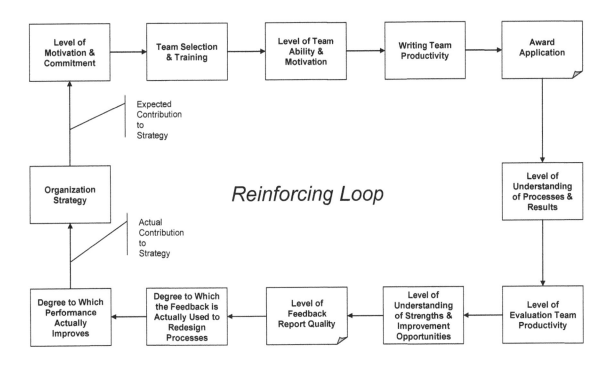

Adapted from Latham 1997, p. 283.

To build quality into the learning cycle, the organization should begin with the deliverables and work backwards. The transformation of the organization and improved performance are the ultimate deliverables of the learning cycle. It is through transformation that the organization achieves performance excellence. The quality of the transformation is dependent not only on leading change but also on the quality of the design and redesign of the processes. The quality of the process design or redesign is dependent on the quality of the diagnosis, which is influenced by the quality of the documented key factors, processes, and results (Latham, 1997). The quality of the description, or award application, is determined by the writing process and the talents of the team.

621

The learning cycle is a reinforcing loop. Organizations that invest adequate talent and time into the process reap the benefits of improved performance if they focus on the business processes that drive their competitiveness. That improvement, typically, motivates them to invest even more talent and time. This cycle continues and creates an improvement or learning curve that can be exponential. On the other hand, organizations that delegate the project and do not invest time and talent will get what they paid for, which is little (or marginal) improvement in performance. This is a "self-fulfilling prophecy," as lack of improvement often results in disappointment and even less investment in time and talent. The lesson here is simple - either invest the time and talent of the best and brightest to work on the assessment and improvement, or don't start the journey.

The organization diagnosis process is focused on three key writing activities and deliverables:

1. The first task is to develop explicit descriptions of the organization context, systems and scorecard – **the Organizational Profile.**
2. Second, the task is to assess the organization systems – **Categories 1 – 6.**
3. Finally, reporting the results and developing qualitative strengths and opportunities for improvement.

Once the assessment document is developed, an assessment can be performed at several levels:

1. A 'paper' assessment based on the written document.
2. An assessment based on the questions in the **ASSESSMENT** portions of this book – This full 150+ questionnaire is included in the CD ROM, included with this book.
3. A 'site visit' assessment from an internal group.
4. A 'site visit' assessment from an external group, such as a Baldrige or State Award assessment team.

The Diagnosis Process

Plotting a course for improvement requires two points of reference - the organization's current position or "as is" design and the desired position or "to be" design. The diagnosis phase is designed to document and evaluate the current position and is composed of seven phases:

1. **Leaders engaged at all levels** - understand the performance excellence model and plan the journey;

2. **Writing team** – select and develop a capable and motivated writing team;

3. **Organized and analyzed data** - storyboard the application;

4. **Review** the storyboards with the senior leader champions;

5. **Documented processes and results** - document the qualitative descriptions of the key factors, management systems and processes, and the associated quantitative results;

6. **Award application** – develop a formal award style application document;

7. **Evaluate** the processes and results - identify strengths, opportunities for improvement; and

8. **Identify** the maturity levels for each process and results section (a.k.a. scoring).

Before "launching" into a full-blown assessment many organizations use the diagnostic questions introduced in the 28 process Areas to Address (In Categories 1 – 6 such as 2.1b, etc.) in Part 3 and the 8 results Areas to Address in Part 4 (Category 7 such as 7.1c) to provide a quick look at the status of their processes and results. The full set of questions is located in one file on the CD-ROM. The questions are intended to be a relatively simple model that can be used to approximate the scoring level of an organization or to give an early indication of where the organization can improve. It is not intended to be comprehensive assessment or to replace a full Baldrige Criteria for Performance Excellence (CPE) assessment. Since it is based on individual perceptions and not hard facts, it is not as rigorous or precise as a comprehensive assessment. It does, however, provide a preliminary quick assessment to better understand where the leaders and employees feel the greatest opportunities for improvement lie and is well worth the relatively small amount of time required.

For a more detailed, comprehensive, and valid assessment, the organization can follow the traditional assessment and evaluation processes described in this chapter.

The steps to write an application, and perform an assessment:

1. Leaders engaged at all levels

The first deliverable is to develop leaders at all levels who are engaged in the performance excellence process. **They <u>do not</u> have to become Criteria for Performance Excellence (CPE) experts,'** but engaged leaders understand the performance excellence model, the maturity levels, and their role in the process. They are not afraid to <u>read</u> the criteria and <u>ask questions</u> about the aspects they do not understand. These are leaders who understand Dr. Deming's point that if something goes wrong it is most likely a system issue and not a people issue. These, leaders must plan the assessment and improvement effort, resource that effort with the right people, and establish goals and timetables which build and maintain momentum.

The biggest hurdle in some organizations is for key leaders to transition from an attitude of 'shortcomings are bad – and must be hidden' to an attitude of shortcomings are 'opportunities for improvement (OFIs) are good, because if we can identify them we can improve them (systematically).' Once an organization's leaders make this transition there are few limits to the levels of performance the organization can achieve.

2. Senior Leadership Team Workshop

To support needed change, leaders must be engaged at all levels. Leaders cannot support something they do not understand. The confused mind says, "No!" If the leaders and people do not understand the change, they will resist all efforts to move in the new direction. Consequently, the first assessment should be accomplished by the senior leadership team. This initial "table-top" assessment not only educates the leadership team about the performance excellence criteria, but also gets the ball rolling and identifies real opportunities for improvement. This first table-top assessment typically takes one to two days.

In addition to training in the CPE model and the process of assessment and improvement, successful organizations invest in clearly defining the following topics and training all leaders in:

1. roles and responsibilities of leaders at all levels to lead the performance excellence change;

2. leadership skills at all levels; and

3. leadership operating principles (the ability to translate beliefs into actions).

3. Calibrate Leaders on the CPE Maturity Levels (Scoring Scales)

The maturity levels or scoring scales for the CPE model are not like the scoring scales with which most people are familiar. All our lives we have been taught that somewhere around 70% is average. For example, in school a score of 70% is the minimum score for a "C" letter grade. In contrast, a score of 70% is highly refined maturity level in the CPE process. In fact, if the organization is 60-70% in all areas, it is a role model and a good candidate for the award. The maturity scales are designed to serve the continuous improvement process for many years. In fact, no organization that we are familiar with has "maxed" the scale in all, or even many, areas. Key steps in the calibration process include:

1. Discuss scoring with the leaders, and calibrate them to understand the level most companies achieve based on a 1000 point scale. Although there are no 'absolutes' the following scoring scale is representative of a general level:

    a. Average Government Agency = 80 - 150 points

    b. Average Company = 150 - 200 points

    c. State Winners = 400 + points

    d. Baldrige Winners = 600 + points

2. Focus the leadership on performance improvement vs. achieving a high score/maturity level.

3. **If leaders focus on the score, they will always be dissatisfied with the process because it is radically different from any other scoring system.**

4. **If leaders focus on improvement, they will always be thrilled with the process because it will provide a limitless supply of Opportunities for Improvement (OFIs) to help make the organization better.**

5. Bottom line - The leadership focus should be on using the process to be more competitive in the marketplace.

4. Ensure That Leaders Understand Their Role(s) In The Process

The learning cycle must be led, and the leaders must be role models - if the leaders aren't learning, no one else in the organization will either. There are at least eight key roles and responsibilities:

1. The senior leaders must own the assessment process.

2. They must understand what is/is not a systematic process.

3. They must understand that:

    a. a systematic process is repeatable, but managing a company with leadership opinion (tribal knowledge) is not repeatable and

    b. the systematic processes the leaders help to establish and improve may be their legacy after they leave the organization.

4. They must freely discuss the Opportunities for Improvement (OFIs) generated by the assessment, without focusing on the past path, but focus on the future – Fix the OFI, don't just argue about 'who's fault it is.'

5. They must discuss their views on the Opportunities for Improvement.

6. They must discuss their views on using this assessment tool to improve the organization.

7. They must remove any barriers for the writing team when the writers cannot remove these barriers themselves.

8. They must develop rules for writing an assessment document, such as:

    a. this assessment and writing process is owned by the senior leaders;

    b. the strengths and gaps are owned by the entire organization;

    c. do not shoot the messenger;

    d. **leaders, and others who have not been trained in the criteria, can advise the writing team (and even write draft inputs to the writing team), but they <u>do not write</u> the final portions of the document;**

    e.   the writers have a fixed schedule for the various draft steps, and the schedule will not change for any one leader who is not available;

    f.   the senior leaders are responsible for reviewing the various drafts. Hence, they are responsible for getting on the writing team's calendar, and not vice versa;

    g.   the writers are representing the leadership team and need access to all material requested by the criteria; and

    h.   the senior leaders need to get their staff and the entire organization committed.

5. Assessment Planning

The path to performance excellence consists of developing all three organizational competencies:

1. Strategic Leadership (Items 1.1, 1.2, 2.1, and 2.2);

2. Execution Excellence (Items 3.1, 3.2, 6.1, and 6.2); and

3. Organizational Learning and Support (Items 5.1, 5.2, 4.1 and 4.2).

Note: Each group also takes care of the associated results items. See Part 4 Organization Scorecard for a diagram that depicts the results areas related to the three competencies.

Additionally, it involves people at all levels - senior leaders, internal performance excellence staff, leaders at all levels, and employees throughout the organization. These key players need to clearly understand and be trained in the following topics:

1. components of a master integrated plan;

2. approaches to developing a master plan; and

3. developing a realistic master plan.

A framework, such as the one shown on the next page, is one way to organize the competencies, activities and key players.

Each organization will want to modify the framework for its own organizational structure, and preferences.

6. Develop The Overall Plan

	Strategic Leadership	Execution Excellence	Organizational Learning
Senior Leadership	• Leadership team owns the journey • Leadership team sets the direction and participates in the journey • Leadership Table Top Assessment • Leadership System • Strategic Planning System • Customer Knowledge • Leader Development	• Executive sponsors for each main group of processes • Align People and Processes with the strategy and mission of the organization • Develop People System • Process System • Customer Relationships	• Develop an approach to learning at the senior/strategic level • Scorecard (run the business and change the business) • Analysis • Org Performance Review
Performance Excellence Staff	• Master Project Plan • Project Management • Organizational Profile • SL Writing Planning • SL Writing Workshop • SL Writing • SL Evaluation • SL Improvement Planning • SL Improvement Implementation	• EE Writing Planning • EE Writing Workshop • EE Writing • EE Evaluation • EE Improvement Planning • EE Improvement Implementation	• OL Writing Planning • OL Writing Workshop • OL Writing • OL Evaluation • OL Improvement Planning • OL Improvement Implementation
All Employees	• Understand the journey and how they contribute • Understand how they contribute to the organizations strategy	• Define their own SIPOC flows • Process Management • People Development	• Process Measurement • Analysis • Process Improvement

Legend: SL = Senior Leader;   OL = Operating Leader;   EE = Employees.

When modifying this matrix for your organization, include individuals who may be absent from the formal leadership hierarchy, but are key at influencing others throughout the organization. These 'decision influencers' may play a key role in a successful journey. Without their support, change initiatives may fail and you may never know why. Once senior leaders are "on board" and supporting the journey, the next step is to identify and develop a capable and motivated writing team.

7. Ensure A Capable And Motivated Writing Team

The next step is to establish a capable and motivated writing team. Research and experience suggest that the level of capability and the motivation of the writing team members are two of the most influential factors to a quality self-assessment or award application.

8. Select the Writing Team

The first step toward establishing a capable and motivated writing team is to select the best and brightest in the organization to be on the team. If the best and brightest do not write the document, the quality of the document produced will suffer along with the perceived credibility of the document in the eyes of senior leaders. If senior leaders do not view the document as credible, their motivation to use it for improvement suffers.

Refer back to the reinforcing loop discussion in the introduction to the journey.

Ideally the writing team includes:

1. Overall Team Leader

    a. One person

    b. A backup team leader for instances when the team leader is absent

2. Champions for each Competency

    a. Strategic Leadership, Execution Excellence, and Organizational Learning

    b. Three people - one per competency area

3. Writers for the Individual Processes and Results Areas

    a. The number here can vary widely depending on the type and size of the organization and the nature of the organization design and distribution of key people

    b. Often, there are 3 to 4 writers for each competency area, for a total of 9-12 people

4. Editors

    a. Two editors

    b. Editors need the same training as the writers

5. Graphics and Publishing

    a. Graphics are an important part of the document and are literally worth more than a thousand words. Getting the graphics right is part art and part science and writing teams often enlist the help of a specialist in this area.

    b. Publishing a clear and well formatted document is also part art and part science and writing teams often engage a specialist in this area as well.

Once the writing team is selected, the next step is to assess their capabilities.

9. Assess the Writing Team's Capabilities

Using a simple tool, such as a *fishbone* diagram, assess the capability of the writing team and develop a plan to address any gaps in their knowledge, skills, and abilities. The idea here is not for every team member to possess all qualifications. However, the entire team should possess them collectively.

Team Capability Fishbone (Cause and Effect) Diagram

Source: Adapted from Latham 1997, p. 206.

10. Ensure That The Writing Team Members and Other Key Stakeholders Understand the Level of Commitment Required

One of the biggest challenges faced by the individual team member is the dilemma of having two (or more) jobs and bosses while serving on the temporary assessment team. Typically, the part of the organization that provided the individual to the team also expects the individual to continue with regular job responsibilities. If not handled properly, this conflict can result in mediocre performance at both jobs and an overworked disgruntled employee.

If the team member is supportive of what the team is trying to achieve, their boss MUST also be supportive. The boss should understand what the commitment entails.

1. The team member was chosen because of their value to the organization.

2. The team member was chosen because of their experience. Being a part of an assessment writing team is not a good developmental assignment. The person should already know the organization and know where the information can be found.

3. The levels of time, thought, writing, assessment demands which will be placed on the person.

4. The hours the person will need to work on the assessment will be significant. This will not allow them to give their existing job 40+ hours per week in addition to the assessment responsibilities.

5. The fact that the person will be assessing the entire organization and not their traditional functional area. They will need access to all of the information required by the criteria and will not just be asking questions as if they were still 'Joe from Accounting.'

Once the boss understands the level of commitment necessary to succeed, the boss should discuss these issues with the team member to develop a mutual understanding of and agreement on the needs, demands, and the approach to mitigate unfavorable consequences for any party. The individual team members face pressures from both the assessment team and their regular job.

Multiple Pressures on the Individual Team Members

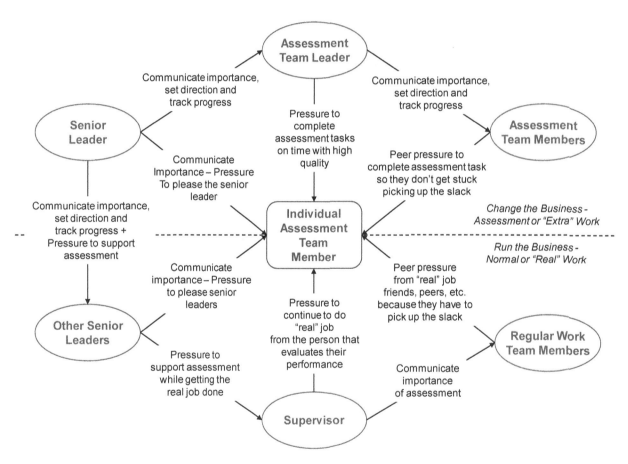

Source: Adapted from Latham 1997, p. 181.

Clearly defined agreements as well as commitment are necessary for the individual to have enough time to do a quality job. It is neither fair nor effective to ask people to devote additional time and effort if they are not viewed favorably for their commitment, effort, and results.

11. Finalize the Writing Team

According to research and experience, four things will determine the quality of the documented processes and results (for an award application):

1. The time available to complete the writing task.

2. The experience and capability of the team.

3. The productivity of the team (productivity is driven primarily by qualifications and motivation).

4. The support given to the team (clerical support, their boss's support, the access to process and data from the organization, etc.).

No training process can make up for selecting a poorly qualified team. Training can enable a talented team, but it cannot create talent or experience and it certainly cannot create desire or motivation to learn through an assessment process. Consequently, team selection is critical to a successful documentation of processes and results. If this project is not important enough to require the best and brightest, the organization should re-evaluate whether they want to complete this assessment. Again, refer back to the reinforcing loop discussion.

12. Train the Writing Team

An organization cannot write a CPE-based application unless they have people who have been trained in the CPE model, criteria, and writing style (such as writing to ADLI for Categories 1-6).

Experience has shown that *writer* training needs to emphasize different aspects of the application process than the traditional *examiner* training. Examiner training helps the examiners calibrate on the scoring and the examination process. Writer training helps the writer to understand how to answer the various CPE questions:

1. The criteria for performance excellence.

2. The process of assessment.

3. The organizational processes.

4. What to write:

    *   In the Organizational Profile

    *   In The Process Categories (Categories 1-6), and the meaning of:

        *   Approach

        *   Deployment

        *   Learning

        *   Integration

    *   In the Results Category (Category 7), and the meaning of:

        *   Levels

        *   Trends

        *   Comparisons

        *   Integration

    *   How to link Approach, Deployment, Results

5. How to work as a team in completing the document.

This training goes well beyond traditional examiner training or what an examiner needs to know. There is an old saying that "it is easier to be a critic than a playwright." Along those same lines, it is easier to be an examiner than it is to be a member of the writing team.

13. Train Other Key People

In addition to the writers, others in the organization need to understand the CPE model as well. This understanding does not necessarily have to be in-depth, depending upon the person's organizational responsibilities:

1. **Leadership** (at all levels) need a <u>basic</u> understanding of the criteria (at the Category and Item Level, and the processes required), and clear guidance on responsibilities during the writing (and performance improvement) process.

2. **Key Manager**s need to be <u>comfortable with what the criteria means</u> and how they relate to the policies, procedures, practices, systems, and process of the organization. This group should include the supervisors of the writers, so they can understand the commitment the writers are making.

3. **Subject Matter Experts** (SMEs) need a <u>basic</u> understanding of the criteria in their area of expertise.

4. **Editors** need to understand the <u>criteria and the linkages</u> that should be reflected in the final document.

With a capable and motivated writing team that has support from the key stakeholders (e.g., bosses), the team is ready to collect, organize, and analyze data that describes current processes and results.

14. Organize and Analyze Data

The third deliverable in this process is organized and analyzed data to support the actual writing of the document (or award application). The idea here is to avoid writing any "pretty" paragraphs until all the data is in place, organized, understood, and aligned. Only then will the team be ready to write well-developed paragraphs that summarize the processes and results in a way that is internally consistent throughout the document.

15. Develop the Organizational Profile

After the writers are trained, their first task is to document the organization's key factors and write the Organizational Profile. Writing an organization profile includes several steps:

1. Complete the key factors worksheets for profile Areas to Address P.1a, P.1b, P.2a, P.2b, and P.2c (on the CD-ROM Worksheets that accompany the BUG book).

2. Establish agreement on the definitions used in the Organizational Profile for key aspects of the business, such as customers, customer segments, customer requirements (by segment), employee groups (and the requirements for each group), external challenges, etc.

3. Identify Organizational Profile gaps.

4. Assign each gap to an owner (for the Organizational Profile this is typically one of the senior leaders) early in the writing process and a due-date to "fill the gap."

5. Write the Organizational Profile.

6. Seek approval of the Organizational Profile from the senior leadership team and other key decision makers.

The Organizational Profile sets the stage for alignment of the organization's key factors with processes and results. For example, the profile identifies the customer groups and their requirements. These same groups and requirements should be consistent throughout the document (award application) including areas such as 3.1 Customer Engagement, 3.2a Voice of the Customer, and 7.2a Customer-Focused Results (where the results must be broken-down by customer segment).

16. Document the Big 6 Anchor Systems

When documenting the processes, the team should start at the highest level of abstraction and work down to greater detail. This approach helps save time and effort because writers can stop when they reach enough detail for their purposes and it provides the context or "home" to go to when they get lost in the details of sub-processes.

Based on the key processes discussed earlier in this book, the current design of the Big 6 key systems should be storyboarded. If these systems do not yet exist, the conceptual design should be created at this time. Big 6 systems include the following:

1. Leadership System
2. Strategic Planning System
3. Customer Listening and Response System
4. Data Analysis and Use System
5. Workforce Evaluation System
6. Process Management System

Once the Big 6 Anchor Systems are documented, the team is ready to move on to story-board the other 20+ critical systems as described earlier in this book. These MUST be defined based on current practices or the team will be writing what they 'wish' the organization did compared to what is actually being done. Once these are defined, the team can move on to the individual Area to Address worksheets. Documenting these processes is discussed in step below in more detail.

17. Complete the Process and Results Worksheets

Completing the worksheets described in this book and provided electronically on the CD-ROM (included), is the first step toward collecting and organizing the data needed to write the first draft. When completed, these worksheets are designed to represent all facets of the CPE model. The team will then have the data it needs to write the summary paragraphs that make up the award application.

The data for the worksheets ideally comes from a variety of sources and represents multiple perspectives in the organization. Using multiple methods and sources to obtain the data (triangulation) will help increase the validity of the document and reduce bias. It probably comes as no surprise that senior leaders of many organizations often have a different perspective of the organization and how it works than do the middle managers or the employees on the front-line. In order to capture and integrate these multiple perspectives, the team should make sure to use multiple sources of data (leaders, managers, employees, etc.); employ multiple methods of data collection (interviews, document reviews, observations, etc.); and use multiple assessors, which is already built into deliverable #2, a capable and motivated writing team.

As you have probably already suspected, triangulation has its price. The more the team triangulates its sources and methods, the greater the validity and lower the bias, but the cost is greater in both time and effort. Consequently, there is an economic decision to be made - how much triangulation is worth the additional cost? In other words, where is the point of diminishing returns?

Reducing Bias and Increasing Validity

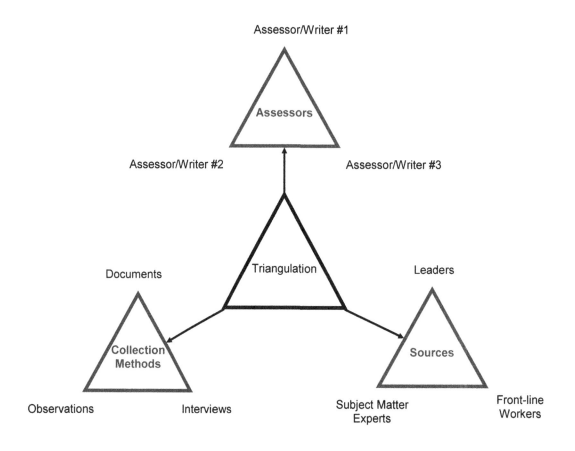

Source: Adapted from Latham 1997, p. 86.

18. Define the Processes - SIPOC

As part of completing the worksheets, the team will identify many processes through out the organization. Based on the Big 6 Anchor Systems, the completed worksheets expand the level of detail and identify other critical systems and processes. A systematic approach to accomplishing this consists of four steps.

1. Agree on the organization's enterprise model and main value chain (these are the activities that most directly produce the products and services that are consumed by external customers.

2. Agree on the key work processes including the key processes found in the various Areas to Address.

3. Identify key processes that the organization does not currently have defined.

4. Develop a plan to storyboard the processes that do not already exist.

For each major process identified, the team will need to document the key requirements, process steps, and measures. To fully understand the flow of a process, the team will need to document the process including inputs and outputs. This approach is often called a SIPOC, which stands for: **S**upplier – **I**nput – **P**rocess – **O**utput – **C**ustomer.

SIPOC Model

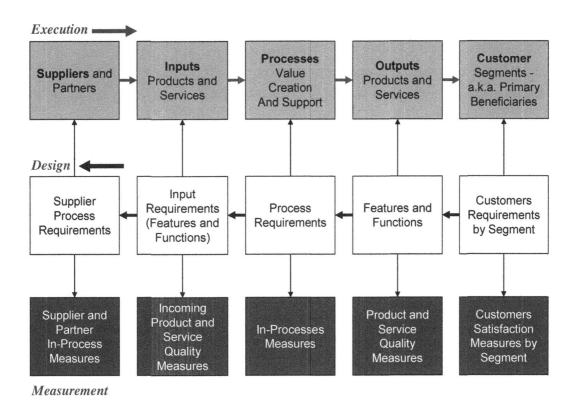

The requirements, the flow or value chain, and the measures need to be documented for each of the five SIPOC stages. This approach helps the organization to identify gaps in the current knowledge of requirements, the process steps, and in the metrics used to assess performance. In addition to completing a 3 x 5 SIPOC table for each major process, an accompanying flow chart will add much to the understanding of the process and how it works.

19. Story-Board the Application

Based on the information documented up to this point, the team will need to complete the following steps:

1. Review each sentence in the criteria, and what the organizational answer is to respond to that part of the criteria.

    a. This MUST be in process terms where what the organization does is clearly documented. It cannot be in terms which are general, not consistent throughout the organization, or 'glowing flowery' terms which the writing team wishes was the case, but is not founded in reality.

b. The Worksheets for the 2015 – 2016 Criteria For Performance Excellence (CPE) are on the CD-ROM included with this book. They are in unprotected MS Word files so the users can change them and complete the boxes with their own information.

2. Identify gaps between what the criteria calls for, and what the organization does. These are the descriptions in step 1, above. The worksheets make it easy to identify what information is missing;

3. Determine if the information to fill the gaps exists in the organization - in other words, is it a real gap or a gap in information;

a. If it is a gap in the information, and not what the organization is doing, additional Subject Matter Experts (SMEs) may be needed;

4. Identify other barriers to completing the worksheets and SIPOC documents; and

5. Identify linkages between the various areas and align the information to ensure an internally consistent document.

In completing this story-board, NIST has some advice to keep in mind for the "Process Items" (Categories 1 through 6) that include questions that begin with the word 'how.'

Process Items include questions that begin with the word "how." Responses should outline your key process information that addresses approach, deployment, learning, and integration. Responses lacking such information, or merely providing an example, are referred to in the Scoring Guidelines as "anecdotal information."

Understanding the meaning of <u>how</u> is described as:

In responding to questions in process items that begin with how, give information on your key processes with regard to approach, deployment, learning, and integration (ADLI; see the Scoring System, page 30). Responses lacking such information, or merely providing an example, are referred to in the scoring guidelines as anecdotal information. (Note: Anecdotal Information scores 0 – 5%).

Show that approaches are systematic. Systematic approaches are repeatable and use data and information to enable learning. In other words, approaches are systematic if they build in the opportunity for evaluation, improvement, innovation, and knowledge sharing, thereby enabling a gain in maturity.

Show deployment. In your responses, summarize how your approaches are implemented in different parts of your organization.

Show evidence of learning. Give evidence of evaluation and improvement cycles for processes, as well as the potential for innovation. Show that process improvements are shared with other appropriate units of your organization to enable organizational learning.

Show integration. Integration is alignment and harmonization among processes, plans, measures, actions, and results. This harmonization generates organizational effectiveness and efficiencies. Showing alignment in the process items and tracking corresponding measures in the results items should improve organizational performance. In your responses, show alignment in four areas:

• **In the Organizational Profile**, make clear what is important to your organization.

• **In Strategy** (category 2), including the strategic objectives, action plans, and core competencies, highlight your organization's areas of greatest focus and describe how you deploy your strategic plan.

> • **In describing organizational-level analysis and review**
> (item 4.1), show how you analyze and review performance
> information as a basis for setting priorities.

> • **In Strategy** (category 2) **and Operations** (category 6),
> highlight the work systems and work processes that
> are key to your organization's overall performance.

(NIST, 2015 - 2016, pp. 36 - 37)

Understanding the meaning of <u>what</u>:

Two types of questions in Process Items begin with the word "what." The first type of question requests basic information on key processes and how they work. Although it is helpful to include who performs the work, merely stating who does not permit diagnosis or feedback.

The second type of question requests information on what your key findings, plans, objectives, goals, or measures are. These latter questions set the context for showing alignment and integration in your performance management system. For example, when you identify key strategic objectives, your action plans, some of your performance measures, and some results reported in Category 7 are expected to relate to the stated strategic objectives.   (NIST, 2015 - 2016, p. 37)

20. Review the Story-Boards with the Executive Leaders (Champions)

Depending on how much the senior leaders have been involved in writing team activities, review of the story-boards might be the first opportunity to inform them of the writing team's progress. It is also an opportunity for the champions (the senior leaders assigned to each category or competency) to give the writing team their inputs and help the writers remove any barriers to the writing process. At a minimum, the following topics should be addressed:

1. Gaps in the critical systems (Category 1 – 6 processes);
2. Gaps in the data;
3. Gaps in linking the data to processes:
4. Barriers to collecting the data to fill the gaps;
5. Ideas as to how to remove the barriers;
6. Identification of any "Hot Buttons"; and
7. Questions and concerns.

Once the data are collected, organized, and analyzed for each Area to Address, the team is now ready to start outlining and writing the actual document (award application).

21. Documented Processes and Results

The fourth deliverable in the diagnosis phase is a concise document of the processes and results that address each area in the criteria. This document can also serve as the award application and should be no longer than 50 pages.

22. Write the First Draft of the Self-Assessment or Award Application Document

The first draft of the award application document should be written, edited, and reviewed with the champions. Note that there is an optimum time between drafts. The 1st, 2nd, and 3rd (final) drafts should be 7-10 calendar days apart. Experience has shown that four days is not enough time to perform adequate research, then come back to the document and make the needed changes. On the other hand, three weeks is too much time. The writers will return to their other job responsibilities and come back lacking

the fresh perspective with which they began. In short, too much time between drafts deteriorates the quality of the document. Moreover, organizations who insist on three weeks between drafts most often find no significant difference between the draft and the final.

23. Review and Refine (Develop Second Draft)

The second draft of the award application should also be written, edited, and reviewed with the senior leader champions. The second draft should be significantly more refined than the first draft, and it should include feedback comments from the champions after the first draft.

24. Walk-the-Walls and Review Each Story-Board to Ensure Linkages

Once the final document is prepared, it is quite helpful to put the pages up on a wall to perform one final review. This tactic allows several people to read the document and allows two people (working in unison) to check the linkages referenced in the document. For example, if one part of the application references another part (and all high-performing organizations have these linkages) one person can read the application and ask the other person to check to see if the linkage in question is where it should be.

25. Make the Final Revisions to the Document

The writers will revise the final document based on the results of walking the walls and the story-board review.

26. Assess the Application and Make Final Edits

An editor should be involved in a final check of the linkages found in the walk-the-walls exercise and should ensure that appropriate changes are made. There is a saying that "there are two types of award applications - perfect ones and completed ones." At some point, the team will have to decide to let the document go to press. All applications have a few silly typos. It should not reflect on the diligence of the organization, but only on the difficulty to keep Murphy's Law at bay while you are writing a complex 50 page document.

27. Award Application

If the organization is applying for an award, there are a few publishing steps to accomplish.

Get the Required Number of Copies Printed

1. Do not forget copies for internal use;

2. Do not forget "modified" copies for restricted use outside the company. These copies frequently have some of the results (the results which are particularly sensitive competitively) taken out; and

3. Get tabs printed on both sides.

28. Proof-Read One Copy

Proofreading at least one copy can help assure that something did not go wrong with all copies.

29. Thumb Through <u>All</u> Copies that Will Be Used

It is amazing what can go wrong in simply printing a document. Even when in-house and reputable organizations are used, pages can be missing, sections can be upside down, and a wide range of other maladies can occur despite best efforts and intentions. An old truism of preparing an application is 'the one document with problems will be the one you send to your CEO.'

Each document that will be used externally or sent to an internal leader should be checked.

30. Mail the Application Copies to the Appropriate Organization by their Deadline

31. Celebrate the Completion of the Document

It is important to celebrate the completion of the documentation phase of the diagnosis process. The participants at this point have learned more about the organization in the past few months than they probably learned in the past few years. Once the key factors, processes, and results are documented, the next step is to evaluate the processes and results.

32. Evaluate the Processes and Results

Once the assessment document (award application) is complete, the next step is to evaluate the processes and results. This evaluation produces qualitative comments that describe the strengths and the opportunities for improvement in the writing of the document itself as well as in the organizational processes and results.

The methods to accomplish the evaluation and feedback are divided into three types (external, internal, and combined), each with its own strengths and weaknesses. The external options include: (a) higher headquarters or parent organization examination; (b) national, state, and local award programs; (c) external consultant(s); or (d) a peer organization (e.g., another division) evaluation. Internal options include having the assessors score the report themselves or setting up an internal examiner team composed of organization members not involved with the assessment. This is a good job for the senior leader team. The combined option combines one or more of each type (internal and external).

According to AT&T (1992), "some companies (Cadillac and Xerox, for example) have found that formal feedback corroborates and expands on internal findings but rarely contradicts them or provides information that dramatically redirects improvement efforts. If external examiners are used their feedback should be systematically compared with the internal assessment results to determine whether there are additional areas for improvement" (p. 29). While external feedback might not be dramatically different from internal feedback, it does tend to point out more opportunities for improvement in a less varnished way than internal assessments. In addition, organizations sometimes do not realize or recognize how good they actually are and external feedback can identify strengths that the organization had not given itself credit for. Most organizations use a combined approach. The output of the evaluation phase consists of qualitative comments that detail the strengths and opportunities for each CPE Items. These comments, along with the summary document (award application), are then used to determine the level of maturity.

33. Identify the Maturity Levels (Scores)

Maturity levels are determined for each of the CPE Items. As described earlier in the chapter titled Maturity Models, there are two maturity models (scoring scales) - one for processes and one for results. The process maturity level is determined by considering the four dimensions of ADLI - approach, deployment, learning, and integration. Results maturity is determined based on the four dimensions of levels, trends, comparisons, and completeness. The application document (process and results descriptions), qualitative comments (strengths and opportunities for improvement), and the maturity levels for the CPE Items are the three key inputs to the design/redesign process described in the next chapter.

34. Prioritize Opportunities for Improvement

Tang and Bauer (1995) propose that if an organization is much better at strategy than they are at execution, or vice versa, there is an imbalance, and the organization is off track. For example, if the organization is great at market strategies but lousy at execution, they will experience the "boom bust curve." In this situation, they will get many initial sales due to high expectations, but they will lose business when they cannot deliver on those expectations. The other side of the "coin" is when the organization can execute well, but they are not offering products and services that meet the customers' needs. In this case, as the old saying goes, "they may be the best buggy whip maker in the market but there isn't much demand." The lesson is that organizations should set priorities to balance the development of the strategic leadership and execution excellence competencies. In addition, if organizational learning is lagging behind, ability for improvement is limited. The goal is to determine where the organization is on all three dimensions, prioritize based on the gaps, then get back on track where all three competencies are developed together.

This Glossary of Key Terms defines and briefly describes terms used throughout book that are important to key performance management concepts. The majority of this glossary was taken directly from the Baldrige Criteria (NIST, 2013-2014, pp. 47 - 54). The definitions have been slightly edited and some definitions added for use with this book.

Where the term being defined is in italics (or where part of the definition is in italics) the italicized part of the definition has been provided by the author (or in one case, from Wikipedia), and is not endorsed by the Malcolm Baldrige National Quality Award Office.

Action Plans

The term "action plans" refers to specific actions that respond to short- and longer-term strategic objectives. Action plans include details of resource commitments and time horizons for accomplishment. Action plan development represents the critical stage in planning when strategic objectives and goals are made specific so that effective, organization-wide understanding and deployment are possible. In the Criteria, deployment of action plans includes creating aligned measures for all departments and work units. Deployment also might require specialized training for some employees or recruitment of personnel.

An example of a strategic objective for a supplier in a highly competitive industry might be to develop and maintain a price leadership position. Action plans could entail designing efficient processes and creating an accounting system that tracks activity-level costs, aligned for the organization as a whole. Deployment requirements might include work unit and team training in setting priorities based on costs and benefits. Organizational-level analysis and review likely would emphasize productivity growth, cost control, and quality.

Alignment

The term "alignment" refers to consistency of plans, processes, information, resource decisions, actions, results, and analyses to support key organization-wide goals. Effective alignment requires a common understanding of purposes and goals. It also requires the use of complementary measures and information for planning, tracking, analysis, and improvement at three levels: the organizational level, the key process level, and the work unit level.

Analysis

The term "analysis" refers to an examination of facts and data to provide a basis for effective decisions. Analysis often involves the determination of cause-effect relationships. Overall organizational analysis guides the management of work systems and work processes toward achieving key business results and toward attaining strategic objectives. Despite their importance, individual facts and data do not usually provide an effective basis for actions or setting priorities. Effective actions depend on an understanding of relationships, derived from analysis of facts and data.

Anecdotal

The term "anecdotal" refers to process information that lacks specific methods, measures, deployment mechanisms, and evaluation, improvement, and learning factors. Anecdotal information frequently uses examples and describes individual activities rather than systematic processes. An anecdotal response to how senior leaders deploy performance expectations might describe a specific occasion when a senior leader visited all of the organization's facilities. On the other hand, a systematic process might describe the communication methods used by all senior leaders to deliver performance expectations on a regular basis to all organizational locations and workforce members, the measures used to assess the effectiveness of the methods, and the tools and techniques used to evaluate and improve the communication methods.

Approach

The term "approach" refers to the methods used by an organization to address the Baldrige Criteria Item requirements. Approach includes the appropriateness of the methods to the Item requirements and to the organization's operating environment, as well as how effectively the methods are used. Approach is one of the dimensions considered in evaluating Process Items.

Balancing Value

A key challenge to an organization will frequently include balancing the differing expectations of the various stakeholder groups. To meet the sometimes conflicting and changing aims that balancing value implies, organizational strategy (normally in the environmental scan phase of strategy development) should explicitly include key stakeholder requirements. This will help the organization develop strategies (and the associated plans and actions) which are aligned to maximize the overall stakeholder benefit, and to achieve what the leaders of the organization intended to achieve.

This does not mean that all stakeholders will get anything they want. It does mean that the leadership needs to start with the stakeholder requirements, and determine the most effective/innovative way to serve the needs of multiple stakeholders. During the planning the balance intended by the leaders (between the stakeholder requirements and how they will/will not be met) should be linked to the beliefs of the organization (e.g., mission, vision, values), and the needs of the multiple stakeholders. The balanced intended should be the balance planned, the balance resourced, the balance deployed, the balanced reviewed (during performance reviews), and the balance achieved.

Basic Requirements

The term "basic requirements" refers to the topic Criteria users need to address when responding to the most central concept of an Item. Basic requirements are the fundamental theme of that Item (e.g., your approach for strategy development for Item 2.1). In the Criteria, the basic requirements of each Item are presented as the Item title question. This presentation is illustrated in the Item format.

Benchmarks

The term "benchmarks" refers to processes and results that represent best practices and performance for similar activities, inside or outside an organization's industry. Organizations engage in benchmarking to understand the current dimensions of world-class performance and to achieve discontinuous (non-incremental) or "breakthrough" improvement.

Benchmarks are one form of comparative data. Other comparative data organizations might use include industry data collected by a third party (frequently industry averages), data on competitors' performance, and comparisons with similar organizations that are in the same geographic area or that provide similar products and services in other geographic areas.

Big Data

For all organizations, turning data into knowledge and knowledge into useful strategic insights is the real challenge of big data. While the volume of data an organization must assimilate and use in decision making may vary widely, all organizations are faced with using data from different sources and of varying quality. This presents challenges in data validation, frequently exacerbated when the data being validated include numerics, text, and video or other formats. Organizations must deal increasingly with more sophisticated data analytics and issues of data integrity. Challenges to cybersecurity enhance the pressures on organizations and increase the need for organizational sophistication. User demands increase the need for speed and availability of data. In 2015, the Criteria incorporate an enhanced focus on data analytics, data integrity, and cybersecurity.

Blind Spot

The term "blind spot" refers to an area which is not being addressed by the organization which is an obscuration of the visual field (or environmental scan) during the planning and implementation of actions. A particular blind spot is the place in the 'visual' field which is not being addressed. If an organization does not address a blind spot, there is some level of risk to the organization or to organizational performance – a blind spot is something that could potentially interfere with organizational performance and strategy.

Blind spots can be something the organization is unaware of, something they are aware of or even something they understand. In any event, however, a decision to act to remove or mitigate the blind spot has not been made, and actions have not been taken.

Once a decision to act is made, the organization should monitor the progress of the actions to determine whether the intended effect of removing or mitigating the risk has occurred. If action is not taken, the organization may still want to monitor the blind spot to ensure the level of risk, which the blind spot represents, does not change to an unacceptable level.

For example: known blind spots can be areas which the organization is aware of, but they have not taken action to mitigate the risk because of a conscious leadership decision that the risk is acceptable. Additionally, some known blind spots can be of a nature that the organization does not know what to do about them, or cannot do anything about them.

Unknown blind spots are areas of risk the organization is not aware of. Frequently these are addressed with the used of specific external experts who can make the organization aware of risks that were previously unknown.

Capability, Workforce

See "workforce capability."

Capacity, Workforce

See "workforce capacity."

Change Management

Organizational change is difficult and generally disruptive to the organization and its people. It requires dedication and commitment. The strategic imperatives and decisions about change have been a focus of past updates to the Criteria. The roadblock many organizations face is that designing change is much easier than the dedication and commitment required to implement, fully deploy, and sustain changes. Revisions to the 2015–2016 Criteria emphasize the ability to accomplish these tactical aspects of change.

Climate Change

While some organizations have a greater opportunity than others to contribute to eliminating the sources of climate change, no organization is immune to its impacts. This is true of all types and sizes of businesses, nonprofit organizations, and government entities. Increasingly severe storms, massive snows, flooding, and power outages potentially affect supply chains, the ability to work, productivity, and the ability to move around. These events increase the need for aid from social service and government agencies. For all organizations, the impacts of climate change are about managing risk, making choices, and building acceptable redundancies and alternatives into performance management systems, while not building overcapacity and wasteful systems. These contingencies are addressed in the 2015–2016 Criteria.

Collaborators

The term "collaborators" refers to those organizations or individuals who cooperate with your organization to support a particular activity or event or who cooperate on an intermittent basis when short-term goals are aligned or are the same. Typically, collaborations do not involve formal agreements or arrangements. See also the definition of "partners."

Core Competencies

The term "core competencies" refers to your organization's areas of greatest expertise. Your organization's core competencies are those strategically important capabilities that are central to fulfilling your mission or provide an advantage in your marketplace or service environment. Core competencies frequently are challenging for competitors or suppliers and partners to imitate, and they may provide a sustainable competitive advantage. Core competencies may involve technology expertise, unique service offerings, a marketplace niche, or particular business acumen (e.g., business acquisitions).

Customer

The term "customer" refers to actual and potential users of your organization's products, programs, or services (referred to as "products" in the Criteria). Customers include the end users of your products, as well as others who might be their immediate purchasers or users. These others might include distributors, agents, or organizations that further process your product as a component of their product. The Criteria address customers broadly, referencing current and future customers, as well as the customers of your competitors.

Customer-driven excellence is a Baldrige Core Value embedded in the beliefs and behaviors of high-performing organizations. Customer focus impacts and should integrate an organization's strategic directions, its work systems and work processes, and its business results.

See the definition of "stakeholders" for the relationship between customers and others who might be affected by your products.

Customer Engagement

The term "customer engagement" refers to your customers' investment in or commitment to your brand and product offerings. It is based on your ongoing ability to serve their needs and build relationships so they will continue using your products. Characteristics of customer engagement include customer retention and loyalty, customers' willingness to make an effort to do business with your organization, and customers' willingness to actively advocate for and recommend your brand and product offerings.

Customer Group

Customer groups (P.1b[2]) might be based on common expectations, behaviors, preferences, or profiles. Within a group there may be customer segments based on differences and commonalities within the group. (2009-2010 Baldrige Criteria, Page 5, Note 4)

For most purposes, the term "customer group" in the criteria has replaced the term "customer segment' in subsequent versions of the criteria. See the definition of 'Segment."

Customer Segment

The term "customer group" in the criteria has replaced the term "customer segment' in previous versions of the criteria. See the definition of 'Segment" and the definition of "Customer Group."

Cycle Time

The term "cycle time" refers to the time required to fulfill commitments or to complete tasks. Time measurements play a major role in the Criteria because of the great importance of time performance to improving competitiveness and overall performance. "Cycle time" refers to all aspects of time performance. Cycle time improvement might include time to market, order fulfillment time, delivery time, changeover time, customer response time, and other key measures of time.

Deployment

The term "deployment" refers to the extent to which an approach is applied in addressing the requirements of a Baldrige Criteria Item. Deployment is evaluated on the basis of the breadth and depth of application of the approach to relevant work units throughout the organization.
Deployment is one of the dimensions considered in evaluating Process Items. For further description, see the Scoring System.

Diversity

The term "diversity" refers to valuing and benefiting from personal differences. These differences address many variables, including race, religion, color, gender, national origin, disability, sexual orientation, age and generational preferences, education, geographic origin, and skill characteristics, as well as differences in ideas, thinking, academic disciplines, and perspectives.

The Baldrige Criteria refer to the diversity of your workforce hiring and customer communities. Capitalizing on both provides enhanced opportunities for high performance; customer, workforce, and community satisfaction; and customer and workforce engagement.

Effective

The term "effective" refers to how well a process or a measure addresses its intended purpose. Determining effectiveness requires (1) the evaluation of how well the process is aligned with the organization's needs and how well the process is deployed or (2) the evaluation of the outcome of the measure used.

Embedded Core Belief

A term used by some organizations to describe the one belief which is so key it is at the top of every thought, process, plan, measure and action. This is part of an organization's DNA. This is beyond core values. This helps give an organization a singular focus on something which is key to their short- and longer-term survivability or differentiation.

For example – survivability: in a heavy industrial environment, an embedded core belief might be safety. To violate this could mean loss of life.

For example – differentiation: in a business which is not typically known for honest business dealings. The organization could differentiate themselves with 'integrity' as an embedded core belief. To violate this could mean loss of brand image and differentiation in the marketplace.

An embedded core belief is, typically, an area where very little, if any, empowerment is given. You do not consciously violate the embedded core belief and stay with the organization. If this intentionally happens, the disconnect between the organizational beliefs and a personal behavior would be too great.

Empowerment

The term "empowerment" refers to giving people the authority and responsibility to make decisions and take actions. Empowerment results in decisions being made closest to the "front line," where work-related knowledge and understanding reside.

Empowerment is aimed at enabling people to satisfy customers on first contact, to improve processes and increase productivity, and to improve the organization's performance results. An empowered workforce requires information to make appropriate decisions; thus, an organizational requirement is to provide that information in a timely and useful way.

Engagement, Customer

See "customer engagement."

Engagement, Workforce

See "workforce engagement."

Enterprise Systems Model

The term "Enterprise Systems Model" (or ESM) refers to a depiction of the flow of an organization which shows the major systems. These include the "work systems" which refer to how the work of your organization is accomplished (see the definition of work systems); the "guidance systems" which refer to how the work of your organization (in your work systems) is directed, led, and managed (see the definition of guidance systems; and the "support systems" which refer to how the work of your organization (in your work systems) is supported (see the definition of support systems.)

An Enterprise Systems Model is frequently used to show how the work of the organization is delivered to the external customer, and is led and supported. Typically the listening to the external customer is an input to the guidance systems, which can change how the organization is guided.

An Enterprise Systems Model can be broken down to: 1) individual systems; 2) processes under each of the systems; and 3) one or more levels of sub-processes down to an appropriate level. Each system or process is typically owned by an individual in the organization, who has the responsibility to define, measure, stabilize and improve it (see the definition of Systematic Process).

Ethical Behavior

The term "ethical behavior" refers to how an organization ensures that all its decisions, actions, and stakeholder interactions conform to the organization's moral and professional principles. These principles should support all applicable laws and regulations and are the foundation for the organization's culture and values. They distinguish "right" from "wrong."

Senior leaders should act as role models for these principles of behavior. The principles apply to all people involved in the organization, from temporary members of the workforce to members of the board of directors, and need to be communicated and reinforced on a regular basis. Although there is no universal model for ethical behavior, senior leaders should ensure that the organization's mission and vision are aligned with its ethical principles. Ethical behavior should be practiced with all stakeholders, including the workforce, shareholders, customers, partners, suppliers, and the organization's local community.

While some organizations may view their ethical principles as boundary conditions restricting behavior, well-designed and clearly articulated ethical principles should empower people to make effective decisions with great confidence.

Excellence

See "Performance Excellence."

Goals

The term "goals" refers to a future condition or performance level that one intends to attain. Goals can be both short- and longer-term. Goals are ends that guide actions. Quantitative goals, frequently referred to as "targets," include a numerical point or range. Targets might be projections based on comparative or competitive data. The term "stretch goals" refers to desired major, discontinuous (non-incremental) or "breakthrough" improvements, usually in areas most critical to your organization's future success.

Goals can serve many purposes, including:

- clarifying strategic objectives and action plans to indicate how you will measure success
- fostering teamwork by focusing on a common end
- encouraging "out-of-the-box" thinking (innovation) to achieve a stretch goal
- providing a basis for measuring and accelerating -progress

Governance

The term "governance" refers to the system of management and controls exercised in the stewardship of your organization. It includes the responsibilities of your organization's owners/shareholders, board of directors, and senior leaders. Corporate or organizational charters, bylaws, and policies document the rights and responsibilities of each of the parties and describe how your organization will be directed and controlled to ensure (1) accountability to owners/shareholders and other stakeholders, (2) transparency of operations, and (3) fair treatment of all stakeholders. Governance processes may include the approval of strategic direction, the monitoring and evaluation of the CEO's performance, the establishment of executive compensation and benefits, succession planning, financial auditing, risk management, disclosure, and shareholder reporting. Ensuring effective governance is important to stakeholders' and the larger society's trust and to organizational effectiveness.

Guidance Systems

The term "guidance systems" refers to how the work of your organization (in your work systems) is directed, led, and managed. Guidance systems are typically internal to the organization. These systems can include systems for leadership, planning, governance, legal, ethical, community support, and improvement. Guidance systems will direct, lead or manage your workforce, your key suppliers and partners, your contractors, your collaborators, and other components of the supply chain needed to support the work systems which produce and deliver your products and services.

Guidance systems may also be called Management Systems, but are NOT the same as a Leadership System, which is only one of the Guidance Systems needed.

Health Care Services

All services delivered by your organization that involve professional clinical/medical judgment, including those delivered to patients and to the community. Health care services also include services that are not considered clinical or medical, such as admissions, food services, and billing.

High-Performance

Ever-higher levels of overall organizational and individual performance, including
quality, productivity, innovation rate, and cycle time. High performance results in improved service and value for customers and other stakeholders.

Approaches to high performance vary in their form, their function, and the incentive systems used. High performance stems from and enhances workforce engagement. It involves cooperation between the management and the workforce, which may involve workforce bargaining units; cooperation among work units, often involving teams; empowerment of your people, including personal accountability; and workforce input into planning. It may involve learning and building individual and organizational skills; learning from other organizations; creating flexible job design and work assignments; maintaining a flattened organizational structure, where decision making is decentralized and decisions are made closest to the front line; and effectively using performance measures, including comparisons. Many organizations encourage high performance with monetary and nonmonetary incentives based on factors such as organizational performance, team and individual contributions, and skill building. Also, approaches to high performance usually seek to align your organization's structure, core competencies, work, jobs, workforce development, and incentives.

How

The term "how" refers to the systems and processes that an organization uses to accomplish its mission requirements. In responding to "how" questions in the Process Item requirements, process descriptions should include information such as approach (methods and measures), deployment, learning, and integration factors. *Responses lacking such information, or merely providing an example, are referred to in the Scoring Guidelines as "anecdotal information."*

Indicators

See "measures and indicators."

Innovation

The term "innovation" refers to making meaningful change to improve products, processes, or organizational effectiveness and to create new value for stakeholders. Innovation involves the adoption of an idea, process, technology, product, or business model that is either new or new to its proposed application. The outcome of innovation is a discontinuous or breakthrough change in results, products, or processes.

Successful organizational innovation is a multistep process that involves development and knowledge sharing, a decision to implement, implementation, evaluation, and learning. Although innovation is often associated with technological innovation, it is applicable to all key organizational processes that would benefit from change, whether through breakthrough improvement or a change in approach or outputs. It could include fundamental changes in organizational structure or the business model to more effectively accomplish the organization's work.

Integration

The term "integration" refers to the harmonization of plans, processes, information, resource decisions, actions, results, and analyses to support key organization-wide goals. Effective integration goes beyond alignment and is achieved when the individual components of a performance management system operate as a fully interconnected unit.

Integration is one of the dimensions considered in evaluating both Process and Results Items. For further description, see the Scoring System.

See also the definition of "alignment."

Intelligent Risks

Opportunities for which the potential gain outweighs the potential harm or loss to your organization's sustainability if you do not explore them. Taking intelligent risks requires a tolerance for failure and an expectation that innovation is not achieved by initiating only successful endeavors. At the outset, organizations must invest in potential successes while realizing that some will lead to failure.

The degree of risk that is intelligent to take will vary by the pace and level of threat and opportunity in the industry. In a rapidly changing industry with constant introductions of new products, processes, or business models, there is an obvious need to invest more resources in intelligent risks than in a stable industry. In the latter, organizations must monitor and explore growth potential and change but, most likely, with a less significant commitment of resources.

See also strategic opportunities.

Key

The term "key" refers to the major or most important elements or factors, those that are critical to achieving your intended outcome. The Baldrige Criteria, for example, refer to key challenges, key plans, key work processes, and key measures—those that are most important to your organization's success. They are the essential elements for pursuing or monitoring a desired outcome.

Knowledge Assets

The term "knowledge assets" refers to the accumulated intellectual resources of your organization. It is the knowledge possessed by your organization and its workforce in the form of information, ideas, learning, understanding, memory, insights, cognitive and technical skills, and capabilities. Your workforce, software, patents, databases, documents, guides, policies and procedures, and technical drawings are repositories of your organization's knowledge assets. Knowledge assets are held not only by an organization but reside within its customers, suppliers, and partners, as well.

Knowledge assets are the "know-how" that your organization has available to use, to invest, and to grow. Building and managing its knowledge assets are key components for your organization to create value for your stakeholders and to help sustain a competitive advantage.

Leadership System

The term "leadership system" refers to how leadership is exercised, formally and informally, throughout the organization; it is the basis for and the way key decisions are made, communicated, and carried out. It includes structures and mechanisms for decision making; two-way communication; selection and development of leaders and managers; and reinforcement of values, ethical behavior, directions, and performance expectations.

An effective leadership system respects the capabilities and requirements of workforce members and other stakeholders, and it sets high expectations for performance and performance improvement. It builds loyalties and teamwork based on the organization's vision and values and the pursuit of shared goals. It encourages and supports initiative and appropriate risk taking, subordinates organizational structure to purpose and function, and avoids chains of command that require long decision paths. An effective leadership system includes mechanisms for the leaders to conduct self-examination, receive feedback, and improve.

The term "leader," as it is used in reference to the Leadership System, refers to all leaders at any level in the organization. This is not only limited the top leaders (the head of the organization and that person's direct reports – which are referred to as "Senior Leadership"), but includes every leader supervising at least one other person. In some organizations key positions are considered leaders even if they do not supervise, and in other organizations all employees are considered leaders.

Learning

The term "learning" refers to new knowledge or skills acquired through evaluation, study, experience, and innovation. The Baldrige Criteria include two distinct kinds of learning: organizational and personal. Organizational learning is achieved through research and development, evaluation and improvement cycles, workforce and stakeholder ideas and input, best-practice sharing, and benchmarking. Personal learning is achieved through education, training, and developmental opportunities that further individual growth.

To be effective, learning should be embedded in the way an organization operates. Learning contributes to a competitive advantage and sustainability for the organization and its workforce. For further description of organizational and personal learning, see the related Core Value and Concept.

Learning is one of the dimensions considered in evaluating Process Items. For further description, see the Scoring System.

Levels

The term "levels" refers to numerical information that places or positions an organization's results and performance on a meaningful measurement scale. Performance levels permit evaluation relative to past performance, projections, goals, and appropriate comparisons.

Measures and Indicators

The term "measures and indicators" refers to numerical information that quantifies input, output, and performance dimensions of processes, products, programs, projects, services, and the overall organization (outcomes). Measures and indicators might be simple (derived from one measurement) or composite.

The Criteria do not make a distinction between measures and indicators. However, some users of these terms prefer "indicator" (1) when the measurement relates to performance but is not a direct measure of such performance (e.g., the number of complaints is an indicator of dissatisfaction but not a direct measure of it) and (2) when the measurement is a predictor ("leading indicator") of some more significant performance (e.g., increased customer satisfaction might be a leading indicator of market share gain).

Mission

The term "mission" refers to the overall function of an organization. The mission answers the question, "What is this organization attempting to accomplish?" The mission might define customers or markets served, distinctive or core competencies, or technologies used.

Multiple Requirements

The term "multiple requirements" refers to the individual questions Criteria users need to answer within each Area to Address. These questions constitute the details of an Item's requirements. They are presented in black text under each Item's Area(s) to Address.

Overall Requirements

The term "overall requirements" refers to the topics Criteria users need to address when responding to the central theme of an Item. Overall requirements address the most significant features of the Item requirements. In the Criteria, the overall requirements of each Item are presented in one or more introductory sentences printed in bold.

Partners

The term "partners" refers to those key organizations or individuals who are working in concert with your organization to achieve a common goal or to improve performance. Typically, partnerships are formal arrangements for a specific aim or purpose, such as to achieve a strategic objective or to deliver a specific product.

Formal partnerships are usually for an extended period of time and involve a clear understanding of the individual and mutual roles and benefits for the partners.
See also the definition of "collaborators."

Patient

The person receiving health care, including preventive, promotional, acute, chronic, rehabilitative, and all other services in the continuum of care. Other terms used for patient include member, consumer, client, and resident.

Performance

The term "performance" refers to outputs and their outcomes obtained from processes, products, and customers that permit evaluation and comparison relative to goals, standards, past results, and other organizations. Performance can be expressed in nonfinancial and financial terms.
The Baldrige Criteria address four types of performance: (1) product, (2) customer-focused, (3) financial and marketplace, and (4) operational.

> **"Product performance"** refers to performance relative to measures and indicators of product and service characteristics important to customers. Examples include product reliability, on-time delivery, customer-experienced defect levels, and service response time. For nonprofit organizations, "product performance" examples might include program and project performance in the areas of rapid response to emergencies, at-home services, or multilingual services.

> **"Customer-focused performance"** refers to performance relative to measures and indicators of customers' perceptions, reactions, and behaviors. Examples include customer retention, complaints, and customer survey results.

> **"Financial and marketplace performance"** refers to performance relative to measures of cost, revenue, and market position, including asset utilization, asset growth, and market share. Examples include returns on investments, value added per employee, debt-to-equity ratio, returns on assets, operating margins, performance to budget, the amount in reserve funds, cash-to-cash cycle time, other profitability and liquidity measures, and market gains.

> **"Operational performance"** refers to workforce, leadership, organizational, and ethical performance relative to effectiveness, efficiency, and accountability measures and indicators. Examples include cycle time, productivity, waste reduction, workforce turnover, workforce cross-training rates, regulatory compliance, fiscal accountability, and community involvement. Operational performance might be measured at the work unit level, key work process level, and organizational level.

Performance Excellence

The term "performance excellence" refers to an integrated approach to organizational performance management that results in (1) delivery of ever-improving value to customers and stakeholders, contributing to organizational sustainability; (2) improvement of overall organizational effectiveness and capabilities; and (3) organizational and personal learning. The Baldrige Criteria for Performance Excellence provide a framework and an assessment tool for understanding organizational strengths and opportunities for improvement and thus for guiding planning efforts.

Defining success is a moving target. The definition of success for organizations of all types (profit seeking, non-profit, and government) is continuously changing and increasingly complex. From the mid-1940s to the 1970s the limited global competition allowed business leaders in the United States to focus mainly on financial results. The "party" ended around 1980 when Xerox woke up to a situation where the Japanese were selling copiers in the US for what it was costing Xerox to make them (Kotter and Heskett, 1992). During the 1980s, quality became a key success factor and was directly linked to market and ultimately financial success. In the beginning many proposed that high quality was simply too expensive. However, we eventually discovered that high quality = reduced cost and increased market share or as Phillip Crosby wrote in a book by the same title - Quality is Free! As the service industry and in particular the knowledge worker industries increased in size and importance they discovered that talented passionate people are also a key to high quality and financial performance. During the 1990s successful organizations became quite good at "connecting the dots" or as FedEx called it - "people, service, profit" (AMA 1991). The "bar" is being raised once again to include sustainable results in three key areas - financial, environmental, and societal or as Elkington, Emerson, and Beloe (2006) call it - the triple bottom line.

Performance Projections

The term "performance projections" refers to estimates of future performance. Projections may be inferred from past performance, may be based on competitors' or similar organizations' performance that must be met or exceeded, may be predicted based on changes in a dynamic environment, or may be goals for future performance. Projections integrate estimates of your organization's rate of improvement and change, and they may be used to indicate where breakthrough improvement or innovation is needed. While performance projections may be set to attain a goal, they also may be predicted levels of future performance that indicate the challenges your organization faces in achieving a goal. Thus, performance projections serve as a key management planning tool.

Process

Linked activities with the purpose of producing a product (or service) for a customer (user) within or outside your organization. Generally, processes involve combinations of people, machines, tools, techniques, materials, and improvements in a defined series of steps or actions. Processes rarely operate in isolation and must be considered in relation to other processes that impact them. In some situations, processes might require adherence to a specific sequence of steps, with documentation (sometimes formal) of procedures and requirements, including well-defined measurement and control steps.

In the delivery of services, particularly those that directly involve customers, *process* is used more generally to spell out what delivering that service entails, possibly including a preferred or expected sequence. If a sequence is critical, the process needs to include information that helps customers understand and follow the sequence. Such service processes also require guidance for service providers on handling contingencies related to customers' possible actions or behaviors.

In knowledge work, such as strategic planning, research, development, and analysis, process does not necessarily imply formal sequences of steps. Rather, process implies general understandings of competent performance in such areas as timing, options to include, evaluation, and reporting. Sequences might arise as part of these understandings.

Process is one of the two dimensions evaluated in a Baldrige-based assessment. This evaluation is based on four factors: approach, deployment, learning, and integration. For further description, see the Scoring System.

oductivity

he term "productivity" refers to measures of the efficiency of resource use.

Although the term often is applied to single factors, such as the workforce (labor productivity), machines, materials, energy, and capital, the productivity concept applies as well to the total resources used in producing outputs. The use of an aggregate measure of overall productivity allows a determination of whether the net effect of overall changes in a process—possibly involving resource trade-offs—is beneficial.

Purpose

The term "purpose" refers to the fundamental reason that an organization exists. The primary role of purpose is to inspire an organization and guide its setting of values. Purpose is generally broad and enduring. Two organizations in different businesses could have similar purposes, and two organizations in the same business could have different purposes.

RCD

*The term "RCD" is a term used for mapping processes. It stands for **Really Crummy Draft**.*

If someone is asked to map a process, they will stress out and not deliver the process map in a reasonable (or even over an extended) time. If you tell them, however, "I only need a really crummy draft (RCD)" then they can map a process very quickly. Once the RCD is developed, it can be modified and improved quickly, giving a finished result in less time, and with more participation (and ownership), than if one person was 'tasked' to develop a perfect process map.

Results

Outputs and outcomes achieved by your organization in addressing the requirements of a Baldrige Criteria Item. Results are evaluated on the basis of current performance; performance relative to appropriate comparisons; the rate, breadth, and importance of performance improvements; and the relationship of results measures to key organizational performance requirements. For further description, see the Scoring System.

Results are on the two dimensions evaluated in a Baldrige-based assessment. This evaluation is based on four factors: levels, trends, comparisons, and integration. For further description, see the Scoring System.

Segment

The term "segment" refers to a part of an organization's overall customer, market, product offering, or workforce base. Segments typically have common characteristics that can be grouped logically. In Results Items, the term refers to disaggregating results data in a way that allows for meaningful analysis of an organization's performance. It is up to each organization to determine the specific factors that it uses to segment its customers, markets, products, and workforce.

Understanding segments is critical to identifying the distinct needs and expectations of different customer, market, and workforce groups and to tailoring product offerings to meet their needs and expectations. As an example, market segmentation might be based on distribution channels, business volume, geography, or technologies employed. Workforce segmentation might be based on geography, skills, needs, work assignments, or job classifications.

Senior Leaders

The term "senior leaders" refers to an organization's senior management group or team. In many organizations, this consists of the head of the organization and his or her direct reports.

Stakeholders

The term "stakeholders" refers to all groups that are or might be affected by an organization's actions and success. Examples of key stakeholders might include customers, the workforce, partners, collaborators, governing boards, stockholders, donors, suppliers, taxpayers, regulatory bodies, policy makers, funders, and local and professional communities.
See also the definition of "customer."

Strategic Advantages

The term "strategic advantages" refers to those marketplace benefits that exert a decisive influence on an organization's likelihood of future success. These advantages frequently are sources of an organization's current and future competitive success relative to other providers of similar products. Strategic advantages generally arise from either or both of two sources: (1) core competencies, which focus on building and expanding on an organization's internal capabilities, and (2) strategically important external resources, which are shaped and leveraged through key external relationships and partnerships.

When an organization realizes both sources of strategic advantage, it can amplify its unique internal capabilities by capitalizing on complementary capabilities in other organizations.

See the definitions of "strategic challenges" and "strategic objectives" below for the relationship among strategic advantages, strategic challenges, and the strategic objectives an organization articulates to address its challenges and advantages.

Strategic Challenges

The term "strategic challenges" refers to those pressures that exert a decisive influence on an organization's likelihood of future success. These challenges frequently are driven by an organization's future competitive position relative to other providers of similar products. While not exclusively so, strategic challenges generally are externally driven. However, in responding to externally driven strategic challenges, an organization may face internal strategic challenges.

External strategic challenges may relate to customer or market needs or expectations; product or technological changes; or financial, societal, and other risks or needs. Internal strategic challenges may relate to an organization's capabilities or its human and other resources.

See the definitions of "strategic advantages" and "strategic objectives" for the relationship among strategic challenges, strategic advantages, and the strategic objectives an organization articulates to address its challenges and advantages.

Strategic Objectives

The term "strategic objectives" refers to an organization's articulated aims or responses to address major change or improvement, competitiveness or social issues, and business advantages. Strategic objectives generally are focused both externally and internally and relate to significant customer, market, product, or technological opportunities and challenges (strategic challenges). Broadly stated, they are what an organization must achieve to remain or become competitive and ensure long-term sustainability. Strategic objectives set an organization's longer-term directions and guide resource allocations and redistributions. See the definition of "action plans" for the relationship between strategic objectives and action plans and for an example of each.

Strategic Opportunities

Prospects that arise from outside-the-box thinking, brainstorming, capitalizing on serendipity, research and innovation processes, nonlinear extrapolation of current conditions, and other approaches to imagining a different future.

The generation of ideas that lead to strategic opportunities benefits from an environment that encourages nondirected, free thought. Choosing which strategic opportunities to pursue involves consideration of relative risk, financial and otherwise, and then making intelligent choices (*intelligent risks*).

See action plans for the relationship between strategic objectives and action plans and for an example of each.

See also intelligent risks.

Support Systems

The term "support systems" refers to how the work of your organization (in your work systems) is supported. Support systems can be internal to the organization or external (such as a corporate HR department providing HR services for a division, or subcontracting your IT). Support systems may involve your workforce, your key suppliers and partners, your contractors, your collaborators, and other components of the supply chain needed to support the work systems which produce and deliver your products and services.

Support systems, by themselves, cannot ensure that an organization is a success. They are critical systems, however, and, if not effectively planned, integrated and executed, can ensure that the organization fails.

Sustainability

The term "sustainability" refers to your organization's ability to address current business needs and to have the agility and strategic management to prepare successfully for your future business, market, and operating environment. Both external and internal factors need to be considered. The specific combination of factors might include industry wide and organization-specific components.

Sustainability considerations might include workforce capability and capacity, resource availability, technology, knowledge, core competencies, work systems, facilities, and equipment. Sustainability might be affected by changes in the marketplace and customer preferences, changes in the financial markets, and changes in the legal and regulatory environment. In addition, sustainability has a component related to day-to-day preparedness for real-time or short-term emergencies.

In the context of the Baldrige Criteria, the impact of your organization's products and operations on society and the contributions you make to the well-being of environmental, social, and economic systems are part of your organization's overall societal responsibilities. Whether and how your organization addresses such considerations also may affect its sustainability.

Operational sustainability typically includes the organization verifying that risks associated with money, data, facilities, equipment, workforce, critical skills, and supply chain have been mitigated, or contingency/recovery plans are in place. Strategic sustainability will depend upon these same factors, plus the effectiveness of the strategy and the quality of leadership and leadership development.

According to the Brundtland Commission, "Sustainable development is development that meets the needs of the present without compromising the ability of future generations to meet their own needs."

Systematic

The term "systematic" refers to approaches that are well-ordered, are repeatable, and use data and information so learning is possible. In other words, approaches are systematic if they build in the opportunity for evaluation, improvement, and sharing, thereby permitting a gain in maturity. For use of the term, see the Scoring Guidelines.

Systematic Process

A systematic process, typically, is a process where the steps undertaken are:

> ***Defined*** *(how the organization does something - the steps are defined to a level where all parties involved and/or outsiders can understand the sequence of activities, who is involved, and what happens in each step);*
> ***Measured*** *- each of the steps has measures (these can be in-process measures or end-of - process measures) - which indicate whether or not steps and/or the entire process is on track;*
> ***Stabilized*** *- this means that each step of the process and/or the entire process is reliable or repeatable, and can give consistent results to the organization;*
> ***Improved*** *– each of the processes has improvement and feedback cycles (where each time you go through the process there is a learning cycle which can be used at the beginning of that process the next time it is repeated).*

Transformational Change

A fundamental shift in the operations, services or approach of an organization. A transformational change may not require a shift in the mission, vision, or values of an organization, but typically does require a shift in the focus, plans, measures or behaviors. This shift in the culture of an organization is a result in a change in the strategy and processes that the organization has used in the past. A transformational change is designed to be organization-wide and is enacted over a period of time.

Transparency (from Wikipedia for Corporate Transparency)

Corporate transparency describes the extent to which a corporation's actions are observable by outsiders. This is a consequence of regulation, local norms, and the set of information, privacy, and business policies concerning corporate decision making and operations openness to employees, stakeholders, shareholders and the general public. From the perspective of outsiders, transparency can be defined simply as the perceived quality of intentionally shared information from the corporation.

Recent research suggests there are three primary dimensions of corporate transparency: information disclosure, clarity, and accuracy. To increment transparency, corporations infuse greater disclosure, clarity, and accuracy into their communications with stakeholders. For example, governance decisions to voluntarily share information related to the firm's ecological impact with environmental activists indicate disclosure; decisions to actively limit the use of technical terminology, fine print, or complicated mathematical notations in the firm's correspondence with suppliers and customers indicate clarity; and decisions to not bias, embellish, or otherwise distort known facts in the firm's communications with investors indicate accuracy. The strategic management of transparency therefore involves intentional modifications in disclosure, clarity, and accuracy to accomplish the firm's objectives.

Trends

The term "trends" refers to numerical information that shows the direction and rate of change for an organization's results. Trends provide a time sequence of organizational performance.

A minimum of three historical (not projected) data points generally is needed to begin to ascertain a trend. More data points are needed to define a statistically valid trend. The time period for a trend is determined by the cycle time of the process being measured. Shorter cycle times demand more frequent measurement, while longer cycle times might require longer time periods before meaningful trends can be determined.

Examples of trends called for by the Criteria include data related to product performance, customer and workforce satisfaction and dissatisfaction results, financial performance, marketplace performance, and operational performance, such as cycle time and productivity.

Value

The term "value" refers to the perceived worth of a product, process, asset, or function relative to cost and to possible alternatives.

Organizations frequently use value considerations to determine the benefits of various options relative to their costs, such as the value of various product and service combinations to customers. Organizations need to understand what different stakeholder groups value and then deliver value to each group. This frequently requires balancing value for customers and other stakeholders, such as your workforce and the community.

Values

The term "values" refers to the guiding principles and behaviors that embody how your organization and its people are expected to operate. Values reflect and reinforce the desired culture of an organization. Values support and guide the decision making of every workforce member, helping the organization accomplish its mission and attain its vision in an appropriate manner. Examples of values might include demonstrating integrity and fairness in all interactions, exceeding customer expectations, valuing individuals and diversity, protecting the environment, and striving for performance excellence every day.

Vision

The term "vision" refers to the desired future state of your organization. The vision describes where the organization is headed, what it intends to be, or how it wishes to be perceived in the future.

Voice of the Customer

Your process for capturing customer-related information. Voice-of-the-customer processes are intended to be proactive and continuously innovative to capture stated, unstated, and anticipated customer requirements, expectations, and desires. The goal is to achieve customer engagement. Listening to the voice of the customer might include gathering and integrating various types of customer data, such as survey data, focus group findings, warranty data, and complaint data, that affect customers' purchasing and engagement decisions.

Work Processes

The term "work processes" refers to your most important internal value creation processes. They might include product design and delivery, customer support, supply chain management, business, and support processes. They are the processes that involve the majority of your organization's workforce and produce customer, stakeholder, and stockholder value.

Your key work processes frequently relate to your core competencies, to the factors that determine your success relative to competitors, and to the factors considered important for business growth by your senior leaders.

Work Systems

The term "work systems" refers to how the work of your organization is accomplished. Work systems involve your workforce, your key suppliers and partners, your contractors, your collaborators, and other components of the supply chain needed to produce and deliver your products and your business and support processes. Your work systems coordinate the internal work processes and the external resources necessary for you to develop, produce, and deliver your products to your customers and to succeed in your marketplace.

Decisions about work systems are strategic. These decisions involve protecting and capitalizing on core competencies and deciding what should be procured or produced outside your organization in order to be efficient and sustainable in your marketplace.

Workforce

The term "workforce" refers to all people actively involved in accomplishing the work of your organization, including paid employees (e.g., permanent, part-time, temporary, and telecommuting employees, as well as contract employees supervised by the organization) and volunteers, as appropriate. The workforce includes team leaders, supervisors, and managers at all levels.

Workforce Capability

The term "workforce capability" refers to your organization's ability to accomplish its work processes through the knowledge, skills, abilities, and competencies of its people.

Capability may include the ability to build and sustain relationships with your customers; to innovate and transition to new technologies; to develop new products and work processes; and to meet changing business, market, and regulatory demands.

Workforce Capacity

The term "workforce capacity" refers to your organization's ability to ensure sufficient staffing levels to accomplish its work processes and successfully deliver your products to your customers, including the ability to meet seasonal or varying demand levels.

Workforce Engagement

The term "workforce engagement" refers to the extent of workforce commitment, both emotional and intellectual, to accomplishing the work, mission, and vision of the organization. Organizations with high levels of workforce engagement are often characterized by high-performing work environments in which people are motivated to do their utmost for the benefit of their customers and for the success of the organization.

In general, members of the workforce feel engaged when they find personal meaning and motivation in their work and when they receive positive interpersonal and workplace support. An engaged workforce benefits from trusting relationships, a safe and cooperative environment, good communication and information flow, empowerment, and performance accountability. Key factors contributing to engagement include training and career development, effective recognition and reward systems, equal opportunity and fair treatment, and family friendliness.

Note:

The Baldrige Criteria – 2015 – 2016 Criteria for Performance Excellence, is the property of the Baldrige Performance Excellence Program, U.S. Department of Commerce, National Institute of Standards and Technology.

This book is designed to educate people about the Baldrige Criteria and serves as a supplemental guide to the Baldrige Criteria booklet itself.

A copy of the full criteria can be obtained by visiting the Baldrige Program Website: *www.nist.gov/baldrige/publications/criteria.cfm*

AMA (1991). *Blueprints for Service Quality*. New York: AMA Membership Publications Division.

Appleby, C. A., Harshman, C. L., & Latham, J. R. (2009). *Baldrige CEO Attitudes and Motivations: Developing a Model of Excellence.* Loveland: Monfort Institute at the University of Northern Colorado.

Baptist (2003). *Baptist Hospital Inc.: 2003 Baldrige Award Application Summary.*

Bass, B. M. (1990). *Bass & Stogdill's Handbook of Leadership: Theory, Research, & Managerial Applications.* New York: Free Press.

Becker, B. E., Huselid, M. A., & Ulrich, D. (2001). *The HR Scorecard: Linking People, Strategy, and Performance.* Boston: Harvard Business School Press.

Beckhard, R., & Harris, R. T. (1987). *Organizational Transitions: Managing Complex Change* (2nd ed.). Reading Massachusetts: Addison-Wesley.

Bemowski, K., & Stratton, B. (1995). How Do People Use the Baldrige Award Criteria. *Quality Progress,* 43 - 47.

BI (2000). *BI 1999 Application Summary*. Paper presented at the Quest for Excellence XII, Washington, D.C.

Branch-Smith (2003). *Branch-Smith Printing 2002 Application Summary*. Paper presented at the Quest for Excellence XV, Washington, D.C.

Bronson (2006). *Bronson Methodist Hospital 2005 Application Summary*. Paper presented at the Quest for Excellence, Washington D.C.

Chugach (2002). *Chugach School District 2001 Application Summary*. Paper presented at the Quest for Excellence XIV, Washington, D.C.

Clarke (2002). *Clarke American Checks, Inc. 2001 Application Summary*. Paper presented at the Quest for Excellence XIV, Washington, D.C.

Collins, J. (2001). *Good to Great: Why Some Companies Make the Leap...and Others Don't*. (1st ed.). New York: HarperCollins.

Deming, W. E. (1986). *Out of the Crisis*. Cambridge, MA: MIT CAES.

Deming, W. E. (1994). *The New Economics: For Industry, Government, Education* (2nd ed.). Cambridge, MA: Massachusetts Institute of Technology Center for Advanced Engineering Study (MIT CAES).

Drucker, P. F. (1985). *Innovation and Entrepreneurship: Practice and Principles* (First ed.). New York: Harper & Row.

Duncan, W. J., Ginter, P. M., & Swayne, L. E. (1998). Competitive advantage and internal organizational assessment. *Academy of Management Executive*, 12(3), 6 - 16.

Elkington, J., Emerson, J., & Beloe, S. (2006). The Value Palette: A Tool for Full Spectrum Strategy. *California Management Review*, 48(2), 6-28.

Evans, J. R., & Ford, M. W. (1997). Value-Driven Quality. *Quality Management Journal*, 4(4), 19 - 31.

Evans, J. R., & Jack, E. P. (2003). Validating Key Results Linkages in the Baldrige Performance Excellence Model. *Quality Management Journal*, 10(2), 7-24.

Ford, M. W., & Evans, J. R. (2001). Baldrige Assessment and Organizational Learning: The Need for Change Management. *Quality Management Journal*, 8(3), 9 - 25.

Forrester, J. W. (1975). *Collected Papers of Jay W. Forrester*. Portland: Productivity Press.

Fry, K. (2005, March). Q. What Makes a Well-Designed Product? *MacAddict*, 10, 31.

GSAM (2011). *Advocate Good Samaritan Hospital 2010 Application Summary*. Paper presented at the Quest for Excellence Conference, Washington, D.C.

Grant, J. H. (2007). Advances and Challenges in Strategic Management. *International Journal of Business*, 12(1), 11-31.

Hamilton, B. A. (2003). *Assessment of Leadership Attitudes About The Baldrige National Quality Program*: NIST.

Heaphy, M. S., & Gruska, G. F. (1995). *The Malcolm Baldrige National Quality Award: A Yardstick for Quality Growth*. Reading, MA: Addison-Wesley.

Hendricks, K. B., & Singhal, V. R. (1997). Does implementing an effective TQM program actually improve operating performance? Empirical evidence from firms that have won quality awards. *Management Science*, 43(9), 1258-1274.

Heskett, J. L., Sasser, E., & Schlesinger, L. A. (1997). *The Service Profit Chain: How Leading Companies Link Profit and Growth to Loyalty, Satisfaction, and Value*. New York: Free Press.

Imai, M. (1986). *KAIZEN: The Key to Japan's Competitive Success* (First ed.). New York: McGraw-Hill.

Jacob, R., Madu, C. N., & Tang, C. (2004). An Empirical Assessment of the Financial Performance of Malcolm Baldrige Award Winners. *The International Journal of Quality and Reliability Management*, 21(8), 897-914.

Jenks (2005). *Jenks Publlic Schools: 2005 Baldrige Award Application Summary*.

Kaplan, R. S., & Norton, D. P. (1996). *The Balanced Scorecard: Translating Strategy into Action*. Boston: Harvard Business School Press.

KARLEE (2001). *KARLEE Company, Inc. 2000 Application Summary*. Paper presented at the Quest for Excellence XIII, Washington D. C.

Knotts, U. S. J., Parrish, L. G., & Evans, C. R. (1993). What Does the U.S. Business Community Really Think About the Baldrige Award? *Quality Progress*, 49 - 53.

Kotter, J. P., & Heskett, J. L. (1992). *Corporate Culture and Performance*. New York: The Free Press.

Latham, J. R. (1997). *A Qualitative and Quantitative Analysis of Organizational Self-Assessment At U.S. Air Force Wings Using Baldrige-Based Nonprescriptive Criteria*. Unpublished PhD Dissertation, Walden University, Minneapolis.

Latham, J. R. (2008). Building Bridges Between Researchers And Practitioners: A Collaborative Approach To Research In Performance Excellence. *Quality Management Journal*, 15(1), 19.

Michalko, M. (1998). Cracking Creativity: The Secrets of Creative Genius. Berkeley: Ten Speed Press.

Monfort (2005). *Monfort College of Business 2004 Application Summary*. Paper presented at the Quest for Excellence, Washington D. C. .

Motorola (2003). *Motorola Commercial, Government and Industrial Solutions Sector 2002 Application Summary*. Paper presented at the Quest for Excellence XV, Washington, D.C.

NIST. (2009). *Malcolm Baldrige National Quality Award: Criteria for performance excellence 2009-2010*. Gaithersburg, Maryland: NIST - National Institute of Standards and Technology.

NIST. (2011). *Malcolm Baldrige National Quality Award: Criteria for performance excellence 2011-2012*. Gaithersburg, Maryland NIST - National Institute of Standards and Technology.

NIST. (2013). *Malcolm Baldrige National Quality Award: Criteria for performance excellence 2013 - 2014*. Gaithersburg, Maryland NIST - National Institute of Standards and Technology.

NMMC (2007). *North Mississippi Medical Center 2006 Application Summary*. Paper presented at the Quest for Excellence, Washington D.C.

Pfeffer, J., & Sutton, R. I. (2006). *Hard Facts, Dangerous Half-Truths and Total Nonsense: Profiting from Evidence-Based Management*. Boston: Harvard Business School Press.

Porter, M. E. (1985). *Competitive Advantage: Creating and Sustaining Superior Performance*. New York: The Free Press.

Poudre (2008). *Poudre Valley Health System: 2008 Baldrige Award Application Summary*.

Prahalad, C. K., & Hamel, G. (1990). The Core Competence of the Corporation. *Harvard Business Review*, 68(3), 79-91.

PRO-TEC (2007). *PRO-TEC Coating Company: 2007 Baldrige Award Application*.

PRSD (2002). *Pearl River School District 2001 Application Summary*. Paper presented at the Quest for Excellence XIV, Washington, D.C.

Quinn, R. E. (1996). *Deep Change: Discovering the Leader Within*. San Francisco: Jossey-Bass.

Richland (2006). *Richland College 2005 Application Summary*. Paper presented at the Quest for Excellence Conference, Washington, D.C.

Ritz-Carlton (2000). *Ritz-Carlton Hotel Company, L.L.C. 1999 Application Summary.* Paper presented at the Quest for Excellence XII, Washington, D.C.

RWJ (2004). *Robert Wood Johnson University Hospital Hamilton: 2004 Baldrige Award Application Summary.*

Senge, P. M. (2006). *The fifth discipline: The art and practice of the learning organization.* New York: Currency Doubleday.

Sharp (2007). *Sharp HealthCare: 2007 Baldrige Award Application Summary.*

SSM (2003). *SSM Health Care 2002 Application Summary.* Paper presented at the Quest for Excellence XV, Washington, D.C.

StLukes (2004). *St Lukes 2003 Application Summary.* Paper presented at the Quest for Excellence, Washington, D.C.

Tang, V., & Bauer, R. (1995). *Competitive Dominance: Beyond Strategic Advantage and Total Quality Management.* New York: Van Nostrand Reinhold.

UWStout (2002). *University of Wisconsin-Stout 2001 Application Summary.* Paper presented at the Quest for Excellence XIV, Washington, D.C.

Wikipedia, definition of *Transparency* (Corporate Transparency).

Wu, K.-C. (1928). *Ancient Chinese Political Theories.* Shanghai, China: The Commercial Press, Limited.